# Delphi Graphics and Game Programming Exposed! with DirectX

### For versions 5.0-7.0

## John Ayres

Wordware Publishing, Inc.

**Library of Congress Cataloging-in-Publication Data**

Ayres, John.
Delphi graphics and game programming exposed! : with DirectX / by John Ayres.
    p.  cm.
Includes bibliographical references and index.
ISBN 1-55622-637-3 (pbk)
1. Computer games—programming.  2. DirectX.  3. Computer graphics
4. Delphi (Computer file)  I. Title.

QA76.76.C672 A97     1999              99-050392
794.8'15268--dc21                     CIP

ISBN 1-55622-637-3
10 9 8 7 6 5 4 3 2
9912

Delphi is a registered trademark of Inprise Corp.
DirectX is a registered trademark of Microsoft Corp.
Other product names mentioned are used for identification purposes only and may be trademarks of their respective
companies.

Some sounds used in examples and on the CD are from "A Zillion Sounds 2.0" Copyright 1994-98, BeachWare Inc.
SpriteLib Graphics used in examples and illustrations Copyright 1998 by Ari Feldman, SpriteLib License Number
206.104.70.55-905268432

All inquiries for volume purchases of this book should be addressed to Wordware Publishing, Inc., at
the above address. Telephone inquiries may be made by calling:

(972) 423-0090

# *Dedication*

To my first child, Cassandra Marie Ayres. She and my wife were still part of each other during most of the production of this book, and as I write this, her "birth day" draws alarmingly near. I've never known such panic and such joy as children bring to their parents. It will be good to experience the world again through her eyes, as I intend to vicariously relive my childhood through her as best I can. Only a parent knows how the emotions of panic, alarm, joy, and jubilation can intermingle and become one; may your children bring you the same emotional gratification. Hero, mentor, role model, playmate, dance partner, confidant, keeper of secrets, and healer of wounds—to me, all these things add up to Fatherhood. I hope to live up to my daughter's expectations of a father, and may she grow to be more than the sum of her parents.

# Contents

# Contents

# Contents

# Contents

# *Foreword*

Welcome to *Delphi Graphics and Game Programming Exposed! with DirectX*. This excellent book is a joy to read. It takes a difficult subject, game programming, breaks it down into its constituent parts, and renders each facet of the whole in clear, engaging language. The text sparkles like a well-cut stone, and the code lights the way for programmers who want to explore new territory in the world of game programming.

This book introduces programmers to the key facts they need to know to create games with Borland Delphi. It carefully describes graphics programming, DirectX programming, gathering user input, playing sounds and music, programming game hardware, and discovering the right architecture for a robust game.

Many technical books are bought simply because they cover an important subject. For those who love games and graphics, certainly this book meets that requirement. However, the text is given a certain additional luster because its author crafted it so carefully. Over the last few years John Ayres has been slowly developing a reputation as one of the major voices in Delphi programming. The high quality of the books that he works on and the talks that he gives have made him a figure of significant stature to Delphi developers.

When John explains a subject, it stays explained. He writes in well-formed sentences and creates logically structured paragraphs that combine to form the framework of a text that fully elucidates a subject. Some programmers have the skills necessary to write great code, but lack the knowledge of how to craft a useful text that comprehensibly encapsulates their knowledge. Other programmers are gifted with the prerequisite writing skills, but they lack a deep knowledge of their subject. John is gifted in both areas, and as a result his work is interesting, well thought out, and easy to understand.

Because of my love for the Delphi programming environment, I'm particularly pleased that this text does such a fine job of showing how to take advantage of what's best in the Object Pascal language, the Delphi VCL, and Borland's many high-performance tools. Delphi is one of the great, if not the greatest, programming environments ever created. John shows you the right way to take advantage of all that raw power to build robust games that will stand the test of time.

Delphi is indeed one of the best tools available for creating computer games, and John Ayres rises to the challenge of his subject by creating a lucid, easy to understand text that covers the full range of relevant technology. A number of excellent programmers have done much to advance the Delphi programming world. These people include the translator of the DirectX headers: Erik Unger; Delphi R&D members Chuck Jazdzewski and Danny Thorpe; Delphi Games Creator programmers Paul Bearne, John Pullen, and Jeff Kurtz; and DelphiX creator Hiroyuki Hori. To that list of names we can now add John Ayres, who has created an excellent resource of use to all Delphi programmers who aspire to write high-quality game and graphics code.

Charlie Calvert
Borland Developer Relations

# Acknowledgments

While this book may bear only one name on the cover, it is the result of input from many people who made its production possible. In an effort to recognize the contributions of those who helped bring this book to life, I would like to acknowledge and give thanks to the following:

First and foremost, I must thank Erik Unger for his excellent translation of the DirectX headers. Without his dedication to the furthering of Delphi games programming, this book simply would not have been possible. He constantly strives to stay abreast of new DirectX developments, and makes new DirectX headers available almost as soon as Microsoft releases an update. He also has many other headers available for both OpenGL and the Glide API. I hope to shake your hand someday at an Inprise convention somewhere.

I must also mention Ari Feldman, who was generous enough to create the freeware sprite library SpriteLib. SpriteLib is included on the CD, and many of the images from this library are used in the examples and illustrations throughout the book. Ari Feldman's creation allowed me to include some quality artwork whereas little stick men and solid polygons would've been used in its absence.

Additionally, John Marshall provided some of the graphic artwork gracing the examples in the chapter on bitmap manipulation and special effects. John is an awesome artist, and it's an honor and a pleasure to have his work in this book.

Thanks to the folks at Beachware who were generous enough to donate 50 excellent sound effects from their *A Zillion Sounds 2.0* CD. This CD contains thousands of sound effects in WAV format that are perfect for use in many games, from button clicks to explosions and laser blasts. Beachware also offers many other CDs filled with textures and musical interludes that you will find useful in your gaming endeavors. Take a look at http://www.beachware.com.

I must also thank David Strahan. An extraordinary musician, he provided several MIDI music compositions used in some of the examples.

I also owe a debt of gratitude to Eric Best, Mark Harwell, Jeff Amano, and Dr. Jim Beckett for putting up with this extracurricular activity of mine while in the middle of many, many time-critical projects, and for providing me with a nice, quiet place to write on my off hours.

Wordware Publishing deserves a big salute. Jim Hill, Russ Stultz, Beth Kohler, and all the fine people there do a wonderful job. Without Wordware Publishing, many of the more specialized Delphi books would never be published. These more targeted titles help the Delphi community to grow and foster a sense of maturity; may other publishers take note.

Of course, no acknowledgment would be complete without mentioning the people who brought us Delphi: Inprise. Inprise is starting to recognize the existence of the many game programmers out there interested in Delphi. Indeed, both Danny Thorpe and Charlie Calvert (native Borlanders) are big proponents of DirectX programming with Delphi. At last year's Inprise convention, I gave a very successful presentation on Delphi games programming, I believe the first one ever, and I've been invited to repeat it this year. I hope that this increased awareness of Delphi game programmers results in more direct support for DirectX and other core gaming APIs.

I would also like to mention Kenneth Harrison, Mike Tobin, and Burleigh Wood, three great friends of mine who served as sounding boards for my ideas and tolerated my absences from many multiplayer gaming sessions while I wrote. Burleigh even loaned me his force feedback joystick so I could write the force feedback chapter. They took time out of their schedules to look over several of the examples herein, and I appreciate their feedback and criticisms.

Many of you may have heard of the JEDI Project by now. This is an international organization of Delphi developers who are dedicated to converting API headers so that Delphi programmers worldwide have access to a greater range of Windows functionality. The members of this organization, through their many e-mails and discussion threads, provided many of the answers to tough dilemmas experienced while researching many of DirectX's nuances. For more information on the JEDI Project, see the page at the back of the book.

The Delphi Developers of Dallas user group was also very helpful in times of need. I gave many lectures and presentations based on the subject material for this book, and the questions and feedback of the membership helped to solidify and fine-tune many of the topics contained herein.

And were it not for the efforts of the growing community of Delphi game programmers, this book would have had no inspiration. Their efforts are slowly fostering acceptance of Delphi within the gaming industry. Indeed, there are several games being published that are written in Delphi, many of which use either freeware Delphi DirectX components or Erik's DirectX headers included with this book. Keep it up; the next game of the year just might have a "Powered by Delphi" logo somewhere in the About box.

Finally, I must give thanks to my family for putting up with the late nights and long hours it took to finish this project. I owe my wife special thanks and gratitude; she was pregnant with our first child during the course of this activity. Even though she denies it, I know that I've neglected her, and yet she still gives me her unconditional love. Without her constant support and encouragement, I would not have had the patience or desire to continue when the going got tough. Thanks, baby.

# *Introduction*

In the beginning, there was darkness. In this Age of Innocence, the unwashed masses practiced the art of entertainment with small pieces of paper bearing symbolic images of kings, queens, and jesters. Sometimes, they used minute pieces of metal and plastic, shaped like various real-world objects, moving them about on large, colored cardboard sheets in accordance with the runes inscribed upon small white cubes. To the casual observer, all was content, but in the minds of the newest generation born of this age, there was a yearning for more. Unbeknownst to the world, this yearning grew, and soon these young pioneers began working in the dark recesses of colleges and universities to bring about a change that would alter the course of history in ways no learned scholar could have ever imagined. Brandishing vacuum tube sabers and using arcane words of power such as RAM, ROM, Bit, and Byte, these acolytes of technology brought forth a new creation known as the Computer. But, their new creation was naive, and lacked intelligence or sophistication; to control it, they had to use a mystical, magical language known as Code. Thus, the Art was born, and a new era had begun.

The First Age was marked by the genesis of immense, hulking beasts that required enormous resources to sustain life. These new life forms were rare, but typically stood several stories tall and required incredible life support systems to maintain an agreeable environment. These giants were moody and possessed little intelligence, but through great effort, they could be trained to perform incredible feats, for their day. The digital landscape was dotted with few of these behemoths, and their trainers were monk-like in their dedication. Unable to break free of their confines due to the immense size of their charges, these monks were forced to toil maddeningly long hours. Their torturous task of preparing the vegetarian meal of holy leaves consumed by these monsters had them working late into the night, and the Art required to create these holy leaves was arcane indeed.

These monks practiced the great Art in the same dark recesses from whence it was conceived, and the Art grew. The once young pioneers had become pedantic, wizened old masters. These old wizards were still rebellious and, yearning for a new form of entertainment, they used the Art in ways that the Powers That Be felt were unproductive. Away from the watchful eyes of their overseers, they shaped the Art in ways that previously existed only in their dreams.

In the dark hours of the morning, these masters used the Art to coax the new creations into providing their long-sought-after entertainment, and they played games such as Tic-Tac-Toe and Pong. Several of these wizards used the Art to create much more sophisticated forms of entertainment, and played games such as Checkers and Chess with their silicon automatons. In the wake of the First Age, walking in the shadow of the evolving Art, a new form of the Art began to grow.

Like dinosaurs, the reign of these behemoths was relatively short-lived. A new catalyst known as the Corporation had used the knowledge learned in the First Age to effect an evolutionary step known as the Home PC. Thus, the Second Age began.

In the Second Age, the pantheon of overlord gods began to form, controlling the evolution of this new creation from on high. Deities known as Gates and Jobs worked their mystical creation power behind the curtains of reality, but their new creations were protozoan in nature. A step back from their massive predecessors, these new single-cell machines were much less sophisticated and powerful, and teetered on the edge of extinction almost as soon as they had appeared. However, these new creatures had become visible to the unwashed masses, and began to elicit their attention. At first, few of the Untrained could afford to adopt one as a pet, but their popularity grew, and soon many of these creations made their homes on desktops in homes and businesses. The Art, still arcane in nature, had begun to emerge from its dark recesses, and several of the Untrained began to delve into its mystical powers.

The Net, the once-dark netherworld populated solely by the wizards and masters of the Art, has now become a tourist attraction, replete with amusement parks, rest stops, and gift shops. Rumors of new CPUs with speeds in excess of 1,000 MHz are being whispered in the dark corners of cyber cafés and coffee shops. Thus, we stand at the dawn of yet another New Age. As the sun breaks over the distant horizon, its golden, shimmering rays cascading over the silicon juggernaut that stands before us, the prospects of the future are at once both exciting and frightening.

Thus, our journey begins.

## The Purpose of This Book

The primary goal of this book is to teach readers graphics and game programming using 8-bit color images under DirectX in the Delphi environment.

The majority of the book is dedicated to the mechanics of creating a game in Delphi, and will therefore be concerned mainly with exactly how to do something, such as fast flicker-free animation. Some parts address more theoretical issues, such as game design, and are very light in their coverage. Other parts are at a more intermediate level, such as artificial intelligence and optimization techniques. The techniques discussed in this book are very practical and can be put to use right away, as opposed to being academic theory. The goal is to give the Delphi games programmer the tools he/she needs to start competing in the shareware games market right away. This book will not cover marketing, package design, distribution, or other topics that do not deal directly with creating the game.

Due to the popularity of DirectX in the game programming industry, this book does not cover anything related to OpenGL. However, Wordware publishes an excellent OpenGL book aimed at Delphi programmers titled *Delphi Developer's Guide to OpenGL* (ISBN 1-55622-657-8). Although this book is DirectX-specific, some chapters may include code examples that run directly under Windows in order to illustrate a complex topic more clearly. This book is concerned with high-performance graphics programming under DirectX, and as such will concentrate only on full-screen, exclusive mode DirectX programming techniques.

This book will not, as others have, create a "framework" from which examples are drawn, nor will it create wrappers or attempt to hide the low-level DirectX API. This is so that readers become familiar with DirectX, not some artificial abstraction layer that might not work for their purposes. The closest to a "framework" that we'll get in this book is the creation of a baseline application that simply gets a page flipping, full-screen DirectDraw application up and running, including mouse support. This was done in order to simplify the creation of all the examples included in the book, but it certainly doesn't shield the developer from any of the nuances or pitfalls of DirectX programming. If you want to do game programming, you have to get in bed with the operating system, the API, and the hardware.

## Conventions

Descriptive text that details steps for implementing or using a specific technique, or narrative text that explains an algorithm or theory, uses a font style similar to the one used for this sentence. Text that contains program code uses a monospaced font style similar to the code snippet below:

```
{draw the paddle graphic to the back buffer}
SrcRect := Rect(252, 500, 339, 506);
FBackBuffer.BltFast(XPos, YPos, FGraphics, SrcRect,
                    DDBLTFAST_NOCOLORKEY OR DDBLTFAST_WAIT);
```

Additionally, the text contains several callouts that point out a specific detail or area of note that the developer should be aware of. These include notes, tips, cautions, and glossaries.

### Notes

These are general points of interest that detail specific items the developer should keep in mind when using the described techniques.

### Tips

Tips are general suggestions or hints for improving a specific technique. Tips may also point out an alternative to some specific detail of a technique or algorithm.

### Cautions

A caution callout alerts the developer to specific hazards with a technique or algorithm that could potentially crash the application or the system. These are specific details of which the developer should be keenly aware.

### Glossary

Being somewhat of an introductory text for game programming, and as the vast majority of readers of this book will have little to no game programming knowledge, glossary callouts identify specific words or phrases that are commonly used in the game programming industry. Game programming, like many specialty areas, tends to have a language all its own, and these glossary items will help the novice user get up to speed on the various jargon and technical terms used when describing game programming techniques.

## What This Book Is

This book is a tutorial that explains DirectX programming within the Delphi environment. Unfortunately, there are not very many professional Delphi programmers working with DirectX, and there are fewer still who have full-time jobs making games using Delphi. The vast majority of Delphi programmers who will likely pick up this book are application and database programmers professionally, but dabble in game programming at night as a hobby or just to satisfy their curiosity. Thus, this book is aimed at those programmers who are curious and interested in game programming, but have little to no experience. As such, the chapters are arranged in a "how-to" style so that you can easily learn about one aspect of DirectX or another. Additionally, those chapters that deal with DirectX-specific components have a subtle reference layout, so that you can go back and easily find a specific detail about a particular DirectX component or function.

This book could be considered an introductory text for game programmers. To this end, it concentrates on the most common DirectX core components, such as DirectDraw, DirectSound, and DirectInput. Although it covers some advanced techniques, such as force feedback, it is aimed primarily at 2D sprite-based graphics techniques, and does not cover 3D techniques or Direct3D. The techniques herein can be used in scientific or other types of visualization applications, but it is slanted toward game programming.

## What This Book is Not

By necessity, this book is not a tutorial on the use of Delphi or the lexical constructions of the Object Pascal language. This book is also not a DirectX reference. The reference documentation that ships with the DirectX SDK is pretty good, and definitely expansive. Any decent DirectX reference would span many volumes. While many of the more common DirectX function calls are examined in detail, you would be wise to download the DirectX SDK so you can have the full reference documentation at your disposal.

Additionally, since we are concerned only with creating high-performance game and graphics applications, this book does not cover windowed DirectX programming techniques or overlays. Plus, so we can squeeze the maximum amount of performance out of the widest range of hardware, we focus only on 8-bit color video modes, and do not discuss non-palettized video modes.

## Reader Requirements

This book assumes that the reader is familiar with the Delphi IDE and with Object Pascal programming in general. It also helps to have a working knowledge of Windows API programming. While some graphics programming experience is helpful, it is not necessarily a requirement.

## Software Requirements

The applications in this book were tested using Delphi 3, 4, and 5 running under Windows 95 and 98. DirectX is not fully supported under Windows NT, so while some of the examples may work under Windows NT, most will not, and none were tested.

The examples in this book make use of the excellent DirectX header files written by Erik Unger for the JEDI project. You will find these files off of the root of the CD-ROM in a directory labeled DXSDK. This directory should be copied to your hard drive, and you will need to add the path to this directory to Delphi's library path. This can be accomplished by clicking the Tools | Environment Options menu item in the Delphi IDE, selecting the Library tab, and clicking on the button next to the Library Path edit box. Adding the path to the DXSDK in this dialog box and clicking OK should allow Delphi to find the necessary files when compiling the examples.

**Note:** You <u>must</u> add the path to the DXSDK directory to Delphi's Library Path before any of the examples will compile.

## Hardware Requirements

All examples were tested on a Pentium 450 with 32 MB of ram and an 8 MB video card. While this is, at the time of this writing, a respectably advanced machine, the examples should run on anything from Pentium 166 with 16 MB of RAM and a 2 MB video card or higher. Additionally, you will need a sound card and speakers for the examples using sound or music output, as well as a joystick or similar device for examples that retrieve input from game devices. Obviously, you will need a force feedback joystick in order to use any of the examples from the force feedback chapter.

## Chapter Organization

Due to the "how-to" nature of this book, the chapters have been arranged in a way to facilitate an interesting read from cover to cover. However, this book could also be used as a limited reference manual, so the chapters have been arranged in a somewhat logical order to keep similar topics together.

The first few chapters serve as a basic introduction to game programming. Several common concepts and terms are explained early on so as to facilitate an easier understanding of the topics to come. Basic game application architecture is also discussed, including some entry-level graphics programming techniques using regular Windows GDI function calls. DirectX is also introduced at this point, specifically covering DirectDraw.

Many intermediate techniques are then covered. These include techniques for use of the system palette as well as many sprite drawing and manipulation techniques. User input is then covered in some detail, including reading input from keyboard, mouse, and game controllers, such as joysticks, using DirectInput. Force feedback is covered to some extent, although this is a more advanced and specialized topic. Sound and music programming is discussed, examining various ways to output sound and music through both DirectSound and Windows multimedia functions.

Advanced topics include various ways to optimize game applications, as well as artificial intelligence techniques. Several more specific algorithms are covered that detail how to manipulate bitmaps and create graphical special effects. Most of these techniques are wrapped up into a case study application that highlights how these pieces come together to form a complete game. Installation of DirectX is also covered.

# Chapter Summaries

**Chapter 1: The Lure of Game Programming** looks at game programming in general, and examines why the game programming industry is so special in the world of computer science.

**Chapter 2: The Anatomy of a Game** looks at what goes into a game from a high-level perspective. It divides game applications into three constituent parts and examines each in detail.

**Chapter 3: Basic Graphics Programming** introduces the reader to basic concepts in graphics programming. Several Windows GDI graphics programming techniques are discussed in order to prepare the reader for more advanced topics.

**Chapter 4: An Introduction to DirectX** introduces the reader to the world of DirectX programming. DirectX is examined in a general manner, and then DirectDraw is discussed in detail.

**Chapter 5: Palettes** looks at palette control and manipulation from a DirectX application.

**Chapter 6: Sprite Techniques** examines how 2-D sprites work. Several different techniques are discussed, including sprite animation and collision detection.

**Chapter 7: Input Techniques** discusses the various methods for reading input from external devices. The keyboard, joystick, and mouse peripherals are discussed in detail, examining how input can be received using both Win32 API functions as well as DirectInput.

**Chapter 8: Force Feedback** examines the force feedback API and how it can be used to create tactile feedback on hardware devices.

**Chapter 9: Sound and Music** looks at what it takes to output sound and music from a game application. Using both Windows multimedia functions as well as DirectSound, this chapter examines digital audio output, MIDI music output, and CD audio output.

**Chapter 10: Optimization Techniques** discusses various methods to optimize and enhance the performance of applications. These include Delphi compiler settings as well as programmatic techniques.

**Chapter 11: Special Effects** discusses how the Lock method of a DirectDraw surface gives developers incredible control over visual images. Several techniques are discussed for bitmap manipulation as well as dynamic image creation.

**Chapter 12: Artificial Intelligence Techniques** looks at various methods for implementing simplistic reasoning and logic functions for game antagonists. Such topics include finite state machines and pathing techniques.

**Chapter 13: Putting It All Together** takes many of the techniques discussed throughout the book and puts them together to form a full, working game called Delphi Blocks.

**Appendix: Installing DirectX** contains a short but concise explanation of how the DirectSetup API simplifies the process of installing DirectX to a user's machine.

**Glossary** contains an alphabetical listing of all of the glossary entries introduced throughout the book.

# CHAPTER 1: *The Lure of Game Programming*

## THIS CHAPTER COVERS THE FOLLOWING TOPICS:

- The good and bad side of the game programming industry in general
- The requirements of a game development language
- The advantages and disadvantages of using Delphi as a game development platform
- Opportunities within the game programming industry
- The types of games currently under production

What pushes the advance of computing technology more than any other influence? Computer games. What provides a never-ending stream of content for dozens of colorful, flashy magazines? Computer games. What do hundreds of thousands, perhaps millions, of people play in their spare time for entertainment and competition? Computer games. What do the technologically adept talk about in newsgroups, in person, and in e-mail? Computer games. What inspires producers to create major motion pictures that flop at the box office and embarrass the people that both worked on them and created the original concept from which they were spawned? Computer games.

Well, perhaps the computer gaming buzz isn't quite that bad, but the computer gaming industry is a multibillion dollar industry that grows every year, and is filled with enough strife, antagonism, competition, and tactical warfare to fill several novels. Tens of thousands of web sites are dedicated to both the production and play of computer games. Dozens of magazines exist that also cover both sides of the gaming coin. Dozens of books have been written on game programming, such as this one, and even more books cover strategies and tactics for playing specific games. The gaming industry is very competitive and dynamic, and by this very nature, a little hostile. Gaming companies are formed and disbanded at an alarming rate, with new ones being born as others, both old and new, die miserable deaths.

As is true with just about anything in this world, the gaming industry comes with a light side and a dark side. There are many things about the gaming industry that would make most programmers cower in fear, yet there are just as many alluring attributes that serve as a powerful seduction towards pursuing a career in it. Although this book is not geared toward dwelling on the negative aspect of such things, let's start by taking a reality check and examining the dark side of the game programming industry. Then we'll look at why the light side is so attractive to intrepid and enthusiastic programmers.

# The Dark Side of the Game Programming Industry

Game programming and the gaming industry in general have several negative aspects that may dissuade the casual programmer from doing much more than dabbling in it as a hobby. The items we're about to examine should not be considered an exhaustive list of condemning attributes, nor should they be considered a list of excuses for not pursuing a dream. As a purchaser of this book, you're at least a little curious about game programming, and perhaps considering a career change. Don't let these things convince you otherwise. Use the discussion of the following topics merely as food for thought to keep your hopes and plans in perspective.

## Difficult Learning Curve

Computer games push manufacturers to produce better, faster hardware because it is very difficult to produce some gaming effects that perform adequately enough to be believable. Although the PC is now capable of supporting some very intense graphics engines, it was never designed to do so. Without the assistance of dedicated hardware, some games would not be possible without very clever programming solutions.

They say knowledge is power, and that isn't more true than in the game programming industry. A new algorithm for shading or texture mapping more polygons in a shorter amount of time can mean the difference between a best-selling game (and thus a profitable company) or a flop (and thus layoffs, bankruptcy, and failed businesses). Because of this, game programmers and gaming companies tend to guard game programming techniques as if it were a matter of national security. Application programmers benefit from the assistance that Delphi (or MFC) gives them, and they can almost always find some example of how to accomplish their goal somewhere on the web or in a book. Game programmers, on the other hand, are often left to their own devices when attempting to solve a problem. Sure, one can usually find a basic example of how to accomplish a desired effect, but only if it has been done before and the technology is a few months old.

**Microsoft Foundation Classes (MFC):** Microsoft's object-oriented component hierarchy, similar to Delphi's VCL.

By its very nature, in order to create a commercial quality game that can compete with other games on a retail shelf, the programmers must employ advanced mathematical equations, professional quality music and sound, and highly detailed and artistic graphical images. Application programmers, on the other hand, usually have demands no greater than knowledge of client/server programming techniques, middleware, and database methodologies. These demands are by no means easy, but the knowledge for accomplishing these feats is usually more attainable than what a game programmer is called upon to know.

## Long Hours

Everyone logs extended time at the keyboard when under crunch mode. However, game programmers tend to be in crunch mode longer and more often than application programmers. This is often due to promises that the marketing department makes that the engineering department is required to keep. Because the gaming industry is so volatile, game applications need to be completed and out the door before a competitor releases a similar title. This requires game programmers to put in long hours; 16-hour days as a norm are not unheard of. Crunch mode for application programmers typically means 10- to 12-hour days. For the game programmer, it typically means that they sleep in their cube for an hour or two each night, shower at work (if they're lucky enough to have one), and get to go home after the title passes quality control.

 **Tip:** If you're touring a company's offices during an interview, look for cots or blankets in people's cubes. That's a good indication of the type of hard work and dedication you'll be expected to demonstrate.

## Corporate Instability

The gaming industry is dynamic and cutthroat. Because there are so many game companies out there, with more appearing daily, competition is fierce. As technology marches on, generating better, more powerful machines, the demands on gamers rise at an ever increasing rate. The incredible burden on game developers to keep up with the demands of consumers, as well as to keep ahead of competitors, causes the production costs of mainstream game titles to approach that of Hollywood movies. The result is an ever narrowing profit margin.

Unfortunately, this tends to translate into a need for game companies to continually crank out best-selling titles. Extremely large game companies can afford a bad title or two, but smaller companies may be dramatically affected by bad sales of even a single title. This is especially true for startups; if that first title doesn't at least break even, it may be impossible to even meet employee payroll requirements, let alone to find enough capital or investors to fund further projects. Even companies that have been around for years could suddenly find themselves in financial stress after only a few bad games.

With the exception of only a few large gaming companies, this volatility seems to be the norm rather than the exception. This is all the more obvious by the number of computer gaming businesses that come and go daily. The end result is that gaming companies tend to be unstable, and are not a good place to go if you want a job that you can work at until retirement.

# The Light Side of the Game Programming Industry

In stark contrast to its negative aspects, the game programming industry exhibits a number of positive aspects that fuel its continued growth. The game programming industry in general is very exciting, in part due to its dynamic nature, but mostly because of the people you can meet and the technology you will work with.

## Fun and Rewarding

What sounds more exciting: creating a client/server application for tracking customer purchases and transactions (complete with reports and custom querying capabilities), or creating a first-person adventure game that lets you run through castles and destroy evil demons? If you chose the client/server application, close this book right now. Perhaps the coolest and most seductive trait of game programming is that you can use your imagination in creative ways not possible with application programming.

As opposed to conforming to Windows user interface guidelines, the game programmer can create highly specialized and flashy user interface elements that are both fun to code and exciting to behold. Creating buildings, cities, continents, and worlds to explore is tremendously entertaining for both the programmer and the user. While creating a tool that allows someone to accomplish a job quickly and efficiently is rewarding, creating a diversion that immerses one into a world of exploration and wonder for hours on end is even more so.

## Fame and Fortune

A good gaming engine is the holiest of holy grails in the programming industry. Pretty much anyone could make a client/server database if they wanted to (given the right training and education), but few can create a game the likes of Quake, Tomb Raider, or Wing Commander. Those that do, however, are elevated to the status of rock star, and are worshiped by thousands of adoring fans. It's always nice to be complimented for your work, perhaps even developing a reputation for quality products and performance amongst your peers. However, actually having groupies and fans takes the meaning of "good job" a bit further.

Another intriguing aspect of game programming is that it is one of the last remaining industries where individuals have the potential to make a lot of money in a short amount of time. With the continued growth of the Internet, it is feasible for a developer to create a game and make tons of money by selling it online. It may also be possible to sell a completed game to a gaming company, netting a nice large chunk or a share of royalties over time, but this practice is in a decline. Success stories of this nature are more the exception than the rule, but the potential does exist for a hard-working, dedicated game programmer to transform his or her labor of love into a cash cow.

**Tip:** If you're lucky, your company will agree to give you a cut of the royalties of any game you work on. Unfortunately, this is a rare and vanishing benefit, but could potentially make you a lot of money if the game sells well.

## The People

A psychology major could probably write a doctoral thesis on how the personalities of people in their chosen industry seem to be very similar. This at least seems true of those in the programming profession. What this means is that you'll most likely be working with people of similar interests, usually resulting in friendships and group social activities. Many gaming companies double as sites for late-night Dungeons and Dragons sessions, impromptu multiplayer Quake tournaments, and any number of other fun recreational activities. People in the game programming industry tend to be intelligent and have a good sense of humor, and in general are very enjoyable to work with.

## Game Programming, In Delphi?

When most people hear about Delphi, they think of rapid database application development. They think of its uses in the corporate environment as a wonderful tool for making myriad database accessing applications, a task for which it is indeed well suited. They compare it to other RAD tools like Visual Basic and PowerBuilder, contrasting their relative strengths and weaknesses in data access, speed, scalability, etc. This attitude has been prevalent since Delphi 1, and is indeed one of the reasons Delphi has done so well. Unfortunately, most people do not consider Delphi to be a viable choice for any other type of application development. Considering the fact that Delphi is built on a long line of well-used Pascal compilers, has full access to the Windows API, creates actual executable binary code, and shares the same back-end linker with Inprise's excellent C++ product, Delphi is indeed capable of doing much more than just enterprise-wide database applications.

In the game programming industry, the dominant language in the U.S. is C/C++. Let's think for a moment why that may be the case. Specifically, let's consider what could arguably be the most important attributes that a development language must offer in order for it to be considered a viable platform for games development.

1. It must compile fast, natively executable code. C/C++ offers this, and indeed you can find benchmarks that supposedly prove which compiler offers the fastest code. However, Delphi uses the same back-end linker that C++ Builder uses, and its compiled code is as fast as that of C++ Builder. Besides, the most computationally intensive parts of gaming applications are usually written in hand-optimized assembly in order to gain the maximum speed advantage. C/C++ may have a few lexical tricks that allow one to squeeze an extra clock cycle or two out of a few instructions, but you can accomplish the same task in Delphi with creative programming efforts. In the speed department, some C/C++ compilers may create faster compiled code than Delphi, but you can always make up for it where it counts using hand-optimized assembly (just like the C/C++ boys do). Remember, a Pentium 166 with 16 MB of RAM is considered obsolete by today's standards, so these marginal speed advantages offered by some C/C++ compilers are much less important than they used to be. The bottom line is that Delphi is as fast as most C/C++ compilers when it comes to the natively compiled form of raw code, and when speed is absolutely essential, Delphi can compile hand-optimized assembly language as well as any C/C++ compiler.

2. It must offer true pointer access to memory. As with C/C++, it's quite easy in Delphi to create a pointer, point it to some location in memory, and commence reading or writing as necessary. Like C/C++, Delphi also allows you to perform pointer arithmetic, moving the location to which the pointer points. This is a very powerful technique which, when used incorrectly, can cause spectacular system-wide crashes. C/C++ does not have any advantages over Delphi when it comes to using pointers.

3. It must offer the ability to manage memory allocation. This goes hand in hand with the ability to use pointers. Game applications typically push the limit on the hardware, and some must specifically manage the memory used by the application in order to realize maximum performance. Like C/C++, Delphi offers many ways to allocate memory, from the automatic memory management offered by the VCL, all the way to Pascal commands for memory management and Windows API functions for allocating and deallocating memory.

4. It must offer full access to operating system resources. Again, just like C/C++, Delphi has full, open access to the entire Windows API. Indeed, Delphi can use any DLL or type library to which it has an import unit. This is one area where C/C++ does have an advantage over Delphi. Since Windows is written in C/C++, DLLs and other resources created by Microsoft and other third-party developers typically have header units for C/C++

access before someone translates it into a Delphi unit. However, thanks to the efforts of the JEDI Project and other individuals, Delphi import units for hundreds of APIs are becoming available to the general public. Typically, Delphi will probably always be one step behind on access to the latest technologies. However, it's not too difficult a task to convert C/C++ headers into Delphi units, and you can usually find the converted unit on the Web or buy one from a Delphi vendor.

Most people will argue that there are several more attributes by which a development language must be judged before determining if it is a viable games development platform. As we've discussed, Delphi meets or exceeds all expectations for the above requirements, and could probably do the same for any other requirement that one could think of. Pascal is an old language; it's been around for quite a while, and is mature, stable, and proven.

It's unfortunate that many people still think of Pascal as a beginner's language, fit for little more than hobby applications. This is probably due to the irrational Western mentality that if something looks complex, or if it is hard to understand, it must be powerful. Bear in mind that a high-level language like C/C++ or Pascal is just an interface to assembly language that is easier for humans to understand. Each language has a few small advantages over the other, but ultimately an application written in either language is transformed into a final assembly language form. The only differences lay in how this transformation is accomplished by the compiler, and Delphi's compiler can create assembly language that competes with the best of them.

## Delphi as a Games Development Platform

So, Delphi is indeed a viable game development platform. What, then, can we expect to encounter when developing a game using Delphi? Delphi's incredible debugging features will be almost unusable if you are creating a DirectX game, primarily because of how DirectX monkeys with the display hardware. However, certain aspects of how the VCL encapsulates the Windows API will take a lot of the drudgery out of DirectX programming, and will indeed make some tasks extremely easy. Most notably, the TBitmap object will be very useful for loading graphics into DirectX memory blocks, and the TCanvas object can be quite handy when performing standard GDI functions, such as outputting text to the screen. Of course, if you will be using Delphi to create non-DirectX games, the full power of the debugging features as well as the GDI encapsulation will make the task of programming a game just as easy as that of developing a database application. In this book, we will focus on creating DirectX games, and we will examine how the VCL can make some aspects of DirectX programming almost trivial.

As a whole, Delphi offers many advantages over other game development platforms. Every language has advantages and disadvantages over every other, which is why there are so many languages to choose from. While the following discussion is by no means an exhaustive look at Delphi versus C/C++, Delphi does have some specific advantages and disadvantages when compared to C/C++ that merit further investigation.

## Advantages

This is a truly opinionated and arguable statement, but Delphi's Object Pascal is a much better language than C/C++ for two reasons: It is not as arcane, and it is much stronger typed. While it is possible to write easily understandable code in C/C++, it is just as easy to write code that is completely unintelligible and unmanageable. C/C++ has a precompiler that allows one to redefine function names (among other things). While this can be quite useful in some instances, if used indiscriminately it can lead to a major headache when trying to decipher what a piece of code accomplishes. C/C++ has many other language constructs that allow one to write very archaic instructions decipherable only by its author or a C/C++ guru. The primary reason this is important is because, in today's development shops, a section of code may be written by one programmer but modified or updated by several others. It is an incredible waste of time and energy if a programmer tasked with the responsibility of updating a section of code has to spend several hours just determining what it does. The archaic quality of C/C++ code, which can be worsened by arrogant or apathetic programmers, tends to make the arduous task of modifying existing code very difficult, if not impossible. Alternatively, Pascal syntax is closer to regular English, and although it is possible to write some very arcane Pascal code, it is typically much easier to understand from a glance than C/C++. Some will argue that C/C++ was written by programmers for programmers, resulting in the greatly abbreviated lexical tokens perpetuating the language. While it is true that this may save a few keystrokes, in the opinion of this writer, Pascal syntax is much easier to understand from a brief glance and its format and construction make it much easier to decipher an algorithm from its implementation.

This goes along with the strong typing imposed by Pascal compilers. Pascal is used as a beginner's language in universities and colleges because it forces programmers to write in a very structured, easily understood manner. The result is that programmers are forced to develop good programming practices. C/C++'s language structure is much more open and unrestricted. While this does allow one to perform some lexical tricks that may be difficult to reproduce in Delphi, it can result in code containing bugs that are very difficult to find. Delphi's strongly typed compiler helps find logical errors and mistakes that may have compiled without so much as a warning in a C/C++ compiler. Writing Delphi code is never bug free, but the strong typing imposed by its compiler helps the programmer find some bugs faster than would be possible with the same code in a C/C++ compiler.

Another great advantage to using Delphi is the overall attitude of the Delphi community at large. Overall, the Delphi community has a very helpful attitude.

There are literally thousands of Delphi sites featuring thousands and thousands of free objects, code tips, and applications with source code. There are dozens of sites available that deal specifically with Delphi game programming, and there are several freely available game programming examples and objects, complete with source code. The JEDI Project, the Delphi Games Creator, and DelphiX are just a few examples of the type of free source code that one can obtain when searching the Web for Delphi game programming knowledge (many of these are contained on the accompanying CD). While you can find just as many (if not more) resources for C/C++ game programming, the Delphi community has an overall helpful attitude, indicative of the type of Delphi programmers that exist in the world.

## Disadvantages

The biggest disadvantage that one may face when pursuing Delphi game programming is in the lack of knowledge available in the industry. Almost every book you see discussing game programming will contain examples written in C/C++. Fortunately, the algorithms discussed in these books can be implemented in just about any language, but the code examples will be almost worthless unless you have a working knowledge of C/C++. This may require the aspiring Delphi game programmer to take a course or two in C/C++ in order to gain the knowledge to put the examples in the myriad of C/C++ game programming books to work in Object Pascal. Unfortunately, the result is an increased learning curve for future Delphi game programmers. It is interesting to note that when Delphi appeared several prominent figures in the game programming industry took note of its abilities and even heralded it as the next great game development platform. The editor of a major gaming industry periodical even predicted that the best games of the coming year would be written in Delphi. This same periodical, and others, have run several articles illustrating game programming techniques using Delphi, written by some of the most visible programmers in the Delphi industry (most notably Charlie Calvert). Hopefully in the future we will see more books written about game programming in Delphi, spreading the knowledge of game application algorithms and generating more jobs for the Delphi games programmer.

Another major disadvantage already touched upon is the fact that Delphi programmers will probably have slower access to the newest programming technologies than C/C++ programmers. We can use DirectX technology as the perfect example. Microsoft has seen fit not to include a type library for the DirectX COM objects. Had a type library been included, Delphi could directly import the library and offer developers immediate access to all of the functions and procedures offered by DirectX. Instead, Delphi developers must translate the C/C++ headers that define the function calls, constants, and data structures by hand. This is a very onerous, time-consuming task, prone to errors that may be difficult to fix. Unfortunately, this means that most Delphi programmers must either write an import unit themselves or wait for one to be made available (for free or for purchase) before using the latest technologies. Thanks to the efforts of the JEDI Project and the individuals participating in it, many technologies previously out of reach of Delphi programmers are now becoming available. Indeed, Erik Unger, a JEDI Project participant, wrote the DirectX import units around which this book is based. Hopefully in the future we will see more cooperation between Microsoft and Inprise, which will result in immediate access to the latest technology by Delphi programmers.

## Opportunities

The game programming industry is as competitive and hostile as the movie production industry. Venture capitalists and investors are quick to throw millions of dollars—more than $2.5 billion a year— at promising startups in hopes of grabbing a piece of the pie. Production costs of games typically average in the millions, and game companies rise and fall almost as frequently as most people change socks. In such a volatile environment, how can one expect to make any progress without being trampled?

Fortunately, the gaming industry is one of the few industries in which someone can compete from their garage or home office. For example, take the game Solitaire, a standard game shipping with Windows. Solitaire is arguably the most popular game in existence today. Probably everyone who has ever taken a look at Windows has played it at least once, and there are many who play it daily. This is a simple game that by no means pushes the envelope of technology, yet it offers an addictive, entertaining pastime that many people enjoy. A similar phenomenon, Tetris, has been copied and cloned to the point where you can find freeware Delphi Tetris components ready to be dropped on a form for instant gaming satisfaction. Theoretically, if Solitaire and Tetris can be such runaway hits, anyone with a good idea that translates into a simplistic game can do just as well.

For example, take a look at Deer Hunter. It's a relatively simplistic game using technology that is well documented, yet it is one of the best-selling games in recent history. It took the developers three months to complete, and it is certainly nothing that would be beyond the reach of a Delphi developer. Its concept is simple, it's aimed at the mass market, and the price point is right (it runs for about $20).

With the global distribution available in the form of the Internet, and third-party companies offering the ability to take credit card orders for your software (for a nominal fee or percentage), it is possible for even the most remote programmer to compete with the big boys. The market for game software is much more open than the vertical markets (such as exist for word processors and spread sheets), and has a wider audience than that available for niche markets. Although you may not get rich from selling a $5 shareware game, you could become quite wealthy by selling several $5 to $10 games.

As a reality check, bear in mind that the process of making games is no longer a one-man operation. Most games consist of good programming, good graphics, and good sound, and the combination of programmer, artist, and musician would be the equivalent of a modern-day Renaissance man. Indeed, to compete with such games as Quake, Wing Commander, or StarCraft, a team of several programmers, artists, content writers, game designers, actors, musicians, and sound engineers would be required to make a serious effort. Even for the most simplistic game, the talents of an artist should be sought out for all but the most elementary of graphical resources. Although it is possible to compete from one's garage, employing the talents of several individuals may be required to meet the demands of your users.

## Untapped Markets

The most actively pursued market for games are males from age 16 to 25 who buy several games a year. These are what you would call "hard-core gamers," and are the type of individuals who buy games like Quake, Tomb Raider, and Command & Conquer. This market is the most competitive, results in the biggest profit margin, and is pretty tied up by all of the big names in the game programming industry. It is these types of people who demand games that would require the aforementioned team of people to make any serious effort to create.

Are males ages 16 to 25 the only demographic to which games should be marketed? Certainly not. There are many untapped age groups and individuals that potentially offer an even greater market share of the gaming industry.

### Children

Children's software can be big business, with companies like Microsoft and others offering software that interacts with animatronic dolls or other devices. However, given the wide range of age groups and the commensurate knowledge to be learned at these ages, a plethora of software can be aimed at this group that combines education with entertainment. Several big-name companies are starting to dominate in this market, but there is still a lack of software for certain age groups that could be filled by the enthusiastic Delphi game programmer.

### Females

Women and girls use computers just as much as men and boys do, yet there is an incredible void in available software aimed specifically at this group. In a very generalized manner of speaking, most gaming software aimed at males is violent, bloody, and very fast paced. Taking into account that there are exceptions for every rule, this type of software typically does not interest most females. A huge untapped market exists for game software aimed specifically at women and younger girls, and any research into recent articles in gaming magazines can turn up scores of discussions and analyses of the types of games that would do well with this group.

### Casual Gamers

This group is starting to receive a lot of press coverage. A seemingly elusive and hard to reach group, the casual gamer is one who uses his or her computer for entertainment, but does not play the games aimed at hard-core gamers. These people like Solitaire and Tetris, and include everyone from housewives/househusbands taking a break while the baby sleeps to business people looking for something to do during lunch. Typically, this group doesn't like games that require long commitments, as you would see in games like Shogo or Final Fantasy. They like games that you can play quickly, something you can drop into and out of during lunch or a quick break. Many people are now trying to market to this group, and some are having better luck than others. This group presents the largest potential, as there are many more housewives/househusbands and business people out there than there are hard-core gamers.

**Note:** For a look at some professional games written in Delphi targeted for this market, visit http://www.gametropolis.com.

# Types of Games

There are almost as many game type categories as there are games. Limited only by the imagination of the programmer, a game can take literally any form, as long as it is entertaining and interactive. There are probably many more game genres left to be discovered by inventive programmers than what is listed here. When Id came out with Wolfenstein 3D, and later Doom, an entirely new category was launched that spawned many successful imitations. Games such as Dune 2 and WarCraft heralded the real-time strategy genre, perhaps even more popular than first-person shooters. Below is an arbitrary categorization of different game genres, discussing the features typically implemented in a game of that category. Delphi, like C/C++, is adequately suited for producing games that fit into any category.

### Real-Time Strategy

This genre, made popular by games such as Dune 2 and Command & Conquer, is one of the most prevalent in the industry. Real-time strategy games are typically war games that require the user to manage various units and other resources, attacking opponents and gathering supplies while the computer (or other human opponents) does the same. This action takes place in real time, meaning that everyone's activity occurs simultaneously and continuously, and while the player is gathering resources in one area, other units owned by that player may be under attack somewhere else. Games such as StarCraft, Command & Conquer, and Myth all fall under this category.

## Turn-Based Strategy

This category is similar to real-time strategy, in that these games are typically war games where the user manages various units and resources. However, unlike real-time strategy games, the action in a turn-based strategy game does not happen simultaneously. One player takes a turn ordering units to attack, defend, or gather supplies, while all other players wait. When the current player is finished, the next player in line takes a turn. Games such as X-Com and Civilization fall under this category.

## First-Person Shooters

By far the most popular of all games, first-person shooters place the user in a virtual world, offering a first-person perspective of the surroundings and featuring freedom of movement and interaction with the virtual environment. These games typically have a multiplayer aspect, and offer a feature known as deathmatch. In a deathmatch, players usually hunt each other down in a virtual game of tag. Highly addictive and incredibly entertaining, games in this category are usually the most complex and competitive of all games in the entire industry. Games such as Quake, Halflife, and X-Wing vs. Tie Fighter fall under this category.

## Adventure Games

While some first-person shooters could arguably be categorized under this heading, adventure games typically portray a virtual world with the player depicted in a third-person environment, usually in an isometric perspective. Interaction with the environment is usually very detailed and extensive, and a complex plot line gets the player involved in the story around which the game is based. Games such as the Ultima series and Fallout are in this category.

## Action Games

This broad category involves games that have more action than substance, such as pinball games and arcade style games. Quick action is the focus of these games, and while there may be a little bit of a plot line or "purpose," it usually serves as little more than a thin justification for the action taking place. These "twitch" games are fun, highly addictive, and do not require long-term commitment. Games such as Asteroids and Missile Command fall under this category.

## Puzzle Games

Another broad category, puzzle games are games of logic that challenge players to exercise their cerebral muscles. Typically, they are abstract games that involve various fundamental abilities such as pattern matching or color grouping. This category includes games such as Tetris or Lose Your Marbles.

## Sports Games

Arguably a category all its own, sports games are computerized simulations of various real-world sports. Several big development houses have created some very realistic simulations of various sports, going so far as to include current rosters of professional athletes, their likenesses, and an estimation of their talents. Games such as NHL 99, Madden 99, and BFL fall under this category.

## Board and Card Games

Perhaps the most common category for casual game programmers, this category is composed of games that could be played with cards, dice, or similar real-world gaming instruments. Typically, they simulate well-known games such as chess, checkers, or poker. These games are typically the easiest for first- time game programmers to create, as they tend to have well-defined rules that translate into well-structured algorithms, and their graphical requirements are not as severe as those of other games. Games such as FreeCell and Monopoly are in this category.

## Simulations

More a software toy than a game, these are applications that attempt to simulate some real-world process as precisely and accurately as possible. They tend to be very detailed, and while fun, typically require a long-term commitment from the player in order to obtain maximum gaming pleasure. This commitment is required in order to see the simulation grow from a beginning or newborn stage into a mature, elder stage. Games such as Sim City and Sim Tower fall under this category.

# Windows, Delphi, and Games

It goes without saying that Windows 95/98 is the most popular platform for computer games. Delphi, as we've discussed, is as powerful and capable as C/C++ when it comes to making games (or any type of Windows application, for that matter). Given the fact that there are many open markets as yet untapped by the big names in the gaming industry, there exists a huge potential for the enthusiastic and dedicated Delphi game programmer to compete and make a profit. Although this book won't show you how to design or market your game, it will show you the basics of game and graphics programming that will serve as a starting point for a future in game programming.

## Summary

In this chapter, we discussed several aspects about game programming in general and Delphi in particular as it relates to game programming. When contemplating a game application concept or analyzing Delphi as a game development platform, it is important to keep these points in mind:

■ As is true with just about anything in this world, the gaming industry comes with a light side and a dark side. There are many things about the gaming industry that would make most programmers cower in fear, yet there are just as many alluring attributes that serve as a powerful seduction towards pursuing a career in it. In general, the game programming industry is plagued by difficult learning curves, long hours, and an unstable business environment. However, programming games can be a lot of fun and very rewarding, and can earn the successful individual a substantial amount of notoriety and wealth.

■ When most people hear about Delphi, they think of rapid database application development. They think of its uses in the corporate environment as a wonderful tool for making myriad database accessing applications, a task for which it is indeed well suited. However, in the game programming industry, the dominant language in the U.S. is C/C++. If the most important attributes for a language to be considered a viable game development platform are fast, natively executable code, true pointer access to memory, memory allocation, and access to operating system resources, Delphi easily meets or exceeds all of these requirements. Ultimately, Delphi is as capable a game development platform as any other language, including C/C++.

■ As a whole, Delphi offers many advantages over other game development platforms. Every language has advantages and disadvantages over every other, which is why there are so many languages to choose from. In general, the Object Pascal language is much more readable than C/C++, and its strong typing typically results in decreased debug time. There are also many free resources available to the Delphi programmer, and several enthusiastic mailing lists, web sites, and organizations dedicated to helping Delphi programmers at all experience levels. Unfortunately, most of the current game programming knowledge exists in the form of C/C++ examples, requiring the potential Delphi game programmer to have at least a passing knowledge of C/C++ in order to grow and learn new game programming algorithms. Delphi programmers also typically do not have immediate access to new technologies introduced by Microsoft due to lack of type libraries and Object Pascal import units.

■ The game programming industry is as competitive and hostile as the movie production industry. Venture capitalists and investors are quick to throw millions of dollars—more than $2.5 billion a year—at promising startups in hopes of grabbing a piece of the pie. Fortunately, the gaming industry is one of the few industries in which someone can compete from their garage or home office. Games such as Solitaire, Deer Hunter, and Tetris are very popular and successful, even though they don't push the envelope of current technology. With the global distribution available in the form of the Internet, and third-party companies offering the ability to take credit card orders for your software (for a nominal fee or percentage), it is possible for even the most remote programmer to compete with the big boys. Untapped markets such as the homebound, children, women, and casual gamers represent a potentially huge opportunity for enterprising Delphi game programmers.

■ There are almost as many game type categories as there are games. Limited only by the imagination of the programmer, a game can take literally any form, as long as it is entertaining and interactive. In general, games can be segregated into the following categories: real-time strategy, turn-based strategy, first-person shooters, adventure, action, puzzle, sports, board and card games, and simulations. Delphi is suited for creating games that fit into any of these categories.

# CHAPTER 2: *The Anatomy of a Game*

Application design is an art unto itself. Several books have been written on the topic of effectively designing an application. Indeed, in the computer industry one can even specialize in such a discipline (if you're a programmer, you probably know someone with the title of "Chief Architect" who only designs applications and no longer writes any code). Application design can be childishly simple or diabolically complex, depending on the task the final application must perform.

However, from a purely academic perspective, all computer applications pretty much do the same thing: receive input, process it, and create output. In typical business applications, the input comes from either a device (commonly a mouse or keyboard) or a database connection, the processing typically involves mathematical calculations, and the output generally results in either a spreadsheet style of data display or (more excitingly) a colorful graph. By contrast, game applications must accept input from several different devices, processing the input by moving onscreen objects around, performing collision detection, playing sound and music as the situation demands, and deciding if missiles are fired or something has died. A game application's output involves drawing the results of these frantic calculations to the screen.

Game application architecture can vary as wildly as business application architecture. However, all games must perform similar actions, usually in a common order. In this chapter, we examine the various components that make up a typical game application. We will study an arbitrary application architecture that can be used for games, and we will discuss the individual subsystems of this architecture, focusing on the functionality they provide to the overall game application. The focus on this chapter is on the theory of game application construction, and as such presents very little actual code examples. However, several pseudo-code listings will be illustrated that encapsulate the techniques discussed in this chapter. Additionally, a simplistic game example is included on the CD for this chapter that demonstrates this architectural theory in a more real-world implementation.

# Game Dissection: The Vital Organs

Games can be incredibly complex, with several different subsystems performing any number of functions that control the overall application. Many developers may feel a little overwhelmed by all the details that go into creating a game. However, like most things in life, game programming is not nearly as complex as one might at first imagine. It's certainly not an easy discipline; one must be very skilled in their talents and have the ability to apply them in creative ways in order to produce new and exciting effects and gaming environments. Fortunately, dozens of books have been written that discuss various game programming techniques in many genres, from 2-D turn-based board games to 3-D fast action, first-person shooters. Anything that one person can learn, another person can learn as well; game programming is a constant quest for new knowledge and new techniques, which gives the field one of its many enticements.

The many game programming books on the market (this one included) typically deal with very specific game programming techniques that demonstrate how some particular game environment or effect can be produced. This allows one to learn specific talents in specific areas, possibly specializing if so desired. While game programming is as varied and diversified as business applications programming, when viewed from a high-level standpoint all games can be reduced to three necessary parts: graphics, sound, and input.

## Graphics

With the exception of user interactivity, graphics are probably the most important part of a game in today's market. Game developers are now using software that was once only used by movie and television production houses to develop graphics for games, and the results are nothing short of amazing. Tools such as TrueSpace, LightWave, and SoftImage, which have all been used to create outstanding special effects for both movies and television, are a necessity for serious game graphics production. Almost any major game includes several animated sequences (usually produced by one of these tools), some of which are on par with action sequences seen in a major motion picture. Game element graphics have also seen amazing improvement over the last several years, with many interactive elements starting their lives as high-resolution 3-D models. However, as important as good graphics are to today's games, it is equally important to realize that just because a game has good graphics, it does not mean it is fun to play. Too many games are made with the theory that if you put in good graphics, users will buy it. Graphics are important for that first impression when a potential consumer picks up the box to have a look, and indeed for the continued enjoyment of the game, but graphics should functionally act as only a complement to the overall game design and playability.

Game graphics can further be broken down into two elements: background graphics and interactive images, or sprites.

## Background Graphics

Background graphics set the mood for a game. Usually, they define the environment in which the game world is set, and they provide a reference point for the user. Typically, background graphics are static, and represent objects that the user either cannot or rarely interacts with. For example, background graphics include the vehicle fuselage of a cockpit in a flight simulator, the radar control console casing in a real-time strategy game, or the surface over which puzzle pieces slide in a pattern matching game. Sometimes, background images may animate in some way, providing more realism to the environment and enhancing the overall gameplay experience (for example, moving the heads of spectators in a tennis game).

## Interactive Images

The most important graphical element of any game are those graphics with which the user interacts. Either by directly controlling the movement and actions of a specific graphical element, or by indirectly affecting the movement and actions of graphical elements through the direct manipulation of other graphical elements, it is these interactive images that represent the actual game play. Typically called sprites, these images generally move about the screen, animating as they change position from place to place.

**sprite:** An image that animates and moves around the screen in some fashion. Typically associated with images that the user can interact with, either directly or through interaction with other sprites.

Sprites take many forms, and serve as a powerful element for increasing realism and improving a user's overall enjoyment of the game. For example, sprites include asteroids in a space game, attacking orcs in a war game, and even your brave soldiers who are about to get butchered by the attacking orcish hordes. Sprites can even be used solely for improved background animation, such as birds flying overhead or vultures picking at the remains of dead orcs and human soldiers.

> **Note:** Creating art for games can be difficult if you're not an artist and do not have access to one. However, there are several freeware art libraries available on the web that contain sprite images. Check out the SpriteLib sprite graphics library by Ari Feldman on the accompanying CD.

## Sound

Sounds in a game application can add depth and richness that is simply impossible to achieve with graphics alone. Sound immerses a player in the world represented by the game, increasing both the realism and the enjoyment of the experience. Technically speaking, it is possible to create a game without sounds of any kind. However, such a game, while possibly enjoyable, will have a feeling of incompleteness and will leave the user with the impression that something is missing.

Just as graphics have progressed from their once-primitive lines and flat polygons, game sound creation has become a specialty field in its own right. Indeed, it is now common for well-known rock musicians to provide music for today's hottest games. Larger game companies are hiring Hollywood sound designers to create realistic sound effects. Even some movie and television production houses are now selling their sound effect libraries for use in game applications.

Game sounds can be broken into two component parts: sound effects and music.

### Sound Effects

Good sound effects can add great depth to any game. An Asteroids clone might be fun enough to play without sound effects, but when you add the whine of laser blasts, the explosions of destroyed asteroids, the thrust of acceleration, and some blips and whirs to go along with normal UI elements such as buttons and menus, the game takes on a whole new dimension. Hearing the scrape of metal as your hero unsheathes his sword and a solid thud as the orcish leader's head falls to the ground after being severed adds both realism and drama to a game. Such a sequence would not be nearly as effective without the accompanying sound effects.

More importantly, sound effects can give the user audible clues as to changing game states. The typical game screen is busy enough, with the user trying desperately to outrun marauding pirates while avoiding cannon fire and shallow water and rocks. Sound effects can relate important information to the player, freeing her up to attend to the situation at hand instead of scanning the game interface to make sure that some critical system isn't on the verge of destruction. For example, a space flight simulator may feature a ship with a shield rating. As the user flies around trying to avoid destruction while accumulating the maximum number of kills, the shield readout must be continually checked to make sure that the ship is still safe from harm. Implementing a sound effect such as a voice saying "Shields Low" will both free the user from a repetitive task as well as induce a sense of urgency when the user hears the sound effect. Another example of this type of audible clue is the typical "We're under attack" heard in real-time strategy games. This frees the user from constantly scanning the map, which can quickly become a tiring chore, if not impossible. Even simple clicks or beeps on buttons and menus can greatly add to the realism and enjoyment of a game.

**Note:** Magazines and books that cover the movie industry, particularly the special effects field, sometimes contain information on how to make sound effects. These same techniques can be used to create awesome sound effects for games.

## Music

Like sound effects, music can add a tremendous amount of depth to a game. Music helps to define the mood for a game, and can work wonders for building tension during climactic moments, a sense of euphoria after a victory, or a sense of melancholy after a defeat. The best games use music that changes with the context of the game, building a sense of anticipation during slow moments just before an ambush, and changing to a heart-pounding rhythm during the attack. The best example of the effective use of music to evoke emotions is in movies. Pay attention to how ballads can produce a feeling of romance or loss, and how anthems can just as effectively make you feel king of the world. A game that can use music as effectively as a movie will generally provide a greater level of enjoyment for its users.

Unlike the other constituent elements of a game application, music may not always be an appropriate addition. While it may add depth to some games, it may be distracting or even a bit annoying in others. An upbeat, urgent rhythm played with electric guitars may be almost essential to a fast-paced aerial dogfight game, but the user may prefer total silence when playing a deeply tactical game such as chess. Thus, it is usually a good practice to include an option to turn off music (or even sound effects).

## User Input

User input is by far the most important part of any game. It is the reason that a game is played in the first place. Without a means of providing some sort of interface so that the user can interact with the game elements, the game is little more than an elaborate animation. The entertainment value of a game comes from this user/game element interaction. If the user wanted to watch a non-interactive animation, she would have watched TV or gone to the movies.

Providing a natural means of user interaction is a very important part in the overall design of a game. While a game may be pretty to look at and pleasant to listen to, if it is difficult to use, it won't be used long. The most appropriate means of user interaction will depend on the type of game. Obviously, flight simulators would best be controlled through a joystick of some sort, while games with lots of moving pieces that can be repositioned freely should probably use the mouse. For other games, the keyboard may be the most natural means of user interaction. Regardless of the most appropriate input device, it is good practice to support input from a wide variety of input devices. This gives users more control over what feels intuitive to them, as some may feel more comfortable using the keyboard over the mouse, and vice versa.

User input can be broken down into two parts: standard input devices and peripheral input devices.

## Standard Input Devices

Since games must provide some method for the user to interact with the game world, it would be nice to know if the end user's machine had a specific input device attached. Fortunately, it would be a rare occurrence indeed to find a machine that did not come with both a mouse and a keyboard as standard attachments. For many games, this combination of input devices works best, and most games may not need any other type of input device. Therefore, it is pretty safe to assume that the user will have at least the mouse and the keyboard available as input devices. Most, if not all, games now support both of these devices, in addition to others.

## Peripheral Input Devices

Peripheral input devices consist of game controllers that are not standard equipment with new computers. Such devices include joysticks, game pads, rudder pedals, and a plethora of other types of input devices of every shape and size. These devices are generally suited for use with "twitch" style games that require good hand-eye coordination, such as flight simulators or first-person shooters. However, several of the more esoteric devices may provide a much more intuitive feel for the user, as opposed to using just a plain keyboard or mouse or joystick. Fortunately, most of these devices are accessed programmatically in a very standard way. This allows the developer to support several devices using the same code base, although some specialty devices may require slightly different coding methods to support their use. As stated above, it is a good practice to support a wide variety of peripheral input devices so that the user will have a choice as to which device feels the most comfortable.

# Real-Time Event-Driven Programming

Anyone who has done any amount of serious work in Delphi is now intimately familiar with the event-driven model of application programming. Delphi developers routinely write event handlers, either by creating them manually through the IDE or by hooking them up programmatically in code. It's an inescapable practice, and it makes application coding and debugging both faster and easier.

Game programming, under Delphi or any language, is similar to application programming in many ways, but it is fundamentally different in a few areas. While object-oriented game programming shares the practice of hooking up events, there's a slight twist to this model that is required for supporting the types of games that are commonly created today.

The model most programmers, especially Delphi programmers, are now very familiar and comfortable with is known as event-driven programming. The application is written in such a way that its functionality is triggered by external events. These events can take the form of programmatic signals from other applications or devices, but for the most part, these events are triggered from user input. Until some event is triggered, it simply sits there waiting for an event to fire. For example, consider a word processor. It might have a few events that are triggered from a programmatic source, such as an autosave function fired off of a timer event. However, if you open a word processor and do nothing, it will simply sit there until the user either presses a keyboard button or activates something with the mouse. Event-driven programming is a very effective and useful method by which very robust applications can be effectively written.

Game applications, on the other hand, are in continuous motion. Events are constantly being fired based on the current game world situation, and the application continues to process with or without user input. This is the most fundamental difference between game programming and application programming, and is known as the real-time event-driven model. The game application cannot sit there and wait until the user moves the joystick before continuing. The user expects enemy ships and objects to be in constant motion, and would probably be surprised if they were not killed in some spectacular way if they just sat there. Sure, some games are written with the same event-driven model as regular applications, such as a Solitaire game, a chess game, or some other turn-based game. However, arcade-style action games that exhibit constant motion must be written using the real-time event-driven model.

**Note:** It is possible to use Delphi's input events such as OnKeyDown to provide event-driven input to a game. However, while this may work for some games, this is generally not the best approach. We'll look at more desirable techniques in Chapter 7, Input Techniques.

# Basic Game Architecture

There are probably as many different ways to design and architect game application code as there are game applications themselves. Each game will have unique and individual requirements based on the style of game and what it does. However, most games must perform similar tasks, usually in a similar order. With this in mind, let's examine an arbitrary game architecture that will support the real-time event-driven model as discussed above.

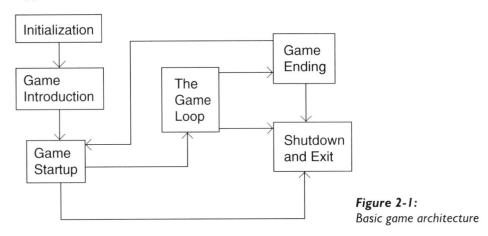

*Figure 2-1:*
*Basic game architecture*

Basically, every game can be divided into six different modules:

■ Initialization

■ Game Introduction

■ Game Startup

■ The Game Loop

■ Game Ending

■ Shutdown and Exit

Typically, the Initialization and Game Introduction modules are performed at the start of program execution, and usually only run once. The user is then presented with the Game Startup module, which generally contains code for letting the user customize the game in some manner. The Game Loop module is then entered, which contains the primary logic for the game. When the game is over, the Game Ending module presents the user with information on their game performance, and then jumps back into the Game Startup module. The Shutdown and Exit module is finally called when the user wishes to discontinue the game and shut it down.

## Initialization

The initialization module is responsible for setting up the beginning game state. It allocates needed memory, initializes global variables, creates lookup tables, and loads resources such as graphics, sound, and music files. Typically, the initialization module will display a splash screen at the beginning of the initialization code so that the user has something to look at. This is an especially good practice if game initialization takes a while; otherwise the user may suspect that the application has frozen or stopped executing.

In Delphi applications, the developer has a number of areas where initialization code can be located. The main form's OnCreate event is the most obvious location, but such code can also be placed in the OnActivate event or even in the initialization section of the unit. The initialization module typically contains code that is only run once at the beginning of application startup. Any variables that will be reset when a new game is started, such as the player's score or starting level, should be modified in the game startup module.

 **Caution:** Pay attention to any dynamically created objects or dynamically allocated memory, and make sure to free these upon termination. Games that leak resources and cause the user to reboot the machine after play are not looked upon favorably.

## Introduction

The introduction module is responsible for introducing the player to the game and welcoming them into the game world. Typically, this takes the form of some sort of animated introduction. Most games, especially those constructed by professional game production houses, will display an elaborate animated sequence that gives a little background to the game and sets the overall mood. Some opening sequences are as good as action movie trailers, and may even feature live actors. The goal with these introductory animations is to immediately pull the player into the game world by eliciting the appropriate emotions and generally getting them into the right mood. Even a simple text display of a short story can be effective if written correctly. Usually, the game will provide a method by which the user can view the introduction again if they so desire, to review the overall game goals and objectives or to simply experience some cool animation again.

While introductory animations are important for setting the mood and the story, it is equally important to remember that all introductions, no matter how cool, will become boring at some point. Some games will only show the introduction when the game is executed for the very first time. Introductory sequences will slow down users who play the game often, so it is important to remember to provide some method to skip the introduction, such as a keypress.

**Tip:** Always allow users to bypass any animation sequence by pressing a hot key.

## Game Startup

The game startup module is responsible for two things. First, it should reset any variables that need to be initialized when a new game is started, such as a player's score, their level, the number of lives left, etc. Second, game startup should allow the user to customize the game in any way supported. For example, game startup should include the code that allows the user to select which input device will be used, what side he'll be playing, or other game-specific options.

## The Game Loop

The game loop module is the focal point of the game application. It contains the primary game logic, and executes the code that creates the game environment and controls all game objects. Its primary responsibility is processing user input and rendering the game output.

The game loop itself is a set of actions that are performed in rapid succession. These actions are performed over and over in a loop, updating the screen to reflect the current state of the game world. These actions are performed with or without any input from the user. Each pass through the game loop updates the screen one time, and represents one frame of animation. The code located in the game loop usually receives the most attention throughout the development cycle of a game, as this code must be highly optimized to run fast enough to achieve an acceptable game speed.

What should be in the loop? That depends on the specific game, and varies on an individual basis. However, most game loops perform similar functions. The game loop is examined more closely below.

## Game Ending

The game ending module is responsible for reporting to the player their overall game performance. This can take many forms, from a simple display of high scores to a summary of several different game statistics, or even an ending animation displaying a different scenario dependent upon whether the user won or lost. Whatever the method, the game ending module should let the user know that the game is over, and provide them with a choice to either start a new game or exit. If the user wishes to play another game, it should give control to the game startup module; otherwise it should execute the shutdown and exit module.

## Shutdown and Exit

The shutdown and exit module is responsible for de-initializing variables and terminating the game application. It should free any dynamically allocated resources that were created in the initialization module, delete any temporary files, and generally ensure that the application will terminate without memory leaks or other artifacts. If the game offers the user a method by which it can be saved, it is usually a good idea to ask the user if they wish to save the current game before exiting. This will avoid frustrated and angry users who have spent several hours playing the game just to have their efforts destroyed by accidentally choosing the wrong option.

**Tip:** Always ask the user if they wish to save the game before exiting (if game saving is supported).

This module should be reachable from several different points in the game. At any time, a user may want to end the game and exit the application, and this should be obtainable from the game startup, game loop, and game ending modules. Typically, several different methods are employed that allow the user to exit the game. For example, there is usually a button or menu item in the game startup and game ending modules that will exit the game. Hot keys are usually available from within the game loop that either give control to the shutdown and exit module or return the user to the game ending or game startup modules so that they can exit from there.

# The Game Loop

As mentioned above, the actual game loop is usually the focal point of a game application. The game loop is where all of the action takes place. It processes a series of instructions over and over as quickly as possible to produce the on-screen images that reflect the current state of the game. This processing continues with or without user interaction, and is precisely the method by which the real-time event-driven model discussed previously is implemented.

Technically speaking, a game loop is responsible for three things: retrieving input, updating game objects, and rendering a new frame of animation. Of course, there's a lot more to a game loop than this oversimplified description suggests. What actually occurs in a game loop is very arbitrary and will depend on the needs of the individual game. However, all games perform similar tasks, usually in a similar order. Expanding upon the three tasks listed above, Figure 2-2 illustrates an example game loop that might be found in a simple action arcade game.

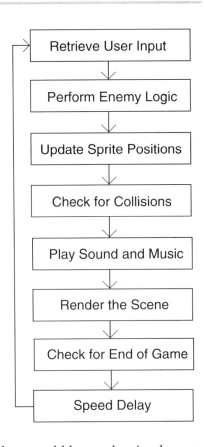

*Figure 2-2:*
*A simplistic game loop*

There are several different techniques by which this game loop architecture could be implemented. In the examples in this book, we will be implementing the primary game loop inside the Application.OnIdle event. This technique is used for several reasons. First, the main game loop will automatically be entered whenever the application becomes idle (after initializing everything in the OnCreate or OnActivate form event handlers or the initialization section of the unit). Second, the application object controls when the OnIdle event is called, meaning that any standard Windows events will be processed and the application never needs to call Application.ProcessMessages. Third, it's simply an easy, Delphi-centric technique for implementing the game loop that should be easy to understand and reproduce.

Alternatively, a while..do or repeat..until loop could be used to implement the game loop. The advantages of this technique are that the developer will have more control over the application, and it will run a little faster than the OnIdle technique. The application could even exit the game loop for some reason, perhaps to display a simple options screen that didn't need the complex animation capabilities afforded by the game loop. The disadvantages to this method of game loop implementation are that these types of loops are generally a little harder to work with when trying to support general Windows events. Application.ProcessMessages must certainly be called at some point within the loop so that standard Windows messages can be handled. Also, the variable controlling the loop's execution must be set so that the loop can exit before the application can terminate; simply calling Close or Application.Terminate will not work. Using this technique can result in little issues such as these that interfere with the normal operation of a Windows application. They can usually be handled with minor workarounds, however, so using a loop such as this may be advantageous depending on the type of game being produced. The following listing demonstrates an implementation of the arbitrary game loop using a while..do loop.

**Listing 2-1:** *Arbitrary game loop example*

```
procedure GameLoop;
var
  TimeStart: Longint;    // used to time the length of one loop iteration
begin

  {this while..do loop will continue processing the same commands in
   rapid succession until instructed to exit from the loop}
  while GameRunning do
  begin

    {record the current time upon starting the loop}
    TimeStart := GetCurrentTime;

    {retrieve input from the user by accessing whichever input device
     the user has chosen}
    RetrieveInput;

    {perform any enemy artificial intelligence and other logic
     associated with game elements not controlled by the user}
    PerformEnemyAI;

    {iterate through all sprites, updating their positions accordingly,
     taking into account user input and enemy AI calculations}
    UpdateSpritePositions;

    {check for any collisions between objects that would result in a
     change in the current game state, such as missiles colliding with a
     target or the player's sprite impacting a wall or other object}
    CheckForCollisions;

    {start any sound effects needed, based on collision detection or
     other game states}
    StartSounds;

    {start any music needed, again based on collision detection or other
     game states}
    StartMusic;

    {all processing has been completed, so draw the current state of the
     game to the screen}
    DrawFrame;

    {determine if the game is still running, based on whether the player
     has died or some other deciding threshold has been reached}
    GameRunning := IsGameOver;

    {determine how long this cycle has taken; if it has been too short,
     pause for the difference so that the game does not run too fast}
```

```
    If GetCurrentTime-TimeStart<TimingValue then
        Pause(GetCurrentTime-TimeStart);

    {process any Windows messages that are waiting}
    Application.ProcessMessages;

  end;  // repeat this process over and over until the game has ended
end;
```

As a matter of practice, several of these tasks may be combined or performed simultaneously. For example, since an application must iterate through every game object to update its position, it would be practical to draw each object as its position is updated. Also, collisions usually result in an object being destroyed or its course being altered, so appropriate sound effects could be started at the time of the collision detection. The point is that these steps represent an arbitrary game loop, and may be rearranged or combined (or even split apart) as the individual circumstances warrant.

Even with this expanded view of a game loop implementation, many of the details attended to within the loop are not fully exposed. Throughout this book, we will examine many game examples that contain highly varied game loops, containing various functions as required by the individual game type. Later chapters will discuss in depth the tasks performed by an individual game example's game loop, but for now, let's examine an overview of what each segment is responsible for within our arbitrary game loop.

## Retrieve User Input

Retrieving user input involves reading the input values from whatever device is supported or that the user has chosen, and translating that information into a form relevant to the control of the game. Most Delphi applications typically handle user input through event handlers, such as OnKeyDown or OnMouseMove. For business applications and even most strategy or turn-based games, this method is fine. However, fast action arcade games typically require more control over the process, and handling user input through events may impede or interfere with the proper execution of the game.

Thus, most games use a polling technique for retrieving user input. Polling involves directly accessing the device at a specific point within the game loop and reading its data. Theoretically, this polling could take place at any time, but it usually occurs at the beginning of the game loop so that the most recent movement can be reflected in the next frame of animation. Direct polling gives the application developer precise control over the processing of input, and can even allow the detection of multiple input events simultaneously (i.e., check if two keys are pressed at the same time).

**polling:** A method for retrieving input or checking some data value manually (as opposed to letting a separate thread check it automatically), usually repeated often at regular intervals.

The primary drawback to the direct polling technique is that user input events can get lost if the polling happens infrequently. This is generally a symptom of a slow game loop, where a large amount of processing takes place before the input device is again polled.

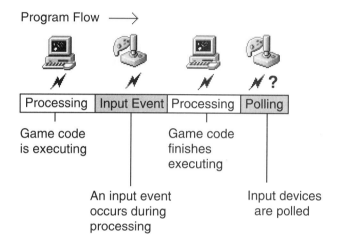

*Figure 2-3:* Missing a user input event

One method to remedy this situation is to conduct device polling at several different places throughout the game loop, and then process the sum of the movement data when it is time to update game world objects. However, another more accurate technique is to buffer user input events. To perform this technique efficiently, a separate thread must be utilized to perform the device polling and event queuing. Fortunately, DirectX provides several methods that make this technique viable, and we'll examine a demonstration of this in the chapter on input techniques.

Once the input has been retrieved, it is translated into events that are meaningful in the context of the game. For example, if the joystick button was pressed, the function for starting a missile or a bullet volley would be called. How the input is translated is, of course, dependent on the type of game itself. The result of such user actions will be apparent after the sprite updating segment has been called and the next frame of animation has been drawn to the screen.

## Perform Antagonist AI and Other Game Logic

In this segment, algorithms that control the behavior of enemy units or other non-player units are performed, with the results being used to update the appropriate sprite positions or to execute any other appropriate actions. This may include deciding if an enemy spacecraft pursues the player or flees, but it also includes other, perhaps more mundane, decision making processes that affect other parts of the game. For example, background sprites that are never interacted with during the game may contain a little logic for changing their animation so that it does not appear repetitive.

This segment may run some very complex code depending on the type of game and its objectives. Some games, such as chess, may have a very advanced thinking engine that examines the current configuration of the board and makes a movement decision based upon the prediction of the next move that the opponent may make. Other games, such as real-time strategy war games, may have several smaller decision engines that determine the most direct route a unit may take to its destination. In general, this segment executes the artificial intelligence code that determines how the game objects will react to the actions of the player.

 **artificial intelligence (AI):** The concept of cognitive software that thinks and reacts to situations in a sentient manner. In relation to game programming, this is the section of code responsible for determining the actions and reactions of game protagonists in relation to the actions and reactions of the player.

Artificial intelligence is a specialty area in its own right, and some game companies hire programmers specifically for their AI expertise. Some AI techniques are well documented and are easy to implement, such as chasing or evading the player or converging on a specific position. Others, such as natural speech generation or pattern recognition, are very difficult to implement and are either closely guarded trade secrets or the province of advanced academic research.

## Update Sprite Positions

The positions of all game objects are updated in this segment. Their velocities are added to their current positions, which are then usually checked to make sure that they are still within the boundaries of the game world. This segment is where the results of user input and artificial intelligence logic are realized. A ship is accelerated or turned according to how the user moved the joystick, and enemy soldiers and cannons are advanced forward or animated per the decisions of the artificial intelligence segment.

Since all objects in the game world need to be updated, the game loop typically iterates through each object, one at a time, applying the position translations as required. The game loop itself needs to run as quickly as possible, so other actions that are performed for each game object are typically executed in this segment as well. The most common action performed at the same time as position updating is probably drawing the sprite image into an offscreen buffer. However, other actions may include collision detection, artificial intelligence processing, or other functions. The process of actually drawing the sprite, as well as other sprite specific procedures, will be examined in Chapter 6, Sprite Techniques.

## Check for Collisions

The collision detection segment is necessary for determining if two sprites or game objects have collided, and the action that is a result thereof. Most games are driven off of events where two sprites come into contact. For example, when a bullet that was fired several frames ago finally touches the enemy ship at which it was targeted, something should happen.

There are hundreds of different methods by which to detect if two or more objects have collided. Some games may require that every object be checked against every other object; others may be interested in the collision between only certain types of objects. Whatever the case, collision detection algorithms vary in complexity according to the task they must perform and the number of objects involved. Accuracy is also an area of great variation. Some may detect only a close collision, and may not be very accurate at all. Others may go as far as comparing the pixels of each bitmap at a certain frame of animation and at a certain position within the game world to see if any pixels actually overlap (a highly accurate method indeed). Speed also becomes a very important issue with the collision detection scheme put into production, as the more accurate the collision detection, typically the slower it will run. Collision detection algorithms will be covered in the chapter on sprite techniques.

## Start Sound Effects

Games would tend to get boring without sound effects to accompany the actions of various game objects. The responsibility of this segment is to commence the output of various sound effects as warranted by the actions of both the user and the game controlled objects. Technically speaking, sound effect playback will probably be handled during other segments of the game loop. For example, when the user presses a button to fire a missile the user input retrieval segment will probably call a function that both starts the missile object as well as commences the playback of an appropriate sound effect. Other sound effects, such as idle background chatter or other appropriate noises that would be generated from non-interactive game objects, will probably be started when the artificial intelligence section makes one of these objects perform some action. Any other sound effects not handled by an appropriate segment, such as ambient sounds or user interface activation sounds, may be generated from this segment. We will see techniques for sound effect output in Chapter 9, Sound and Music.

## Start Music

As with sound effects, music enhances the gaming experience, and this segment is responsible for starting musical output or changing the tune of the existing output. Again, music playback may be handled by another, more appropriate segment. However, music is commonly used to reflect the overall mood or state of the game. As such, this segment would be responsible for examining the current state as it would reflect from the user's standpoint, and start or change the music as appropriate. For example, a neutral musical interlude may be output when the user is just flying along to the next waypoint. This could be changed, on the fly, to a more intense, urgent musical number when the user goes into combat. It could be changed to an even more intense score if the player or enemy is heavily damaged, and finally an appropriate tune could be played based on the user's victory or defeat. This segment would need to perform the necessary actions to determine the current state of the game, playing a specific musical piece as appropriate. The chapter on sound and music contains examples of musical score playback techniques.

## Render the Next Frame

This segment is responsible for the most important part of the game loop, that of displaying the current state of the game from the user's perspective in graphical form. Depending on the complexity of the game, this may simply entail drawing two-dimensional bitmap images to the screen, or rendering a complex, realistic view based on the positions of three-dimensional models. Of all the segments in a game loop, this segment has the greatest variety of implementations. Like all game programming topics, some techniques are well documented, such as simple sprite output or even three-dimensional raycasting or rendering techniques. Other techniques, such as true three-dimensional space rendering, are trade secrets and are poorly documented, if at all.

Typically, rendering a frame of animation starts by drawing the background. This may be as simple as a game board or something more complex, like a textured, scaled wall. Sprite images are then drawn over this background. All of this drawing generally takes place in an offscreen graphical buffer. After all drawing and rendering has been completed, this buffer is then blasted to the screen, at which point it becomes visible as the next frame of animation. As sprite positions are modified, their images drawn to reflect these new positions, and the results displayed to the screen in rapid succession, the illusion of animation is achieved. DirectX provides several methods for performing graphical output, both simplistic and complex.

## Check for Game End

At some point, the current state of the game needs to be compared with a known state to see if a state change is in order. For example, if all of the player's lives have been used up, the game is over. Additionally, when all of the enemy creatures have been eliminated or the exit is found, the current level has ended and it is time to advance to the next level of difficulty.

Advanced games may potentially contain several states that affect how the overall game loop is processed. For example, when a level is completed, the game may go into a temporary intermission state where, instead of performing the normal gameplay animation, it displays a summary of the previous level's accomplishments as well as the name or number of the next level being entered. A discussion of expanding the game loop to support different game states is covered below.

## Speed Delay

The one constant in the computer industry is that machines will only get faster and faster as time marches on. Therefore, a game that plays at an acceptable speed today may be too fast to be humanly playable on a new machine six months from now. To ensure that the game runs at a specific speed on every machine, this segment determines if enough time has passed since the rendering of the last frame to constrain the game to a specific speed.

One technique for controlling the speed of a game is to time the duration of the processing of the current animation frame. A starting time is recorded at the beginning of the game loop. At the end of the loop, this starting time is subtracted from the current time. If the result is less than a specific amount of time that will constrain the game speed to a certain rate, the execution is paused for the difference.

This results in a game that should run at a constant speed on any machine equal to or faster than the minimum recommended system for the game. The sprite techniques chapter and other chapters throughout this book contain implementations of timing algorithms for controlling game speed.

**Note:** To accommodate slower systems, some games perform timing tests to see how fast animation can be performed. If it is slower than a certain threshold, the game may compensate by dropping animation frames or turning off some features. The result will be a scaled-down, probably less attractive version of the game, but it has the advantage of running on older systems, which may be a selling point for the customer.

# Game States

The game loop example detailed above provides the application with a framework that makes game animation and user input control easy and intuitive for the developer. However, it is not as robust as it needs to be for real-world applications. How many games jump right into the action immediately upon launching them? Most games display some sort of mission briefing or demonstration while waiting for the user to actually start a game. Typically, action games will also display some sort of information when a user has completed a level. Still others allow the user to input their name when a game has ended.

We have examined games in terms of the general tasks that are performed. Additionally, games can be examined from the standpoint of their current mode of execution. When a game is first launched, it is considered to be in one mode of execution, but when a new game is started and the user is actually playing, it is in a totally different mode of execution.

Our current game loop does not support this functionality. What is needed is a technique by which the game can be put into specific modes of execution, or states. For example, when the game is first launched, it should be initialized to a demo state. Other states, such as an intermission state or a game over state, will control what parts of the game loop are executed, and will display the appropriate output.

To extend our game loop, we will assume that it supports a game with five states:

■ Demo

■ Playing

■ Intermission

■ Paused

■ Game Over

Each different state would involve executing code appropriate only for that state. Through each iteration of the game loop, the current state is checked, and an appropriate set of functions is executed that produces output (and retrieves input) commensurate with that state.

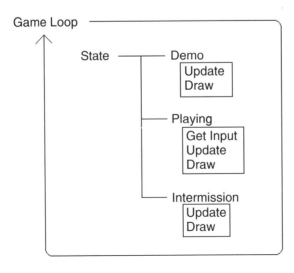

*Figure 2-4:*
*Controlling the game through states*

This could be implemented by using a case statement. The game states could be represented as an enumerated type. Then, when the game loop is executed, the case statement would jump to the appropriate code for the current state. The game state could then be set elsewhere as dictated by user input or the results of game object actions, which would subsequently change the output of the game loop on the next iteration. For example, if collision detection results in the destruction of the final enemy, the current level could be advanced and the game state set to Intermission. After the collision detection code and the rest of the game loop for the current state has finished, the next iteration through the game loop will flow through the Intermission section of code. Listing 2-2 demonstrates a possible implementation of this technique.

**Listing 2-2:** *Game state implementation*

```
type
  TGameState = (gsDemo, gsPlaying, gsIntermission, gsPaused, gsGameOver);

var
  GameState: TGameState;

      .
      .
      .

procedure GameLoop;
begin
  while GameRunning do
    case GameState of
      gsDemo :          begin
                          {demo code}
                        end;
      gsPlaying :       begin
                          {game play code}
                        end;
      gsIntermission :  begin
                          {intermission code}
                        end;
      gsPaused :        begin
                          {paused code}
                        end;
      gsGameOver :      begin
                          {game over code}
                        end;
    end;
end;
```

This technique requires the case statement to be executed over and over. If this becomes a speed issue, this technique could be modified such that each case statement entry jumps to a function that contains its own internal loop. That internal loop would then continue until the game state changes. When this occurs, the internal loop exits, and the main game loop must be called again to switch execution into another function with its own internal loop. This modification is illustrated in Figure 2-5. Technically, an internal loop may simply display a static graphic and then pause for an appropriate period of time, such as for an intermission, instead of performing some sort of animation loop. However, static screens are usually pretty boring.

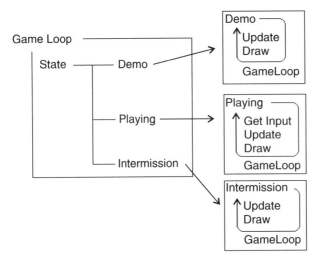

**Figure 2-5:**
*A modified game state looping architecture*

Designing a game application in this manner allows it to be controlled in a very logical and ordered manner. The state of a game can flow from one state to another as appropriate, changing between logical states and ultimately creating a circuit or loop from game beginning through game play to game end and back again. For example, games may start in the demo state, switching into the playing state when a user starts a game. This state will move back and forth between the paused state and the intermission state as the user finishes levels and plays the game. Ultimately, the user will finish the game or will die, at which point the state will switch to the game over state, and finally back to the demo state, where the entire process can be restarted anew. Figure 2-6 illustrates the flow of game logic through a typical game loop constructed in this manner.

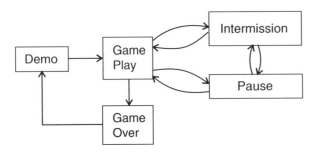

**Figure 2-6:**
*The flow of game states*

Each state's code is responsible for supplying specific output or retrieving specific input, as appropriate for the intention of that state. Some games may have more states than others; other games may not use this design at all, opting for another, more applicable control method. Even so, whether a game uses this technique or not, the execution of a game can be described in terms of states.

## The Demo State

This state typically provides some sort of animation while waiting for the user to start a new game. This may take the form of simple animations within user interface controls (such as animated images on buttons) or something more complex. This state could even be used to play the opening animation sequence introducing players to the game.

Some games provide a demonstration of game play as the background animation. This is certainly a popular technique with hot first-person shooters, and even with most action arcade-like games. Displaying a demonstration of actual game play can whet users' appetites for the game and help to familiarize them with the environment before actually diving in.

To appropriately show a demonstration of game play, this state must run some code elements of the state that is used for actual game play. Artificial intelligence routines could be used to simulate the input of a user and generate some interesting animation. Alternatively, input from an actual game session could be saved to an output file. If designed correctly, the functions that interpret user input could take their values from either a user input device or this digitized user input file. Thus, the demo state would simply open this file and begin streaming the data to the input routines, resulting in an exact duplication of the player's movements and actions.

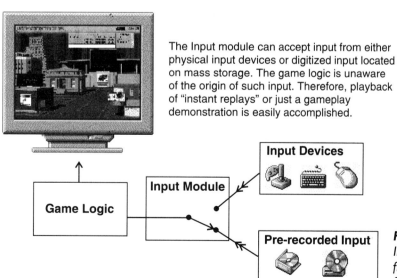

The Input module can accept input from either physical input devices or digitized input located on mass storage. The game logic is unaware of the origin of such input. Therefore, playback of "instant replays" or just a gameplay demonstration is easily accomplished.

**Figure 2-7:**
*Input coming from devices or files*

This technique has many benefits. For one, the developer can control exactly what the user will see in the demonstration, which could avoid accidentally showing off hidden rooms or other surprises. Additionally, the developer could digitize walkthroughs that could then be used in separate game hint packages. Also, this method lends itself directly to instant replay functionality, highly desirable in sports and racing games.

## The Playing State

This state is responsible for the code that makes up the actual game play. All of the segments of the previous game loop presented above will be found here, such as user input processing, sprite updating, and screen drawing. The code run in this state will probably look similar to the example game loop implementation previously discussed.

## The Intermission State

When a user has completed a level (or a series of levels or a mission), games usually enter a type of intermission state. In this state, a report is given to the user that, depending on the type of game, details the user's accomplishments in the completed level. Such things as the number of kills, the number of secrets found or unnoticed, and the accuracy of shots are typically highlighted, as is the number of the next level or the name of the next mission. Sometimes, even an animation will be used to provide a transition from one level to the next, especially if a "chapter" of the game has been completed and an entirely new set of environments and enemies are about to be introduced. Intermission states only last a short while, setting the game state to playing once the intermission state is over.

 **Tip:** It is a good practice to provide a hot key or some other mechanism whereby a user can skip the intermission state and proceed directly back to the playing state.

## The Paused State

The paused state is simply a suspension of game play. All game object logic and processing should be halted, including the output of sound effects and possibly even the output of music. Typically, pausing a game should simply toggle between the paused state and the playing (or intermission) state. Pausing a game should usually have no effect during a demo or game over state. Paused states are generally entered through either a hot key activation or by interacting with a user interface control (such as a button or menu item).

### The Game Over State

In the game over state, an expanded report of the user's accomplishments throughout the course of the game could be displayed. This includes the information displayed during the intermission state as it applies to the overall game achievements. End game animations could also be played, perhaps varying the exact animation dependent upon whether the player won or lost. The game over state usually only lasts for a short amount of time, perhaps only a little longer than the intermission state, before proceeding to the demo state.

## Case Study

In order to further demonstrate the concepts discussed in this chapter, we should examine the case study provided on the CD in this chapter's directory. It is a game titled Shoot 'em, where the player simply fires at oncoming enemy spaceships. It is a simple game using simple graphics, but it should serve as an example of implementing several of the topics we just covered. This is not a complete game, and many of the tasks required by a commercial quality game have been left out (such as sound and music output) so as not to complicate the code. The architecture used in this example game will be the basis for examples to come.

Of particular interest to this chapter is the game loop itself. The example implements a simplistic game loop similar to the first loop architecture we've discussed. It is state driven, and throughout the code you can see where this state is modified and how it affects the overall game processing. This game loop is embodied in the DrawSurfaces procedure. Take a look at this procedure to get a taste of how to implement an actual game loop.

This case study example is presented in its entirety to get you familiar with the types of examples demonstrated throughout the book. There are several programming techniques implemented in this example that we have yet to discuss, such as sprite manipulation. This example also contains some DirectX initialization code that we haven't yet discussed. Peruse the first part of the example to get familiar with the function calls that we'll be exploring in subsequent chapters. Beginning with the DrawSurfaces procedure, we see some techniques that we've outlined in this chapter. This example also demonstrates how to logically control such entities as sprites and background animation elements with arrays. Later in the book, we'll extend this to a more general approach for controlling game entities.

**Listing 2-3:** *The Shoot 'em example game*

```
unit ShootEmU;

{*****************************************************************************

    Shoot Example Application

    Author: John Ayres

    Like most examples in the book, this one takes advantage of the baseline
    DirectX application code.  It implements a very simplistic game in order
    to demonstrate basic game architecture. The architecture of a game is
    arbitrary and will in part be determined by the type of game being
    created. However, most games share similar tasks in order to generate
    a frame of animation, and this example should serve to familiarize
    the user with some of the more common gaming application tasks.


    *****************************************************************************


    Copyright © 1999 by John Ayres, All Rights Reserved

    This example utilizes sprites from the freeware sprite library
    SpriteLib by Ari Feldman.

    Sprite lib sprites Copyright (c) 1998 by Ari Feldman. Check out
    http://www.chromewave.com

    This code is freeware and can be used for any personal or commercial
    purposes without royalty or license.  Use at your own risk.

    *****************************************************************************}


interface

uses
  Windows, Messages, SysUtils, Classes, Graphics, Controls, Forms, Dialogs,
  DDraw;

{these constants are used to modify specific attributes of the DirectX
 application, such as the color of the main form, the requested resolution,
 etc.}
const
  DXWIDTH     = 640;
  DXHEIGHT    = 480;
  DXCOLORDEPTH = 8;
  BUFFERCOUNT = 1;
  COOPERATIVELEVEL = DDSCL_FULLSCREEN or DDSCL_ALLOWREBOOT or
                     DDSCL_ALLOWMODEX or DDSCL_EXCLUSIVE;
  SURFACETYPE     = DDSCAPS_COMPLEX or DDSCAPS_FLIP or DDSCAPS_PRIMARYSURFACE;
```

```
const
  {this user-defined message is used to start the flipping loop}
  WM_DIRECTXACTIVATE = WM_USER + 200;

  {the player's ship index}
  PLAYERSHIPIDX = 0;

  {the total number of ships}
  NUMSHIPS = 5;

  {the total number of bullets}
  NUMBULLETS = 19;

  {the total number of explosions}
  NUMEXPLOSIONS = 5;

  {the total number of stars}
  NUMSTARS = 100;

type
  {tracks the overall game state}
  TGameState = (gsDemo, gsPlaying, gsIntermission);

  {our base sprite class}
  TSprite = class
  public
    XPos, YPos,
    XVel, YVel,
    NumFrames,
    CurFrame,
    FrameWidth, FrameHeight,
    XFrameStartOffset, YFrameStartOffset: Integer;
    BoundBox,
    CollisionBox: TRect;
    Living: Boolean;
    CurAnimTime,
    AnimThreshold: LongWord;

    procedure Move; virtual;
    procedure Draw; virtual;
  end;

  {our star class, descended from sprites}
  TStar = class(TSprite)
  public
    Color: Byte;

    procedure Move; override;
    procedure Draw; override;
  end;
```

```
{the explosion class, also descended from sprites}
TExplosion = class(TSprite)
public
  procedure Move; override;
end;

{the form class}
TfrmDXAppMain = class(TForm)
  procedure FormCreate(Sender: TObject);
  procedure FormDestroy(Sender: TObject);
  procedure FormKeyDown(Sender: TObject; var Key: Word;
    Shift: TShiftState);
  procedure FormActivate(Sender: TObject);
private
  { Private declarations }

  {flips back to the GDI surface to display the exception error message}
  procedure ExceptionHandler(Sender: TObject; ExceptionObj: Exception);

  {the main rendering loop}
  procedure AppIdle(Sender: TObject; var Done: Boolean);

  {intercepts certain messages to provide appropriate functionality}
  procedure AppMessage(var Msg: TMsg; var Handled: Boolean);

  {flips the DirectX surfaces}
  procedure FlipSurfaces;

  {restores any lost surfaces}
  procedure RestoreSurfaces;

  {draws the contents of surfaces}
  procedure DrawSurfaces;
public
  {tracks the overall game state}
  GameState: TGameState;

  {tracks the level and score, number of ships left to destroy before
   advancing to the next level, and the number of lives the player has left}
  Level,
  Score,
  NumShipsToNextLevel,
  LivesLeft: Integer;

  {timing variable for pausing in the intermission mode}
  TimeAccum: Longint;

  {indicates if the player can shoot or not}
  CanShoot: Boolean;

  {tracks all of the living ships}
```

```
    Ships: array[0..NUMSHIPS] of TSprite;

    {tracks all of the living player bullets}
    PlayerBullets: array[0..NUMBULLETS] of TSprite;

    {tracks all of the living enemy bullets}
    EnemyBullets: array[0..NUMBULLETS] of TSprite;

    {tracks all of the living explosions}
    Explosions: array[0..NUMEXPLOSIONS] of TExplosion;

    {tracks all of the living stars}
    Stars: array[0..NUMSTARS] of TStar;

    {these are various procedures that initialize certain variables and
     generalize control of certain elements of the game}
    procedure StartEnemy;
    procedure StartExplosion(XPos, YPos: Integer);
    procedure StartBullet(XPos,YPos,XVel,YVel: Integer;PlayerBullet: Boolean);
    procedure ResetPlayer;
    procedure ResetAll;
    procedure PlayerShipKilled;

    procedure NewGame;
  end;


var
  frmDXAppMain: TfrmDXAppMain;

  {the main DirectDraw interface}
  FDirectDraw: IDirectDraw4;

  {the interfaces for the primary and back buffer surfaces and bitmap image}
  FPrimarySurface,
  FBackBuffer,
  FGraphicsImage: IDirectDrawSurface4;

  {the palette interface}
  FPalette: IDirectDrawPalette;


implementation

uses
  DXTools, DDUtil, MMSystem, gensuppt;

{$R *.DFM}
```

```
{ *-->>  BASELINE APPLICATION CODE <<--* }


{ - the callback function used to ensure that the selected graphics mode -
  - is supported by DirectX                                             - }
function EnumModesCallback(const EnumSurfaceDesc: TDDSurfaceDesc2;
                                 Information: Pointer): HResult; stdcall;
begin
  {if the height, width, and color depth match those specified in the
   constants, then indicate that the desired graphics mode is supported}
  if (EnumSurfaceDesc.dwHeight = DXHEIGHT) and
     (EnumSurfaceDesc.dwWidth = DXWIDTH) and
     (EnumSurfaceDesc.ddpfPixelFormat.dwRGBBitCount = DXCOLORDEPTH) then
    Boolean(Information^) := TRUE;

  Result := DDENUMRET_OK;
end;


{ -> Events Hooked to the Application <- }

{ - this event is called when an exception occurs, and simply flips back -
  - to the GDI surface so that the exception dialog box can be read      - }
procedure TfrmDXAppMain.ExceptionHandler(Sender: TObject;
                                         ExceptionObj: Exception);
begin
  {disconnect the OnIdle event to shut off the rendering loop}
  Application.OnIdle := nil;

  {if the DirectDraw object was successfully created, flip to the GDI surface}
  if Assigned(FDirectDraw) then
    FDirectDraw.FlipToGDISurface;

  {display the exception message}
  MessageDlg(ExceptionObj.Message, mtError, [mbOK], 0);

  {reconnect the OnIdle event to reenter the rendering loop}
  Application.OnIdle := AppIdle;
end;

{ - handles certain messages that are required to make DirectX function -
  - properly within Delphi                                             - }
procedure TfrmDXAppMain.AppMessage(var Msg: TMsg; var Handled: Boolean);
begin
  case Msg.Message of
    WM_ACTIVATEAPP:
      {unhook the OnIdle event when the application is being deactivated.
       this will stop all rendering}
      if not Boolean(Msg.wParam) then
        Application.OnIdle := nil
      else
```

```
          {upon activating the application, send ourselves the user-defined
            message}
          PostMessage(Application.Handle, WM_DIRECTXACTIVATE, 0, 0);
    WM_DIRECTXACTIVATE:
      begin
        {upon activating, restore all surfaces (reloading their memory as
          necessary), hook up the OnIdle event, and redraw the contents of
          all surfaces}
        RestoreSurfaces;
        Application.OnIdle := AppIdle;
        DrawSurfaces;
      end;
    WM_SYSCOMMAND:
      begin
        {do not allow a screen saver to kick in}
        Handled := (Msg.wParam = SC_SCREENSAVE);
      end;
  end;
end;


{ -> Form Events <- }

{ - initialize essential form properties - }
procedure TfrmDXAppMain.FormCreate(Sender: TObject);
var
  iCount: Integer;
begin
  Randomize;

  {set up the application exception handler}
  Application.OnException := ExceptionHandler;

  {initialize form properties;  note that the FormStyle property must be
    set to fsStayOnTop}
  BorderStyle := bsNone;
  BorderIcons := [];
  FormStyle    := fsStayOnTop;
  Color        := clBlack;
  Cursor       := crNone;

  {initialize the game state to demo}
  GameState := gsDemo;

  {create all of the star objects}
  for iCount := 0 to NUMSTARS do
  begin
    {create the star}
    Stars[iCount] := TStar.Create;

    {set its position}
```

```
      Stars[iCount].XPos := Random(DXWIDTH);
      Stars[iCount].YPos := Random(DXHEIGHT);

      {set its velocity. stars are only going to move from the top of the screen
       to the bottom, so we're only concerned with the horizontal velocity}
      Stars[iCount].XVel := 0;
      Stars[iCount].YVel := Random(5)+1;

      {set the color of the star based on its velocity}
      case Stars[iCount].YVel of
        1..2  : Stars[iCount].Color := 252;
        3..4  : Stars[iCount].Color := 251;
        5     : Stars[iCount].Color := 255;
      end;
    end;
end;

{ - provides essential cleanup functionality - }
procedure TfrmDXAppMain.FormDestroy(Sender: TObject);
var
  iCount: Integer;
begin
  {disengage our custom exception handler}
  Application.OnException := nil;

  {remember, we do not have to explicitly free the DirectDraw objects, as they
   will free themselves when they go out of context (such as when the
   application is closed)}

  for iCount := 0 to NUMSTARS do
    Stars[iCount].Free;
end;

{ - this method initializes DirectX and creates all necessary objects - }
procedure TfrmDXAppMain.FormActivate(Sender: TObject);
var
  {we can only get a DirectDraw4 interface from the DirectDraw interface, so we
   need a temporary interface}
  TempDirectDraw: IDirectDraw;

  {structures required for various methods}
  DDSurface: TDDSurfaceDesc2;
  DDSCaps: TDDSCaps2;

  {flag used to determine if the desired graphics mode is supported}
  SupportedMode: Boolean;
begin
  {if DirectDraw has already been initialized, exit}
  if Assigned(FDirectDraw) then exit;

  {create a temporary DirectDraw object. this is used to create the
```

```
                desired DirectDraw4 object}
DXCheck( DirectDrawCreate(nil, TempDirectDraw, nil) );

try
  {we can only get a DirectDraw4 interface through the QueryInterface
   method of the DirectDraw object}
  DXCheck( TempDirectDraw.QueryInterface(IID_IDirectDraw4, FDirectDraw) );
finally
  {now that we have the DirectDraw4 object, the temporary DirectDraw
   object is no longer needed}
  TempDirectDraw := nil;
end;

{set the cooperative level to that defined in the constants}
DXCheck( FDirectDraw.SetCooperativeLevel(Handle, COOPERATIVELEVEL) );

{hook up the application message handler}
Application.OnMessage := AppMessage;

{call EnumDisplayModes and verify that the desired graphics mode is
 indeed supported}
FillChar(DDSurface, SizeOf(TDDSurfaceDesc2), 0);
DDSurface.dwSize    := SizeOf(TDDSurfaceDesc2);
DDSurface.dwFlags   := DDSD_HEIGHT or DDSD_WIDTH or DDSD_PIXELFORMAT;
DDSurface.dwHeight := DXHEIGHT;
DDSurface.dwWidth   := DXWIDTH;
DDSurface.ddpfPixelFormat.dwSize := SizeOf(TDDPixelFormat_DX6);
DDSurface.ddpfPixelFormat.dwRGBBitCount := DXCOLORDEPTH;
SupportedMode := FALSE;
DXCheck( FDirectDraw.EnumDisplayModes(0, @DDSurface, @SupportedMode,
                                      EnumModesCallback) );

{if the desired graphics mode is not supported by the DirectX drivers,
 display an error message and shut down the application}
if not SupportedMode then
begin
  MessageBox(Handle, PChar('The installed DirectX drivers do not support a '+
                           'display mode of: '+IntToStr(DXWIDTH)+' X '+
                           IntToStr(DXHEIGHT)+', '+IntToStr(DXCOLORDEPTH)+
                           ' bit color'), 'Unsupported Display Mode Error',
                           MB_ICONERROR or MB_OK);
  Close;
  Exit;
end;

{set the display resolution and color depth to that defined in the constants}
DXCheck( FDirectDraw.SetDisplayMode(DXWIDTH, DXHEIGHT, DXCOLORDEPTH, 0, 0) );

{initialize the DDSurface structure to indicate that we will be creating a
 complex flipping surface with one backbuffer}
FillChar(DDSurface, SizeOf(TDDSurfaceDesc2), 0);
```

```
    DDSurface.dwSize  := SizeOf(TDDSurfaceDesc2);
    DDSurface.dwFlags := DDSD_CAPS or DDSD_BACKBUFFERCOUNT;
    DDSurface.ddsCaps.dwCaps := SURFACETYPE;
    DDSurface.dwBackBufferCount := BUFFERCOUNT;

    {create the primary surface object}
    DXCheck( FDirectDraw.CreateSurface(DDSurface, FPrimarySurface, nil) );

    {indicate that we want to retrieve a pointer to the backbuffer (the surface
     immediately behind the primary surface in the flipping chain) }
    FillChar(DDSCaps, SizeOf(TDDSCaps2), 0);
    DDSCaps.dwCaps := DDSCAPS_BACKBUFFER;

    {retrieve the surface}
    DXCheck( FPrimarySurface.GetAttachedSurface(DDSCaps, FBackBuffer) );

    {load the palette from the bitmap to be used and attach it to the
     primary surface}
    FPalette := DDLoadPalette(FDirectDraw, ExtractFilePath(ParamStr(0))+
    'SpriteImgs.bmp');
    DXCheck( FPrimarySurface.SetPalette(FPalette) );

    {load the bitmap image containing the background and animation frames}
    FGraphicsImage := DDLoadBitmap(FDirectDraw, ExtractFilePath(ParamStr(0))+
                      'SpriteImgs.bmp');

    {indicate which color in the bitmap is transparent}
    DXCheck( DDSetColorKey(FGraphicsImage, $00000000) );

    {initialize the surfaces with the images}
    DrawSurfaces;

    {post a message that will hook up the OnIdle event and start the main
     rendering loop}
    PostMessage(Handle, WM_ACTIVATEAPP, 1, 0);
end;


{ -> Form Methods <- }

{ - this method is called in order to flip the surfaces - }
procedure TfrmDXAppMain.FlipSurfaces;
var
  DXResult: HResult;
begin
  {perform the page flip. note that the DDFLIP_WAIT flag has been used,
   indicating that the function will not return until the page flip has been
   performed. this could be removed, allowing the application to perform other
   processing until the page flip occurs. however, the application will need to
   continuously call the Flip method to ensure that the page flip takes place}
```

```
      DXResult := FPrimarySurface.Flip(nil, DDFLIP_WAIT);

    {if the surfaces were lost, restore them. on any other error, raise an
     exception}
    if DXResult = DDERR_SURFACELOST then
      RestoreSurfaces
    else if DXResult <> DD_OK then
      DXCheck(DXResult);
end;

{ - this method is called when the surface memory is lost  -
  - and must be restored.  surfaces in video memory that   -
  - contain bitmaps must be reinitialized in this function - }
procedure TfrmDXAppMain.RestoreSurfaces;
begin
  {restore the primary surface, which in turn restores any implicit surfaces}
  FPrimarySurface._Restore;

  {restore the bitmap image's surface}
  FGraphicsImage._Restore;

  {reload the bitmap into the surface}
  DXCheck( DDReLoadBitmap(FGraphicsImage, ExtractFilePath(ParamStr(0))+
                          'SpriteImgs.bmp') );
end;

{ - this method is continuously called by the application, and provides -
  - the main rendering loop.  this could be replaced by a custom        -
  - while..do loop                                                    - }
procedure TfrmDXAppMain.AppIdle(Sender: TObject; var Done: Boolean);
begin
  {indicates that the application should continuously call this method}
  Done := FALSE;

  {if DirectDraw has not been initialized, exit}
  if not Assigned(FDirectDraw) then Exit;

  {draw surface content and flip the surfaces}
  DrawSurfaces;
  FlipSurfaces;
end;

{ - this method is called when the contents of the surfaces need to be  -
  - drawn. it will be continuously called by the AppIdle method, so any  -
  - rendering or animation could be done within this method            - }
procedure TfrmDXAppMain.DrawSurfaces;
var
  SourceRect,
  ISectRect: TRect;
  iCount, iCount2: Integer;
  SurfaceDC: HDC;
```

```
  WorkCanvas: TCanvas;
begin
  {erase the last frame of animation}
  ColorFill(FBackBuffer, $00000000, nil);

  {draw all of the background stars. the stars are a background animation
   that are unaffected by any game state, so we always draw them}
  for iCount := 0 to NUMSTARS do
  begin
   Stars[iCount].Move;
   Stars[iCount].Draw;
  end;

  {perform various actions based on the current game state}
  case GameState of
    gsDemo : begin
                {in the demo state, we simply want to draw some text on the screen}
                WorkCanvas := TCanvas.Create;
                FBackBuffer.GetDC(SurfaceDC);

                {draw the game's title and instructions}
                try
                  WorkCanvas.Handle := SurfaceDC;

                  WorkCanvas.Font.Size := 52;
                  WorkCanvas.Font.Name := 'Arial';
                  WorkCanvas.Font.Style := [fsBold, fsItalic];
                  WorkCanvas.Font.Color := clRed;
                  WorkCanvas.Brush.Style := bsClear;
                  WorkCanvas.TextOut(DXWIDTH div 2 -
                                (WorkCanvas.TextWidth('Shoot ''em') div 2),
                                DXHEIGHT div 2 -
                                (WorkCanvas.TextHeight('Shoot ''em') div 2),
                                'Shoot ''em');

                  WorkCanvas.Font.Size := 14;
                  WorkCanvas.Font.Name := 'Arial';
                  WorkCanvas.Font.Style := [fsBold];
                  WorkCanvas.Font.Color := clWhite;
                  WorkCanvas.Brush.Style := bsClear;
                  WorkCanvas.TextOut(DXWIDTH div 2 - (WorkCanvas.
                                TextWidth('Press Enter to begin') div 2),
                                DXHEIGHT - (WorkCanvas.
                                TextHeight('Press Enter to begin')) - 15,
                                'Press Enter to begin');
                finally
                  WorkCanvas.Handle := 0;
                  FBackBuffer.ReleaseDC(SurfaceDC);
                  WorkCanvas.Free;
                end;
```

```
                            {when the user presses the Enter key, initialize a new
                            game, and change the game state}
                            if (GetAsyncKeyState(VK_RETURN) and $8000) = $8000 then
                               NewGame;
                    end;
           gsIntermission : begin
                               {in the intermission state, we want to draw the current
                                level on the screen for only a few seconds before
                                changing the game state}

                               {record the current time}
                               if TimeAccum = -1 then
                                  TimeAccum := timeGetTime;

                               {draw the current level on the screen}
                               WorkCanvas := TCanvas.Create;
                               FBackBuffer.GetDC(SurfaceDC);

                               try
                                  WorkCanvas.Handle := SurfaceDC;

                                  WorkCanvas.Font.Size := 52;
                                  WorkCanvas.Font.Name := 'Arial';
                                  WorkCanvas.Font.Style := [fsBold, fsItalic];
                                  WorkCanvas.Font.Color := clRed;
                                  WorkCanvas.Brush.Style := bsClear;
                                  WorkCanvas.TextOut(DXWIDTH div 2 - (WorkCanvas.
                                           TextWidth('Level '+IntToStr(Level)) div 2),
                                           DXHEIGHT div 2 - (WorkCanvas.
                                           TextHeight('Level '+IntToStr(Level)) div 2),
                                           'Level '+IntToStr(Level));
                               finally
                                  WorkCanvas.Handle := 0;
                                  FBackBuffer.ReleaseDC(SurfaceDC);
                                  WorkCanvas.Free;
                               end;

                               {if we have been displaying this for more than 3 seconds,
                                reset certain variables and change the game state}
                               if timeGetTime-TimeAccum>3000 then
                               begin
                                  ResetPlayer;
                                  TimeAccum := -1;
                                  GameState := gsPlaying;
                               end;
                            end;
           gsPlaying : begin
                          {in the playing state, the user is actively playing the
                           game. this section will contain the game logic for
                           moving the player and performing enemy AI}
```

```
{retrieve user input}
if Ships[PLAYERSHIPIDX] <> nil then
begin
  {move left or right when cursor keys are pressed}
  if (GetAsyncKeyState(VK_RIGHT) and $8000) = $8000 then
    Ships[PLAYERSHIPIDX].XPos := Ships[PLAYERSHIPIDX].XPos+4;
  if (GetAsyncKeyState(VK_LEFT) and $8000) = $8000 then
    Ships[PLAYERSHIPIDX].XPos := Ships[PLAYERSHIPIDX].XPos-4;

  {make sure the player does not go beyond the
   screen boundaries}
  if Ships[PLAYERSHIPIDX].XPos < 0 then
    Ships[PLAYERSHIPIDX].XPos := 0;
  if Ships[PLAYERSHIPIDX].XPos>DXWIDTH-Ships[PLAYERSHIPIDX].
                             FrameWidth then
    Ships[PLAYERSHIPIDX].XPos:=DXWIDTH-Ships[PLAYERSHIPIDX].
                             FrameWidth;

  {fire a shot when the spacebar is pressed. the CanShoot
   variable is used here to force the player to release the
   spacebar before another shot can be fired}
  if ((GetAsyncKeyState(32) and $8000) = $8000) and
     (CanShoot) then
  begin
    StartBullet(Ships[PLAYERSHIPIDX].XPos+
               (Ships[PLAYERSHIPIDX].FrameWidth div 2)-5,
               Ships[PLAYERSHIPIDX].YPos, 0, -8, TRUE);
    CanShoot := FALSE;
  end
  else
  if (GetAsyncKeyState(32) and $8000) = 0 then
    CanShoot := TRUE;
end;

{some enemy AI. this is incredibly simplistic, but it
 simply creates an enemy ship at a random interval. the
 frequency of enemy ship generation increases as the
 level increases, making the game harder}
if Random(1000) < 5 * Level then
  StartEnemy;

{move all of the bullets}
for iCount := 0 to NUMBULLETS do
begin
  {move player bullets}
  if PlayerBullets[iCount] <> nil then
  begin
    {update the bullet based on velocity}
    PlayerBullets[iCount].Move;

    {collision detection. we must determine if this
```

```
           bullet has collided with an enemy ship}
           for iCount2 := PLAYERSHIPIDX+1 to NUMSHIPS do
             if (Ships[iCount2] <> nil) and
                (IntersectRect(ISectRect,
                               PlayerBullets[iCount].CollisionBox,
                               Ships[iCount2].CollisionBox)) then
             begin
               {indeed, the bullet did strike an enemy ship.
                we should create an explosion, increment the
                player's score, and destroy both the bullet and
                the enemy ship}
               StartExplosion(Ships[iCount2].XPos,
                              Ships[iCount2].YPos);
               Inc(Score, Level * 5);
               PlayerBullets[iCount].Living := FALSE;
               Ships[iCount2].Living := FALSE;

               {the level increases when the player has destroyed
                a certain number of enemy ships, so we must
                record this kill}
               Dec(NumShipsToNextLevel);
             end;

           {if the bullet is still alive, draw it; otherwise
            destroy it}
           if PlayerBullets[iCount].Living then
             PlayerBullets[iCount].Draw
           else
           begin
             PlayerBullets[iCount].Free;
             PlayerBullets[iCount] := nil;
           end;
        end;

        {now, we move enemy bullets}
        if EnemyBullets[iCount] <> nil then
        begin
          {update the bullet based on velocity}
          EnemyBullets[iCount].Move;

          {as with the player bullets, we must determine if an
           enemy bullet has collided with the player's ship}
          if (Ships[PLAYERSHIPIDX] <> nil) and
             (IntersectRect(ISectRect,
                            EnemyBullets[iCount].CollisionBox,
                            Ships[PLAYERSHIPIDX].CollisionBox))then
          begin
            {indeed, the enemy bullet has collided with the
             player's ship, destroying it. we should create an
             explosion and destroy both the enemy bullet and the
             player's ship}
```

```
              StartExplosion(Ships[PLAYERSHIPIDX].XPos,
                        Ships[PLAYERSHIPIDX].YPos);
          EnemyBullets[iCount].Living := FALSE;
          Ships[PLAYERSHIPIDX].Living := FALSE;

          {we want the player to see the explosion, so we must
           wait an appropriate amount of time before changing
           the game state}
          TimeAccum := timeGetTime;
        end;

        {if the enemy bullet is still alive, draw it; otherwise
         destroy it}
        if EnemyBullets[iCount].Living then
          EnemyBullets[iCount].Draw
        else
        begin
          EnemyBullets[iCount].Free;
          EnemyBullets[iCount] := nil;
        end;
      end;

    {game state AI.  again, this is very simplistic, but if the
     user has destroyed a certain amount of enemy ships
     (based on the level), the level increases. as the level
     increases, the number of enemy ships that the user is
     required to destroy also increases. this results in the
     game getting harder and harder as the player progresses}
    if NumShipsToNextLevel <= 0 then
    begin
      Inc(Level);
      NumShipsToNextLevel := 5 * Level;
      ResetAll;

      {since we've increased the game level, we should go to
       intermission to inform the player of what has happened}
      GameState := gsIntermission;
      Break;
    end;
  end;

  {update and draw any explosions}
  for icount := 0 to NUMEXPLOSIONS do
    if Explosions[iCount] <> nil then
    begin
      {although explosions don't really move, they
       animate, and in the interest of similarity,
       they have a Move method like other sprites}
      Explosions[iCount].Move;

      {explosions are short lived. if the explosion is
```

```
                         still living (and thus animating), draw it; otherwise
                         destroy it}
                      if Explosions[iCount].Living then
                        Explosions[iCount].Draw
                      else
                      begin
                        Explosions[iCount].Free;
                        Explosions[iCount] := nil;
                      end;
                   end;

     {now move all of the ships}
     for iCount := 0 to NUMSHIPS do
       if Ships[iCount] <> nil then
       begin
         {some enemy specific code...}
         if iCount > PLAYERSHIPIDX then
         begin
           {we should also detect if an enemy ship has collided
            with the player's ship...}
           if (Ships[PLAYERSHIPIDX] <> nil) and
              (IntersectRect(ISectRect,Ships[iCount].CollisionBox,
               Ships[PLAYERSHIPIDX].CollisionBox)) then
           begin
             {if indeed the player and enemy ships have collided,
              we should start two explosions and kill both ships}
             StartExplosion(Ships[PLAYERSHIPIDX].XPos,
                            Ships[PLAYERSHIPIDX].YPos);
             StartExplosion(Ships[iCount].XPos,
                            Ships[iCount].YPos);
             Ships[iCount].Living := FALSE;
             Ships[PLAYERSHIPIDX].Living := FALSE;

             {this kill should count towards the total amount
              required to advance a level}
             Dec(NumShipsToNextLevel);

             {as before, we need to determine if the player has
              increased to the next level.  however, the player
              has just died, so we don't want to immediately
              change the game state}
             if NumShipsToNextLevel <= 0 then
             begin
               Inc(Level);
               NumShipsToNextLevel := 5 * Level;
             end;

             {we want the player to see the explosion, so we must
              wait an appropriate amount of time before changing
              the game state}
             TimeAccum := timeGetTime;
```

```
          end
          else
          begin
            {there was no collision with the player's ship,
             so perform some very simplistic AI. this will
             randomly change the horizontal velocity of the
             ship, and randomly fire a bullet at the player}
            if Random(1000) < 10 then
              Ships[iCount].XVel := 0-Ships[iCount].XVel;

            if Random(1000) < 50 then
              StartBullet(Ships[iCount].XPos+
                          (Ships[iCount].FrameWidth div 2)-5,
                          Ships[iCount].YPos, 0, 8, FALSE);
          end;
        end;

        {update the ship's position based on velocity}
        Ships[iCount].Move;

        {if the ship is still living, draw it, otherwise
         destroy it}
        if Ships[iCount].Living then
          Ships[iCount].Draw
        else
        begin
          Ships[iCount].Free;
          Ships[iCount] := nil;
        end;
      end;

  {display the number of ships left}
  for iCount := 0 to LivesLeft-1 do
  begin
    SourceRect := Rect(392, 48, 422, 70);
    FBackBuffer.BltFast(500+(iCount*30)+5, 455,
                        FGraphicsImage, SourceRect,
                        DDBLTFAST_SRCCOLORKEY or
                        DDBLTFAST_WAIT);
  end;

  {display the score}
  WorkCanvas := TCanvas.Create;
  FBackBuffer.GetDC(SurfaceDC);

  try
    WorkCanvas.Handle := SurfaceDC;

    WorkCanvas.Font.Size := 10;
    WorkCanvas.Font.Name := 'Arial';
    WorkCanvas.Font.Color := clWhite;
```

```
                        WorkCanvas.Brush.Style := bsClear;
                        WorkCanvas.TextOut(5, 465, 'Score: '+IntToStr(Score));
                      finally
                        WorkCanvas.Handle := 0;
                        FBackBuffer.ReleaseDC(SurfaceDC);
                        WorkCanvas.Free;
                      end;

                      {if our timing variable has been initialized, the player
                       has been killed. thus, we check to see if an appropriate
                       amount of time has passed before resetting certain
                       variables and reinitializing the player. this allows
                       players to see the ship exploding when it collides with
                       a missile or an enemy ship}
                      if (TimeAccum > -1) and (timeGetTime-TimeAccum>2000) then
                      begin
                        PlayerShipKilled;
                      end;
                  end;
      end;
end;



{ -> Deletable Events <- }

///
{ - as a matter of convenience this framework will terminate when the -
  - Escape key is pressed, but this should probably be deleted and     -
  - replaced with your own terminate methods                           - }
procedure TfrmDXAppMain.FormKeyDown(Sender: TObject; var Key: Word;
  Shift: TShiftState);
begin
  if Key = VK_ESCAPE then
    Close;
end;
///


{ *-->>  END BASELINE APPLICATION CODE <<--* }


{ TSprite }

procedure TSprite.Draw;
var
  SourceRect: TRect;

  DestY: Integer;
begin
  {if it is time to increment the current frame...}
```

```
    if timeGetTime - CurAnimTime > AnimThreshold then
    begin
      {increment the frame of animation}
      Inc(CurFrame);

      {roll it over if necessary}
      if CurFrame>=NumFrames then
        CurFrame := 0;

      {record the time}
      CurAnimTime := timeGetTime;
    end;

    {draw the next animation frame into the backbuffer}
    SourceRect := Rect(XFrameStartOffset+(FrameWidth*CurFrame),
                       YFrameStartOffset, XFrameStartOffset+
                       (FrameWidth*CurFrame)+FrameWidth,
                       YFrameStartOffset+FrameHeight);

    {if the sprite is fully on screen...}
    if (YPos >= 0) and (YPos <= DXHEIGHT-FrameHeight) then
      {draw it to the screen}
      FBackBuffer.BltFast(XPos, YPos, FGraphicsImage, SourceRect,
                          DDBLTFAST_SRCCOLORKEY OR DDBLTFAST_WAIT)
    else
    begin
      {...otherwise, it is partially hidden at the top or bottom, so determine
       the rectangular portion of the sprite that is visible}
      if YPos < 0 then
      begin
        DestY := 0;
        SourceRect := Rect(SourceRect.Left, SourceRect.Top-YPos,
                           SourceRect.Right, SourceRect.Bottom);
      end
      else
      begin
        DestY := YPos;
        SourceRect := Rect(SourceRect.Left, SourceRect.Top, SourceRect.Right,
                           SourceRect.Top+(DXHEIGHT-YPos));
      end;

      {copy the image portion to the screen}
      FBackBuffer.BltFast(XPos, DestY, FGraphicsImage, SourceRect,
                          DDBLTFAST_SRCCOLORKEY OR DDBLTFAST_WAIT);
    end;
end;

procedure TSprite.Move;
begin
  {move the sprite according to its horizontal velocity}
  XPos := XPos + XVel;
```

```
     YPos := YPos + YVel;

     {clip the sprite to the boundaries of the screen}
     if XPos > DXWIDTH-FrameWidth then
     begin
       XPos := DXWIDTH-FrameWidth;
       XVel := 0-XVel;
     end;
     if XPos < 0 then
     begin
       XPos := 0;
       XVel := 0-XVel;
     end;

     {update its bounding box}
     CollisionBox := Rect(XPos+BoundBox.Left, YPos+BoundBox.Top,
                          XPos+BoundBox.Right, YPos+BoundBox.Bottom);

     {if the sprite has gone off the top or bottom of the screen, it is dead}
     if (YPos < 0-FrameHeight) or (YPos > DXHEIGHT) then
       Living := FALSE;
end;

{ TExplosion }

procedure TExplosion.Move;
begin
  {explosions don't actually move, but an explosion's lifespan is over when
   it has played all of its frames}
  if CurFrame+1 >= NumFrames then
    Living := FALSE;
end;

{ TStar }

procedure TStar.Move;
begin
  {stars only move vertically, so update their position}
  YPos := YPos + YVel;

  {clip them to the boundaries of the screen, wrapping around if necessary}
  if YPos < 0 then
    YPos := DXHEIGHT;
  if YPos >= DXHEIGHT then
    YPos := 0;
end;

procedure TStar.Draw;
var
  SurfaceDesc: TDDSurfaceDesc2;
begin
```

```
{lock the backbuffer}
SurfaceDesc.dwSize := SizeOf(TDDSurfaceDesc2);
FBackBuffer.Lock(nil, SurfaceDesc, DDLOCK_SURFACEMEMORYPTR or DDLOCK_WAIT,0);

{color the appropriate pixel in the backbuffer using the star's color. this
 is a very fast way to plot individual pixels}
try
  Byte(Pointer(Longword(SurfaceDesc.lpSurface)+
              (YPos*SurfaceDesc.lPitch+XPos))^) := Color;
finally
  {the buffer must be unlocked before it can be flipped}
  FBackBuffer.Unlock(nil);
end;
end;

procedure TfrmDXAppMain.NewGame;
begin
  {initialize game variables}
  Level := 1;
  Score := 0;
  LivesLeft := 3;
  NumShipsToNextLevel := 5;

  {reset all sprites}
  ResetAll;

  {go to intermission}
  GameState := gsIntermission;
end;

procedure TfrmDXAppMain.StartBullet(XPos, YPos, XVel, YVel: Integer;
  PlayerBullet: Boolean);
var
  iCount: Integer;
begin
  {if we're starting a player bullet}
  if PlayerBullet then
  begin
    {find an open slot in the bullets array}
    for iCount := 0 to NUMBULLETS do
      if PlayerBullets[iCount] = nil then
      begin
        {create a new bullet}
        PlayerBullets[iCount] := TSprite.Create;

        {initialize the bullet sprite's properties}
        PlayerBullets[iCount].NumFrames := 1;
        PlayerBullets[iCount].CurFrame := 0;
        PlayerBullets[iCount].FrameWidth := 10;
        PlayerBullets[iCount].FrameHeight := 17;
        PlayerBullets[iCount].XFrameStartOffset := 372;
```

```
          PlayerBullets[iCount].YFrameStartOffset := 48;
          PlayerBullets[iCount].BoundBox := Rect(0, 0, 10, 17);
          PlayerBullets[iCount].Living := TRUE;
          PlayerBullets[iCount].XPos := XPos;
          PlayerBullets[iCount].YPos := YPos;
          PlayerBullets[iCount].XVel := XVel;
          PlayerBullets[iCount].YVel := YVel;
          PlayerBullets[iCount].CurAnimTime := timeGetTime;
          PlayerBullets[iCount].AnimThreshold := 10000;

          {this bullet has been created, we can exit}
          Break;
        end;
    end
    else
    begin
      {otherwise, search for an open slot in the enemy bullets array}
      for iCount := 0 to NUMBULLETS do
        if EnemyBullets[iCount] = nil then
        begin
          {create the bullet}
          EnemyBullets[iCount] := TSprite.Create;

          {initialize the bullet sprite's properties}
          EnemyBullets[iCount].NumFrames := 1;
          EnemyBullets[iCount].CurFrame := 0;
          EnemyBullets[iCount].FrameWidth := 10;
          EnemyBullets[iCount].FrameHeight := 10;
          EnemyBullets[iCount].XFrameStartOffset := 382;
          EnemyBullets[iCount].YFrameStartOffset := 51;
          EnemyBullets[iCount].BoundBox := Rect(0, 0, 10, 10);
          EnemyBullets[iCount].Living := TRUE;
          EnemyBullets[iCount].XPos := XPos;
          EnemyBullets[iCount].YPos := YPos;
          EnemyBullets[iCount].XVel := XVel;
          EnemyBullets[iCount].YVel := YVel;
          EnemyBullets[iCount].CurAnimTime := timeGetTime;
          EnemyBullets[iCount].AnimThreshold := 10000;

          {this bullet has been created, we can exit}
          Break;
        end;
    end;
end;

procedure TfrmDXAppMain.StartEnemy;
var
  iCount: Integer;
begin
  {search for an open slot in the ships array. notice that the player's ship
   is always located at the first index, so we skip it}
```

```
          for iCount := PLAYERSHIPIDX+1 to NUMSHIPS do
            if Ships[iCount] = nil then
            begin
              {create the sprite}
              Ships[iCount] := TSprite.Create;

              {initialize the sprite properties}
              Ships[iCount].NumFrames := 3;
              Ships[iCount].CurFrame := 0;
              Ships[iCount].FrameWidth := 62;
              Ships[iCount].FrameHeight := 36;
              Ships[iCount].XFrameStartOffset := 186;
              Ships[iCount].YFrameStartOffset := 0;
              Ships[iCount].BoundBox := Rect(3, 3, 59, 33);
              Ships[iCount].Living := TRUE;
              Ships[iCount].XPos := Random(DXWIDTH - 61)+1;
              Ships[iCount].YPos := -36;
              Ships[iCount].XVel := Random(6)-3;
              Ships[iCount].YVel := Random(4)+1;
              Ships[iCount].CurAnimTime := timeGetTime;
              Ships[iCount].AnimThreshold := 100;

              {the sprite was created, we can exit}
              Break;
            end;
end;

procedure TfrmDXAppMain.StartExplosion(XPos, YPos: Integer);
var
  iCount: Integer;
begin
  {search for an open slot in the explosions array}
  for iCount := 0 to NUMEXPLOSIONS do
    if Explosions[iCount] = nil then
    begin
      {create the explosion sprite}
      Explosions[iCount] := TExplosion.Create;

      {initialize the sprite properties}
      Explosions[iCount].NumFrames := 6;
      Explosions[iCount].CurFrame := 0;
      Explosions[iCount].FrameWidth := 62;
      Explosions[iCount].FrameHeight := 47;
      Explosions[iCount].XFrameStartOffset := 0;
      Explosions[iCount].YFrameStartOffset := 48;
      Explosions[iCount].Living := TRUE;
      Explosions[iCount].XPos := XPos;
      Explosions[iCount].YPos := YPos;
      Explosions[iCount].CurAnimTime := timeGetTime;
      Explosions[iCount].AnimThreshold := 100;
```

```
            {the sprite was created, we can exit}
            Break;
        end;
end;

procedure TfrmDXAppMain.ResetAll;
var
  iCount: Integer;
begin
  {free all of the ships}
  for iCount := 0 to NUMSHIPS do
  begin
    Ships[iCount].Free;
    Ships[iCount] := nil;
  end;

  {free all of the bullets}
  for iCount := 0 to NUMBULLETS do
  begin
    PlayerBullets[iCount].Free;
    PlayerBullets[iCount] := nil;

    EnemyBullets[iCount].Free;
    EnemyBullets[iCount] := nil;
  end;

  {free all of the explosions}
  for iCount := 0 to NUMEXPLOSIONS do
  begin
    Explosions[iCount].Free;
    Explosions[iCount] := nil;
  end;

  {reset the pause timer}
  TimeAccum := -1;
end;

procedure TfrmDXAppMain.ResetPlayer;
begin
  {make sure the player ship is created}
  if not Assigned(Ships[PLAYERSHIPIDX]) then
    Ships[PLAYERSHIPIDX] := TSprite.Create;

  {initialize the player ship sprite properties}
  Ships[PLAYERSHIPIDX].NumFrames := 3;
  Ships[PLAYERSHIPIDX].CurFrame := 0;
  Ships[PLAYERSHIPIDX].FrameWidth := 62;
  Ships[PLAYERSHIPIDX].FrameHeight := 48;
  Ships[PLAYERSHIPIDX].XFrameStartOffset := 0;
  Ships[PLAYERSHIPIDX].YFrameStartOffset := 0;
  Ships[PLAYERSHIPIDX].BoundBox := Rect(3, 3, 59, 45);
```

```
    Ships[PLAYERSHIPIDX].Living := TRUE;
    Ships[PLAYERSHIPIDX].XPos := DXWIDTH div 2;
    Ships[PLAYERSHIPIDX].YPos := DXHEIGHT-Ships[PLAYERSHIPIDX].FrameHeight-20;
    Ships[PLAYERSHIPIDX].XVel := 0;
    Ships[PLAYERSHIPIDX].YVel := 0;
    Ships[PLAYERSHIPIDX].CurAnimTime := timeGetTime;
    Ships[PLAYERSHIPIDX].AnimThreshold := 100;

    {indicate that the player can now shoot}
    CanShoot := TRUE;
end;

procedure TfrmDXAppMain.PlayerShipKilled;
begin
    {decrement the number of lives}
    Dec(LivesLeft);

    {reset all of the sprites}
    ResetAll;

    {if the player has no more lives left, go to demo; otherwise go to
     intermission}
    if LivesLeft < 0 then
      GameState := gsDemo
    else
      GameState := gsIntermission;
end;

end.
```

## Summary

In this chapter, we discussed the most important and most basic issues involved in designing game application software. When designing the architecture of game application software, it is important to keep these points in mind:

■ Every game, no matter how complex, can be broken down into three constituent parts: graphics, sound, and user input.

■ The specific architecture of a game will vary widely depending on the type of game and its inherent functionality. Even so, most games usually perform similar tasks in a similar order. From a high-level standpoint, game software can be thought of in terms of six elements that perform necessary tasks: Initialization, Game Introduction, Game Startup, the Game Loop, Game Ending, and Shutdown and Exit.

■ The game loop is usually the focal point of a game application, and is where all of the action takes place. It processes a series of instructions over and over as quickly as possible to produce the on-screen images that reflect the current state of the game. This processing continues with or without user interaction. It can be implemented in a variety of ways, and must perform several different tasks as rapidly as possible. Technically speaking, a game loop is responsible for three things: retrieving input, updating game objects, and rendering a new frame of animation. Additionally, it must perform collision detection, enemy AI, and other tasks commensurate with the specific type of game.

■ Games can be examined from the standpoint of their current mode of execution, or state. A state based gaming architecture allows the game to be controlled in a more logical and ordered manner. The state of a game can flow from one state to another as appropriate, changing between logical states and ultimately creating a circuit from game beginning through game play to game end and back again. In general, games can be considered to execute in five different states: Demo, Playing, Intermission, Paused, and Game Over.

# CHAPTER 3: *Basic Graphics Programming*

**THIS CHAPTER COVERS THE FOLLOWING TOPICS:**

- Graphical elements, such as pixels, lines, and polygons
- Video mode resolutions and color depth, and the difference between palettized and non-palettized video modes
- Device contexts and their use
- Using the TCanvas object for graphical output
- Essential bitmap techniques
- Color palettes

Like other industries, the computer industry has matured to the point that it can be thought of in terms of specialties. There are specialists in hardware installation, technical support, client/server architecture, etc. Some fields, such as programming, are further divided. Programming offers many areas of specialization, including database programming, speech recognition, or even communications. Of these, graphics programming is one of the most fun, rewarding, and sought-after specialties. All client-side applications that interact directly with the user make some use of graphics programming techniques, be they simple GDI commands for drawing basic Windows interface elements or full-fledged, 3-D rendered landscapes in games. At some point, any programmer working on an application to be used by end users will need to have some knowledge of graphical programming techniques.

This book's primary focus is on high-performance graphics and games programming using DirectX. Although the techniques discussed throughout the book are advanced by their very nature, the neophyte to graphics programming should not be ignored. Many people have used Delphi solely for client/server database applications or business related programs, and are just now experimenting with its broader range of functionality. There have been several shareware games written in Delphi, and retail games created with Delphi, while rare, are starting to emerge. Thus, many readers of this book are probably new to graphics programming, and may be a little fearful of the advanced topics presented in the coming chapters.

To this end, this chapter has been dedicated to acclimating the Delphi programmer to terms and concepts common in graphics programming. Although no one concept is discussed in any great depth, after reading this chapter, the casual Delphi programmer will be familiar with many of the terms and concepts that will be expounded upon in later chapters. This should give Delphi programmers a good base of knowledge to prepare them for the graphics programming techniques to come. Readers who are familiar with basic graphics programming topics, such as pixels, lines, polygons, bitmaps, and using the TCanvas object, may want to skip ahead to the next chapter, which introduces DirectX. However, if you're not familiar with these topics, read on.

# The Graphical Device Interface

One of the fundamental pieces of Windows is the Graphical Device Interface, or the GDI. This important subsystem is responsible for all of the graphical output displayed to the screen during a Windows session. The GDI subsystem is accessed through a wide variety of functions and procedures. Buttons, lines, scroll bars, application windows themselves, even text, are all drawn by these GDI functions and procedures.

**Graphical Device Interface (GDI):** The Windows subsystem responsible for all graphical output during a Windows session.

One of Window's strongest attributes is its device independence, or its ability to be run on a wide variety of hardware combinations. Due to this requirement, the GDI's primary purpose is to provide a mechanism by which an application can output graphical content without the programmer being concerned about what type of hardware upon which the application will be running. It accomplishes this goal superbly; it is incredibly easy to draw lines, buttons, bitmaps, etc., without being concerned with hardware.

Unfortunately, as a direct consequence of this device independence, the GDI is notorious for its slow performance. Even with this reputation, the GDI is very useful when creating tools for games. While most games today are written in DirectX, it is very common for the game programmers to write tools under regular Windows using the GDI. Strictly speaking, while games run faster under DirectX, it's usually quicker to write the tools used to build the game using good ol' Windows and the GDI. The tools themselves rarely need the performance achievable with DirectX, and the incredible richness of the GDI API makes it simple and quick to produce the tools. It is now common for games to include some of the tools used in its creation, such as level editors. However, today's incredibly fast processors and Windows accelerated video cards are making this speed issue less of a problem. Although many would argue that a commercial quality game could not be accomplished using standard GDI techniques, several commercial and shareware games have been successfully created using nothing more than an intelligent application of GDI programming techniques.

**Figure 3-1:**
*Games using GDI techniques*

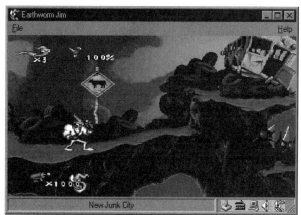

*Earthworm Jim for Windows 95*
*by Activision*

*Pitfall: The Mayan Adventure*
*by Activision*

*Mission:Moon by*
*Beckett Interactive*

Later in the chapter, we'll explore how Delphi and the TCanvas class unlock the power of the GDI and make it incredibly easy for the application developer to take advantage of some very powerful graphics programming techniques. First, however, we need to cover a number of concepts that are critical to understanding graphics programming.

# Graphical Elements

To begin exploring the topic of graphics programming, one must be familiar with a number of terms that describe various graphical elements. Like any specialty, graphics programming has its share of jargon, much of which will be discovered throughout the pages of this book. However, there are several terms that describe concepts in just about every application of graphics programming. These are: the pixel, the line, polygons, and bitmaps.

## *Pixels*

When the GDI displays an image to the screen, whether it's an application window, a button, text, etc., it draws the graphic in a series of different colored dots. As these dots are drawn to the screen, they eventually form an image that is recognizable to the user. This dot is called a pixel, and it is the smallest graphic that can be drawn to the screen. This action of "drawing" individual colored dots to the computer screen happens so fast (usually) that it appears instantaneous to the viewer.

**pixel:** The smallest, single element in a graphical image or on the display surface.

The entire computer screen can be thought of as a grid of dots, or pixels. The size of this grid determines the video mode resolution, and the number of colors in which an individual pixel can be drawn determines the color depth (more on this later).

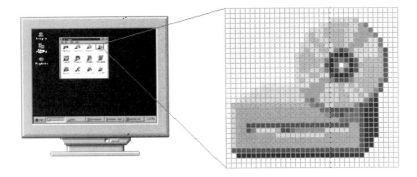

*Figure 3-2:*
*The screen is composed of dots, or pixels*

## Lines

Next to pixels, lines are the most common graphical element seen in user interfaces. The GDI uses lines of different colors to simulate the beveled surfaces common in Windows user interfaces. Of course, lines have several thousand other practical uses, from representing scales and rulers to graphs and other more complex graphical content. Strictly speaking, a line is simply a collection of pixels arranged in a linear fashion.

**line:** A collection of pixels, usually arranged in a linear or connecting configuration.

Lines have a mathematical discipline all their own, known as geometry. The study of lines and the mathematics that manipulate them is almost a fundamental requirement for any serious graphics programming. Even if the application will not be strictly output lines, it is sometimes useful to utilize geometry (and trigonometry, see below) to produce incredibly realistic scene generation. We'll see more of this when we cover ray casting engines later in the book.

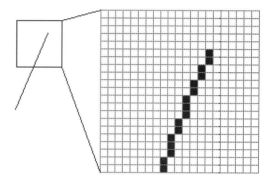

**Figure 3-3:**
*A line is a collection of pixels*

## Polygons

Polygons are quite prevalent in the world of 2-D graphics programming. Buttons are usually square or rectangular in shape, and it's not uncommon to see controls or graphics that are triangular, pentagonal, or configured into some other shape. Simply put, a polygon is a collection of lines, connected at the end to form some sort of closed shape.

**polygon:** A collection of lines, arranged in such a way that the ends are connected to form a continuous, closed shape.

Circles, ovals, and curves can be lumped into this category. The concept of polygons is absolutely critical to 3-D programming. Like lines, polygons are governed by a mathematical discipline known as trigonometry (actually, trigonometry and geometry are almost joined at the hip, and I use the relationship to lines and polygons loosely). Trigonometry is the study of angles, and this coupled with polygonal shapes allows the creation of incredibly realistic 3-D environments. We'll see some examples of this later in the book.

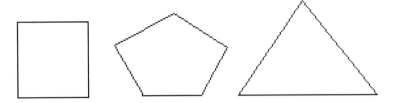

**Figure 3-4:**
*A polygon is a collection of lines*

## Bitmaps

Computer graphics would quickly get boring if only lines and polygons could be used to construct a scene in a game or an interface for a business application. The human brain has incredible pattern recognition skills, and utilizing this in a game or user interface can bring to life exotic locales or make a business application easy and intuitive to use. Take a look at the Windows desktop or any business application, and the prevalent use of icons and other graphical metaphors to indicate a function. Generally speaking, these can be considered bitmaps. Like lines, a bitmap is a collection of pixels arranged in such a way that they represent a picture.

**bitmap:** A collection of pixels arranged in a rectangular configuration in such a way that they form a recognizable shape, such as a picture or texture.

Digitized photos, the little images of floppy disks, printers, and pieces of paper on buttons in a business application, and the texture on the walls of the latest 3-D first-person shooter are all considered bitmaps. To coin a cliché, a picture is indeed worth a thousand words, and their liberal use in games and applications can result in several hundred, or perhaps even thousands, of bitmap images in use in any one program. By their very nature, bitmaps consume lots of memory, but few serious applications can succeed without employing them.

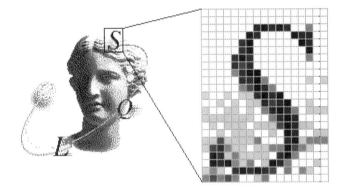

**Figure 3-5:**
*A bitmap is a collection of pixels*

## Graphical Element Classifications

Apart from the basic graphical elements described above, conversations in graphical programming sometimes indicate a broader subdivision of graphic types. Graphical output can generally be divided into two classifications: raster and vector. It is rare to hear about game applications being described as one or the other, but it is very common to discuss graphically based business applications or tools in terms of a raster-based or vector-based application.

### Raster Graphics

Raster graphics are images that are composed of individual pixels statically arranged in such a way as to represent a picture or image. Realistically, this refers to images such as icons and bitmaps.

**raster graphics:** Graphics that are composed of a collection of pixels that together form a picture or image. Generally refers to bitmaps, icons, and other such graphical types.

In general, raster graphics are very resolution dependent, and tend to lose resolution when scaled to a different size. The algorithms necessary for scaling or rotating raster graphics are generally very complex, and the quality of the results varies wildly depending upon the implementation.

The most common raster graphic file format is the humble Windows bitmap. Bitmaps can be created using the Paint application that comes with Windows. Delphi contains an Images directory that includes several bitmap files to be used as button glyphs or backgrounds within applications.

### Vector Graphics

Vector graphics are images that are described as a series of connected points in a virtual 2-D or 3-D grid. This type of graphic includes lines, polygons, circles, and curves. TrueType fonts, being described by a collection of connected points, are also considered to be vector graphics.

**vector graphics:** Graphics that are represented by a series of connected points in a virtual 2-D or 3-D Cartesian (or similar) coordinate system. Generally refers to lines, polygons, curves, and other such graphical types.

Unlike raster graphics, vector graphics are resolution independent, and can be scaled to any size without degradation of image quality. Although somewhat complex, the algorithms for scaling and rotating vector graphics are well documented and easily implemented, and the quality of the results is identical from implementation to implementation.

A common vector graphic file format is the Windows metafile. Its most prevalent use is with clip art type graphics that come with word processors and presentation programs. Because of its resolution independence, clip art stored in this format can be enlarged or shrunk as the user requires.

# Video Mode Resolutions and Color Depth

Discussions of graphics programming usually start from a consideration of what resolution the video driver is currently in, and how many colors are available in which to draw the graphics. These two concepts are directly related, and are generally referred to in a combined sense as the video mode.

**video mode:** The video hardware state which dictates the display resolution and number of available colors for graphical output.

These two items will have a profound effect on the graphics programming techniques involved in drawing the graphical elements previously discussed. Both the resolution and the color depth of the current video mode will affect the perceived quality of the displayed graphical images. The greater the resolution and color depth, the more realistic and detailed the displayed graphics will become. However, on the downside, higher resolution and deeper color depth mean greater memory usage and slower speed.

## Resolution

The resolution of the current video mode controls how many pixels can be displayed on the screen.

**resolution:** A measurement of the number of pixels displayed on the screen.

As the resolution increases, more and more pixels are available for displaying graphics. This will directly affect the perceived size of graphical images. This is especially true for raster graphics, as vector graphics can be adjusted accordingly. For example, if a bitmap image is 50 pixels by 50 pixels in size, it will appear larger when displayed at its original resolution when the video mode is set to 800 x 600 pixels than it will when the video mode is set to 1024 x 768 pixels. As illustrated in Figure 3-6, a fixed size bitmap image will appear smaller in higher resolution video modes because individual pixels must be smaller in order to fit more of them onto the screen.

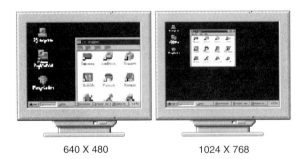

640 X 480          1024 X 768

**Figure 3-6:**
*Two different display resolutions*

Supported resolutions are dependent upon the video card installed in the machine, the video driver, and the monitor upon which the output is displayed. The video driver and video card dictate the video modes available for use. However, occasionally the monitor connected to the machine will be unable to handle the new video mode.

**Caution:**  Switching to a video mode that is unsupported by the monitor can potentially damage it, and should be avoided.

Perhaps the most common display resolution employed by desktop machines today is 800 pixels wide and 600 pixels high. However, it is usually wise to develop for the smallest common denominator in order to take advantage of a broader market (and subsequent revenue potential). Thus, many developers create games based on a 640 x 480 resolution. Generally speaking, it is harder to write code that will support a wide variety of resolution sizes. Nevertheless, the extra effort that allows users to take advantage of new equipment usually pays off, and makes your customers very happy.

## Color Depth

The color depth of the current video mode controls how many colors in which an individual pixel can be drawn. Color depth is measured in bits per pixel, meaning that the more bits used to describe a color, the more colors there are available in which to draw a pixel.

**color depth:** A measurement of the number of bits per pixel required to describe the color of an individual pixel.

The color depth of the current video mode will affect the techniques used to draw graphics more so than the display resolution. Color depth determines if the video mode will be palettized or non-palettized (discussed below). As this affects how pixels are stored, different techniques must be employed when drawing graphics. As the bits per pixel increase, the number of colors available for each individual pixel increases, but so does the amount of memory required to hold a bitmap. The following table summarizes common color depths and the amount of colors available per pixel under each:

*Table 3-1:* Color depth versus available colors

| Bits Per Pixel | Number of Colors Available |
|---|---|
| 4 | 16 colors |
| 8 | 256 colors |
| 16 | 65,536 colors (high color mode) |
| 24 | 16,777,216 colors (true color mode) |
| 32 | 16,777,216 colors plus 256 levels of transparency (true color) |

Color depths of only 4 bits per pixel are no longer used for games. Perhaps the most common color depth used in games is 8 bits per pixel, as this makes it very easy to manipulate individual pixels in a bitmap, or to move large amounts of pixels around in memory. However, thanks to hardware acceleration, faster processors, and other advances, higher color depths are starting to be used in more games. 16-bit color games are becoming more prevalent, but 24-bit and 32-bit color depths are still too slow to be used for games that run on anything other than today's higher end PCs.

## Video Board Memory

Apart from the video modes supported by the video driver and the graphics card itself, available video modes are further restricted by the amount of video RAM available on the graphics card. Only video RAM can be used support various video modes, and as the resolution and color depth of a video mode increase, so does the amount of video RAM required to support it. For example, a video mode of 800 x 600 pixels at a color depth of 8 bits per pixel requires 480,000 bytes, almost half a MB. If a video mode requires more memory than is available on the video card, it cannot be supported. For example, a video mode of 1024 x 760 at 16 bits per pixel cannot be supported unless the video card has at least 1,572,864 bytes of RAM available. This will become much more important later when we discuss DirectX surfaces.

## The Components of a Color

When discussing pixel colors and color depth, it is important to understand how colors are represented internally. The color of every pixel drawn to the screen is determined by three components: a red intensity, a blue intensity, and a green intensity. As these intensities increase or decrease, the color of an individual pixel is affected accordingly. Each intensity can have a minimum value of 0, and a maximum value of 255. If the intensity of each component is 0, the resulting color is black, while if each component is at 255, the resulting color is white. This gives a maximum of 16,777,216 colors, well beyond the scope of what the human eye can accurately detect from shade to shade. This is referred to as RGB color, standing for red, green, and blue, respectively.

**RGB color:** Refers to the method by which colors are represented, usually in the form of a red, green, and blue component, respectively.

Most of the time, colors are used in this RGB format. However, occasionally colors will be used in a reverse format (BGR), depending on which GDI functions are being used.

## Palettized Modes

Four and eight bits-per-pixel color depths are the only palettized video modes. As 4 bits-per-pixel color depths are no longer used for games, we will discuss only 8 bits-per-pixel color depths. At 8 bits-per-pixel, each pixel can assume a value between 0 and 255. These values act as an index into what can be considered a 256-entry array known as the color palette. Now, each entry in this array contains an 8-bit value for the blue, green, and red intensity of a color. In effect, this gives 8 bits-per-pixel color depths access to 16,777,216 potential colors, but only 256 of them can be shown at one time.

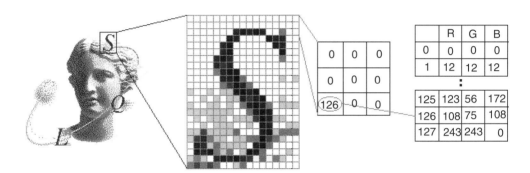

**Figure 3-7:**
*An 8 bits-per -pixel bitmap's pixels act as indices into a color palette*

There are many things to consider when working with 8 bits-per-pixel color modes. A major disadvantage to this mode is that all bitmaps to be displayed simultaneously must be drawn using the same palette. This requires a lot of careful planning on the part of art production, and can limit the creativity of artists and the variety of artwork that can be displayed on screen. Bitmaps that are drawn using one palette but displayed on a device in which a different palette is currently being used, will have unpredictable results.

A bitmap's pixels could be mapped to the closest approximation of the appropriate color in the current palette, but this process is slow, usually produces inadequate results, and is not appropriate for fast action games. Different palettes can be used between scenes, however, which can reduce this effect. However, 8 bits-per-pixel video modes give the greatest speed advantage, and a tremendous number of colors can potentially be used while taking up the least amount of RAM. Up to four pixels can be moved simultaneously by using 32-bit memory movement instructions, allowing bitmaps to be moved about at blindingly fast speeds.

Another major advantage comes from palette animation. If colors within the palette are moved about, or cycled, every pixel drawn using that color is affected simultaneously and automatically. This can be used for various special effects, such as flowing water or lighting. Palette animation is not available under non-palettized video modes. Since this book is concerned with high-performance games and graphics programming, all examples will use only 8 bits-per-pixel video modes in order to squeeze out as much speed as possible.

## Non-palettized Modes

16, 24, and 32 bits-per-pixel video modes directly store the color value for each pixel. This color value is encoded according to the bits-per-pixel used, and can vary from video board to video board. In general, 16 bits-per-pixel color depths use five bits to describe each of the red, green, and blue intensities of a color. 24 bits-per-pixel uses a full eight bits to describe each intensity, and 32 bits-per-pixel uses the same format with eight extra bits used as a translucency value.

Non-palettized video modes have the advantage of total freedom to display any number of bitmaps simultaneously, without worrying about color problems or palette management. The downside to this is that more memory is required for both display and bitmap storage, and games tend to run slower as it requires longer to move a bitmap from one place in memory to another. This book will concentrate on using only 8 bits-per-pixel color depths, so any further discussion of non-palettized video modes is beyond our scope.

# Graphics Output Techniques

As stated above, the GDI provides the primary functions and procedures by which graphics can be drawn to the screen. There are literally hundreds of functions and procedures, and covering all of them is well beyond the scope of this book. However, we will discuss a number of the most common GDI graphical output functions and will look at several examples that demonstrate their use.

## The Device Context

A device context represents a surface upon which graphical output can be drawn. Specifically, a device context represents the surface of an output device such as a monitor, printer, or plotter, and gives the developer access to modify its appearance. This access is accomplished through the specific device's device driver.

 **device context (DC):** Represents the surface of an output device such as a monitor, printer, or plotter, allowing the application to perform graphical output.

Under regular Windows programming, the device context provides the only way to render graphics to the screen. Device contexts can be used with Direct-Draw functions to make certain tasks easier, as we'll see in later chapters. Most, if not all, GDI API functions require a handle to the device context upon which the specified graphical operation will be performed. Device contexts represent certain areas on the screen, from the surface of a control (such as a button) to the entire surface of a window or even the screen itself. To retrieve a handle to a device context, an application calls the GetDC function, passing it the handle of the window whose surface is to be drawn upon. It is very important to call the ReleaseDC function when the application is finished drawing its output, as neglecting to release the device context can cause Windows to lock up. Fortunately, we will not need to be concerned much with device contexts, as the TCanvas object encapsulates the functionality of the device context and makes graphical output much easier.

## Painting on the Canvas

Objects derived from TGraphicControl and TCustomControl provide a TCanvas property for performing graphical output. This allows the developer to determine the appearance of the control. The TCanvas object, as an encapsulation of the device context, contains numerous methods for drawing graphics, making the use of most GDI function calls unnecessary. However, when using GDI API functions that are not encapsulated by the TCanvas object, the Handle property can be used in parameters that require a handle to a device context. Lines, polygons, even individual pixels can be drawn on the surface of a TCanvas object with relative ease. Again, like the device context, the TCanvas object represents the surface of a window, such as a control or the application window itself. Thus, when anything is drawn on the canvas, it will appear on screen in the position of the control or window which it represents.

**Note:** Graphics output is controlled by specifying a horizontal and vertical coordinate, with the horizontal coordinate increasing from left to right and the vertical coordinate increasing from top to bottom. Since the TCanvas object represents an individual window or control, the origin of its coordinates is relative to the window or control it represents. Thus, the coordinate 0, 0 will be in the upper left-hand corner of the window or control it represents, which may or may not be the upper left-hand corner of the physical screen.

Now let's examine some techniques for drawing graphics. These techniques will be concerned with drawing graphics primitives, or simple lines, dots, and polygons. These simplistic techniques demonstrate how easy it is to use the TCanvas encapsulation of a device context for performing graphical output. They all use the Canvas property of the main form for the drawing surface.

## Pens and Brushes

TCanvas objects contain several properties, two of which are extremely important when performing graphical output: the Pen property and the Brush property. The Pen property determines the characteristics of lines drawn on the TCanvas, such as a line's thickness and color. The Brush property determines the appearance of the interiors of polygons, such as the color and pattern. Using the TPen and TBrush objects, several pens and brushes can be constructed by the application and assigned to the appropriate properties when necessary. However, most of the time, it is sufficient to simply change the properties of the TCanvas as needed.

## Drawing Pixels

The Pixels property of the TCanvas object gives the application access to individual pixels of the surface. This is accessed like a two-dimensional array, with the first index acting as the horizontal coordinate and the second index acting as the vertical coordinate. The Pixels property reports or receives a color in the form of a TColor type (which is an RGB color value, regardless of the video mode). The following example demonstrates using the Pixels property of a TCanvas object to draw random pixels.

**Listing 3-1:** *Using the Pixels property*

```
procedure TfrmPixelDemo.TimerTimer(Sender: TObject);
var
  iCount: Integer;
begin
  {draw 100 random pixels in a random RGB color}
  for iCount := 0 to 99 do
    Canvas.Pixels[Random(ClientWidth),Random(ClientHeight)] := RGB(Random(256),
                                                                    Random(256),
                                                                    Random(256));
end;
```

Unfortunately, this method of accessing individual pixels of an image is incredibly slow, and should never be used for fast graphical output.

*Figure 3-8:*
*Drawing individual pixels*

## Drawing Lines

Lines are drawn using the attributes set by the Pen property. The PenPos property determines the current position of the pen or the starting point of any drawing operation that uses the pen (such as drawing lines). This position can be modified by directly setting the PenPos property or by calling the MoveTo method. The LineTo method is called to actually draw the line, from the position indicated by the PenPos property to the position passed in the LineTo method. This pen position is updated to the coordinates passed to the LineTo position after the line is drawn. The following example demonstrates how to use these methods to draw various lines of random length, color, and width.

*Listing 3-2: Using the MoveTo and LineTo methods*

```
procedure TfrmLineDemo.TimerTimer(Sender: TObject);
begin
  {set a random pen color and width}
  Canvas.Pen.Color := RGB(Random(256), Random(256), Random(256));
  Canvas.Pen.Width := Random(5);

  {draw a line between two random points}
  Canvas.MoveTo(Random(ClientWidth), Random(ClientHeight));
  Canvas.LineTo(Random(ClientWidth), Random(ClientHeight));
end;
```

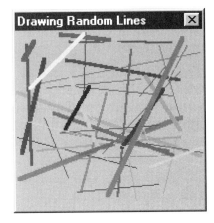

*Figure 3-9:*
*Drawing random lines*

## Drawing Polygons

Polygons are drawn using the attributes set by both the Pen and Brush properties. The Pen property determines the outline of the polygon, and the Brush property determines how the polygon is filled. Several methods exist that draw polygons of different shapes, from rectangles to circles. The Polygon method can be used to draw polygons of any arbitrary shape simply by passing it an open array of TPoint structures. The following example demonstrates how to use several polygon drawing methods to draw polygons of various shapes and colors.

**Listing 3-3:** *Using various polygon drawing methods*

```
procedure TfrmPolygonDemo.TimerTimer(Sender: TObject);
type
  {enumerated type representing several standard polygon drawing routines}
  TPolyType = (ptChord, ptEllipse, ptPie, ptRectangle, ptRoundRect);
var
  X1, X2, X3, X4, Y1, Y2, Y3, Y4: Integer;
begin
  {initialize a set of random coordinates}
  X1 := Random(ClientWidth);
  X2 := Random(ClientWidth);
  X3 := Random(ClientWidth);
  X4 := Random(ClientWidth);

  Y1 := Random(ClientHeight);
  Y2 := Random(ClientHeight);
  Y3 := Random(ClientHeight);
  Y4 := Random(ClientHeight);

  {set the brush to a random RGB color}
  Canvas.Brush.Color := RGB(Random(256), Random(256), Random(256));

  {draw a random polygon}
  case TPolyType(Random(Ord(ptRoundRect)+1)) of
    ptChord     : Canvas.Chord(X1, Y1, X2, Y2, X3, Y3, X4, Y4);
    ptEllipse   : Canvas.Ellipse(X1, Y1, X2, Y2);
    ptPie       : Canvas.Pie(X1, Y1, X2, Y2, X3, Y3, X4, Y4);
    ptRectangle : Canvas.Rectangle(X1, Y1, X2, Y2);
    ptRoundRect : Canvas.RoundRect(X1, Y1, X2, Y2, X3, Y3);
  end;
end;
```

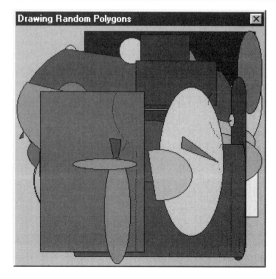

**Figure 3-10:**
*Drawing random polygons*

## *Drawing Text*

Perhaps the most common use of TCanvas graphical output techniques is for drawing text. The Font property of the TCanvas object determines the attributes of the text, including its typeface, size, and style. The TextOut method is used to draw the specified string at the indicated coordinates. These coordinates denote the top left corner of the text string. The following example demonstrates how to use the TextOut method to draw randomly colored text at random positions on the form.

*Tip:* By setting the Style property of the canvas's Brush property to bsClear, the background behind text will be transparent. This allows images underneath the text to show through, and is useful for drawing text on top of bitmap images.

*Listing 3-4:* Using the TextOut method

```
procedure TfrmTextDemo.TimerTimer(Sender: TObject);
begin
  {set a random text color}
  Canvas.Font.Color  := RGB(Random(256), Random(256), Random(256));

  {set a random text size}
  Canvas.Font.Size   := Random(10)+5;

  {set the text typeface}
  Canvas.Font.Name   := 'Arial';
  {set the brush style to clear so that the image behind the text
   will be visible}
  Canvas.Brush.Style := bsClear;

  {draw text at a random coordinate}
  Canvas.TextOut(Random(ClientWidth), Random(ClientHeight), 'Delphi Graphics');
end;
```

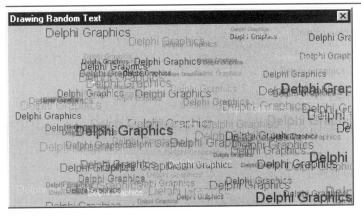

*Figure 3-11:*
*Drawing random text*

# Bitmap Essentials

It is quite possible for one to create a really engaging and entertaining game using nothing but line and polygon drawing techniques. However, if such graphical output were used in all games, everything would look very similar, and there would be little visual variety. In order to achieve the desired visual quality and variety that would be necessary in almost any game, bitmaps must be used.

Bitmaps come in many varieties, from two color to true color, and in many different formats, such as the Windows BMP format, JPEG, TIFF, GIF, etc. Each format presents its own benefits and weaknesses, and each is useful under specific circumstances. Obviously, the only format native to Windows is the Windows BMP format. This format can easily by accessed by low-level Windows API functions as well as Delphi VCL objects and functions, so the BMP format is the one on which we will focus.

## Bitmap Types: DDB and DIB

Most bitmap formats have subformats that allow an image to be stored similarly to the original format but with slight modifications, and the Windows bitmap format is no exception. Typically, subformats come about as a result of updated technology. New technology may contain enhanced functionality that was not available when the original format was created. Thus, subformats are born containing attributes that allow the image to take advantage of the new technological achievements. Windows bitmaps come in two flavors: DDB and DIB.

### Device-Dependent Bitmaps

The device-dependent bitmap, or DDB, is an older bitmap format and is kept around solely for backward compatibility. This format is so named because it is very dependent on the device upon which it is displayed for certain information. The DDB format does not store any color palette information or resolution information, storing only its width, height, color depth, and array of pixels that make up the image. DDBs always use the system color palette when they are displayed. Coupled with the lack of original resolution information, it is very difficult to accurately display a DDB in its original form on anything other than the original device upon which it was created. Additionally, the image itself can only be modified through the use of GDI functions. The storage and display of a DDB is handled natively by the video driver and video hardware. Naturally, this makes the use and display of DDBs very fast, but they are not very flexible.

 **device-dependent bitmap (DDB):** An older bitmap image format that stores only height, width, color depth, and image pixels.

### Device-Independent Bitmaps

The device-independent bitmap, or DIB, stores all the information required to accurately display the image on any device. Such information includes the color palette for the image, the resolution of the device upon which the bitmap was originally created, and a data compression flag. The pixels defining the DIB image are also directly accessible to the developer, making this format incredibly flexible. The DIB bitmap format describes a standardized pixel format, making the storage and display of such images a responsibility of generic GDI functions and global memory. As such, the use and display of DIBs is not quite as fast as DDBs, but their flexibility more than makes up for the loss in speed.

**device-independent bitmap (DIB):** A flexible bitmap image format that includes all necessary information to accurately reproduce the image on any device.

## The TBitmap Object

The Delphi TBitmap object encapsulates the functionality of both the DDB and DIB image formats. By default, when a TBitmap object is created, it holds an image in the DDB format. When a bitmap is loaded into it, the image will be stored in the DIB format. The TBitmap object contains many useful properties and methods that make the manipulation of bitmap images incredibly easy.

### Loading Images

Using regular GDI calls to simply load an image from a file may take half a dozen lines of code or more. With the TBitmap object, a simple call to its LoadFromFile method will load the image data and its palette, at which point the bitmap is ready for use. If the image is stored in a resource attached to the executable (or a DLL), the TBitmap's LoadFromResourceID or LoadFromResourceName methods give the developer flexibility in determining how the image is extracted from the resource. These methods alone more than justify the use of a TBitmap object over hard-core GDI function calls.

### Displaying Images

The TBitmap object itself does not contain any methods that deal directly with its display. This functionality lies in the domain of the TCanvas object. There are several methods by which a bitmap can be displayed, and they all have similar ancestors in the form of GDI function calls. The act of copying bitmap pixels to the screen for display is known as a bitblt, or blit.

**bitblt:** bit block transfer. Pronounced "blit," this is the act of copying the pixels of a bitmap image onto the screen or other graphical output surface for display.

The easiest TCanvas method available for displaying an image is Draw. It simply takes three parameters: a horizontal and vertical position of the upper left-hand corner of the image and the image object itself. This draws the entire image with its upper left-hand corner located at the specified coordinate. Other methods include CopyRect, which allows only a portion of an image to be drawn (scaling as necessary), and StretchDraw, which allows the image to be drawn larger or smaller than its original size. Listing 3-5 illustrates loading a bitmap and displaying it on the surface of a form.

***Listing 3-5:*** *Loading and displaying a bitmap image*

```
procedure TForm1.FormCreate(Sender: TObject);
begin
  {create the bitmap object}
  Bitmap := TBitmap.Create;

  {load in a bitmap image}
  Bitmap.LoadFromFile(ExtractFilePath(ParamStr(0))+'Athena.bmp');
end;

procedure TForm1.FormDestroy(Sender: TObject);
begin
  {free the bitmap object}
  Bitmap.Free;
end;

procedure TForm1.FormPaint(Sender: TObject);
begin
  {display the bitmap using the Draw method}
  Canvas.Draw(8, 24, Bitmap);

  {display the bitmap using the CopyRect method}
  Canvas.CopyRect(Rect(192, 24, 344, 104),Bitmap.Canvas,Rect(62, 39, 111, 74));

  {display the bitmap using the StretchDraw method}
  Canvas.StretchDraw(Rect(8, 184, 352, 264), Bitmap);
end;
```

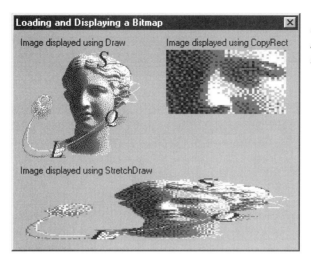

*Figure 3-12:*
*An image displayed using several different methods*

### Direct Pixel Access

One of the biggest benefits of using a DIB over a DDB is the fact that individual pixels can be directly accessed. This makes feasible many advanced graphical rendering techniques, such as ray casting. Accessing the individual pixels of a DDB (and even using the Pixels property of a TCanvas) is incredibly slow and could never be used for such advanced graphical output techniques.

To access individual pixels using the TBitmap object, the ScanLine property must be used. The ScanLine property is an indexed property that requires a row number and returns a pointer to the block of memory that contains the specified rows of pixels. The actual format of the information stored in this block of memory is dependent upon the value of the TBitmap's PixelFormat property. The PixelFormat value reflects the number of bits required to describe one pixel in the image. Refer to the color depth topic discussed previously for more information on bits-per-pixel and its relation to the number of colors an image can contain. Thus, it is very important to know how the image information is stored before accessing it.

Since this book is primarily concerned with 256-color images and graphical modes, assume that a TBitmap object has been loaded with a 256-color bitmap image. A variable of type PByteArray can be used to access the pixels pointed to by the ScanLine property. PByteArray is defined as a pointer to an array of bytes. The result of accessing the ScanLine property is assigned to our PByteArray variable, at which point the individual pixels can be accessed by a simple index into the array. Since a 256-color bitmap defines one pixel as 8 bits, or a byte, using a PByteArray variable allows the developer to access individual pixels correctly. If the image were of any other color depth, a different approach to accessing the pixels would need to be used. Listing 3-6 demonstrates accessing individual pixels through the ScanLine property.

*Listing 3-6:* Accessing individual pixels through the ScanLine property

```
procedure TForm1.Button1Click(Sender: TObject);
var
  Bitmap: TBitmap;
  Pixels: PByteArray;
  iBand, iRow, iCol: Integer;
  DrawColor: Byte;
begin
  {create the bitmap object}
  Bitmap := TBitmap.Create;

  {initialize the appropriate properties so we can access individual pixels
   in a known way}
  Bitmap.Width  := 169;
  Bitmap.Height := 128;
  Bitmap.PixelFormat := pf8Bit;

  {create 8 horizontal bands of alternating colors}
  DrawColor := 19;
  for iBand := 0 to 7 do
  begin
    {flip-flop the color. this is an 8 bit image, so we specify the color
     as an index into the palette.}
    if DrawColor = 16 then
      DrawColor := 19
    else
      DrawColor := 16;

    {each band is comprised of 16 rows of color}
    for iRow := 0 to 15 do
    begin
      {retrieve a pointer to the row of pixels}
      Pixels := Bitmap.ScanLine[(iBand*16)+iRow];

      {set each pixel in the row to the specific color}
      for iCol := 0 to Bitmap.Width-1 do
        Pixels[iCol] := DrawColor;
    end;
  end;

  {draw the bitmap to the screen}
  Canvas.Draw(8, 8, Bitmap);

  {free the bitmap}
  Bitmap.Free;
end;
```

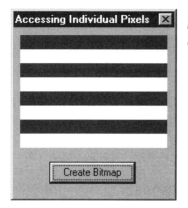

*Figure 3-13:*
*Individually painted pixels*

## Raster Operations

In addition to simply copying bitmap pixels from place to place, certain functions can modify exactly how the pixels are drawn onto their destination according to a specified setting. This is known as a raster operation, or ROP, and it determines how the pixels from the source, the destination, and the destination device context's selected brush are combined. The pixels are combined using boolean operations.

**raster operation (ROP):** A Boolean function performed on pixels when they are copied from bitmap to bitmap that determines how the pixels from the source, the destination, and the destination device context's selected brush are combined.

There are 256 total raster operations, each producing a different output based on the Boolean operator used and the order in which pixels are combined. Of these, only 16 are commonly used in Windows graphics programming. There are several GDI functions, such as BitBlt and StretchBlt, that allow a developer full access to all 256 raster operations. Using the Delphi VCL, the CopyMode property of the TCanvas object specifies the raster operation to be used, and can be set to one of 16 constants that represent the 16 most commonly used raster operations.

Raster operations are incredibly useful under certain circumstances. They can be used to easily implement specific special effects which, without raster operations, would be more difficult to implement otherwise. For example, using raster operations, it is very easy to simulate transparent pixels in a bitmap when it is displayed over a background. This effect and others could be implemented using any one of a hundred different techniques, but raster operations make their implementation fast and simple.

## Simulating Transparency

Perhaps the most common function performed by the graphical output code of a game is to display one bitmap over another, with the pixels of the background showing through the "transparent" pixels of the displayed bitmap or sprite. Without transparency, every sprite image would have to be rectangular, or the resulting animation would look horrible. Figure 3-14 graphically illustrates the importance of transparency.

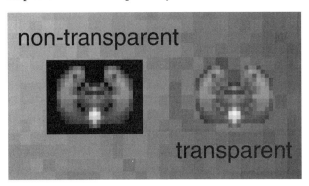

**Figure 3-14:**
*The effect of transparency*

The easiest method by which sprites can be transparently drawn to the background is known as masking. Masking uses two bitmaps for each sprite image, as each bitmap will be used with a different raster operation when the sprite is drawn.

**masking:** The act of using two bitmaps, an AND bitmap and an OR bitmap, along with raster operations to draw one bitmap over another while simulating transparent pixels in the source bitmap.

This method is precisely what happens when an application sets a TBitmap object's Transparent property to True and then calls TCanvas.Draw. This is a very convenient encapsulation in Delphi. However, the only drawback is that the transparent color is either the color of the pixel in the bottom leftmost pixel of the bitmap or is specified in the TBitmap's TransparentColor property, depending on the value of its TransparentMode property. The result is that this specified transparent color cannot be used elsewhere in the image, and unless proper care is taken when constructing the image, the result may not be what is expected. Using the direct approach as explained below gives the developer more control over the appearance of the final image. Figure 3-15 displays the difference between using the TransparentColor property and using the technique described below.

The two sprite images consist of an AND mask and an OR mask. The OR mask is the actual sprite image as it should appear in the destination. The only requirement for the OR mask is that pixels that should be transparent must be totally black (this must be palette slot zero for 256 color images). The AND mask is a monochrome bitmap consisting of only black and white. The black areas should match those of the actual sprite image in the OR mask, and the white areas represent pixels that should be transparent (opaque, or sprite image pixels, must be palette slot 0, and transparent pixels must be palette slot 255). Figure 3-16 illustrates a sprite image (the OR mask) and its accompanying silhouette (the AND mask).

Drawn after setting the TBitmap's Transparent property to True.

Drawn using direct masking techniques.

**Figure 3-15:**
*Using the TBitmap. Transparent property versus the direct approach*

AND Mask

OR Mask

**Figure 3-16:**
*A sprite AND and OR mask*

Drawing a sprite image with transparent pixels requires two steps. First, the AND mask is drawn to the destination bitmap using a boolean AND raster operation. The white pixels (representing the transparent areas) have a binary value of 11111111 for 256-color images (a decimal value of 255, the last palette slot). Higher color depths will result in a binary value of all ones. When this binary value is ANDed with the colors of the pixels in the destination image, the result is the color of the pixels in the destination image, thereby preserving the destination image data. The black pixels (representing opaque image data), on the other hand, have a binary value of 00000000. When ANDed with the destination image, the result is black. Effectively, this creates a "cutout" area in the destination image where the actual sprite image will appear.

The second step is to draw the OR mask to the destination bitmap using a boolean OR raster operation. The black pixels of the OR mask (representing the transparent areas), when ORed with the destination, will preserve the destination image data, just as the white pixels did in the first step. The actual sprite image data, when ORed with the destination, will be combined with the black "cutout" area produced from the first step. Thus, the sprite image data will be preserved. This results in a perfectly copied sprite with the background image showing through the transparent areas. Figure 3-17 demonstrates the results of each step in the process.

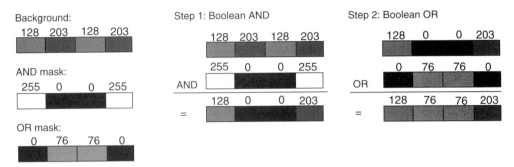

***Figure 3-17:***
*Using masks with raster operations*

The result, while perhaps not blindingly fast, should be more than adequate under most circumstances, if there are not a large amount of sprites on the screen. This technique is easy to implement, but it does require double the storage space for sprite images. The following example demonstrates how this technique is implemented.

***Listing 3-7:*** *Implementing masking techniques*

```
procedure TForm1.FormPaint(Sender: TObject);
begin
  {copy the background image to the destination}
  Canvas.Draw(480, 48, imgBackground.Picture.Bitmap);

  {combine the AND mask image with the background image in the destination
   using a boolean AND operation. this carves out an area for the final
   foreground image}
  Canvas.CopyMode := cmSrcAnd;
  Canvas.Draw(480+((imgBackground.Width div 2)-(imgAndMask.Width div 2)),
              48+((imgBackground.Height div 2)-(imgAndMask.Height div 2)),
              imgAndMask.Picture.Bitmap);

  {copy the result of step one into the 'background' image used for step 2}
  Canvas.CopyMode := cmSrcCopy;
  Canvas.CopyRect(Rect(8, 288, 248, 468), Canvas, Rect(480, 48, 720, 228));
  {copy the 'background' image resulting from step 1 into the destination}
  Canvas.CopyRect(Rect(480, 288, 720, 468), Canvas, Rect(8, 288, 248, 468));

  {combine the OR mask image with the result from step 1 in the destination
   using a boolean OR operation.  this copies the foreground image into the
```

```
    area carved out by step 1 while preserving the pixels around it, thereby
    creating the illusion of transparency.}
  Canvas.CopyMode := cmSrcPaint;
  Canvas.Draw(480+((imgBackground.Width div 2)-(imgAndMask.Width div 2)),
              288+((imgBackground.Height div 2)-(imgAndMask.Height div 2)),
              imgORMask.Picture.Bitmap);
end;
```

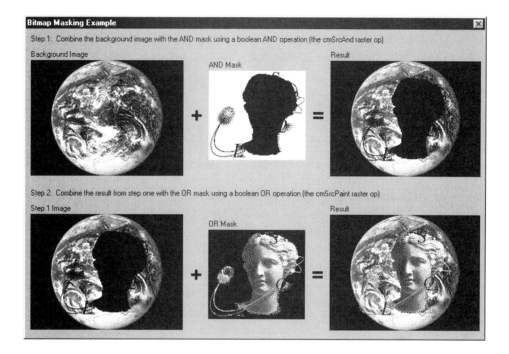

*Figure 3-18:*
*The transparently displayed image*

# Palettes

As previously discussed, working under palettized video modes provides a number of advantages and disadvantages. Palettized modes can be a real pain at times, requiring careful planning on the part of art production and special considerations on the part of the programmer. However, the advantages of working under a 256-color video mode usually outweigh the disadvantages, primarily because it is a very speedy mode to work under, and palette animation can be used for special effects.

The Windows palette manager is a difficult beast to tame. There are many nuances to working in a palettized mode under Windows, making the creation of games using regular GDI functions difficult indeed. As this book's primary topic is game and graphics programming using DirectX, we will not cover palettes in the depth required for making non-DirectX games. However, it is useful to cover a few of the most basic palette topics in order to prepare the reader for DirectX palettes covered in a later chapter.

## Logical vs. System Palettes

There are two different kinds of palettes used by the Windows operating system: the system palette and logical palettes. The system palette is a Windows-maintained global palette containing all of the colors that can be displayed. The first and last ten palette entries are reserved for the system, and contain the 20 static colors that are used for drawing specific user interface elements, such as window title bars, borders, and 3-D user interface elements. The remaining 236 colors can be set in the application.

Logical palettes are created by the application and contain the colors that the application would like to use. When the application specifies the palette it wishes to use, the Windows palette manager merges the logical palette with the current system palette. It accomplishes this by examining each entry in the logical palette and mapping it to an existing entry in the system palette, if a particular color exists in both palettes. If no matching entry is found, the color in the logical palette is placed into the first unused entry in the system palette. If an existing entry is not found and there are no more unused palette slots, the Windows palette manager maps the color to the closest approximation in the system palette. This continues until all colors in the logical palette have been merged with the colors in the system palette.

A logical palette must be selected into a device context before it can be used. If the specified device context identifies an active window, the logical palette is treated as a foreground palette and the Windows palette manager will mark all non-static entries in the system palette as unused. This allows the logical palette to potentially replace all non-static colors of the system palette. If the device context does not identify an active window, the logical palette is treated as a background palette, and can set unused palette slots only if any remain after the foreground palette has been merged.

The palette information stored in a DIB bitmap file can be considered a logical palette. Delphi takes care of most palette-specific concerns automatically, as the TBitmap object will load a bitmap's palette and put it into use. In the next chapter, we will learn how to load a palette from a bitmap and use it to initialize the DirectX palette.

**Note:** The TBitmap object has a property called Palette. This property is the handle to the bitmap's logical palette, and can be used in any GDI function that manipulates logical palettes.

## Using a Palette

Delphi encapsulates a large portion of the Windows API, making Windows programming easy and fun. Unfortunately, not everything in the Windows API has been conveniently simplified in this manner, and this includes palette functionality. This means that in order to use palettes, one must use low-level Windows API calls throughout most of the process.

In order to begin using a custom palette, a logical palette must first be made. First, variables of type PLogPalette and HPALETTE must be declared. The PLogPalette is a pointer to a logical palette structure, which contains a member for the palette version, a member for the number of palette entries, and then an array of type TPaletteEntry. The TPaletteEntry type is a structure that contains fields for the red, green, and blue components of a color, and a flag indicating how the entry is to be used. The PLogPalette variable is initialized to the appropriate values, including the desired colors, and is then passed to the CreatePalette function. This returns a handle to the newly created palette, which is then assigned to the HPALETTE variable. At this point, the palette can be selected into a device context using the SelectPalette function. If using a bitmap, the palette handle can be directly assigned to the TBitmap.Palette property. To actually merge the logical palette with the system palette so the new colors can be used, call the RealizePalette function. When the application no longer needs the logical palette, it should be deleted by calling the DeleteObject function. The following example demonstrates creating a logical palette to draw a red gradient fill.

*Figure 3-19:*
*The custom palette*

*Listing 3-8:* Using custom palettes

```
type
  TForm1 = class(TForm)
    procedure FormCreate(Sender: TObject);
    procedure FormPaint(Sender: TObject);
    procedure FormDestroy(Sender: TObject);
  private
    { Private declarations }
    FormPalette: HPALETTE;          // a handle to a logical palette
  public
    { Public declarations }
    function GetPalette: HPALETTE; override;
  end;

{Whoops! Delphi incorrectly imports the GetSystemPaletteEntries function.
 Here's the correct declaration that gives all of the functionality available
 with this API function}
function GetSystemPaletteEntries(DC: HDC; StartIndex, NumEntries: UINT;
                                PaletteEntries: Pointer): UINT; stdcall;

var
  Form1: TForm1;

implementation

{$R *.DFM}

function TForm1.GetPalette: HPALETTE;
begin
  {when something requests the palette of the form
   pass it back the new logical palette}
  Result := FormPalette;
end;

{link in the GetSystemPaletteEntries function}
function GetSystemPaletteEntries; external gdi32
        name 'GetSystemPaletteEntries';

procedure TForm1.FormCreate(Sender: TObject);
var
  ThePalette: PLogPalette;   // a logical palette definition structure
  iLoop: Integer;            // general loop counter
begin
  {get enough memory to hold the colors in the first 10 system
   palette slots, plus 32 of our own. this memory is temporary,
   and is no longer needed once the palette is created.}
  GetMem(ThePalette, SizeOf(TLogPalette)+42*SizeOf(TPaletteEntry));

  {initialize the palette version number}
```

```
      ThePalette^.palVersion := $300;

      {we will have a total of 42 entries in our palette}
      ThePalette^.palNumEntries := 42;

      {get the first 10 system palette entries}
      GetSystemPaletteEntries(Form1.Canvas.Handle, 0, 10,
                             @(ThePalette^.palPalEntry));

      {we only want 32 new palette entries, and we want them to start
       immediately after the first 10 system palette entries. by retrieving
       the first 10 system palette entries, when we realize our new palette,
       the first 10 logical palette entries will be mapped to the first 10
       system palette entries, and our palette entries will follow}
      for iLoop := 0 to 31 do
      begin
        {create a gradient red palette}
        ThePalette^.palPalEntry[iLoop+10].peRed   := 255-((255 div 32)*iLoop);
        ThePalette^.palPalEntry[iLoop+10].peGreen := 0;
        ThePalette^.palPalEntry[iLoop+10].peBlue  := 0;
        {do not match this palette entry to any other palette entry}
        ThePalette^.palPalEntry[iLoop+10].peFlags := PC_NOCOLLAPSE;
      end;

      {create the palette}
      FormPalette := CreatePalette(ThePalette^);

      {free the temporary memory}
      FreeMem(ThePalette, SizeOf(TLogPalette)+42*SizeOf(TPaletteEntry));
    end;

    procedure TForm1.FormPaint(Sender: TObject);
    var
      OldPalette: HPALETTE;        // a handle to the previous palette
      iLoop: Integer;              // general loop control variable
    begin
      {select our new logical palette into the device context}
      OldPalette := SelectPalette(Canvas.Handle, FormPalette, FALSE);

      {map our logical palette into the system palette}
      RealizePalette(Canvas.Handle);

      {display a red gradient}
      for iLoop := 0 to 31 do
      begin
        Canvas.Brush.Color := $01000000 or iLoop+10;
        Canvas.FillRect(Rect(10, iLoop*10+16, 260, (iLoop*10)+36));
      end;

      {select the previous palette back into the device context}
      SelectPalette(Canvas.Handle, OldPalette, FALSE);
```

```
end;

procedure TForm1.FormDestroy(Sender: TObject);
begin
  {we no longer need the logical palette, so delete it}
  DeleteObject(FormPalette);
end;
```

# Further Adventures in Windows Programming

The rest of this book could be dedicated to Windows GDI programming techniques without ever exhausting the subject. Indeed, several such books have been written that cover Windows graphics programming in much greater detail than that presented here. Our goal with this book is to study DirectX programming techniques under Delphi, so further discussion of GDI programming techniques is beyond our scope. However, if you would like more information concerning graphics programming under Windows, consult the following titles:

> *Black Art of Windows Game Programming* (ISBN 1-87873-995-6, Waite Group Press)
> *Delphi 2 Multimedia Adventure Set* (ISBN 1-88357-764-0, Coriolis Group)
> *The Tomes of Delphi 3: Win32 Core API* (ISBN 1-55622-610-1, Wordware Publishing)

Several more books that cover graphics programming, both Windows-specific and general algorithms, are listed in the bibliography at the end of the book. The remainder of this book will be dedicated to creating high-speed games using DirectX techniques.

# Summary

In this chapter, we discussed several basic topics in graphics programming. Although all of the examples demonstrated these topics using normal Windows GDI function calls, the concepts and theories presented apply to graphics programming in general. When coding a graphically intensive application under Windows, it is important to keep these points in mind:

■ The GDI subsystem is responsible for all of the graphical output displayed to the screen during a Windows session. One of Windows' strongest attributes is its device independence, or its ability to be run on a wide variety of hardware combinations. Due to this requirement, the GDI's primary purpose is to provide a mechanism by which an application can output graphical content without the programmer being concerned about what type of hardware upon which the application will be running. Unfortunately, as a direct consequence of this device independence, the GDI is notorious for its slow performance. Even so, the GDI is very useful when creating tools for games, and some commercial games have been written using little more than generic GDI function calls.

■ One must be familiar with a number of terms that describe various common graphical elements. Such graphical elements include pixels, lines, polygons, and bitmaps. A pixel is defined as the smallest, single element in a graphical image or on the display surface. Lines are a collection of pixels, usually arranged in a linear configuration. A collection of lines, arranged in such a way that the ends are connected to form a continuous, closed shape, is known as a polygon. A bitmap is a collection of pixels arranged in a rectangular configuration in such a way that they form a recognizable shape, such as a picture or texture.

■ Discussions of graphics programming usually start from a consideration of what resolution the video driver is currently in and how many colors are available in which to draw the graphics. These two concepts are directly related, and are generally referred to in a combined sense as the video mode. Both the resolution and the color depth of the current video mode will affect the perceived quality of the displayed graphical images. The greater the resolution and color depth, the more realistic and detailed the displayed graphics will become. However, on the downside, higher resolution and deeper color depth mean greater memory usage and slower speed.

■ The color of every pixel drawn to the screen is determined by three components: a red intensity, a blue intensity, and a green intensity. As these intensities increase or decrease, the color of an individual pixel is affected accordingly. Each intensity can have a minimum value of 0 and a maximum value of 255. If the intensity of each component is 0, the resulting color is black, while if each component is at 255, the resulting color is white. This gives a maximum of 16,777,216 colors. This is referred to as RGB color, denoting red, green, and blue, respectively.

■ Four and eight bits-per-pixel color depths are the only palettized video modes. At 8 bits-per-pixel, each pixel can assume a value between 0 and 255. These values act as an index into what can be considered a 256-entry array known as the color palette. Each entry in this array contains an 8-bit value for the blue, green, and red intensity of a color. Palettized display modes require careful planning of art resources, but are very fast and allow for palette animation special effects. By contrast, 16, 24, and 32 bits-per-pixel video modes directly store the color value for each pixel. This color value is encoded according to the bits-per-pixel used, and can vary from video board to video board. Non-palettized video modes have the advantage of total freedom to display any number of bitmaps simultaneously, without worrying about color problems or palette management. The downside to this is that more memory is required for both display and bitmap storage, and games tend to run slower as it requires longer to move a bitmap from one place in memory to another.

■ A device context represents a surface upon which graphical output can be drawn. Specifically, a device context represents the surface of an output device such as a monitor, printer, or plotter, and gives the developer access to modify its appearance. Fortunately, we will not need to be concerned much with device contexts, as the TCanvas object encapsulates the functionality of the device context and makes graphical output much easier.

■ Bitmaps come in many varieties, from two color to true color, and in many different formats. The native Windows bitmap format is easy to use, and comes in two subformats: DDB and DIB. The device-dependent bitmap, or DDB, is an older bitmap format and is kept around solely for backward compatibility. The device-independent bitmap, or DIB, stores more information than a DDB and can accurately be reproduced on any output device. The use and display of DIBs is not quite as fast as DDBs, but their flexibility more than makes up for the loss in speed. Fortunately, the TBitmap object encapsulates the functionality of both the DDB and DIB image formats, making bitmap manipulation easy.

■ There are many nuances to working in a palettized mode under Windows, making the creation of games using regular GDI functions difficult. There are two different kinds of palettes used by the Windows operating system: the system palette and logical palettes. The system palette is a Windows-maintained global palette containing all of the colors that can be displayed. Logical palettes are created by the application, and contain the colors that the application would like to use.

# CHAPTER 4: *An Introduction to DirectX*

Now that we've covered some basic graphics programming techniques, it's time to dive into what really makes game programming under Windows a reality: DirectX. When DirectX was initially introduced, it was not well received among game programmers. People feared that Microsoft was trying to force them into a game development architecture that would potentially render useless any proprietary graphics techniques. Fortunately, this was not Microsoft's aim, and after DirectX was looked over and evaluated by the gaming industry at large, it was embraced, and has now become the standard low-level programming interface around which games are now created. While it is possible to create some cool games using various GDI functions, to make games that will compete in today's market the savvy Delphi programmer must use the DirectX API.

# What is DirectX?

To put it technically, DirectX is really nothing more than a series of DLLs which give the developer access to low-level hardware while still maintaining some level of device independence. More specifically, DirectX is comprised of a number of COM objects which are implemented in the aforementioned DLLs. These COM objects provide the primary interface to system-level hardware in an object-oriented, language-independent fashion. The overall COM architecture allows the DirectX development team to expand and advance DirectX functionality without affecting applications written with earlier versions of DirectX. In essence, developers can now write games with all the power available under DOS while still maintaining the device independence of the Windows operating system.

In practice, DirectX programming is a lot like using Delphi VCL objects without the benefit of a visual environment. Various DirectX objects are instantiated and initialized, and sometimes linked with other DirectX objects through various method calls. Unlike the VCL, however, DirectX uses several very complex data structures as parameters in many methods. The DirectX API itself is huge, spread across numerous subsystems and various objects within those subsystems. We'll examine several of these subsystems closely throughout the remainder of this book.

## The Promise of DirectX

Developing games in a DOS environment can be a nightmare. The multitude of new hardware devices pouring out of hardware vendors had dramatically differing interfaces, making it difficult indeed to support more than a handful of devices in any one game. A high-level operating system like Windows, on the other hand, offers many benefits to game developers, such as consistent programming interfaces to new devices, simplified installation and configuration features, and extensive built-in functionality. However, before the advent of DirectX, this level of abstraction in the Windows environment posed a serious performance penalty that was unacceptable in any fast-action, high-performance game.

The DirectX development team's goal was to create a low-level architecture that would provide developers with the hardware control they need at the speed they demanded, while still retaining Windows' device-independent benefits. This was to be accomplished without imposing a restrictive high-level design architecture. First and foremost, DirectX had to be fast in order to allow game developers to create the high-performance, adrenaline-pumping action games demanded by hard-core game players. DirectX applications must also coexist peacefully with other Windows applications, such as spreadsheets and word processors. Therefore, DirectX promises three things to developers: fast execution, minimal style restraints, and a level of abstraction that will provide benefits from future hardware.

## Speed

One of the things that makes DirectX so fast is that it takes advantage of hardware acceleration whenever possible. If a hardware device directly supports a certain function within its electronics, such as copying an image from one area in memory to another, the DirectX drivers send the function call directly to the hardware (which is probably where the "Direct" moniker was derived). This results in blindingly fast performance.

Another benefit to hardware acceleration is true multitasking capabilities. Any DirectX function that is supported in hardware will return immediately after the function is called, even before the task of that function is carried out. This allows the CPU to continue processing application instructions while other hardware is carrying out the previous command. For example, if the display hardware supports moving an image from one area to another, the application can instruct the hardware to perform this task while asynchronously performing game logic calculations.

## Minimal Style Restraints

By its very nature, DirectX is a very low-level application programming interface. Game developers have spent a lot of time and money in creating innovative techniques for performing graphical output, techniques which can make one game stand apart from the others. If this competitive edge were to be threatened, many game developers would never have taken a second look at DirectX. Therefore, instead of creating a general gaming library that imposed high-level restrictions in how a game is put together, DirectX acts as a general enhancement to the Windows operating system. This results in many low-level function calls that provide power and speed while not insisting that developers create games "the right way." While this may not exactly automate certain tasks, it does allow for the greatest level of creativity and ingenuity when designing new games while affording the developer a certain level of device independence.

## Abstraction

The level of abstraction provided by the Windows operating system allows DirectX to take advantage of hardware advances as they become available. The DirectX interfaces were not designed merely to support the currently available hardware; they were designed in such a way that developers can take advantage of new hardware benefits when they are introduced. This shifts the burden of providing support for new hardware from the developers to the hardware manufacturers themselves. In many cases, when users purchase some new hardware device, all that is required for their existing DirectX games to take advantage of new benefits is to download the latest DirectX drivers. For example, when MMX technology was introduced, DirectX drivers were updated to support the new features. If a user downloaded and installed the new DirectX drivers, existing games would immediately and transparently take advantage of the new technology.

## Benefits and Drawbacks of DirectX Programming

For the most part, DirectX delivers exceptionally on all of its promises. It does indeed give developers a high-performance interface to system-level hardware while maintaining the benefits of the Windows operating system. DirectX offers the game programmer many benefits over using GDI functions, indeed many benefits that weren't even available under DOS. Even so, there are a few drawbacks to using DirectX over GDI, especially in the Delphi environment. While none of the drawbacks are truly serious, Delphi developers should be aware of both the advantages and disadvantages of using DirectX over traditional Windows programming techniques.

### Benefits

***Speed***   As we've already discussed, DirectX allows the game developer to squeeze the maximum performance out of applications. Performing just about any game application task is substantially faster than employing similar GDI functions. In fact, DirectX offers some functionality that would be very difficult and time consuming to emulate using the multimedia API.

***Greater Control***   DirectX gives applications incredible control over some things that would be impossible, impractical, or difficult under GDI. Such tasks as direct memory access to bitmapped graphics or audio data (in either hardware or system memory) and full control over the color palette (without the annoying GDI remapping of colors) are now possible through DirectX.

***Feature Emulation***   Many features for which hardware acceleration is unavailable are emulated in DirectX. This provides the developer with a certain minimal framework of functionality that is guaranteed to exist with or without hardware support. While this may result in some loss of performance, software emulation of hardware features is implemented using very low-level multimedia API functions and assembly language, and in many cases is almost as fast as the hardware implementation. Most of the standard features have a software emulation, such as copying image data from one memory area to another or mixing sound buffers on the fly.

### Drawbacks

***Difficult Debugging***    DirectX applications are simply harder to debug than traditional Windows applications. Most high-performance games are written in a full-screen video mode, and in a full-screen video mode, you can't set breakpoints and step through your code. There are other debugging techniques you can use to get around this limitation, but once an application initializes a full-screen video mode, most of Delphi's awesome debugging features are completely useless.

***Few Delphi Examples***    DirectX has, until recently, been solely the domain of C/C++ programmers. As such, most examples are written in C/C++. All of the DirectX documentation is certainly written for C/C++. Unfortunately, Delphi programmers may be required to learn at least a nominal amount of C/C++ before taking advantage of the DirectX documentation and numerous DirectX books and references that are available. Fortunately, several companies and individuals have written numerous DirectX libraries for Delphi, and there are several Delphi-specific DirectX programming web sites now available. Hopefully, this will result in an increase of DirectX documentation and references for the ambitious Delphi game programmer.

***Steep Learning Curve***    Even in its most recent incarnation, DirectX is still a fairly new API. As such, one must usually perform several steps in order to perform certain actions, especially when initializing many of the DirectX subsystems. The programmer is usually required to perform these steps in a very specific order, and unless the programmer is very familiar with how certain DirectX functionality is implemented, it may be very difficult to get things working initially. This, coupled with the fact that the DirectX API is huge and there are few Delphi examples, usually results in a rather step learning curve for first-time game programmers.

## The DirectX Architecture

The DirectX API itself, in the form of various COM objects and their methods, acts as an interface into the DirectX drivers. On the back side, the DirectX drivers can be thought of as two separate systems: the hardware abstraction layer (HAL) and the hardware emulation layer (HEL).

**HAL:** hardware abstraction layer; the DirectX drivers responsible for direct interface to hardware capabilities.

**HEL:** hardware emulation layer; the DirectX drivers responsible for emulating certain functionality if not present in hardware.

The HAL represents the hardware itself. When a DirectX object is created, it interrogates the HAL about hardware capabilities. The HEL, on the other hand, represents the software emulation of certain features. If an application asks a DirectX object to perform a certain task, it will be performed in hardware if the HAL indicates that the capability exists. Otherwise, the task will be performed in software if the HEL supports the emulated feature. Some features would be very slow to emulate in software, and thus may not be available in the HEL. These features will simply be unavailable to the application unless the HAL indicates they are present in the hardware. The HAL provides developers with hardware acceleration when available, and the HEL fills in where it can to provide a consistent, base set of features.

It is important to note that, for the most part, this is completely transparent to developers. Unless a developer is using a feature that is specifically implemented in hardware and not emulated by the HEL (such as overlays), an application need not be concerned if hardware support is present or not. However, an application can query DirectX to see if specific features are implemented in hardware or are emulated. An application can then use this knowledge to optimize various game functions, taking advantage of those functions that are specifically supported by the hardware and using a different approach for those functions that are too slow when emulated. This allows game developers to write applications that take advantage of available hardware under various configurations while still functioning adequately under all configurations.

## DirectX Components

DirectX is comprised of many components. Indeed, it seems as if new DirectX components are added every day, and there are sure to be more and more in subsequent versions. While the inventive game developer could potentially make use of all of these DirectComponents, there are only a few that are essential for game development. In this book, we will specifically look at the DirectDraw, DirectSound, and DirectInput components.

### DirectDraw

The DirectDraw component is responsible for all graphical output to the screen. DirectDraw objects provide functionality for such tasks as tear-free animation using page flipping techniques, access to graphical coprocessors, display memory management, and color palette manipulation. It is the core component of DirectX, and serves as the foundation for other DirectX components, such as Direct3D.

### DirectSound

The DirectSound component is responsible for digitized audio playback. It provides stereo and 3-D sound functionality and sound card memory management. It allows the developer to asynchronously play any number of sounds, mixing them on the fly and automatically converting their format to that of the primary sound output stream.

### DirectInput

The DirectInput component is responsible for providing the application with data retrieved from any type of input device. This not only includes the mouse and keyboard, but joysticks, flightsticks, rudder pedals, steering wheels, and other devices that have yet to be invented. DirectInput also supports output devices, such as force feedback peripherals.

### Other DirectX Components

There are several other DirectX components that are of particular interest to game developers, but are not quite as essential as the previous three. Several of these components may be required depending on the type of game being produced, and certainly any game could be enhanced by taking advantage of the functionality represented by these components. This is not an exhaustive list by any means, but game developers may want to further investigate the following components:

**DirectPlay** – Provides transport-independent messaging services between multiple computers. This is an essential component for multiplayer games, and includes functionality for organizing and launching a multiplayer game session.

**DirectSetup** – Provides automated installation of DirectX drivers.

**Direct3D** – Provides three-dimensional graphics rendering functionality. This component is segregated into low-level and high-level interfaces, which provide varying levels of control and expedience.

**DirectMusic** – Provides playback of MIDI music compositions. This component allows developers to directly control the exact sound of each instrument, and includes the ability to mix separate MIDI compositions on the fly to achieve context-sensitive musical transitions.

## DirectX and Delphi

Now that we know what DirectX is, we need to know what is required in order to use DirectX under the Delphi environment. Unfortunately, Delphi programmers do not enjoy the automatic access to DirectX resources that C/C++ developers do. If Microsoft were to include a type library along with the DirectX DLLs, it would be a simple task indeed to import the type library and immediately begin using the DirectX COM objects. Alas, this is not the case, and accessing DirectX functionality is the first obstacle that enthusiastic Delphi game developers must face.

## The DirectX SDK

As a C/C++ developer, you would simply need to purchase the DirectX SDK from Microsoft and install its accompanying files to begin developing DirectX applications. As a Delphi developer, however, there is no need to purchase the DirectX SDK. All that is required is the DirectX redistributable files available for free download from Microsoft's DirectX web site, or from the many commercial games that include them.

However, it may be worth your while to purchase the DirectX SDK, as it includes many benefits. The most important thing you will gain by purchasing the SDK is the DirectX documentation. As this book is not a reference manual, it will not discuss many of the nuances of DirectX programming that are available in the hundreds of pages of DirectX documentation. Dozens of examples are also available in the SDK which, although written in C/C++, are valuable references for investigating some of DirectX's more powerful features. The SDK also includes a DirectX control panel applet that allows you to control numerous global settings that may be helpful during debugging.

Perhaps most importantly, the DirectX SDK includes information on the files that can be distributed with your applications. While you can always suggest that your users visit the Microsoft web site to download the DirectX files if they do not already have them installed, it is a wise practice to always include all required files and DLLs with your applications. Therefore, you will need to be aware of the many legal requirements for bundling the DirectX redistributables with your applications. For more information about the DirectX SDK, check out **http://www.microsoft.com/directx/resources/devdl.htm**. You can order the DirectX SDK for a nominal fee by visiting **http://www.microsoft.com/directx/ sdkcdorder.asp**.

## Project JEDI

If you have the DirectX end user redistributable files installed (which you probably do if you've played any recent games), all you will need are the Delphi import files converted from the original DirectX C/C++ header files. All code in this book is based around the Project JEDI DirectX header files written by Erik Unger. Project JEDI (Joint Endeavor of Delphi Innovators) is a nonprofit organization composed of Delphi programmers all over the world. Their goal is to convert C/C++ header files for various APIs into Delphi import units, thus giving Delphi developers everywhere access to the same programming resources as their C/C++ cousins.

Erik's header files are a raw conversion of the original C/C++ headers, supporting DirectX 6 under Delphi 4. This gives Delphi developers the exact same functionality as would be available under C/C++. This is not a library that automates certain tasks; it is a hard-core unit containing the same low-level objects and methods that the C/C++ programmers use. This book is aimed at teaching the reader how to program DirectX, not how to use some arbitrary

DirectX library. Thus, these units were the perfect choice. Indeed, after reviewing several of the DirectX examples used throughout this book, you should be able to comprehend most C/C++ examples, as the DirectX method calls are the same. This book, and the companion CD, contain the latest version of Erik's header files at the time of publication. However, to get more information about the header files, some examples, and the latest version, check out **http:// www.delphi-jedi.org/DelphiGraphics/jedi-index.htm.**

Erik Unger's headers give Delphi developers access to DirectDraw, DirectSound, DirectInput, DirectPlay, DirectSetup, and Direct3D. This is the full functionality available under all of these DirectX subsystems, including force feedback and 3-D sound. The DXTools unit accompanying the files also includes several utility functions, such as testing the return results of DirectX methods and performing matrix manipulations. Throughout the course of this book, we will develop a utility unit converted from a C/C++ utility unit shipping with the DirectX SDK that simplifies several menial tasks such as loading a bitmap, a WAV file, or a palette. Later in this chapter, we will begin to use our utility unit and Erik's header files to create a baseline DirectX application from which all other examples in this book are based.

**Tip:** While the latest headers at the time of the writing were used for all of the book's examples, it is quite possible that the headers will have gone through several more versions by the time this book goes to print. The examples in this book will compile with the headers included on the CD, but you should get the latest headers from the JEDI page to have access to all the newest features. Bear in mind that the book examples may require a little adjustment when used with the new headers, as method declarations may have changed.

## Other Components and Headers

Fortunately, the Delphi gaming community is starting to see a rise in the number of available DirectX headers and components. Some are freely available, others you must purchase, but all of them give the Delphi developer a little more functionality than the raw headers accompanying this book.

### DelphiX

A freeware component suite written by Hiroyuki Hori, DelphiX comes complete with source code and gives the developer access to DirectDraw, Direct3D, DirectSound, DirectInput (including force feedback support), and DirectPlay. There are several cool components in this suite which allow the developer to bundle graphics and sound into compressed libraries, and includes some awesome alpha blending functionality. The examples clearly demonstrate some of the advanced techniques capable with DelphiX, and there are several freeware tools available that make editing sound and graphics libraries easy. For more information, check out **http://www.ingjapan.or.jp/hori/indexe.html**.

### The Delphi Games Creator (DGC)

Another freeware component suite, the DGC gives developers access to DirectDraw, DirectSound, DirectPlay, and DirectInput. Written by John Pullen, Paul Bearne, and Jeff Kurtz, the DGC comes complete with source code. The DGC also comes with editors for bundling sound and graphics into libraries, and will map all images in a graphics library to a single palette. Palette cycling and cool transition effects are just some of the added functionality available with this component suite. It also includes a scrolling map component and editor for making tile-based map engines. One of the first and oldest freeware DirectX component suites, the DGC has a large following, and is suitable for private or commercial DirectX applications. For more information, check out **http://www.ex.ac.uk/~PMBearne/DGC.html**.

### RingZero GDK

Created by Systems Advisory Group Enterprises, Inc., the RingZero GDK and RingZero 3D are component suites that give the Delphi developer access to DirectDraw, DirectSound, DirectPlay, DirectInput, and Direct3D. Although these component suites must be purchased, you gain the benefit of technical support and continuing updates (which may or may not always be available with freeware components). Source code is also available. These component suites are very easy to use, and can expedite the creation of a DirectX game if you are impatient or have a pressing deadline. Unfortunately, as of this writing, these components only support DirectX 5, and can only be used under Delphi 2 or 3. However, by the time this book reaches store shelves, RingZero may be compatible with Delphi 4 and DirectX 6. For more information, check out **http://www.sage-inc.com**.

## A DirectDraw Tutorial

DirectX has hopefully been installed to your machine by now, and we have the units required to give us access to DirectX components and functionality. At this point, we can begin exploring the world of DirectX programming and all of its nuances, pitfalls, and rewards.

DirectDraw is the core, most fundamental DirectX component, and as such, is a good starting point for a discussion of DirectX programming. We will go over a good number of DirectDraw concepts, many of which are mirrored in other DirectX components. Several of the methods called and tasks performed by the DirectDraw objects are very similar, if not exact, to those of other DirectX components, such as DirectSound and DirectInput. The learning curve discussed earlier starts here, as there are quite a few concepts to explain.

## Features

DirectDraw offers many features above and beyond what is available through the Win32 API. As with all DirectX components, DirectDraw gives the developer more control over graphical output than the Windows API, while providing incredible performance not attainable using GDI functions. DirectDraw provides the following features and many more for powerful Windows game programming:

■ Direct access to image memory, whether located in system or display memory

■ The ability to specify the location of surface memory (i.e., system or display memory)

■ Hardware acceleration for many graphical functions

■ Screen resolution and color depth changing on the fly

■ Direct control over the system palette (in full-screen mode)

■ Powerful page-flipping methods for incredibly fast animation

In the following sections we will see how DirectDraw is used to change the display mode and color depth, how bitmaps are loaded into usable DirectDrawSurfaces, and how page-flipping animation is implemented.

## Functional Overview

DirectX programming primarily consists of creating parent objects, namely objects that represent specific DirectX components, and then using these objects to create child objects that represent a specific functionality. The following illustration and discussion outline actions that will become familiar when we cover other DirectX components.

DirectDraw programming consists of creating a DirectDraw object and several DirectDrawSurface objects. The DirectDraw object itself acts as a liaison between the application and the display driver. Through the DirectDraw object, we can change the display resolution and color depth as well as create individual DirectDrawSurface and DirectDrawPalette objects.

Individual DirectDrawSurface objects represent display buffer memory. This can be either offscreen storage for image data or the visible display itself. The application uses these surface objects to communicate directly with the video hardware, either through direct memory access of image data or methods that access hardware acceleration. Surfaces provide methods to copy image data to and from each other, performing various operations on the image data such as scaling or ignoring transparent pixels. DirectDrawSurface objects encapsulate much of the power provided by DirectDraw.

DirectDrawPalette objects hold color data for images that are stored in a palettized format. They also represent the application's interface directly to the display hardware's palette. DirectDrawPalette objects will be covered in more detail in the next chapter.

## COM Fundamentals

DirectX objects are COM based, consequently involving all of the associated benefits and drawbacks of using COM objects. Microsoft's Component Object Model (COM) is a huge beast, not unlike that of the VCL. A full-fledged discussion of COM is beyond the scope of this book, and unnecessary for the purposes of DirectX programming. However, there are a few COM theories that we must understand before delving into the heart of DirectX programming.

Working with DirectX objects has some similarities to working with other COM objects, but there are a few differences. The primary difference that most experienced COM programmers will discover is the fact that DirectX objects do not need to be created by using the CoCreateInstance function. Other COM objects frequently used in a traditional COM application, such as IClassFactory, are also unnecessary. All DirectX objects are created through custom function calls that return an instantiated COM object. For example, the DirectDrawCreate function is used to create an instantiated IDirectDraw object (more on this later). If you've never worked with COM objects before, this takes some of the confusion out of the loop, and is similar to creating traditional VCL objects in code.

A COM object can almost be thought of as a VCL object with no properties, only methods. The methods of a COM object are known as an interface. A COM object can have more than one interface, and it can be extended by added new interfaces, similar to deriving a new component from an ancestor. However, the COM standard dictates that an interface can never change. The result of this is that older code is guaranteed to work with newer COM objects, as the original interfaces will still be implemented and available. For this reason, you will see several different types of interface declarations in the DirectX header files. As each new version of DirectX comes out, offering new functionality, an entirely new interface must be created to support this functionality. However, you can rest assured that your DirectX game will still work when DirectX 7, 8, 9, etc., are introduced in the future.

An interesting feature implemented by COM allows applications to query a COM object to see if it implements a particular interface. This allows your application to be extremely flexible when implementing certain features. For example, force feedback is a newer addition to DirectInput functionality. Your application, upon startup, could query the DirectInput objects to see if they support the interface required to implement force feedback output. If they do not, indicating that the game is running on a machine with an older version of DirectX, you could simply bypass the part of your code that implemented force feedback. However, if the force feedback interface is available, your application can make full use of its features. In this way, game applications can be very robust, taking advantage of special features only on those machines that have them available, while still running acceptably on older machines without those features. We will see an example of this later in this chapter when we discuss how to detect what version of DirectX the user has installed.

## Reference Counting

One fundamental concept in COM is the idea of lifetime management. COM was implemented with the idea that several users, or clients, could potentially use the exact same COM object, thus saving memory and resources. Therefore, the COM objects themselves implement a method of reference counting. Essentially, COM objects keep a count of how many times they are being used. When they are created, this count is initialized to 1. When a new client wishes to use the COM object, this reference count is incremented. When a client no longer needs the COM object and it goes out of scope, such as when an application terminates, the reference count is decremented. When the reference count reaches 0, the object knows it can free itself.

This reference count incrementing and decrementing is accomplished by calling the AddRef and Release methods implemented in all COM objects. However, fortunately for Delphi developers, Delphi takes care of this automatically and, for the most part, transparently. Reference counting does add some esoteric nuances to using COM objects that are not present when using VCL objects. As a Delphi DirectX developer, don't worry about explicitly freeing DirectX objects after they are created; they will free themselves when they go out of scope or when the application terminates. For more information on general COM programming concepts, look at *Delphi 4 Developer's Guide* by Teixeira and Pacheco (ISBN 0-672-31284-0) or *Delphi Developer's Handbook* by Cantu, Lam, and Gooch (ISBN 0-782-11987-5).

## GUID

COM objects are identified by a unique number known as a GUID, pronounced "goo-id" or "gwid" (like "squid"), which stands for globally unique identifier. Without going into too much detail, Microsoft provides an API call that generates a GUID that is completely unique; it is guaranteed to be unique if the machine on which the GUID was created has a network card installed. The concept of what a GUID is or how it is used is only important to the DirectX developer in that GUIDs are used to identify many individual objects and devices, such as specific DirectX objects (such as memory surfaces or sound buffers) and specific drivers (such as a particular video driver or device). We will be using GUIDs throughout every example in the book.

## Surfaces

Perhaps the single, most important concept in DirectDraw programming is that of the surface. A surface is directly analogous to Delphi's TBitmap or TCanvas object. It represents a virtual "picture" upon which graphical output can be drawn. In reality, a surface is a linear chunk of memory that is managed as if it were rectangular. Surfaces have width and height, among many other properties. The memory for a surface can be located in a number of places, but primarily it will be found in system memory or in the memory on the display card itself.

There are many, many different types of surfaces, some of which are very specialized for a particular purpose. Surfaces can be used specifically for 3-D rendering, or for storing textures used in 3-D rendering; they can be set up to receive live video feeds, or perhaps to store only transparency information (known as the alpha channel). For the purposes of this book, we will be concerned with only three different types: the primary surface, the backbuffer surface, and off-screen surfaces.

**alpha channel:** A component of color that records levels of transparency/opacity as opposed to actual color data.

### The Primary and Backbuffer Surfaces

Technically speaking, these are really the same type of surface. The primary surface represents the image that the user sees on the display screen. Anything drawn onto the primary surface is immediately displayed. The backbuffer surface has the same capabilities and format of the primary surface, and is used in an animation technique known as page flipping (more on this below).

### Off-screen Surfaces

An off-screen surface, as it will be used in this book, is simply a surface in memory that is never directly displayed on the screen. Typically the same format as the primary and backbuffer surfaces, off-screen surfaces are generally used for storing background graphics and sprite animation frames. They can also be used as work surfaces for composing a graphical image. The image in these surfaces is then copied onto the primary or backbuffer surfaces to be displayed. We'll see an example of this later in the chapter.

## Page Flipping

Page flipping is an incredibly powerful technique for producing flicker-free animation. The term "page flipping" comes from the inspiration for this animation technique—that of traditional cartoon animation. Cartoons (and movies, for that matter) create the illusion of animation by displaying to the viewer a series of images, one after the other. Someone can create a crude animation by taking a stack of paper, drawing an image on each page, and then flipping through it rapidly. This is the architecture of page flipping animation. The idea is to create two surfaces, the primary surface and the backbuffer surface. The next frame of animation is composed on the backbuffer surface, and then it is "flipped" to the display screen. This updates the entire display screen in one fell swoop, resulting in a flickerless animation.

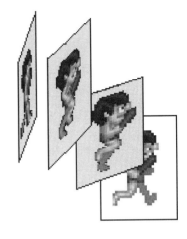

This page flipping animation architecture is incredibly easy to implement under DirectX. Just about every video card available supports this in hardware, making it incredibly fast. Therefore, we will use this page flipping technique for nearly every animation and game example throughout the book. We will see how to initialize and implement page flipping in the examples to follow.

*Figure 4-1:*
*Page flipping animation*

## Resolution, Color Depth, and Video Memory

We discussed resolution, color depth, and video memory quite a bit in Chapter 3, Basic Graphics Programming. That discussion is just as relevant to DirectDraw programming as it was to GDI graphics programming. However, under DirectDraw, the developer has much more control over the resolution and color depth. This also affects how the memory represented by a surface is directly accessed. To simplify matters, we will be concerned only with 256-color palettized display modes. A number of different display modes may be available under DirectX, and we'll demonstrate how to retrieve a list of the available display modes shortly.

## Windowed Versus Full-Screen

Perhaps the most powerful aspect of DirectDraw programming is that the application can have control over the entire display screen, known as a full-screen application. However, DirectDraw also allows a developer to take advantage of DirectDraw capabilities for drawing graphics in a regular window while sharing desktop space with other windows. This is known as windowed mode. Generally speaking, it is more difficult to support a windowed DirectDraw application than it is to support a full-screen mode. A windowed DirectDraw application requires a DirectDrawClipper object (not covered in this book), and must handle a number of other requirements typical of a traditional GDI graphical application, such as dealing with a shared palette. We are concerned only with high-performance game programming, so this book will only demonstrate full-screen DirectDraw applications. This will greatly simplify the code, and will provide us with the greatest amount of control and power. The distinction between windowed and full-screen is known as the cooperative level, and will be covered in more detail below.

## Initializing DirectDraw

We've covered several COM and DirectDraw programming concepts, so now it's time to see them in action. There are several tasks the application is required to perform before DirectDraw can be instantiated and the display mode modified. Some of these tasks are optional, some are not. DirectDraw, and DirectDraw surfaces, are instantiated by performing the following:

- Enumerating display devices
- Creating the DirectDraw object
- Enumerating the supported display modes
- Setting the cooperative level
- Setting the display mode
- Creating surfaces

### Enumerating Display Devices

While it is safe to assume that most machines only have one display device attached, the latest version of Windows does allow multiple monitors and other display devices (such as virtual reality headsets) to be installed simultaneously. Although it is not strictly necessary, it may be good practice to allow the user to pick the display device on which to display the DirectDraw application. However, for the examples in the book, we will only be concerned with the primary display device.

The function DirectDrawEnumerateEx is used to list all available display devices. It is a callback function that will call the specified function once for each installed display HAL it finds. The first device enumerated will be the primary display device; any others attached to the system will follow. The DirectDrawEnumerateEx function is declared as:

```
function DirectDrawEnumerateEx(
lpCallback: TDDEnumCallbackEx;   // the address of the callback function
lpContext: Pointer;              // an application-specific value
dwFlags: DWORD                   // scope flags
): HResult; stdcall;             // returns a DirectX error code
```

The first parameter is the address of the function that is called for each enumerated device. The second parameter is a pointer to an application-defined value, such as a pointer to a TList or perhaps just a variable, and can be set to nil if not needed. The last parameter is a series of flags that control the scope of the enumeration. The callback function itself is defined as:

```
function TDDEnumCallbackEx(
lpGUID: PGUID;                    // a pointer to the device GUID
lpDriverDescription: PAnsiChar;   // the device description
lpDriverName: PAnsiChar;          // the device name
lpContext: Pointer;               // the application-specific value
Monitor: HMonitor                 // a handle to the monitor
): BOOL; stdcall;                 // returns TRUE or FALSE
```

The first three parameters of this function are the most interesting. The lpGUID parameter will contain the GUID for the specific device. This GUID must be stored, as it must be used later for creating the DirectDraw object. The lpDriverDescription and lpDriverName parameters contain the textual description and name of the enumerated device. These can be presented to the user in a list of devices, allowing them to choose the desired display object. The lpContext parameter simply contains the pointer passed to the initial DirectDrawEnumerateEx function. The last parameter will be zero in most cases, and can be ignored. The callback function must return a value of TRUE to continue the enumeration; returning FALSE signals the function to stop enumerating devices.

The following example demonstrates enumerating all available display devices.

**Listing 4-1:** *Enumerating display devices*

```
implementation

uses
  DDraw;

function EnumDevices(lpGUID: PGUID; lpDriverDescription: PAnsiChar;
      lpDriverName: PAnsiChar; lpContext: Pointer;
      Monitor: HMonitor): BOOL; stdcall;
begin
  {add the name and description of the enumerated device. here, we would
   need to store the GUID for the device so it would be available when
   the user selected the desired display device}
  TStringList(lpContext).Add(lpDriverName+' - '+lpDriverDescription);

  {continue enumeration}
  Result := TRUE;
end;

procedure TForm1.FormCreate(Sender: TObject);
```

```
begin
  {enumerate all attached display devices}
  DirectDrawEnumerateEx(EnumDevices, lbxDevices.Items, 0);
end;
```

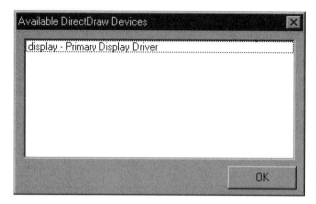

*Figure 4-2:*
*The list of attached display devices*

## Creating the DirectDraw Object

The first truly required step in initializing a DirectDraw application is to create the DirectDraw object itself. To create the DirectDraw object, call the DirectDrawCreate function, which is defined as:

```
function DirectDrawCreate(
lpGUID: PGUID;              // the GUID of the DirectDraw device
out lplpDD: IDirectDraw;    // the IDirectDraw object to be instantiated
pUnkOuter: IUnknown         // unused, set to nil
): HResult; stdcall;        // returns a DirectX error code
```

The first parameter takes the GUID of the selected device. It can be set to nil to create a DirectDraw object associated with the primary display device, or it can be set to a GUID as retrieved from device enumeration above. Additionally, it can be set to DDCREATE_HARDWAREONLY or DDCREATE_EMULATIONONLY to only use the HAL or HEL, respectively. This allows the developer to perform testing and debugging against emulated or hardware accelerated features. The second parameter takes a pointer to the IDirectDraw object. When this function returns, this object will be instantiated. The last parameter is used for COM aggregation, and must be set to nil as it is currently unsupported.

**Caution:** It is possible to create multiple DirectDraw objects, but this is unadvisable. Each DirectDraw object is independent of the others, and surfaces and other child objects cannot be shared between them.

Now, this function will only return an instantiated IDirectDraw object, but since we are concerned with DirectX 6 functionality, we need to get an instantiated IDirectDraw4 object. Thus, we should create a temporary IDirectDraw object, and once this is instantiated, we can use the QueryInterface method of the object to retrieve an instantiated IDirectDraw4 object. The temporary object can then be released by setting it to nil. We'll illustrate the creation of an IDirectDraw4 object below.

**Note:** Delphi's AS operator can be used to accomplish the same thing. However, use of the QueryInterface method is a little less abstract.

## *Enumerating the Supported Display Modes*

It is typically much harder to create an application that supports multiple display modes. As discussed in the previous chapter, changing display modes modifies the size of graphics as they are displayed on screen, and changes the amount of screen area that must be filled with graphics. This puts an additional requirement on the programmer to determine how graphics will be displayed in different modes (if they are to be scaled, stretched, etc.), and may put additional requirements on artists if they must develop additional graphics to support different resolutions and color depths. However, allowing the user to choose which display mode works best on their system is a good practice, as the user can then tune the game to achieve acceptable speeds. Even if your game will support only one graphic mode, it is useful to determine if the machine supports this mode. Our examples will be concerned with only one specific display mode in order to simplify the code, but we still need to enumerate the available display modes to ensure that the machine can handle the application.

Enumerating display modes is similar to enumerating display devices. After the IDirectDraw4 object is created, we can call its EnumDisplayModes method to enumerate all display resolutions and color depths supported by the display driver. The EnumDisplayModes method is defined as:

```
function EnumDisplayModes(
dwFlags: DWORD;                                 // scope flags
lpDDSurfaceDesc: PDDSurfaceDesc2;               // a surface description structure
lpContext: Pointer;                             // an application-defined value
lpEnumModesCallback: TDDEnumModesCallback2      // the callback function
): HResult;                                     // returns a DirectX error code
```

The first parameter is a series of flags that determine how the display modes are enumerated, and can be set to zero. The second parameter is a pointer to a TDDSurfaceDesc2 structure that contains information defining the types of display modes to be enumerated. We can use this to enumerate only specific types of display modes, such as all 800 x 600 modes or all palettized display modes. Setting this parameter to nil will enumerate all supported display modes. The third parameter is a pointer to an application-defined value, and the last parameter is a pointer to the callback function itself. The callback function is defined as:

```
function TDDEnumModesCallback2(
const lpDDSurfaceDesc: TDDSurfaceDesc2;    // a surface description record
lpContext: Pointer                         // the application-defined value
): HResult;                                // returns a DirectX error code
```

The first parameter contains a TDDSurfaceDesc2 structure initialized with information about the enumerated display device. This includes information such as the width, height, and color depth. The second parameter contains a pointer to the application-defined value. This function must return DDENUMRET_OK to continue the enumeration; DDENUMRET_CANCEL will stop the enumeration.

The TDDSurfaceDesc2 object is complex, and is used in a number of different IDirectDrawSurface4 methods. The TDDSurfaceDesc2 structure is defined as:

```
TDDSurfaceDesc2 = packed record
  dwSize: DWORD;                             // size of the TDDSurfaceDesc structure
  dwFlags: DWORD;                            // flags indicating valid members
  dwHeight: DWORD;                           // surface height
  dwWidth: DWORD;                            // surface width
  case Integer of
  0: (
    lPitch : LongInt;                        // distance to start of next row
  );
  1: (
    dwLinearSize : DWORD;                    // optimized surface size
    dwBackBufferCount: DWORD;                // number of backbuffers
    case Integer of
    0: (
      dwMipMapCount: DWORD;                  // number of mip-map levels
      dwAlphaBitDepth: DWORD;                // depth of alpha buffer
      dwReserved: DWORD;                     // reserved
      lpSurface: Pointer;                    // pointer to surface memory
      ddckCKDestOverlay: TDDColorKey;        // color key for destination overlays
      ddckCKDestBlt: TDDColorKey;            // color key for destination blt
      ddckCKSrcOverlay: TDDColorKey;         // color key for source overlays
      ddckCKSrcBlt: TDDColorKey;             // color key for source blt
      ddpfPixelFormat: TDDPixelFormat;       // pixel format description
      ddsCaps: TDDSCaps2;                    // surface capabilities
      dwTextureStage: DWORD;                 // multitexture cascade stage
    );
    1: (
      dwRefreshRate: DWORD;                  // refresh rate
    );
  );
end;
```

The following listing illustrates creating an IDirectDraw4 object and enumerating all supported display modes.

***Listing 4-2:*** *Creating IDirectDraw and enumerating display modes*

```
var
  Form1: TForm1;
  FDirectDraw: IDirectDraw4;

implementation

function EnumModesCallback(const lpDDSurfaceDesc: TDDSurfaceDesc2;
                           lpContext: Pointer): HResult; stdcall;
begin
  {list the height, width, and color depth of the enumerated display mode}
  TStringList(lpContext).Add(IntToStr(lpDDSurfaceDesc.dwWidth)+' X '+
                    IntToStr(lpDDSurfaceDesc.dwHeight)+', '+
                    IntToStr(lpDDSurfaceDesc.ddpfPixelFormat.dwRGBBitCount)+
                    ' bits/pixel');

  {continue enumeration}
  Result := DDENUMRET_OK;
end;


procedure TForm1.FormCreate(Sender: TObject);
var
  {we can only get a DirectDraw4 interface from the DirectDraw interface, so we
   need a temporary interface}
  TempDirectDraw: IDirectDraw;
begin
  {create a temporary DirectDraw object. this is used to create the
   desired DirectDraw4 object}
  DirectDrawCreate(nil, TempDirectDraw, nil);

  try
    {we can only get a DirectDraw4 interface through the QueryInterface
     method of the DirectDraw object}
    TempDirectDraw.QueryInterface(IID_IDirectDraw4, FDirectDraw);
  finally
    {now that we have the desired DirectDraw object, the temporary DirectDraw
     object is no longer needed}
    TempDirectDraw := nil;
  end;

  {begin enumerating supported display modes}
  FDirectDraw.EnumDisplayModes(0,nil, lbxDisplayModes.Items, EnumModesCallback);
end;
```

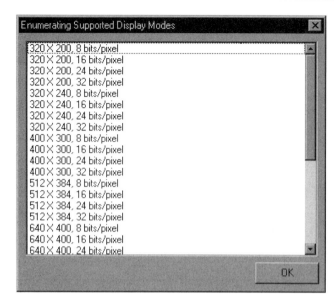

**Figure 4-3:**
*Supported display modes*

## Setting the Cooperative Level

As discussed earlier, the cooperative level determines if the application runs in full-screen mode or if it will share the desktop with other windows. Basically, it determines how the application will work with other applications. The concept of cooperative level is also found in other DirectX components.

Setting the cooperative level requires a simple call to the IDirectDraw4's SetCooperativeLevel method, which is defined as:

```
function SetCooperativeLevel
(hWnd: HWND;                 // a handle to the main window
dwFlags: DWORD              // flags controlling the cooperative level
): HResult;                 // returns a DirectX error code
```

The first parameter is a handle to the application's main window. The second is a series of flags that specify the actual cooperative level. For our discussion, we should pass DDSCL_EXCLUSIVE and DDSCL_FULLSCREEN, which indicates that our application will be responsible for maintaining the entire display. We'll see an example of its use below.

## Setting the Display Mode

Here's where the real action takes place. We've created the IDirectDraw4 object, allowed the user to select a display mode or determined that our predefined display mode is supported, and we've set the cooperative level. All that's left is to actually change the display mode itself. This is accomplished through

IDirectDraw4's SetDisplayMode method. The SetDisplayMode method is defined as:

```
function SetDisplayMode(
dwWidth: DWORD;              // the desired width, in pixels
dwHeight: DWORD;            // the desired height, in pixels
dwBPP: DWORD;               // the color depth, in bits
dwRefreshRate: DWORD;       // the refresh rate
dwFlags: DWORD              // control flags
): HResult;                 // returns a DirectX error code
```

The first and second parameters specify the desired width and height of the display, in pixels, and it must match a supported display mode as returned by the EnumDisplayModes function. The third parameter indicates the number of bits that describe an individual pixel's color, and again this must match a supported display mode. The refresh rate and flags parameters can both be set to zero. When this function is called, the display mode is immediately switched to the mode specified. The screen will likely go blank, you'll hear some clicking, and then the display hardware will reset to the specified mode.

Now, before we can set the display mode, DirectDraw makes some demands of the main window that must be met before either the SetCooperativeLevel or the SetDisplayMode methods will work. According to the DirectX documentation, the window whose handle is sent to the SetCooperativeLevel method must not have any border, and must be a stay-on-top window. This can be accomplished in Delphi by setting the form's BorderStyle to bsNone and the FormStyle to fsStayOnTop in the form's OnCreate event. Only then will the SetDisplayMode method work correctly.

The following example demonstrates setting the cooperative level and switching the display mode.

**Listing 4-3:** *Setting the display mode to full screen*

```
var
  Form1: TForm1;
  FDirectDraw: IDirectDraw4;

implementation

procedure TForm1.FormCreate(Sender: TObject);
begin
  {initialize form properties.  note that the FormStyle property must be
   set to fsStayOnTop}
  BorderStyle := bsNone;
  BorderIcons := [];
  FormStyle   := fsStayOnTop;
end;

procedure TForm1.FormActivate(Sender: TObject);
```

```
var
  {we can only get a DirectDraw4 interface from the DirectDraw interface, so we
   need a temporary interface}
  TempDirectDraw: IDirectDraw;
begin
  {create a temporary DirectDraw object. this is used to create the
   desired DirectDraw4 object}
  DirectDrawCreate(nil, TempDirectDraw, nil);

  try
    {we can only get a DirectDraw4 interface through the QueryInterface
     method of the DirectDraw object}
    TempDirectDraw.QueryInterface(IID_IDirectDraw4, FDirectDraw);
  finally
    {now that we have the desired DirectDraw object, the temporary DirectDraw
     object is no longer needed}
    TempDirectDraw := nil;
  end;

  {set the cooperative level}
  FDirectDraw.SetCooperativeLevel(Handle, DDSCL_FULLSCREEN or DDSCL_EXCLUSIVE);

  {set the display resolution and color depth}
  FDirectDraw.SetDisplayMode(640, 480, 8, 0, 0);
end;
```

**Note:** You'll notice that the DirectDraw initialization code has been moved to the form's OnActivate event. We've found this is a more appropriate place to put initialization code, and the examples throughout the rest of the book will expound upon the code placed in this method.

The result of this example is a bit surprising. The form itself was still visible, albeit in a full-screen mode, and the mouse cursor was still able to manipulate objects on the form. This is possible because the GDI is still outputting graphical images, and by default the memory area to which the GDI is rendering is still visible when the DirectDraw application sets its display mode. This can be useful when a DirectDraw application needs to start up and display an interface to the user that is easily put together using regular Delphi controls.

## Page Flipping

At this point, we can instantiate DirectDraw and adjust the display hardware's display mode, but not much else. We still can't draw anything to the screen, making any sort of animation very difficult. We need to modify our DirectDraw code so it supports the page flipping architecture discussed earlier. In order to accomplish this, we must first create a primary surface and an attached backbuffer surface.

## Creating Surfaces

We will create the primary and backbuffer surfaces simultaneously, creating what is known as a complex surface. A complex surface is one surface with a series of separate surfaces that are implicitly attached to it. These surfaces are arranged in a linear fashion. Typically, page flipping applications create only two surfaces (the primary and one backbuffer). However, some applications may need three or more.

**Note:** The primary surface and all backbuffers <u>must</u> reside in video memory. Thus, the number of backbuffers that can be created is dependent upon the size of the surfaces, the color depth, and the available display memory.

The primary surface is always visible to the user. Animation is accomplished by drawing any graphical output to the backbuffer surface, which is offscreen. When the next frame of animation needs to be displayed, the backbuffer surface memory and the primary surface memory change places (or flip). Only the memory referenced by these two objects change; no other attributes or other attached objects are affected. Your BackBuffer object will <u>always</u> point to the backbuffer surface, and your PrimarySurface object will <u>always</u> point to the primary surface. This is illustrated below.

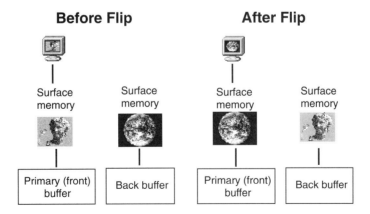

**Figure 4-4:**
*Page flipping the primary and backbuffer surfaces*

We can create the primary and backbuffer surfaces by calling the IDirectDraw4 method CreateSurface. The CreateSurface method is defined as:

```
function CreateSurface(
var lpDDSurfaceDesc: TDDSurfaceDesc2;     // a surface description structure
var lplpDDSurface: IDirectDrawSurface4;   // the IDirectDrawSurface4 object
pUnkOuter: IUnknown                       // unused, set to nil
): HResult;                               // returns a DirectX error code
```

The first parameter is a data structure that defines the type of surface we wish to create. The second parameter is a pointer to the IDirectDrawSurface4 object that is instantiated by the function. The last parameter is used for COM aggregation and should be set to nil.

The TDDSurfaceDesc2 structure is a very complex data structure as we examined above, but for the purposes of this function, we are concerned only with a few members. To begin, we should initialize all members of the surface by calling FillChar(DDSurface, SizeOf(TDDSurfaceDesc2), 0). We need to indicate that we are interested in the capabilities and buffer count members of this structure, so we need to set its dwFlags member to DDSD_CAPS or DDSD_BACKBUFFERCOUNT (by ORing the values, we combine them). We then must set its ddsCaps.dwCaps member to DDSCAPS_COMPLEX or DDSCAPS_FLIP or DDSCAPS_PRIMARYSURFACE. The DDSCAPS_COMPLEX flag indicates we are creating a complex surface with implicitly attached surfaces, DDSCAPS_FLIP indicates this will be a flipping structure, and DDSCAPS_PRIMARYSURFACE indicates that the root surface in the flipping structure will be the primary surface. We must also set the dwBackBufferCount to indicate how many backbuffers we will need. In our case, we can set this to one. Finally, we must set the dwSize member to SizeOf(TDDSurfaceDesc2).

**Caution:** DirectX methods use lots and lots of very complex data structures. These data structures may vary from version to version, and some methods may use only specific members of any particular structure. It is imperative that any data structure with a member denoting its size <u>must</u> have this member initialized by calling SizeOf. Failing to perform these two requirements can lead to failed method calls.

When this method returns, the IDirectDrawSurface4 object will point to the primary surface. However, we really want to perform all of our animation on the backbuffer surface, so we must instantiate an object to point to this surface. This is accomplished through the IDirectDrawSurface4's GetAttachedSurface method. When this method is called on a complex surface with implicitly attached surfaces, it instantiates an IDirectDrawSurface4 object to point to the specified surface. The GetAttachedSurface method is defined as:

```
function GetAttachedSurface(
var lpDDSCaps: TDDSCaps2;                      // surface capabilities
var lplpDDAttachedSurface: IDirectDrawSurface4 // a surface object
): HResult;                                    // returns an error code
```

The first parameter is a TDDSCaps2 structure whose dwCaps member must be set to DDSCAPS_BACKBUFFER. The second parameter is an IDirectDrawSurface4 object that will be set to point to the backbuffer surface when the function returns. This function returns the first attached surface whose capabilities match those defined in the function call. In our case, we receive a pointer to our only backbuffer surface. The TDDSCaps2 structure is defined as:

```
TDDSCaps2 = packed record
  dwCaps: DWORD;          // capabilities flags
  dwCaps2 : DWORD;        // more capability flags
  dwCaps3 : DWORD;        // yet more capability flags
  dwCaps4 : DWORD;        // still more capability flags
end;
```

The use of the CreateSurface and GetAttachedSurface functions will be demonstrated below.

## Rendering with GDI

We've created a page flipping surface structure that will demonstrate DirectDraw's animation capabilities, but unless we actually draw something to the screen, we won't be able to tell if anything is happening when we actually flip the surfaces. Let's cover a cool DirectDraw and Delphi trick that will make some tasks incredibly easy.

The IDirectDrawSurface4 object contains a method called GetDC which returns a handle to a GDI device context. This allows us to use any GDI function call to render graphics, or text, directly onto the surface. If we create a TCanvas object and set its handle to the value returned by GetDC, we can take full advantage of all TCanvas methods. This is a very powerful Delphi technique that can make graphics programming incredibly simple. The GetDC method is defined as:

```
function GetDC(
var lphDC: HDC              // a variable that receives the DC
): HResult;                 // returns a DirectX error code
```

The only parameter to this method is a variable that will receive the device context handle for the surface.

After we are through using the device context, we must release it before performing any DirectDraw methods that work on the surface, such as flipping or copying surface memory to or from the surface in question. We accomplish this by calling the IDirectDrawSurface4 method ReleaseDC, which is defined as:

```
function ReleaseDC(
hDC: Windows.HDC            // a variable containing the DC to release
): HResult;                 // returns a DirectX error code
```

This method's only parameter must be set to the device context handle returned from the previous call to GetDC.

 **Caution:** It is <u>absolutely imperative</u> that every call to GetDC be matched with a call to ReleaseDC. When a device context is retrieved, the normal execution of Windows is put on hold. Therefore, any code between GetDC and ReleaseDC must execute as quickly as possible, as messages and other system events could get backed up. Also, any other DirectDraw methods that work directly on the surface must not be called until the device context has been released. Therefore, it is good practice to use a try..finally block, putting the ReleaseDC call in the Finally part to ensure that the device context is released. Otherwise, your system <u>will</u> crash violently.

Any GDI function or TCanvas method can be used for rendering graphics to a surface. Bear in mind that you will be suffering from GDI's sluggishness, but you may be able to reuse proprietary GDI graphics rendering methods and leverage your former development investments. Specifically, we'll be using these techniques to perform text output in a number of examples. We will also examine how this makes the process of loading and displaying bitmaps incredibly simple.

## Flipping the Surfaces

OK, we've created our complex flipping structure, we've drawn some text on the front and backbuffer in order to differentiate them, now we're ready for action. To actually flip the contents of the surfaces, call the Flip method of the primary surface object. The Flip method is defined as:

```
function Flip(
lpDDSurfaceTargetOverride: IDirectDrawSurface4;   // surface to flip
dwFlags: DWORD                                     // wait flags
): HResult;                                        // returns an error code
```

Typically, the first parameter is set to nil as the default behavior is to flip to the next buffer in the chain. However, if there is more than one backbuffer, this parameter can be set to the particular buffer in order to flip it to the screen. The last parameter is set to either zero or DDFLIP_WAIT. If it is set to zero, the function immediately returns, regardless if the flip operation could be set up. If the DDFLIP_WAIT flag is specified, the function does not return until the flip operation occurs. Setting this parameter to zero allows the application to perform extra processing while waiting for the display hardware to set up the flip operation. However, the Flip method must continuously be called in order to set up the flip operation. If the flip operation could not be set up, this function will return DDERR_WASSTILLDRAWING. In most cases, it is easiest to set this parameter to DDFLIP_WAIT, which is the flag we will use in the examples throughout this book.

The following example demonstrates the creation of the primary and backbuffer surfaces, rendering using GDI functions, and page flipping.

***Listing 4-4:*** *A simple page flipping application*

```
var
  Form1: TForm1;
  FDirectDraw: IDirectDraw4;

  FPrimarySurface,
  FBackBuffer: IDirectDrawSurface4;

implementation

procedure TForm1.FormCreate(Sender: TObject);
begin
  {initialize form properties.  note that the FormStyle property must be
   set to fsStayOnTop}
  BorderStyle := bsNone;
  BorderIcons := [];
  FormStyle   := fsStayOnTop;
  Color       := clBlack;

  {turn off the cursor}
  ShowCursor(FALSE);
end;

procedure TForm1.FormActivate(Sender: TObject);
var
  {we can only get a DirectDraw4 interface from the DirectDraw interface, so we
   need a temporary interface}
  TempDirectDraw: IDirectDraw;

  {structures required for various methods}
  DDSurface: TDDSurfaceDesc2;
  DDSCaps: TDDSCaps2;

  {these variables are used in GDI rendering}
  TempCanvas: TCanvas;
  SrfcDC: HDC;
begin
  {create a temporary DirectDraw object. this is used to create the
   desired DirectDraw4 object}
  DirectDrawCreate(nil, TempDirectDraw, nil);

  try
    {we can only get a DirectDraw4 interface through the QueryInterface
     method of the DirectDraw object}
```

```
      TempDirectDraw.QueryInterface(IID_IDirectDraw4, FDirectDraw);
finally
  {now that we have the desired DirectDraw object, the temporary DirectDraw
   object is no longer needed}
  TempDirectDraw := nil;
end;

{set the cooperative level}
FDirectDraw.SetCooperativeLevel(Handle, DDSCL_FULLSCREEN or DDSCL_EXCLUSIVE);

{set the display resolution and color depth}
FDirectDraw.SetDisplayMode(640, 480, 8, 0, 0);

{initialize the DDSurface structure to indicate that we will be creating a
 complex flipping surface with one backbuffer}
FillChar(DDSurface, SizeOf(TDDSurfaceDesc2), 0);
DDSurface.dwSize  := SizeOf(TDDSurfaceDesc2);
DDSurface.dwFlags := DDSD_CAPS or DDSD_BACKBUFFERCOUNT;
DDSurface.ddsCaps.dwCaps := DDSCAPS_COMPLEX or DDSCAPS_FLIP or
                            DDSCAPS_PRIMARYSURFACE;
DDSurface.dwBackBufferCount := 1;

{create the primary surface object}
FDirectDraw.CreateSurface(DDSurface, FPrimarySurface, nil);

{indicate that we want to retrieve a pointer to the backbuffer (the surface
 immediately behind the primary surface in the flipping chain) }
FillChar(DDSCaps, SizeOf(TDDSCaps2), 0);
DDSCaps.dwCaps := DDSCAPS_BACKBUFFER;

{retrieve the surface}
FPrimarySurface.GetAttachedSurface(DDSCaps, FBackBuffer);

{create a temporary canvas object and retrieve an HDC for the primary surface}
TempCanvas := TCanvas.Create;
FPrimarySurface.GetDC(SrfcDC);
try
  {set the canvas's handle to the surface's DC}
  TempCanvas.Handle := SrfcDC;

  {clear the surface to black}
  TempCanvas.Brush.Color := clBlack;
  TempCanvas.FillRect(Rect(0, 0, 640, 480));

  {draw some lime colored text}
  TempCanvas.Font.Color := clLime;
  TempCanvas.TextOut(100, 100, 'Primary Surface. Press Escape to close');
finally
  {don't forget to release the DC}
  TempCanvas.Handle := 0;
  FPrimarySurface.ReleaseDC(SrfcDC);
```

```
  end;

  {get the backbuffer's DC}
  FBackBuffer.GetDC(SrfcDC);
  try
    {set up the canvas, and clear the backbuffer to blue}
    TempCanvas.Handle := SrfcDC;
    TempCanvas.Brush.Color := clBlue;
    TempCanvas.FillRect(Rect(0, 0, 640, 480));

    {draw some yellow colored text}
    TempCanvas.Font.Color := clYellow;
    TempCanvas.TextOut(200, 200, 'Backbuffer Surface. Press Escape to close');
  finally
    {release the DC and destroy the temporary canvas object}
    TempCanvas.Handle := 0;
    FBackBuffer.ReleaseDC(SrfcDC);
    TempCanvas.Free;
  end;

  {commence flipping}
  FlipClock.Enabled := TRUE;
end;

procedure TForm1.FlipClockTimer(Sender: TObject);
begin
  {flip the contents of the primary and backbuffer surfaces}
  FPrimarySurface.Flip(nil, DDFLIP_WAIT);
end;
```

## Displaying Bitmaps

The ability to draw text, or even lines and polygons, into a surface is cool, but to really create anything visually exciting, we need to be able to display bitmaps. DirectDraw, unfortunately, does not have any built-in functionality for loading a bitmap, but using GDI techniques and Delphi's TBitmap object, we can easily remedy the situation.

The most common application for loading a bitmap is to store background or sprite images off screen, which will later be copied into the primary or, most likely, the backbuffer surface. Therefore, the first order of business is to create the off-screen surface, which will hold the bitmap image. Again, we will use the CreateSurface method. However, this time we will initialize the dwFlags member of the TDDSurfaceDesc2 structure to DDSD_CAPS or DDSD_HEIGHT or DDSD_WIDTH. We must then set the dwWidth and dwHeight members to the desired width and height of the surface, typically reflecting the width and height of the bitmap image. Finally, we set the ddsCaps.dwCaps member to

DDSCAPS_OFFSCREENPLAIN, indicating that this is a plain, off-screen surface. The color depth of the surface will match that of the primary surface.

**Caution:** You cannot create an off-screen surface wider than the primary surface in video memory unless the hardware specifically supports it. We cover retrieving the hardware capabilities below. However, you can create off-screen surfaces wider than the primary surface in system memory.

## Surface Memory Location

When creating a surface, the application can request that the memory for a surface be allocated from a specific area. This allows an application to create surfaces, and thus load bitmaps, into memory on the display hardware, or to system memory. Video memory has the advantage of being incredibly fast when copied into another surface also located on the video memory; display memory has the advantage of being directly accessed by the CPU faster than video memory. When creating a surface, the following four flags can be combined with other flags in the ddsCaps.dwCaps member of the TDDSurfaceDesc2 structure, thereby controlling where the memory for the surface is located.

*Table 4-1: Memory location flags*

| Flag | Memory Location |
| --- | --- |
| DDSCAPS_LOCALVIDMEM | Conventional video memory. Must be combined with DDSCAPS_VIDEOMEMORY. |
| DDSCAPS_NONLOCALVIDMEM | Accelerated Graphics Port (AGP) display memory. Must be combined with DDSCAPS_VIDEOMEMORY. |
| DDSCAPS_VIDEOMEMORY | Video memory. |
| DDSCAPS_SYSTEMMEMORY | System memory. |

**Note:** DDSCAPS_NONLOCALVIDMEM is applicable only to AGP hardware, and only if the DirectDraw driver for that hardware supports it. You can determine if AGP is supported by DirectDraw by retrieving the hardware capabilities as discussed below.

You do not have to indicate a memory location for surfaces. By default, surfaces will be created in video memory. When video memory is depleted, or a surface is too big to fit into what's left, it is automatically created in system memory. However, if a location is specified in the CreateSurface call and there is not enough memory, it will fail.

## *Loading and Displaying the Bitmap*

Actually loading the bitmap is quite easy. We simply create a TBitmap object and use its LoadFromFile method to pull the bitmap into memory. Of course, we must still somehow copy the bitmap into our off-screen surface. This is where the previous information about GDI comes in. Using GDI, we can retrieve a device context for our off-screen surface and use the GDI BitBlt function to copy the bitmap into the surface itself. Alternatively, we can create another TCanvas object, assign the surface's device context to the TCanvas's handle, and use the TCanvas.Draw method to copy the bitmap into the surface. With that accomplished, we can release the surface's device context and destroy the TBitmap object. This is illustrated in Listing 4-5.

## *Blitting Surfaces*

OK, now that the bitmap has been loaded into our off-screen surface, which should be located in display memory if there was enough room, we need to copy it from the off-screen surface onto our primary surface for display. Usually we would copy it into the backbuffer surface as part of our animation rendering engine, but for this example, we will simply copy it directly to the primary surface.

To copy one portion of a surface into another surface, we use the IDirectDrawSurface4's BltFast method. The BltFast method is defined as:

```
function BltFast(
dwX: DWORD;                        // the destination horizontal coordinate
dwY: DWORD;                        // the destination vertical coordinate
lpDDSrcSurface: IDirectDrawSurface4; // the source surface
var lpSrcRect: TRect;              // the rectangular area on the source
dwTrans: DWORD                     // transfer flags
): HResult;                        // returns a DirectX error code
```

The first two parameters determine the horizontal and vertical coordinates where the source surface area will be copied onto the destination surface. The third parameter is a pointer to the source surface, and the fourth parameter defines the rectangular area in the source surface that is to be copied onto the destination surface. The last parameter contains a series of flags that control certain aspects about the transfer. In particular, the DDBLTFAST_WAIT flag can be specified to indicate that the function should not return until the copying has been accomplished. Other flags indicate transparency options, but these will be covered in the chapter on sprite techniques.

If the resulting bitmap looks somewhat corrupted, don't worry. Our current example makes no use of palettes, and thus the resulting appearance of the bitmap will be at the mercy of the current contents of the system palette. We will examine palettes at length in the next chapter.

**Listing 4-5:** *Loading and displaying a bitmap*

```
var
  Form1: TForm1;
  FDirectDraw: IDirectDraw4;

  FPrimarySurface,
  FBitmap: IDirectDrawSurface4;

Implementation

procedure TForm1.FormActivate(Sender: TObject);
var
  {we can only get a DirectDraw4 interface from the DirectDraw interface, so we
   need a temporary interface}
  TempDirectDraw: IDirectDraw;

  {structures required for various methods}
  DDSurface: TDDSurfaceDesc2;

  {these variables are used in GDI rendering}
  TempCanvas: TCanvas;
  SrfcDC: HDC;

  {the bitmap object}
  TempBitmap: TBitmap;

  {defines the area to be copied}
  SrcRect: TRect;
begin
  {create a temporary DirectDraw object. this is used to create the
   desired DirectDraw4 object}
  DirectDrawCreate(nil, TempDirectDraw, nil);

  try
    {we can only get a DirectDraw4 interface through the QueryInterface
     method of the DirectDraw object}
    TempDirectDraw.QueryInterface(IID_IDirectDraw4, FDirectDraw);
  finally
    {now that we have the desired DirectDraw object, the temporary DirectDraw
     object is no longer needed}
    TempDirectDraw := nil;
  end;

  {set the cooperative level}
  FDirectDraw.SetCooperativeLevel(Handle, DDSCL_FULLSCREEN or DDSCL_EXCLUSIVE);

  {set the display resolution and color depth}
  FDirectDraw.SetDisplayMode(640, 480, 8, 0, 0);
```

```
{initialize the DDSurface structure to indicate that we will be creating a
 primary surface}
FillChar(DDSurface, SizeOf(TDDSurfaceDesc2), 0);
DDSurface.dwSize   := SizeOf(TDDSurfaceDesc2);
DDSurface.dwFlags := DDSD_CAPS;
DDSurface.ddsCaps.dwCaps := DDSCAPS_PRIMARYSURFACE;

{create the primary surface object}
FDirectDraw.CreateSurface(DDSurface, FPrimarySurface, nil);

{create a temporary canvas object and retrieve an HDC for the primary
 surface}
TempCanvas := TCanvas.Create;
FPrimarySurface.GetDC(SrfcDC);
try
  {set the canvas's handle to the surface's DC}
  TempCanvas.Handle := SrfcDC;

  {clear the surface to black}
  TempCanvas.Brush.Color := clBlack;
  TempCanvas.FillRect(Rect(0, 0, 640, 480));
finally
  {don't forget to release the DC}
  TempCanvas.Handle := 0;
  FPrimarySurface.ReleaseDC(SrfcDC);
end;

{create the temporary bitmap}
TempBitmap := TBitmap.Create;

{load the bitmap}
TempBitmap.LoadFromFile(ExtractFilePath(ParamStr(0))+'Athena.bmp');

{initialize the attributes for the surface}
FillChar(DDSurface, SizeOf(TDDSurfaceDesc2), 0);
DDSurface.dwSize    := SizeOf(TDDSurfaceDesc2);
DDSurface.dwFlags   := DDSD_CAPS or DDSD_HEIGHT or DDSD_WIDTH;
DDSurface.dwWidth   := TempBitmap.Width;
DDSurface.dwHeight := TempBitmap.Height;
DDSurface.ddsCaps.dwCaps := DDSCAPS_OFFSCREENPLAIN;

{create the desired DirectDraw surface object}
FDirectDraw.CreateSurface(DDSurface, FBitmap, nil);

{retrieve a DC for the bitmap surface}
FBitmap.GetDC(SrfcDC);
try
  TempCanvas.Handle := SrfcDC;

  {draw the bitmap onto the surface using GDI functions}
  TempCanvas.Draw(0, 0, TempBitmap);
```

```
finally
  {cleanup}
  TempCanvas.Handle := 0;
  FBitmap.ReleaseDC(SrfcDC);
  TempCanvas.Free;
end;

{record the size of the surface (same as the bitmap), as this will be needed
 when we copy the surface into the primary surface}
SrcRect := Rect(0, 0, TempBitmap.Width, TempBitmap.Height);

{destroy the bitmap object}
TempBitmap.Free;

{blit the off-screen surface onto the primary surface, thus displaying
 the bitmap}
FPrimarySurface.BltFast(50, 50, FBitmap, SrcRect, DDBLTFAST_WAIT);
end;

procedure TForm1.FormKeyDown(Sender: TObject; var Key: Word;
  Shift: TShiftState);
begin
  if Key = VK_ESCAPE then
    Close;
end;
```

## Lost Surfaces

DirectX applications, even under exclusive, full-screen mode, must still coexist gracefully with other Windows applications. This means that users are free to Alt+Tab into and out of a DirectX application into other Windows applications. When a full-screen DirectX application is Alt+Tabbed out of, it is automatically minimized by DirectDraw, and the GDI resumes normal output in the original display mode. This has serious implications for surfaces located in display memory. When the GDI takes over in a situation like this, all display memory is reallocated to the GDI itself, thus wiping out anything stored in a surface located in display memory. When the DirectDraw application is returned to, any methods that manipulate display memory surfaces are likely to return a DDERR_SURFACELOST error.

When this error is detected, it is a simple matter to restore the surface's memory. Simply call the Restore method of the IDirectDrawSurface4 object in question. The Restore method is defined as:

```
function Restore: HResult;                // returns a DirectX error code
```

This will restore the memory allocated for that surface, and further methods that manipulate that surface will no longer fail until the surface's memory is lost again. However, the contents of that surface may be undefined, and must be restored. Thus, your application should contain a function that initializes the contents of all surfaces that can be called again and again in the event that surface memory is lost.

**Note:** This only applies to surfaces stored in video memory; system memory surfaces and their content will never be lost. You will need to restore the primary surface memory, which in turn implicitly restores the memory of all attached surfaces (such as the backbuffer).

## Retrieving DirectDraw Capabilities

DirectX was written so that a developer can take advantage of certain hardware features if they are available, such as overlays or the ability to create off-screen surfaces wider than the primary surface. We can determine what features are available by calling the IDirectDraw4's GetCaps method. The GetCaps method is defined as:

```
function GetCaps(
var lpDDDriverCaps: TDDCaps;         // hardware capabilities
var lpDDHELCaps: TDDCaps             // emulated capabilities
): HResult;                          // returns a DirectX error code
```

The first parameter returns a TDDCaps structure outlining the capabilities supported by the hardware itself, and the second parameter returns a similar structure detailing capabilities that are emulated. The hardware capabilities will vary depending on the available hardware, but the emulated capabilities will remain the same regardless of the hardware (but dependent on the version of DirectDraw installed). These structures are huge, and contain just about anything the developer or application would need to know about available features. The following example illustrates how the members of the individual structures are queried to determine the existence of a particular feature.

*Listing 4-6: Retrieving DirectDraw capabilities*

```
procedure TForm1.FormCreate(Sender: TObject);
var
  {we can only get a DirectDraw4 interface from the DirectDraw interface, so we
   need a temporary interface}
  TempDirectDraw: IDirectDraw;

  {hardware and emulated capability structures}
  HALCaps, HELCaps: TDDCaps;
begin
  {create a temporary DirectDraw object. this is used to create the
   desired DirectDraw4 object}
  DirectDrawCreate(nil, TempDirectDraw, nil);
```

```
try
  {we can only get a DirectDraw2 interface through the QueryInterface
   method of the DirectDraw object}
   TempDirectDraw.QueryInterface(IID_IDirectDraw4, FDirectDraw);
finally
  {now that we have the desired DirectDraw object, the temporary DirectDraw
   object is no longer needed}
   TempDirectDraw := nil;
end;

{initialize the capabilities structures}
FillChar(HALCaps, SizeOf(TDDCaps), 0);
FillChar(HELCaps, SizeOf(TDDCaps), 0);
HALCaps.dwSize := SizeOf(TDDCaps);
HELCaps.dwSize := SizeOf(TDDCaps);

{retrieve the hardware and software capabilities}
FDirectDraw.GetCaps(HALCaps, HELCaps);

{display several pieces of information}
SysInfo.Items.Add('Total Video Memory: '+IntToStr(HALCaps.dwVidMemTotal
                   div 1000)+' KB');
SysInfo.Items.Add('');

{hardware caps}
SysInfo.Items.Add('Hardware Capabilities');
SysInfo.Items.Add('——————————————-');

if (HALCaps.dwCaps and DDCAPS_BLT) = DDCAPS_BLT then
  SysInfo.Items.Add('Hardware accelerated blits');

if (HALCaps.dwCaps and DDCAPS_BLTCOLORFILL) = DDCAPS_BLTCOLORFILL then
  SysInfo.Items.Add('Hardware accelerated color fills');

if (HALCaps.dwCaps and DDCAPS_BLTQUEUE) = DDCAPS_BLTQUEUE then
  SysInfo.Items.Add('Asynchronous hardware blits');

if (HALCaps.dwCaps and DDCAPS_BLTSTRETCH) = DDCAPS_BLTSTRETCH then
  SysInfo.Items.Add('Hardware stretch blits');

if (HALCaps.dwCaps2 and DDCAPS2_CERTIFIED ) = DDCAPS2_CERTIFIED  then
  SysInfo.Items.Add('Microsoft certified driver');

if (HALCaps.dwCaps2 and DDCAPS2_NONLOCALVIDMEM ) = DDCAPS2_NONLOCALVIDMEM  then
  SysInfo.Items.Add('AGP video card');

if (HALCaps.dwCKeyCaps and DDCKEYCAPS_SRCBLT) = DDCKEYCAPS_SRCBLT   then
  SysInfo.Items.Add('Hardware accelerated source color key blits');

SysInfo.Items.Add('');
SysInfo.Items.Add('');
```

```
{emulated caps}
SysInfo.Items.Add('Emulated Capabilities');
SysInfo.Items.Add('————————————————-');

if (HELCaps.dwCaps and DDCAPS_BLT) = DDCAPS_BLT then
  SysInfo.Items.Add('Emulated blits');
if (HELCaps.dwCaps and DDCAPS_BLTCOLORFILL) = DDCAPS_BLTCOLORFILL then
  SysInfo.Items.Add('Emulated color fills');

if (HELCaps.dwCaps and DDCAPS_BLTQUEUE) = DDCAPS_BLTQUEUE then
  SysInfo.Items.Add('Emulated asynchronous blits');

if (HELCaps.dwCaps and DDCAPS_BLTSTRETCH) = DDCAPS_BLTSTRETCH then
  SysInfo.Items.Add('Emulated stretch blits');

if (HELCaps.dwCaps2 and DDCAPS2_CERTIFIED ) = DDCAPS2_CERTIFIED  then
  SysInfo.Items.Add('Microsoft certified driver');

if (HELCaps.dwCaps2 and DDCAPS2_NONLOCALVIDMEM ) = DDCAPS2_NONLOCALVIDMEM  then
  SysInfo.Items.Add('Emulated AGP video card');

if (HELCaps.dwCKeyCaps and DDCKEYCAPS_SRCBLT) = DDCKEYCAPS_SRCBLT   then
  SysInfo.Items.Add('Emulated source color key blits');
end;
```

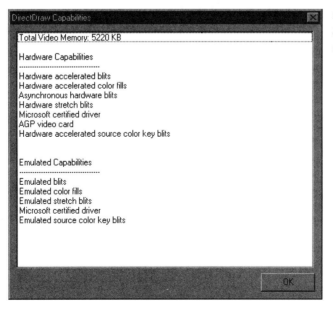

*Figure 4-5:*
*Some supported
DirectDraw features*

# The DirectX Baseline Application

In an effort to expedite the creation of DirectX applications, this book contains a baseline DirectX application that instantiates DirectDraw, sets up a page flipping architecture, and implements a high-speed rendering loop that can attain the highest animation speed possible. This is implemented by providing an event handler for the TApplication's OnIdle event. The OnIdle event is called whenever the application becomes idle; if the Done parameter of this method is set to False, this event will continuously be called by the application, providing a perfect spot for a rendering loop. There are stubbed out methods for drawing surface content and restoring surface content in the event that it is lost. A number of constants are defined at the top of the main unit that control the display resolution and color depth, as well as the cooperative level and the flags for the complex flipping surface. The indicated display resolution and color depth is checked to see if it is supported before setting the display mode. It will also shut off the rendering loop automatically when the application is Alt+Tabbed out of, and restart it when Alt+Tabbed back into. Theoretically, all one must do is load off-screen surfaces in the area indicated in the Activate method, flesh out the RestoreSurfaces method to restore any off-screen surface memory, and complete the DrawSurfaces method to render animation to the backbuffer surface. The act of flipping the surfaces is carried out by the rest of the application. The Escape key will exit the application and return to Windows.

Bear in mind that this is a general architecture meant to assist the reader in quickly getting a DirectX application up and running. It also provides a standardized framework from which every other example throughout the rest of this book will be based, cutting down on the amount of code that must be illustrated in example listings. This is not the best architecture for every game. Indeed, you may need to alter it dramatically depending on the requirements of your application. However, the baseline application tries to be as unimposing as possible, taking care of standard functionality while providing plenty of room for application-specific logic. What follows is a complete listing of the baseline application. Future examples will be based on this application, and thus will not contain any of the code for initializing DirectDraw; code listings will only contain code pertinent to the current discussion. This baseline application will run as is, but the output will be a black screen. However, it is a simple task to implement code in the DrawSurfaces method that will output animation to the screen, and we will see many examples of this in the coming chapters.

**Listing 4-7:** *The DirectX baseline application*

```
unit DDrawSkelU;

{*************************************************************************
    Skeleton DirectDraw Application
```

```
      Author: John Ayres
      This is a bare bones DirectDraw application that creates a primary surface
      with one backbuffer and implements a continuous flip between them. It
      contains some minimal error checking code as well as an application
      exception handling routine that flips back to the GDI surface so that
      exception messages can be seen. The Application.OnIdle event is used to
      implement the loop that flips the surfaces. This uses a large chunk of
      CPU time (which is ok in a game), but could potentially be replaced
      with a While..Do loop or some other looping architecture.

      This baseline code is used throughout the book as a starting point for
      examples. It was designed to be easily extensible, and should provide
      all of the initialization and startup code that you will need for your
      own DirectX applications.
      Code that is marked by '///' can and should be replaced by your own code.


 *************************************************************************


      Copyright © 1999 by John Ayres, All Rights Reserved

      This code is freeware and can be used for any personal or commercial
      purposes without royalty or license.  Use at your own risk.

 *************************************************************************}

interface

uses
  Windows, Messages, SysUtils, Classes, Graphics, Controls, Forms, Dialogs,
  DDraw;

{these constants are used to modify specific attributes of the DirectX
 application, such as the resolution and color depth}
const
  DXWIDTH      = 640;
  DXHEIGHT     = 480;
  DXCOLORDEPTH = 8;
  BUFFERCOUNT  = 1;
  COOPERATIVELEVEL = DDSCL_FULLSCREEN or DDSCL_ALLOWREBOOT or DDSCL_ALLOWMODEX
                     or DDSCL_EXCLUSIVE;
  SURFACETYPE      = DDSCAPS_COMPLEX or DDSCAPS_FLIP or DDSCAPS_PRIMARYSURFACE;

const
  {this user-defined message is used to start the flipping loop}
  WM_DIRECTXACTIVATE = WM_USER + 200;

type
  TfrmDXAppMain = class(TForm)
    procedure FormCreate(Sender: TObject);
    procedure FormDestroy(Sender: TObject);
    procedure FormKeyDown(Sender: TObject; var Key: Word;
```

```
      Shift: TShiftState);
    procedure FormActivate(Sender: TObject);
  private
    { Private declarations }

    {flips back to the GDI surface to display the exception error message}
    procedure ExceptionHandler(Sender: TObject; ExceptionObj: Exception);

    {the main rendering loop}
    procedure AppIdle(Sender: TObject; var Done: Boolean);

    {intercepts certain messages to provide appropriate functionality}
    procedure AppMessage(var Msg: TMsg; var Handled: Boolean);

    {flips the DirectDraw surfaces}
    procedure FlipSurfaces;

    {restores any lost surfaces}
    procedure RestoreSurfaces;

    {draws the contents of surfaces}
    procedure DrawSurfaces;
  public
    { Public declarations }
  end;

var
  frmDXAppMain: TfrmDXAppMain;

  {the main DirectDraw interface}
  FDirectDraw: IDirectDraw4;

  {the interfaces for the primary and backbuffer surfaces}
  FPrimarySurface,
  FBackBuffer: IDirectDrawSurface4;

implementation

uses
  DXTools;

{$R *.DFM}

{ *-->>  BASELINE APPLICATION CODE <<--* }

{ - the callback function used to ensure that the selected graphics -
  - mode is supported by DirectX                                  - }
function EnumModesCallback(const EnumSurfaceDesc: TDDSurfaceDesc2;
                        Information: Pointer): HResult; stdcall;
begin
  {if the height, width, and color depth match those specified in the
```

```
                   constants, then indicate that the desired graphics mode is supported}
        if (EnumSurfaceDesc.dwHeight = DXHEIGHT) and
           (EnumSurfaceDesc.dwWidth = DXWIDTH) and
           (EnumSurfaceDesc.ddpfPixelFormat.dwRGBBitCount = DXCOLORDEPTH) then
          Boolean(Information^) := TRUE;

      Result := DDENUMRET_OK;
    end;


    { -> Events hooked to the application <- }

    { - this event is called when an exception occurs, and simply flips back -
      - to the GDI surface so that the exception dialog box can be read      - }
    procedure TfrmDXAppMain.ExceptionHandler(Sender: TObject;
                                              ExceptionObj: Exception);
    begin
      {disconnect the OnIdle event to shut off the rendering loop}
      Application.OnIdle := nil;

      {if the DirectDraw object was successfully created, flip to the GDI surface}
      if Assigned(FDirectDraw) then
        FDirectDraw.FlipToGDISurface;

      {display the exception message}
      MessageDlg(ExceptionObj.Message, mtError, [mbOK], 0);

      {reconnect the OnIdle event to reenter the rendering loop}
      Application.OnIdle := AppIdle;
    end;

    { - this method is continuously called by the application, and provides  -
      - the main rendering loop.  this could be replaced by a custom          -
      - while..do loop                                                       - }
    procedure TfrmDXAppMain.AppIdle(Sender: TObject; var Done: Boolean);
    begin
      {indicates that the application should continuously call this method}
      Done := FALSE;

      {if DirectDraw has not been initialized, exit}
      if not Assigned(FDirectDraw) then Exit;

      {note that at this point game logic could be inserted that controls things
       like sprite movement and collision detection}

      {draw surface content and flip the surfaces}
      DrawSurfaces;
      FlipSurfaces;
    end;

    { - handles certain messages that are required to make DirectX function  -
```

```
                                                                   - }
  - properly within Delphi
procedure TfrmDXAppMain.AppMessage(var Msg: TMsg; var Handled: Boolean);
begin
  case Msg.Message of
    WM_ACTIVATEAPP:
      {unhook the OnIdle event when the application is being deactivated.
       this will stop all rendering}
      if not Boolean(Msg.wParam) then
        Application.OnIdle := nil
      else
        {upon activating the application, send ourselves the user-
         defined message}
        PostMessage(Application.Handle, WM_DIRECTXACTIVATE, 0, 0);
    WM_DIRECTXACTIVATE:
      begin
        {upon activating, restore all surfaces (reloading their memory as
         necessary), hook up the OnIdle event, and redraw the contents of
         all surfaces}
        RestoreSurfaces;
        Application.OnIdle := AppIdle;
        DrawSurfaces;
      end;
    WM_SYSCOMMAND:
      begin
        {do not allow a screen saver to kick in}
        Handled := (Msg.wParam = SC_SCREENSAVE);
      end;
  end;
end;



{ -> Form Events <- }

{ - initialize essential form properties - }
procedure TfrmDXAppMain.FormCreate(Sender: TObject);
begin
  {set up the application exception handler}
  Application.OnException := ExceptionHandler;

  {initialize form properties.  note that the FormStyle property must be
   set to fsStayOnTop}
  BorderStyle := bsNone;
  BorderIcons := [];
  FormStyle   := fsStayOnTop;
  Color       := clBlack;
  Cursor      := crNone;

  {turn off the mouse cursor}
  ShowCursor(FALSE);
end;
```

```
{ - provides essential cleanup functionality - }
procedure TfrmDXAppMain.FormDestroy(Sender: TObject);
begin
  {disengage our custom exception handler}
  Application.OnException := nil;

  {display the mouse cursor}
  ShowCursor(TRUE);

  {remember, we do not have to explicitly free the DirectX objects,
   as they will free themselves when they go out of context (such as
   when the application is closed)}
end;

{ - this method initializes DirectX and creates all necessary objects - }
procedure TfrmDXAppMain.FormActivate(Sender: TObject);
var
  {we can only get a DirectDraw4 interface from the DirectDraw interface, so we
   need a temporary interface}
  TempDirectDraw: IDirectDraw;

  {structures required for various methods}
  DDSurface: TDDSurfaceDesc2;
  DDSCaps: TDDSCaps2;

  {flag used to determine if the desired graphics mode is supported}
  SupportedMode: Boolean;
begin
  {if DirectDraw has already been initialized, exit}
  if Assigned(FDirectDraw) then exit;

  {create a temporary DirectDraw object. this is used to create the
   desired DirectDraw4 object}
  DXCheck( DirectDrawCreate(nil, TempDirectDraw, nil) );

  try
    {we can only get a DirectDraw4 interface through the QueryInterface
     method of the DirectDraw object}
    DXCheck( TempDirectDraw.QueryInterface(IID_IDirectDraw4, FDirectDraw) );
  finally
    {now that we have the DirectDraw4 object, the temporary DirectDraw
     object is no longer needed}
    TempDirectDraw := nil;
  end;

  {hook up the application message handler}
  Application.OnMessage := AppMessage;

  {call EnumDisplayModes and verify that the desired graphics mode
   is indeed supported}
  FillChar(DDSurface, SizeOf(TDDSurfaceDesc2), 0);
```

```
DDSurface.dwSize    := SizeOf(TDDSurfaceDesc2);
DDSurface.dwFlags   := DDSD_HEIGHT or DDSD_WIDTH or DDSD_PIXELFORMAT;
DDSurface.dwHeight := DXHEIGHT;
DDSurface.dwWidth  := DXWIDTH;
DDSurface.ddpfPixelFormat.dwSize := SizeOf(TDDPixelFormat_DX6);
DDSurface.ddpfPixelFormat.dwRGBBitCount := DXCOLORDEPTH;
SupportedMode := FALSE;
DXCheck( FDirectDraw.EnumDisplayModes(0, @DDSurface, @SupportedMode,
                                      EnumModesCallback) );

{if the desired graphics mode is not supported by the DirectX drivers,
 display an error message and shut down the application}
if not SupportedMode then
begin
  MessageBox(Handle, PChar('The installed DirectX drivers do not support a '+
             'display mode of: '+IntToStr(DXWIDTH)+' X '+
             IntToStr(DXHEIGHT)+', '+IntToStr(DXCOLORDEPTH)+' bit color'),
             'Unsupported Display Mode Error', MB_ICONERROR or MB_OK);
  Close;
  Exit;
end;

{set the cooperative level to that defined in the constants}
DXCheck( FDirectDraw.SetCooperativeLevel(Handle, COOPERATIVELEVEL) );

{set the display resolution and color depth to that defined in the constants}
DXCheck( FDirectDraw.SetDisplayMode(DXWIDTH, DXHEIGHT, DXCOLORDEPTH, 0, 0) );

{initialize the DDSurface structure to indicate that we will be creating a
 complex flipping surface with one backbuffer}
FillChar(DDSurface, SizeOf(TDDSurfaceDesc2), 0);
DDSurface.dwSize   := SizeOf(TDDSurfaceDesc2);
DDSurface.dwFlags := DDSD_CAPS or DDSD_BACKBUFFERCOUNT;
DDSurface.ddsCaps.dwCaps := SURFACETYPE;
DDSurface.dwBackBufferCount := BUFFERCOUNT;

{create the primary surface object}
DXCheck( FDirectDraw.CreateSurface(DDSurface, FPrimarySurface, nil) );

{indicate that we want to retrieve a pointer to the backbuffer (the surface
 immediately behind the primary surface in the flipping chain) }
FillChar(DDSCaps, SizeOf(TDDSCaps2), 0);
DDSCaps.dwCaps := DDSCAPS_BACKBUFFER;

{retrieve the surface}
DXCheck( FPrimarySurface.GetAttachedSurface(DDSCaps, FBackBuffer) );

{at this point, offscreen buffers and other surfaces should be created. other
 DirectDraw objects should be created and initialized as well, such as
 palettes. the contents of all offscreen surfaces should also be initialized
 at this point}
```

```
    {post a message that will hook up the OnIdle event and start the main
      rendering loop}
    PostMessage(Handle, WM_ACTIVATEAPP, 1, 0);
end;


{ -> Form Methods <- }

{ - this method is called in order to flip the surfaces - }
procedure TfrmDXAppMain.FlipSurfaces;
var
  DXResult: HResult;
begin
  {perform the page flip. note that the DDFLIP_WAIT flag has been used,
    indicating that the function will not return until the page flip has been
    performed. this could be removed, allowing the application to perform other
    processing until the page flip occurs. however, the application will need
    to continuously call the Flip method to ensure that the page flip takes
    place}
  DXResult := FPrimarySurface.Flip(nil, DDFLIP_WAIT);

  {if the surfaces were lost, restore them. on any other error,
    raise an exception}
  if DXResult = DDERR_SURFACELOST then
    RestoreSurfaces
  else if DXResult <> DD_OK then
    DXCheck(DXResult);
end;

{ - this method is called when the surface memory is lost  -
  - and must be restored.  surfaces in video memory that   -
  - contain bitmaps must be reinitialized in this function - }
procedure TfrmDXAppMain.RestoreSurfaces;
begin
  {restore the primary surface, which in turn restores any implicit surfaces}
  FPrimarySurface._Restore;

  {here you should reload any bitmaps stored in video memory surfaces}
end;

{ - this method is called when the contents of the surfaces need to be  -
  - drawn. it will be continuously called by the AppIdle method, so any  -
  - rendering or animation could be done within this method         - }
procedure TfrmDXAppMain.DrawSurfaces;
begin
end;


{ -> Deletable Events <- }
```

*///*

```
{ - as a matter of convenience this framework will terminate when the -
  - Escape key is pressed, but this should probably be deleted and   -
  - replaced with your own terminate methods                    - }
procedure TfrmDXAppMain.FormKeyDown(Sender: TObject; var Key: Word;
  Shift: TShiftState);
begin
  if Key = VK_ESCAPE then
    Close;
end;
///


{ *-->>  END BASELINE APPLICATION CODE <<--* }

end.
```

## DirectX Result Codes

Just about every DirectX function and method returns an HResult, a 32-bit number that maps to a DirectX error code. There are hundreds of error codes, all of which are located in the DDraw unit. These codes can be translated into a textual form by calling the DXErrorString function located in the DXTools unit. The DXTools unit also contains a procedure called DXCheck that will raise an exception if a DirectX function returns any error code other than DD_OK.

In theory, every call to any DirectX method should be wrapped with this DXCheck function. In practice, this may be impractical, but you should always check the results of any extremely critical methods, such as blits, flips, and initialization code. Methods such as these can cause an application to waltz off into limbo if they fail and are not gracefully handled, so checking the result code is very important for a robust application.

The DXErrorString function can be incredibly useful when debugging a DirectX application. The result of this function could be written out to a disk-based text file, and later examined if the DirectX application crashes. This tends to happen often when developing DirectX applications, and due to the fact that you cannot step through your code or use any of Delphi's awesome debugging features, this is a useful, if sloppy, debugging technique.

## Retrieving the DirectX Version

Most commercial DirectX applications ship with a version of the DirectX runtime redistributables. The developer knows that the application will be using either the version installed with the application or a more recent version installed by other applications or the operating system. However, sometimes it is necessary to determine which version of DirectX is installed before initializing objects, particularly if the application is to be distributed without the DirectX run-time redistributables, such as on floppy or over the Internet.

Specifically, you should not be checking for an overall DirectX version, but instead you should check for the availability of specific interfaces. As we've seen, the QueryInterface method implemented in every COM object can determine if a specific interface is supported. Using this method, you can determine if certain features are supported on the target machine. For example, if the IDirectDraw4 interface is not available, you know that you're working with a version of DirectDraw older than 6. By querying for other interfaces, you can determine if 3-D sound or force feedback devices are supported. Using the QueryInterface method is much more reliable than checking the drive for the existence and time stamp of particular files.

Additionally, DirectSetup features a method for retrieving the current version of DirectX that is installed on the machine. See Appendix A for complete information about DirectSetup and how to retrieve the current version of DirectX.

## Summary

In this chapter, we discussed several DirectX and DirectDraw topics. The examples built from initializing DirectDraw all the way to implementing a general page flipping architecture and displaying bitmaps. DirectX programming in general is a very complex topic, filled with many nuances with which the developer must become familiar. We covered DirectDraw programming to a minor degree in order to illustrate this point, and as a foundation upon which the rest of the book's knowledge will be built. When coding a DirectX application, and using DirectDraw in particular, it is important to keep these points in mind:

■ The DirectX development team's goal was to create a low-level architecture that would provide developers with the hardware control they need at the speed they demanded, while still retaining Windows' device-independent benefits. This was to be accomplished without imposing a restrictive high-level design architecture. Therefore, DirectX promises three things to developers: fast execution, minimal style restraints, and a level of abstraction that will provide benefits from future hardware.

■ DirectX delivers exceptionally on all of its promises, and offers many benefits, such as speed, control, and feature emulation. However, DirectX programming has a number of drawbacks, such as difficult debugging, few Delphi-specific examples, and a steep learning curve. The developer must determine if the benefits and advantages offered by DirectX outweigh the drawbacks and disadvantages for the specific functionality required by the application.

■ The DirectX API itself, in the form of various COM objects and their methods, acts as an interface into the DirectX drivers. On the back side, the DirectX drivers can be thought of as two separate systems: the hardware abstraction layer (HAL) and the hardware emulation layer (HEL). The HAL represents the hardware itself. The HEL, on the other hand, represents the software emulation of certain features. It is important to note that, for the most part, this is completely transparent to developers.

■ DirectX is comprised of many components. While the inventive game developer could potentially make use of all of these components, there are only a few which are essential for game development: DirectDraw, DirectSound, and DirectInput. Other components that may be useful in a particular game include DirectPlay, DirectSetup, Direct3D, and DirectMusic.

■ Under Delphi, you do not necessarily need the DirectX SDK; you only need the DirectX redistributables that are installed with the DirectX SDK or almost any commercially available game. However, the DirectX SDK includes a number of debugging and control panel utilities that can be useful, and is the only source for the DirectX API documentation. In this book, we use the DirectX headers from the JEDI project, translated by Erik Unger. However, there are several other commercial and shareware/freeware DirectX components and headers that can dramatically decrease the production time for a DirectX project under Delphi.

■ DirectX objects are COM based, consequently involving all of the associated benefits and drawbacks of using COM objects. Working with DirectX objects has some similarities to working with other COM objects, but there are a few differences. The primary difference is the fact that DirectX objects do not need to be created by using the CoCreateInstance function. All DirectX objects are created through custom function calls that return an instantiated COM object. A COM object can almost be thought of as a VCL object with no properties, only methods. The methods of a COM object are known as an interface. A COM object can have more than one interface, and it can be extended by added new interfaces, similar to deriving a new component from an ancestor. However, the COM standard dictates that an interface can never change. COM objects determine when they can destroy themselves, and thus do not need to be freed by the creating application. A unique identifier called a GUID is used to distinguish individual COM objects.

■ Perhaps the single most important concept in DirectDraw programming is that of the surface. A surface is directly analogous to Delphi's TBitmap or TCanvas object. It represents a virtual "picture" upon which graphical output can be drawn. In reality, a surface is a linear chunk of memory that is managed as if it were rectangular. Surfaces have width and height, among many other properties. The memory for a surface can be located in a number of places, but primarily it will be found in system memory or in the memory on the display card itself. There are many different types of surfaces, some of which are very specialized for a particular purpose. For the purposes of this book, we will be concerned with only three different types: the primary surface, the backbuffer surface, and off-screen surfaces.

■ Page flipping is an incredibly powerful technique for producing flicker-free animation. The term "page flipping" comes from the inspiration for this animation technique, that of traditional cartoon animation. Cartoons (and movies, for that matter) create the illusion of animation by displaying to the viewer a series of images, one after the other. Someone can create a crude animation by taking a stack of paper, drawing an image on each page, and then flipping through it rapidly. This is the architecture of page flipping animation. The idea is to create two surfaces, the primary surface and the backbuffer surface. The next frame of animation is composed on the backbuffer surface, and then it is "flipped" to the display screen. This updates the entire display screen in one fell swoop, resulting in a flickerless animation.

■ There are several tasks an application is required to perform before DirectDraw can be instantiated and the display mode modified. Some of these tasks are optional, some are not. The application may want to enumerate all attached display devices, although this is not specifically required. After the user picks an enumerated display device, or if the application simply decides to go with the primary display device, the DirectDraw object can be created. Supported display modes can then be enumerated; while not specifically required, the display mode into which the display hardware is switched must be a supported mode, which can be verified by enumerating supported display modes. The cooperative level can then be set, determining if the application will run full screen or windowed. Finally, setting the display mode causes the hardware to switch over to the indicated resolution and color depth. Bear in mind that certain requirements are imposed on the main window before the display mode can be set properly.

■ A device context handle can be retrieved from a surface, allowing the application to use GDI rendering functions. When combined with a TCanvas object, the full power of Delphi's built-in graphical rendering functionality can be brought to bear. However, the sluggishness of the GDI will also be present. It is very important that any device contexts retrieved be released before performing any DirectDraw functions that manipulate the surface.

■ Bitmaps can be easily loaded and stored into a surface by using the TBitmap object combined with the drawing capabilities of a TCanvas object and a device context retrieved from a surface.

■ The memory associated with surfaces located in display memory can be lost if the user Alt+Tabs out of the application. When the DirectDraw application receives focus again, it must call the Restore method of any display memory surfaces, including the primary surface. Their contents will be undefined, so they must be reinitialized by reloading bitmaps or redrawing graphics.

■ DirectX was written so that a developer can take advantage of certain hardware features if they are available, such as overlays or the ability to create off-screen surfaces wider than the primary surface. We can determine what features are available by calling the IDirectDraw4's GetCaps method.

■ Just about every DirectX function and method returns an HResult, a 32-bit number that maps to a DirectX error code. There are hundreds of error codes, all of which are located in the DDraw unit. These codes can be translated into a textual form by calling the DXErrorString function located in the DXTools unit. You should always check the results of any extremely critical methods, such as blits, flips, and initialization code. Methods such as these can cause an application to waltz off into limbo if they fail and are not gracefully handled, so checking the result code is very important for a robust application.

■ Sometimes it is necessary to determine which version of DirectX is installed before initializing objects, particularly if the application is to be distributed without the DirectX run-time redistributables, such as on floppy or over the Internet. Specifically, you should not be checking for an overall DirectX version, but instead you should check for the availability of specific interfaces. The QueryInterface method implemented in every COM object can determine if a specific interface is supported.

# CHAPTER 5: *Palettes*

**THIS CHAPTER COVERS THE FOLLOWING TOPICS:**

■ The definition of a color palette

■ The creation and use of the IDirectDrawPalette object

■ Palette animation

Game programmers tend to have mixed feelings about palettized display modes. On one hand, you've got special animation effects and superior performance benefiting you from using a palettized display mode. On the other hand, you've got graphic resource management nightmares, an extra layer of indirection and complexity, and a limited resource in the form of color. With the increasing speed of today's hardware, someday the performance boost available with palettized display modes will not outweigh the benefits of using 16-bit or 32-bit color modes. However, at this point, creating games in a 256-color palettized display mode still has many advantages over the higher color depth modes. Since this book discusses techniques for game and graphics programming under 256 video modes, we should examine how DirectX handles color palettes in a little more depth.

In this chapter, we will examine how palettes are supported under DirectDraw in full-screen exclusive mode. We covered color depth and palettes back in Chapter 3, Basic Graphics Programming, and palettes still work very much the same way under DirectX. For the sake of completeness (in case you skipped Chapter 3), we'll briefly examine what a color palette is and how it works. Then we'll dive right into creating DirectDraw palettes, how they are used, and some special effects you can accomplish with them. If you read the basic graphics programming chapter, skip ahead to the section on the IDirectDrawPalette object.

# What is a Palette?

A color palette is a mechanism by which a potentially large range of colors can be displayed without using enormous amounts of memory. Four and eight bits-per-pixel color depths are the only palettized video modes. As 4 bits-per-pixel color depths are no longer used for games, we will discuss only 8 bits-per-pixel color depths. At 8 bits-per-pixel, each pixel can assume a value between 0 and 255. These values act as an index into what can be considered a 256-entry array known as the color palette. Now, each entry in this array contains an 8-bit value for the blue, green, and red intensity of a color. In effect, this gives 8 bits-per-pixel color depths access to 16,777,216 potential colors, but only 256 of them can be shown at one time. When a bitmap is displayed, the video hardware looks at the 8-bit pixel value, and using that value as an index into the 256-entry color table, it draws a pixel using the red, green, and blue intensities stored in the indicated color table entry.

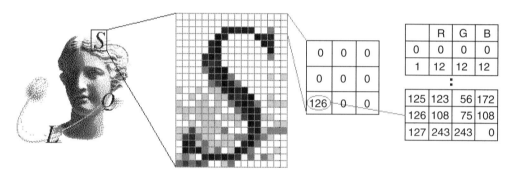

*Figure 5-1:*
*An 8 bits-per-pixel bitmap's pixels act as indices into a color palette*

There are many things to consider when working with 8 bits-per-pixel color modes. A major disadvantage to this mode is that all bitmaps to be displayed simultaneously must be drawn using the same palette. This requires a lot of careful planning on the part of art production, and can limit the creativity of artists and the variety of artwork that can be displayed on screen. Bitmaps that are drawn using one palette but displayed on a device in which a different palette is currently being used will have unpredictable results. A bitmap's pixels could be mapped to the closest approximation of the appropriate color in the current palette, but this process is slow, usually produces inadequate results, and is not appropriate for fast action games. Different palettes can be used between scenes, however, which can reduce this effect.

However, 8 bits-per-pixel video modes give the greatest speed advantage, and a tremendous number of colors can potentially be used while taking up the least amount of RAM. Up to four pixels can be moved simultaneously by using

32-bit memory movement instructions, allowing bitmaps to be moved about at blindingly fast speeds. Another major advantage comes from palette animation. If colors within the palette are moved about, or cycled, every pixel drawn using that color is affected simultaneously and automatically. This can be used for various special effects, such as flowing water or lighting. Palette animation is not available under non-palettized video modes. Since this book is concerned with high-performance games and graphics programming, all examples will use only 8 bits-per-pixel video modes in order to squeeze out as much speed as possible.

# The IDirectDrawPalette Object

Using DirectDraw, an application has direct access to the display card's hardware palette registers. In order to set the palette entries of the display hardware, the developer must use the IDirectDrawPalette object. Of all the DirectX objects, the palette object is perhaps the easiest to manipulate and use. It has only a few methods, and using the object is very straightforward.

## Creating the Palette Object

The CreatePalette method of the IDirectDraw object is called to actually create the IDirectDrawPalette object. This simple function takes only a few parameters, and is declared as:

```
function CreatePalette (
dwFlags: DWORD;                           // control flags
lpColorTable: pointer;                    // a pointer to an array of
                                          // TPaletteEntry structures
var lplpDDPalette: IDirectDrawPalette;    // a pointer to the new
                                          // IDirectDrawPalette object
pUnkOuter: IUnknown                       // COM aggregation
): HResult;                               // returns an error code
```

The first parameter takes a series of constants that can be combined using the OR boolean operator to indicate the type of palette being created and some of its capabilities. In particular, 2-, 4-, 16-, or 256-entry palettes can be created by specifying the appropriate flags. Since we're primarily interested in 256-color display modes, we'll using the DDPCAPS_8BIT flag to indicate that we want 256 entries in the palette. The third parameter takes a pointer to a variable of type IDirectDrawPalette that will hold the instantiated palette object when this function returns. The final parameter will be used in the future for COM aggregation. For now, we'll always set this parameter to nil.

The second parameter is really the heart of this function. It is a pointer to an array of palette entry structures that contain the colors used to initialize the palette. In our case, this will be an array of 256 entries. These structures are of type TTrueColor, and are defined as:

```
TTrueColor = record
  case integer of
    1 : (Data : DWORD);        // the color as a 32-bit value
    2 : (R,G,B,A : byte);      // red, green, blue, and alpha intensities
end;
```

This structure contains members for the red, green, and blue components of a color, defining a 24-bit RGB color value. The final member is useful only under windowed DirectX and with Direct3D, so we will not be concerned with it.

**Note**  Incidentally, the TPaletteEntry data structure type could also be used. It is defined somewhat differently, but it is the same size as this structure, and its members map to the same members of the TTrueColor structure.

## Defining Palette Colors

It would be easy enough for an application to programmatically define all of the colors in the palette. We could simply iterate through all entries in the color table array, setting the red, green, and blue values as necessary to create the desired palette. While this is certainly a workable approach, and is desirable in the case where a custom color gradient effect needs to be achieved, most often an application's palette needs to be initialized with the colors used in a bitmap.

Fortunately for us, we're using Delphi, which makes this whole problem incredibly easy to solve. To start, we'll need to create a TBitmap object, and use it to load in the bitmap whose palette we wish to use. Then, we'll use the GDI function GetPaletteEntries to retrieve all of the bitmap's palette entries. The GetPaletteEntries function is defined as:

```
GetPaletteEntries(
Palette: HPALETTE;         // a handle to a logical palette
StartIndex: UINT;          // the starting palette index
NumEntries: UINT;          // the number of palette entries to retrieve
PaletteEntries: Pointer    // a pointer to an array of TPaletteEntry structures
): UINT;                   // returns the number of palette entries retrieved
```

The first parameter takes a handle to a logical palette, which we can simply set to the Palette property of the TBitmap object we've just created. The second parameter indicates the index of the first palette slot we would like to retrieve. The third parameter indicates the number of palette slots to retrieve. The final parameter is a pointer to an array of TPaletteEntry structures which will receive the palette data.

The cool thing here is that we can pass this function the same array of TTrueColor structures that we'll use in the call to CreatePalette. The entire procedure only takes a few lines of code, and looks something like this:

```
var
  Palette: array[0..255] of TTrueColor;
  DDPalette: IDirectDrawPalette;
  TempBitmap: TBitmap;
begin
  {create the temporary bitmap}
  TempBitmap := TBitmap.Create;

  try
    {load the bitmap, and extract its palette}
    TempBitmap.LoadFromFile('c:\somebitmap.bmp');
    GetPaletteEntries(TempBitmap.Palette, 0, 256, Palette);

    {create the palette object}
    DDraw.CreatePalette(DDPCAPS_8BIT, @Palette, DDPalette, nil);
  finally
    TempBitmap.Free;
  end;
end;
```

This creates an IDirectDrawPalette object that is initialized with the palette stored in the specified bitmap. We've encapsulated this functionality in the DDUtil unit on the companion CD in the function DDLoadPalette. You can simply call this function, passing it a pointer to the DirectDraw object and the path and filename of the bitmap whose palette you wish to use, and it returns an instantiated IDirectDrawPalette object. This makes palette creation and initialization a one-line function call.

 **Caution:** By default, only 254 palette entries in an 8-bit palette can be used. DirectDraw predefines palette slot 0 as black and palette slot 255 as white. You can use all 256 entries by specifying the DDPCAPS_ ALLOW256 flag in the first parameter of the call to CreatePalette. However, some video cards use palette slot 0 to define the overscan color, the color of the area around the usable display area. Some versions of Windows NT won't allow this slot to be changed at all. Changing palette slot 0 may cause some unpredictable effects on some video cards, so don't use the DDPCAPS_ALLOW256 flag unless absolutely necessary.

 **overscan:** The area on a monitor that borders the usable display area.

## Using the Palette Object

Actually using a palette object is almost as simple as creating one. We use the SetPalette method of the IDirectDrawSurface4 object to associate a palette with a palettized surface. When a palette is associated with a surface, its color table is inserted into the hardware color registers, instantly changing the color of any displayed pixels. The only parameter this function takes is a pointer to the IDirectDrawPalette object that was created earlier. The SetPalette method is defined as:

```
function SetPalette (
lpDDPalette: IDirectDrawPalette      // a pointer to an IDirectDrawPalette object
): HResult;                          // returns a DirectX error code
```

The only parameter to this method is a pointer to the IDirectDrawPalette object we've created. Only the palette associated with the primary surface will affect the actual hardware palette registers. Thus, you must attach the newly created palette to the primary surface before the new colors take effect. Palettes can actually be attached to any palettized surface, and the same palette can be attached to more than one surface, but only the palette attached to the primary surface will actually affect the display.

**Note:** If a surface becomes lost and must be restored, any attached palettes are unaffected, and do not need to be reconnected after a surface is restored. Additionally, palettes do not move when surfaces are flipped, so it is unnecessary to attach palettes to both a primary surface and backbuffer.

If an IDirectDrawPalette object is not attached to the primary surface, the current entries in the hardware palette (left over from the last application) will be used. This usually results in bitmaps and graphics that appear garbled or corrupted. Therefore, unless your graphics will only be using the standard 20 Windows colors (left in the palette if the last application ran was a regular Windows application), you should always instantiate and attach a new palette object to the primary surface.

The following examples illustrate what happens when a bitmap is displayed with and without associating a palette with the primary surface. When an IDirectDrawPalette object is created, initialized with the bitmap's palette, and associated with the primary surface, the displayed bitmap appears as it did when it was created. In the second example, the bitmap is shown without associating any sort of palette with the primary surface. The results will be unpredictable, and will depend largely upon whatever application last modified the palette registers.

***Listing 5-1:*** *Displaying a bitmap with a palette*

```
var

    .
    .
    .

  FPalette: IDirectDrawPalette;

    .
    .
    .

procedure TfrmDXAppMain.FormActivate(Sender: TObject);
var

    .
    .
    .

{the array of palette entries}
  Palette: array[0..255] of TTrueColor;

  {our temporary bitmap}
  TempBitmap: TBitmap;
begin

    .
    .
    .

  {retrieve the surface}
  DXCheck( FPrimarySurface.GetAttachedSurface(DDSCaps, FBackBuffer) );

  {create the temporary bitmap}
  TempBitmap := TBitmap.Create;

  try
    {load the bitmap, and extract its palette}
    TempBitmap.LoadFromFile(ExtractFilePath(ParamStr(0))+'Background.bmp');
    GetPaletteEntries(TempBitmap.Palette, 0, 256, Palette);

    {create the palette object}
    DXCheck( FDirectDraw.CreatePalette(DDPCAPS_8BIT or DDPCAPS_ALLOW256,
                                       @Palette, FPalette, nil) );
  finally
    {free our temporary bitmap object}
    TempBitmap.Free;
  end;
```

```
{attach the palette to the primary surface so that it takes affect}
DXCheck( FPrimarySurface.SetPalette(FPalette) );

{at this point, offscreen buffers and other surfaces should be created. other
 DirectDraw objects should be created and initialized as well, such as
 palettes. the contents of all surfaces should also be initialized at this
 point}
FBackground := DDLoadBitmap(FDirectDraw, ExtractFilePath(ParamStr(0))+
                     'Background.bmp');

{copy the bitmap to both the primary surface and the backbuffer}
Source := Rect(0, 0, DXWIDTH, DXHEIGHT);
FPrimarySurface.BltFast(0, 0, FBackground, Source, DDBLTFAST_NOCOLORKEY or
                     DDBLTFAST_WAIT);
FBackBuffer.BltFast(0, 0, FBackground, Source, DDBLTFAST_NOCOLORKEY or
                     DDBLTFAST_WAIT);

      .
      .
      .

end;
```

**Listing 5-2:** *Displaying a bitmap without a palette*

```
procedure TfrmDXAppMain.FormActivate(Sender: TObject);
var

      .
      .
      .

begin

      .
      .
      .

   {retrieve the surface}
   DXCheck( FPrimarySurface.GetAttachedSurface(DDSCaps, FBackBuffer) );

   {at this point, offscreen buffers and other surfaces should be created. other
    DirectDraw objects should be created and initialized as well, such as
    palettes. the contents of all surfaces should also be initialized at this
    point}
   FBackground := DDLoadBitmap(FDirectDraw, ExtractFilePath(ParamStr(0))+
                        'Background.bmp');
```

```
{copy the bitmap to both the primary surface and the backbuffer}
Source := Rect(0, 0, DXWIDTH, DXHEIGHT);
FPrimarySurface.BltFast(0, 0, FBackground, Source, DDBLTFAST_NOCOLORKEY or
                        DDBLTFAST_WAIT);
FBackBuffer.BltFast(0, 0, FBackground, Source, DDBLTFAST_NOCOLORKEY or
                        DDBLTFAST_WAIT);
    .
    .
    .
end;
```

## Disconnecting Palettes

You can disconnect any palette from a surface by simply calling the SetPalette method again with a parameter of nil. However, you can directly attach a new palette to a surface without disconnecting any current palette first. When a palette is connected to a surface, its reference count is incremented by one. Attaching the same palette to other surfaces increases the reference count, but attaching the same palette to the same surface again does not increase it.

## Palettes and GDI Functions

When mixing GDI functions with DirectX, GDI functions will use whatever palette is attached to the primary surface at the time the function is called. We must be cautious, since the functions we have examined that load a bitmap into a surface take advantage of the TBitmap object, which ultimately uses GDI functions for drawing the bitmap. If there is not currently a palette attached to the primary surface, the current hardware palette will be used. By default, GDI will remap bitmap bits to the closest matching colors available when the bitmap is copied to a surface's DC. Sometimes, the results are acceptable. However, if you subsequently attempt to attach a palette to the primary surface, the bitmap bits will have been translated by GDI and will not match up with the palette entries, resulting in visual garbage. When loading bitmaps using surface DCs and the TBitmap object, always load and attach the bitmap's palette to the primary surface first.

**Note:** Unlike graphics programming under GDI, there is no color conversion performed when blitting a bitmap from one surface to another. All pixels will be interpreted in terms of the destination surface's palette. Therefore, you need only attach a palette object to the primary surface.

# Palette Animation

Apart from the blitting speed benefits realized from having only 8 bits per pixel, palette animation is another great benefit of palettized display modes. Palette animation is a cheap yet powerful method for achieving effects that would be very slow under higher video modes. Animations such as running water and fades are easily implemented using palette animation; the same trick would require constant blitting under non-palettized video modes. We'll examine a cool text effect achievable through palette animation, as well as a generic screen transition where a bitmap fades in and out.

## *Animating the Palette*

Palette animation works by replacing the color value of a specific color table entry with another value. This instantly changes the color of any pixel drawn using that color table entry to the new color. There are two methods of accomplishing this. The first method requires the creating of multiple palette objects. Each palette object contains different color values in the specific color table entries to be animated. To achieve the animation, you simply call the SetPalette method of the primary surface in a continuous loop, changing the palette object used each time. While this will work, it essentially changes all 256 color registers each time, thus making it somewhat slow. It is uncommon to change all 256 color registers during each iteration of a palette animation, so this method is not recommended.

The second method is a more practical solution in that it is generally faster and doesn't waste as many resources as multiple palette objects would. It takes advantage of two methods of the IDirectDrawPalette object: the GetEntries and the SetEntries methods. The GetEntries method is defined as:

```
function GetEntries (
dwFlags: DWORD;            // not currently used, set to 0
dwBase: DWORD;            // the starting entry
dwNumEntries: DWORD;      // the number of entries to retrieve
lpEntries: pointer        // a pointer to an array of TPaletteEntry structures
): HResult;               // returns an error code
```

This function fills the array of TPaletteEntry structures specified in the fourth parameter with the color values of the palette's entries, starting from the entry specified in the second parameter. We can modify these color values as necessary, and then place them back into the palette using the SetEntries method, which is defined as:

```
function SetEntries (
dwFlags: DWORD;            // not currently used, set to 0
dwStartingEntry: DWORD;   // the starting entry
dwCount: DWORD;           // the number of entries to set
```

```
lpEntries: pointer          // a pointer to an array of TPaletteEntry structures
): HResult;                 // returns an error code
```

This function simply sets the color values in the palette to those specified in the array of TPaletteEntry structures specified in the fourth parameter, starting from the entry specified in the second parameter. When this action is performed on a palette attached to the primary surface, the colors of pixels drawn using these palette entries are immediately changed, and palette animation has occurred.

**Note:** When using this method to change a range of color entries, it is faster to change several entries that are adjacent (i.e., entries 5, 6, 7, 8, 9), as opposed to changing non-contiguous color entries (i.e., 13, 57, 73, 109).

It would be easy to demonstrate this technique by filling the screen with a color, say palette slot 5, and then using GetEntries and SetEntries in a loop to continuously change the color in entry 5. Similarly, if displaying a bitmap with a lot of pixels drawn using palette slot 5, this technique could change all of those pixels instantly. This could be useful for creating several variations of a monster using only one bitmap. In level one, the monster could be blue, but in level two, you can change the color table entry to red, and using the same bitmap, display a red version of the monster, perhaps indicating that it is a little tougher.

To demonstrate the technique of palette animation, we're going to do something a little more ambitious. Since the GetEntries and SetEntries methods allow us to change a range of color entries, it would be cool if we could draw a bitmap using a color gradient, and then rotate those color entries so the gradient appears to move. Using this technique is also a good way to implement moving water effects.

We start by loading our bitmap in and displaying it. Then, in our main animation loop, we use GetEntries to retrieve the range of color values to be modified. We then save the value in the last entry, slide all the other entries up one, and place the saved entry in the first spot. This rotates the color entries as illustrated in Figure 5-2.

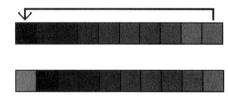

*Figure 5-2:*
*Rotating color entries*

We then place the modified entries back into the palette by calling SetEntries. The bitmap used in this example is simply the words "Delphi Rocks" drawn using a red gradient. Rotating the palette entries using this technique makes the gradient appear to move, and results in a very cool text animation effect. Listing 5-3 shows the heart of the example code that performs the actual palette animation.

**Listing 5-3:** *Animating a palette*

```
procedure TfrmDXAppMain.DrawSurfaces;
var
  {our palette slots to be modified}
  Entries: array[0..29] of TTrueColor;

  {a temporary palette slot holder}
  Temp: TTrueColor;

  {loop variable}
  iCount: Integer;
begin
  {retrieve the range of palette entries to be animated}
  FPalette.GetEntries(0, 9, 30, @Entries);

  {rotate the color entries up one, moving the last palette
   slot into the first slot}
  Temp := Entries[29];
  for iCount := 29 downto 1 do
    Entries[iCount] := Entries[iCount-1];
  Entries[0] := Temp;

  {place the rotated entries into the palette. this will cause
   the colors in the displayed image to change, creating the illusion
   of movement}
  FPalette.SetEntries(0, 9, 30, @Entries);
end;
```

## Screen Transitions

As another use for palette animation, let's examine a very clean, professional screen transition effect known as the fade. A fade is a cinematic effect where an image slowly appears from a solid color, such as black or white.

 **fade:** A transition effect where an image slowly appears out of a solid color, such as black or white.

Unlike the previous technique, we'll be performing palette animation on all 256 entries in the palette so that the entire image is affected (however, you could use only a subset of the entries in the palette to fade only portions of the image, but that's beyond the scope of this exercise). We must start by retrieving the entire color table into a permanent array that will hold all of the color's original values. The trick to this technique is in setting the values of a "work" array to a percentage of the values stored in the permanent, or "original colors" array, and then setting the palette's colors to the work array's values. We could simply change the red, green, and blue color components by a constant value, but that would make some colors fade in and out faster than others, causing the image to appear to change as it fades in or out. By setting the individual color elements as a percentage of the original value for that entry, we achieve a smooth transition effect. To fade in from black, the work array values are started at zero, and then gradually increased until they reach the original values. Fading out just reverses the procedure. Listing 5-4 demonstrates the heart of this technique.

**Tip:** Most games require a standardized palette such that all graphics are based on the same palette. If you are creating a game that features many different screens, you could create all backgrounds and artwork with individual palettes for each screen. Then, you could use the fade in/out screen transition and change the palette based on the new screen. This would allow you to use multiple palettes in a game, providing for a richer depth of color.

**Listing 5-4:** *Performing screen transitions*

```
procedure TfrmDXAppMain.FadeEffect(FadeIn: Boolean);
const
  STEPS = 100;     // we want 100 fade steps
var
  iCount, iCount2: Integer;
begin
  {if we are fading in from black...}
  if FadeIn then
  begin
    for iCount := 0 to STEPS do
    begin
      {modify the 'work' palette to a percentage of each original palette's
       color value, based on our current step}
      for iCount2 := 0 to 255 do
      begin
        AnimPalette[iCount2].R := Trunc(OrgPalette[iCount2].R*(iCount/STEPS));
        AnimPalette[iCount2].G := Trunc(OrgPalette[iCount2].G*(iCount/STEPS));
        AnimPalette[iCount2].B := Trunc(OrgPalette[iCount2].B*(iCount/STEPS));
        AnimPalette[iCount2].A := 0;
      end;

      {plug the palette into the hardware, causing the colors to take effect}
      FPalette.SetEntries(0, 0, 256, @AnimPalette);

      {pause for a fraction of a second}
      Sleep(10);
    end;
  end
  else
```

```
{if we are fading out to black...}
begin
  for iCount := 0 to STEPS do
  begin
    {modify the 'work' palette to a percentage of each original palette's
     color value, based on our current step. notice this is opposite from
     the previous block}
    for iCount2 := 0 to 255 do
    begin
      AnimPalette[iCount2].R := OrgPalette[iCount2].R-
                               Trunc(OrgPalette[iCount2].R*(iCount/STEPS));
      AnimPalette[iCount2].G := OrgPalette[iCount2].G-
                               Trunc(OrgPalette[iCount2].G*(iCount/STEPS));
      AnimPalette[iCount2].B := OrgPalette[iCount2].B-
                               Trunc(OrgPalette[iCount2].B*(iCount/STEPS));
      AnimPalette[iCount2].A := 0;
    end;

    {plug the palette into the hardware, causing the colors to take effect}
    FPalette.SetEntries(0, 0, 256, @AnimPalette);

    {pause for a fraction of a second}
    Sleep(10);
  end;
end;
end;
```

## Summary

In this chapter, we discussed how the IDirectDrawPalette object provides an application with hardware palette management functionality within an exclusive, full-screen DirectDraw environment. Keep these points in mind when programmatically manipulating the hardware palette:

■ The hardware palette is only used under palettized display modes. Thus, you will only be concerned with the palette when creating 256-color games.

■ Palettes give us access to a large range of colors while keeping memory requirements to a minimum. This also improves application performance as moving pixels between surfaces is very efficient. Under palettized display modes, we also have access to palette animation, which makes certain special effects easy to implement.

■ The colors in the palette could be defined programmatically, but typically they are initialized from the palette of a bitmap containing graphics used in the game.

■ By default, only 254 palette entries can be used. DirectDraw predefines palette slot 0 as black and palette slot 255 as white. You can use all 256 entries by specifying the DDPCAPS_ALLOW256 flag in the first parameter of the call to CreatePalette. However, bear in mind that some video cards use palette slot 0 to define the overscan color, the color of the area around the usable display area.

■ If a surface becomes lost and must be restored, any attached palettes are unaffected, and do not need to be reconnected after a surface is restored.

■ Palettes do not move when surfaces are flipped, so it is unnecessary to attach palettes to both a primary surface and backbuffer.

■ Only the palette associated with the primary surface will affect the actual hardware palette registers. Thus, you must attach the newly created palette to the primary surface before the new colors take effect. Palettes can actually be attached to any palettized surface, and the same palette can be attached to more than one surface, but only the palette attached to the primary surface will actually affect the display. If a palette is not attached to the primary surface, the current entries in the hardware palette (left over from the last application) will be used.

■ When mixing GDI functions with DirectX, GDI functions will use whatever palette is attached to the primary surface at the time the function is called.

# CHAPTER 6: *Sprite Techniques*

As we discussed in Chapter 2, The Anatomy of a Game, the most important graphical elements of any game are those graphics with which the user interacts, known as sprites. Sprites are such an integral part of any game that knowledge of their implementation and utilization is paramount. Sprites provide the animated elements of a game that make the gaming environment come alive. These can take the form of images that the player directly interacts with, such as a spaceship, or background elements that are non-interactive yet provide animation that makes the environment richer, deeper, and more believable. Without sprites, all you would have is a static bitmap, which would be quite boring.

The natural discussion of sprite implementation also leads to such sprite related issues as collision detection. With the exception of the most simplistic, most games need to detect when one sprite comes into contact with another. This would be important when, say, a missile launched from your ship comes into contact with a space-borne hunk of rock. Most players would expect the game to replace the rock with several smaller rocks and increment their score. Thus, it is important to understand the techniques by which sprite collision can be detected.

In this chapter, we examine several techniques for implementing sprites, discussing animation and movement as well as collision detection and timing issues.

# The Illusion of Animation

The method by which a game displays an animated image on the video screen has actually been around for many decades, even before computers were a household item. Indeed, if you have any knowledge of how movies or cartoons work, you already know the fundamentals of sprite animation.

The basic premise is simple. A series of images is required, where each image shows the character or object to be animated in a slightly different position than the image before it, like a filmstrip. Each image is known as a frame.

**frame:** A single image in a series of images to be animated.

When each image is rapidly displayed one after another, the human brain expects to see smooth motion, and any gaps in movement from one frame to another (provided it is not too large) will be automatically filled in. In essence, it's really nothing more than a complex visual illusion.

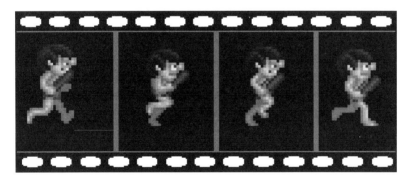

*Figure 6-1:*
*Movie frames*

Creating the illusion of animated images using the computer is almost identical to this technique. Instead of a filmstrip, a series of bitmaps is constructed in which each bitmap contains an image of the character or object in a slightly different position. If each bitmap is copied to the video screen in rapid succession, the illusion of animation will be achieved. This is known as frame animation.

**frame animation:** The process of producing animation by rapidly displaying a series of images depicting an object or character in slightly different positions each frame.

Unlike a filmstrip, which contains images of a scene in its entirety, the series of bitmaps to be animated usually contains only an image of the sprite itself. In fact, these images usually only contain images of the sprite in different positions without regard to its actual location in the scene. Location is controlled by other methods, which we'll see shortly. Of course, a series of bitmaps that does depict an entire scene could be used under special circumstances, such as showing an opening animation or perhaps an animation when the user is moving from one level to another. However, for the purposes of this chapter, we will examine only sprite animation techniques.

## Constructing the Animation Frames

The first step that is required is to create the series of bitmaps that will depict the animated object or character. As explained above, each bitmap should display the object or character in a slightly different position. You could store these as individual bitmap files, but the most common practice is to store all of these images in one bitmap, with each frame of the animation in the correct sequence, one after another. Another common practice is to make all frames of the animation equal in size. This simplifies the code when copying the image from the bitmap to the screen, as demonstrated in the example to follow.

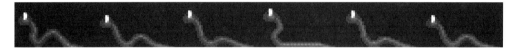

**Figure 6-2:** *An animated image bitmap*

## Producing the Animation

The actual process of producing animation is simple. We start by defining a variable that will hold the current frame number, starting at 0. Through each iteration of the game loop, we increment the frame number by 1. If it goes beyond the actual number of frames, reset it to 0. Then, we copy the appropriate frame out of the bitmap onto the screen, using this frame number as an index.

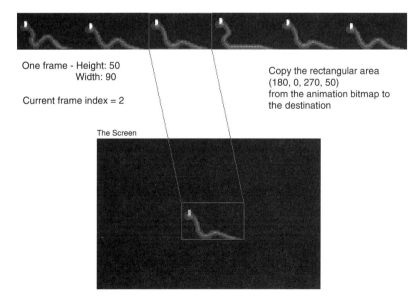

One frame - Height: 50
Width: 90

Current frame index = 2

Copy the rectangular area (180, 0, 270, 50) from the animation bitmap to the destination

The Screen

**Figure 6-3:** *Producing animation*

Since each frame of the animation is exactly the same size, it is very easy to calculate the appropriate place in the bitmap from which to copy the image. Assuming that we've arranged our frames horizontally in the bitmap, we only need to compute the X offset within the bitmap at which to start and end the copy. These are calculated using the following formulas:

```
XStart := FrameNum * WidthOfOneFrame;
XEnd := XStart + WidthOfOneFrame;
```

These offsets can easily be used with the Blt or BltFast methods of the IDirectDrawSurface object to copy the correct frame to the backbuffer. Incrementing the frame number each iteration through the game loop causes a new frame of the animation to be displayed each time. If this occurs in rapid succession, and the bitmaps are displayed at the same spot, we achieve the illusion of animation, as the example below illustrates.

*Listing 6-1: Simple frame animation*

```
procedure TfrmDXAppMain.DrawSurfaces;
var
  SourceRect: TRect;      // determines the area to copy from in the source bitmap
  SrfcDC: HDC;            // these two are used to make text drawing easier
  TempCanvas: TCanvas;
begin
  {increment the overall frame number}
  Inc(FFrameNum);

  {start the frame number from the beginning if it goes beyond the
   number of frames in the animation}
  if FFrameNum > 5 then
    FFrameNum := 0;

  {blit the entire snake frame bitmap to illustrate the animation frames}
  SourceRect := Rect(0, 0, 540, 50);
  FBackBuffer.BltFast(50, 75, FImages, SourceRect,
                  DDBLTFAST_NOCOLORKEY OR DDBLTFAST_WAIT);

  {blit the current frame of the animation}
  SourceRect := Rect(FFrameNum*90, 0, (FFrameNum*90)+90, 50);
  FBackBuffer.BltFast(275, 215, FImages, SourceRect,
                  DDBLTFAST_NOCOLORKEY OR DDBLTFAST_WAIT);

  .
  .
  .

end;
```

# The Illusion of Motion

Creating the illusion of animation was simple enough. However, even the most complex and beautifully rendered animation would quickly get boring if it stayed in the same spot. So, how do we go about moving the animated sprite across the screen to produce a more interesting and believable animation?

Again, the process is quite simple. On the most primitive level, when the application prepares to draw the next frame of animation, simply change the horizontal or vertical coordinate (or both) at which the image will be drawn into the destination. If these coordinates keep changing, the animated image will be drawn at different positions, creating the illusion of motion.

## *Sprite Attributes*

Before we begin, a few items of information need to be tracked for each sprite. In particular, its current X (horizontal) and Y (vertical) coordinate must be tracked so the application knows where to draw the sprite. A horizontal and vertical velocity could also be stored. These velocities would indicate the number of pixels to move the sprite, and would be added to the X and Y coordinates on each iteration through the game loop. If we also tracked the current frame of animation, the number of frames in the animation, and a pointer to the bitmap or DirectDraw surface containing the sprite images, we could create a basic sprite object that might look like this:

```
TSprite = class
  FXPos, FYPos,                 // tracks the current position
  FXVel, FYVel,                 // tracks the velocity
  Height, Width,                // sprite frame height and width
  FCurFrame,                    // tracks the current frame number
  FFrameNum: Integer;           // tracks the number of frames
  FImages: IDirectDrawSurface4; // a pointer to the sprite images
end;
```

## *The Animation Cycle*

The effect we want to produce is the image of an object moving across the screen in a believable manner. To achieve this illusion of motion, we will tackle the process of animation by breaking it into three distinct steps: erasing the sprite image, updating the sprite position, and drawing the sprite image.

If we simply move the sprite and continue to draw it on the screen without ever erasing it, the previous sprite images will still be visible, ruining the animation effect. We want our animation to look like a single object moving about as one would expect to see in a cartoon or movie. Thus, the first thing we must do is erase the previous sprite image. For this example, we will simply clear the entire surface by performing a color fill using the Blt method. The IDirectDrawSurface4's Blt method is defined as:

```
function Blt(
lpDestRect: PRect;                    // the destination rectangle
lpDDSrcSurface: IDirectDrawSurface4;  // the source surface
lpSrcRect: PRect;                     // the source rectangle
dwFlags: DWORD;                       // control flags
lpDDBltFx: PDDBltFX                   // a pointer to a TDDBltFX structure
): HResult;                           // returns a DirectX error code
```

The first parameter describes the rectangular area in the destination surface to which the image data is copied. The second parameter identifies the surface whose image data is being copied. The third parameter describes the rectangular area in the source surface from which the image data is copied. Note that if these rectangular areas are not the same size, the resulting image will be scaled as required. The fourth parameter is a series of flags indicating which members of the final parameter are valid and generally control the behavior of the blit. The final parameter is a pointer to a TDDBltFX structure. This rather large and complex structure contains information for various special graphical effects, such as color fills and raster operations. We'll see an example of this function's use to perform a color fill in Listing 6-2.

**Note:** In the DDUtil unit, we've created a function called ColorFill that uses the Blt method to fill a region with a color. You specify a surface, the color in the form of a TColor, and a rectangular region to be filled (or nil to fill the entire surface). This allows the developer to fill an area with a solid color using only one line of code.

Next, we simply add the horizontal and vertical velocities to the horizontal and vertical coordinates of the sprite. At this point, we may do some simple calculations to see if the sprite has moved off screen or out of bounds, and adjust its velocities accordingly. We then increment the frame number and draw the appropriate frame of the sprite image at the new coordinates. Figure 6-4 illustrates this process.

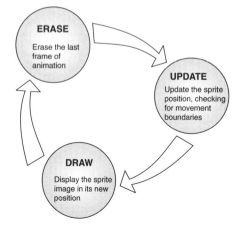

*Figure 6-4:*
*The animation cycle*

The value of the sprite velocities should take into account the type of animation being performed. If the animation is a top-down view of a ship flying in space, the horizontal and vertical velocities could be adjusted to make the sprite move all around the screen. However, if the animation is a side view of a walking character, we would probably only want to adjust the horizontal velocity (unless, of course, the character is jumping). The velocity value must also be adjusted to make the animation look more believable (i.e., a character would move faster when running than when walking).

Implementing this animation method is little more than an extension of the previous frame animation example, as the following listing demonstrates.

*Listing 6-2:* Simple sprite movement

```
procedure TfrmDXAppMain.DrawSurfaces;
var
  SourceRect: TRect
  SrfcDC: HDC;
  TempCanvas: TCanvas;
  BltFx: TDDBltFx;
begin
  {erase the last frame of animation by using a simple color fill to
   'black out' the entire backbuffer surface}
  FillChar(BltFx, SizeOf(TDDBltFx), 0);
  BltFx.dwSize := SizeOf(TDDBltFx);
  BltFx.dwFillColor := 0;
  FBackBuffer.Blt(nil, nil, nil, DDBLT_COLORFILL or DDBLT_WAIT, @BltFx);

  {increment the frame number and update the sprite's position}
  with FSprite do
  begin
    Inc(FCurFrame);

    {make sure we roll over the frame number as necessary}
    if FCurFrame > FFrameNum then
      FCurFrame := 0;

    {add the velocities to the positions. our sprite will only move
     horizontally, so we do not need to bother with the vertical values}
    FXPos := FXPos + FXVel;

    {see if the sprite is moving offscreen, and adjust
     its position accordingly}
    if FXPos < 0 then
      FXPos := DXWIDTH - 90;

    {blit the current frame}
    SourceRect := Rect(FCurFrame*90, 0, (FCurFrame*90)+90, 49);
    FBackBuffer.BltFast(FXPos, FYPos, FImages, SourceRect,
                    DDBLTFAST_SRCCOLORKEY OR DDBLTFAST_WAIT);
```

```
        end;

            .
            .
            .

        end;
```

## Transparency Issues

So far, the examples we've seen all demonstrate sprite animation against a solid black background. This may work for some games, but what if we wanted to have some sort of cool background graphic behind our sprites, like a starfield or perhaps a forest, mountains, or other type of setting? This not only makes the overall animation more visually stimulating, but it improves its believability and makes the overall gaming experience more realistic. To do this, we need to draw the frames of the sprite image using some technique for displaying the background through the parts of the sprite image that are supposed to be transparent. Figure 6-5 illustrates the difference between a sprite image being displayed with and without transparent pixels.

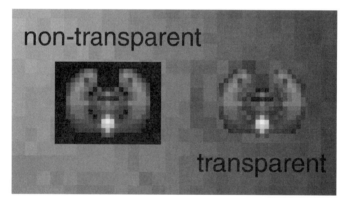

**Figure 6-5:**
*Sprite transparency*

Implementing transparency such as this is another broad topic in graphics programming that's been widely studied. There are probably hundreds, if not thousands, of methods to display a graphic with transparent areas. The trick is to do it as quickly as possible so it won't negatively affect the performance of the game. We will examine a few of the most common techniques used to display graphics with transparent pixels. These will include DirectDraw color keying and direct pixel checking.

**Tip:** You can potentially optimize your application by including several different methods for blitting graphics in the game engine. It is perfectly normal
to have one blitting function for graphics with no transparency (i.e., tiled
graphics such as floors, or textures), a separate general blitting function
for sprites with transparent pixels, and then perhaps a highly optimized
assembly blitter that's used for displaying graphics when optimum speed is
required. The point is that you do not have to use only one blitting technique for all graphics in your game engine; use many blitting techniques for
optimization and greater application performance.

## Color Keying

Color keying is the DirectX way of implementing transparency. With color keying, you specify a color that will be transparent. When DirectDraw blits this
graphic onto the background, any pixels whose color matches that of the color
key will not be drawn to the destination. Thus, the background will "show
through" those pixels, as if they were transparent. The effect is similar to a technique that film makers use called blue screen. In a blue screen effect, an actor
stands in front of a solid blue background. Later, the film is combined with a
background image, which shows through all of the blue areas. Blue, in this case,
is considered the color key.

Color keying is very easy to implement in DirectX. It's supported by the HEL,
so you know it will always work, and if supported by the hardware, it's incredibly fast. The only drawback to color keying is in the fact that every pixel in your
image that is the color of the color key will be transparent. Thus, that color cannot be used for anything opaque in the image. However, the loss of one useful
color out of 256 is easy to live with.

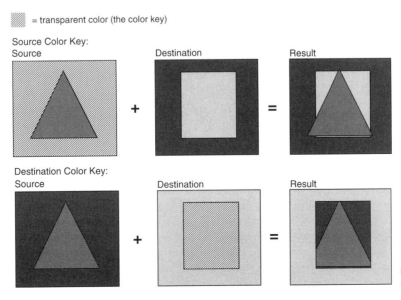

**Figure 6-6:**
*Color keying*

Under DirectX, there are actually two types of color keys: source and destination. In source color keying, the source image (the image to be copied) is the one containing the transparent pixels. When the source image is copied onto the destination image, the color keyed pixels in the source image are replaced by the pixels in the destination. With destination color keys, the destination image is the one containing the transparent pixels. When the source image is copied onto the destination image, the color keyed pixels in the destination are replaced by the pixels in the source.

In our examples, we will cover only source color keying, as destination color keying is not supported by the HEL and requires hardware support.

### Setting a Color Key

We specify a color key by calling the IDirectDrawSurface4's SetColorKey method. SetColorKey is defined as:

```
function SetColorKey (
dwFlags: DWORD;                  // indicates the type of color key
lpDDColorKey: PDDColorKey        // the transparent color(s)
): HResult;                      // returns a DirectX error code
```

The first parameter takes a flag that indicates the behavior of the color key. For our purposes, we'll set this to DDCKEY_SRCBLT, indicating a source color key. The second parameter is a pointer to a TDDColorKey structure that defines the color or colors to be interpreted as transparent. The TDDColorKey record is defined as:

```
TDDColorKey = packed record
  dwColorSpaceLowValue: DWORD;    // low boundary of color space
  dwColorSpaceHighValue: DWORD;   // high boundary of color space
end;
```

The values of these fields are specified in the color format of the surface. Since we're using 256-color (or palettized) surfaces, we simply indicate the index of the color that we wish to be transparent. This record structure allows us to define a range of colors that will be transparent. This is primarily useful when working with video data, as shadows and other slight variations in color due to digitizing the video result in a background that will be a range of colors as opposed to one single color. Game artwork should usually be drawn with only one transparent color, and for our purposes, we will define only one color as transparent by setting both record elements to the same value.

In our examples, we'll only set the color key of surfaces that contain source images to be blitted over a background, such as sprite images. For example, to set the color key of an arbitrary surface to palette index 0, we only need a few lines of code:

```
var
  ColorKey: TDDColorKey;
begin
  ColorKey.dwColorSpaceLowValue  := 0
  ColorKey.dwColorSpaceHighValue := 0

  DirectDrawSurface.SetColorKey(DDCKEY_SRCBLT, @ColorKey);
end;
```

**Note:** We have implemented a function in the DDUtil unit called
DDSetColorKey that allows the developer to set the color key for a surface in one line of code. This function was translated from a similar
function in the DirectX SDK. You simply pass in the surface and a color in
the form of a TColor. The function uses a complex technique for matching
the specified color to a format appropriate for the pixel format of the surface, so the function can be used for surfaces of any color depth.

## Using Color Keys

Now that we have our color key set up, we can extend the previous sprite example to display the sprite image over a background. After we load the sprite
images, we set their color key as described above. Then, when we actually draw
the sprite using the BltFast method, we specify the DDBLTFAST_SRCCOLORKEY
in its dwTrans parameter to indicate that the source surface has a color key that
should be taken into account during the blit.

Additionally, we must also load the image to be used as our sprite background. Now, as discussed previously, during the animation cycle we must erase
the last frame of the sprite animation. Instead of simply filling the entire surface
with black as we did previously, this time we'll draw the background image into
the backbuffer. The background image will fill the entire backbuffer, and thus
will erase the last frame of animation.

**Listing 6-3:** *Sprite transparency through color keying*

```
procedure TfrmDXAppMain.FormActivate(Sender: TObject);
var

  .
  .
  .

  {the color key record}
  ColorKey: TDDColorKey;
begin

  .
  .
```

```
        .

  {create a palette based on the sprite bitmap}
    FPalette := DDLoadPalette(FDirectDraw,
  ExtractFilePath(ParamStr(0))+'SnakeFrames.bmp');

    {attach the palette to the primary surface so that it takes effect}
    DXCheck( FPrimarySurface.SetPalette(FPalette) );

    {load in the bitmap containing the background and sprite images}
    FImages := DDLoadBitmap(FDirectDraw, ExtractFilePath(ParamStr(0))+
                            'SnakeFrames.bmp');

    {load the background bitmap}
    FBackground := DDLoadBitmap(FDirectDraw, ExtractFilePath(ParamStr(0))+
                                'Background.bmp');

    {initialize the color key record...}
    ColorKey.dwColorSpaceLowValue  := 0;
    ColorKey.dwColorSpaceHighValue := 0;

    {...and set the source color key}
    FImages.SetColorKey(DDCKEY_SRCBLT, @ColorKey);

    {initialize the sprite object}
    FSprite := TSprite.Create;
    FSprite.FXPos := DXWIDTH - 90;
    FSprite.FYPos := 215;
    FSprite.FXVel   := -1;
    FSprite.FYVel   := 0;
    FSprite.FCurFrame := 0;
    FSprite.FFrameNum := 5;
    FSprite.FImages := FImages;


    .
    .
    .


end;

procedure TfrmDXAppMain.DrawSurfaces;
var
  SourceRect: TRect
begin
  {erase the last frame of animation}
  SourceRect := Rect(0, 0, DXWIDTH, DXHEIGHT);
  FBackBuffer.BltFast(0, 0, FBackground, SourceRect,
                    DDBLTFAST_NOCOLORKEY OR DDBLTFAST_WAIT);

  {increment the frame number and update the sprite's position}
  with FSprite do
```

```
begin
  Inc(FCurFrame);

  {rollover the frame number as necessary}
  if FCurFrame > FFrameNum then
    FCurFrame := 0;

  {add the velocities to the positions. our sprite will only move
   horizontally, so we do not need to bother with the vertical values}
  FXPos := FXPos + FXVel;

  {see if the sprite is moving offscreen, and adjust
   its position accordingly}
  if FXPos < 0 then
    FXPos := DXWIDTH - 90;

  {blit the current frame, taking into account a source color key}
  SourceRect := Rect(FCurFrame*90, 0, (FCurFrame*90)+90, 49);
  FBackBuffer.BltFast(FXPos, FYPos, FImages, SourceRect,
                      DDBLTFAST_SRCCOLORKEY OR DDBLTFAST_WAIT);
  end;
end;
```

## Pixel Checking

A somewhat more direct way of implementing transparency, this method draws the sprite image one pixel at a time. As it is drawing individual pixels, it checks the pixel it will be drawing to see if its color matches the specified transparent color. If so, it skips drawing that pixel entirely; otherwise it draws the pixel into the destination.

Implementing this method is a bit more involved than color keying. By its very nature, it is pointer intensive and requires some creative pointer manipulation. It also requires more intimate knowledge of the pixel format of both the source and destination surfaces. It is slower than color keying, but through clever optimization can be as fast as non-hardware assisted color keying. However, the biggest benefit that a developer will see from this method is that it allows the creation of incredible special effects, such as lighting and translucency.

### Locking a Surface

This method requires direct access to the memory that contains both the source bitmap and the destination, which is usually the backbuffer surface. Using normal GDI functions, this would be impossible. This is one of the things that makes DirectDraw so attractive to game developers.

To retrieve a pointer to surface memory, we must use the Lock method of the IDirectDrawSurface4 object. Using this method, we can access the entire surface memory or provide the coordinates for accessing only a specific rectangular area of the memory. The Lock method is defined as:

```
function Lock (
lpDestRect: PRect;                    // the surface region to lock
out lpDDSurfaceDesc: TDDSurfaceDesc2; // a TDDSurfaceDesc2 structure
dwFlags: DWORD;                       // indicates locking behavior
hEvent: THandle                       // unused
): HResult;                           // returns a DirectX error code
```

The first parameter indicates the rectangular area of the surface to lock; specifying nil in this parameter locks the entire surface. The second parameter is a TDDSurfaceDesc2 structure that will be initialized with relevant details about the surface. In particular, the lpSurface member of this structure will contain a pointer to the upper left pixel of the surface memory. Other members of this structure will contain additional information about the surface, such as its height, width, and stride. The third parameter is a series of flags controlling access to the locked memory, such as read-only or write-only. The final parameter is unused and should be set to zero.

As an example, the code for retrieving a pointer to our backbuffer memory would look something like:

```
var
  BackSurfaceDesc: TDDSurfaceDesc2;
begin
  {initialize the size member}
  BackSurfaceDesc.dwSize := SizeOf(TDDSurfaceDesc2);

  {lock the backbuffer memory}
  FBackBuffer.Lock(nil,BackSurfaceDesc,DDLOCK_WAIT or DDLOCK_SURFACEMEMORYPTR,0)
```

**Note:** It is very important to always set the size member of any record structure that has one before using it in any function call.

As with all DirectX functions, it is usually a good practice to check the return code from a call to the Lock method. The DDLOCK_WAIT flag will cause the Lock method to wait until the surface is available and no longer being accessed by the hardware blitter. However, if the surface is locked by another thread or process, this function will return immediately with a DDERR_SURFACEBUSY error regardless of the DDLOCK_WAIT flag.

### Accessing the Memory

When the Lock method returns, the lpSurface member of the TDDSurfaceDesc2 structure will contain a pointer to the surface memory. Exactly how this is used depends entirely on the pixel format of the surface. Since all of our examples deal with 256-color palettized display modes, pixels will be stored as bytes.

Therefore, if we typecast the lpSurface member as a pointer to a byte, writing a value at the location reference by this pointer will change one byte on the surface, and thus one pixel in the image the surface contains.

In practice, it is useful to access this pointer as a pointer to an array of bytes. This allows us to access horizontal bytes as if they were stored in a one-dimensional array. Although perhaps not immediately obvious, the process is simple. We'll need to create a new data type that is declared as an array of byte with only one element, and another data type that is a pointer to this previous type, like so:

```
TBytePtr = array[0..0] of Byte;
PBytePtr = ^TBytePtr;
```

Then, if we set a variable of type PBytePtr to the value of the lpSurface member, we can easily reference the surface memory as an array of bytes:

```
var
  BackMem: PBytePtr;
begin
  BackMem := PBytePtr(BackSurfaceDesc.lpSurface);
```

### Drawing the Sprite

We must lock both the backbuffer surface and the surface containing the sprite images. Once this is done, we iterate through each row of the sprite, and each pixel in the row. For each pixel in the current row being drawn, we check to see if it is equal to the specified transparent color. If it is not, we go ahead and set the appropriate pixel in the destination memory to the value of the pixel being checked. If it is indeed equal to the transparent color, we simply move on to the next pixel in the row. The following example demonstrates an implementation of this technique.

**Listing 6-4:** *Drawing a sprite with transparent pixels*

```
procedure TfrmDXAppMain.DrawSurfaces;
var
  SourceRect: TRect
  BackSurfaceDesc,
  SpriteSurfaceDesc: TDDSurfaceDesc2;
  BackMem, SpriteMem: PBytePtr;
  Row, Col: Integer;
begin
  {erase the last frame of animation}
  SourceRect := Rect(0, 0, DXWIDTH, DXHEIGHT);
  FBackBuffer.BltFast(0, 0, FBackground, SourceRect,
                  DDBLTFAST_NOCOLORKEY OR DDBLTFAST_WAIT);

  {increment the frame number and update the sprite's position}
```

```
with FSprite do
begin
  Inc(FCurFrame);

  {rollover the frame number as necessary}
  if FCurFrame > FFrameNum then
    FCurFrame := 0;

  {add the velocities to the positions. our sprite will only move
   horizontally, so we do not need to bother with the vertical values}
  FXPos := FXPos + FXVel;

  {see if the sprite is moving offscreen, and adjust
   its position accordingly}
  if FXPos < 0 then
    FXPos := DXWIDTH - 90;

  {—begin blitting the current frame—}

  {we need to lock both the backbuffer surface and the sprite image
   surface, so begin by locking the backbuffer}
  BackSurfaceDesc.dwSize := SizeOf(TDDSurfaceDesc2);

  {we're going to lock the entire surface}
  DXCheck(FBackBuffer.Lock(nil, BackSurfaceDesc,
          DDLOCK_WAIT or DDLOCK_SURFACEMEMORYPTR, 0));

  {initialize the byte array pointer to point at the locked memory}
  BackMem := PBytePtr(BackSurfaceDesc.lpSurface);

  {increment this pointer to the position in the buffer at which the
   sprite should be displayed (based on the sprite's position)}
  BackMem := Pointer(Longint(BackMem)+FXPos+(FYPos*BackSurfaceDesc.lPitch));

  {now, lock the sprite surface}
  SpriteSurfaceDesc.dwSize := SizeOf(TDDSurfaceDesc2);

  {again, we'll lock the entire surface}
  DXCheck(FImages.Lock(nil, SpriteSurfaceDesc,
          DDLOCK_WAIT or DDLOCK_SURFACEMEMORYPTR, 0));

  {initialize the byte array pointer to point at the locked memory}
  SpriteMem := PBytePtr(SpriteSurfaceDesc.lpSurface);

  {increment this pointer to the position of the current sprite frame}
  SpriteMem := Pointer(Longint(SpriteMem)+(FCurFrame*90));

{iterate through each row of pixels in the sprite image (our sprite image is
 90 X 50) }
for Row := 0 to 49 do
begin
```

```
    {iterate through each pixel in the current row}
    for Col := 0 to 89 do
      {if the pixel in the sprite image is not 0 (the transparent color),
       copy it into the destination surface}
      if SpriteMem^[Col] <> 0 then
        BackMem^[Col] := SpriteMem^[Col];

    {move to the next row in the sprite and backbuffer surface memory}
    Inc(BackMem, BackSurfaceDesc.lPitch);
    Inc(SpriteMem, SpriteSurfaceDesc.lPitch);
  end;
  ****************************************************************************

    {we have now copied the sprite, so unlock the surface memory}
    FBackBuffer.Unlock(nil);
    FImages.Unlock(nil);
  end;
end;
```

Of special consideration is the part in the rendering loop (the DrawSurfaces method) where the pointers to the backbuffer and sprite surface memory are incremented to point to the next row:

```
{move to the next row in the sprite and backbuffer surface memory}
Inc(BackMem, BackSurfaceDesc.lPitch);
Inc(SpriteMem, SpriteSurfaceDesc.lPitch);
```

Among the values returned by the call to the Lock method is the surface's pitch, or stride. This value is the actual distance between two pixels that are vertically adjacent. It is a result of storing memory that is logically arranged in rectangular fashion, but is actually accessed linearly. Often, the pitch is the same as the width of the surface, as one might expect. However, never assume that the pitch is constant, even for different surfaces in the same video memory. Always use the lPitch value to move vertically between rows.

**Caution:** Some display cards can organize memory differently than others, and the resolution and color depth can have dramatic effects on how memory is accessed directly. Therefore, always increment the row by using the lPitch value.

## *Unlocking a Surface*

With every call to the Lock method, a call to the Unlock method must be made. This allows the locked surface to be accessed again by other threads and processes, and most importantly by the hardware. A surface cannot be blitted or otherwise manipulated by the hardware unless it has been unlocked. After calling Unlock, any pointers to the surface memory will no longer be valid.

Therefore, it is necessary to call Lock again during the next rendering cycle to retrieve a valid pointer to surface memory. The Unlock method of IDirectDrawSurface4 is defined as:

```
function Unlock (
lpRect: PRect              // the previously locked rectangular area
: HResult;                 // returns a DirectX error code
```

The only parameter defines the rectangular area that was passed to the initial Lock method. It is possible to lock multiple rectangular, overlapping areas simultaneously. Thus, DirectDraw needs to know which rectangular area to unlock, and the values for this parameter must match those passed to the original Lock method. Pass nil here if you used nil in the Lock method to lock the entire surface.

**Caution:** When accessing surface memory, it is very important to complete rendering quickly and unlock the surface as soon as possible. This is because Windows is effectively stopped between the calls to Lock and Unlock. This can cause things to get backed up rather quickly, causing all sorts of nasty side effects, like system hangs. This won't occur when locking surfaces explicitly created in surface memory, but always try to use tight, efficient code when locking a surface and always remember to call the Unlock method when you no longer require direct memory access.

## Collision Detection

All games, at some point, must deal with the situation in which one sprite touches another. For some games, this may be when a bullet strikes an alien or when an animated mouth collides with a glowing white pellet to eat it. A game application must determine when these situations happen, and this is where collision detection comes in.

There exist as many different methods to perform collision detection as there do methods to draw a sprite. Many articles have been written on this subject, exploring the nuances of checking large amounts of sprites against each other and the optimizations required to perform such techniques in a timely fashion. In most cases, however, sprite collision can be detected using one of two techniques: bounding boxes and pixel overlap comparisons.

### Bounding Boxes

The bounding box method of collision detection works by defining a rectangular region around the sprite, its "bounding box." To determine if a collision with another sprite has occurred, the application simply determines if their bounding box rectangles intersect. If indeed the rectangles intersect, a collision has occurred and the game application can respond accordingly, as shown in the following illustration.

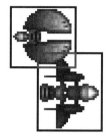
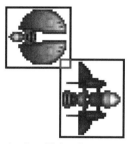

a: Sprite bounding box collision

b: A collision is reported where none has occurred

c: Shrinking the size of bounding boxes increases collision accuracy

*Figure 6-7:*
*Sprite bounding boxes*

Notice that in Figure 6-7b, the intersected rectangles would indicate that a collision has occurred, although clearly the sprites are not touching. This is the inherent drawback to using bounding boxes, in that many times during close calls a collision may be flagged when in fact the sprites never touched. Shrinking the size of the bounding boxes to where they do not encapsulate the entire sprite diminishes this error, as shown in Figure 6-7c. However, the reverse effect can occur, where two sprites have collided although no collision was detected. For the most part, it is better to err on the side of the player and allow the infrequent true collisions to go unresolved. However, for some games where precise collision detection is required, it is necessary to actually check the pixels of one image with the pixels of another to see if they overlap, as we examine shortly.

**Tip:** It is possible to use two or more bounding boxes for a sprite, thereby providing a more accurate approximation of the sprite's surface. The GDI also contains many functions to create regions of different shapes and sizes, including circular and polygonal, which can then be used to detect collisions more accurately.

Windows has highly optimized routines that make manipulating rectangles a breeze. In particular, the IntersectRect function determines if two rectangles overlap and returns a rectangle that defines the area of intersection. The IntersectRect function is defined as:

```
IntersectRect(
var lprcDst: TRect;        // the rectangle receiving the intersection coordinates
const lprcSrc1: TRect;     // the first rectangle
const lprcSrc2: TRect      // the second rectangle
: BOOL;                    // returns TRUE or FALSE
```

The first parameter is a rectangle that will receive the coordinates of the intersection between the rectangles specified in the last two parameters. If the rectangles do not intersect, the first parameter will be set to all zeroes and the function returns FALSE.

The following example demonstrates how to use bounding boxes to determine if two sprites have collided.

***Listing 6-5:*** *Bounding box collision detection*

```
procedure TfrmDXAppMain.DrawSurfaces;
var
  Intersection, Area: TRect;
  iCount: Integer;

  {this function moves and draws a sprite}
  procedure MoveSprite(var Sprite: TSprite);
  var
    SrfcDC: HDC;
    TempCanvas: TCanvas;
  begin
    {move the sprite, checking for horizontal and vertical screen boundaries}
    Sprite.FXPos := Sprite.FXPos + Sprite.FXVel;


      .
      .
      .


    {update the sprite's bounding box based on its new position}
    Sprite.Boundary := Rect(Sprite.FXPos, Sprite.FYPos,
                            Sprite.FXPos+Sprite.Width,
                            Sprite.FYPos+Sprite.Height);

    {draw the sprite transparently}
    Area := Rect (0, 0,  Sprite.Width, Sprite.Heigh);
    FBackBuffer.BltFast(Sprite.FXPos, Sprite.FYPos, Sprite.FImages,
                    Area, DDBLTFAST_SRCCOLORKEY or DDBLTFAST_WAIT);

    {draw a red border around the sprite to display its bounding box}


      .
      .
      .


  end;

begin
  {erase the previous animation frame}
  Area := Rect (0, 0, DXWIDTH, DXHEIGHT);
  FBackBuffer.BltFast(0, 0, FBackground, Area,
                    DDBLTFAST_NOCOLORKEY or DDBLTFAST_WAIT);
```

```
{move and draw the sprites}
for iCount := 0 to 1 do
  MoveSprite(Sprites[iCount]);

{if any of the sprite's bounding boxes intersect, signal a collision. real
  world examples would generally require checking many rectangles against
  each other}
if IntersectRect(Intersection, Sprites[0].Boundary, Sprites[1].Boundary) then
  Messagebeep(0);
end;
```

## Pixel Overlap Comparison

The bounding box method of collision detection can easily be extended to provide very accurate pixel level collision detection. Basically, a standard bounding box collision detection is performed. It is necessary that the bounding boxes of the sprites be the same dimensions as the sprite images (actually, they could be different, but the resulting offset math makes the pixel offset determinations cumbersome). Once a collision has occurred, it is necessary to determine the exact rectangular intersection area, which is conveniently reported by the IntersectRect function. The coordinates of the upper left corner of the rectangle are subtracted from the coordinates of the upper left corner of each of the sprite image positions. This will give a starting offset of the intersection rectangle relative to the sprites. From this starting offset within the sprite images, a simple embedded loop is used to walk through the pixels in each sprite image, comparing the colors of the pixels in the relative position of each sprite as determined by the intersection rectangle. If any non-transparent pixels match up, then the sprites overlap and a collision has occurred, as illustrated below.

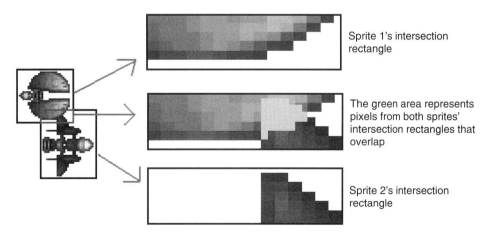

Sprite 1's intersection rectangle

The green area represents pixels from both sprites' intersection rectangles that overlap

Sprite 2's intersection rectangle

***Figure 6-8:*** *Pixel level collision detection*

This algorithm provides very accurate collision detection. Due to its nature, we must directly access the surface memory as we covered above. This is a slow collision detection technique, but it could possibly be optimized using assembly language. However, for small numbers of sprites, the performance penalty is minimal. The following example demonstrates pixel-accurate collision detection.

**Listing 6-6:** *Collision detection at the pixel level*

```
procedure TfrmDXAppMain.DrawSurfaces;
var
  Intersection, Area: TRect;
  iCount: Integer;
  Sprite1SurfaceDesc,
  Sprite2SurfaceDesc: TDDSurfaceDesc2;
  Sprite1Mem, Sprite2Mem: PBytePtr;
  iRow, iCol: Integer;
  SrfcDC: HDC;
  Hit: Boolean;



  {this function moves and draws a sprite}
  procedure MoveSprite(var Sprite: TSprite);
  var
    SrfcDC: HDC;
    TempCanvas: TCanvas;
  begin

      .
      .
      .

  end;

begin
  {erase the previous animation frame}
  FBackBuffer.BltFast(0, 0, FBackground, Rect(0, 0, DXWIDTH, DXHEIGHT),
                  DDBLTFAST_NOCOLORKEY or DDBLTFAST_WAIT);

  {move and draw the sprites}
  for iCount := 0 to 1 do
    MoveSprite(Sprites[iCount]);

  {retrieve the intersection of the sprite's bounding boxes. if there is
   indeed an intersection, compare the pixels in intersecting areas of each
   sprite. if the AND of any two pixels is greater than 0 (our transparent
   pixel value is 0, so two overlapped image pixels will return a value
   greater than 0), then there was indeed a pixel level collision.}
  if IntersectRect(Intersection, Sprites[0].Boundary, Sprites[1].Boundary) then
  begin
```

```
{at this point, the bounding boxes have collided, so we need to prepare to
 access the sprite surfaces. we will lock the entire surface of each
 sprite}
Sprite1SurfaceDesc.dwSize := SizeOf(TDDSurfaceDesc2);
DXCheck(FShip1.Lock(nil, Sprite1SurfaceDesc,
                    DDLOCK_WAIT or DDLOCK_SURFACEMEMORYPTR, 0));

{initialize the byte array to the intersected
 rectangular area of the sprite}
Sprite1Mem := PBytePtr(Sprite1SurfaceDesc.lpSurface);
Sprite1Mem := Pointer(Longint(Sprite1Mem)+
                      ((Intersection.Top-Sprites[0].FYPos)*
                      Sprite1SurfaceDesc.lPitch+
                      (Intersection.Left-Sprites[0].FXPos)));

{lock the other sprite's surface}
Sprite2SurfaceDesc.dwSize := SizeOf(TDDSurfaceDesc2);
DXCheck(FShip2.Lock(nil, Sprite2SurfaceDesc,
        DDLOCK_WAIT or DDLOCK_SURFACEMEMORYPTR, 0));

{and initialize the other byte array to the intersected
 rectangular area of the sprite}
Sprite2Mem := PBytePtr(Sprite2SurfaceDesc.lpSurface);
Sprite2Mem := Pointer(Longint(Sprite2Mem)+
                      ((Intersection.Top-Sprites[1].FYPos)*
                      Sprite2SurfaceDesc.lPitch+
                      (Intersection.Left-Sprites[1].FXPos)));

{begin determining if a collision has taken place.}
Hit := FALSE;
for iRow := 0 to (Intersection.Bottom-Intersection.Top)-1 do
  for iCol := 0 to (Intersection.Right-Intersection.Left)-1 do
    {if the pixels in the intersected rectangular areas of
     both sprites is something other than a transparent
     pixel, a collision has occurred}
    if Sprite1Mem^[iRow*Sprite1SurfaceDesc.lPitch+iCol] and
       Sprite2Mem^[iRow*Sprite2SurfaceDesc.lPitch+iCol] > 0 then
      Hit := TRUE;

{visually indicate any collisions}
FBackBuffer.GetDC(SrfcDC);
try
  if Hit then
    TextOut(SrfcDC, 10, 460, 'Collision!', Length('Collision!'));
finally
  FBackBuffer.ReleaseDC(SrfcDC);
end;

{we no longer need access to surfaces, so unlock them}
FShip1.Unlock(nil);
FShip2.Unlock(nil);
```

```
        end;
end;
```

# Animation Issues

Apart from getting sprites to move and animate, game developers are confronted with dozens of sprite-based issues, depending on the type of game. Complex sprites may have hundreds of animation frames, segregated into different actions, all of which must be triggered at the appropriate time by the game state. Collision detection may be a big issue, made even worse by large amounts of sprites that can move around in a virtual world several times the size of the screen. These and other animation issues are sure to appear as you develop your Delphi game masterpiece.

There are a few animation issues that are fairly common among different games, and generally have straightforward resolutions. You've probably noticed that our previous sprite examples demonstrating animation ran incredibly fast, so fast that the animation was unbelievable. This is an issue of timing. Implementing a method to slow down the animation of a sprite is very elementary, and is little more than an extension of our previous sprite movement algorithm.

Another topic to consider is the concept of z-order, or depth. Some games may exhibit many sprites in which collision is infrequent or unimportant. In this instance, it is important to consider which sprites should be drawn first, as the order in which sprites are drawn will connote depth to the viewer. Those sprites that are farthest away should naturally be drawn under those sprites that are closer. Again, implementing such functionality is relatively straightforward.

**z-order:** The position along the z, or third-dimensional, axis. This is an imaginary axis that runs perpendicular to the screen, and gives the illusion of depth.

## Timing

In order to slow down sprite animation, the current frame number should not be incremented each time through the game loop. Instead, it should be incremented only at specific intervals. To implement this technique, we need to add two members to our sprite object: one for the current interval measurement and one for a threshold amount. When this current interval measurement exceeds the threshold, we can increment the frame counter.

Technically, we could set the threshold amount to an integer value, and then increment the current interval measurement each time through the game loop. However, this would make the speed of the sprite animation contingent on the speed of the game. A more efficient method would be to base the speed of animation on an elapsed time amount. This would constrain the animation to a specific rate that would be constant on all machines.

We can do this by setting our threshold amount to a specific time interval, measured in milliseconds. Our current interval measurement would then be set to the system time of the last increment of the frame number. In the game loop, we then check to see if the amount of time indicated in the threshold has elapsed since the last increment of the frame number. If so, we increment the frame number and reset the current interval measurement. The following example demonstrates this technique.

***Listing 6-7:*** *Accurate sprite animation timing*

```
type
  {the sprite class}
  TSprite = class
    FXPos, FYPos,                    // tracks the current position
    FXVel, FYVel,                    // tracks the velocity
    FCurFrame,                       // tracks the current frame number
    FFrameNum: Integer;              // tracks the number of frames
    FImages: IDirectDrawSurface4;    // a pointer to the sprite images
    FCurTime,                        // tracks a timing value
    FTimeThreshold: LongWord;        // holds the animation timing threshold
  end;

procedure TfrmDXAppMain.FormActivate(Sender: TObject);
var



    .
    .
    .



begin

    .
    .
    .


  {initialize the sprite object}
  FSprite := TSprite.Create;
  FSprite.FXPos := DXWIDTH - 90;
  FSprite.FYPos := 215;
  FSprite.FXVel  := -1;
  FSprite.FYVel  := 0;
  FSprite.FCurFrame := 0;
  FSprite.FFrameNum := 5;
  FSprite.FImages := FImages;

  {retrieve the current system time to initialize the timing algorithm}
  FSprite.FCurTime := timeGetTime;
```

```
    {we want the sprite to animate every 100 milliseconds}
    FSprite.FTimeThreshold := 100;

       .
       .
       .

end;

procedure TfrmDXAppMain.DrawSurfaces;
var

       .
       .
       .

begin
  {erase the last frame of animation by using a simple color fill to
   'black out' the entire backbuffer surface}
  FillChar(BltFx, SizeOf(TDDBltFx), 0);
  BltFx.dwSize := SizeOf(TDDBltFx);
  BltFx.dwFillColor := 0;
  FBackBuffer.Blt(nil, nil, nil, DDBLT_COLORFILL or DDBLT_WAIT, @BltFx);

  {increment the frame number and update the sprite's position}
  with FSprite do
  begin
    {if the elapsed time since the last frame number increment
     is greater than our threshold amount...}
    if timeGetTime - FCurTime > FTimeThreshold then
    begin
      {animate the sprite by incrementing the frame number}
      Inc(FCurFrame);

      {make sure we roll over the frame number as necessary}
      if FCurFrame > FFrameNum then
        FCurFrame := 0;

      {store the current system time}
      FCurTime := timeGetTime;
    end;

       .
       .
       .

end;
```

## Z-Order

As stated above, the z-order of a sprite is its position along an imaginary third-dimensional axis. Some games may feature foreground sprites and background sprites, while others may have sprites that move closer to and farther from the user, scaling as appropriate in a pseudo three-dimensional viewpoint. In games like these, drawing sprites in the correct order becomes an important issue.

However, actually accomplishing this illusion of depth is quite simple. Essentially, the application needs to draw the sprites starting with the farthest from the user and ending with the closest. As you draw the nearer sprites, their images will obscure those farther away, giving the illusion of depth. This is known as the painter's algorithm; the technique is illustrated below.

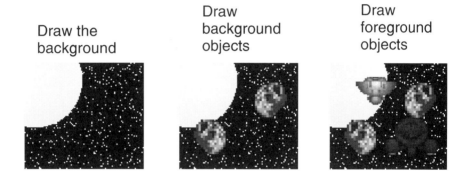

**Figure 6-9:** *The painter's algorithm*

We've already implemented the painter's algorithm in a very simplistic way by drawing the background behind the sprites before drawing them. In a more complex, real-world application, the z-order of the sprites themselves must be taken into account. We can accomplish this by simply adding another member to our sprite object for tracking this z-order.

In practice, we'll need to move the sprites and then sort them by z-order before drawing. The sorting step is necessary in order to draw the sprites in the correct order. Any well-documented, high-performance sorting algorithm will do. In the following example, we don't employ any sort of real sorting algorithm for the sake of code simplicity. However, the example does demonstrate a simple z-ordering mechanism. Sprites that are moving downward have a higher, or closer, z-order than those moving upward. Implementing scaling to draw the sprites larger when they are closer and smaller when they are farther away would improve the illusion.

*Listing 6-8:* Drawing sprites according to z-order

```
type

   .
   .
   .

{the sprite class}
  TSprite = record
    FXPos, FYPos,              // tracks the current position
    FXVel, FYVel,              // tracks the velocity
    Height, Width,             // sprite frame height and width
    FCurFrame,                 // tracks the current frame number
    FFrameNum: Integer;        // tracks the number of frames
    FImages: IDirectDrawSurface4;  // a pointer to the sprite images
    FCurTime,                  // tracks a timing value
    FTimeThreshold: LongWord;  // holds the animation timing threshold
    ZOrder: Integer;           // the sprite depth
  end;

var

   .
   .
   .

  Sprites: array[0..1] of TSprite;
  ZOrderIndex: array[0..1] of Integer;

implementation

   .
   .
   .

procedure TfrmDXAppMain.FormActivate(Sender: TObject);
begin

   .
   .
   .

{initialize the first spaceship}
  with Sprites[0] do
  begin
    Width := 61;
    Height := 56;

    FXPos := DXWIDTH div 2;
```

```
      FYPos := DXHEIGHT;

      FYVel := 3;

      FImages := FShip1;

      ZOrder := 0;
   end;

   {initialize the second spaceship}
   with Sprites[1] do
   begin
     Width := 60;
     Height := 74;

     FXPos := DXWIDTH div 2;
     FYPos := 0;

     FYVel := -3;

     FImages := FShip2;

     ZOrder := 1;
   end;

   .
   .
   .

end;

   .
   .
   .

procedure TfrmDXAppMain.DrawSurfaces;
var
  iCount: Integer;
  Area: TRect;

  {this function moves a sprite}
  procedure MoveSprite(var Sprite: TSprite);
  begin
    Sprite.FYPos := Sprite.FYPos + Sprite.FYVel;
    if Sprite.FYPos<0 then
    begin
      Sprite.FYPos := 0;
      Sprite.FYVel := 0-Sprite.FYVel;

      {we've only got 2 z-order values, so flip it when the sprite
       hits a boundary}
```

```
          Sprite.ZOrder := 1-Sprite.ZOrder;
      end
      else
      if Sprite.FYPos>DXHEIGHT-Sprite.Height then
      begin
        Sprite.FYPos := DXHEIGHT-Sprite.Height;
        Sprite.FYVel := 0-Sprite.FYVel;

        Sprite.ZOrder := 1-Sprite.ZOrder;
      end;
   end;

begin
  {erase the previous animation frame}
  Area := Rect(0, 0, DXWIDTH, DXHEIGHT);
  FBackBuffer.BltFast(0, 0, FBackground, Area,
                      DDBLTFAST_NOCOLORKEY or DDBLTFAST_WAIT);

  {move the sprites}
  for iCount := 0 to 1 do
    MoveSprite(Sprites[iCount]);
  {perform some really simplistic z-order sorting}
  if Sprites[0].ZOrder > Sprites[1].ZOrder then
  begin
    ZOrderIndex[0] := 0;
    ZOrderIndex[1] := 1;
  end
  else
  begin
    ZOrderIndex[0] := 1;
    ZOrderIndex[1] := 0;
  end;

  {now that the sprites are sorted per their z-order, draw them starting
   with the farthest sprite. this will result in a layered graphic with
   distant sprites being obscured by closer sprites}
  for iCount := 0 to 1 do
    FBackBuffer.BltFast(Sprites[ZOrderIndex[iCount]].FXPos,
                        Sprites[ZOrderIndex[iCount]].FYPos,
                        Sprites[ZOrderIndex[iCount]].FImages,
                        Rect(0, 0, Sprites[ZOrderIndex[iCount]].Width,
                             Sprites[ZOrderIndex[iCount]].Height),
                        DDBLTFAST_SRCCOLORKEY or DDBLTFAST_WAIT);
end;
```

# Summary

In this chapter, we discussed several techniques for implementing sprites and sprite animation. We looked at various DirectDraw methods for implementing transparency, and we also took a look at what is required for detecting collisions between two sprites. We also lightly covered some of the more common animation issues facing developers. When writing sprite manipulation code, it is important to keep these points in mind:

■ The most important graphical elements of any game are those graphics with which the user interacts. Sprites provide the animated elements of a game that make the gaming environment come alive. These can take the form of images that the player directly interacts with, such as a spaceship, or background elements that are non-interactive yet provide animation that makes the environment richer, deeper, and more believable

■ To produce the illusion of animation, a series of images is required, where each image shows the character or object to be animated in a slightly different position than the image before it, like a filmstrip. When each image is rapidly displayed one after another, the human brain expects to see smooth motion, and any gaps in movement from one frame to another will be automatically filled in.

■ To produce the illusion of motion, when the application prepares to draw the next frame of animation, simply change the horizontal or vertical coordinate at which the image will be drawn into the destination. If these coordinates keep changing, the animated image will be drawn at different positions.

■ A few items of information need to be tracked for each sprite. In particular, its current x and y coordinate must be tracked so the application knows where to draw the sprite. A horizontal and vertical velocity could also be stored. These velocities would indicate the number of pixels to move the sprite, and would be added to the x and y coordinates on each iteration through the game loop. It should also track the current frame of animation, the number of frames in the animation, and a pointer to the bitmap or DirectDraw surface containing the sprite images.

■ The process of standard sprite animation is accomplished by following three distinct steps: erasing the sprite image, updating the sprite position, and drawing the sprite image.

■ In order to make sprite images more believable, they must contain pixels that are rendered transparently so that the background shows through. This can be accomplished through color keying, or through a more direct approach by drawing each pixel individually and skipping those pixels that are transparent.

■ When using the Lock method to access surface memory directly, remember to always call the Unlock method before using the surface in other method calls.

■ All games, at some point, must deal with the situation when one sprite touches another. For some games, this may be when a bullet strikes an alien or when an animated mouth collides with a glowing white pellet to eat it. In most cases, sprite collision can be detected using one of two techniques: bounding boxes and pixel overlap comparisons.

■ Bounding box collision detection works by defining a rectangular region around the sprite, its "bounding box." To determine if a collision with another sprite has occurred, the application simply determines if their bounding box rectangles intersect

■ After determining the rectangular intersection area between two sprites, we can access the sprite image surfaces and compare the pixels that are within this intersection rectangle. If any non-transparent pixels overlap, we have a pixel overlap collision. This method is very accurate, but tends to be slow.

■ Sprite animation should be regulated to make it look more believable. We can accomplish this by incrementing the current frame number only at specific intervals.

■ Games with multiple layers of sprites must take into account the sprites' z-order. Sprites should be sorted by z-order and drawn starting with the farthest sprites. This will result in closer sprites obscuring sprites that are farther from the viewer, giving an illusion of depth.

# CHAPTER 7: *Input Techniques*

An excellent graphics engine is important to the popularity and enjoyment of a game. The sound effects and music that are synchronized to the action on screen are also imperative. However, think of the most enjoyable game you've ever played, and consider what it would be like if you had no way of interacting with the game elements. It would be like watching a movie, at best. How about if you could interact with the game through only a single button on the keyboard, or perhaps with only the movement of the mouse cursor? Your actions would be limited indeed, as would your enjoyment of the game. As with graphics and sound, user input is a vital piece of overall game development that merits serious consideration.

User input functionality is something most developers, and game players, take for granted. Even so, the method by which a game player interacts with the game can have a profound effect on how skillfully the player navigates the game's environment, and consequently the overall enjoyment of the game. Some game types naturally lean towards certain types of input devices; flight simulators tend to "feel right" when played with a joystick, whereas real-time strategy games are usually best played with the mouse. The supported devices allowing the user to provide game input, and how those devices are implemented in terms of how they manipulate game elements, can make or break a game.

In this chapter, we examine various techniques for retrieving user input through a variety of devices. Regular Windows API functions will be briefly touched upon, as our discussion will focus on how DirectInput provides developers with a responsive and powerful interface to any input device available.

# Human/Computer Interaction

Human/computer interaction is the concept of how humans and machines, typically computers, interact with one another in a method that is meaningful and intelligible to both. Entire volumes have been written on techniques to make human/computer interaction more intuitive, including both input techniques themselves as well as the presentation of the interface. While the majority of this concept is beyond the scope of this book, certain elements are relative to our discussion of user input techniques.

**human/computer interaction:** The concept of techniques and methods by which humans and machines, primarily computers, exchange information.

Exactly how user input will be translated into game element manipulation is dependent on the game itself. Flight simulators need input that affects the direction of flight, or perhaps even the selection and use of a weapon. Strategy games, by contrast, need input that determines which token is selected and its direction of movement or combat. These concepts will be accounted for when the game itself is designed. Perhaps the most important consideration for user input is the device by which the user will interact with the machine and, more specifically, the game.

## Input Devices

Technically speaking, today's machines have a wide variety of devices by which they can receive input from users. Some of the more exotic input devices, such as speech recognition, are becoming available to the average computer user, and may one day replace many, or all, of the standard input devices currently in use. While it may be a good marketing hook to provide support for some of these more esoteric input devices, all games should provide support for standard input devices found on almost every machine. These standard input devices consist of the keyboard, the mouse, and game controllers.

### Keyboard

It would be hard to imagine any computer in today's market that doesn't come with a keyboard. The keyboard has been the standard input device since the dawn of the home PC, and it is safe to assume that it will be available for input when your game is executed. Retrieving keyboard input is easy and very straightforward, and can provide a very intuitive interface for almost any game.

## Mouse

The mouse is another standard input device available on just about every machine. While not quite as old as the keyboard, the mouse is just as necessary and probably more important for user input, thanks to Windows. Since our games will be using DirectX, and will thus be restricted to the Windows platform, we can assume that the mouse will be available for input when the game is executed. Retrieving mouse input is almost as easy and straightforward as retrieving keyboard input, and like the keyboard, it provides a very intuitive interface for certain types of games.

## Game Controllers

About five years ago, this category would probably have been called simply Joysticks. However, in the recent past, a multitude of input devices has been created that are aimed specifically at providing intuitive input for various games. Rudder pedals, steering wheels, gamepads, throttles, and all manner of sundry and arcane input devices are now available, making some games much more enjoyable to play. Even the standard joystick has become incredibly complex, with many sporting impressive arrays of buttons, switches, sliders, and even tactile responses known as force feedback.

**force feedback:** A method by which an input device can output tactile feedback to the user through various actuator motors.

Strictly speaking, a game cannot automatically assume that any type of game controller is hooked up to the machine, as game controllers have not yet become a standard input device shipped with new machines. It is good programming practice to provide an alternative form of input in the absence of a more appropriate input device, even if this input interface is somewhat cumbersome or even awkward. Retrieving input from various game controllers is necessarily more difficult than retrieving input from the mouse or keyboard, primarily because of the sheer number and variety of available game controllers. However, if a game lends itself to input from a specific type of game controller, such as a steering wheel for driving games, then the game should provide support for the most appropriately intuitive input device.

# Input Considerations

Even though the developer has determined which input devices will be supported and how they interact with game elements, individual users may find this structure somewhat restrictive based on their particular preferences. To accommodate those who feel your perfect interface could use some improvement, it is important to allow the user to change the configuration of input methods to their desired taste, within the structure of the input interface.

Perhaps the easiest to implement, and the most effective in terms of user configuration preferences, is a method by which users can redefine which keys or buttons perform which actions. This could be accomplished by presenting the user with a dialog box containing all available actions and the keys or buttons to which those actions are mapped. This should include keys on the keyboard and buttons on both the mouse and joystick. For example, the trigger button on a joystick may be used to fire a round of bullets in a flight simulator game, by default. However, the user may be more comfortable performing this action with another button. Allowing for the remapping of input methods in this way lets the individual user customize the game to his or her preferences, thus making it more enjoyable to a wider audience.

**Tip:** For an excellent example of an implementation of this technique, take a look at games like Quake and Halflife.

# DirectInput

DirectInput is the DirectX component responsible for providing user input from all manner of input devices, such as keyboards, mice, and game controllers. As with other DirectX components, the DirectInput API is large, and has its own set of requirements and nuances.

For some devices, DirectInput programming is almost trivial. For others, it is incredibly complex. DirectInput's complexity comes from the fact that it was designed to provide input from future game controllers that have not yet been invented. This forward thinking allows developers to provide support for new game controllers without having to rely on a new version of DirectInput. This support comes at the price of obscurity and complexity, but the marketing hook of supporting the latest input device may well be worth the effort. Fortunately, standard input devices such as the mouse and keyboard are relatively easy to interface with. Even joysticks and similar game controllers, while more complex, are not absolutely arcane in their implementation.

## Features

DirectInput offers many features above and beyond what is available through the Win32 API. As with all DirectX components, DirectInput gives the developer more control over user input than the Windows API, while also providing an improvement in performance. DirectInput provides the following features of specific interest to game developers:

■ Responsive input retrieval directly from input device hardware

■ Support for almost any input device, including mice, keyboards, joysticks, and other game controllers

■ Access to force feedback devices for providing tactile output

■ Support for multiple input devices attached to the machine, such as two or more keyboards or mice

Later in this chapter we will see how DirectInput is used to retrieve user input from the keyboard, the mouse, and standard game controllers such as joysticks.

## Functional Overview

Similar to DirectDraw, DirectInput programming consists of creating a DirectInput object and several DirectInputDevice objects. The DirectInput object itself acts as a liaison between the application and input device drivers. Individual DirectInputDevice objects represent the application's interface directly to input hardware or, more specifically, that hardware's device driver. The DirectInput object is used to create individual DirectInputDevice objects, which can then be queried to determine the specific capabilities of the device.

The DirectInputDevice object is used to communicate with all input devices. In other words, there is not a separate object type for communicating with keyboards, mice, or joysticks; they are all interfaced through a DirectInputDevice object. This is one of the reasons why DirectInput programming can be complex. The individual methods of a DirectInputDevice object all work with input devices in similar ways according to the context of the type of device. For example, you set device properties through a single function call, yet the properties themselves are dependent upon the device. You can set the range of motion returned from a joystick as a property, but this wouldn't make any sense if you tried to do the same with a keyboard.

However, at the same time that this type of interface introduces a level of complexity, communicating with different devices is very similar in form from device to device. After you've grasped a particular concept with one device, it is very easy to apply that knowledge to other devices. This may result in what appears to be some redundancy when we discuss individual devices later in the chapter. However, the information reported by these methods is dependent on the device we are communicating with, making these concepts uniquely different depending on the context in which they are used.

### Buttons and Axes

Where DirectInput is concerned, a button is considered to be any switch that has an on and off position. There is no distinction made between buttons on a mouse, keyboard, or joystick. Bear in mind that just because a device is referred to as a button, it does not necessarily have to be physically represented as a button. A device on a game controller that has a specific on and off position may take the form of a physical toggle switch, but will be treated by DirectInput as a button.

Conversely, an axis has a range of positions where its value is affected by the physical movement of a device in some particular direction. Like buttons, axes do not necessarily have a specific physical representation. Joysticks and mice are objects that, generally speaking, represent two axes. However, sliders and dials on joysticks or game controllers and the wheel on a Microsoft IntelliMouse are also axes. Rudder pedals, steering wheels, and flight yokes are other examples of controllers that represent axes.

In similar fashion, an axis does not necessarily have an association with any particular direction in space. Joysticks and mice report movement along the x and y axes, which may translate into the movement of a pointer or a change in the direction of flight. However, in the context of a specific game, this information may be used to indicate the depth at which an object is placed or the circular rotation of a dial. This points out that just because an axis may have a specific name, its value is meaningful only in the context in which it is used and does not have to map to any physical direction or movement.

While many devices report movement along various axes, the measurement of this movement is dependent on the type of device reporting it. Some devices report axis movement as a relative measurement, which others report it as an absolute measurement.

***Relative Measurement***   Some axes can move an infinite distance in a particular direction, and lack a default or "rest" position. An example of this type of axis measurement would be that reported by a mouse. Therefore, the values returned by this type of device are meaningful only in relation to the last measurement taken from the device.

***Absolute Measurement***   Other axes can physically only move a specific distance. This would include the movement of the joystick or the movement of dials and sliders on a game controller. These values are typically measured from a fixed point and have a specific range.

**Note:**  DirectInput does allow the developer to redefine a relative axis to report absolute data and vice versa. The employment and implications of this technique are dependent on the context of the application itself.

## Immediate and Buffered Data

Since DirectInput communicates directly with device hardware, it does not return the state of axis movement or button presses with Windows messages. Instead, there are two flexible methods by which the application can retrieve the state of an input device: immediate and buffered.

Buffered data retrieval simulates the mechanism by which Windows reports input. Individual input events are stored in a buffer, which takes the form of an array of data structures containing the various axis movement values or button clicks. When you create a DirectInputDevice object for a particular input device, there is an additional step required in order to initialize the device to store information in this buffer.

Immediate data retrieval does not report a stream of singular events, but returns the current state of the device at the time of the function call. This will be reported in an initialized data structure dependent upon the specific device type, and can include information on the entire device or only for a specific object on that device, such as a button. There is no additional setup required to retrieve immediate data from a device.

Either of these data retrieval methods are perfectly acceptable depending on the requirements of the individual application. Indeed, both could be used simultaneously. However, it is generally most useful to utilize buffered data retrieval for relative data measurements and immediate data retrieval for absolute data measurements. We will see examples of both later in the chapter.

### Polling and Event Notification

The "when" of retrieving input data may be as important as the "how." In what seems to be a recurring theme throughout this book, DirectInput provides two choices: polling and event notification.

Polling involves checking the state of the input device at the time that the input is needed. Typically, this is performed in the game loop. The state of the device may be checked only once, or perhaps multiple times, and is usually returned in the form of immediate data. Since the device is only checked at specific intervals, it is possible for the user to manipulate the device between checks, thus resulting in lost input. Polling may seem like a throwback to the days of DOS game programming. Indeed, it is similar, but polling for new input data is incredibly easy to implement, and in most cases is adequate for precise input measurement.

Event notification, on the other hand, is very similar to event-driven programming. This is a mechanism by which DirectInput will notify the application when new input data is available, and is best paired with buffered data retrieval. While this method of retrieving input can be very powerful, it is much more difficult to implement and involves the use of threads, Win32 event objects, and critical sections. We will see examples of both later in the chapter.

### Cooperative Levels

As discussed in the DirectDraw tutorial, a cooperative level determines how the application works with other applications. As with other DirectX components, DirectInput gives the developer a choice as to how the application will share input devices with other applications, in terms of who can gain access to the device and if input can be retrieved based on application focus.

The first measurement of cooperative level determines when your application has access to data from the device, known as foreground or background access. Foreground access means that your application will have access to input data only when its main window has focus. Background access allows your application to retrieve input data whether it has focus or not; input data is available at all times, even if the application is minimized. Foreground mode is the most common for games and other applications. Nevertheless, you may need to use background mode if the application requires access to the device when a dialog box is open.

The second measurement of cooperative level is based on exclusivity, which determines if only a single application has access to a device. Applications that acquire a device in non-exclusive mode can retrieve input from that device unless another application acquires it exclusively. When a device is acquired exclusively, only the acquiring application can receive input from that device. In non-exclusive mode, other applications can acquire the device in non-exclusive or exclusive mode. In exclusive mode, other applications can only retrieve the device in non-exclusive mode. Thus, only one application at a time can have exclusive access to a device. For some devices, such as force feedback, this is a necessity, as two applications sending force feedback effects simultaneously could confuse the user and possibly damage the hardware.

When specifying a cooperative level, the application must indicate either foreground or background in addition to either exclusive or non-exclusive access. The following table summarizes the two cooperative level measurements and their implications for the current application and others in the system.

*Table 7-1:* DirectInput cooperative levels

| Measurement | Implications | Validity |
|---|---|---|
| Non-Exclusive/Background | Other applications can acquire the device exclusively or non-exclusively; input data is available at all times | All devices except force feedback |
| Non-Exclusive/Foreground | Other applications can acquire the device exclusively or non-exclusively; input data is available only when application has focus | All devices except force feedback |
| Exclusive/Background | Other applications can acquire the device non-exclusively; input data is available at all times | All devices except keyboards |
| Exclusive/Foreground | Other applications can acquire the device non-exclusively; input data is available only when application has focus | All devices except keyboards |

Bear in mind that Windows requires exclusive access to the keyboard at all times, so that functions such as Alt+Tab and Ctrl+Alt+Delete are always available. Thus, an application can only obtain non-exclusive access to the keyboard. Conversely, Windows can only use the mouse in an exclusive mode, and thus loses access to the mouse when another application acquires it exclusively. This means that when an application acquires the mouse in an exclusive mode, the mouse cursor will disappear and Windows will no longer generate mouse messages.

There is a small performance gain when acquiring the mouse in exclusive mode, since mouse messages are not being generated. However, there is no particular performance advantage to exclusive over non-exclusive cooperative levels for other devices.

 **Tip:** It is standard practice to inform users to close all other applications before starting your game. It is doubtful that users would try to play two or more games at once, so you should generally set the cooperative level to exclusive/foreground.

### Device Acquisition

Once a device is set up, the application cannot receive input data until it instructs DirectInput that it is ready to do so. This process is known as acquiring the device. Once a device is acquired, input data can be retrieved in whatever manner desired as discussed above. Successfully acquiring the device is dependent on the cooperative level specified by the application and by those of other applications using DirectInput, as we just illustrated.

However, bear in mind that a device can be forcibly unacquired by the application. This may happen when another application receives focus or acquires the device in exclusive mode (again dependent on the cooperative level of both applications and who acquired the device first). In this instance, any method that returns input data will return a value of DIERR_INPUTLOST or DIERR_NOTACQUIRED. You will need to check for this error value in your application, possibly attempting to reacquire the device until successful. You may also deliberately unacquire the device, such as when Windows needs the mouse in order to give the user access to menus.

## Initializing DirectInput

As with other DirectX components, several steps are required in order to set up DirectInput and begin interfacing with user input devices. In general, most of these steps are required to read data from keyboards, mice, and game controllers. We will cover these steps in a broad sense here in order to familiarize you with them. They will be covered again more precisely when we look at retrieving data from specific input devices. DirectInput, and DirectInput devices, are instantiated by performing the following:

■ Creating the DirectInput object

■ Enumerating input devices

■ Creating the input device

■ Setting the data format

■ Setting the cooperative level

■ Setting device properties

■ Acquiring the device

## Creating the DirectInput Object

The first step in retrieving data from an input device is to create the DirectInput object itself. Creating the DirectInput object involves calling the DirectInputCreate function, which is defined as:

```
function DirectInputCreate(
hinst: THandle;              // the application instance handle
dwVersion: DWORD;            // DirectInput version number
out ppDI: IDirectInput;      // the IDirectInput object to be instantiated
punkOuter: IUnknown          // unused, set to nil
): HResult; stdcall;         // returns a DirectX error code
```

The first parameter is a handle to the calling application's instance. The second parameter indicates the DirectInput version number. Most applications should simply set this parameter to DIRECTINPUT_VERSION (a constant defined in the DInput.pas file). However, if an earlier version number is indicated, DirectInput will emulate that version. This is useful if you had no need for newer DirectInput functionality, such as force feedback. The third parameter takes a pointer to the IDirectInput object. When this function returns, this object will be instantiated. The last parameter is used for COM aggregation, and must be set to nil as it is currently unsupported.

**Caution:** If indicating an earlier version in the call to DirectInputCreate, the application must use the data structures compatible with this earlier version. Note that this will also affect the value to which the dwSize member of these structures must be initialized.

## Enumerating Input Devices

Technically speaking, this step is not required if your application will only support keyboard and mouse input devices. It may be useful if the target machine has more than one keyboard or mouse attached, but you can still tell

DirectInput to create objects that represent the primary keyboard and mouse. However, game controllers are another story. Since there are no primary or default game controllers, applications that wish to support joysticks, steering wheels, etc., must obtain individual GUIDs for these objects through enumeration.

The EnumDevices method of the IDirectInput object is used to list all available input devices. It is a callback function that will call the specified function once for each type of device attached to the system as indicated by the scope flags. The EnumDevices method is defined as:

```
function EnumDevices(
dwDevType: DWORD;                           // indicates the type to enumerate
lpCallback: TDIEnumDevicesCallbackA;        // the callback function
pvRef: Pointer;                             // an application-defined value
dwFlags: DWORD                              // flags controlling the scope
): HResult;                                 // returns a DirectX error code
```

The first parameter is a flag indicating the type of devices to enumerate. This can be set to zero to enumerate all devices, DIDEVTYPE_MOUSE to enumerate mice, DIDEVTYPE_KEYBOARD to enumerate keyboards, or DIDEVTYPE_JOYSTICK to enumerate game controllers. The second parameter is a pointer to the callback function itself. The third parameter is a pointer to an application-defined value. The final parameter is a series of flags that further restrict the enumeration. This can be set to DIEDFL_ATTACHEDONLY to restrict enumeration to attached devices and/or DIEDFL_FORCEFEEDBACK to enumerate only force feedback devices. The callback function is defined as:

```
function TDIEnumDevicesCallbackA(
var lpddi: TDIDeviceInstance;               // a device description record
pvRef: Pointer                              // the application-defined value
): BOOL; stdcall;                           // returns TRUE or FALSE
```

The first parameter contains a TDIDeviceInstance structure initialized with information about the enumerated input device. The second parameter contains a pointer to the application-defined value. This function must return TRUE to continue the enumeration; FALSE will stop the enumeration.

The TDIDeviceInstance structure passed into this callback function contains everything necessary for presenting the user with a list of choices, as well as creating an input object of the desired type. The TDIDeviceInstance structure is defined as:

```
TDIDeviceInstance = packed record
  dwSize: DWORD;                                              // size of structure
  guidInstance: TGUID;                                        // object instance GUID
  guidProduct: TGUID;                                         // object product GUID
  dwDevType: DWORD;                                           // device type flag
  tszInstanceName: Array [0..MAX_PATH-1] of WideChar;         // instance name string
  tszProductName: Array [0..MAX_PATH-1] of WideChar;          // product name string
```

```
    guidFFDriver: TGUID;                    // force feedback driver
    wUsagePage: WORD;                       // HID usage page code
    wUsage: WORD;                           // HID usage page
  end;
```

An application could display a list of available input devices based on the instance name and product name available from the TDIDeviceInstance structure. If the instance GUID was stored along with this information, the application could create an input device using the GUID of the associated device that the user selected. The following example demonstrates creating an IDirectInput object and enumerating all attached game controllers.

*Listing 7-1: Creating an IDirectInput object and enumerating game controllers*

```
var
  Form1: TForm1;
  FDirectInput: IDirectInput;

implementation

function EnumInputDevs(var lpddi: TDIDeviceInstance; pvRef: Pointer): Integer;
        stdcall;
begin
  {display the instance name and product name of the enumerated game device}
  TStringList(pvRef).Add(lpddi.tszInstanceName+' - '+lpddi.tszProductName);

  {continue enumeration}
  Result := 1;
end;


procedure TForm1.FormActivate(Sender: TObject);
begin
  {create the DirectInput object}
  DirectInputCreate(hInstance, DIRECTINPUT_VERSION, FDirectInput, nil);

  {enumerate all attached game devices}
  FDirectInput.EnumDevices(DIDEVTYPE_JOYSTICK, EnumInputDevs,
                        lbxJoysticks.Items, DIEDFL_ATTACHEDONLY);
end;
```

At this point, the method calls for creating and initializing input device objects are the same, but the arguments passed into these methods are different depending on the input device itself. We will cover them briefly here, but we will wait to demonstrate any examples until we get to the sections where we demonstrate reading input data from various devices.

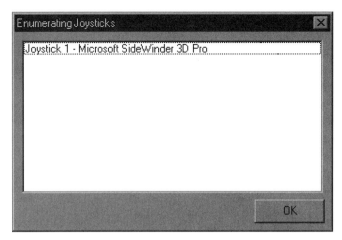

**Figure 7-1:**
*Attached game devices*

### Creating the Input Device

The DirectInput object has been created, and we've presented the user with a list of input devices from which one device has been selected. Given this device's instance GUID, we can now create an IDirectInputDevice object representing the device. We create this object by calling IDirectInput's CreateDevice method. The CreateDevice method is defined as:

```
function CreateDevice(
rguid: PGUID;                             // the device instance GUID
var lplpDirectInputDevice: IDirectInputDevice;  // the IDirectInputDevice object
pUnkOuter: IUnknown                       // unused, set to nil
): HResult;                               // returns a DirectX error code
```

The first parameter is the instance GUID for the desired input device. For game controllers, this should be a GUID retrieved from device enumeration. For the primary keyboard, you can use GUID_SysKeyboard, and for the primary mouse, you can use GUID_SysMouse. The second parameter is a pointer to the IDirectInputDevice object. When this function returns, this object will be instantiated. The final parameter is used for COM aggregation and should be set to nil.

This function will only return an instantiated IDirectInputDevice object, but if we wish to use force feedback devices, we need to get an instantiated IDirectInputDevice2 object. We should probably retrieve an IDirectInputDevice2 object anyway, as some game controllers have a special requirement for retrieving data, as explained below. Thus, we should create a temporary IDirect-InputDevice object, and once this is instantiated, we can use the QueryInterface method of the object to retrieve an instantiated IDirectInputDevice2 object. The temporary object can then be released by setting it to nil.

## Setting the Data Format

Once the device has been created, you must instruct DirectInput as to the format in which input data should be reported. This step is required, as input data from a mouse, for example, would be completely different than that retrieved from the keyboard or a joystick. You may be asking, why should we do this if DirectInput knows what kind of device we just created? Again, this is part of DirectInput's open architecture. Setting the data format in this manner allows the developer to declare a custom data format for new devices not yet created. We'll see an example of this later when we cover game controllers. Actually, setting the data format is quite easy, and requires calling the IDirectInputDevice's SetDataFormat method. The SetDataFormat method is defined as:

```
function SetDataFormat(
var lpdf: TDIDataFormat              // a data format structure
): HResult;                          // returns a DirectX error code
```

The only parameter to this method is a variable of type TDIDataFormat. The TDIDataFormat structure is a complicated beast due to this open architecture. Fortunately, there are several standard, predefined data formats that we can use for communicating with just about any input device. For the keyboard, we can set this parameter to c_dfDIKeyboard; the mouse uses c_dfDIMouse. Joysticks supposedly could use either c_dfDIJoystick or c_dfDIJoystick2 (for advanced game controllers and force feedback). However, in practice, we have found that neither of these data structures seem to work correctly. Game controllers come in all shapes and sizes and can have a wide variety of buttons, axes, sliders, POV hats, etc. Therefore, creating a custom data structure on the fly based on the type of objects available on the device usually provides better results. We'll see an example of this later in the chapter when we discuss game controllers.

**POV hat:** The point-of-view (POV) hat is a device that typically rests on the top of a joystick, and can be used to indicate a viewing direction separate from movement direction.

The value passed to this function ultimately determines the data structure used when retrieving immediate data from any particular device. The parameters of the GetDeviceState method (covered below in the individual sections for each different device) are directly affected by the value passed to SetDataFormat. Each of the predefined values for SetDataFormat correspond to the following data structures that must be subsequently used in the call to GetDeviceState when retrieving immediate data.

**Table 7-2:** *Data formats and their data structures*

| Format | Structure |
| --- | --- |
| c_dfDIKeyboard | TDIKeyboardState |
| c_dfDIMouse | TDIMouseState |
| c_dfDIJoystick * | TDIJoyState |
| c_dfDIJoystick2 * | TDIJoyState2 |

\* Don't use these; use the technique for building a custom data format later in the chapter.

### Setting the Cooperative Level

We are almost ready to begin using the device, so now it is time to set the cooperative level. The cooperative levels and their ramifications were explained above. Setting the cooperative level requires a call to the IDirectInputDevice's SetCooperativeLevel method. The SetCooperativeLevel method is defined as:

```
function SetCooperativeLevel(
hwnd: HWND;                    // a handle to the application window
dwFlags: DWORD                 // cooperative level flags
): HResult;                    // returns a DirectX error code
```

The first parameter is the handle to the application's main window. This lets Windows and DirectInput know the application to which the input data should be sent. The second parameter is a combination of flags indicating the desired cooperative level. This must be set to one of each from DISCL_BACKGROUND/ DISCL_FOREGROUND and DISCL_EXCLUSIVE/DISCL_NONEXCLUSIVE.

### Setting Device Properties

This step may be optional depending on the type of input device and the method by which input data is retrieved (i.e., immediate or buffered). However, some devices have certain properties that must be initialized before data can be retrieved from them. For example, joysticks must have their axes ranges set before they can return meaningful input data. Also, if you intend on using buffered data retrieval, you must set the size of the buffer. Setting device properties is accomplished by calling the IDirectInputDevice's SetProperty method. The SetProperty method is defined as:

```
function SetProperty(
rguidProp: TRefGUID;           // property identifier
var pdiph: TDIPropHeader       // the property data structure
): HResult;                    // returns a DirectX error code
```

This is another method where DirectInput's open architecture results in complexity. The first parameter identifies which property of the device to set. The value of this parameter is very dependent on the type of the device. For instance, it would be meaningless to set the range of an axis for a keyboard device. This parameter could be a GUID provided by the manufacturer of the device that identifies some specific property. Fortunately, however, there are several predefined values that we can use for setting specific properties. Perhaps the most common value passed to this parameter is DIPROP_BUFFERSIZE, which indicates we wish to set the size of the buffer for buffered data retrieval.

The second parameter is a pointer to a TDIPropHeader data structure. Here's where the complexity comes in. This parameter is a little misleading, because the method actually takes a pointer to whatever data structure is defined for the particular property being set. This could be some huge, custom data structure as defined by the product manufacturer. The only requirement is that the data structure must begin with a TDIPropHeader structure, which lets DirectInput know just how big the main structure is and the object on the device (such as an axis) whose properties are being set. Fortunately, most properties require only a single DWORD of information (such as buffer size) or perhaps two LongWords (in the case of ranges). The TDIPropHeader structure itself is defined as:

```
TDIPropHeader = packed record
  dwSize: DWORD;              // the size of the main structure
  dwHeaderSize: DWORD;       // the size of the TDIPropHeader structure
  dwObj: DWORD;              // the device object identifier
  dwHow: DWORD;              // indicates how to identify the device object
end;
```

The first member of this structure identifies the size of the overall structure. The second member should be set to the size of the TDIPropHeader structure. The third member identifies the device object (such as an axis) whose property is being set. There are a number of predefined identifiers that we will use to set various properties, and we'll see examples of this later in the sections on mouse and joystick programming. This member could be set to zero if a property that affects the entire device is being set, such as the buffer size. The last member tells DirectInput how the dwObj member is interpreted. This should be set to DIPH_DEVICE in the case of properties that affect the entire device. For individual device objects, there are two methods by which these objects can be identified. In this book, we will be concerned only with the offset method, so we should set this last member to DIPH_BYOFFSET.

DirectInput defines two standard structures that are most commonly used with SetProperty. The TDIPropDWord structure is used for setting properties that take only a single DWORD of information (such as buffer size), and the TDIPropRange structure is used for setting properties requiring two LongWords (such as ranges). The TDIPropDWord structure is defined as:

```
TDIPropDWord = packed record
 diph: TDIPropHeader;       // the TDIPropHeader structure
  dwData: DWORD;            // the value for the DWORD property
end;
```

The TDIPropRange structure is defined as:

```
TDIPropRange = packed record
  diph: TDIPropHeader;          // the TDIPropHeader structure
  lMin: Longint;                // the minimum range value
  lMax: Longint;                // the maximum range value
end;
```

We'll see examples using the SetProperty method with these two data structures later in the chapter.

**Note:** Device properties can be retrieved by using the GetProperty method, which takes the exact same parameters.

### Acquiring the Device

The input device has been set up, and we are now ready to begin retrieving data. As explained above, we must acquire the device, which is accomplished by calling IDirectInputDevice's Acquire method. This simple method is defined as:

```
function Acquire: HResult;          // returns a DirectX error code
```

Subsequent calls to Acquire, once the device has been acquired, have no effect. A device can similarly be unacquired by calling the Unacquire method, which also takes no parameters.

# Retrieving Input Data

While the steps required for initializing and setting up DirectInput and DirectInputDevices are similar for every device, exactly how the input data is retrieved and extracted varies from device to device. This will also depend on whether you will be using immediate data retrieval or buffered data retrieval. This leads to subtle nuances in which initialization steps are required, and how the data returned from certain methods is interpreted.

In this section, we will take a look at examples for reading input data from three standard devices: the keyboard, the mouse, and the joystick. Each is similar in implementation, but there are differences that warrant a closer inspection. At the same time, we will also demonstrate both immediate data retrieval and buffered data retrieval. While we will only implement one or the other method of data retrieval in each example to simplify the code, immediate or buffered data retrieval can be used for any input device.

One thing to consider when developing your game application is if the complexity of DirectInput is even warranted. The Windows API contains numerous powerful functions that allow the user to read input from the keyboard, the mouse, or even game controllers. There is no support for force feedback, but if your application only requires a very simple interface to input devices, you may want to stick with standard Windows messages, or perhaps the Win32 API. In the following examples, we will demonstrate simplistic methods for reading input from devices using Win32 API functions before delving into the more complex DirectInput methods. Which you choose will be totally dependent on the type of game and the performance it will require, but either or both techniques are perfectly acceptable.

## Keyboard Input

Of all input devices, the keyboard is perhaps the least complex. Having been the standard for input since almost the dawn of computers themselves, reading keyboard input is very straightforward and easy.

DirectInput approaches the keyboard not as a text input device, but as a gamepad with many buttons (according to the DirectInput documentation). As such, you gain the benefit of being able to differentiate between the left and right versions of identical keyboard buttons, such as Shift, Alt, and Ctrl. However, DirectInput completely ignores such control panel settings as repeat rate and other keyboard properties. Thus, pressing a key registers as a single key press, regardless of how long it has been held down. Similarly, releasing a key also registers as a singular event. Therefore, you must specifically write your code to respond to a key being held down, starting when a key press is noted and ending when the key has been detected as released (if necessary).

### Windows Functions

Windows provides developers with the GetAsyncKeyState function, which is very similar to retrieving immediate keyboard data using DirectInput. GetAsyncKeyState simply indicates if a specific key is pressed or released at the time of the function call. GetAsyncKeyState is defined as:

```
function GetAsyncKeyState(
vKey: Integer           // a virtual key code
): SHORT;               // returns a key press state code
```

This function's only parameter takes a virtual key code, such as VK_LEFT for the left cursor key. It returns a 16-bit value that indicates, if the most significant bit is set, the specified key is currently pressed. For applications that only require a modicum of keyboard input, this function may be more than adequate. The following example demonstrates the use of this function.

***Listing 7-2:*** *Retrieving keyboard input through GetAsyncKeyState*

```
procedure TForm1.Timer1Timer(Sender: TObject);
begin
  {poll the keyboard to check the state of various keys. the program can
    respond to multiple keys changing states simultaneously}
```

```
   if (GetAsyncKeyState(VK_LEFT) and $8000) = $8000 then
     shpLeft.Brush.Color := clRed
   else
     shpLeft.Brush.Color := clMaroon;

   if (GetAsyncKeyState(VK_RIGHT) and $8000) = $8000 then
     shpRight.Brush.Color := clRed
   else
     shpRight.Brush.Color := clMaroon;

   if (GetAsyncKeyState(VK_UP) and $8000) = $8000 then
     shpUp.Brush.Color := clRed
   else
     shpUp.Brush.Color := clMaroon;

   if (GetAsyncKeyState(VK_DOWN) and $8000) = $8000 then
     shpDown.Brush.Color := clRed
   else
     shpDown.Brush.Color := clMaroon;
end;
```

Unfortunately, this method cannot distinguish between left and right versions of certain keyboard keys, such as Shift, Alt, etc. Although easy to implement, it must still go through the Windows operating system to retrieve input data, which for many games may be too slow. For the best response times and total keyboard input control, we must use DirectInput.

## *DirectInput Initialization*

We must follow most of the steps outlined above to initialize DirectInput to receive keyboard data. In most cases, we only need to determine if a particular button is being pressed at a specific time, so immediate data retrieval is the perfect solution. This being the case, initialization of DirectInput is very straightforward.

The first order of business is creating the DirectInput object. We can then immediately create an IDirectInputDevice object for the primary keyboard using the GUID_SysKeyboard value. Since it's not likely that the keyboard will have force feedback capabilities, we'll skip querying for an IDirectInputDevice2 object. We must then set the data format to c_dfDIKeyboard, the standard keyboard data format. We'll set the cooperative level for foreground, non-exclusive, and finally acquire the device so we can retrieve data. That's all there is to initializing DirectInput for immediate keyboard data retrieval. These steps are illustrated in the example below.

**Note:** Remember, the keyboard cannot be acquired in an exclusive cooperative level.

*Listing 7-3: Initializing DirectInput for keyboard data retrieval*

```
{create the DirectInput object}
DirectInputCreate(hInstance, DIRECTINPUT_VERSION, FDirectInput, nil);

{create the DirectInputDevice object for the primary keyboard}
FDirectInput.CreateDevice(@GUID_SysKeyboard, FDirectInputDevice, nil);

{set the data format for keyboard data}
FDirectInputDevice.SetDataFormat(c_dfDIKeyboard);

{set the appropriate cooperative level}
FDirectInputDevice.SetCooperativeLevel(Handle, DISCL_FOREGROUND or
                                       DISCL_NONEXCLUSIVE) );

{acquire the keyboard}
FDirectInputDevice.Acquire;
```

## Reading Input Data

Retrieving immediate data from any device involves a single call to the
IDirectInputDevice's GetDeviceState method. This method returns a snapshot of
the state of the device at the time the function was called, including all pressed
keys, axis movements, etc. The GetDeviceState function is defined as:

```
function GetDeviceState(
cbData: DWORD;              // the size of the data structure
lpvData: Pointer            // a pointer to the appropriate data structure
): HResult;                 // returns a DirectX error code
```

Remember the call to the SetDataFormat method? This indicated to DirectInput
the structure in which to report device data. The value passed to SetDataFormat
indicates the data structure to be passed into GetDeviceState in the lpvData
parameter. For keyboards, we use the TDIKeyboardState structure. The first
parameter must be set to the size of this data structure.

The TDIKeyboardState structure itself is simply a 256-entry array of bytes.
Each entry corresponds to a specific key on the keyboard. The array can be
indexed using the DIK_* constants defined in the DInput.pas file for each specific key. If the hit bit of this byte is set, the key is currently down; otherwise it
is up.

Therefore, to retrieve the current state of all keyboard keys, we simply call
the GetDeviceState method of the IDirectInputDevice object we just created and
check the high bit of the keys with which we are concerned. We must check for

input data each time we need it, a technique known as polling as we discussed when we looked at polling versus event notification. The following example demonstrates this technique.

**Listing 7-4:** *Retrieving immediate keyboard input data*

```
procedure TfrmDXAppMain.DrawSurfaces;
var
  KeyboardState: TDIKeyboardState;
  SourceRect: TRect;
begin

.
.
.

  {retrieve the current state of the keyboard as immediate data}
  FDirectInputDevice.GetDeviceState(SizeOf(KeyboardState), @KeyboardState);

  {if any of the cursor keys are held down, display an appropriate graphic}
  if (KeyboardState[DIK_UP] and $80) = $80 then
  begin
    SourceRect := Rect(0, 110, 110, 110+110);
    FBackBuffer.BltFast(265, 75, FImage, SourceRect, DDBLTFAST_NOCOLORKEY or
                        DDBLTFAST_WAIT);
  end;

  if (KeyboardState[DIK_DOWN] and $80) = $80 then
  begin
    SourceRect := Rect(2*110, 110, (2*110)+110, 110+110);
    FBackBuffer.BltFast(265, 295, FImage, SourceRect, DDBLTFAST_NOCOLORKEY or
                        DDBLTFAST_WAIT);
  end;

  if (KeyboardState[DIK_LEFT] and $80) = $80 then
  begin
    SourceRect := Rect(3*110, 110, (3*110)+110, 110+110);
    FBackBuffer.BltFast(155, 185, FImage, SourceRect, DDBLTFAST_NOCOLORKEY or
                        DDBLTFAST_WAIT);
  end;

  if (KeyboardState[DIK_RIGHT] and $80) = $80 then
  begin
    SourceRect := Rect(110, 110, 110+110, 110+110);
    FBackBuffer.BltFast(375, 185, FImage, SourceRect, DDBLTFAST_NOCOLORKEY or
                        DDBLTFAST_WAIT);

  end;
end;
```

## Mouse Input

The other standard input device, the mouse, is probably used in just about every type of game for allowing the user to choose options and to set up game parameters. While it is almost as easy to read mouse data as it is the keyboard, there are certain nuances that must be considered.

The mouse returns data for up to three buttons and up to three axes. Since DirectInput works directly with the mouse driver, any control panel settings for the mouse are ignored, such as button swapping. However, the application could check on the status of button swapping by calling GetSystemMetrics(SW_SWAPBUTTON). The axis data returned by the mouse is relative by nature, as the mouse can move infinitely in any direction. These values are arbitrary and not based on screen coordinates, control panel settings, etc. The x-axis and y-axis values returned by the mouse correspond to the horizontal and vertical movements of the physical device; mouse wheel values will be reported as a z-axis. As in the windowed world, mouse travel to the left or away from the user is negative, and right or toward the user is positive.

DirectInput allows you to retrieve axis movement, but it does not provide a mouse cursor (under exclusive mode). This must be implemented in the application itself. This is certainly not a difficult task, as you know where to draw the mouse cursor by the x-axis and y-axis values you've retrieved (as they pertain to your application). This allows you to implement elaborate animated mouse cursors using techniques as discussed in the chapter on sprites. The animation could even be context sensitive based on the position of the cursor or the current game state. The only thing to keep in mind is that you will want to draw the mouse cursor as the last step of your rendering process so it is not obscured by other graphics.

**Note:** Setting a non-exclusive cooperative level will display a mouse cursor, but it will flicker horribly in a page flipping architecture such as that used throughout this book. It is usually best to acquire the mouse exclusively and implement your own mouse cursor drawing functionality.

One drawback to drawing the mouse cursor in this manner is that its responsiveness will be very dependent on the frame rate of the application itself. For example, say the user starts the game on a very slow machine, and it has a frame rate of about five frames per second. If you draw your mouse cursor at the end of the rendering loop, it will be very jerky and unresponsive, and could make leaving the game very difficult indeed. In order to combat this dependence on the game's overall frame rate, we will be implementing a multithreaded solution for drawing the mouse cursor.

This multithreaded architecture will also be useful for detecting available mouse input through event notification. This technique involves the use of

Windows event objects as well as a critical section for thread synchronization. This complex architecture will be covered in more detail below.

## Windows Functions

Windows provides developers with the GetCursorPos function, which is very similar to retrieving immediate mouse data for the cursor position using DirectInput. The GetAsyncKeyState function can be used to retrieve the current state of mouse buttons. The GetCursorPos function is defined as:

```
function GetCursorPos(
var lpPoint: TPoint                    // receives coordinates of cursor
): BOOL;                               // returns TRUE or FALSE
```

This function's only parameter is a TPoint variable that receives the horizontal and vertical coordinate of the mouse cursor's current position. For applications that only require a modicum of mouse input, this function may be more than adequate. The following example demonstrates the use of this function.

***Listing 7-5:** Retrieving mouse input through GetCursorPos*

```
procedure TForm1.Timer1Timer(Sender: TObject);
var
  CursorPos: TPoint;
begin
  {retrieve the position of the mouse cursor}
  GetCursorPos(CursorPos);

  {the retrieved position is in screen coordinates, so we must convert them
   to client coordinates}
  CursorPos := ScreenToClient(CursorPos);

  {draw the background into the offscreen buffer, erasing the last 'frame'}
  Offscreen.Canvas.Draw(0, 0, Background);

  {now, transparently draw our custom mouse cursor into the offscreen buffer.
   note that we've moved the 'hotspot' so that it will be in the center of the
   cursor}
  BitBlt(Offscreen.Canvas.Handle, CursorPos.X-16, CursorPos.Y-16,
         CursorAND.Width, CursorAND.Height, CursorAND.Canvas.Handle, 0, 0,
         SRCAND);
  BitBlt(Offscreen.Canvas.Handle, CursorPos.X-16, CursorPos.Y-16,
         CursorOR.Width, CursorOR.Height, CursorOR.Canvas.Handle, 0, 0,
         SRCPAINT);

  {finally, draw the new frame of animation onto the screen}
  Canvas.Draw(0, 0, Offscreen);
end;
```

One drawback with GetCursorPos is that it reports the position of the mouse in relation to the screen, and thus is an absolute measurement as it reports values in the range of 0, 0 to screen width, screen height. This may be fine for some games, but others may require the infinite resolution and quicker response offered by DirectInput.

## DirectInput Initialization

We must follow most of the steps outlined above to initialize DirectInput to receive mouse data. Since we are dealing with a stream of relative axis values, we will use the buffered method of input data retrieval. Therefore, unlike the keyboard, we must set certain properties of the device to initialize this buffer. Due to our multithreaded architecture, we have a few more tasks to complete, some of which are not directly related to DirectInput.

**Note:** Retrieving immediate mouse data is similar to retrieving immediate keyboard data, and will return the cumulative sum of all axes movements since the last call to GetDeviceState.

The first order of business is creating the DirectInput object. We can then immediately create an IDirectInputDevice object for the primary mouse using the GUID_SysMouse value. Since it's not likely that the mouse will have force feedback capabilities, we'll skip querying for an IDirectInputDevice2 object. We must then set the data format to c_dfDIMouse, the standard mouse data format. We'll then set the cooperative level for foreground, exclusive. These steps are illustrated below.

**Listing 7-6:** *Initializing DirectInput for mouse data retrieval*

```
{create the DirectInput object}
DirectInputCreate(hInstance, DIRECTINPUT_VERSION, FDirectInput, nil);

{create the DirectInputDevice object for the primary mouse}
FDirectInput.CreateDevice(@GUID_SysMouse, FMouseDevice, nil);

{set the data format for mouse data}
FMouseDevice.SetDataFormat(c_dfDIMouse);

{set the appropriate cooperative level}
FMouseDevice.SetCooperativeLevel(Handle,DISCL_FOREGROUND or DISCL_EXCLUSIVE);
```

With this accomplished, we should now set the size of the buffer that will hold our mouse input data. This property takes only a simple DWORD of information, so we can use a TDIPropDWord structure in our call to SetProperty. After initializing the appropriate size members, we should set the diph.dwObj member to zero and the diph.dwHow member to DIPH_DEVICE, indicating that this property affects the entire device. Setting the dwData member to 64 indicates we want to set the buffer size to hold 64 "data packets" (this number is arbitrary, and can be higher or lower as dictated by the application requirements). Thus, our buffer will be capable of holding 64 individual instances of mouse input, be that axis movement, button presses, etc. If we do not retrieve and flush this buffer before this limit is reached, any subsequent input data will be lost. This process is illustrated below.

**Listing 7-7:** *Setting the size of the buffer*

```
procedure TfrmDXAppMain.FormActivate(Sender: TObject);
var

  .
  .
  .

  {the mouse property structure}
  MouseProp: TDIPropDWord;
begin

  .
  .
  .

  {initialize our property structure}
  MouseProp.diph.dwSize := SizeOf(TDIPropDWord);
  MouseProp.diph.dwHeaderSize := SizeOf(TDIPropHeader);
  MouseProp.diph.dwObj := 0;
  MouseProp.diph.dwHow := DIPH_DEVICE;
  MouseProp.dwData := 64;            // we want 64 data 'packets'

  {set the size of the buffer property}
  DXCheck( FMouseDevice.SetProperty(DIPROP_BUFFERSIZE, MouseProp.diph) );
```

**Event Notification**   As we've previously discussed, DirectInput has a method known as event notification where it can signal the application that an input event has occurred on some device. This releases the application from the requirement of polling the device through every iteration of the game loop, but it introduces some serious implications.

This technique works by using a Windows event object. Basically, an event is little more than a flag that exists in a "signaled" or "non-signaled" state, and is used for thread synchronization. Using the IDirectInputDevice's SetEventNotification method you can pass the device an event, which will be set to a signaled state when new input is available.

The only way this is useful is in a call to one of the Win32 API wait functions. These functions halt execution of a thread until the event object passed into the function becomes signaled. This is useless in a single-threaded application, as it would halt the execution of the primary thread unless the mouse is moving, making for a boring game indeed. This is why we must use this technique in a multithreaded application. We'll see one of these wait functions in action below.

We will actually want to create two events, one which is passed to DirectInput to signal the availability of new mouse input and one to signal the thread to terminate. We can create these events using the Win32 API function CreateEvent, which is defined as:

```
function CreateEvent(
lpEventAttributes: PSecurityAttributes;   // pointer to security attributes
bManualReset: BOOL;                       // flag for manual reset event
bInitialState: BOOL;                      // flag for initial state
lpName: PChar                             // name of the event object
): THandle;                               // returns a handle of the event object
```

For our purposes, we can set the first parameter to nil, and the second and third parameters to FALSE. We can set the final parameter to an appropriate name for the event, but it is unimportant to our application. These events will be stored in an array for easy management. We will also create a TCriticalSection object, which we will use to synchronize the main thread and our secondary input thread. Using the critical section object will be covered below when we read the mouse data from the buffer.

Now that we've created our events, we need to tell DirectInput which event to signal when mouse input becomes available. This is accomplished by calling the IDirectInputDevice's SetEventNotification method, defined as:

```
function SetEventNotification(
hEvent: THandle                    // a handle to the event to be signaled
): HResult;                        // returns a DirectX error code
```

The only parameter to this method is the handle of the event to be signaled, which we just created above. The following example demonstrates the setup required for initializing event notification.

**Listing 7-8:** *Initializing event notification*

```
{create our events, one for indicating new mouse input data, one for
 indicating that the application is terminating}
FMouseEvents[MOUSEEVENT] := CreateEvent(nil, FALSE, FALSE, 'MouseEvent');
FMouseEvents[QUITEVENT] := CreateEvent(nil, FALSE, FALSE, 'QuitEvent');

{create our critical section synchronization object}
FCritSec := TCriticalSection.Create;

{set the event notification}
DXCheck( FMouseDevice.SetEventNotification(FMouseEvents[MOUSEEVENT]) );
```

***Secondary Thread Creation*** Now that the critical section and events have been set up, we need to create our secondary thread. This second thread is where we will perform all input data retrieval. We used the File | New menu to create a new TThread object, using the Execute method as the location for our code that retrieves mouse input. We'll examine the details of this code below when we cover reading input data. To actually create the thread, we call our TThread object's Create method, passing its only parameter a value of TRUE to indicate we want the thread to be suspended upon creation. The thread should be suspended as we have not yet acquired the mouse. We then set its Priority property to tpTimeCritical, indicating we want it to be immediately responsive, and its FreeOnTerminate property to TRUE, indicating it should free itself when it is terminated. These steps are illustrated in the following listing.

*Listing 7-9: Creating the secondary input thread*

```
{create our secondary input thread}
FMouseThread := TMouseThread.Create(TRUE);

{we want it to be supremely responsive}
FMouseThread.Priority := tpTimeCritical;

{indicate it should free itself when it terminates}
FMouseThread.FreeOnTerminate := TRUE;
```

***Device Acquisition*** Now that the events have been created and set up and the secondary input thread has been initialized, we can acquire the device by calling the Acquire method. As a final step, we must begin executing the input thread by calling the thread's Resume method. We are now finally ready to start retrieving buffered, event-driven mouse input data.

## Reading Input Data

As we previously mentioned, our secondary thread will handle the task of retrieving the input data from the buffer. Thus, all of the code we are about to review is located in the Execute method of our secondary TThread object.

The first item of note in the Execute method concerns the notification events we created. After checking for termination, the very first task we perform in the thread is to call the WaitForMultipleObjects Win32 API function. This function halts execution of the thread until one or more event objects become signaled (known as blocking the thread). The WaitForMultipleObjects function is defined as:

```
function WaitForMultipleObjects(
nCount: DWORD;                   // the number of objects in the array
lpHandles: PWOHandleArray;       // a pointer to an array of object handles
bWaitAll: BOOL;                  // wait flag
```

```
dwMilliseconds: DWORD              // timeout interval
): DWORD;                          // returns an array index
```

We pass in our array of object handles and the number of objects in the array in the first two parameters. We only want the thread to be blocked until either of the events becomes signaled, so we set the third parameter to FALSE. We want the thread to wait indefinitely until one of the events is signaled, so we set the final parameter to INFINITE. This function call will not return until either of the events becomes signaled.

When the function does return, we need to check its return value. We subtract the constant WAIT_OBJECT_0 from this return value to get the index in the array of the object that became signaled. If the Quit event was signaled (indicating we are terminating the application), we should immediately terminate the thread and exit the Execute method. Otherwise, we know it was the mouse event that became signaled, and we are ready to start retrieving mouse input data.

**Note:** We set the Quit event to signaled using the SetEvent Win32 API function in the main form's OnDestroy event. We must also use the CloseHandle Win32 API function to dispose of the event handles we created. See the full example on the CD for details.

Once past this, we make use of our critical section object. A critical section is a device that is used to synchronize access to variables and objects from multiple threads. This is accomplished by calling the TCriticalSection's Enter method. If one thread calls the Enter method of a critical section after another thread has already called it, this second thread is blocked until the first thread calls the TCriticalSection's Leave method. At this point, the other thread becomes unblocked, and any other thread will be blocked in a similar fashion until the current thread calls the Leave method. By using critical sections, we can allow only one thread at a time access to specific variables and objects. This is important, as this secondary input thread will be drawing to the primary DirectDraw surface, and surfaces can only be accessed by one thread at a time. It will also be updating global variables that track the mouse cursor, as well as a list of mouse click events that are used by the primary thread to determine if the user clicked on something interactive.

Now we are ready to being retrieving input data from our buffer. This is accomplished by calling the IDirectInputDevice's GetDeviceData method. The GetDeviceData method is defined as:

```
function GetDeviceData(
cbObjectData: DWORD;               // the size of the device data structure
rgdod: PDIDeviceObjectData;        // a pointer to the device data structure
var pdwInOut: DWORD;               // a variable indicating the number of elements
dwFlags: DWORD                     // data removal flags
```

```
): HResult;                         // returns a DirectX error code
```

The first parameter is set to the size of a TDIDeviceObjectData structure. The second parameter is a pointer to an array of TDIDeviceObjectData structures which, upon return, will contain the buffered device data. The third parameter indicates how many elements to retrieve, and should be equal to or less than the number of elements in the array. When this method returns, it will contain the actual number of elements retrieved. The last parameter indicates if the data should be removed from the buffer. Setting this to zero removes the data from the buffer; a value of DIGDD_PEEK leaves the buffer intact.

**Note:** You do not have to remove the entire contents of the buffer at once. You may remove them one at a time or in similar small increments, if desired.

This method will return one TDIDeviceObjectData structure for each individual input event that has occurred on the device since the last time data was retrieved. This means there is one event for a button press, one for a button release (even if it was the same button), one for <u>every</u> individual movement along *each* axis, etc. This is why it is important to set the buffer size to an appropriate number, as it is easy to overflow the buffer if a lot of activity is occurring.

The TDIDeviceObjectData structure contains all the information necessary to report any input event on the specific device. The TDIDeviceObjectData structure is defined as:

```
TDIDeviceObjectData = packed record
  dwOfs: DWORD;                     // the device object identifier
  dwData: DWORD;                    // the data
  dwTimeStamp: DWORD;               // when the event occurred
  dwSequence: DWORD;                // the event sequence number
end;
```

The first member, dwOfs, indicates what actually caused the input. This value is very specific to the type of device being used. In the case of buffered keyboard data, this value will be one of the DIK_* key values. For mice, this could be DIMOFS_X, DIMOFS_Y, or DIMOFS_Z to indicate movement along one of the axes, or DIMOFS_BUTTON0, DIMOFS_BUTTON1, or DIMOFS_BUTTON0 to indicate a change of state in one of the mouse buttons. There are similar DIJOFS_* values defined for various buttons and axes on joysticks. The dwData member contains the data for the input event, and again is very specific to both the device and the object on that device that signaled the input event. In the case of one of the axes, dwData will contain either relative or absolute axis movement, in arbitrary units. In the case of buttons, if the high bit is set, the button was pressed; if it is clear, the button was released.

If we enter a loop to retrieve one input event at a time, we can examine all of these members and update various global variables accordingly. In our example on the CD, we add any axis movement to global mouse cursor variables, and then ultimately clip them to the boundaries of our DirectDraw screen resolution. While our example is concerned only with button presses, we do store each mouse button press in a list of button press objects, storing the location of the press and the button that was pressed. We can use this later in our application logic to determine if the user clicked on an interactive game element.

*Tip:* The dwTimeStamp member of this structure indicates when the input event actually occurred. The time stamps from subsequent events could potentially be used to determine if the user double-clicked on some item. The dwSequence number, on the other hand, indicates the chronological sequence in which input events where obtained. This is useful for determining the order of input from two separate devices, as DirectInput never assigns the same sequence number for events from different devices, even if they have the same time stamp. This might come in handy if developing a multiplayer game where two people can play from the same machine.

All of this new functionality has been added to our baseline application so we can easily create DirectX applications with mouse support. While we are not going to cover it here, this new baseline application contains some additional code for drawing the mouse cursor on the primary surface from the secondary input thread. This solves the problem we noted earlier about the mouse cursor dependency on the animation frame rate. The following listing illustrates using the event notification and buffered data retrieval methods for obtaining mouse input data.

*Listing 7-10: Retrieving buffered mouse input data*

```
interface

type

    .
    .
    .

  {this class is used to track click events}
  TMouseData = class
  public
    XPos, YPos: Integer;
    Button: TMouseButton;

    constructor Create(X, Y: Integer; MButton: TMouseButton);
  end;
```

```
var
  CurX, CurY, OldX, OldY: Integer;       // the mouse position variables
  MouseClickList: TList;                 // the list of click events
  FCritSec: TCriticalSection;            // syncronization object
  FMouseEvents: TWOHandleArray;          // events array

const
  {we're using a 32 X 32 pixel mouse cursor image}
  CURSORWIDTH = 32;
  CURSORHEIGHT = 32;

  {our animated mouse cursor has 8 frames}
  NUMFRAMES = 8;

implementation

constructor TMouseData.Create(X, Y: Integer; MButton: TMouseButton);
begin
  {create and initialize the mouse data object for a click event}
  XPos := X;
  YPos := Y;
  Button := MButton;
end;

procedure TMouseThread.Execute;
var
  EventNum: Integer;
  NumElements: DWORD;
  DeviceData: TDIDeviceObjectData;
  DataResult: HRESULT;
  SourceRect,
  DirtyRect: TRect;
begin
  {continuously perform this code until terminated}
  while not Terminated do
  begin
    {wait until one of the events becomes signaled}
    EventNum := WaitForMultipleObjects(2, @FMouseEvents, FALSE, INFINITE);

    {was the quit event signaled?  if so, terminate}
    if EventNum-WAIT_OBJECT_0 = QUITEVENT then
    begin
      Terminate;
      Break;
    end;

    {we are about to use global variables, so enter the critical section}
    FCritSec.Enter;

    {store the current mouse cursor coordinates}
    OldX := CurX;
```

```
OldY := CurY;

{begin retrieving buffered data}
while TRUE do
begin
  {we only want to retrieve one element at a time}
  NumElements := 1;

  {retrieve the buffered data}
  DataResult := FMouseDevice.GetDeviceData(SizeOf(TDIDeviceObjectData),
                                    @DeviceData, NumElements, 0);

  {if we retrieved data, update global variables}
  if (DataResult = DI_OK) and (NumElements = 1) then
  begin
    case DeviceData.dwOfs of
      {update mouse cursor positions}
      DIMOFS_X        : CurX := CurX + DeviceData.dwData;
      DIMOFS_Y        : CurY := CurY + DeviceData.dwData;
      {update our list of click events}
      DIMOFS_BUTTON0  : MouseClickList.Add(TMouseData.Create(CurX, CurY,
                                                      mbLeft));
      DIMOFS_BUTTON1  : MouseClickList.Add(TMouseData.Create(CurX, CurY,
                                                      mbRight));
    end;
  end
  else
    {if there were no move input events to retrieve, continue}
    Break;
end;

{clip the global mouse cursor positions to the extents of our
 screen resolution}
if CurX < 0 then
  CurX := 0;
if CurX > DXWIDTH-CURSORWIDTH then
  CurX := DXWIDTH-CURSORWIDTH-1;
if CurY < 0 then
  CurY := 0;
if CurY > DXHEIGHT-CURSORHEIGHT then
  CurY := DXHEIGHT-CURSORHEIGHT-1;

{if the mouse position has changed...}
if not ((CurX = OldX) and (CurY = OldY)) then
begin
  {draw the mouse cursor if the old and new positions do not overlap...}
  if (ABS(CurX - OldX)>= CURSORWIDTH) or
     (ABS(CurY - OldY)>= CURSORHEIGHT) then
  begin
    {erase the old cursor}
```

```
      SourceRect := Rect(NUMFRAMES*CURSORWIDTH, 0, NUMFRAMES*CURSORWIDTH+
                         CURSORWIDTH, CURSORHEIGHT);
      FPrimarySurface.BltFast(OldX, OldY, FMouseCursors, SourceRect,
                              DDBLTFAST_NOCOLORKEY or DDBLTFAST_WAIT);

      {save area under new cursor location}
      SourceRect := Rect(CurX, CurY, CurX+CURSORWIDTH, CurY+CURSORHEIGHT);
      FMouseCursors.BltFast(NUMFRAMES*CURSORWIDTH, 0, FPrimarySurface,
                            SourceRect, DDBLTFAST_NOCOLORKEY or
                            DDBLTFAST_WAIT);

      {draw new cursor}
      SourceRect := Rect(FCursorFrame*CURSORWIDTH, 0, (FCursorFrame*
                         CURSORWIDTH)+CURSORWIDTH, CURSORHEIGHT);
      FPrimarySurface.BltFast(CurX, CurY, FMouseCursors, SourceRect,
                              DDBLTFAST_NOCOLORKEY or DDBLTFAST_WAIT);
  end
  else
  {...or draw the mouse cursor if the old and new positions do overlap}
  begin
    {copy the dirty rectangle to the scratch buffer}
    UnionRect(DirtyRect, Rect(OldX, OldY, OldX+CURSORWIDTH,
                              OldY+CURSORHEIGHT),
              Rect(CurX, CurY, CurX+CURSORWIDTH, CurY+CURSORHEIGHT));
    FMouseScratch.BltFast(0, 0, FPrimarySurface, DirtyRect,
                          DDBLTFAST_NOCOLORKEY or DDBLTFAST_WAIT);

    {erase the old cursor from the scratch buffer}
    SourceRect := Rect(NUMFRAMES*CURSORWIDTH, 0, NUMFRAMES*CURSORWIDTH+
                       CURSORWIDTH, CURSORHEIGHT);
    FMouseScratch.BltFast(OldX-DirtyRect.Left, OldY-DirtyRect.Top,
                          FMouseCursors, SourceRect, DDBLTFAST_NOCOLORKEY or
                          DDBLTFAST_WAIT);

    {save the area under the new cursor}
    SourceRect := Rect(CurX-DirtyRect.Left, CurY-DirtyRect.Top, (CurX-
                       DirtyRect.Left)+CURSORWIDTH, (CurY-
                       DirtyRect.Top)+CURSORHEIGHT);
    FMouseCursors.BltFast(NUMFRAMES*CURSORWIDTH, 0, FMouseScratch,
                          SourceRect, DDBLTFAST_NOCOLORKEY or
                          DDBLTFAST_WAIT);

    {draw new cursor into scratch buffer}
    SourceRect := Rect(FCursorFrame*CURSORWIDTH, 0, (FCursorFrame*
                       CURSORWIDTH)+CURSORWIDTH, CURSORHEIGHT);
    FMouseScratch.BltFast(CurX-DirtyRect.Left, CurY-DirtyRect.Top,
                          FMouseCursors, SourceRect, DDBLTFAST_NOCOLORKEY or
                          DDBLTFAST_WAIT);

    {draw scratch buffer back to primary buffer}
    SourceRect := Rect(0, 0, DirtyRect.Right-DirtyRect.Left,
```

```
                              DirtyRect.Bottom-DirtyRect.Top);
           FPrimarySurface.BltFast(DirtyRect.Left, DirtyRect.Top, FMouseScratch,
                              SourceRect, DDBLTFAST_NOCOLORKEY or
                              DDBLTFAST_WAIT);
        end;
      end;

      {we are finished using global variables, so we can now leave
       the critical section}
      FCritSec.Leave;
    end;
end;
```

## Game Controller Input

Game controller input programming can be both fun and complex. The fun comes from the fact that game controllers can be of almost any shape and size, and tend to resemble non-computer input devices such as steering wheels, rudder pedals, flight yokes, etc. This incredible variety is also the cause of the complexity. Since game controllers can have almost any number of axes, buttons, sliders, etc., the developer never knows the exact configuration of an attached controller without deducing what is available programmatically. This leads to a level of complexity not found in similar code for interfacing with keyboards and mice.

Game controllers can return a wide range of information. Data for up to three axes can be returned, including their rotation, velocity, acceleration, and force (with the existence of force feedback). Additionally, the state of two sliders, four POV hats, and 128 buttons can also be retrieved. By default, all of the axis information returned from game controllers is absolute, as most axes can move only so far in either direction. However, these values are arbitrary and not based on screen coordinates, etc. Like the mouse, axis data corresponds to the physical movement of the device. However, since game controllers can be almost any shape, the sign of these values and their relation to the direction of physical movement on the device is dependent upon the device itself (such as rotation of an axis). Also unlike the mouse, game controllers do take into account control panel settings, such as calibration. Therefore, you do not have to worry about writing specific code for calibrating a game controller before retrieving its state.

**Tip:** To run the control panel application for game controllers to begin calibration (or any control panel associated with any DirectInputDevice, for that matter), simply call IDirectInputDevice's RunControlPanel method, passing zero in its two parameters. This allows users to easily calibrate game controllers from within your game.

Game controller input programming has a number of additional nuances that one must be aware of. As stated earlier, the predefined data format structure for joysticks and game controllers does not seem to work appropriately. Thus, in the examples below, we will enumerate all objects on an input device (such as axes, buttons, etc.) and create a custom data format. This will provide support for a wider range of game controllers (theoretically, all game controllers) and will result in more robust and stable code.

### Additional Game Controller Considerations

Above and beyond what is required to set up buffered data retrieval, game controllers require that the developer set up additional properties for each axis before input data can be retrieved. Specifically, the range of values for each axis must be set, as well as their deadzone and saturation levels.

*Range*   A minimum and maximum range must be set for each axis. These values are completely arbitrary; DirectInput will scale the data returned from the driver to fit within this range, but these values are meaningful only within the context in which they are used. The center position of the axis will be the center of this specified range.

*Deadzone*   The deadzone indicates an area around the center of an axis in which the axis can move, yet the position will be reported as the lowest value within the range. This allows a joystick to wander around a little in the center without reporting movement. This can be useful for setting sensitivity levels. This deadzone range is not subtracted from the overall range; DirectInput compresses the range values into a smaller part of the physical range of the axis. The deadzone value is always between 0 and 10,000, indicating a percentage of the overall range of axis travel in hundredths of degrees. For example, a value of 2,000 indicates we wish the first 20 percent of the physical range of axis travel to fall within the deadzone. This range is based on the center position of the axis, with one-half of the range on either side.

*Saturation*   Saturation is similar to the deadzone in that it defines an area at the extent of axis travel in which the axis can move but the position will be reported as the highest value within the range. Again, this can be useful for setting sensitivity levels. However, some joysticks may only report the highest range values when the stick is moved to a diagonal position. Like the deadzone, saturation values are always between 0 and 10,000 (hundredths of degrees), and indicate the percentage of physical axis travel at which the highest range values will be reported. For example, a value of 9,000 indicates that the saturation zone begins at 90 percent of the physical range of axis travel (the last 10 percent of axis travel will fall within the saturation zone). Again, this range is based on the center position of the axis, and the range values themselves are compressed into the remaining part of the physical axis range.

**Caution:** It is possible to set a saturation and a deadzone that completely obscure discrete axis measurements (i.e., saturation and deadzone can be set such that axis values will only be reported as the minimum or maximum value in the specified range).

 **Note:** Axes on a game pad do not report discrete values; they only report values at the central and extreme ends of the specified range.

## Game Controller Objects

Game controllers come with a variety of objects with which the user can provide input data. These objects include axes, POVs, and buttons. Although most game controllers exhibit input objects that are not available on the keyboard and mouse, data retrieved from these objects is not unlike that retrieved from more conventional input devices.

***Lateral and Rotational Axes*** Game controller axes come in two flavors: lateral and rotational. A lateral axis moves in a straight line, such as left and right or forward and backward. Conversely, a rotational axis moves in a circular fashion, rotating about the x-, y-, or z-axis. The twisting motion on some joysticks is an example of a rotational axis. The values returned from each axis type is similar, however, and will be within the range specified by the developer.

***POV Hats*** A point-of-view hat is neither a button nor an axis (it has more than two positions but reports values in a fixed range). The data reported by a POV is in polar coordinates, with 0 to the north (or top) and subsequent values increasing in a clockwise direction. These values are reported in hundredths of degrees (i.e., 9000 = 90 degrees). When the POV is centered, the low word of the reported value will be $FFFF. Most POVs have a granularity of 45 or 90 degrees.

 **Caution:** While the GetProperty method of IDirectInputDevice can be used to retrieve the granularity, some game controller devices report this information incorrectly.

***Buttons*** Game controller button state is reported exactly as keyboard or mouse buttons: If the high bit of the low word is set, the button is down; otherwise it is up.

## Windows Functions

Windows provides several functions to developers for determining game controller capabilities and retrieving input data. For the most part, these functions are incredibly powerful and can report almost as much data as their DirectInput counterparts. For most applications, these functions may supply all the required power.

**Note:** MMSystem must be added to the Uses clause of any unit employing these functions.

Game controller capabilities can be retrieved by using the joyGetDevCaps function. joyGetDevCaps is defined as:

```
joyGetDevCaps(
uJoyID: UINT;          // the game controller identifier
lpCaps: PJoyCaps;      // a TJoyCaps structure
uSize: UINT            // the size of the TJoyCaps structure
): MMRESULT;           // returns an error condition
```

The first parameter is a constant indicating the game controller whose properties are to be retrieved. The second parameter points to a TJoyCaps structure, a rather large structure containing information such as the minimum and maximum range values of axes, the number of buttons on the controller, etc. The final parameter must be set to the size of the TJoyCaps structure. Developers should use this function first to determine what objects are available on the device before retrieving input data.

The actual state of all objects on the game controller is retrieved by using the joyGetPosEx structure. joyGetPosEx is defined as:

```
joyGetPosEx(
uJoyID: UINT;          // the game controller identifier
lpInfo: PJoyInfoEx     // a TJoyInfoEx structure
): MMRESULT;           // returns an error condition
```

The first parameter is a constant indicating the game controller whose state is to be retrieved (presumably the same value passed to the joyGetDevCaps function). The second value is a pointer to a TJoyInfoEx structure. This structure defines the state of up to six axes (three axes and their rotations), 32 buttons, and one POV. The following example demonstrates how this function can report the state of a game controller. Figure 7-2 shows the output.

***Listing 7-11:*** *Retrieving game controller input through joyGetPosEx*

```
procedure TfrmJoyTestBed.GetJoyInfoPoll;
var
   CrossHairX,
   CrossHairY: Integer;
   iCount: Integer;
   JoyPos: TJoyInfoEx;
begin
   {poll the joystick for its status, retrieving information for up to 32 buttons
```

```
  and 6 axis positions}
  JoyPos.dwSize := SizeOf(TJoyInfoEx);
  JoyPos.dwFlags := JOY_RETURNALL;
  joyGetPosEx(JOYSTICKID1, @JoyPos);

  {retrieve the coordinates of the X, Y axis relative to the panel}
  CrossHairX := JoyToRelative(0, pbCrossHairSurface.Width, JoyCaps.wXmin,
                              JoyCaps.wXmax, JoyPos.wXpos);

  CrossHairY := JoyToRelative(0, pbCrossHairSurface.Width, JoyCaps.wYmin,
                              JoyCaps.wYmax, JoyPos.wYpos);


  {draw the X, Y axis crosshair}
  DrawCrossHair(CrossHairX, CrossHairY);

  {draw the Point Of View direction}
  if (JoyCaps.wCaps and JOYCAPS_HASPOV) = JOYCAPS_HASPOV then
    DrawPOV(JoyPos.dwPOV);

  {draw the position of additional axes}
  if (JoyCaps.wCaps and JOYCAPS_HASZ) = JOYCAPS_HASZ then
    shpZBarPos.Width := JoyToRelative(0, pnlZBar.Width, JoyCaps.wZmin,
                                      JoyCaps.wZmax, JoyPos.wZpos);

  if (JoyCaps.wCaps and JOYCAPS_HASR) = JOYCAPS_HASR then
    shpRBarPos.Width := JoyToRelative(0, pnlRBar.Width, JoyCaps.wRmin,
                                      JoyCaps.wRmax, JoyPos.dwRpos);

  if (JoyCaps.wCaps and JOYCAPS_HASU) = JOYCAPS_HASU then
    shpUBarPos.Width := JoyToRelative(0, pnlUBar.Width, JoyCaps.wUmin,
                                      JoyCaps.wUmax, JoyPos.dwUpos);

  if (JoyCaps.wCaps and JOYCAPS_HASV) = JOYCAPS_HASV then
    shpVBarPos.Width := JoyToRelative(0, pnlVBar.Width, JoyCaps.wVmin,
                                      JoyCaps.wVmax, JoyPos.dwVpos);

  {test the joystick buttons}
  for iCount := 0 to 31 do
    if (ButtonLights[iCount]<>nil) then
      if Longbool(JoyPos.wButtons and Trunc(Power(2, iCount))) then
        ButtonLights[iCount].Brush.Color := clRed
      else
        ButtonLights[iCount].Brush.Color := clMaroon;
end;
```

Unfortunately, some game controllers have objects that provide input that joyGetPosEx simply cannot detect. Additionally, there is no Win32 API support for force feedback capabilities. These functions can allow a developer to rapidly implement game controller support, and may be useful for prototyping.

However, for the best response times, support for any game controller, and force feedback functionality, developers must use DirectInput.

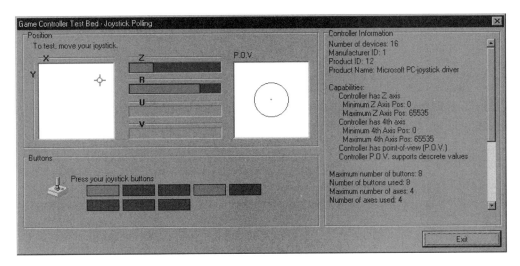

**Figure 7-2:** *Win32 joystick input*

## DirectInput Initialization

We must follow most of the steps outlined above to initialize DirectInput to receive game controller data. However, since there is no system game controller and we are required to set up our own data format, there are several additional steps that must be taken.

As always, we start by creating the DirectInput object. We must know the exact instance GUID of the game controller device before a DirectInputDevice object can be created, so we must enumerate the attached game controllers. Therefore, we call the EnumDevices method, passing it a type of DIDEVTYPE_JOYSTICK to indicate that we wish to enumerate game controllers. Usually there is only one game controller connected to the system. However, you may wish to create a list of all attached devices and present it to the user, as we explained earlier in the chapter. Once the instance GUID of the game controller is known, we can create the input device by calling the CreateDevice method. We need to use the Poll method, which is only available in the IDirectInputDevice2 interface, so we'll need to use QueryInterface to retrieve the appropriate object.

Now that we've created the device, we can retrieve its capabilities. We need to know how many buttons, axes, etc., this controller has; this and other information can be retrieved by calling the GetCapabilities method of the IDirectInputDevice object. GetCapabilities is defined as:

```
function GetCapabilities(
var lpDIDevCaps: TDIDevCaps                    // a TDIDevCaps structure
```

```
): HResult;                              // returns a DirectX error code
```

The only parameter to this method is a pointer to a TDIDevCaps structure. This structure describes the capabilities of the queried device, and is defined as:

```
TDIDevCaps = packed record
  dwSize: DWORD;                         // the size of the structure
  dwFlags: DWORD;                        // device flags
  dwDevType: DWORD;                      // device type identifier
  dwAxes: DWORD;                         // number of axes
  dwButtons: DWORD;                      // number of buttons
  dwPOVs: DWORD;                         // number of POVs
  dwFFSamplePeriod: DWORD;               // force feedback sample period
  dwFFMinTimeResolution: DWORD;          // force feedback time resolution
  dwFirmwareRevision: DWORD;             // firmware version
  dwHardwareRevision: DWORD;             // hardware version
  dwFFDriverVersion: DWORD;              // device driver version
end;
```

Apart from the various members that denote the number of available objects, the dwFlags member may be of particular interest. This member contains a combination of flags that denote various attributes of the overall device. You can check to see if this member contains DIDC_ATTACHED, indicating that a game controller is physically attached to the machine. Checking it for DIDC_FORCEFEEDBACK indicates that the device supports force feedback.

In addition to retrieving the capabilities of the overall input device, we may also want to retrieve information on a specific object on that device. This is accomplished by calling the IDirectInputDevice's GetObjectInfo method. GetObjectInfo is defined as:

```
function GetObjectInfo(
var pdidoi: TDIDeviceObjectInstance;     // a TDIDeviceObjectInstance structure
dwObj: DWORD;                            // object identifier
dwHow: DWORD                             // object identification method
): HResult;                              // returns a DirectX error code
```

The first parameter takes a pointer to a TDIDeviceObjectInstance structure that will contain information about the desired object when the function returns. The second parameter is the device object identifier whose information we wish to retrieve. The final parameter should be set to DIPH_BYOFFSET. The TDIDeviceObjectInstance structure is another large structure that we will use again later when we construct our custom data format. The TDIDeviceObjectInstance structure is defined as:

```
TDIDeviceObjectInstance = packed record
  dwSize: DWORD;                         // size of the structure
  guidType: TGUID;                       // object type GUID
  dwOfs: DWORD;                          // offset (also object identifier)
  dwType: DWORD;                         // object type
```

```
    dwFlags: DWORD;                          // attribute flags
    tszName: Array [0..MAX_PATH-1] of CHAR;  // object name
    dwFFMaxForce: DWORD;                     // maximum force magnitude
    dwFFForceResolution: DWORD;              // force resolution
    wCollectionNumber: WORD;                 // link collection number
    wDesignatorIndex: WORD;                  // designator index
    wUsagePage: WORD;                        // usage page
    wUsage: WORD;                            // usage
    dwDimension: DWORD;                      // dimensional units
    wExponent: WORD;                         // dimension exponent
    wReserved: WORD;                         // reserved
end;
```

Incidentally, this method can be used to simply detect the existence of a specific object. If the return value is not DI_OK for a specific object, then we know it doesn't exist on the input device. The following example demonstrates creating the object, retrieving device capabilities, and using the aforementioned technique to determine if any rotational axes are available on the device.

***Listing 7-12:*** *Creating the input device and querying capabilities*

```
procedure TestForRotationalAxis(Offset: Integer; AxisName: string;
                                Panel: TPanel; Shape: TShape);
var
  ObjectInst: TDIDeviceObjectInstance;
begin
  {we will be retrieving information on a device object, so prepare a
   data structure}
  FillChar(ObjectInst, SizeOf(TDIDeviceObjectInstance), 0);
  ObjectInst.dwSize := SizeOf(TDIDeviceObjectInstance);

  {this simply determines if the specified object exists. we are using this
   here to specifically test for rotational axes (see where this function
   is called), but we could also use it to determine the existence of
   other axes or even buttons}
  if FDirectInputDevice.GetObjectInfo(
     ObjectInst, Offset, DIPH_BYOFFSET) = DI_OK then
  with frmJoyTestBed.memControllerInfo.Lines do
  begin
    Add('      '+AxisName+' rotational axis');
    Panel.Color := clMaroon;
  end
  else
  begin
    Panel.Color := clBtnFace;
    Shape.Width := 0;
  end;
end;

procedure TfrmJoyTestBed.FormActivate(Sender: TObject);
```

```
var
  FJoyList: TStringList;
  iCount: Integer;

  DevCaps: TDIDevCaps;

  TempDevice: IDirectInputDevice;

       .
       .
       .

begin
  {create the DirectInput object}
  DirectInputCreate(hInstance, DIRECTINPUT_VERSION, FDirectInput, nil);

  {create a list to hold information on each available game controller}
  FJoyList := TStringList.Create;

  {enumerate attached game controllers}
  FDirectInput.EnumDevices(DIDEVTYPE_JOYSTICK, EnumInputDevs, FJoyList,
                           DIEDFL_ATTACHEDONLY);

  {we'll add this information to a list box in a dialog box, and display this
   to the user so they can choose their desired input controller}
  frmDevices := TfrmDevices.Create(Self);
  for iCount := 0 to FJoyList.Count-1 do
    frmDevices.lbxJoyDevices.Items.Add(FJoyList[iCount]);
  frmDevices.ShowModal;

  {create the input device based on the input controller specified by the user}
  DXCheck( FDirectInput.CreateDevice(PGUID(FJoyList.Objects[0])^, TempDevice,
                                     nil) );

  {close this dialog box, and delete the list of GUIDs}
  frmDevices.Release;
  for iCount := 0 to FJoyList.Count-1 do
    Dispose(PGUID(FJoyList.Objects[0]));
  FJoyList.Free;

  {we need the new version of the input device interface, so retrieve it}
  try
    DXCheck(TempDevice.QueryInterface(IDirectInputDevice2, FDirectInputDevice));
  finally
    TempDevice := nil
  end;

  {retrieve the capabilities of this device}
  DevCaps.dwSize := SizeOf(DevCaps);
  FDirectInputDevice.GetCapabilities(DevCaps);
```

```
          .
          .
          .
{determine if the controller is unplugged}
if (DevCaps.dwFlags and DIDC_ATTACHED) <> DIDC_ATTACHED then
  ShowMessage('Controller is unplugged');

{create button indicators}
for iCount := 0 to DevCaps.dwButtons-1 do
begin
  ButtonLights[iCount]              := TShape.Create(GroupBox2);
  ButtonLights[iCount].Left         := 96+((iCount mod 5)*(49+5));
  ButtonLights[iCount].Top          := 48+((iCount div 5)*(17+5));
  ButtonLights[iCount].Width        := 49;
  ButtonLights[iCount].Height       := 17;
  ButtonLights[iCount].Brush.Color  := clMaroon;
  ButtonLights[iCount].Parent       := GroupBox2;
end;

{indicate if a POV is available}
if DevCaps.dwPOVs > 0 then
begin
  Label9.Enabled := TRUE;
  Panel2.Color := clWhite;
end
else
begin
  Label9.Enabled := FALSE;
  Panel2.Color := clBtnFace;
end;

{display controller capabilities}
with DevCaps, memControllerInfo.Lines do
begin
  Add('Number of buttons: '+IntToStr(dwButtons));
  Add('Number of axes: '+IntToStr(dwAxes));
  Add('Number of POVs: '+IntToStr(dwPOVs));
  Add('');
  Add('Rotational Axes:');

  TestForRotationalAxis(DIJOFS_RX, 'RX', pnlRXBar, shpRXBarPos);
  TestForRotationalAxis(DIJOFS_RY, 'RY', pnlRYBar, shpRYBarPos);
  TestForRotationalAxis(DIJOFS_RZ, 'RZ', pnlRZBar, shpRZBarPos);
 end;

          .
          .
          .

end;
```

***Setting the Data Format*** Now that the device has been created and its capabilities have been determined, we need to set the data format. As mentioned earlier, we must generate our own data format programmatically to ensure that the greatest number of input devices are supported. We begin by declaring a variable of type TDIDataFormat. TDIDataFormat is defined as:

```
TDIDataFormat = packed record
  dwSize: DWORD;                    // size of this structure
  dwObjSize: DWORD;                 // size of a TDIObjectDataFormat structure
  dwFlags: DWORD;                   // attribute flags
  dwDataSize: DWORD;                // size of data packet
  dwNumObjs: DWORD;                 // number of objects in the array
  rgodf: PDIObjectDataFormat;       // array of TDIObjectDataFormat structures
end;
```

This structure carries information that describes a device's data format. The first member should be set to the size of the TDIDataFormat structure. The second member is set to the size of a TDIObjectDataFormat structure. The third member is a series of flags that describe certain attributes of the data format. For our purposes, we can set this member to DIDF_ABSAXIS to indicate that axes measurements are absolute. The fourth member indicates the size of the data packet returned from the driver. This value must be a multiple of 4, and must exceed the largest offset value for an object's data in the packet. For our purposes, we'll set this to the size of the TDIJoyState2 structure. The fifth member indicates the number of objects that are in the sixth member, which is a pointer to an array of TDIObjectDataFormat structures. The TDIObjectDataFormat structure is defined as:

```
TDIObjectDataFormat = packed record
  pguid: ^TGUID;        // object GUID
  dwOfs: DWORD;         // object offset
  dwType: DWORD;        // object type
  dwFlags: DWORD;       // attribute flags
end;
```

The TDIObjectDataFormat structure contains information about a specific object on the input device, such as an individual axis or button. The first member is the object's unique identifying GUID. The second member is the object's offset within the data packet. This is also the object identifier that we have used in other methods. The third member indicates the object type (such as a button or axis), and the final member contains attribute flags for the object.

After we initialize the first four members of the TDIDataFormat structure, we must begin building the array of TDIObjectDataFormat structures for each object on the device. To do this, we must employ the EnumObjects method. EnumObjects works the same as all other enumeration functions in that it calls a callback function once for each object on the input device. The EnumObjects method is defined as:

```
function EnumObjects(
lpCallback: TDIEnumDeviceObjectsCallbackA;    // the callback function
pvRef: Pointer;                               // application-defined value
dwFlags: DWORD                                // enumeration flags
): HResult;                                    // returns a DirectX error code
```

The first parameter is a pointer to the callback function, the second parameter is a pointer to an application-defined value, and the final parameter is a series of flags that control the scope of enumeration. For our purposes, we'll set this final parameter to DIDFT_ALL to indicate we wish to enumerate all devices. The callback function itself must be defined as:

```
function TDIEnumDeviceObjectsCallbackA(
var lpddoi: TDIDeviceObjectInstance;    // a TDIDeviceObjectInstance structure
pvRef: Pointer                          // the application-defined data
): BOOL; stdcall;                        // returns TRUE or FALSE
```

The first parameter is an initialized TDIDeviceObjectInstance structure containing all the information we need about this specific object. The only other parameter is a pointer to the application-defined value. This callback function should return TRUE to continue enumeration or FALSE otherwise.

As we are enumerating, for each object, we can save the GUID, offset, and type as reported from the TDIDeviceObjectInstance structure into our array of TDIObjectDataFormat structures. We also must keep a count of the number of objects found.

When enumeration completes, we will have a correctly initialized TDIDataFormat structure, complete with an array of correctly initialized TDIObjectDataFormat structures. This entire data structure is then sent to the SetDataFormat method to finally set the correct data format for the game controller. This is illustrated in the following example.

**Listing 7-13:** *Setting the data format*

```
procedure SetDataFormat;

  function DIEnumDeviceObjectsProc(const peff: TDIDeviceObjectInstance;
                                   pvRef: Pointer): HRESULT; stdcall;
  begin
    {if the offset is not beyond the indicated data size... (useful if
    we were to use the TDIJoyState data structure instead) }
    if peff.dwOfs<FDataFormat.dwDataSize then
    begin
      {save the type GUID for this object}
      FDataFormatGUIDs[FDataFormat.dwNumObjs] := peff.guidType;

      {add the object information to our custom made data format}
      with FDataFormatObjects[FDataFormat.dwNumObjs] do
      begin
```

```
            pguid := @FDataFormatGUIDs[FDataFormat.dwNumObjs];
            dwOfs := peff.dwOfs;
            dwType := peff.dwType;
            dwFlags := 0;
        end;

        {if this object is an axis, store it in our axis list}
        if (peff.dwType and DIDFT_AXIS) > 0 then
        begin
          FAxisList[NumAxes] := peff.dwOfs;
          Inc(NumAxes);
        end;

        {increment the number of objects found}
        Inc(FDataFormat.dwNumObjs);
      end;

    {continue enumeration}
    Result := DIENUM_CONTINUE;
  end;

begin
  {enumerate all objects on this input device. this will build our custom data
   structure programmatically with the correct information for each object}
  FDirectInputDevice.EnumObjects(@DIEnumDeviceObjectsProc, nil, DIDFT_ALL);

  {set the data format for the input device}
  DXCheck( FDirectInputDevice.SetDataFormat(FDataFormat) );
end;

procedure TfrmJoyTestBed.FormActivate(Sender: TObject);
var

    .
    .
    .

begin

    .
    .
    .

  {initialize our axis tracking variable}
  NumAxes := 0;

  {now we need to begin creating the data format structure and setting the
   data format, so we must initialize the overall data format structure}
  with FDataFormat do
  begin
    dwFlags := DIDF_ABSAXIS;
```

```
      dwDataSize := SizeOf(TDIJoyState2);
      dwSize := SizeOf(FDataFormat);
      dwObjSize := SizeOf(TDIObjectDataFormat);
      dwNumObjs := 0;
      rgodf := @FDataFormatObjects;
    end;

    {create and set a data format specifically made for this device}
    SetDataFormat;

      .
      .
      .

end;
```

***Setting Axis Properties***   With the data format set, we are now ready to start setting various properties for all of the axes.

As discussed above, we must set the range, deadzone, and saturation for each axis. To accomplish this task, we'll need variables of type TDIPropRange for the range and TDIPropDWord for the deadzone and saturation. As we illustrated in the mouse example, we must initialize the various size members of this structure. Unlike the mouse example, however, we will set the dwObj members of both structures to the object identifier for each individual axis. We could set this to DIPH_DEVICE, setting the properties for all axes on the device, but we may want to set different ranges, deadzones, and saturations for each device. For the TDIPropRange structure, we'll set the lMin and lMax members to –1,000 and 1,000, respectively. For the TDIPropDWord structure, we'll set the dwData member to 1,000 for deadzone properties (indicating 10 percent deadzone), and 9,000 for saturation properties (indicating that the last 10 percent is saturation). We can then call the SetProperty method once for each axis and each property. Once this is complete, we can finally set our cooperative level and acquire the device so we can start retrieving input. This is illustrated in the following listing.

***Listing 7-14:*** *Setting axis properties*

```
procedure TfrmJoyTestBed.FormActivate(Sender: TObject);
var
  iCount: Integer;
  RangeProp: TDIPropRange;
  DataProp: TDIPropDWord;

    .
    .
    .
```

```
begin

    .
    .
    .

  {we must now set the range for each axis, so initialize a range
   property structure}
  RangeProp.diph.dwSize := SizeOf(TDIPropRange);
  RangeProp.diph.dwHeaderSize := SizeOf(TDIPropHeader);
  RangeProp.diph.dwHow := DIPH_BYOFFSET;
  RangeProp.lMin := -1000;
  RangeProp.lMax := 1000;

  {we must also set deadzones and saturations for each axis, so
   initialize a DWord property structure}
  DataProp.diph.dwSize := SizeOf(TDIPropDWord);
  DataProp.diph.dwHeaderSize := SizeOf(TDIPropHeader);
  DataProp.diph.dwHow := DIPH_BYOFFSET;

  {for each axis...}
  for iCount := 0 to NumAxes-1 do
  begin
    {set its range...}
    RangeProp.diph.dwObj := FAxisList[iCount];
    DXCheck( FDirectInputDevice.SetProperty(DIPROP_RANGE, RangeProp.diph) );

    {its deadzone... (this value is in 100ths of a percent}
    DataProp.dwData := 1000;
    DataProp.diph.dwObj := FAxisList[iCount];
    DXCheck( FDirectInputDevice.SetProperty(DIPROP_DEADZONE, DataProp.diph) );

    {and its saturation (this value is also in 100ths of a percent}
    DataProp.dwData := 9000;
    DXCheck( FDirectInputDevice.SetProperty(DIPROP_SATURATION, DataProp.diph));
  end;

    .
    .
    .


  {set the cooperative level}
  DXCheck( FDirectInputDevice.SetCooperativeLevel(Handle, DISCL_EXCLUSIVE or
                                             DISCL_FOREGROUND) );

  {finally, acquire the device so we can start retrieving information}
  DXCheck( FDirectInputDevice.Acquire );
  {enable the timer that retrieves the controller state}
  tmrJoyPoll.Enabled := TRUE;
end;
```

### *Reading Input Data*

Compared to setting up DirectInput for game controllers, actually reading their input data is rather simple.

Game controllers usually do not generate hardware interrupts. As such, Windows (and the device driver) is not informed that an input event has occurred on the device. Thus, for almost all game controllers, the Poll method must be called to instruct the driver to retrieve device information before the application can retrieve the device's state. The Poll method takes no parameters. If a game controller does not require polling, this method has no effect. Therefore, it's usually a good practice to always call the Poll method regardless of the game controller or its driver.

Once this is done, the application can call the GetDeviceState method, passing in a pointer to a TDIJoyState2 structure. Although you can use buffered data techniques, most applications can get by with retrieving immediate game controller data. The TDIJoyState2 structure is defined as:

```
TDIJoyState2 = packed record
  lX: Longint;                          // x-axis position
  lY: Longint;                          // y-axis position
  lZ: Longint;                          // z-axis position
  lRx: Longint;                         // x-axis rotation
  lRy: Longint;                         // y-axis rotation
  lRz: Longint;                         // z-axis rotation
  rglSlider: Array [0..1] of Longint;   // extra axes positions
  rgdwPOV: Array [0..3] of DWORD;       // POV directions
  rgbButtons: Array [0..127] of BYTE;   // 128 buttons
  lVX: Longint;                         // x-axis velocity
  lVY: Longint;                         // y-axis velocity
  lVZ: Longint;                         // z-axis velocity
  lVRx: Longint;                        // x-axis angular velocity
  lVRy: Longint;                        // y-axis angular velocity
  lVRz: Longint;                        // z-axis angular velocity
  rglVSlider: Array [0..1] of Longint;  // extra axes velocities
  lAX: Longint;                         // x-axis acceleration
  lAY: Longint;                         // y-axis acceleration
  lAZ: Longint;                         // z-axis acceleration
  lARx: Longint;                        // x-axis angular acceleration
  lARy: Longint;                        // y-axis angular acceleration
  lARz: Longint;                        // z-axis angular acceleration
  rglASlider: Array [0..1] of Longint;  // extra axes accelerations
  lFX: Longint;                         // x-axis force
  lFY: Longint;                         // y-axis force
  lFZ: Longint;                         // z-axis force
  lFRx: Longint;                        // x-axis torque
  lFRy: Longint;                        // y-axis torque
  lFRz: Longint;                        // z-axis torque
  rglFSlider: Array [0..1] of Longint;  // extra axes forces
end;
```

This rather large structure defines the state of every object on the game controller. The position and rotation of various axes is easily retrievable, as is the state of buttons, POVs, etc. The following listing illustrates how to retrieve the current state of a game controller.

***Listing 7-15:*** *Retrieving immediate game controller input data*

```
procedure TfrmJoyTestBed.tmrJoyPollTimer(Sender: TObject);
var
  DevState: TDIJoystate2;
  iCount: Integer;
begin
  {more often than not, game controllers do not generate hardware
   interrupts. thus, we have to poll the device driver in order to
   get the current state of the device.}
  FDirectInputDevice.Poll;

  {retrieve the state of all objects on the device}
  DXCheck( FDirectInputDevice.GetDeviceState(SizeOf(DevState), @DevState) );

  {we're assuming here that the game controller has an X and Y axis
   (as joysticks and gamepads do), so draw a crosshair}
  DrawCrossHair((DevState.lX + 1000) div 20, (DevState.lY + 1000) div 20);

  {draw slider bars for any other axes}
  for iCount := 2 to NumAxes-1 do
    case FAxisList[iCount] of
      DIJOFS_Z  : shpZBarPos.Width  := (DevState.lZ + 1000) div 20;
      DIJOFS_RX : shpRXBarPos.Width  := (DevState.lRx + 1000) div 20;
      DIJOFS_RY : shpRYBarPos.Width  := (DevState.lRy + 1000) div 20;
      DIJOFS_RZ : shpRZBarPos.Width  := (DevState.lRz + 1000) div 20;
    end;

  {if a POV is available (availability of which should probably be placed
   in a global variable as opposed to checking the enabled state of a
   label), then draw a crosshair}
  if Label9.Enabled then
    DrawPov(DevState.rgdwPOV[0]);

  {test the joystick buttons}
  for iCount := 0 to 127 do
  if ButtonLights[iCount] <> nil then
    if (DevState.rgbButtons[iCount] and $80) = $80 then
      ButtonLights[iCount].Brush.Color := clRed
    else
      ButtonLights[iCount].Brush.Color := clMaroon;
end;
```

# Summary

In this chapter, we discussed several techniques for retrieving user input data from various input devices. We examined both common Win32 API functions and their DirectInput counterparts for reading the state of keyboard, mice, and game controller devices. We also covered various techniques for retrieving this data, including immediate and buffered data as well as polling and event notification. When coding user input data routines using DirectInput or Win32 API functions, it is important to keep these points in mind:

■ Input is one of the three fundamental parts of a game, and as such is important to overall game enjoyment. Exactly how user input will be translated into game element manipulation is dependent on the game itself. Flight simulators need input that affects the direction of flight, or perhaps even the selection and use of a weapon. Strategy games, by contrast, need input that determines which token is selected and its direction of movement or combat.

■ Input devices go beyond the standard mouse and keyboard. There are now a wide variety of peripheral game controllers in all shapes and sizes. Rudder pedals, steering wheels, gamepads, throttles, and all manner of sundry and arcane input devices are now available, making some games much more enjoyable to play. Even the standard joystick has become incredibly complex, with many sporting impressive arrays of buttons, switches, sliders, and even tactile responses known as force feedback.

■ An important user input consideration is support for user configurable controls. Even though the developer has determined which input devices will be supported and how they interact with game elements, individual users may find this structure somewhat restrictive based on their particular preferences.

■ DirectInput is the DirectX component responsible for providing user input from all manner of input devices, such as keyboards, mice, and game controllers. DirectInput offers many features above and beyond what is available through the Win32 API. As with all DirectX components, DirectInput gives the developer more control over user input than the Windows API, while also providing an improvement in performance.

■ Similar to DirectDraw, DirectInput programming consists of creating a DirectInput object and several DirectInputDevice objects. The DirectInput object itself acts as a liaison between the application and input device drivers. Individual DirectInputDevice objects represent the application's interface directly to input hardware, or more specifically, that hardware's device driver.

■ Where DirectInput is concerned, a button is considered to be any switch that has an on and off position. There is no distinction made between buttons on a mouse, keyboard, or joystick. An axis has a range of positions where its value is affected by the physical movement of a device in some particular direction. Some axes can move an infinite distance in a particular direction, and are measured in relative values. Other axes can physically move only a specific distance, and are measured in absolute values.

■ Buffered data retrieval simulates the mechanism by which Windows reports input. Individual input events are stored in a buffer, which takes the form of an array of data structures containing the various axis movement values or button clicks. Immediate data retrieval does not report a stream of singular events, but returns the current state of the device at the time of the function call.

■ Polling involves checking the state of the input device at the time that the input is needed. Typically, this is performed in the game loop. Event notification, on the other hand, is very similar to event-driven programming. This is a mechanism by which DirectInput will notify the application when new input data is available, and is best paired with buffered data retrieval.

■ As discussed in the DirectDraw tutorial, a cooperative level determines how the application works with other applications. As with other DirectX components, DirectInput gives the developer a choice as to how the application will share input devices with other applications, in terms of who can gain access to the device and if input can be retrieved based on application focus. Bear in mind that Windows requires exclusive access to the keyboard at all times, so that functions such as Alt+Tab and Ctrl+Alt+Delete are always available. Thus, an application can only obtain non-exclusive access to the keyboard.

■ Once a device is set up, the application cannot receive input data until it instructs DirectInput that it is ready to do so. This process is known as acquiring the device. Bear in mind that a device can be forcibly unacquired by the application. This may happen when another application receives focus or acquires the device in exclusive mode.

■ Several steps are required in order to set up DirectInput and begin interfacing with user input devices. In general you must create the DirectInput object, enumerate input devices, create the input device, set the data format, set the cooperative level, set device properties, and then acquire the device.

■ While the steps required for initializing and setting up DirectInput and DirectInputDevices are similar for every device, exactly how the input data is retrieved and extracted varies from device to device. This will also depend on whether you will be using immediate data retrieval or buffered data retrieval. This leads to subtle nuances in which initialization steps are required, and how the data returned from certain methods is interpreted.

■ Retrieving keyboard data is the easiest. The GetAsyncKeyState Win32 API function could potentially be used if the full power of DirectInput was not needed. However, you would not be able to differentiate between left and right versions of certain keys, such as Shift or Ctrl.

■ Mouse data is best retrieved using a buffer coupled with event notification. This requires setting up a secondary thread and using critical sections to synchronize variable access. The Win32 API function GetCursorPos function could potentially be used instead, but this function reports absolute values relative to the screen.

■ Game controller data input retrieval is very complex. We must set up a custom data format, but this complexity results in support for a wider range of devices. We must also set up the range, deadzone, and saturation properties for each axis. We could use the joyGetPosEx function, but this function only supports up to six axes and 32 buttons, and has no support for force feedback.

# CHAPTER 8: *Force Feedback*

Cutting-edge computer games offer an entertainment experience very similar to Hollywood movies. Such games feature almost photo-realistic environments, complete with appropriate lighting, 3-D sound effects, and music to enhance the emotional impact. However, consider how much more realistic and immersive a gaming experience would be if you could feel the blow of your axe against an enemy's armor, or the resistance of gravity and air as you wheel your jet fighter through a tight turn. This is what force feedback technology is all about.

Force feedback allows the game developer to add the illusion of mass and momentum to game elements previously only represented as dots of colored light. Like sound and music, it adds an intangible realistic element to a game that could not be accomplished otherwise. Force feedback support appeared in DirectX 5, and since then, game manufacturers have slowly implemented force feedback support into their products. Like sound and music, no game absolutely requires force feedback in order to make it entertaining. On the other hand, unless you're making a game like Solitaire, it would be crazy to ignore the exciting functionality this new technology offers; it is certainly a requirement for action games to actively compete in the retail market.

The force feedback API is part of DirectInput. At the time of this writing, force feedback functionality is available primarily on joysticks and a few wheels, but the technology is designed to work with devices of any shape and size. The result is a very flexible yet complex system. For our purposes, we will focus our discussion of force feedback as it applies to joysticks, but keep in mind that the concepts to follow can be applied to any type of force feedback device.

***Tip:*** These examples were written and tested specifically on the Microsoft SideWinder® Force Feedback Pro joystick, but they should work on any force feedback device with an x- and y-axis.

# Features

Force feedback has no equivalent in the Win32 API world, and as such cannot be compared to any existing functionality. As we've discussed, the purpose of force feedback is to provide the user with tactile output based on conditions within the game world. This is accomplished through either an active push on one or more of the axes supported by the device, or through some form of resistance along those axes when the user manipulates the device. Considering this, DirectInput's force feedback functionality provides the following features of interest to game developers:

■ Several different standard effects representing a wide range of tactile responses

■ Device-specific effects implemented by the device driver (when available)

■ Modification of effects on the fly (when available)

■ Creation of customized effects

■ Triggered effects controlled by the device

In the following sections we will discuss how the Delphi game developer can take advantage of each of these features to create tactile feedback that provides a new level of realism to game environments.

# Functional Overview

In order to begin using force feedback, the application must already have an initialized IDirectInputDevice2 object. An elaborate data structure is then initialized depending on the type of effect desired. IDirectInputDevice2 uses this initialized data structure to create an IDirectInputEffect object.

The IDirectInputEffect object represents the developer's direct interface to the force feedback hardware. This is not to be confused with the functionality provided by the IDirectInputDevice2 object; IDirectInputDevice2 is responsible for communicating user input from the device, whereas IDirectInputEffect is responsible for outputting tactile feedback responses to the device. Through the IDirectInputEffect interface, the application can query the force feedback hardware's capabilities, start and stop the effect, modify the effect on the fly, and control other aspects of the force feedback hardware itself.

Once an effect is created, it must be downloaded to the device. This typically happens automatically, as we'll discuss below. The act of downloading an effect tells the driver to prepare the effect for playback. How this is accomplished is determined by the driver, but typically the effect's parameters are placed into hardware memory so that the device will not need to communicate with the system in response to axis movement and button presses. However, a device can only handle a finite number of effects, and may return a DIERR_DEVICEFULL error. The workaround is to simply unload another, hopefully unused, effect and then try again.

Once an effect is created, it must be explicitly started. Effects can play infinitely or for a specified amount of time, and can be stopped if necessary. Alternatively, when the effect is being created, it can be associated with a button on the device. The device driver will then start the effect when the button is pressed. Triggered effects such as this will stop when the effect duration has been reached or when the button is released, whichever comes first. This functionality is totally independent of the application. Some devices even support repeating an effect while the button is held down, perfect for re-creating the kickback of a machine gun or other automatic weapon.

# Basic Concepts

When discussing force feedback effects, it is necessary to understand several general concepts as they apply to the effect itself. These concepts define the action of the effect, such as its strength and direction. Such concepts include kinetic forces, conditions, magnitude, coefficient, gain, duration, sample period, axes, direction, and envelope.

## Kinetic Force

A kinetic force is an effect that actively pushes on one or more axes. This push can be in a single direction or in alternating directions such as occurs with periodic effects. This active push is applied regardless of the position or movement of the axis (or axes). An example of this is a push on the joystick in the direction of the user to simulate recoil from firing a rocket.

**kinetic force:** An active push on one or more axes on a force feedback device.

**Note:** Force feedback devices are required to have a safety feature installed that prevents the playback of effects unless the user is actively gripping the device. This helps avoid potential injury that might occur if the user is trying to pick up the device while a kinetic force effect is playing.

## Condition

Unlike a kinetic force, a condition is a resistance or force that is applied to one or more axes in response to their movement or position. For example, the self-centering effect that a force feedback joystick automatically exhibits is a condition that tries to move the stick back to its center position. Another example would be to apply a dampening effect to the stick in order to re-create the resistance of moving around in an underwater environment. There are currently four different types of conditions, which we'll cover in more detail shortly.

**condition:** A resistant force applied to one or more axes on a force feedback device in response to the movement or position of those axes.

## Magnitude

Magnitude is a measurement of the strength of a kinetic force, relative to the total maximum force that can be output by the device. The magnitude of a force can be expressed as an integer value between –10,000 and 10,000, where positive values represent a force in one direction and negative values represent the same force in the opposite direction. The DI_FFNOMINALMAX constant defined by the DInput unit, initialized to 10,000, represents the total maximum force that can be exerted by the device on any given axis. This constant allows the developer to define the magnitude of a force as a percentage of the total maximum force available on the device (i.e., DI_FFNOMINALMAX div 2 would be 50 percent of the maximum available force).

**magnitude:** A measurement of the strength of a kinetic force output by a force feedback device, relative to the total maximum force available on the device itself.

## Coefficient

Coefficient is conceptually similar to magnitude, except that it is a measurement of the strength of resistance to movement along an axis. Like magnitude, this value is expressed as an integer between –10,000 and 10,000, where positive values represent resistance and negative values represent acceleration (i.e., it has the effect of pulling along the direction of motion). Again, it is best to use the DI_FFNOMINALMAX constant to define a coefficient as a percentage of the total maximum force.

**coefficient:** A measurement of the strength of resistance output by a force feedback device in response to the movement of an axis, relative to the total maximum force available on the device itself.

**Note:** In the case of a spring condition (discussed later in this chapter), a negative coefficient has the effect of pushing the axis away from the defined neutral point.

## Duration

Duration defines how long the effect will play, measured in microseconds. The constant DI_SECONDS, found in the DInput unit, can be used to define the duration in terms of one-second intervals (or fractions thereof). The constant INFINITE can also be used to indicate an effect with no duration. This type of effect will play until explicitly stopped or the IDirectInputEffect object is freed. In the case of triggered effects, playback is stopped when the duration expires or the button is released.

**Tip:** An infinite duration is typically used for condition effects or periodic forces; it typically doesn't make sense to specify an infinite duration for a constant or ramp force.

## Sample Period

Sample period defines the interval between actual changes in the strength of a force, measured in microseconds. Setting this to a large value will cause the strength of the effect to be adjusted fewer times over the course of its duration, which may cause a ratcheting sensation. Setting this value to zero allows for the smoothest change in relative force strength.

## Gain

Gain acts as a scaling factor for magnitudes and coefficients. It is expressed as a value between 0 and 10,000, indicating the percentage by which to scale the magnitude or coefficient. For example, 10,000 indicates no scaling, whereas 5,000 indicates 50 percent of the specified magnitude or coefficient. Gain can be applied to the entire device or only to individual effects. The DI_FFNOMINALMAX constant can again be used here to easily define a scaling factor as a percentage of the nominal value.

**gain:** A scaling factor for magnitudes and coefficients, measured in hundredths of a percent.

**Note:** Use the SetProperty method of the IDirectInputDevice interface in order to set the gain for the entire device.

## Axes

Axes determine what axis (or axes) of movement on the force feedback device will be affected by the force feedback effect. This also indirectly determines the available directions for an effect, depending on how many axes will be affected by the force feedback output. Of course, the axes available are totally dependent on the type of device. For example, most force feedback joysticks allow output along the x and y axes, as shown below. Other devices, such as steering wheels, may define these axes differently. Axes can be identified by using the DIJOFS_* constants.

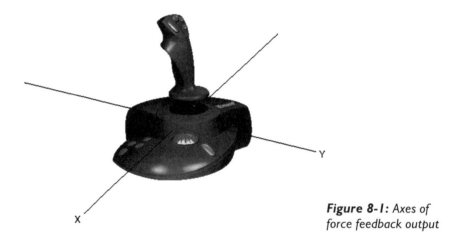

**Figure 8-1:** *Axes of force feedback output*

## Direction

Direction can be a complicated concept when it comes to force feedback. Bear in mind that the force feedback API was designed to work not only with such devices as joysticks, but with other devices like steering wheels, throttle controls, and devices that can move in three dimensions. In a nutshell, direction determines the bearing of an effect along an axis (or axes) when its magnitude or coefficient values are positive. Negative values act in the opposite of the defined direction.

Single axis directions are easily handled, as you can simply control the sign of the magnitude or coefficient in order to define the direction. In the case of multiple axes, however, there are three available coordinate systems: spherical, polar, and Cartesian. The Cartesian coordinate system may be useful if force feedback is being used in conjunction with Direct3D. The spherical coordinate system is necessary for defining the direction of an effect on three or more axes of movement. Since our discussion is focused on joystick programming, however, we'll use the polar coordinate system. The polar coordinate system is perhaps the easiest to use, as it requires only the compass direction of the force, measured in hundredths of a degree. The DI_DEGREES constant is defined in the DInput unit, and can be used to easily specify a direction in terms of degrees.

Bear in mind that the direction of a force is in terms of the direction from which the force originates. For example, a force from the north would push the stick toward the user, and would thus have a direction of zero. A force from the west, pushing the stick to the right, would have a direction of 90 * DI_DEGREES. The following illustration graphically explains the concept of direction as it applies to a joystick.

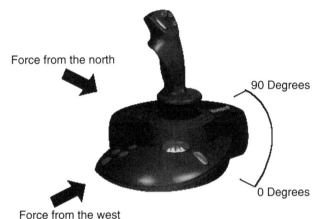

Force from the north

90 Degrees

0 Degrees

Force from the west

*Figure 8-2: Force feedback direction*

## Envelope

An envelope is a set of values that modify the magnitude of a force at the beginning and end of playback, and can be applied to all forces except conditions. This allows a developer to define the attack and fade of a force, like a musical note. We'll examine envelopes in greater detail later in the chapter.

**envelope:** A series of values that shape a force at the beginning and end of playback.

# Force Feedback Effects

Force feedback effects are divided into six different categories: conditions, constant forces, periodic forces, ramp forces, device-specific effects, and custom forces. Each one of these is defined by an overall basic effect structure, which describes certain global attributes for the effect such as duration and direction, and a more type-specific structure, which describes very specific effect attributes depending on its category. Some of these categories even have subtypes. This makes for a rather complex system, but it should be more than adequate for just about any tactile feedback desired.

## Base Effect Structure

All force feedback effects are defined by a primary structure called TDIEffect. This structure is used when creating the effect as well as modifying the effect after it has been created. This complex structure defines the overall parameters of the effect and includes members that hold other structures that further define the effect, and are dependent on the type of effect desired. The TDIEffect structure is defined as:

```
TDIEffect = packed record
  dwSize : DWORD;                        // the size of the structure, in bytes
  dwFlags : DWORD;                       // indicates the directional coordinate
                                         //    system and axes/button identification
  dwDuration : DWORD;                    // duration of the effect in microseconds
  dwSamplePeriod : DWORD;                // the sample period, in microseconds
  dwGain : DWORD;                        // the gain for the specific effect
  dwTriggerButton : DWORD;               // trigger button identifier
  dwTriggerRepeatInterval : DWORD;       // repetition interval, in microseconds
  cAxes : DWORD;                         // number of axes involved in the effect
  rgdwAxes : ^DWORD;                     // array of axis identifiers
  rglDirection : ^longint;               // array of direction bearings
  lpEnvelope : PDIEnvelope;              // pointer to a TDIEnvelope structure
  cbTypeSpecificParams : DWORD;          // the size of the structure in the
                                         //    lpvTypeSpecificParams member
  lpvTypeSpecificParams : pointer;       // pointer to type-specific data structure
end;
```

As usual with all DirectX data structures, the dwSize member should be set to SizeOf(TDIEffect). The dwFlags member indicates both the directional coordinate system as well as the method by which axes and buttons are to be identified. For our purposes, we'll use the values DIEFF_POLAR to indicate a polar coordinate system and DIEFF_OBJECTOFFSETS to indicate button and axis data format offsets (using the OR operator to combine them). Most of the other members, such as duration, sample period, and gain, correspond directly to the concepts covered earlier, and should be set accordingly. The dwTriggerButton member indicates the button that will start the effect. This member can be set to a button offset (i.e., DIJOFS_BUTTON1) or DIEB_NOTRIGGER, indicating that the effect is not triggered. Assigning a value to dwTriggerRepeatInterval will cause the effect to be repeated as long as the button is held down (if supported). The cAxes member should be set to the number of axes involved in the effect, and the rgdwAxes member should point to an array of DWORDs, with each member holding a DIJOFS_* constant for each individual axis. The rglDirection member is a pointer to an array of longints that define the direction of the effect. There must be cAxes members in this array, but for the polar coordinate system, the bearing is stored in the first member, and the last member (remember, we're only using two axes) is set to zero. The lpEnvelope member points to a TDIEnvelope structure, which we'll discuss in more detail shortly. Finally, the cbTypeSpecificParams should be set to the size, in bytes, of the data structure pointed to by the lpvTypeSpecificParams member. This data structure is dependent on the type of desired effect; we'll take a closer look at each effect type below, and examine their individual type-specific parameter data structures.

**Note:** If two or more effects are assigned to a button, the last one down-loaded to the device will be the one triggered.

***Supported Effect Parameters*** Unfortunately, some members of the TDIEffect structure may be unsupported by some drivers. For example, a specific driver may not allow an effect to be associated with a trigger, or it may not support repeated playback of triggered effects. However, the application can use the GetEffectInfo method of the IDirectInputDevice2 interface to determine which TDIEffect parameters are supported. The GetEffectInfo method is defined as:

```
function GetEffectInfo(
var pdei: TDIEffectInfoA;          // effect information structure
const rguid: TGUID                 // effect GUID
) : HResult;                       // returns a DirectX error code
```

The rguid parameter should be set to the GUID of the effect for which information is requested (these GUIDs are listed below when we get to creating the effect). The pdei parameter should be set to a variable of type TDIEffectInfoA. When this method returns, the TDIEffectInfoA structure will be initialized with all of the relevant information concerning the specified effect. The TDIEffectInfoA structure is defined as:

```
TDIEffectInfoA = packed record
  dwSize : DWORD;                        // size of the structure in bytes
  guid : TGUID;                          // the effect GUID
  dwEffType : DWORD;                     // effect type flags
  dwStaticParams : DWORD;                // supported parameter flags
  dwDynamicParams : DWORD;               // dynamically modifiable parameters
  tszName : array [0..MAX_PATH-1] of CHAR; // effect name
end;
```

The dwStaticParams member contains a series of flags that indicate which members of the TDIEffect structure are supported. These flags are listed in Table 8-1. If you combine each flag with the dwStaticParams member using a Boolean AND operation, you can easily determine which TDIEffect members are supported by the driver. However, it is not always necessary to determine if a specific member is supported or not. If a member of this structure is not supported, it will simply be ignored by the driver. Therefore, you could go ahead and assign values to specific members and never worry about getting an error when you create the effect. On the other hand, you'll probably need to know if an effect can be assigned to a trigger button and if this effect can be repeated if that is integral to game play, and find an appropriate alternative if this functionality is not supported.

*Table 8-1: Supported TDIEffect member flags*

| Flag | Supported TDIEffect Member |
|---|---|
| DIEP_DURATION | dwDuration |
| DIEP_SAMPLEPERIOD | dwSamplePeriod |
| DIEP_GAIN | dwGain |
| DIEP_TRIGGERBUTTON | dwTriggerButton |
| DIEP_TRIGGERREPEATINTERVAL | dwTriggerRepeatInterval |
| DIEP_AXES | cAxes, rgdwAxes |
| DIEP_DIRECTION | rglDirection |
| DIEP_ENVELOPE | lpEnvelope |

The dwSize member, of course, must be set to SizeOf(TDIEffectInfoA) before calling the GetEffectInfo method. The guid member contains the GUID of the effect, and the tszName member contains the name of the effect type. The dwEffType member will contain a series of DIEFT_* flags indicating the effect type. You may want to check this member, as if it contains the DIEFT_DEADBAND, DIEFT_FFATTACH, DIEFT_FFFADE, DIEFT_POSNEGCOEFFICIENTS, DIEFT_POSNEGSATURATION, or DIEFT_SATURATION flags, the effect supports the lDeadBand parameter (covered below under condition effects), the attack and fade envelope parameters, positive and negative coefficient values (covered below under condition effects), positive and negative saturation values (also covered below under conditions), and saturation of condition effects, respectively.

Incidentally, dwDynamicParams also contains a series of DIEP_* flags that indicate which members of the TDIEffect structure can be changed dynamically while the effect is playing. This allows an application to modify an effect on the fly to reflect changes in the game world or to create more complex effects. We'll look at an example of modifying an effect on the fly later in this chapter. The following listing demonstrates how the GetEffectInfo method can be used to determine which members of the TDIEffect structure are supported.

*Listing 8-1: Determining supported effect parameters*

```
var
  frmSupFxParams: TfrmSupFxParams;

  FDirectInput: IDirectInput;
  FDirectInputDevice: IDirectInputDevice2;

  {these are used to create our on-the-fly device data format}
  FDataFormat: TDIDataFormat;
```

```
            FDataFormatObjects: array[0..255] of TDIObjectDataFormat;
            FDataFormatGUIDs: array[0..255] of TGUID;

            {these just track present axes}
            FAxisList: array[0..255] of Integer;
            NumAxes: Integer;

implementation

uses DXTools, frmDevicesU;


function EnumInputDevs(var lpddi: TDIDeviceInstance; pvRef: Pointer): Integer;
                                                                      stdcall;
var
  TempGuid: PGuid;
begin
  {we must save this guid in a separate list for use later when we
   create the device}
  New(TempGuid);
  TempGuid^ := lpddi.guidInstance;

  {display device information}
  TStringList(pvRef).AddObject(lpddi.tszInstanceName+'-'+lpddi.tszProductName,
                               TObject(TempGuid));

  {continue enumeration}
  Result := 1;
end;


procedure SetDataFormat;

  function DIEnumDeviceObjectsProc(const peff: TDIDeviceObjectInstance;
    pvRef: Pointer): HRESULT; stdcall;
  begin
    {if the offset is not beyond the indicated data size... (useful if
     we were to use the TDIJoyState data structure instead) }
    if peff.dwOfs<FDataFormat.dwDataSize then
    begin
      {save the type GUID for this object}
      FDataFormatGUIDs[FDataFormat.dwNumObjs] := peff.guidType;

      {add the object information to our custom made
       data format}
      with FDataFormatObjects[FDataFormat.dwNumObjs] do
      begin
        pguid := @FDataFormatGUIDs[FDataFormat.dwNumObjs];
        dwOfs := peff.dwOfs;
        dwType := peff.dwType;
        dwFlags := 0;
```

```
      end;

      {if this object is an axis, store it in our axis list}
      if (peff.dwType and DIDFT_AXIS) > 0 then
      begin
        FAxisList[NumAxes] := peff.dwOfs;
        Inc(NumAxes);
      end;

      {increment the number of objects found}
      Inc(FDataFormat.dwNumObjs);
    end;

  {continue enumeration}
  Result := DIENUM_CONTINUE;
  end;

begin
  {enumerate all objects on this input device. this will build our custom data
   structure programmatically with the correct information for each object}
  FDirectInputDevice.EnumObjects(@DIEnumDeviceObjectsProc, nil, DIDFT_ALL);

  {set the data format for the input device}
  DXCheck( FDirectInputDevice.SetDataFormat(FDataFormat) );
end;

procedure TfrmSupFxParams.FormActivate(Sender: TObject);
var
  FJoyList: TStringList;
  iCount: Integer;

  TempDevice: IDirectInputDevice;

  RangeProp: TDIPropRange;
  DataProp: TDIPropDWord;

  EffectInfo: TDIEffectInfoA;
begin
  {create the DirectInput object}
  DirectInputCreate(hInstance, DIRECTINPUT_VERSION, FDirectInput, nil);

  {create a list to hold information on each available game controller}
  FJoyList := TStringList.Create;

  {enumerate attached game controllers}
  //*** may want to cull out only those with force feedback here
  FDirectInput.EnumDevices(DIDEVTYPE_JOYSTICK, EnumInputDevs, FJoyList,
                           DIEDFL_ATTACHEDONLY);

  {we'll add this information to a list box in a dialog box, and display this
   to the user so they can choose their desired input controller}
```

```
frmDevices := TfrmDevices.Create(Self);
for iCount := 0 to FJoyList.Count-1 do
  frmDevices.lbxJoyDevices.Items.Add(FJoyList[iCount]);
frmDevices.ShowModal;

{create the input device based on the input controller specified by the user}
DXCheck( FDirectInput.CreateDevice(PGUID(FJoyList.Objects[0])^,
                                   TempDevice, nil) );

{close this dialog box, and delete the list of GUIDs}
frmDevices.Release;
for iCount := 0 to FJoyList.Count-1 do
  Dispose(PGUID(FJoyList.Objects[0]));
FJoyList.Free;

{we need the new version of the input device interface, so retrieve it}
try
  DXCheck(TempDevice.QueryInterface(IDirectInputDevice2,FDirectInputDevice));
finally
  TempDevice := nil
end;

{now we need to begin creating the data format structure and setting the
 data format, so we must initialize the overall data format structure}
with FDataFormat do
begin
  dwFlags := DIDF_ABSAXIS;
  dwDataSize := SizeOf(TDIJoyState2);
  dwSize := SizeOf(FDataFormat);
  dwObjSize := SizeOf(TDIObjectDataFormat);
  dwNumObjs := 0;
  rgodf := @FDataFormatObjects;
end;

{create and set a data format specifically made for this device}
SetDataFormat;

{we must now set the range for each axis, so initialize a range
 property structure}
RangeProp.diph.dwSize := SizeOf(TDIPropRange);
RangeProp.diph.dwHeaderSize := SizeOf(TDIPropHeader);
RangeProp.diph.dwHow := DIPH_BYOFFSET;
RangeProp.lMin := -1000;
RangeProp.lMax := 1000;

{we must also set deadzones and saturations for each axis, so
 initialize a DWord property structure}
DataProp.diph.dwSize := SizeOf(TDIPropDWord);
DataProp.diph.dwHeaderSize := SizeOf(TDIPropHeader);
DataProp.diph.dwHow := DIPH_BYOFFSET;
```

```
{for each axis...}
for iCount := 0 to NumAxes-1 do
begin
  {set its range...}
  RangeProp.diph.dwObj := FAxisList[iCount];
  DXCheck( FDirectInputDevice.SetProperty(DIPROP_RANGE, RangeProp.diph) );

  {its deadzone... (this value is in 100ths of a percent)}
  DataProp.dwData := 1000;
  DataProp.diph.dwObj := FAxisList[iCount];
  DXCheck( FDirectInputDevice.SetProperty(DIPROP_DEADZONE, DataProp.diph) );

  {and its saturation (this value is also in 100ths of a percent)}
  DataProp.dwData := 9000;
  DXCheck( FDirectInputDevice.SetProperty(DIPROP_SATURATION,DataProp.diph));
end;

{set the cooperative level.}
DXCheck( FDirectInputDevice.SetCooperativeLevel(Handle, DISCL_EXCLUSIVE or
                                                DISCL_FOREGROUND) );

{finally, acquire the device so we can start retrieving information}
DXCheck( FDirectInputDevice.Acquire );

{initialize the effect information structure}
FillChar(EffectInfo, SizeOf(TDIEffectInfoA), 0);
EffectInfo.dwSize := SizeOf(TDIEffectInfoA);

{retrieve effect information for constant forces}
FDirectInputDevice.GetEffectInfo(EffectInfo, GUID_ConstantForce);

{begin displaying supported TDIEffect parameters}
lbxEffectInfo.Items.Add('Effect Name: '+EffectInfo.tszName);
lbxEffectInfo.Items.Add('');
lbxEffectInfo.Items.Add('Supported TDIeffect Members:');

if (EffectInfo.dwStaticParams and DIEP_DURATION) = DIEP_DURATION then
  lbxEffectInfo.Items.Add('    dwDuration');
if (EffectInfo.dwStaticParams and DIEP_SAMPLEPERIOD) =
    DIEP_SAMPLEPERIOD then
  lbxEffectInfo.Items.Add('    dwSamplePeriod');
if (EffectInfo.dwStaticParams and DIEP_GAIN) = DIEP_GAIN then
  lbxEffectInfo.Items.Add('    dwGain');
if (EffectInfo.dwStaticParams and DIEP_TRIGGERBUTTON) =
    DIEP_TRIGGERBUTTON then
  lbxEffectInfo.Items.Add('    dwTriggerButton');
if (EffectInfo.dwStaticParams and DIEP_TRIGGERREPEATINTERVAL) =
    DIEP_TRIGGERREPEATINTERVAL then
  lbxEffectInfo.Items.Add('    dwTriggerRepeatInterval');
if (EffectInfo.dwStaticParams and DIEP_AXES) = DIEP_AXES then
  lbxEffectInfo.Items.Add('    cAxes');
```

```
    if (EffectInfo.dwStaticParams and DIEP_DIRECTION) = DIEP_DIRECTION then
      lbxEffectInfo.Items.Add('      rglDirection');
    if (EffectInfo.dwStaticParams and DIEP_ENVELOPE) = DIEP_ENVELOPE then
      lbxEffectInfo.Items.Add('      lpEnvelope');
end;
```

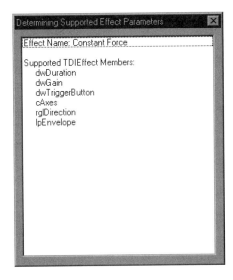

*Figure 8-3:* Microsoft SideWinder Force Feedback Pro supported parameters

## Conditions

As we've discussed, conditions are force feedback effects that respond to the position or motion of an axis. Condition effects are divided into four subtypes: spring, friction, damper, and inertia, all of which produce similar but subtly different tactile feedback sensations.

All condition effects use a TDICondition structure for their type-specific parameters. The TDICondition structure is defined as:

```
TDICondition = packed record
  lOffset : longint;                    // effect offset
  lPositiveCoefficient : longint;       // positive offset coefficient
  lNegativeCoefficient : longint;       // negative offset coefficient
  dwPositiveSaturation : DWORD;         // positive offset max force output
  dwNegativeSaturation : DWORD;         // negative offset max force output
  lDeadBand : longint;                  // inactive region
end;
```

Each condition subtype makes use of specific members of this structure, as we'll examine below. Unlike other effects, conditions can accept an array of TDICondition structures in the lpvTypeSpecificParams member of the TDIEffect structure. Each TDICondition structure defines condition parameters for each axis, with each TDICondition structure in the array matching up to the axis specified in the rgdwAxes member at the same index. When using an array of

TDICondition structures in this manner, the cbTypeSpecificParams member of the TDIEffect structure must be set to SizeOf(TDICondition) multiplied by the number of members in the array. We'll see an example of this later in the chapter.

***Spring*** A spring condition causes the device to exert a force on an axis when it is moved away from a central location. This central location is defined by the lOffset member. A value of 0 puts this point at the center of the axis. The lOffset member can be set to values ranging from –10,000 to 10,000 (or you can use the DI_FFNOMINALMAX constant again), with negative values to the left and positive values to the right, relative to the axis.

The lPositiveCoefficient indicates the strength of the force exerted on the axis when it is moved to the farthest position from the defined central location. This force is increased from 0 to lPositiveCoefficient as the axis is moved, giving a sensation of increased resistance as the axis is moved farther and farther away from the neutral point. Again, the lPositiveCoefficient can be set to values in the range –10,000 to 10,000, with positive values pushing the axis toward the central location and negative values pulling the axis away from the central location. If the driver supports negative coefficients, the lNegativeCoefficient member can be set to values within this range, which can be used to indicate a different amount of force to be applied when the axis is moved to the negative side of the central location. If negative coefficients are not supported, the positive coefficient is used.

The lDeadBand member defines an area around the central location in which the axis can move before any amount of force is applied. The saturation values define a similar area at the farthest distance of the axis, with the negative saturation value indicating an area on the negative side of the central location. As with coefficients, if negative saturation values are not supported, the positive saturation value is used. dwPositiveSaturation, dwNegativeSaturation, and lDeadBand members can be set in the range of 0 to 10,000, indicating a percentage of the range of travel in hundredths of a percent.

**Note:** The lDeadBand member may not be supported by some drivers.

***Friction*** The friction condition causes the device to exert a constant force on an axis as the axis is moved, regardless of its position. The lPositiveCoefficient member indicates the strength of this force, with values ranging from –10,000 to 10,000. Positive values indicate a push on the axis in the opposite direction of its movement, giving a resistant sensation, and negative values indicate a pull on the axis in the direction of its movement, giving an accelerating sensation. The lOffset, lNegativeCoefficient, dwPositiveSaturation, dwNegativeSaturation, and lDeadBand members are ignored.

***Damper*** The damper condition causes the device to exert a force on an axis in proportion to its velocity of movement. In other words, the faster the axis is moving, the more force is exerted. The lPositiveCoefficient member indicates the maximum force applied, with values in the range of –10,000 to 10,000. Like friction, positive values indicate a push on the axis in the opposite direction of its movement, and negative values indicate a pull on the axis in the direction of its movement.

The lOffset member is used to define a central point very similar to the spring condition. However, this central point is in relation to the axis' velocity, with a value of 0 indicating no velocity. A value other than 0 will cause a force to be applied to the axis even when it is not moving. The saturation and deadband parameters act in a similar manner in relation to velocity, and can be used to indicate a minimum and maximum velocity range in which force would be exerted on the axis.

***Inertia*** The inertia condition is very similar to the damper condition, except that force is exerted in proportion to the acceleration of an axis. In other words, no force will be applied if the axis is moving at a steady velocity. Like the damper condition, the lPositiveCoefficient member is used to indicate the maximum force, with positive values causing resistance and negative values causing acceleration. Also like the damper condition, the lOffset can be used to define a central point relative to the acceleration of the axis, with non-zero values generating acceleration. Saturation and deadband work in a similar manner.

## Constant Forces

A constant force is simply a push on an axis at a given magnitude. It is the simplest of all force feedback effects, and as such, it has a very simple type-specific data structure. Constant forces use a TDIConstantForce structure for their type-specific parameters, which is defined as:

```
TDIConstantForce = packed record
  lMagnitude : longint;                  // the strength of the force
end;
```

The only member of this structure, lMagnitude, indicates the strength of the force in the range –10,000 to 10,000. Positive values push the axis in the direction indicated by the rglDirection member of the TDIEffect structure; negative values push the axis in the opposite direction.

## Ramp Forces

A ramp force creates a steadily increasing or decreasing push on an axis over the duration specified by the dwDuration member of the TDIEffect structure. Ramp forces use a TDIRampForce structure for their type-specific parameters, which is defined as:

```
TDIRampForce = packed record
  lStart : longint;              // the starting force magnitude
  lEnd : longint;                // the ending force magnitude
end;
```

As with constant forces, the lStart and lEnd members indicate the strength of the force in the range –10,000 to 10,000, with positive values pushing the axis in the indicated direction and negative values pushing in the opposite direction.

**Note:** The dwDuration member of the TDIEffect structure cannot be set to INFINITE for ramp forces.

## Periodic Forces

A periodic effect causes a force to be applied to an axis in an oscillating manner. This is also known as a wave effect, as the magnitude and direction of a force changes over time. Similar to conditions, periodic forces are divided into sub-types: sine, triangle, sawtooth up, sawtooth down, and square. These produce alternating forces on an axis in a manner suggested by their name, as indicated by the following illustration.

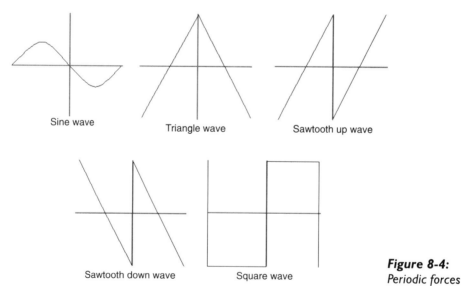

Sine wave Triangle wave Sawtooth up wave

Sawtooth down wave Square wave

*Figure 8-4:*
*Periodic forces*

All periodic effects use a TDIPeriodic structure for their type-specific parameters. The TDIPeriodic structure is defined as:

```
TDIPeriodic = packed record
  dwMagnitude : DWORD;           // the absolute force magnitude
  lOffset : longint;             // neutral wave position
  dwPhase : DWORD;               // force start position
```

```
   dwPeriod : DWORD;                            // wave frequency
end;
```

The dwMagnitude member indicates the absolute magnitude of the force to be exerted on the axis, in a range of 0 to 10,000. While the force is playing, this magnitude will steadily cycle between this value through the negative of this value and back again, creating a push on the axis in alternating directions. The manner in which this cycling takes effect is determined by the force type, as indicated in Figure 8-4. For example, a sine force would cycle the magnitude, and thus direction, of the force in a steady, smooth manner, where a square force would push the axis in alternating directions at the greatest magnitude in a very jarring, immediate manner.

The lOffset member indicates the center of the waveform in relation to the amount of force exerted, and will raise or lower the absolute magnitude of the force appropriately. For example, a value of zero indicates that the waveform will oscillate around zero magnitude. A value of –1,000, however, indicates that the waveform will oscillate around –1,000 magnitude, modifying the positive and negative magnitudes of the waveform accordingly. This is visually illustrated in the figure below.

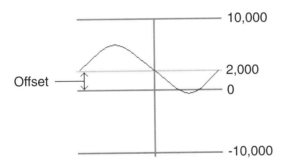

**Figure 8-5:** *Modifying the waveform offset*

**Note:** The sum of dwMagnitude and the absolute value of lOffset cannot exceed 10,000 or DI_FFNOMINALMAX.

The dwPhase member indicates the point at which the waveform should start, and is measured in hundredths of degrees. For example, setting this member to 9,000 for a sine periodic effect shifts the starting point by 90 degrees, and creates a cosine effect. This member is not always supported by all drivers. Finally, the dwPeriod member indicates the frequency of the waveform, measured in microseconds. For most drivers, this value cannot be set above one second, and it will have a minimum practical value based on how fast the motors in the device can reverse their direction.

## Device-Specific Effects

Many force feedback manufacturers provide several effects built in to the device driver. Many of these may be standard effect types, such as ramp forces, constant forces, or conditions, but some may be custom forces. Additionally, some of these forces may have adjustable type-specific parameters. If they have adjustable parameters and are not a custom force, you can use the type-specific parameters structure appropriate for the force type to modify the force during playback. Otherwise, you'll need to get the type-specific parameters structure from the driver documentation if you wish to change an adjustable device-specific custom force on the fly.

Of course, device-specific forces are going to change from device to device, but non-adjustable device-specific forces are perhaps the easiest to use as the application needs to know nothing about them. In order to use a device-specific effect, we must first retrieve a list of available effects; this is accomplished by using the EnumEffects method of the IDirectInputDevice2 interface. The EnumEffects method is defined as:

```
function EnumEffects(
lpCallback: TDIEnumEffectsCallbackA;    // a pointer to the callback function
pvRef: pointer;                          // application-specific data
dwEffType: DWORD                         // flag affecting enumeration
) : HResult;                             // returns a DirectX error code
```

The pvRef parameter is simply a pointer to application-specific data, which will be passed to the callback function. The dwEffType parameter contains a DIEFT_* flag which determines what type of effects are to be enumerated. In our case, we'll use the DIEFT_HARDWARE flag to indicate that we want only hardware-specific effects. The lpCallback parameter is a pointer to the callback function. The callback function itself must be defined as:

```
function TDIEnumEffectsCallbackA(
var pdei: TDIEffectInfoA;          // a TDIEffectInfoA structure
pvRef: pointer                     // a pointer to application-specific data
) : BOOL; stdcall;                 // returns TRUE or FALSE
```

The pdei parameter contains an initialized TDIEffectInfoA structure that has all of the pertinent information about the enumerated effect. In particular, the GUID member of this structure contains the GUID for the enumerated effect, which will need to be recorded for subsequent use when the effect is created. The pvRef parameter simply contains a pointer to the application-defined data specified when the EnumEffects method was called. This callback function should return TRUE to continue enumeration or FALSE to cancel it. Listing 8-2 demonstrates how to use the EnumEffects method to enumerate all device-specific effects that do not have any adjustable type-specific parameters.

*Listing 8-2: Enumerating device-specific effects*

```
var
  FDirectInput: IDirectInput;
  FDirectInputDevice: IDirectInputDevice2;

    .
    .
    .

implementation

uses DXTools, frmDevicesU;

    .
    .
    .

function EnumEffects(var pdei: TDIEffectInfoA; pvRef: pointer) : Integer; stdcall;
begin
  {filter out any effects that have adjustable type-specific parameters}
  if (pdei.dwStaticParams and DIEP_TYPESPECIFICPARAMS) =
      DIEP_TYPESPECIFICPARAMS then
  begin
    Result := 1;
    Exit;
  end;

  {add the name of the effect to the list box}
  frmJoyTestBed.lbxDevEffects.Items.Add(pdei.tszName);

  {continue enumeration}
  Result := 1;
end;

procedure TfrmEnumDevEffects.FormActivate(Sender: TObject);
begin

    .
    .
    .

  {enumerate all hardware-specific effects}
  FDirectInputDevice.EnumEffects(EnumEffects, nil, DIEFT_HARDWARE);
end;
```

**Figure 8-6:** *Microsoft SideWinder Force Feedback Pro device effects*

Like all effects, you'll use a TDIEffect structure when creating device-specific effects. However, some effects may have default values that will be used by the driver whenever certain specific members of the TDIEffect structure are set to a particular value. For example, the Microsoft SideWinder Force Feedback Pro joystick will use default values for the sample period and duration if the dwSamplePeriod and dwDuration members of the TDIEffect structure are set to 1000. Other devices will probably use different values, and may require delving into the driver documentation.

## Custom Forces

If none of the standard effect types provide the tactile feedback sensation desired, you can attempt to create it using a custom force. A custom force is little more than an array of magnitudes. It replays this array of magnitudes as constant forces; each element is played in sequence at a constant interval and in the same direction (which can be reversed by negative magnitudes). Custom forces use the TDICustomForce structure for their type-specific parameters, which is defined as:

```
TDICustomForce = packed record
  cChannels : DWORD;              // number of channels
  dwSamplePeriod : DWORD;         // sample period
  cSamples : DWORD;               // number of elements in sample array
  rglForceData : ^longint;        // pointer to the array of samples
end;
```

The cChannels member indicates how many axes are involved in the force, and results in each sample in the samples array being rotated amongst the axes (i.e., in the case of two axes and a cChannels setting of 2, element 1 applies to the first axis, element 2 to the second, element 3 to the first, etc.). This functionality may not be supported by all drivers.

The dwSamplePeriod member is very similar to the dwSamplePeriod member of the TDIEffect structure. The dwSamplePeriod member of the TDICustomForce structure indicates how long each element in the samples array will play, whereas the dwSamplePeriod in the TDIEffect structure indicates how long DirectInput waits before recalculating the force output by the device. Most devices do not support the dwSamplePeriod member of the TDICustomForce structure, and instead use the dwSamplePeriod member of the TDIEffect structure to determine how long to play each sample. In most cases, both members should be set to the same value to avoid any confusing behavior.

The cSamples member should be set to the number of elements in the array, which is pointed to by the rglForceData member. This array contains a series of longints that define the magnitudes in the range –10,000 to 10,000.

**Note:** Applying an envelope to a custom force may not be supported by all drivers.

# Creating Effects

As usual, a specific series of steps must be taken by the application in order to create a force feedback effect and prepare it for playback. Some of these steps may be optional depending on certain properties of the effect. In general, a force feedback effect is initialized and used by performing the following steps:

■ Create and acquire the DirectInput device

■ Query for force feedback support

■ Initialize a TDIEffect structure and the appropriate type-specific parameters structure

■ Create the effect object

■ Download the effect (sometimes optional)

■ Start the effect (sometimes optional)

■ Stop the effect (sometimes optional)

## Create and Acquire the DirectInput Device

Force feedback is a subsystem of DirectInput. As such, an initialized IDirectInputDevice2 interface must be created before any force feedback functionality can be utilized. Please refer to Chapter 7, Input Techniques, for a detailed explanation of creating an IDirectInputDevice2 object. Specifically, we'll be using the code from that chapter for communicating with the joystick. Other game controllers will function similarly.

## Query for Force Feedback Support

While you could certainly require the user to have a force feedback joystick installed before using your application, it would be much wiser to allow input from any game controller attached to the system, and use force feedback only when it was available on the device. In order to determine if a device supports force feedback, we must call the GetCapabilities method of the IDirectInputDevice2 interface. This method is described in the Input Techniques chapter, but for the sake of completeness, its definition is reprinted here:

```
function GetCapabilities(
var lpDIDevCaps: TDIDevCaps              // a TDIDevCaps structure
): HResult;                              // returns a DirectX error code
```

The only parameter to this method is a pointer to a TDIDevCaps structure. Again, for the sake of completeness, it is defined as:

```
TDIDevCaps = packed record
  dwSize: DWORD;                         // the size of the structure
  dwFlags: DWORD;                        // device flags
  dwDevType: DWORD;                      // device type identifier
  dwAxes: DWORD;                         // number of axes
  dwButtons: DWORD;                      // number of buttons
  dwPOVs: DWORD;                         // number of POVs
  dwFFSamplePeriod: DWORD;               // force feedback sample period
  dwFFMinTimeResolution: DWORD;          // force feedback time resolution
  dwFirmwareRevision: DWORD;             // firmware version
  dwHardwareRevision: DWORD;             // hardware version
  dwFFDriverVersion: DWORD;              // device driver version
end;
```

The only member we're concerned with at this point is the dwFlags member. If this member contains the flag DIDC_FORCEFEEDBACK, then we know that this device supports force feedback functionality. Incidentally, we can check for other DIDC_* flags to determine if the device supports such force feedback parameters as attack and fade (which refer to envelopes), deadband, negative coefficients and saturations, etc.

## Initialize a TDIEffect Structure and the Type-Specific Parameters Structure

Now that we have a device and we know it supports force feedback, it is time to define the type of effect we wish to create. This is accomplished by initializing a TDIEffect structure and a type-specific parameters structure appropriate for the desired effect.

The first thing we should do is initialize the type-specific parameters structure. For example, if we were creating a periodic effect, we would need a TDIPeriodic structure, initialized in the following manner:

```
PeriodicInfo.dwMagnitude := DI_FFNOMINALMAX;
PeriodicInfo.lOffset := 0;
PeriodicInfo.dwPhase := 0;
PeriodicInfo.dwPeriod := DI_SECONDS div 20;
```

This indicates that we want a periodic effect that uses the maximum magnitude available on the device with no offset or phase shift and a relatively quick frequency. This will result in a vibrating effect, which we could potentially use to portray the feel of a powerful weapon such as a chainsaw or machine gun.

***Tip:*** Remember that the overall strength of any effect will be scaled by the gain set for the device.

Next, we need to define the axes on which this effect will be played. We're using the joystick, so we'll indicate that the effect should use both the x- and y-axis. We'll use a small array of DWORDs, indicating the axes themselves using DIJOFS_* flags. We'll also indicate the direction of the effect. In this case, we'll be using the polar coordinate system, so we need a small array of longints (with as many elements as there are in the axis array). We simply need to indicate only the compass bearing of the desired direction in the first element, and set the last element to zero. This is accomplished like so:

```
AxisArray[0] := DIJOFS_X;
AxisArray[1] := DIJOFS_Y;

DirArray[0] := 180*DI_DEGREES;
DirArray[1] := 0;
```

With this completed, we need to initialize the TDIEffect structure. For example:

```
EffectInfo.dwSize := SizeOf(TDIEffect);
EffectInfo.dwFlags := DIEFF_OBJECTOFFSETS or DIEFF_POLAR;
EffectInfo.dwDuration := INFINITE;
EffectInfo.dwSamplePeriod := 0;
EffectInfo.dwGain := DI_FFNOMINALMAX;
EffectInfo.dwTriggerButton := DIJOFS_BUTTON0;
EffectInfo.dwTriggerRepeatInterval := INFINITE;
EffectInfo.cAxes := 2;
EffectInfo.rgdwAxes := @AxisArray;
EffectInfo.rglDirection := @DirArray;
EffectInfo.lpEnvelope := nil;
EffectInfo.cbTypeSpecificParams := SizeOf(TDIPeriodic);
EffectInfo.lpvTypeSpecificParams := @PeriodicInfo;
```

Here, we've indicated that we have an effect of infinite duration, and that we'll be using a polar coordinate system with device objects indicated by offsets. We've set the gain to maximum, so our effect will play with the strongest possible force available on the device (scaled by any gain set for the device itself). We've hooked the effect up to button 0 on the device, so it will automatically play when the user presses the button. A trigger repeat interval of infinite will really have no effect, as the effect will automatically continue to play until the button is released because of the infinite duration. We've also indicated the axes and direction, and we set up the cbTypeSpecificParams and lpvTypeSpecificParams members to indicate the size of and point to our type-specific parameters structure, respectively.

## Create the Effect Object

Now that the effect is completely defined, it needs to be created. The CreateEffect method of the IDirectInputDevice2 interface is used to generate an initialized IDirectInputEffect object. The CreateEffect method is defined as:

```
function CreateEffect(
const rguid: TGUID;              // the effect type guid
lpeff: PDIEffect;                // pointer to a TDIEffect structure
var ppdeff: IDirectInputEffect;  // returns an IDirectInputEffect object
punkOuter: IUnknown              // COM aggregation
) : HResult;                     // returns a DirectX error code
```

The first parameter takes a GUID for the type of effect to be created. This can be either a predefined GUID for standard effects (listed below) or a GUID obtained from calling the EnumEffects method. The second parameter takes a pointer to the TDIEffect structure we initialized above. The third parameter takes a pointer to the IDirectInputEffect object, which will be instantiated when the method returns. The final parameter is used for COM aggregation and should be set to nil.

*Table 8-2:* Predefined effect GUIDs

| GUID | Description |
|---|---|
| GUID_ConstantForce | Constant forces |
| GUID_RampForce | Ramp forces |
| GUID_Square | Square wave periodic forces |
| GUID_Sine | Sine wave periodic forces |
| GUID_Triangle | Triangle wave periodic forces |
| GUID_SawtoothUp | Sawtooth up wave periodic forces |
| GUID_SawtoothDown | Sawtooth down wave periodic forces |
| GUID_Spring | Spring conditions |
| GUID_Damper | Damper conditions |

**Table 8-2:** *Predefined effect GUIDs* (cont.)

| GUID | Description |
|---|---|
| GUID_Inertia | Inertia conditions |
| GUID_Friction | Friction conditions |
| GUID_CustomForce | Custom forces |

## Download the Effect

Once an effect is created, it must be downloaded into the device before it can be played. Downloading an effect is accomplished by calling the Download method of the IDirectInputEffect interface, which is defined as:

```
function Download : HResult;                // returns a DirectX error code
```

Now, it is not always necessary to download an effect. If the input device is in an acquired state when the effect is created, it is downloaded automatically. It is also downloaded automatically whenever the Start method is called (see below). For some effects, such as a triggered effect that was created before the device was acquired, the Download method must be used (as the Start method will not be called for triggered effects). Also, there is a little bit of a lag when an effect is initially downloaded, so explicitly downloading an effect before gameplay starts may reduce any detectable pause the first time an effect is to be played.

As discussed earlier, a DIERR_DEVICEFULL error may be returned when using a force feedback effect. This indicates that the device has reached its maximum number of downloadable force feedback effects, and room must be created before a new effect can be used. An existing effect can be unloaded from a device by calling the Unload method of the IDirectInputEffect interface, which is defined as:

```
function Unload : HResult;  // returns a DirectX error code
```

It is possible to use the DIPROP_FFLOAD flag with the GetProperty method of the IDirectInputDevice2 interface to retrieve the memory load for the device. You'll need to use a TDIPropDWORD structure, and upon returning, the dwData member of this structure will contain a value in the range of 0 to 100, indicating the percentage of device memory in use. Checking this value before downloading a new effect may give you some indication as to whether or not the device will be able to hold the new effect without unloading an existing one.

**Note:** If a device is unacquired (as would happen when another application gained focus), all effects are automatically unloaded. Effects should be downloaded again when the device is reacquired, especially triggered effects for which the Start method will never be called.

## Start the Effect

Once the effect is downloaded, it can be played. Triggered effects are started whenever the specified button is pressed, but non-triggered effects must be explicitly told to begin playing. This is accomplished by calling the Start method of the IDirectInputEffect interface. Note that the input device must be acquired at the exclusive cooperative level before the Start method will succeed. The Start method is defined as:

```
function Start(
dwIterations: DWORD;            // number of times to repeat the effect
dwFlags: DWORD                  // playback flags
) : HResult;                    // returns a DirectX error code
```

The dwIterations parameter indicates how many times to play the effect. This parameter can be set to a positive integer value or to INFINITE, indicating it will continue playing until explicitly stopped. Of course, for effects that have a defined duration of INFINITE, the dwIterations parameter is effectively useless, and some devices do not even support multiple iterations.

The dwFlags parameter indicates how the effect should be played on the device. By default, an effect will be mixed with other effects currently playing on the device when it is started. Setting this flag to DIES_SOLO will stop all other currently playing effects before playing the new effect. The DIES_NODOWNLOAD flag can also be used to indicate that the effect should not automatically be downloaded. This parameter can be set to zero or any combination of these two flags.

**Note:** If the effect is already playing when Start is called, it will stop and be restarted from the beginning.

## Stop the Effect

Effects with a finite duration or those associated with a button will automatically stop when the duration has been reached or the button is released. However, some effects, such as those explicitly started with an infinite duration, will continue to play until the device is unacquired. Sometimes, it may be necessary to stop an effect, and this is where the Stop method of the IDirectInputEffect interface comes in. It is defined as:

```
function Stop : HResult;               // returns a DirectX error code
```

## Case Study

Creating force feedback effects, while somewhat confusing, isn't quite as complicated as other DirectX subsystems. The following listing is a case study example which demonstrates how to create each type of effect. While not particularly robust, this example should serve to demonstrate how the above steps are followed for each effect type.

**Listing 8-3:** *Creating force feedback effects*

```
var

    .
    .
    .

  {these hold all of the different effects}
  PeriodicEffect,
  RampEffect,
  ConstantEffect,
  ConditionEffect,
  DeviceEffect,
  CustomEffect: IDirectInputEffect;

    .
    .
    .

  {global effect info structures}
  AxisArray: array[0..1] of DWORD;
  DirArray: array[0..1] of longint;
  EffectInfo: TDIEffect;

implementation

uses DXTools, frmDevicesU;

    .
    .
    .

function EnumEffects(var pdei: TDIEffectInfoA; pvRef: pointer) : Integer; stdcall;
var
  TempGuid: PGuid;
begin
  {filter out any effects that have adjustable type-specific parameters}
  if (pdei.dwStaticParams and DIEP_TYPESPECIFICPARAMS) =
      DIEP_TYPESPECIFICPARAMS then
  begin
    Result := 1;
    Exit;
  end;

  {create a new guid and save the guid info}
  New(TempGuid);
```

```
    TempGuid^ := pdei.guid;

    {add the name of the effect and its guid to the list box}
    frmEffectTest.lbxDevEffects.Items.AddObject(pdei.tszName, TObject(TempGuid));

    {continue enumeration}
    Result := 1;
end;

    .
    .
    .

procedure TfrmEffectTest.FormActivate(Sender: TObject);
begin

    .
    .
    .

    {set the cooperative level.}
    DXCheck( FDirectInputDevice.SetCooperativeLevel(Handle, DISCL_EXCLUSIVE
                                                    or DISCL_FOREGROUND) );

    {finally, acquire the device so we can start retrieving information}
    DXCheck( FDirectInputDevice.Acquire );

    {initialize the global axis array. we'll set it up to affect the
     X and Y axis of a joystick}
    AxisArray[0] := DIJOFS_X;
    AxisArray[1] := DIJOFS_Y;

    {indicate the direction of the effects. we'll be using polar coordinates
     so we'll indicate a 180 degree direction}
    DirArray[0] := 180*DI_DEGREES;
    DirArray[1] := 0;

    {enumerate all hardware-specific effects}
    FDirectInputDevice.EnumEffects(EnumEffects, nil, DIEFT_HARDWARE);
end;

procedure TfrmEffectTest.btnPeriodicClick(Sender: TObject);
var
    PeriodicInfo: TDIPeriodic;
begin
    {turn off the device effects list box and reset the force feedback device}
    lbxDevEffects.Visible := FALSE;
    FDirectInputDevice.SendForceFeedbackCommand(DISFFC_RESET);

    {set up our periodic effect parameters}
    PeriodicInfo.dwMagnitude := DI_FFNOMINALMAX;
```

```
      PeriodicInfo.lOffset := 0;
      PeriodicInfo.dwPhase := 0;
      PeriodicInfo.dwPeriod := DI_SECONDS div 20;

      {set up general parameters for the periodic effect}
      EffectInfo.dwSize := SizeOf(TDIEffect);
      EffectInfo.dwFlags := DIEFF_OBJECTOFFSETS or DIEFF_POLAR;
      EffectInfo.dwDuration := INFINITE;                  // repeat indefinitely
      EffectInfo.dwSamplePeriod := 0;
      EffectInfo.dwGain := DI_FFNOMINALMAX;
      EffectInfo.dwTriggerButton := DIJOFS_BUTTON0;    // tie it to button 0
      EffectInfo.dwTriggerRepeatInterval := INFINITE;
      EffectInfo.cAxes := 2;
      EffectInfo.rgdwAxes := @AxisArray;
      EffectInfo.rglDirection := @DirArray;
      EffectInfo.lpEnvelope := nil;
      EffectInfo.cbTypeSpecificParams := SizeOf(TDIPeriodic);
      EffectInfo.lpvTypeSpecificParams := @PeriodicInfo;

      {create the periodic effect}
      FDirectInputDevice.CreateEffect(GUID_sine, @EffectInfo, PeriodicEffect, nil);
    end;

    procedure TfrmEffectTest.btnRampClick(Sender: TObject);
    var
      RampInfo: TDIRampForce;
    begin
      {turn off the device effects list box and reset the force feedback device}
      lbxDevEffects.Visible := FALSE;
      FDirectInputDevice.SendForceFeedbackCommand(DISFFC_RESET);

      {set up our ramp effect parameters}
      RampInfo.lStart := -DI_FFNOMINALMAX;
      RampInfo.lEnd := DI_FFNOMINALMAX;

      {set up general parameters for the ramp effect}
      EffectInfo.dwSize := SizeOf(TDIEffect);
      EffectInfo.dwFlags := DIEFF_OBJECTOFFSETS or DIEFF_POLAR;
      EffectInfo.dwDuration := DI_SECONDS div 2;       // half second duration
      EffectInfo.dwSamplePeriod := 0;
      EffectInfo.dwGain := DI_FFNOMINALMAX;
      EffectInfo.dwTriggerButton := DIJOFS_BUTTON0;    // tie it to button 0
      EffectInfo.dwTriggerRepeatInterval := 0;
      EffectInfo.cAxes := 2;
      EffectInfo.rgdwAxes := @AxisArray;
      EffectInfo.rglDirection := @DirArray;
      EffectInfo.lpEnvelope := nil;
      EffectInfo.cbTypeSpecificParams := SizeOf(TDIRampForce);
      EffectInfo.lpvTypeSpecificParams := @RampInfo;

      {create the ramp effect}
```

```
    FDirectInputDevice.CreateEffect(GUID_RampForce, @EffectInfo, RampEffect,nil);
end;

procedure TfrmEffectTest.btnConstantClick(Sender: TObject);
var
  ConstantInfo: TDIConstantForce;
begin
  {turn off the device effects list box and reset the force feedback device}
  lbxDevEffects.Visible := FALSE;
  FDirectInputDevice.SendForceFeedbackCommand(DISFFC_RESET);

  {set up our constant effect parameters}
  ConstantInfo.lMagnitude := DI_FFNOMINALMAX;

  {set up general parameters for the constant effect}
  EffectInfo.dwSize := SizeOf(TDIEffect);
  EffectInfo.dwFlags := DIEFF_OBJECTOFFSETS or DIEFF_POLAR;
  EffectInfo.dwDuration := DI_SECONDS div 2;         // half second duration
  EffectInfo.dwSamplePeriod := 0;
  EffectInfo.dwGain := DI_FFNOMINALMAX;
  EffectInfo.dwTriggerButton := DIJOFS_BUTTON0;      // tie it to button 0
  EffectInfo.dwTriggerRepeatInterval := 0;
  EffectInfo.cAxes := 2;
  EffectInfo.rgdwAxes := @AxisArray;
  EffectInfo.rglDirection := @DirArray;
  EffectInfo.lpEnvelope := nil;
  EffectInfo.cbTypeSpecificParams := SizeOf(TDIConstantForce);
  EffectInfo.lpvTypeSpecificParams := @ConstantInfo;

  {create the constant effect}
  FDirectInputDevice.CreateEffect(GUID_ConstantForce, @EffectInfo,
                                  ConstantEffect, nil);
end;

procedure TfrmEffectTest.btnConditionClick(Sender: TObject);
var
  ConditionInfo: array[0..1] of TDICondition;
  DirArray: array[0..1] of longint;
begin
  {turn off the device effects list box and reset the force feedback device}
  lbxDevEffects.Visible := FALSE;
  FDirectInputDevice.SendForceFeedbackCommand(DISFFC_RESET);

  {for a condition, we don't really want a direction, so empty
   the direction array}
  DirArray[0] := 0;
  DirArray[1] := 0;

  {set up our condition effect parameters for the first axis}
  ConditionInfo[0].lOffset := 0;
  ConditionInfo[0].lPositiveCoefficient := DI_FFNOMINALMAX;
```

```
    ConditionInfo[0].lNegativeCoefficient := DI_FFNOMINALMAX;
    ConditionInfo[0].dwPositiveSaturation := 0;
    ConditionInfo[0].dwNegativeSaturation := 0;
    ConditionInfo[0].lDeadBand := 0;

    {set up our condition effect parameters for the second axis}
    ConditionInfo[1].lOffset := 0;
    ConditionInfo[1].lPositiveCoefficient := DI_FFNOMINALMAX;
    ConditionInfo[1].lNegativeCoefficient := DI_FFNOMINALMAX;
    ConditionInfo[1].dwPositiveSaturation := 0;
    ConditionInfo[1].dwNegativeSaturation := 0;
    ConditionInfo[1].lDeadBand := 0;

    {set up general parameters for the condition effect}
    EffectInfo.dwSize := SizeOf(TDIEffect);
    EffectInfo.dwFlags := DIEFF_OBJECTOFFSETS or DIEFF_POLAR;
    EffectInfo.dwDuration := INFINITE;                 // infinite duration
    EffectInfo.dwSamplePeriod := 0;
    EffectInfo.dwGain := DI_FFNOMINALMAX;
    EffectInfo.dwTriggerButton := DIEB_NOTRIGGER;      // not tied to a button
    EffectInfo.dwTriggerRepeatInterval := 0;
    EffectInfo.cAxes := 2;
    EffectInfo.rgdwAxes := @AxisArray;
    EffectInfo.rglDirection := @DirArray;
    EffectInfo.lpEnvelope := nil;
    {notice that here we've got to indicate the size of the entire array}
    EffectInfo.cbTypeSpecificParams := 2*SizeOf(TDICondition);
    EffectInfo.lpvTypeSpecificParams := @ConditionInfo;

    {create the condition effect}
    FDirectInputDevice.CreateEffect(GUID_Friction, @EffectInfo, ConditionEffect,
                                    nil);

    {start the condition effect, killing all other effects currently playing}
    ConditionEffect.Start(1, DIES_SOLO);
end;

procedure TfrmEffectTest.btnDeviceClick(Sender: TObject);
begin
  {simply make the device effects list box visible}
  lbxDevEffects.Visible := TRUE;
end;

procedure TfrmEffectTest.lbxDevEffectsClick(Sender: TObject);
begin
  if lbxDevEffects.ItemIndex > -1 then
  begin
    {reset the force feedback device}
    FDirectInputDevice.SendForceFeedbackCommand(DISFFC_RESET);

    {set up general parameters for the device-specific effect}
```

```
          EffectInfo.dwSize := SizeOf(TDIEffect);
          EffectInfo.dwFlags := DIEFF_OBJECTOFFSETS or DIEFF_POLAR;
          EffectInfo.dwDuration := DI_SECONDS*2;            // half second duration
          EffectInfo.dwSamplePeriod := 0;
          EffectInfo.dwGain := DI_FFNOMINALMAX;
          EffectInfo.dwTriggerButton := DIJOFS_BUTTON0;    // tied to button 0
          EffectInfo.dwTriggerRepeatInterval := 0;
          EffectInfo.cAxes := 2;
          EffectInfo.rgdwAxes := @AxisArray;
          EffectInfo.rglDirection := @DirArray;
          EffectInfo.lpEnvelope := nil;
          {we only play effects that do not have adjustable type-specific parameters,
           so we indicate such in the TDIEffect structure}
          EffectInfo.cbTypeSpecificParams := 0;
          EffectInfo.lpvTypeSpecificParams := nil;

          {create the device-specific effect}
          FDirectInputDevice.CreateEffect(PGuid(lbxDevEffects.Items.Objects
                     [lbxDevEffects.ItemIndex])^, @EffectInfo, DeviceEffect, nil);
     end;
end;

procedure TfrmEffectTest.btnCustomClick(Sender: TObject);
var
  CustomInfo: TDICustomForce;
  MagnitudeArray: array[0..3] of longint;
begin
  {turn off the device effects list box and reset the force feedback device}
  lbxDevEffects.Visible := FALSE;
  FDirectInputDevice.SendForceFeedbackCommand(DISFFC_RESET);

  {set up our array of magnitudes for the custom effect. this will create
   an increasing oscillation}
  MagnitudeArray[0] := -DI_FFNOMINALMAX div 4;
  MagnitudeArray[1] := DI_FFNOMINALMAX div 2;
  MagnitudeArray[2] := 0-(DI_FFNOMINALMAX div 4) * 3;
  MagnitudeArray[3] := DI_FFNOMINALMAX;

  {set up our custom effect parameters}
  CustomInfo.cChannels := 1;
  CustomInfo.dwSamplePeriod := 100000;
  CustomInfo.cSamples := 4;
  CustomInfo.rglForceData := @MagnitudeArray;

  {set up general parameters for the custom effect}
  EffectInfo.dwSize := SizeOf(TDIEffect);
  EffectInfo.dwFlags := DIEFF_OBJECTOFFSETS or DIEFF_POLAR;
  EffectInfo.dwDuration := INFINITE;                // infinite duration
  EffectInfo.dwSamplePeriod := 100000;              // sample periods the same
  EffectInfo.dwGain := DI_FFNOMINALMAX;
  EffectInfo.dwTriggerButton := DIJOFS_BUTTON0;     // tied to button 0
```

```
EffectInfo.dwTriggerRepeatInterval := 0;
EffectInfo.cAxes := 2;
EffectInfo.rgdwAxes := @AxisArray;
EffectInfo.rglDirection := @DirArray;
EffectInfo.lpEnvelope := nil;
EffectInfo.cbTypeSpecificParams := SizeOf(TDICustomForce);
EffectInfo.lpvTypeSpecificParams := @CustomInfo;

{create the custom effect}
dxcheck(FDirectInputDevice.CreateEffect(GUID_CustomForce, @EffectInfo,
CustomEffect, nil));
end;
```

# Additional Effect Considerations

While this is not meant to be a complete reference to DirectX, there are several more force feedback specific methods that have not been discussed, but may be very useful to applications that incorporate force feedback functionality. In particular, applications may need to determine the status of an effect or the state of the overall force feedback system, send a command to the force feedback system, or modify effect parameters on the fly.

## Retrieving Effect Status

There may be times when the application needs to determine if an effect is currently playing or not. This is easily accomplished by calling the GetEffectStatus method of the IDirectInputEffect interface. The GetEffectStatus method is defined as:

```
function GetEffectStatus(
var pdwFlags : DWORD                  // flags indicating the effect status
) : HResult;                          // returns a DirectX error code
```

The only parameter to this method is a variable that will be initialized to one or more flags. The effect is currently playing if the DIEGES_PLAYING flag is present in the pdwFlags variable.

## Retrieving the Force Feedback System State

Another useful method of the IDirectInputDevice2 interface is the GetForceFeedbackState method. This method returns a series of flags which indicate the overall state of the force feedback device. The GetForceFeedbackState method is defined as:

```
function GetForceFeedbackState(
var pdwOut: DWORD                     // flags indicating overall device state
) : HResult;                          // returns a DirectX error code
```

The pdwOut parameter is simply a variable that, upon return, will be initialized with the flags that indicate the overall force feedback system status. This can be a combination of one or more flags from the following table.

*Table 8-3:* *Force feedback state flags*

| Flag | Description |
|------|-------------|
| DIGFFS_EMPTY | The device has no downloaded effects. |
| DIGFFS_STOPPED | No effects are playing. |
| DIGFFS_PAUSED | All active effects are paused. |
| DIGFFS_ACTUATORSON | Force feedback actuators are enabled. |
| DIGFFS_ACTUATORSOFF | Force feedback actuators are disabled. |
| DIGFFS_POWERON | Power to the force feedback device is available. |
| DIGFFS_POWEROFF | Power to the force feedback device is not available. |
| DIGFFS_SAFETYSWITCHON | The safety switch is on. |
| DIGFFS_SAFETYSWITCHOFF | The safety switch is off, and the device cannot operate. |
| DIGFFS_USERFFSWITCHON | The force feedback switch is on. |
| DIGFFS_USERFFSWITCHOFF | The force feedback switch is off, and force feedback effects cannot be played. |
| DIGFFS_DEVICELOST | The device has been unacquired and must be reacquired. |

## Sending Commands to the Force Feedback System

There are times when it is necessary to send global commands to the force feedback system. For example, if the user pauses the game, it would be nice to pause all playing effects without having to enumerate them all and call Stop for each one, and then restart them when the user resumes play. This can be accomplished through the SendForceFeedbackCommand method of the IDirectInputDevice2 interface. The SendForceFeedbackCommand method is defined as:

```
function SendForceFeedbackCommand(
dwFlags: DWORD                          // the command value
) : HResult;                            // returns a DirectX error code
```

The single parameter of this function takes one value from the following table.

*Table 8-4:* *Force feedback system commands*

| Command | Description |
|---------|-------------|
| DISFFC_RESET | Resets the entire device. All effects are destroyed and must be re-created. |
| DISFFC_STOPALL | All actively playing effects are stopped. |

***Table 8-4:*** *Force feedback system commands* (cont.)

| Command | Description |
|---|---|
| DISFFC_PAUSE | All actively playing effects are paused. When restarted, they continue playing to the remainder of their duration. New effects cannot be started. |
| DISFFC_CONTINUE | Continues playing from a paused state. |
| DISFFC_SETACTUATORSON | Turns force feedback actuators on. |
| DISFFC_SETACTUATORSOFF | Turns force feedback actuators off. Effects can still be played but will be ignored by the device. |

## Modifying an Effect at Run Time

In order to further customize an effect to reflect changes in the game world, an effect can be modified while it is playing, provided that this is supported by the driver. As we examined earlier, we can use the GetEffectInfo method to determine which parameters can be dynamically changed during effect playback. In practice, we can change any of the parameters at any time; the parameters listed in dwDynamicParams indicate those parameters that can be changed without restarting the effect. Changing a parameter that is not included in dwDynamicParams will cause the force feedback system to stop and then restart the effect.

To change an effect's parameters during playback, call the SetParameters method of the IDirectInputEffect interface. The SetParameters method is defined as:

```
function SetParameters(
var peff: TDIEffect;        // a TDIEffect structure with new parameters
dwFlags: DWORD              // control flags
) : HResult;                // returns a DirectX error code
```

The first parameter contains a TDIEffect structure that contains the new values for the effect parameters to be changed. It is not necessary to initialize the entire structure, only those members containing the new effect parameters. The second parameter contains a series of flags that indicate which members of the TDIEffect structure contain the new information. These are the same flags as returned by the GetEffectInfo method, and are listed in Table 8-1. Some additional flags available with this method control the behavior of the force feedback system when the effect is modified. For example, calling the SetParameters method automatically downloads the effect. This can be disabled by including the DIEP_NODOWNLOAD flag in the second parameter. These additional flags are listed below.

*Table 8-5: Parameter flags*

| Flag | Description |
|------|-------------|
| DIEP_NODOWNLOAD | Effect parameters are updated but not downloaded to the device. |
| DIEP_NORESTART | Suppresses restart of an effect. If the effect must be restarted, an error code of DIERR_EFFECTPLAYING is returned, and the effect continues to play with the original parameters. |
| DIEP_START | Starts playing the effect if it is not playing already. |
| DIEP_TYPESPECIFICPARAMS | Indicates that the lpvTypeSpecificParams and cbTypeSpecificParams members of the TDIEffect structure contain new data. |

The following listing demonstrates changing an effect's direction at run time.

*Listing 8-4: Changing effect parameters at run time*

```
var

   .
   .
   .

  {tracks the direction in degrees}
  EffectDir: Integer;

implementation

   .
   .
   .

procedure TfrmJoyTestBed.FormActivate(Sender: TObject);
var

   .
   .
   .

  AxisArray: array[0..1] of DWORD;
  DirArray: array[0..1] of longint;
  EffectInfo: TDIEffect;
  PeriodicInfo: TDIPeriodic;
begin

   .
   .
   .
```

```
  {this effect plays on the X and Y axis}
  AxisArray[0] := DIJOFS_X;
  AxisArray[1] := DIJOFS_Y;

  {initialize the direction}
  EffectDir := 1;
  DirArray[0] := EffectDir*DI_DEGREES;
  DirArray[1] := 0;

  {initialize a periodic effect}
  PeriodicInfo.dwMagnitude := DI_FFNOMINALMAX;
  PeriodicInfo.lOffset := 0;
  PeriodicInfo.dwPhase := 0;
  PeriodicInfo.dwPeriod := DI_SECONDS;;

  {initialize the global effect parameters}
  EffectInfo.dwSize := SizeOf(TDIEffect);
  EffectInfo.dwFlags := DIEFF_OBJECTOFFSETS or DIEFF_POLAR;
  EffectInfo.dwDuration := INFINITE;                 // infinite duration
  EffectInfo.dwSamplePeriod := 0;
  EffectInfo.dwGain := DI_FFNOMINALMAX;
  EffectInfo.dwTriggerButton := DIEB_NOTRIGGER;   // no trigger
  EffectInfo.dwTriggerRepeatInterval := 0;
  EffectInfo.cAxes := 2;
  EffectInfo.rgdwAxes := @AxisArray;
  EffectInfo.rglDirection := @DirArray;
  EffectInfo.lpEnvelope := nil;
  EffectInfo.cbTypeSpecificParams := SizeOf(TDIPeriodic);
  EffectInfo.lpvTypeSpecificParams := @PeriodicInfo;

  {create a sine wave periodic effect}
  FDirectInputDevice.CreateEffect(GUID_sine, @EffectInfo, PeriodicEffect, nil);

  {start the effect, suppressing all other effects on the device}
  PeriodicEffect.Start(1, DIES_SOLO);

  {enable the timer that changes the effect direction}
  tmrDirChanger.Enabled := TRUE;
end;

procedure TfrmJoyTestBed.tmrDirChangerTimer(Sender: TObject);
var
  DirArray: array[0..1] of longint;
  EffectInfo: TDIEffect;
begin
  {increase the effect direction angle}
  Inc(EffectDir, 2);

  {roll the angle over nicely}
  if EffectDir > 360 then
```

```
    EffectDir := 1;

{display the new angle}
lblAngle.Caption := 'Effect Angle: '+IntToStr(EffectDir);

{indicate the new direction}
DirArray[0] := EffectDir*DI_DEGREES;
DirArray[1] := 0;

{set up the effect parameters}
FillChar(EffectInfo, SizeOf(TDIEffect), 0);
EffectInfo.dwFlags := DIEFF_POLAR;
EffectInfo.dwSize := SizeOf(TDIEffect);
EffectInfo.rglDirection := @DirArray;
EffectInfo.cAxes := 2;

{dynamically change the parameters, indicating that the effect
 should not restart. if the device doesn't support this, the change
 will fail, but the effect will continue to play}
PeriodicEffect.SetParameters(EffectInfo, DIEP_DIRECTION or DIEP_NORESTART);
end;
```

# Envelopes

The basic effect types give the developer a wide range of possibilities for creating tactile feedback. Indeed, using custom forces or modifying a force at run time gives us even greater control over the "feel" of the feedback. We can further customize an effect by using an envelope.

An envelope is a method by which a force can be shaped, and is very similar in concept to envelopes in musical terms. Specifically, an envelope describes the starting magnitude for an effect and the amount of time it takes for the magnitude to go from this initial starting point to the magnitude defined by the type-specific parameters of the specific effect. This is known as the attack. Similarly, the envelope also describes the final magnitude of the effect and the amount of time it takes for the magnitude to go from the effect-defined magnitude to this final level. This is known as the fade. These times take place during the entire duration of the effect, so the sum of both times should not exceed this duration. Any remaining time indicates the sustain, and determines how much time the effect is played at the defined magnitude. A visual illustration of an envelope is shown in Figure 8-7.

 **envelope:** A series of values that shape a force at the beginning and end of playback.

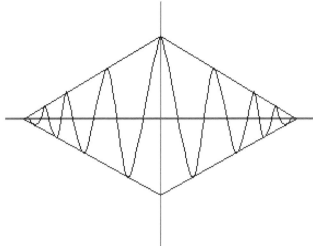

**Figure 8-7:**
*An envelope shaping an effect*

**Note:** Envelopes do not apply to condition effects.

Envelopes are defined by a TDIEnvelope structure. A pointer to this structure is placed in the lpEnvelope member of the TDIEffect structure when an effect is defined. The TDIEnvelope structure is defined as:

```
TDIEnvelope = packed record
  dwSize : DWORD;                  // the size of the structure in bytes
  dwAttackLevel : DWORD;           // the initial magnitude
  dwAttackTime : DWORD;            // the attack duration
  dwFadeLevel : DWORD;             // the ending magnitude
  dwFadeTime : DWORD;              // the fade duration
end;
```

As usual with so many DirectX structures, the dwSize member must be set to SizeOf(TDIEnvelope). The dwAttackLevel member defines the starting magnitude for the effect. Actually, this defines a percentage, in hundredths of a percent, of the maximum available force in the direction of the effect, and thus can be a value between 0 and 10,000. The dwFadeLevel member is very similar, except that it defines the percentage of maximum available force at the end of effect playback. Both dwAttackTime and dwFadeTime define the duration of the attack and fade in microseconds.

**Note:** Neither the attack nor fade levels need to be less than the sustain level. If they are defined greater than the sustain level, the effect will start at a greater level than the sustain and will fall down to it (or vice versa in the case of fade level).

The following example demonstrates applying an envelope to a sine wave periodic force.

***Listing 8-5:** Using an envelope with periodic forces*

```
procedure TfrmJoyTestBed.FormActivate(Sender: TObject);
var

  .
  .
  .

  AxisArray: array[0..1] of DWORD;
  DirArray: array[0..1] of longint;
  EffectInfo: TDIEffect;
  PeriodicInfo: TDIPeriodic;
  Envelope: TDIEnvelope;
begin

  .
  .
  .

  {this effect plays on the X and Y axis}
  AxisArray[0] := DIJOFS_X;
  AxisArray[1] := DIJOFS_Y;

  {initialize the direction}
  DirArray[0] := 180*DI_DEGREES;
  DirArray[1] := 0;

  {initialize a periodic effect}
  PeriodicInfo.dwMagnitude := DI_FFNOMINALMAX;
  PeriodicInfo.lOffset := 0;
  PeriodicInfo.dwPhase := 0;
  PeriodicInfo.dwPeriod := DI_SECONDS div 10;

  {initialize the envelope. this will cause the effect to rise to the
   sustain level and then immediately fall back to 0 magnitude, as the
   entire duration of the effect is only 2 seconds, and both the
   attack and fade time each last a full second}
  Envelope.dwSize := SizeOf(TDIEnvelope);
  Envelope.dwAttackLevel := 0;
  Envelope.dwAttackTime := DI_SECONDS;
  Envelope.dwFadeLevel := 0;
  Envelope.dwFadeTime := DI_SECONDS;

  {initialize the global effect parameters}
  EffectInfo.dwSize := SizeOf(TDIEffect);
  EffectInfo.dwFlags := DIEFF_OBJECTOFFSETS or DIEFF_POLAR;
  EffectInfo.dwDuration := DI_SECONDS * 2;        // infinite duration
```

```
        EffectInfo.dwSamplePeriod := 0;
        EffectInfo.dwGain := DI_FFNOMINALMAX;
        EffectInfo.dwTriggerButton := DIJOFS_BUTTON0;   // tied to button 0
        EffectInfo.dwTriggerRepeatInterval := 0;
        EffectInfo.cAxes := 2;
        EffectInfo.rgdwAxes := @AxisArray;
        EffectInfo.rglDirection := @DirArray;
        EffectInfo.lpEnvelope := @Envelope;
        EffectInfo.cbTypeSpecificParams := SizeOf(TDIPeriodic);
        EffectInfo.lpvTypeSpecificParams := @PeriodicInfo;

        {create a sine wave periodic effect}
        FDirectInputDevice.CreateEffect(GUID_sine, @EffectInfo, PeriodicEffect, nil);
    end;
```

# Summary

In this chapter, we discussed techniques for utilizing force feedback technology. We examined how to use both standard and custom effects, as well as how to modify effects on the fly. We also looked at shaping effects using envelopes. When using force feedback technology in your games, it is important to keep these points in mind:

■ Force feedback is part of the DirectInput subsystem, and was designed to work not only with joysticks but with any type of input device.

■ When discussing force feedback effects, it is necessary to understand several general concepts as they apply to the effect itself. Such concepts include kinetic forces, conditions, magnitude, coefficient, gain, duration, sample period, axes, direction, and envelope.

■ A kinetic force is an effect that actively pushes on one or more axes. This push can be in a single direction or in alternating directions such as occurs with periodic effects.

■ A condition is a resistance or force that is applied to one or more axes in response to their movement or position.

■ Magnitude is a measurement of the strength of a kinetic force, relative to the total maximum force that can be output by the device. The magnitude of a force can be expressed as an integer value between –10,000 and 10,000, where positive values represent a force in one direction and negative values represent the same force in the opposite direction.

■ The DI_FFNOMINALMAX constant is set to 10,000 and represents the total maximum force that can be exerted by the device on any given axis. This constant allows the developer to define the magnitude of a force as a percentage of the total maximum force available on the device.

■ Coefficient is a measurement of the strength of resistance to movement along an axis. Like magnitude, this value is expressed as an integer between –10,000 and 10,000.

■ Duration defines how long the effect will play, measured in microseconds.

■ The constant DI_SECONDS can be used to define the duration in terms of one-second intervals (or fractions thereof).

■ Sample period defines the interval between actual changes in the strength of a force, measured in microseconds.

■ Gain acts as a scaling factor for magnitudes and coefficients. It is expressed as a value between 0 and 10,000, indicating the percentage by which to scale the magnitude or coefficient.

■ Axes determine what axis (or axes) of movement on the force feedback device will be affected by the force feedback effect.

■ Direction determines the bearing of an effect along an axis (or axes) when its magnitude or coefficient values are positive. Negative values act in the opposite of the defined direction.

■ An envelope is a set of values that modify the magnitude of a force at the beginning and end of playback, and can be applied to all forces except conditions.

■ Force feedback effects are divided into six different categories: conditions, constant forces, periodic forces, ramp forces, device-specific effects, and custom forces.

■ All force feedback effects are defined by a primary structure called TDIEffect. This structure is used when creating the effect as well as modifying the effect after it has been created.

■ Each type of effect is defined by different parameters. These parameters are stored in a type-specific parameter data structure which differs from effect to effect.

■ Some members of the TDIEffect structure may be unsupported by some drivers. However, the application can use the GetEffectInfo method of the IDirectInputDevice2 interface to determine which TDIEffect parameters are supported.

■ Some effects must be downloaded to the device after they are created before they can be played. However, if the input device is in an acquired state when the effect is created, it is downloaded automatically. It is also downloaded automatically whenever the Start method is called. For some effects, such as a triggered effect that was created before the device was acquired, the Download method must be used.

■ A DIERR_DEVICEFULL error may be returned when using a force feedback effect. This indicates that the device has reached its maximum number of downloadable force feedback effects, and an existing effect must be unloaded from a device by calling the Unload method.

■ Triggered effects are automatically started when the trigger is pushed, and stopped when the trigger is released. Otherwise, effects must be explicitly started using the Start method. For effects with infinite duration, the Stop method must be called to halt playback.

■ Use the GetEffectStatus method to determine if an effect is currently playing.

■ Use the GetForceFeedbackState method to determine the overall state of the force feedback device.

■ Use the SendForceFeedbackCommand method to send global commands to the force feedback system.

■ The SetParameters method allows a force feedback effect to be modified on the fly.

# CHAPTER 9: *Sound and Music*

Most people discuss games in terms of the technology used for the graphics engine. Hot first-person shooters are discussed in terms of colored lighting, interactive environments, the polygon count of characters, etc. Real-time strategy game discussions feature such terms as computer AI, realism of surface features (such as hills), tactical advantages of weapons, etc. Although rarely the topic of discussion, the importance of the third major piece of a game, sound and music, is not lost on game developers.

Regardless of the technological accomplishment represented by the game's graphics engine, no game is truly complete without some sort of sound effects to bring the environment to life, or a driving soundtrack to set the mood. Would Quake have been as good if you couldn't hear a heavy-breathing mutant around the corner? Would X-Wing have given you the same thrill without the musical fanfare following a completed mission? Indeed, music and sound effects round out a game and add the polish that can make a good game great.

In this chapter, we examine various techniques for incorporating sound effects and music into Delphi games. We will examine using DirectSound for manipulation and playback of sound effects, and we will take a look at regular Windows MCI commands for playing music in both MIDI and Red Book Audio formats.

DirectX 6.1 and above features a DirectX component known as DirectMusic. DirectMusic could potentially revitalize the use of MIDI through its incredible features. It provides an interface for supporting downloadable instrument sounds as well as methods to change the playback of MIDI files on the fly. This can result in context-sensitive musical playback that, supposedly, may never be the same twice. Unfortunately, we were unable to cover DirectMusic in this volume, but look for several articles about its use appearing in trade magazines in the very near future.

# Sound Effects

Sound effects are very important in a game, as they help to immerse the player in the environment depicted by the game's playing area. Viewing an animation of a ship exploding is much more exciting when accompanied by a loud roar. Walking down a dark passageway is much more realistic when the hollow sounds of boot heels on damp stone is heard. Using sound effects in this manner can draw the user into the environment in ways that even the most advanced 3-D engine could never hope to accomplish.

In addition to immersion and suspension of belief, sound effects can give audible clues to the user that indicate a change in the environment. For example, the hum of an engine could be changed to reflect the amount of damage it has taken, providing a correlation to the engine's maximum speed. A low growl or heavy breathing sound could signal the presence of an unknown assailant, heightening the user's tension level and excitement. Even the subtle sounds of clicks and whirs emitted when the game's buttons and sliders are manipulated help make the environment all the more real to the user.

The Windows Multimedia API contains a number of sound output functions. Some are very easy to implement but lack the control that might be required for some games. Most games will need to play several sound effects at once, such as the whine of an engine, laser bursts, and explosions. Playing several sound effects simultaneously is known as mixing, and unfortunately such functionality is not built in to the Windows Multimedia API.

**mixing:** Combining several sounds in real time in such a way that they can be played simultaneously.

Low-level multimedia sound output functions could be used to implement mixing or even manipulate the sounds in real time to create special effects such as echo or reverb. However, such code is difficult to write at best, and just as difficult to debug. Let's examine the easiest method to implement sound output under Windows, and then we'll take a look at how DirectSound provides all the sound output power that a game will ever need.

## Simplistic Sound Effects

Not every game requires the power of full-blown DirectSound implementation. Indeed, if your game uses few sound effects, or does not require the ability to play several sounds simultaneously, it is much easier to implement the sound output functionality built into the Windows API. By far, the easiest yet most flexible function available for playing sound effects is the PlaySound function. The PlaySound function can play audio files in the WAV format, from either a file on disk, a resource, or even an image of the sound in memory. It can play the sound asynchronously, allowing the application to continue processing, and it can play sounds in a continuous loop. This function would be perfect for almost any gaming need except for one major drawback: It cannot play more than one sound at a time. As stated above, low-level audio functions could be used to implement mixing, but this is difficult, and now obsolete thanks to DirectSound. The PlaySound function is defined as:

```
function PlaySound(
pszSound: PChar;          // the sound to be played
hmod: HMODULE;            // a module handle
fdwSound: DWORD           // flags controlling sound playback
): BOOL;                  // returns TRUE or FALSE
```

The first parameter indicates the sound to be played, and can be a filename, an alias, or a resource identifier as specified by the flags in the third parameter. If the first parameter is set to nil, any currently playing WAV is stopped. The second parameter contains the handle of the executable or DLL if the sound to be played is a resource; otherwise it should be set to zero. The final parameter is a series of flags that indicate how to interpret the first parameter as well as how the sound file should be played, such as in a loop.

**Note:** You must include MMSystem in the Uses clause of any unit that will use the PlaySound function.

The following example demonstrates how to use the PlaySound function to play sound effects from various locations.

*Listing 9-1: Playing sound effects with PlaySound*

```
implementation

uses MMSystem;

var
  WaveFile: TMemoryStream;

{$R *.DFM}

{$R WaveRes.res}

procedure TForm1.FormCreate(Sender: TObject);
begin
  {create the image of a WAV file in memory}
  WaveFile := TMemoryStream.Create;
  WaveFile.LoadFromFile('Memory.wav');
end;

procedure TForm1.FormDestroy(Sender: TObject);
begin
  {delete the in memory WAV file}
```

```
    WaveFile.Free;
  end;

procedure TForm1.btnPlayFileClick(Sender: TObject);
begin
  {play a sound from a WAV file}
  PlaySound('File.wav', 0, SND_FILENAME or SND_ASYNC);
end;

procedure TForm1.btnPlayResClick(Sender: TObject);
begin
  {play a sound from a resource (see the WaveRes.rc file for the
   resource script)}
  PlaySound('WaveResource', hInstance, SND_RESOURCE or SND_ASYNC);
end;

procedure TForm1.btnPlayMemClick(Sender: TObject);
begin
  {play a sound from a WAV file image in memory}
  PlaySound(WaveFile.Memory, 0, SND_MEMORY or SND_ASYNC);
end;

procedure TForm1.btnPlayLoopClick(Sender: TObject);
begin
  {play a continuously looping sound from a file}
  PlaySound('Loop.wav', 0, SND_FILENAME or SND_ASYNC or SND_LOOP);

  btnPlayStop.Enabled := TRUE;
end;

procedure TForm1.btnPlayStopClick(Sender: TObject);
begin
  {stop all sound output}
  PlaySound(nil, 0, SND_PURGE);

  btnPlayStop.Enabled := FALSE;
end;
```

As illustrated, it is relatively simple to play a sound file by simply passing the PlaySound function the name of the WAV file. Playing a sound from a resource is almost as simple. The WAV files must be compiled into a resource by using the BRCC32.exe resource compiler included with Delphi (see the WaveRes.rc file in the directory containing the above example on the companion CD). Once this is complete, the resource file is linked into the executable using the $R compiler directive. Then, it's a simple matter of passing the PlaySound function the name of the WAV resource (as opposed to the name of a WAV file), the handle of the module containing the resources (useful for putting WAV resources into DLLs), and the SND_RESOURCE flag.

**Note:** WAV files must be compiled using a resource type of "WAVE" in the resource script file before PlaySound can find them.

Playing sounds from memory is easy enough, and improves the performance of your application as PlaySound does not have to reload the WAV file or resource each time it is called. By using the TMemoryStream object, a WAV file can easily be loaded into memory and passed to the PlaySound function via its Memory property.

Together with the ability to continuously play a sound (by using the SND_LOOP flag) or stop all sound output (by using the SND_PURGE flag), the PlaySound function is relatively powerful. If your game or application will not require the ability to play multiple sounds simultaneously, the PlaySound function will probably provide all the functionality required. However, to optimize sound output performance, play a virtually unlimited number of sounds simultaneously, or produce special effects, DirectSound is the way to go.

## DirectSound

DirectSound is that portion of DirectX that is responsible for the manipulation and playback of digitized sound (music is handled via other API functions described later in the chapter). While not nearly as simplistic as the PlaySound function, the methods in the DirectSound API provide the developer with plenty of audio playback control while not being nearly as difficult as writing your own mixing and manipulation code with low-level audio API calls.

### Features

DirectSound offers many features above and beyond what is available through the Win32 API. As with all DirectX components, DirectSound gives the developer more control over sound output than the Windows API, while also providing an improvement in performance. DirectSound provides the following features of specific interest to game developers:

- Automatic use of hardware acceleration (when available)
- Automatic conversion of WAV formats
- Simultaneous output of a virtually unlimited number of sounds
- Special effects such as panning, volume control, frequency adjustment, and 3-D placement

In the following sections we will discuss how the Delphi game developer can take advantage of each of these features to create rich sound output for applications or games.

## Functional Overview

Similar to DirectDraw, DirectSound programming consists of creating a DirectSound object and several sound buffers. The DirectSound object itself represents the developer's direct interface to the audio hardware. Through the IDirectSound interface, the application can query the audio hardware's capabilities, create sound buffers, and control other aspects of the hardware itself.

Of primary interest to DirectSound programmers is the secondary sound buffer object (or specifically the IDirectSoundBuffer object). A secondary sound buffer object represents a sound, or WAV file, in memory. It is a similar relationship as surfaces are to bitmaps in DirectDraw programming. This memory is typically located in system RAM. However, some sound cards contain hardware RAM for the purpose of accelerating sound output. DirectSound will automatically take advantage of this hardware memory by placing secondary sound buffers in the sound card RAM. All of this is transparent to the developer. The majority of time spent in programming DirectSound will be in creation and manipulation of these secondary sound buffers.

When a secondary sound buffer is played, its sound information is mixed with other secondary sound buffers and placed in the primary buffer. The primary buffer represents the conglomeration of all the sounds that will be played simultaneously, and is constantly streamed out to the sound output hardware. As secondary buffers are mixed into the primary buffer, DirectSound automatically converts their format into that of the primary buffer. This makes it easy for the developer to use sounds in varying formats, such as 8- and 16-bit sound, or sounds recorded at different sampling rates. As this mixing occurs, any special effects are applied to the sound, such as panning, volume, or 3-D positioning. The number of buffers that DirectSound can mix is limited only by processing time.

DirectSound provides a software mixer for combining system memory buffers and hardware buffers into the primary buffer. System memory buffers are always mixed in software, but if a hardware mixer is available, the mixed system buffers are streamed to the hardware mixer, along with the hardware buffers. This elaborate process is illustrated in Figure 9-1.

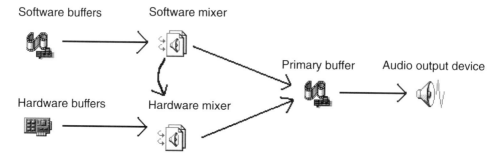

*Figure 9-1:* *DirectSound functional overview*

***Sound Buffers*** As stated above, the majority of time spent when programming DirectSound is in creation and manipulation of secondary sound buffers. The primary sound buffer can also be accessed, allowing the developer to change the primary sound buffer format or even implement custom mixing algorithms. There are a number of attributes and concepts associated with sound buffers that must be explained and understood before they can be put to good use.

***Audio Format*** As of this writing, all sound buffers must contain sound data in the pulse code modulation (PCM) format.

**pulse code modulation (PCM):** An uncompressed audio format; the most common format for Windows WAV files.

Fortunately, this is the most common format for Windows WAV files. Unfortunately, you cannot assume that any file with the .wav extension is in the PCM format. WAV files are also stored in the Resource Interchange File Format (RIFF), which is a complex, variable length file format consisting of header "chunks" followed by data "chunks" of variable length.

**Resource Interchange File Format (RIFF):** A complex, variable length file consisting of variable length "chunks." Each chunk can describe data or a header (which contains a description of the data following it). Commonly used for multimedia file formats, such as WAV files.

The data chunks in WAV files can contain audio data in any number of different formats (you can examine this by opening the Sound Recorder under Accessories and choosing Save As). WAV RIFF files contain a header "chunk" in the form of a TWaveFormatEx structure, which allows the developer to check the format of the WAV file before copying its data into a secondary sound buffer. The TWaveFormatEx structure contains a number of useful pieces of information describing the WAV file, such as the number of channels, the sampling rate, and the number of bits per sample. The TWaveFormatEx structure is defined as:

```
TWaveFormatEx = packed record
  wFormatTag: Word;        // format type, must be WAVE_FORMAT_PCM for
                           //   DirectSound compatibility
  nChannels: Word;         // number of channels (1 = mono, 2 = stereo)}
  nSamplesPerSec: DWORD;   // the sample rate, in hertz (samples per second),
                           //   typically 11025 (telephone quality), 22050 (radio
                           //   quality), or 44100 (CD quality)
  nAvgBytesPerSec: DWORD;  // average transfer rate (nSamplesPerSec*nBlockAlign)
  nBlockAlign: Word;       // bytes per sample (nChannels*nBitsPerSample/8)
  wBitsPerSample: Word;    // number of bits per sample (8 or 16)
  cbSize: Word;            // number of bytes of extra information, can be
                           //   ignored
end;
```

**hertz (Hz):** A measurement of samples per second.

The audio format of secondary buffers will be dictated by the format of the WAV file they contain. However, the primary buffer has a default audio format of 22,050 Hz, 2 channels, 8 bits per sample. DirectSound gives the developer the abilities to change this format, as we'll see shortly.

**Buffer Memory Locations**   When DirectSound creates a secondary sound buffer, it automatically tries to locate the buffer in RAM on the sound card, if available. If there are no hardware buffers available, the sound is stored in system memory. Sound buffers located in hardware have the shortest path to the primary sound buffer, and thus are appropriately suited for sounds that are needed quickly and will be repeated often (such as gunshots), or looped continually (such as an engine hum). Although sound buffers are created in hardware memory by default, the developer can specify the desired memory location of a sound buffer by using specific flags, as described later in this chapter. The number of sound buffers that DirectSound can make are restricted only by available free memory (system memory and sound card hardware memory)

The existence of hardware buffers usually indicates the existence of a hardware mixer. Each hardware buffer takes up one hardware mixing channel (even if the buffer isn't playing), and the number of available hardware buffers is limited by the number of hardware mixing channels. This affects the number of sounds that can be mixed by the hardware mixer. DirectSound will take up the slack by performing any necessary mixing in the software mixer. This will all be transparent to the developer but is useful knowledge when optimizing performance.

**Buffer Types**   Secondary sound buffers come in two flavors: static and streaming. Static buffers are used for short sounds that can be placed into memory in their entirety. These are typically short, often repeated or looping sounds. Streaming buffers are used for large sounds that cannot fit into a reasonably sized block of memory, or for sounds that change often and must by copied into the buffer in pieces as it is playing.

By default, DirectSound tries to create a streaming buffer. However, like the buffer memory location, the developer can indicate a desired buffer type through the use of various flags in the buffer creation function.

**Optimum Buffer Configuration**   Since DirectSound tries to locate secondary sound buffers in hardware memory first, sound buffers should be created in order of importance. This will ensure that the sounds used most often will enjoy the greatest performance. However, to optimize performance, the developer should dictate the type of buffer when one is created, and where it will be placed. In general, static buffers should be used for short, often repeated or looping sounds, and should be placed in hardware memory. Streaming buffers, on the other hand, should be placed in system memory (on ISA cards you have no choice, as hardware streaming buffers are not supported). Locating a streaming buffer in hardware does not eliminate any processing overhead as new audio data is continually moving between hardware and software. Thus, hardware buffers should be reserved only for buffers that are not continually updated.

The exception to this rule is when a sound buffer will be duplicated. DirectSound allows copies of a sound buffer to be created that contain their own play and write pointers but do not copy the actual buffer memory. This is useful when a certain sound will be played multiple times, but you want the user to hear the end of the previous sound while the beginning of the next sound is being played (i.e., the dissipation at the end of a laser burst while the next laser burst is charging). Duplicating a hardware buffer requires using hardware resources that may be needed elsewhere. Indeed, the call to duplicate a hardware buffer will fail if there are an insufficient number of hardware resources available. For this reason, it is better to place static buffers that will be duplicated in system memory. An example of duplicating a sound buffer for this purpose will be demonstrated later in the chapter.

**Buffer Memory Format**    The memory in a DirectSound sound buffer is conceptually circular. Basically, this means that when DirectSound comes to the end of a buffer, it automatically goes back to the beginning. Think of sound buffer memory like the surface of a cylinder, as illustrated by Figure 9-2.

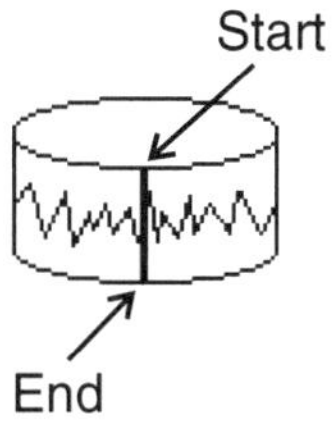

Each buffer contains a play and write pointer into the memory containing the audio data. The current play position indicates the offset of the next byte that will be sent to the mixer. The current write position is located beyond the current play position and indicates the first byte in the buffer at which it is safe to write new data. The data located between the play and write positions is queued for playback and should never be altered. The write position maintains a distance of approximately 15 milliseconds of play time ahead of the play position. Nevertheless, applications should be writing data to the buffer well ahead of the current write position to allow for any delays in moving the data into the buffer. This information is typically useful only when dealing with streaming buffers, as the application must track the point at which it is safe to stream more audio data into the buffer.

*Figure 9-2*
*Sound buffer memory is conceptually circular*

**Audible Focus**    The final important concept when dealing with sound buffers is that of audible focus. When a sound buffer is created, the developer can determine if the sound will continue to be heard when another application receives focus. By default, sounds will not be heard when the application loses focus (although they continue to play silently). A sound buffer can be given Global focus upon creation, indicating that the sound will always be audible unless another application receives focus and obtains exclusive access to the audio hardware (it will continue to play when the application is in the background). Alternatively, a sound buffer can have Sticky focus, indicating that it will be audible unless another application using DirectSound receives focus.

## Initialization

As with DirectDraw, there are several steps the developer must follow to set up DirectSound before loading and playing sound buffers. Some of these steps are somewhat optional, but in general, DirectSound is instantiated by performing the following:

- Enumerating audio devices
- Creating the DirectSound object
- Setting the cooperative level
- Retrieving audio device capabilities
- Setting the format of the primary buffer

***Enumerating Audio Devices***   DirectSound provides a function that returns information for every audio output device with an installed hardware driver detected in the system. As a general rule, it is unnecessary for most applications to enumerate all audio output devices. The user can select a preferred audio output device through the Multimedia control panel applet, and DirectSound should be created using this selection unless there is good reason to do otherwise. However, if the developer wants the application to check all available audio drivers for certain capabilities, or just wishes to provide the user with a list of available audio drivers to choose from, the DirectSoundEnumerate function is used. The DirectSoundEnumerate function is defined as:

```
function DirectSoundEnumerate(
lpDSEnumCallback: TDSEnumCallback;      // a pointer to the callback function
lpContext: Pointer                      // an application-defined value
): HResult;                             // returns a DirectX error code
```

The first parameter is a pointer to a user-defined callback function. DirectSoundEnumerate prepares a list of every installed audio driver and sends information about each one, one at a time, to this user-defined callback function. This information includes the GUID for the device, the description of the device, and the module name of the DirectSound driver for the device. The other parameter is a 32-bit user-defined value (this is defined as a pointer but is intended for application-specific use and is ignored by the function). The TDSEnumCallback callback function itself is defined as:

```
function TDSEnumCallback(
lpGuid: PGUID;                    // the audio device GUID
```

```
lpstrDescription: PAnsiChar;        // a description of the device
lpstrModule: PAnsiChar;             // the module name
lpContext: Pointer                  // the user-defined value
): BOOL;                            // returns TRUE or FALSE
```

The first parameter is the GUID for the enumerated audio device. The second and third parameters contain textual information describing the audio device. The final parameter contains the user-defined value passed to the original DirectSoundEnumerate function. Every time the callback function is called, it should return a value of TRUE to continue the enumeration or FALSE if no other driver information is required.

The first device enumerated by this function is always the preferred audio output device selected by the user, as described above. This device is known as the primary sound driver.

**primary sound driver:** The audio output device selected by the user on the Audio tab of the Multimedia control panel applet.

Actually, this is not a true device enumeration, as no GUID will be returned for this device and the callback function will only receive a description string of "Primary Sound Driver" for the purpose of displaying it in a list. Once the primary sound driver has been enumerated, the callback function is called once for every available sound card.

**Note:** On any system with a sound card, the callback function will be called at least twice: once for the primary sound driver and once for the actual sound card hardware. A GUID will be received on the second and subsequent calls.

The following example demonstrates the use of the DirectSoundEnumerate function to retrieve the names of all available audio drivers installed on the system.

**Listing 9-2:** *Enumerating audio output devices*

```
{the user-defined enumeration function. note that the stdcall keyword must be
 used before Windows can call this function correctly}
function EnumSoundDevices(lpGuid: PGUID;               // the device GUID
                     lpstrDescription: PAnsiChar; // the description
                     lpstrModule: PAnsiChar;      // the module name
                     lpContext: Pointer           // the user-defined info
                     ): BOOL; stdcall;            // stdcall must be used
begin
  {add the description and the module name of the enumerated driver to the
   list box. the first one will be the primary sound driver, and will not
   contain a module name}
```

```
Form1.lbxSoundDevices.Items.Add(lpstrDescription+' - '+lpstrModule);

{indicate that we wish to continue enumeration}
Result := TRUE;
end;

procedure TForm1.FormCreate(Sender: TObject);
begin
  {begin enumerating all available audio drivers}
  DirectSoundEnumerate(EnumSoundDevices, nil);
end;
```

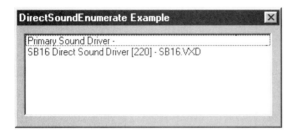

*Figure 9-3*: *The list of drivers retrieved from DirectSoundEnumerate*

**Creating the DirectSound Object** To begin actually using DirectSound functionality, a DirectSound object must be created. This is accomplished by calling the DirectSoundCreate function. The DirectSoundCreate function is defined as:

```
function DirectSoundCreate(
lpGuid: PGUID;             // the sound device GUID
out ppDS: IDirectSound;    // the IDirectSound object to be instantiated
pUnkOuter: IUnknown        // unused
): HResult;                // returns a DirectX error code
```

The first parameter is a pointer to the GUID of the desired audio device (retrieved through enumeration as explained above, or set to nil to indicate the primary sound driver). The second parameter is an IDirectSound interface which will be instantiated when the function returns. The final parameter is used for COM aggregation and should be set to nil.

**Caution:** It is possible to create multiple DirectSound objects, but this is unadvisable. When an additional DirectSound object is created, its cooperative level (explained below) overrides that of any previously created objects. A single DirectSound object should be created for the duration of the application.

**Setting the Cooperative Level** Once the DirectSound object is created, the application should immediately set its cooperative level. The cooperative level determines how the audio device will be shared between the current application and others, as well as access to certain functionality. The cooperative level is set by calling the SetCooperativeLevel method of the IDirectSound interface. The SetCooperativeLevel method is defined as:

```
function SetCooperativeLevel(
hwnd: HWND;                  // a window handle
dwLevel: DWORD               // the cooperative level flags
): HResult;                  // returns a DirectX error code
```

The first parameter is a handle to the application's main window. The second parameter contains a series of flags indicating the desired cooperative level. The flags indicating each cooperative level are described in the table below. Most applications will use the Normal cooperative level, as this allows the most compatible operation with other applications that use the sound card. However, games will normally use the Priority or Exclusive levels, as these allow for the most efficient and optimized use of audio hardware. The cooperative levels below are listed in ascending order, and each level has the abilities of all levels below it.

**Table 9-1:** *DirectSound cooperative levels*

| Level | Flag | Abilities | Restrictions |
|---|---|---|---|
| Normal | DSSCL_NORMAL | Can play secondary sound buffers. | Cannot set the format of the primary sound buffer, cannot write to the primary sound buffer, and cannot call the Compact method. |
| Priority | DSSCL_PRIORITY | Can change the format of the primary buffer, has first rights to hardware resources, and can call the Compact method. | |
| Exclusive | DSSCL_EXCLUSIVE | Mutes all sound output from background applications. | |
| Write Primary | DSSCL_WRITEPRIMARY | Can write directly to the primary sound buffer. | Cannot play secondary sound buffers. |

**Note:** When using DirectDraw in conjunction with DirectSound, the window handle passed to the SetCooperativeLevel method of the IDirectSound object must also be sent to the SetCooperativeLevel of the IDirectDraw4 object.

***Retrieving Audio Device Capabilities*** Most applications will be concerned with simply creating a DirectSound object and several secondary buffers, and outputting sound, letting DirectSound take care of the details. However, when creating high-performance, CPU-intensive games, it may be necessary to take a more active role in defining how the system will use available hardware resources. This is where the GetCaps method of the IDirectSound object comes in handy. The GetCaps method is defined as:

```
function GetCaps(
var lpDSCaps: TDSCaps                  // a TDSCaps structure
): HResult;                            // returns a DirectX error code
```

The only parameter for this function is a TDSCaps structure that is initialized with the capabilities of the audio device when the function returns. Several members of this structure, such as the dwMaxHwMixingAllBuffers, dwMaxHwMixingStaticBuffers, and dwTotalHwMemBytes members, can be used to optimize performance by determining what sounds can be placed in hardware buffers in the most efficient manner. Unfortunately, some members of this structure may not be universally supported by all drivers, and the values returned by some members may just be estimates. The best way to use the GetCaps method is to call it after creating each hardware sound buffer.

**Note:** The dwSize member of the TDSCaps structure must be initialized to SizeOf(TDSCaps) before calling the GetCaps method.

Of particular interest to the game programmer is the value of the dwFlags member. This member contains a combination of one or more flags that indicate device capabilities. Specifically, if the DSCAPS_EMULDRIVER flag is included in this value, a DirectSound driver is not actually present in the system, and all DirectSound functionality is being emulated. This means that no hardware acceleration is available, secondary sound buffers can only be created in system memory, and playback latency will be higher. See the example program in Listing 9-3 for a list of available flags.

The TDSCaps structure is defined as:

```
TDSCaps = packed record
  dwSize: DWORD;                        // the size of the structure, in bytes
  dwFlags: DWORD;                       // capability flags
  dwMinSecondarySampleRate: DWORD;      // minimum sample rate for secondary
                                        //    buffers in hardware
  dwMaxSecondarySampleRate: DWORD;      // maximum sample rate for secondary
                                        //    buffers in hardware
  dwPrimaryBuffers: DWORD;              // number of primary buffers (always 1)
  dwMaxHwMixingAllBuffers: DWORD;       // maximum number of hardware buffers
  dwMaxHwMixingStaticBuffers: DWORD;    // maximum number of static hardware
                                        //    buffers
```

```
        dwMaxHwMixingStreamingBuffers: DWORD;  // maximum number of streaming hardware
                                                  buffers
        dwFreeHwMixingAllBuffers: DWORD;        // number of free hardware buffers
        dwFreeHwMixingStaticBuffers: DWORD;     // number of free static hardware
                                                  buffers
        dwFreeHwMixingStreamingBuffers: DWORD;// number of free streaming hardware
                                                  buffers
        dwMaxHw3DAllBuffers: DWORD;             // maximum number of 3-D hardware
                                                  buffers
        dwMaxHw3DStaticBuffers: DWORD;          // maximum number of 3-D static hardware
                                                  buffers
        dwMaxHw3DStreamingBuffers: DWORD;       // maximum number of 3-D streaming
                                                  hardware buffers
        dwFreeHw3DAllBuffers: DWORD;            // number of free 3-D hardware buffers
        dwFreeHw3DStaticBuffers: DWORD;         // number of free 3-D static hardware
                                                  buffers
        dwFreeHw3DStreamingBuffers: DWORD;      // number of free 3-D streaming hardware
                                                  buffers
        dwTotalHwMemBytes: DWORD;               // total hardware memory, in bytes
        dwFreeHwMemBytes: DWORD;                // free hardware memory, in bytes
        dwMaxContigFreeHwMemBytes: DWORD;       // largest contiguous block of free
                                                  hardware memory, in bytes
        dwUnlockTransferRateHwBuffers: DWORD;   // rate of data transfer to hardware
                                                  buffers, in kilobytes per second
        dwPlayCpuOverheadSwBuffers: DWORD;      // percentage of CPU cycles used to mix
                                                  software buffers
        dwReserved1: DWORD;                     // reserved, not used
        dwReserved2: DWORD;                     // reserved, not used
end;
```

The following example demonstrates how to create the DirectSound object, set its cooperative level, and retrieve audio hardware capabilities.

*Listing 9-3: Creating DirectSound and retrieving hardware capabilities*

```
procedure TForm1.FormCreate(Sender: TObject);
var
  DXSound: IDirectSound;
  DevCaps: TDSCaps;
begin
  {create the DirectSound object}
  DirectSoundCreate(nil, DXSound, nil);

  {set its cooperative level to the lowest setting, as we only need to
   retrieve device capabilities}
  DXSound.SetCooperativeLevel(Handle, DSSCL_NORMAL);

  {initialize the TDSCaps structure}
  FillChar(DevCaps, SizeOf(TDSCaps), 0);
  DevCaps.dwSize := SizeOf(TDSCaps);
```

```
{retrieve the capabilities of the audio hardware}
DXSound.GetCaps(DevCaps);

{display general device capabilities}
with lbxDevCaps.Items do
begin
  Add('General driver capabilities -');
  Add('');
  if (DevCaps.dwFlags and DSCAPS_CERTIFIED) = DSCAPS_CERTIFIED then
    Add('Driver tested and certified by Microsoft');
  if (DevCaps.dwFlags and DSCAPS_CONTINUOUSRATE) = DSCAPS_CONTINUOUSRATE then
    Add('Supports all sample rates between min and max');
  if (DevCaps.dwFlags and DSCAPS_EMULDRIVER) = DSCAPS_EMULDRIVER then
    Add('No DirectSound driver detected');
  if (DevCaps.dwFlags and DSCAPS_PRIMARY16BIT) = DSCAPS_PRIMARY16BIT then
    Add('Supports 16-bit primary buffer');
  if (DevCaps.dwFlags and DSCAPS_PRIMARY8BIT) = DSCAPS_PRIMARY8BIT then
    Add('Supports 8-bit primary buffer');
  if (DevCaps.dwFlags and DSCAPS_PRIMARYMONO) = DSCAPS_PRIMARYMONO then
    Add('Supports a 1-channel primary buffer');
  if (DevCaps.dwFlags and DSCAPS_PRIMARYSTEREO) = DSCAPS_PRIMARYSTEREO then
    Add('Supports a 2-channel primary buffer');
  if (DevCaps.dwFlags and DSCAPS_SECONDARY16BIT) = DSCAPS_SECONDARY16BIT then
    Add('Supports 16-bit hardware mixed secondary buffers');
  if (DevCaps.dwFlags and DSCAPS_SECONDARY8BIT) = DSCAPS_SECONDARY8BIT then
    Add('Supports 8-bit hardware mixed secondary buffers');
  if (DevCaps.dwFlags and DSCAPS_SECONDARYMONO) = DSCAPS_SECONDARYMONO then
    Add('Supports 1 channel hardware mixed secondary buffers');
  if (DevCaps.dwFlags and DSCAPS_SECONDARYSTEREO)=DSCAPS_SECONDARYSTEREO then
    Add('Supports 2 channel hardware mixed secondary buffers');

  Add('Number of primary buffers: '+IntToStr(DevCaps.dwPrimaryBuffers));
  Add('Software mixing CPU overhead: '+
      IntToStr(DevCaps.dwPlayCpuOverheadSwBuffers)+'%');

  {if the driver is a true DirectSound driver, it can take advantage of any
   hardware acceleration, so display hardware-specific attributes}
  if (DevCaps.dwFlags and DSCAPS_EMULDRIVER)  DSCAPS_EMULDRIVER then
  begin
    Add('');
    Add('');
    Add('Hardware specific capabilities -');
    Add('');
    Add('Minimum secondary hardware buffer sample rate: '+
        IntToStr(DevCaps.dwMinSecondarySampleRate));
    Add('Maximum secondary hardware buffer sample rate: '+
        IntToStr(DevCaps.dwMaxSecondarySampleRate));
    Add('Maximum hardware buffers: '+
        IntToStr(DevCaps.dwMaxHwMixingAllBuffers));
    Add('Maximum static hardware buffers: '+
        IntToStr(DevCaps.dwMaxHwMixingStaticBuffers));
```

```
        Add('Maximum streaming hardware buffers: '+
            IntToStr(DevCaps.dwMaxHwMixingStreamingBuffers));
        Add('Free hardware buffers:'+IntToStr(DevCaps.dwFreeHwMixingAllBuffers));
        Add('Free static hardware buffers: '+
            IntToStr(DevCaps.dwFreeHwMixingStaticBuffers));
        Add('Free streaming hardware buffers: '+
            IntToStr(DevCaps.dwFreeHwMixingStreamingBuffers));
        Add('Maximum 3-D hardware buffers: '+
            IntToStr(DevCaps.dwMaxHw3DAllBuffers));
        Add('Maximum 3-D static hardware buffers: '+
            IntToStr(DevCaps.dwMaxHw3DStaticBuffers));
        Add('Maximum 3-D streaming hardware buffers: '+
            IntToStr(DevCaps.dwMaxHw3DStreamingBuffers));
        Add('Free 3-D hardware buffers: '+IntToStr(DevCaps.dwFreeHw3DAllBuffers));
        Add('Free 3-D static hardware buffers: '+
            IntToStr(DevCaps.dwFreeHw3DStaticBuffers));
        Add('Free 3-D streaming hardware buffers: '+
            IntToStr(DevCaps.dwFreeHw3DStreamingBuffers));
        Add('Total hardware memory: '+IntToStr(DevCaps.dwTotalHwMemBytes)+
            ' bytes');
        Add('Free hardware memory: '+IntToStr(DevCaps.dwFreeHwMemBytes)+'bytes');
        Add('Maximum contiguous free hardware memory: '+
            IntToStr(DevCaps.dwMaxContigFreeHwMemBytes)+' bytes');
        Add('Data transfer rate: '+
            IntToStr(DevCaps.dwUnlockTransferRateHwBuffers)+' kb per second');
    end;
  end;

end;
```

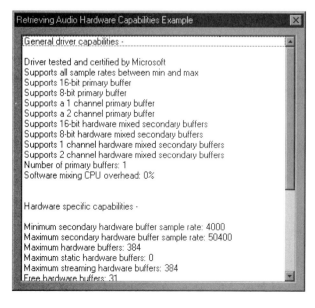

**Figure 9-4:** *The audio hardware capabilities*

***Setting the Format of the Primary Buffer*** As noted above, the primary buffer has a default format of 22,050 Hz, 2 channels, 8 bits per sample. Regardless of the format of any secondary sound buffers, DirectSound converts them on the fly into the format of the primary buffer. This is completely transparent to the developer, and in general, most applications can take advantage of this automatic conversion and never be concerned with the format of any audio data. However, it does take some processing time to do this conversion, and in a high-performance game where no processing time should be wasted, this may be unacceptable. Alternatively, the developer may desire better sound quality than that offered by the default format. Fortunately, DirectSound provides a method by which the format of the primary buffer can be changed as desired by the developer.

**Note:** DirectSound is optimized for 16-bits-per-sample sounds. Therefore, changing the primary sound buffer format for 16-bit sounds can further reduce playback latency and reduce the load on the CPU when processing sound data.

In order to change the format of the primary buffer, a TDSBufferDesc structure (containing buffer description information) must be initialized. This data structure is described later in this chapter, but the dwFlags member must be set to DSBCAPS_ PRIMARYBUFFER, the dwBufferBytes member must be set to 0, and the lpwfxFormat member must be set to nil. Then, the CreateSoundBuffer method of the IDirectSound object is called, passing this data structure as a parameter, to retrieve a pointer to the primary sound buffer object (the CreateSoundBuffer function is discussed in more detail later).

Once a pointer to the primary sound buffer object is retrieved, a TWaveFormatEx structure is initialized to the appropriate settings for the desired primary buffer format. Finally, the SetFormat method of the primary sound is called, passing it the initialized TWaveFormatEx structure. The SetFormat method of IDirectSoundBuffer is defined as:

```
function SetFormat(
const lpcfxFormat: TWaveFormatEx     // a TWaveFormatEx structure
): HResult;                          // returns a DirectX error code
```

At this point, the pointer to the primary sound buffer object can be released, as the new format settings are persistent until the format of the primary sound buffer is again modified.

**Note:** The cooperative level of the DirectSound object must be set to a minimum of DSSCL_PRIORITY before the format of the primary sound buffer can be changed.

In the following example, the sample sound is known to have a format of 44,100 Hz, 2 channels, 16 bits per sample. The format of the primary sound buffer is changed to that of the sample sound to facilitate the most optimum audio playback environment. Several functions not yet discussed are used in the example, but will be explained later in the chapter.

**Listing 9-4:** *Setting the format of the primary sound buffer*

```
var
  DXSound: IDirectSound;
  Sound: IDirectSoundBuffer;

procedure TForm1.FormCreate(Sender: TObject);
var
  BufDesc: TDSBufferDesc;
  Format: TWaveFormatEx;
  PrimeBuf: IDirectSoundBuffer;
begin
  {create the DirectSound object}
  DirectSoundCreate(nil, DXSound, nil);

  {set its cooperative level high enough to allow the application to
   change the format of the primary buffer}
  DXSound.SetCooperativeLevel(Handle, DSSCL_PRIORITY);

  {initialize the buffer description structure to indicate we wish to
   retrieve the primary buffer}
  FillChar(BufDesc, SizeOf(TDSBufferDesc), 0);
  BufDesc.dwSize         := SizeOf(TDSBufferDesc);
  BufDesc.dwFlags        := DSBCAPS_PRIMARYBUFFER;
  BufDesc.dwBufferBytes := 0;
  BufDesc.lpwfxFormat    := nil;

  {retrieve the primary buffer}
  DXSound.CreateSoundBuffer(BufDesc, PrimeBuf, nil);

  {initialize the wave format structure to the desired primary buffer
   format settings. this will be the same format used by the example
   sound, which should have lower playback latency since it no longer
   needs to be converted}
  FillChar(Format, SizeOf(TWaveFormatEx), 0);
  Format.wFormatTag      := WAVE_FORMAT_PCM;
  Format.nChannels       := 2;
  Format.nSamplesPerSec  := 44100;
  Format.wBitsPerSample  := 16;
  Format.nBlockAlign     := (Format.nChannels*Format.wBitsPerSample) div 8;
  Format.nAvgBytesPerSec := Format.nSamplesPerSec*Format.nBlockAlign;

  {set the format of the primary buffer}
```

```
    PrimeBuf.SetFormat(Format);

    {release the primary buffer (it retains the settings just defined)}
    PrimeBuf := nil;

    {load in the example sound}
    Sound := DSLoadSound(DXSound, ExtractFilePath(ParamStr(0))+'Sample.wav',
                         FALSE);
end;

procedure TForm1.Button1Click(Sender: TObject);
begin
  {play the example sound (the primary buffer is now in the same format
   as this sound buffer)}
  Sound.SetCurrentPosition(0);
  Sound.Play(0, 0, 0);
end;
```

## Creating Buffers

Now that DirectSound has been properly instantiated, the application has checked that the sound card provides the desired capabilities, and the format of the primary sound buffer has been changed to match that of the sounds to be played, it is time to start loading and playing sounds.

As with initialization, there are several steps the developer must follow in order to properly create a secondary sound buffer and load it with sound data. Unlike initialization, however, none of these steps are optional, and some are repeated regularly when creating a streaming buffer. In order to load and play a WAV file, the application must perform the following:

■ Describe the format of the WAV file to be played

■ Describe various secondary sound buffer attributes, such as the size of the buffer and any buffer capabilities

■ Create the sound buffer (an IDirectSoundBuffer object) using the above information

■ Copy the sound data from the WAV file into the buffer

■ Play the sound buffer

■ Repeat the last two steps for streaming buffers

By far, the most complex step in initializing a secondary sound buffer is copying the data from a WAV file into the sound buffer itself. Unfortunately, DirectSound does not come with any built-in methods for retrieving audio data from a file or a resource. However, the DirectX SDK comes with several units that contain functions for performing this necessary step, specifically the Wave.C and DSUtil.C units. These units have been converted to Pascal, and live in the form of the DSUtil.pas, DSWaveFiles.pas, and DSWaveResources.pas units. The DSUtil unit contains a function (DSLoadSound, used in the previous example) that will load a sound from a WAV file or a resource, passing back an instantiated IDirectSoundBuffer interface (static sounds only). The DSUtil unit uses functions located in the DSWaveFiles and DSWaveResources units to provide this functionality, and the examples that follow will discuss how to use these functions to initialize sound buffers with sound data.

For the most part, the steps required to load and play a sound are identical for both static and streaming buffers. The primary difference is in how a streaming buffer is continually loaded with new information as it is played. The most common situation, and easiest to follow, is loading and playing static buffers, which is discussed first, followed by streaming buffers.

***Static Buffers*** The first step in creating any secondary sound buffer is to initialize a TWaveFormatEx structure with information concerning the format of the sound buffer. Of course, this information comes from the desired sound itself. As described earlier in the chapter, WAV files are stored in the RIFF file format, which includes the information we are seeking conveniently configured in the TWaveFormatEx format. Parsing WAV file information out of a RIFF file is not too terribly complicated, but is involved enough that it would take several pages just to describe the process. Instead of wasting space describing such an esoteric task, we will use several functions from the DSWaveFiles.pas unit (converted from the original Wave.C unit found in the DirectX SDK) that perform this function. These functions use several of the low-level multimedia input/output functions, and perusing their code may provide useful insight for providing your own wave parsing routines.

To retrieve the desired information, we call the WaveOpenFile function. This function opens the WAV file and initializes a TWaveFormatEx structure (passed in as a variable parameter) with the WAV file's format information. Then we must call the WaveStartDataRead function, which positions a file pointer at the start of the actual sound data within the WAV file, and retrieves the total size of the sound data.

At this point, we are just about ready to create the actual sound buffer object, so we must initialize a TDSBufferDesc structure with information describing what type of sound buffer to create. The TDSBufferDesc structure is defined as:

```
TDSBufferDesc = packed record
dwSize: DWORD;            // the size of the structure, in bytes
dwFlags: DWORD;           // buffer description flags
dwBufferBytes: DWORD;     // the size of the sound buffer, in bytes
dwReserved: DWORD;        // reserved, must be 0
lpwfxFormat: PWaveFormatEx; // a pointer to the TWaveFormatEx structure
end;
```

**Note:** The dwSize member of the TDSBufferDesc structure must be set to SizeOf(TDSBufferDesc) before calling the CreateSoundBuffer method.

For static buffers, the dwBufferBytes member should be set to the total size of the sound data as retrieved by the WaveStartDataRead function. The lpwfxFormat member should point to the TWaveFormatEx structure initialized by the WaveOpenFile function. The most important member of this structure, dwFlags, can be set to a combination of values that determine several things about the sound buffer, including its location in memory and its type. By default, DirectSound tries to create a streaming buffer, so this member must be set to DSBCAPS_STATIC in order to create a static buffer. Also by default, the sound buffer will be located in hardware memory if any is available. The DSBCAPS_LOCHARDWARE flag can be used to force the sound buffer into hardware memory (failing if there is not enough free hardware memory for the buffer), or the DSBCAPS_LOCSOFTWARE flag can be used to force the sound buffer into system memory. Several other flags are available which provide other controls over the buffer, such as panning and volume, which will be explained below.

Now that the buffer description has been initialized, the CreateSoundBuffer method of the IDirectSound object is called. The CreateSoundBuffer method is defined as:

```
function CreateSoundBuffer(
const lpDSBufferDesc: TDSBufferDesc;        // the buffer description
var lpIDirectSoundBuffer: IDirectSoundBuffer;  // the sound buffer object
pUnkOuter: IUnknown                         // unused
): HResult;                                 // returns a DirectX error code
```

The first parameter is the TDSBufferDesc structure that has been initialized as discussed above. The second parameter is an IDirectSoundBuffer object that will be instantiated when the function returns. The final parameter is used for COM aggregation and should be set to nil. This creates a secondary sound buffer that is now ready to receive actual sound data.

In order to start copying audio data from the sound file into the buffer, we must retrieve a pointer directly to the sound buffer memory itself. This is accomplished by calling the Lock method of the IDirectSoundBuffer object (this is similar to calling the Lock method of a DirectDraw surface). The Lock method is defined as:

```
function Lock(
dwWriteCursor,                   // offset of start of lock
dwWriteBytes: DWORD;             // number of bytes to lock
var lplpvAudioPtr1: Pointer;     // first memory pointer
var lpdwAudioBytes1: DWORD;      // number of bytes locked
var lplpvAudioPtr2: Pointer;     // second memory pointer
var lpdwAudioBytes2: DWORD;      // number of bytes locked
```

```
dwFlags: DWORD              // lock control flags
): HResult;                 // returns a DirectX error code
```

The first parameter is the offset, in bytes, of the beginning of the locked memory from the start of the sound buffer. The second parameter indicates how many bytes should be locked. The next four parameters indicate where the buffer is actually locked and how many bytes were locked. These parameters are explained in detail below under streaming buffers. The final parameter can indicate that the entire buffer should be locked, or locking should begin from the position of the Write cursor.

The information returned by this function is, in turn, used in a call to the WaveReadFile function, which actually copies the audio data from the WAV file into the sound buffer. Once the data is copied, the Unlock method of the IDirectSoundBuffer is called to unlock the sound buffer memory, and the WaveCloseReadFile function is called to close the actual WAV file. The Unlock method is defined as:

```
function Unlock(
lpvAudioPtr1: Pointer;      // offset of first lock
dwAudioBytes1: DWORD;       // number of bytes to be unlocked
lpvAudioPtr2: Pointer;      // offset of second lock
dwAudioBytes2: DWORD        // number of bytes to be unlocked
): HResult;                 // returns a DirectX error code
```

The four parameters passed to this function correspond to the pointers and byte lock counts retrieved from the initial Lock method.

The sound buffer has been created and loaded with audio data, and is now ready to be output through the audio hardware. The SetCurrentPosition method of the IDirectSoundBuffer object can be called to set the actual position within the sound data to start the audio playback. The SetCurrentPosition method is defined as:

```
function SetCurrentPosition(
dwPosition: DWORD           // the current position offset
): HResult;                 // returns a DirectX error code
```

The only parameter in this function is the offset, in bytes, from the beginning of the buffer to which the current playing position should be set.

Finally, the Play method is called to actually begin audio playback. The Play method is defined as:

```
function Play(
dwReserved1,                // reserved
dwReserved2,                // reserved
dwFlags: DWORD              // play control flags
): HResult;                 // returns a DirectX error code
```

The first two parameters are unused and should be set to zero. The third parameter can be set to zero to simply play the sound once, or it can be set to DSBPLAY_LOOPING to continuously play the sound. The Stop method can be called to discontinue any sound playback from the buffer (the Stop method has no parameters).

**Note:** Like DirectDraw surfaces, the memory allocated to secondary sound buffers can be lost when another application takes over the sound hardware. In this case, any calls to the Lock or Play methods will return DSERR_BUFFERLOST. The Restore method can be called to reallocate the buffer memory. However, the contents of this memory will be invalid, and the audio data must be recopied into the sound buffer.

The following example demonstrates how to create a static sound buffer, load it with audio data from an external WAV file, and play it.

**Listing 9-5:** *Creating and playing static wave files*

```
var
  DXSound: IDirectSound;
  Sounds: array[0..5] of IDirectSoundBuffer;  // holds all of our sound objects

const
  {the names of the WAV files to be used}
  FileNames: array[0..5] of string = ('bigz05.wav', 'bigzap.wav', 'bloop.wav',
                                       'boingg.wav', 'bwik.wav', 'elslide.wav');
procedure TForm1.FormCreate(Sender: TObject);
var
  iCount: Integer;
begin
  {create the DirectSound object}
  DirectSoundCreate(nil, DXSound, nil);

  {set its cooperative level (we won't change the primary buffer format, so
   a cooperative level of Normal is all that is needed)}
  DXSound.SetCooperativeLevel(Handle, DSSCL_NORMAL);

  {load in the six example sounds}
  for iCount := 0 to 5 do
    LoadSound(FileNames[iCount], Sounds[iCount]);
end;

    .
    .
    .

{this function is used to load a WAV file and initialize an
 IDirectSoundBuffer object with the audio data}
```

```
procedure TForm1.LoadSound(FileName: string; var Buffer: IDirectSoundBuffer);
var
  Audio: PByte;
  Junk: Pointer;
  NumBytesLocked: DWORD;
  JunkBytes: DWORD;
  WaveFormat: PWaveFormatEx;
  mmioHndle: HMMIO;
  ChunkInfo,
  ChunkInfoParent: TMMCKInfo;
  BufDesc: TDSBufferDesc;
begin
  {open the specified WAV file and read its format information}
  WaveOpenFile(PChar(ExtractFilePath(ParamStr(0))+FileName), mmioHndle,
               WaveFormat, @ChunkInfoParent);

  {advance the file pointer to the beginning of audio data, and retrieve the
   size of the buffer required to hold all of the audio data}
  WaveStartDataRead(mmioHndle, @ChunkInfo, @ChunkInfoParent);

  {initialize a buffer description record, including the size of the audio
   data and its format retrieved from the previous two function calls}
  FillMemory(@BufDesc, SizeOf(TDSBufferDesc), 0);
  BufDesc.dwSize := SizeOf(TDSBufferDesc);
  BufDesc.dwFlags := DSBCAPS_STATIC; // could also use DSBCAPS_LOCHARDWARE to
                                     // force the buffer into hardware memory
  BufDesc.dwBufferBytes := ChunkInfo.cksize;
  BufDesc.lpwfxFormat := WaveFormat;

  {create the sound buffer object}
  DXSound.CreateSoundBuffer(BufDesc, Buffer, nil);

  {lock the entire buffer}
  Buffer.Lock(0, 0, Pointer(Audio), NumBytesLocked, Junk, JunkBytes,
              DSBLOCK_ENTIREBUFFER);

  {copy the audio data into the sound buffer object}
  WaveReadFile(mmioHndle, NumBytesLocked, Audio, @ChunkInfo, JunkBytes);

  {unlock the buffer}
  Buffer.Unlock(Audio, NumBytesLocked, nil, 0);

  {close the WAV file. at this point, the IDirectSound buffer has been
   initialized and is ready to be played}
  WaveCloseReadFile(mmioHndle, WaveFormat);
end;

procedure TForm1.Button1Click(Sender: TObject);
begin
  {the Tag property of each button is set to the appropriate index into
   the array of IDirectSoundBuffer objects. when a button is pressed, reset
```

```
          the current position of the appropriate buffer, and start playing it}
          Sounds[TButton(Sender).Tag].SetCurrentPosition(0);
          Sounds[TButton(Sender).Tag].Play(0, 0, 0);
        end;
```

The DSWaveResources.pas unit contains functions similar to those found in the DSWaveFiles.pas unit for loading WAV file information from resources. Internally, dramatically different API functions are called, mainly those used for manipulating resources on a binary level as opposed to multimedia file input/output functions. Specifically, the DSGetWaveResource function is called to initialize both the TDSBufferDesc and the TWaveFormatEx structures. The CreateSoundBuffer method is then called as usual, and the DSFillSoundBuffer function is called to actually copy the audio data into the buffer. The following example demonstrates how to use these functions to create and play static sound buffers from audio data in a resource. This example also demonstrates how to check for a lost sound buffer and restore its contents.

*Listing 9-6: Creating and playing static wave files from resource information*

```
var
  DXSound: IDirectSound;
  Sounds: array[0..5] of IDirectSoundBuffer;  // holds all of our sound objects

const
  {the resource names of the waves to be used}
  ResNames: array[0..5] of PChar = ('bigz05', 'bigzap', 'bloop',
                                    'boingg', 'bwik', 'elslide');

 {this function is used to load a wave resource and initialize an
 IDirectSoundBuffer object with the audio data}
procedure LoadSound(ResName: PChar; var Buffer: IDirectSoundBuffer);
var
  BufDesc: TDSBufferDesc;
  pbWaveData: PByte;
begin
  {empty the buffer description record}
  FillMemory(@BufDesc, SizeOf(TDSBufferDesc), 0);

  {load the wave resource, initializing the format and required buffer size}
  if DSGetWaveResource(0, ResName, BufDesc.lpwfxFormat, pbWaveData,
                    BufDesc.dwBufferBytes) then
  begin
    {initialize the remaining buffer description members}
    BufDesc.dwSize := SizeOf(TDSBufferDesc);
    BufDesc.dwFlags := DSBCAPS_STATIC; // could also use DSBCAPS_LOCHARDWARE to
                                       // force the buffer into hardware memory

    {create the sound buffer object}
    DXSound.CreateSoundBuffer(BufDesc, Buffer, nil);
```

```
      {fill the sound buffer with the audio data from the resource}
      DSFillSoundBuffer(Buffer, pbWaveData, BufDesc.dwBufferBytes);
    end;
end;

{this function is used to restore the contents of an IDirectSoundBuffer object
 when its memory has been lost. it is very similar to the LoadSound function}
procedure ReloadSound(ResName: PChar; var Buffer: IDirectSoundBuffer);
var
  BufDesc: TDSBufferDesc;
  pbWaveData: PByte;
begin
  {empty the buffer description record}
  FillMemory(@BufDesc, SizeOf(TDSBufferDesc), 0);

  {load the wave resource, initializing a pointer to the wave data
   and the size of the data}
  if DSGetWaveResource(0, ResName, BufDesc.lpwfxFormat, pbWaveData,
                       BufDesc.dwBufferBytes) then
  begin
    {restore the buffer's memory}
    Buffer.Restore;

    {fill the sound buffer with the audio data from the resource}
    DSFillSoundBuffer(Buffer, pbWaveData, BufDesc.dwBufferBytes);
  end;
end;

procedure TForm1.Button1Click(Sender: TObject);
begin
  {the Tag property of each button is set to the appropriate index into
   the array of IDirectSoundBuffer objects. when a button is pressed, reset
   the current position of the appropriate buffer, and start playing it}
  Sounds[TButton(Sender).Tag].SetCurrentPosition(0);

  {attempt to play the sound. if the buffer memory has been lost...}
  if Sounds[TButton(Sender).Tag].Play(0, 0, 0) = DSERR_BUFFERLOST then
  begin
    {...restore the sound buffer}
    ReloadSound(ResNames[TButton(Sender).Tag], Sounds[TButton(Sender).Tag]);

    {play the restored sound buffer}
    Sounds[TButton(Sender).Tag].SetCurrentPosition(0);
    Sounds[TButton(Sender).Tag].Play(0, 0, 0);
  end;
end;

procedure TForm1.FormCreate(Sender: TObject);
var
  iCount: Integer;
```

```
begin
  {create the DirectSound object}
  DirectSoundCreate(nil, DXSound, nil);

  {set its cooperative level (we won't change the primary buffer format, so
   a cooperative level of Normal is all that is needed)}
  DXSound.SetCooperativeLevel(Handle, DSSCL_NORMAL);

  {load in the six example sounds}
  for iCount := 0 to 5 do
    LoadSound(ResNames[iCount], Sounds[iCount]);
end;
```

***Streaming Buffers*** As mentioned previously, streaming buffers are used for large sounds that will not fit into a reasonably sized chunk of memory. A good use for streaming buffers would be for playback of digitized dialog, or perhaps a digitized music track. Creating streaming buffers is very similar to creating static buffers. The application must first read in a WAV file (or resource) and retrieve its format. Then, it must set up a TDSBufferDesc structure with the appropriate attributes.

There are two major differences between creating streaming buffers and creating static buffers: the flags used in the buffer description structure and the size of the buffer itself. As you would expect, the dwFlags member of the TDSBufferDesc structure will not contain the DSBCAPS_STATIC flag. However, this member should contain the DSBCAPS_GETCURRENTPOSITION2 flag to ensure the most accurate play position tracking. As for the size of the buffer, instead of setting it to the total size required to hold all of the audio data as in static buffer creation, it is set to a size large enough to hold approximately two seconds worth of audio data. Two seconds is an arbitrary number and depends on the application's specific needs. The actual size of the buffer is dependent on the wave's sample rate and bits per sample (the nAvgBytesPerSec member of the wave's TWaveFormatEx structure should be used).

To actually begin loading data into the buffer, we must first know where the current play and write positions are within the buffer (described earlier under Buffer Memory Format). The GetCurrentPosition method of the IDirectSoundBuffer object retrieves the offset from the beginning of the buffer for both the play and write positions. The GetCurrentPosition method is defined as:

```
function GetCurrentPosition(
lpdwCapturePosition,              // the current play position
lpdwReadPosition: PDWORD          // the current write position
): HResult;                       // returns a DirectX error code
```

The first parameter is set to the current position of the play cursor, as an offset from the beginning of the buffer in bytes. The second parameter is set to the current position of the write cursor, again as an offset in bytes from the beginning of the buffer.

How the data is loaded into the buffer is up to the application. For example, data could be written into the buffer right at the start of the write position (not recommended), or it could be written into the buffer at some point ahead of the current play position. In our examples below, we'll write data into the buffer based on the current play position.

You may have noticed how the Lock method returns two lock start offsets and two bytes locked counts. This is again due to the circular nature of buffer memory. For example, say the buffer is 5,000 bytes long, and the Lock method is called with a starting offset of 3,000 and a request to lock 3,000 bytes. The last 2,000 bytes in the buffer can be locked, but the final 1,000 requested bytes must be locked from the beginning of the buffer. This is why two offsets and two byte counts are returned. Again, depending on how your application copies data into the buffer, these values can be used to continuously copy data into the buffer in a circular format.

All that remains is to play the buffer and determine exactly when to write data into the buffer. We've already seen how a buffer can be played. In the case of streaming buffers, it might be useful to fill the buffer with silence and start playing it immediately, especially if the sound will be looped. Filling the buffer with silence involves simply zeroing out the buffer's memory using the techniques described above for writing data into a buffer.

**Note:** We have a function in the DSUtil unit called FillBufferWithSilence that performs this task.

As for when to write data into the buffer, there are two methods available to the application: polling and notification. Polling involves using the GetCurrentPosition method as described above. GetCurrentPosition is called at regular intervals (like every pass through the game's main loop), writing data into the buffer based on the Play or Write position returned at that moment. The advantages to this method are that it's simple and easy to implement. The disadvantages are that unless polling is performed at regular intervals, the Play position can easily race past the point where new data should have been copied into the buffer, resulting in old data being played back and a generally messed up audio output. The other method, notification, involves using the IDirectSoundNotify interface together with a number of low-level API functions such as CreateEvent and WaitForMultipleObjects to create event objects that are signaled when the Play position reaches certain points within the buffer. The advantage to this method is that it is more efficient than continually calling the GetCurrentPosition method. The disadvantages are that it is much more difficult to set up, requires multiple threads (in some cases), and is consequently more difficult to debug. For our purposes, the polling method will be more than adequate.

The following example demonstrates creating a streaming buffer and writing data into the buffer by polling the current play position.

***Listing 9-7:*** *Creating a streaming buffer*

```
var
  DXSound: IDirectSound;
  Sound: IDirectSoundBuffer;

  WaveFormat: PWaveFormatEx;
  mmioHndle: HMMIO;
  ChunkInfo,
  ChunkInfoParent: TMMCKInfo;

procedure TForm1.FormCreate(Sender: TObject);
var
  Audio: PByte;
  Junk: Pointer;
  NumBytesLocked: DWORD;
  JunkBytes: DWORD;
  BufDesc: TDSBufferDesc;
begin
  {the OnIdle event serves as our game loop as it would in
   DirectDraw examples}
  Application.OnIdle := AppIdle;

  {create the DirectSound object}
  DirectSoundCreate(nil, DXSound, nil);

  {set its cooperative level (we won't change the primary buffer format, so
   a cooperative level of Normal is all that is needed)}
  DXSound.SetCooperativeLevel(Handle, DSSCL_NORMAL);

  {open the specified WAV file and read its format information}
  WaveOpenFile(PChar(ExtractFilePath(ParamStr(0))+'longwave.wav'), mmioHndle,
             WaveFormat, @ChunkInfoParent);

  {advance the file pointer to the beginning of audio data, and retrieve the
   size of the buffer required to hold all of the audio data}
  WaveStartDataRead(mmioHndle, @ChunkInfo, @ChunkInfoParent);

  {initialize a buffer description record, including the size of the audio
   data and its format retrieved from the previous two function calls}
  FillMemory(@BufDesc, SizeOf(TDSBufferDesc), 0);
  BufDesc.dwSize := SizeOf(TDSBufferDesc);
  BufDesc.dwFlags := DSBCAPS_GETCURRENTPOSITION2 or DSBCAPS_LOCSOFTWARE;
  BufDesc.dwBufferBytes := WaveFormat.nAvgBytesPerSec*2;   // 2 seconds worth
  BufDesc.lpwfxFormat := WaveFormat;

  {create the sound buffer object}
```

```
      DXSound.CreateSoundBuffer(BufDesc, Sound, nil);

  {initialize it with silence}
  FillBufferWithSilence(Sound);

  {begin playing the buffer}
  Sound.Play(0, 0, DSBPLAY_LOOPING);
end;

procedure TForm1.FormDestroy(Sender: TObject);
begin
  {disconnect our loop}
  Application.OnIdle := nil;

  {we no longer need to access the WAV file, so close it}
  WaveCloseReadFile(mmioHndle, WaveFormat);
end;

procedure TForm1.AppIdle(Sender: TObject; var Done: Boolean);
const
  LastPlayPos: Integer = 0;
var
  CurPlayPos,
  CurWritePos: Integer;
  StartOffset: Integer;
  Audio,
  Junk: Pointer;
  NumBytesLocked,
  JunkBytes,
  BytesRead: DWORD;
begin
  {setting Done to FALSE indicates that we want the application to
   continuously call this function}
  Done := FALSE;

  {if the DirectSound object has been created...}
  if Assigned(Sound) then
  begin
    {retrieve the play and write positions}
    Sound.GetCurrentPosition(@CurPlayPos, @CurWritePos);

    {since our buffer is only 2 seconds long, WaveFormat.nAvgBytesPerSec
     represents the midpoint of the buffer (1 second)}
    if (CurPlayPos<LastPlayPos) or ((CurPlayPos>=WaveFormat.nAvgBytesPerSec)
    and (LastPlayPos<WaveFormat.nAvgBytesPerSec)) then
    begin
      {wrap around the starting offset as necessary}
      If CurPlayPos>=WaveFormat.nAvgBytesPerSec then
        StartOffset := 0
      else
        StartOffset := WaveFormat.nAvgBytesPerSec;
```

```
    {lock the buffer, preparing it to write out 1 second of data}
    Sound.Lock(StartOffset, WaveFormat.nAvgBytesPerSec, Pointer(Audio),
              NumBytesLocked, Junk, JunkBytes, 0);

    {copy the audio data into the sound buffer object}
    WaveReadFile(mmioHndle, NumBytesLocked, Audio, @ChunkInfo, BytesRead);

    {copy any extra bytes as necessary}
    if BytesRead<NumBytesLocked then
    begin
      WaveStartDataRead(mmioHndle, @ChunkInfo, @ChunkInfoParent);
      WaveReadFile(mmioHndle, NumBytesLocked-BytesRead,
                  Pointer(Longint(Audio)+BytesRead), @ChunkInfo, BytesRead);
    end;

    {unlock the buffer}
    Sound.Unlock(Audio, NumBytesLocked, nil, 0);

    {store the last known playing position}
    LastPlayPos := CurPlayPos;
  end;
  end;
end;
```

---

## Duplicating Buffers

It is quite common in action games to have a short sound that is repeated often, such as gunshots, laser bursts, or even explosions. To play a regular static buffer in its entirety, the SetCurrentPosition method is called to "rewind" the sound, and then the Play method is called to begin audio output. If this sound is to be repeated rapidly, such as when the user is frantically pressing the fire button, the sound may seem to stutter, as each time the sound is replayed the previously playing sound is started from the beginning. The solution would be some method by which this sound buffer can be copied, sharing the sound data with the original buffer but with its own playing position. Fortunately, DirectSound provides a method by which a static buffer can be duplicated.

By calling the DuplicateSoundBuffer method, another IDirectSoundBuffer object is created. This new object has its own play and write pointers, but it shares the audio data with the original sound (as opposed to creating its own sound buffer). It can be played or stopped regardless of the state of the original sound, but since it shares the original buffer, a duplicated buffer should not be locked nor should its data be modified. The DuplicateSoundBuffer method is defined as:

```
function DuplicateSoundBuffer(
lpDsbOriginal: IDirectSoundBuffer;        // the original sound buffer
var lpDsbDuplicate: IDirectSoundBuffer    // the duplicated sound buffer
): HResult;                               // returns a DirectX error code
```

The first parameter is a pointer to the sound buffer that is to be duplicated. The second parameter is an IDirectSoundBuffer object that is instantiated as a copy of the original when the function returns.

Bear in mind that although the sound buffer is not reproduced, duplicating a sound buffer does require some resources. Thus, it is better to locate static buffers to be duplicated in system memory, as duplicating a hardware buffer may require additional hardware resources that are not available or should be used for more efficient purposes.

**Note:** Calling DuplicateSoundBuffer on a hardware buffer will fail when no more (or insufficient) hardware resources are available.

The DirectX SDK comes with an object that encapsulates this buffer duplication, making it easy to manage sounds that must be played multiple times concurrently. While the following example makes no use of any such object, it is easy to see how one could potentially be created to encapsulate the functionality as illustrated. The example demonstrates how to play a single sound multiple times by using the DuplicateSoundBuffer method to create several copies of the sound. For comparison purposes, the original sound can be played as well, illustrating how using the DuplicateSoundBuffer method can help eliminate stutter from sounds played in rapid succession.

*Listing 9-8: Using the DuplicateSoundBuffer method*

```
var
  DXSound: IDirectSound;
  Sound: IDirectSoundBuffer;

  {the array of duplicated sound buffers}
  SoundArray: array[0..5] of IDirectSoundBuffer;

  {stores the current index into the array}
  CurSound: Integer;

procedure TForm1.FormCreate(Sender: TObject);
var
  iCount: Integer;
begin
  {create the DirectSound object}
  DirectSoundCreate(nil, DXSound, nil);

  {set its cooperative level}
  DXSound.SetCooperativeLevel(Handle, DSSCL_NORMAL);

  {load in the example sound}
  Sound := DSLoadSound(DXSound, ExtractFilePath(ParamStr(0))+'Sample.wav',
                       FALSE);
```

```
  {create several duplicates of the original sound}
  for iCount := 0 to 5 do
    DXSound.DuplicateSoundBuffer(Sound, SoundArray[iCount]);

  {set the index to the first element}
  CurSound := 0;
end;

procedure TForm1.Button1Click(Sender: TObject);
begin
  {simply play the original buffer from the beginning. results in a stutter
   if played rapidly}
  Sound.SetCurrentPosition(0);
  Sound.Play(0, 0, 0);
end;

procedure TForm1.Button2Click(Sender: TObject);
begin
  {increment the index and wrap it around if necessary}
  Inc(CurSound);
  if CurSound>5 then
    CurSound := 0;

  {play a duplicated buffer from the beginning}
  SoundArray[CurSound].SetCurrentPosition(0);
  SoundArray[CurSound].Play(0, 0, 0);
end;
```

## Buffer Controls

The IDirectSoundBuffer interface contains several methods by which the application can control certain aspects of the sound. Specifically, an application can control pan, frequency, and volume. This allows a developer to implement several special sound effects that can greatly enhance a game. For example, the pan control can be used to move the sound of an engine whine from side to side as a spaceship crosses the screen. Volume could be used to reduce and finally eliminate an engine whine as a ship moves farther away. The frequency could even be adjusted up or down to indicate the speed of an engine, or perhaps even damage.

Specifically, pan is controlled through the GetPan and SetPan methods, frequency is controlled through the GetFrequency and SetFrequency methods, and volume is controlled through the GetVolume and SetVolume methods. All methods take but a single parameter. Pan and volume are expressed in relative terms, but frequency is expressed in hertz. All attributes have an acceptable range, and pan and volume have a neutral value, which is illustrated in Table 9-2.

The desired sound buffer controls are specified when the IDirectSoundBuffer object is created. As mentioned previously, the dwFlags member of the TDSBufferDesc structure can be set to a combination of values that indicate the memory location of the sound buffer and other attributes. The three flags used to give control of a buffer's pan, frequency, and volume are illustrated in Table 9-2. Additionally, the DBSCAPS_CTRLALL or the DBSCAPS_CTRLDEFAULT flags can be used to indicate that the buffer has access to all controls or the pan, frequency, and volume controls, respectively.

**Caution:** As an issue of performance, buffers with additional controls require additional processing time for real-time modification of the sound data. Therefore, it is suggested that only the specific control flags truly needed for a buffer be used, and the DBSCAPS_CTRLALL or DBSCAPS_CTRLDEFAULT flags should only be used for buffers that actually need all controls.

*Table 9-2: Pan, frequency, and volume ranges and neutral values*

| Control | Flag | Neutral Value | Range |
|---|---|---|---|
| Frequency | DSBCAPS_ CTRLFREQUENCY | None | Software buffers: DSBFREQUENCY_MIN to DSBFREQUENCY_MAX.<br><br>Hardware buffers: dwMinSecondarySample rate to dwMaxSecondarySampleRate (see the GetCaps method) |
| Pan | DSBCAPS_CTRLPAN | DSBPAN_CENTER | DSBPAN_LEFT to DSBPAN_RIGHT |
| Volume | DSBCAPS_CTRLVOLUME | DSBVOLUME_MAX | DSBVOLUME_MIN to DSBVOLUME_MAX |

The following example demonstrates how to create a sound buffer using the pan, volume, and frequency controls, retrieve their settings, and modify their values in real time.

*Listing 9-9: Using buffer controls for special effects*

```
procedure TForm1.FormCreate(Sender: TObject);
var
  Audio: PByte;
  Junk: Pointer;
  NumBytesLocked: DWORD;
  JunkBytes: DWORD;
  WaveFormat: PWaveFormatEx;
  mmioHndle: HMMIO;
```

```
      ChunkInfo,
      ChunkInfoParent: TMMCKInfo;
      BufDesc: TDSBufferDesc;
      Pos: LongInt;
      FreqPos: DWORD;
  begin
    {create the DirectSound object}
    DirectSoundCreate(nil, DXSound, nil);

    {set its cooperative level high enough to allow the application to
     change the format of the primary buffer}
    DXSound.SetCooperativeLevel(Handle, DSSCL_NORMAL);

    {open the WAV file}
    WaveOpenFile(PChar(ExtractFilePath(ParamStr(0))+'Example.wav'), mmioHndle,
                WaveFormat, @ChunkInfoParent);

    {begin reading WAV file data}
    WaveStartDataRead(mmioHndle, @ChunkInfo, @ChunkInfoParent);

    {initialize the sound buffer description structure, indicating the
     controls we wish to use}
    FillMemory(@BufDesc, SizeOf(TDSBufferDesc), 0);
    BufDesc.dwSize := SizeOf(TDSBufferDesc);
    BufDesc.dwFlags := DSBCAPS_STATIC or DSBCAPS_CTRLFREQUENCY or
                       DSBCAPS_CTRLPAN or DSBCAPS_CTRLVOLUME;
    BufDesc.dwBufferBytes := ChunkInfo.cksize;
    BufDesc.lpwfxFormat := WaveFormat;

    {create the sound buffer}
    DXCheck( DXSound.CreateSoundBuffer(BufDesc, Sound, nil) );

    {copy the sound data into the buffer}
    DXCheck( Sound.Lock(0, 0, Pointer(Audio), NumBytesLocked, Junk, JunkBytes,
                       DSBLOCK_ENTIREBUFFER) );
    WaveReadFile(mmioHndle, NumBytesLocked, Audio, @ChunkInfo, JunkBytes);
    DXCheck( Sound.Unlock(Audio, NumBytesLocked, nil, 0) );

    {close the WAV file}
    WaveCloseReadFile(mmioHndle, WaveFormat);

    {initialize the Pan trackbar}
    tbrPan.Min := DSBPAN_LEFT;
    tbrPan.Max := DSBPAN_RIGHT;
    Sound.GetPan(Pos);
    tbrPan.Position := Pos;

    {initialize the Volume trackbar}
    tbrVolume.Min := DSBVOLUME_MIN;
    tbrVolume.Max := DSBVOLUME_MAX;
    Sound.GetVolume(Pos);
```

```
          tbrVolume.Position := Pos;

          {initialize the Frequency trackbar}
          tbrFrequency.Max := DSBFREQUENCY_MAX;
          tbrFrequency.Min := DSBFREQUENCY_MIN;
          Sound.GetFrequency(FreqPos);
          tbrFrequency.Position := FreqPos;

          {begin playing the sound}
          Sound.Play(0, 0, DSBPLAY_LOOPING);
        end;

        procedure TForm1.tbrPanChange(Sender: TObject);
        begin
          {set the Pan position}
          Sound.SetPan(tbrPan.Position);
        end;

        procedure TForm1.tbrVolumeChange(Sender: TObject);
        begin
          {set the Volume position}
          Sound.SetVolume(tbrVolume.Position);
        end;

        procedure TForm1.tbrFrequencyChange(Sender: TObject);
        begin
          {set the Frequency}
          Sound.SetFrequency(tbrFrequency.Position);
        end;
```

## Music

Music, like sound effects, adds depth to a game, giving it a feeling of completeness. Even more than sound effects, music adds mood to a game, and when used effectively can adjust the user's frame of mind as effectively as a movie sound track.

Most games feature music that changes in response to changing conditions within the game. An effective use of music would be to play something eerie and mysterious when exploring catacombs, change to a heart-pounding rock-and-roll piece during the heat of combat, and end with a euphoric anthem to signal victory or a melancholic hymn to signal defeat. The difficulty comes in writing such musical ballads; programmatically outputting the result is easy by comparison.

The topic of musical output, while poorly documented, has been explored by a number of adventurous programmers, and as such there are several techniques for its implementation. One simple technique may be to simply digitize a musical piece and use the methods described above for its playback. Several other techniques involve digitized music compressed in various formats and then uncompressed on the fly as it is output to the audio device. However, for our purposes, we will examine only two common musical output techniques: MIDI and CD audio. Both of these techniques use Win32 MCI API commands, and as such do not make use of DirectX or DirectSound functionality.

> **Tip:** As stated at the beginning of the chapter, the DirectX 6.1 and above SDK contains the new DirectMusic component that brings the power of DirectX to MIDI output. The header files were not available during the production of this book, and thus we were unable to cover them in this chapter. However, the DirectMusic header files are available on the CD accompanying this book.

## MCISendCommand

All of the examples to follow make use of a very powerful Win32 API function called MCISendCommand. This is a high-level command in the Media Control Interface (MCI) subsystem of Windows. The MCISendCommand function is simple in its declaration but very complex in terms of what it can do. You can use the MCISendCommand function to take advantage of any native Windows multimedia functionality, including playback of WAV files, video files, and MIDI and CD music (as we'll see below), and interaction with video recording and playback equipment. Our uses of this function will be limited solely to MIDI and CD audio output, but you should be aware that this is a very powerful and complex function that unfortunately is poorly documented. The MCISendCommand function is defined as:

```
function mciSendCommand(
mciId: MCIDEVICEID;        // the MCI device identifier
uMessage: UINT;            // the command message
dwParam1,                  // command message flags
dwParam2: DWORD            // address of parameter structure
): MCIERROR;               // returns an MCI error code
```

The first parameter to this function is the identifier of the MCI device to which the command should be sent. This is retrieved when the device is first opened. The second parameter is the actual command to be sent to the device. Each command instructs the device to perform a different task, and we'll see several commands in the following examples. The third parameter is a series of flags that are dependent on the type of command sent, and indicate which members of the structure identified by the last parameter contain valid data. In particular, the MCI_WAIT flag is used often to indicate that the function should not return until the command has been carried out. The final parameter takes a pointer to a data structure, again dependent upon the type of command being sent. Some data structures must be initialized, while others are initialized by the function and contain pertinent data when it returns. For some reason, due to the way this function was declared, you must pass the structure's address by typecasting it as a longint. This will be illustrated in the examples to follow.

### Notification

MCISendCommand is asynchronous by nature, and will return immediately unless the MCI_WAIT flag was specified. In this event, you can usually specify the MCI_NOTIFY flag to indicate that the function should notify the application when it has completed. This is accomplished by sending the application an MM_MCINOTIFY message. It is a simple matter to define a handler for this message, and this technique is used in Listing 9-10.

## MIDI

MIDI, or Musical Instrument Digital Interface, is a format for describing musical sound, much the same as the WAV format describes digitized sound. It is an effective means of providing music within a small footprint. Both software for creating MIDI files and freeware or shareware MIDI songs are readily available.

 **MIDI (Musical Instrument Digital Interface):** A digital format for describing music.

In order to implement MIDI music playback, several steps must be followed. With the exception of detecting available hardware, none of these steps are optional. Outputting MIDI music is implemented by performing these tasks:

■ Check for MIDI output hardware existence

■ Open the MIDI output device

■ Set the time format

■ Commence playback

■ Retrieve playback status

■ Close the device

### Check for MIDI Output Hardware Existence

The target machine must have a device capable of outputting MIDI music. It would be very difficult these days to find a sound card that did not also include the ability to output MIDI music. Thus, it is safe to assume that any machine with a sound card is capable of outputting MIDI. However, the developer can use the function midiOutGetNumDevs to determine if there are indeed any devices that can output MIDI music. The midiOutGetNumDevs function takes no parameters and returns a simple integer. If this integer value is greater than zero, at least one hardware device has been found that is capable of MIDI music output.

## Open the MIDI Output Device

The first real step in playing MIDI music is to open the "sequencer" device (the hardware device capable of outputting MIDI music) and the MIDI file that will be played. This requires a variable of the type TMCI_Open_Parms. This data structure describes the device being opened and the file that will be played on the device. The TMCI_Open_Parms data structure is defined as:

```
TMCI_Open_Parms = record
  dwCallback: DWORD;              // a window handle
  wDeviceID: MCIDEVICEID;         // the device identifier
  lpstrDeviceType: PAnsiChar;     // the name of the device
  lpstrElementName: PAnsiChar;    // the name of the element
  lpstrAlias: PAnsiChar;          // a device alias
end;
```

The first member of this structure can be set to the handle of a window which will receive the MM_MCINOTIFY message (if so desired) when the function completes. The second member will be set to the MCI device identifier when the function returns, and should be stored for later use. The third parameter is set to the name of the device; for MIDI file playback, this should be set to 'sequencer.' The fourth parameter is set to the name of the MIDI file, which is opened and prepared for playback when this function returns. The final member contains a device alias and for our purposes can be ignored.

For our purposes, we can also ignore the dwCallback member. Thus, to open the MIDI device and a MIDI file, we must initialize lpstrDeviceType to 'sequencer,' set lpstrElementName to the filename of our MIDI file, and pass the structure to the MCISendCommand function, specifying MCI_OPEN as our command message. For example:

```
{open the MIDI output device, loading the Canyon MIDI song}
OpenParms.lpstrDeviceType  := 'sequencer';
OpenParms.lpstrElementName := 'C:\Windows\Media\Canyon.mid';
MCISendCommand(0, MCI_OPEN, MCI_OPEN_TYPE or MCI_OPEN_ELEMENT or MCI_WAIT,
               LongInt(@OpenParms));

{save a handle to the device}
MCIDeviceID := OpenParms.wDeviceID;
```

When this command returns, the wDeviceID member of TMCI_Open_Parms will contain a device identifier for the opened MIDI sequencer. The application should store this value, as it will be used in all subsequent MCISendCommand function calls.

## Set the Time Format

The MCI subsystem needs to know the time format for playback of various media so it will not come out garbled or trashed. MIDI music is timed by the millisecond, so we must inform MCI to set the time format for playback to milliseconds. This is accomplished by initializing a variable of type TMCI_Set_Parms. The TMCI_Set_Parms structure is defined as:

```
TMCI_Set_Parms = record
  dwCallback: DWORD;                    // a window handle
  dwTimeFormat: DWORD;                  // the time format
  dwAudio: DWORD;                       // audio output channel
end;
```

The first member of this structure can be set to the handle of a window which will receive the MM_MCINOTIFY message (if so desired) when the function completes. The second parameter is a flag that indicates the time format. The final member indicates the audio output channel.

For our purposes, we are only interested in the dwTimeFormat member, which should be set to MCI_FORMAT_MILLISECONDS to indicate a millisecond time format. This initialized structure is then sent to the MCISendCommand function with a command message of MCI_SET. We must also pass in the device ID that we recorded from the previous call to indicate the device whose time format is being set. For example:

```
{set the time format to milliseconds}
SetParms.dwTimeFormat := MCI_FORMAT_MILLISECONDS;
MCISendCommand(MCIDeviceID, MCI_SET, MCI_WAIT or MCI_SET_TIME_FORMAT,
              LongInt(@SetParms));
```

## Commence Playback

The final step simply informs the multimedia system that we wish to play the file. This requires a variable of the type TMCI_Play_Parms. The TMCI_Play_Parms data structure is defined as:

```
TMCI_Play_Parms = record
  dwCallback: DWORD;                    // a window handle
  dwFrom: DWORD;                        // play start position
  dwTo: DWORD;                          // play end position
end;
```

The first member of this structure can be set to the handle of a window which will receive the MM_MCINOTIFY message (if so desired) when the function completes. The second member indicates the position at which to start playback, and the final member indicates the position at which to end playback.

This data structure allows the application to specify the exact position from which to begin playback and an exact position at which to end the playback.

Even though the MCISendCommand function requires a variable of this type, there is no need to initialize any of the members to simply play the MIDI file; it will play it from start to finish by default. The MCI_PLAY command message instructs Windows to begin playback. For example:

```
{commence song playback, indicating that we wish to receive an MM_MCINOTIFY
 message when the playback has completed}
PlayParms.dwCallback := Handle;
MCISendCommand(MCIDeviceID, MCI_PLAY, MCI_NOTIFY, LongInt(@PlayParms));
```

Notice that we set the dwCallback member to the handle of our main window, and indicated that we wished to be notified when the function finishes. If we had used the MCI_WAIT flag, our application would hang until the MIDI file had finished playing. Obviously, this is not acceptable, so we indicated that we would instead like to receive the MM_MCINOTIFY message when the music stops. In our example below, we use this to implement a looping feature.

### Retrieve Playback Status

While certainly not a required step, most applications at some point may need to know the current position of playback. This could be used to change the music according to the context, waiting for playback to reach a specific point so the music can be changed at an appropriate time. We can retrieve the current playback status by using a variable of type TMCI_Status_Parms. TMCI_Status_Parms is defined as:

```
TMCI_Status_Parms = record
  dwCallback: DWORD;                 // a window handle
  dwReturn: DWORD;                   // the status value
  dwItem: DWORD;                     // the status item
  dwTrack: DWORD;                    // length
end;
```

The first member of this structure can be set to the handle of a window which will receive the MM_MCINOTIFY message (if so desired) when the function completes. The second member contains the status value when the function returns. The third member contains a flag indicating the item whose status is to be retrieved. For our purposes, this can be set to MCI_STATUS_POSITION to indicate we wish to retrieve the status of the playback position. The final member indicates the length or number of tracks. The MCI_STATUS command message indicates we wish to retrieve the device's status. For example:

```
{retrieve the current position of the song playback}
StatusParms.dwItem := MCI_STATUS_POSITION;
MCISendCommand(MCIDeviceID, MCI_STATUS, MCI_WAIT or MCI_STATUS_ITEM,
               LongInt(@StatusParms));
```

## Close the Device

When the application terminates or MIDI music playback is no longer required, the MCI device must be closed and released by calling the MCISendCommand with a command message of MCI_CLOSE. The MCI device ID must be passed in to the first parameter, but the last two parameters are unused and should be set to zero.

The following example implements the discussed steps in order to play back a MIDI music file.

**Listing 9-10:** *Playing MIDI music*

```
procedure TfrmMidiExample.FormCreate(Sender: TObject);
begin
  {determine if there are any devices capable of outputting MIDI music}
  if midiOutGetNumDevs<1 then
  begin
    ShowMessage('There are no devices attached to the system capable of '+
                'outputting MIDI music.');
    Application.Terminate;
  end;
end;

procedure TfrmMidiExample.FormClose(Sender: TObject;
  var Action: TCloseAction);
begin
  {make sure that the MIDI device is closed before exiting the program}
  MCISendCommand(MCIDeviceID, MCI_CLOSE, 0, 0);
end;

procedure TfrmMidiExample.btnPlayClick(Sender: TObject);
var
  OpenParms: TMCI_Open_Parms;
  PlayParms: TMCI_Play_Parms;
  StatusParms: TMCI_Status_Parms;
  SetParms: TMCI_Set_Parms;
begin
  {open the MIDI output device, loading the Canyon MIDI song}
  OpenParms.lpstrDeviceType  := 'sequencer';
  OpenParms.lpstrElementName := 'C:\Windows\Media\Canyon.mid';
  MCISendCommand(0, MCI_OPEN, MCI_OPEN_TYPE or MCI_OPEN_ELEMENT or MCI_WAIT,
                LongInt(@OpenParms));

  {save a handle to the device}
  MCIDeviceID := OpenParms.wDeviceID;

  {set the time format to milliseconds}
  SetParms.dwTimeFormat := MCI_FORMAT_MILLISECONDS;
  MCISendCommand(MCIDeviceID, MCI_SET, MCI_WAIT or MCI_SET_TIME_FORMAT,
                LongInt(@SetParms));
```

```
   {retrieve the length of the song}
   StatusParms.dwItem := MCI_STATUS_LENGTH;
   MCISendCommand(MCIDeviceID, MCI_STATUS, MCI_WAIT or MCI_STATUS_ITEM,
                  LongInt(@StatusParms));

   {display this length in terms of minutes and seconds}
   Label1.Caption := Format('%d:%.2d', [StatusParms.dwReturn div 1000 div 60,
                            Trunc(Frac(StatusParms.dwReturn/1000/60)*60)]);

   {commence song playback, indicating that we wish to receive an MM_MCINOTIFY
    message when the playback has completed}
   PlayParms.dwCallback := Handle;
   MCISendCommand(MCIDeviceID, MCI_PLAY, MCI_NOTIFY, LongInt(@PlayParms));

   {enable the playback position polling timer}
   tmrPosition.Enabled := TRUE;
end;

         .
         .
         .


procedure TfrmMidiExample.tmrPositionTimer(Sender: TObject);
var
   StatusParms: TMCI_Status_Parms;
begin
   {retrieve the current position of the song playback}
   StatusParms.dwItem := MCI_STATUS_POSITION;
   MCISendCommand(MCIDeviceID, MCI_STATUS, MCI_WAIT or MCI_STATUS_ITEM,
                  LongInt(@StatusParms));

   {indicate this position in terms of minutes and seconds}
   Label2.Caption := Format('%d:%.2d', [StatusParms.dwReturn div 1000 div 60,
                            Trunc(Frac(StatusParms.dwReturn/1000/60)*60)]);
end;
```

## CD Audio

MIDI offers the advantage of providing large musical scores with minimal space requirements. However, unless the user has a dedicated MIDI sound card (unlikely unless they are a musician), musical sound quality will always be less than perfect. Many games are circumventing this limitation by playing their musical scores directly off of the CD on which the game is distributed. This offers the highest possible sound quality, although the amount of music available to the game will be limited by the number of scores and their length, as CD audio requires much more storage space than MIDI files.

The method by which data and music is stored on the CD varies. In a mixed-mode CD, all executable data must be placed in what a regular CD player would recognize as the first track. Multisession CDs do not have this requirement.

**Caution:** While the application is accessing data from the CD, it cannot play a musical track, and vice versa.

The music data itself is stored on the CD in a format known as Red Book Audio. This format provides for stereo music at the highest quality, and is the format used by the professional music industry to record music onto conventional audio CDs. An interesting side effect to this arrangement is that a CD game taking advantage of Red Book Audio music can be placed into a conventional CD player and played as if it were any regular music CD. The data track will be nothing but white noise, but the musical tracks can be replayed as desired.

**Red Book Audio:** The digital format used to store professional music on conventional audio CDs.

It is important to note that the end user's machine must be set up correctly before it can play CD audio music. This involves installing a small wire that runs directly from the CD to the audio output hardware. While most new machines have this installed automatically, it may not always be available. Also, as an added benefit, this direct connection between the hardware results in true multitasking when playing CD audio. The audio signals are sent directly to the sound output hardware, bypassing the CPU completely. Thus, playing CD audio involves almost no CPU utilization, resulting in almost no performance penalties.

Like MIDI music playback, several steps must be followed in order to initialize and commence the playback of a CD audio track. CD audio playback is implemented by performing these tasks:

- Open the CD device
- Check for the existence of the CD
- Set the time format
- Retrieve the number of tracks and their length
- Commence playback
- Stop playback
- Close the device

### Open the CD Device

If the music for a game is stored on a CD along with the executable code, the target machine must contain a CD-ROM drive in order to use the application. Thus, we do not need to check for the existence of a CD-ROM drive. However, it is good practice to test for the existence of a CD in the drive before attempting to play a track from it. This will be discussed in a moment.

Like MIDI, we must first open the CD device. However, unlike MIDI, we do not need to specify a file. Again, we will need a variable of the type TMCI_Open_Parms, but this time its lpstrDeviceType member must be set to the string 'cdaudio'. For example:

```
{open the cd audio playback device}
OpenParms.lpstrDeviceType := 'cdaudio';
MCISendCommand(0, MCI_OPEN, MCI_OPEN_TYPE or MCI_WAIT, Longint(@OpenParms));

{save a handle to the cd audio device}
MCIDeviceID := OpenParms.wDeviceID;
```

### Check for the Existence of the CD

Once the CD audio device is opened, we can poll it to determine if a CD is actually inserted. To accomplish this, we need a variable of the type TMCI_Status_Parms. The dwItem member of this data structure must be set to MCI_STATUS_MEDIA_PRESENT to indicate that we wish to test for the presence of a CD in the drive. We then call the MCISendCommand function, passing MCI_STATUS in its second parameter. For example:

```
{determine if a CD is present in the drive}
StatusParms.dwItem := MCI_STATUS_MEDIA_PRESENT ;
MCISendCommand(MCIDeviceID, MCI_STATUS, MCI_WAIT or MCI_STATUS_ITEM,
               LongInt(@StatusParms));
```

When this function returns, if the dwReturn member is set to zero, there is no CD present in the drive, and the application should display an error message asking the user to insert the CD, repeating the check as necessary. If the dwReturn member is greater than zero, there is a CD in the drive, although it may not be the game's CD. Each CD contains a unique identifying number that we can use to determine if it is the required CD. The example in Listing 9-11 demonstrates how to extract this identifying number.

### Set the Time Format

Like MIDI, we must inform the MCI subsystem as to the timing format used for playback. Red Book Audio is timed by tracks, minutes, seconds, and frames, where there are 75 frames per second. We will use a variable of type TMCI_Set_Parms, setting its dwTimeFormat member to MCI_FORMAT_TMSF to indicate this unusual timing format. For example:

```
{set the time format for the CD audio device}
SetParms.dwTimeFormat := MCI_FORMAT_TMSF;
MCISendCommand(MCIDeviceID, MCI_SET, MCI_WAIT or MCI_SET_TIME_FORMAT,
               Longint(@SetParms));
```

### Retrieve the Number of Tracks and Their Length

While it's not absolutely necessary to retrieve the number of tracks on a CD, you do need to record the length of each track. More specifically, you must record the length of the very last track for reasons that are explained below. For the purposes of our example, however, we will record the number of tracks on the CD and the length of each so they may be displayed by our CD player example.

We make use of another TMCI_Status_Parms variable, setting its dwItem member to MCI_STATUS_NUMBER_OF_TRACKS to indicate we wish to retrieve the number of tracks. Once this is accomplished, we can then set dwTrack to a specific track number (we'll iterate through each track) and the dwItem member to MCI_STATUS_LENGTH, indicating we wish to retrieve its length. For example:

```
{retrieve the number of tracks on the CD}
StatusParms.dwItem := MCI_STATUS_NUMBER_OF_TRACKS ;
MCISendCommand(MCIDeviceID, MCI_STATUS, MCI_WAIT or MCI_STATUS_ITEM,
              LongInt(@StatusParms));
NumTracks := StatusParms.dwReturn;

{for each track, indicate its length}
for iCount := 1 to NumTracks do
begin
  StatusParms.dwTrack := iCount;
  StatusParms.dwItem := MCI_STATUS_LENGTH;
  MCISendCommand(MCIDeviceID, MCI_STATUS, MCI_WAIT or MCI_STATUS_ITEM or
                MCI_TRACK, LongInt(@StatusParms));
  .
  .
  .
end;
```

### Commence Playback

Once the CD device is opened, and we have determined that a CD does in fact exist, we can play a track. For this, we will need a variable of the type TMCI_Play_Parms. However, we must make use of the dwFrom and dwTo members of this structure in order to indicate the exact desired track to play.

Because of the unusual timing format, we must use the MCI_MAKE_TMSF function to encode an appropriate starting and ending play position. Playing a single track is relatively simple, as we can specify a starting track with an ending track one greater than the starting track. For example:

```
PlayParms.dwFrom := MCI_MAKE_TMSF(1, 0, 0, 0);
PlayParms.dwTo := MCI_MAKE_TMSF(2, 0, 0, 0);
MCISendCommand(MCIDeviceID, MCI_PLAY, MCI_FROM or MCI_TO, Longint(@PlayParms));
```

This indicates that we wish to play track one in its entirety. However, this technique will not work on the last track, since there is not another track beyond it (and setting the from member to a value one greater than the number of tracks on a CD results in an error). Therefore, you must specify the exact length of the track when playing the very last one. This is why we recorded all of the track lengths earlier. We'll see an implementation of this in Listing 9-11.

## Stop Playback

Before another CD track can be played, the currently playing track must be stopped. This is accomplished by simply calling the MCISendCommand function with a command message of MCI_STOP. For example:

```
MCISendCommand(MCIDeviceID, MCI_STOP, MCI_WAIT, 0);
```

## Close the Device

As with MIDI, the MCI device must be closed and released by calling the MCISendCommand with a command message of MCI_CLOSE when the application terminates. The MCI device ID must be passed in to the first parameter, but the last two parameters are unused and should be set to zero.

The following example implements the discussed steps in order to play back Red Book Audio data from a CD.

**Listing 9-11:** *Playing CD Audio tracks*

```
procedure TfrmCDExample.FormCreate(Sender: TObject);
var
  OpenParms: TMCI_Open_Parms;
  StatusParms: TMCI_Status_Parms;
  SetParms: TMCI_Set_Parms;
  InfoParms: TMCI_Info_Parms;

  UniqueID: array[0..255] of char;

  NumTracks,
  iCount: Integer;
begin
  {open the cd audio playback device}
  OpenParms.lpstrDeviceType := 'cdaudio';
  MCISendCommand(0, MCI_OPEN, MCI_OPEN_TYPE or MCI_WAIT, Longint(@OpenParms));

  {save a handle to the cd audio device}
  MCIDeviceID := OpenParms.wDeviceID;

  {determine if a CD is present in the drive}
  StatusParms.dwItem := MCI_STATUS_MEDIA_PRESENT ;
  MCISendCommand(MCIDeviceID, MCI_STATUS, MCI_WAIT or MCI_STATUS_ITEM,
                 LongInt(@StatusParms));
```

```
         if not LongBool(StatusParms.dwReturn) then
         begin
           ShowMessage('No CD is inserted in the CD-ROM drive. Please insert a CD '+
                       'and try again.');
           Application.Terminate;
         end;

         {retrieve and display the unique CD identification number. this is for
          information only, and is not required for playing a track from the CD}
         InfoParms.dwRetSize := 255;
         InfoParms.lpstrReturn := UniqueID;
         MCISendCommand(MCIDeviceID, MCI_INFO, MCI_INFO_MEDIA_IDENTITY or MCI_WAIT,
                       Longint(@InfoParms));
         lblUniqueID.Caption := UniqueID;

         {set the time format for the CD audio device}
         SetParms.dwTimeFormat := MCI_FORMAT_TMSF;
         MCISendCommand(MCIDeviceID, MCI_SET, MCI_WAIT or MCI_SET_TIME_FORMAT,
                       Longint(@SetParms));

         {retrieve the number of tracks on the CD}
         StatusParms.dwItem := MCI_STATUS_NUMBER_OF_TRACKS ;
         MCISendCommand(MCIDeviceID, MCI_STATUS, MCI_WAIT or MCI_STATUS_ITEM,
                       LongInt(@StatusParms));
         NumTracks := StatusParms.dwReturn;

         {for each track, indicate its length}
         for iCount := 1 to NumTracks do
         begin
           StatusParms.dwTrack := iCount;
           StatusParms.dwItem := MCI_STATUS_LENGTH;
           MCISendCommand(MCIDeviceID, MCI_STATUS, MCI_WAIT or MCI_STATUS_ITEM or
                         MCI_TRACK, LongInt(@StatusParms));

           {when polling for length on a specific track, the value returned in the TMSF
            format is not exactly what you would expect. the Track macro returns
            minutes, the Minute macro returns seconds, the Second macro returns frames,
            and the Frame macro returns nothing. notice also that we are saving the
            exact length of each track in the Objects property}
           lbxCDTracks.Items.AddObject('Track '+IntToStr(iCount)+' - '+
                               Format('%d:%.2d',
                               [MCI_TMSF_TRACK(StatusParms.dwReturn),
                               MCI_TMSF_MINUTE(StatusParms.dwReturn)]),
                               TObject(MCI_MAKE_TMSF(
                               iCount,MCI_TMSF_TRACK(StatusParms.dwReturn),
                               MCI_TMSF_MINUTE(StatusParms.dwReturn),
                               MCI_TMSF_SECOND(StatusParms.dwReturn))));
         end;
       end;

       procedure TfrmCDExample.lbxCDTracksDblClick(Sender: TObject);
```

```
var
  PlayParms: TMCI_Play_Parms;
begin
  {the user has indicated that another track should be played. therefore, stop
   any CD audio currently being output}
  MCISendCommand(MCIDeviceID, MCI_STOP, MCI_WAIT, 0);

  {the index of the selected item matches the index of the requested CD audio
   track. however, CD audio track indexes are one-based, and list box indexes
   are zero-based, so we must add a one to the selected item index. this
   indicates the starting track from which to begin playback}
  PlayParms.dwFrom := MCI_MAKE_TMSF(lbxCDTracks.ItemIndex+1, 0, 0, 0);

  {remember that we stored the actual length of each track in the Objects
   property along with the track name? since there is no track following the
   last track on the CD, we cannot tell the device to play the current track
   to the next track. to play the last track on the CD, we must indicate the
   exact length of that track. therefore, if we are playing the last track,
   we extract the track's exact length from the Objects property. otherwise
   we can simply tell it to play to the next track}
  if lbxCDTracks.ItemIndex = lbxCDTracks.Items.Count-1 then
    PlayParms.dwTo := Longint(lbxCDTracks.Items.Objects[lbxCDTracks.ItemIndex])
  else
    PlayParms.dwTo := MCI_MAKE_TMSF(lbxCDTracks.ItemIndex+2, 0, 0, 0);

  {instruct the CD audio device to play the indicated selection}
  MCISendCommand(MCIDeviceID, MCI_PLAY, MCI_FROM or MCI_TO,
                 Longint(@PlayParms));
end;

procedure TfrmCDExample.TimerTimer(Sender: TObject);
var
  StatusParms: TMCI_Status_Parms;
begin
  {poll the CD to determine the position of the current playback}
  StatusParms.dwItem := MCI_STATUS_POSITION;
  MCISendCommand(MCIDeviceID, MCI_STATUS, MCI_WAIT or MCI_STATUS_ITEM,
                 LongInt(@StatusParms));

  {the returned position value is in TMSF format. thus, we must extract the
   appropriate minutes and seconds values}
  lblPosition.Caption := Format('%d:%.2d',
                         [MCI_TMSF_MINUTE(StatusParms.dwReturn),
                          MCI_TMSF_SECOND(StatusParms.dwReturn)]);
end;

procedure TfrmCDExample.FormClose(Sender: TObject; var Action: TCloseAction);
begin
  {the application is terminating, so stop any CD audio playback, and
   close the CD audio device}
  MCISendCommand(MCIDeviceID, MCI_STOP, MCI_WAIT, 0);
```

```
    MCISendCommand(MCIDeviceID, MCI_CLOSE, 0, 0);
end;
```

## Summary

In this chapter, we discussed several techniques for playing both sound effects and music. We examined various DirectSound methods for performing digitized audio playback, including changing the format of the primary buffer as well as duplicating sound buffers. We also covered the steps required to output MIDI music as well as more superior techniques for playing audio tracks from a CD. When coding for sound or music output using DirectSound or Win32 multimedia API functions, it is important to keep these points in mind:

■ Sound effects are very important for game enjoyment, as they not only enhance the believability of the gaming environment but also provide the player with audible clues that indicate changes in the game state.

■ The PlaySound function is incredibly powerful for what it does. It can be used to play sounds from a file, from a resource, or from memory. While it may be adequate under some circumstances, it cannot play multiple sounds simultaneously.

■ DirectSound offers many features above and beyond what is available with Win32 API functions. Hardware acceleration is automatically utilized when available. A virtually unlimited number of sounds can be mixed and played simultaneously, and several special effects can be applied to the output, such as panning, volume control, and frequency adjustment.

■ Similar to DirectDraw, DirectSound programming consists of creating a DirectSound object and several sound buffers. The DirectSound object itself represents the developer's direct interface to the audio hardware. Through the IDirectSound interface, the application can query the audio hardware's capabilities, create sound buffers, and control other aspects of the hardware itself.

■ DirectSound buffers are circular in nature. This is important when dealing with streaming buffers, as accessing buffer memory may require extra steps when starting near the end of the buffer.

■ When DirectSound creates a secondary sound buffer, it automatically tries to locate the buffer in RAM on the sound card, if available. If there are no hardware buffers available, the sound is stored in system memory. Sound buffers located in hardware have the shortest path to the primary sound buffer, and thus are appropriately suited for short sounds that are needed quickly and will be repeated often.

■ Secondary sound buffers come in two flavors: static and streaming. Static buffers are used for short sounds that can be placed into memory in their

354 ■ Chapter 9: Sound and Music

entirety. These are typically short, often repeated or looping sounds. Streaming buffers are used for large sounds that cannot fit into a reasonably sized block of memory or for sounds that change often, and must by copied into the buffer in pieces as it is playing. By default, DirectSound tries to create a streaming buffer.

■ Sound buffers should be created in order of importance. This will ensure that the sounds used most often will enjoy the greatest performance. However, to optimize performance, the developer should dictate the type of buffer when one is created, and where it will be placed. In general, static buffers should be used for short, often repeated or looping sounds, and should be placed in hardware memory. Streaming buffers should be placed in system memory. The exception to this rule is when a sound buffer will be duplicated. Duplicating a hardware buffer requires using hardware resources that may be needed elsewhere. Thus, it is better to place static buffers that will be duplicated in system memory.

■ When a sound buffer is created, the developer can determine if the sound will continue to be heard when another application receives focus. By default, sounds will not be heard when the application loses focus (although they continue to play silently).

■ DirectSound is optimized for 16-bits-per-sample sounds. Therefore, changing the primary sound buffer format for 16-bit sounds can further reduce playback latency and reduce the load on the CPU when processing sound data.

■ The most complex step in initializing a secondary sound buffer is copying the data from a WAV file into the sound buffer itself. Unfortunately, DirectSound does not come with any built-in methods for retrieving audio data from a file or a resource. However, the DSUtil.pas, DSWaveFiles.pas, and DSWaveResources.pas units contain translations from DirectX SDK sound utility functions to copy audio data from a WAV file or a resource into a DirectSound buffer.

■ Music, like sound effects, adds depth to a game, giving it a feeling of completeness. Even more than sound effects, music adds mood to a game, and when used effectively can adjust the user's frame of mind as effectively as a movie sound track.

■ The Windows Media Control Interface features the MCISendCommand function that allows us to easily play both MIDI music and Red Book Audio from CDs. However, DirectX 6.1 and above feature a new DirectX component called DirectMusic that may revolutionize the use of MIDI.

■ The MCISendCommand function is asynchronous by nature, and will return immediately unless the MCI_WAIT flag was specified. In this event, you can usually specify the MCI_NOTIFY flag to indicate that the function should notify the application when it has completed. This is accomplished by sending the application an MM_MCINOTIFY message. It is a simple matter to define a handler for this message.

■ MIDI, or Musical Instrument Digital Interface, is a format for describing musical sound, much the same as the WAV format describes digitized sound. It is an effective means of providing music within a small footprint, and both software for creating MIDI files as well as freeware or shareware MIDI songs are readily available.

■ MIDI musical sound quality is less than perfect. Many games are circumventing this limitation by playing their musical scores directly off of the CD on which the game is distributed. This offers the highest possible sound quality, although the amount of music available to the game will be limited by the number of scores and their length, as CD audio requires much more storage space than MIDI files.

■ Music data is stored on the CD in a format known as Red Book Audio. This format provides for stereo music at the highest quality, and is the format used by the professional music industry to record music onto conventional audio CDs. The end user's machine must be set up correctly before it can play CD audio music. This involves installing a small wire that runs directly from the CD to the audio output hardware, and while most new machines have this installed automatically, it may not always be available.

# CHAPTER 10: *Optimization Techniques*

The technique of optimizing code has been elevated to an art form. With today's more advanced hardware, operating systems, and compilers, typically only the more experienced programmers will be relegated the duty of optimization. One must be intimately familiar with the workings of these three elements to truly be a master optimizer. However, there are several general techniques that are well publicized that can dramatically increase the speed at which an application runs, and you don't have to eat, sleep, and breath assembly code to use them. Fortunately, Delphi helps a lot in the optimization department. There are also a number of Delphi-specific code traps that can dramatically slow down your applications. Optimization is a very broad topic, and there are several books that examine it exhaustively. In this chapter, we will examine a number of both Delphi-related optimization techniques and some general techniques that can be applied in almost any programming language.

**Note:** You should run the examples in this chapter with optimization turned off (under Project | Options | Compiler). The example code is somewhat simplistic, and Delphi's internal optimizations are usually so good that they can further optimize the code. Running the examples with optimization turned off gives you a better idea as to how the illustrated optimization will benefit application performance in a real-world situation. Also note that because the examples are simplistic, the loops within them are generally repeated more times than what would normally be encountered.

# Optimization Theory

While optimization can be considered more an art than a science, there are a few general optimization rules that everyone should follow. The most important step in optimization is knowing where to optimize. After you've determined where the bottlenecks are in application execution, the next step is to evaluate the problem and determine how to optimize the code.

You could take a guess at which part of your code is the slowest, but this method will most likely result in wasted time and increased frustration. The best course of action would be to employ a profiler to time program execution. Profilers generally report the number of times a particular function was called and the average length of execution. Using a profiler can quickly highlight the bottlenecks in an application, indicating a general location where optimization would be most effective.

The freeware Delphi profiler GpProfile is an excellent profiling tool for all 32-bit versions of Delphi, and it comes with source code. At the time of this writing, it is available at **http://members.xoom.com/primozg/gpprofile/ gpprofile.htm**. Additionally, several Delphi tool vendors are working on retail versions of Delphi profilers, which should be available by the time this book reaches store shelves.

**profiler:** A profiler is an application that typically measures application execution time. The level at which an application is timed usually varies, from timing the execution of individual lines to the execution time of functions, procedures, or the overall application.

In general, it is best to ignore optimization until the application is almost complete. Trying to write optimized code from the outset can be very distracting. Concentrate on actually getting the application to run first. Chances are that a developer could spend several hours optimizing a piece of code that is ultimately replaced midway through development. Optimizing code as a last step in the development process ensures that the time will be well spent.

## *Timing Code*

In the absence of a profiler, there are several techniques a Delphi programmer can employ to time the execution of functions and methods. The one employed by the examples in this book involves the use of the timeGetTime function. The timeGetTime function retrieves the time that has elapsed since Windows was started, in milliseconds. Under Windows 95, this has a precision of 1 millisecond. Under Windows NT, the default precision is 5 or more milliseconds, but this can be adjusted by calling the timeBeginPeriod and timeEndPeriod functions.

**Note:** You must include MMSystem in the Uses clause of any unit using the timeGetTime function.

Timing a function involves only three steps: recording the current value of timeGetTime in a variable, running the function code, and then again recording the current value of timeGetTime. The difference of these two values equals the total function execution time, as the following example illustrates.

*Listing 10-1: Using timeGetTime to time function execution*

```
procedure TForm1.Button1Click(Sender: TObject);
var
  StartTime,
  EndTime: LongInt;
begin
  {start tracking the time}
  StartTime := timeGetTime;

  {code to be timed goes here}

  {record the ending time}
  EndTime := timeGetTime;

  {the difference between the starting and ending times gives
   us the overall time required to execute the timed code}
  Label1.Caption := 'Elapse Time: '+IntToStr(EndTime - StartTime);
end;
```

The timeGetTime function should be as accurate as required for just about any profiling needs. However, if more accuracy is required, the QueryPerformanceCounter and QueryPerformanceFrequency functions can be used. These functions give the developer access to the high-resolution performance counter that is present in just about every computer manufactured since the 486 was cutting-edge technology. QueryPerformanceFrequency returns the number of counts per second that the high-resolution timer records, and QueryPerformanceCounter returns the current count. Bear in mind, however, that these functions are useful only for timing very short periods, and cannot be used to time anything that executes for more than one second.

## Examining the Algorithm

Once the bottleneck has been found, the first step in optimizing the code should be to reevaluate the algorithm. Examining the algorithm embodied by the code and finding a better algorithm will typically result in improved performance over that gained by any one particular optimization technique described below.

The classic example is the bubble sort versus the binary sort. Both algorithms achieve the same result—a sorted list. However, the binary sort method is much faster than the bubble sort. Had a developer spent time employing various specific optimization techniques such as using assembly language or lookup tables, the performance of the original code may have been improved, but most likely would have resulted in a lot of wasted time and effort.

## Effective Optimization

Knowing where to begin is probably the hardest part about optimizing code. In general, don't worry about optimizing short pieces of code that are not called very often in the application. For example, if a few lines of code (or even one line) takes two seconds to process but is only called a few times during the entire life of the application, it is not worth examining. If possible, this type of code should be placed where a user will not mind the wait. In the typical game application, this usually involves the loading of game resources such as graphics and sound. This type of code should be executed when an application is starting and a splash screen is being displayed. Code of this nature can also be executed when changing levels or starting a level.

Typically, the best place to begin optimization is within the innermost part of loops. Take, for example, the following pseudo-code:

```
for iCount := 0 to 10 do
begin
  {outer loop code}
  for iCount2 := 0 to 100 do
  begin
    {inner loop code}
  end;
end;
```

If the outer loop code took a total of 100 milliseconds to execute for one iteration, excluding the inner loop, it would take a total of 1000 milliseconds, or one full second, for the entire loop to process (iterating 10 times). If the inner loop code took a total of 10 milliseconds to execute one iteration, it would take a total of 1000 milliseconds to process (iterating 100 times). Since the outer loop code takes longer to execute than the inner loop code (excluding the fact that the inner loop is executed with the outer loop code), one might be tempted to try optimizing the outer loop. The grand total execution time required to process this example is approximately 11 seconds (1 full second for the inner loop, executed 10 times (1 * 10), plus 1 more second for the outer loop). Even though the outer loop takes longer to process than the inner loop, if the total execution time of the outer loop was reduced to even 1 millisecond, the entire process will still take more than 10 seconds to execute. Now, if the inner loop execution time was cut in half (from 10 milliseconds to 5), the total execution time would be reduced from 11 seconds to approximately 6 seconds. That's a big savings. As this example illustrates, the biggest performance enhancements will usually come from optimizing code performed in the innermost loops.

**Tip:** Typical culprits, and places to begin looking for optimization opportunities, usually include loops that redraw the entire screen a pixel at a time as well as manager loops that perform specific actions on each item in a list.

Finally, knowing when to quit is almost as important as knowing where to start. Optimization gurus state that any code, however optimized, could always be optimized further. However, there is a diminishing margin of returns encountered at a certain level of optimization. For example, say a developer spends 10 hours optimizing code, decreasing its execution time by 100 milliseconds. The time spent was probably worth it. Now, if it takes another 5 or 10 hours to reduce the execution time by another 10 milliseconds, the developer's time could probably be better spent elsewhere. At some point, execution time will only be dropping by a few milliseconds, and a decision will need to be made about whether or not the time spent performing the optimization is worth the performance increases.

## Delphi-Specific Optimization Techniques

Delphi itself offers a number of very useful optimization options. The compiler performs quite a few automatic optimizations. There are several other options available that also affect how Delphi generates machine code. All of these options are available on the Compiler tab of the Project Options dialog, accessed using Project| Options.

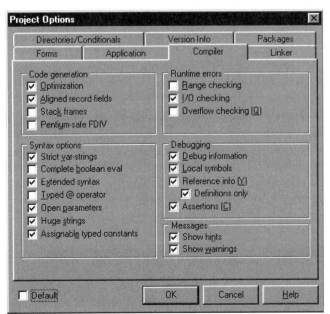

**Figure 10-1:**
*Project options*

**Caution:** If you are not familiar with these settings or have never used them before, Delphi may act in a manner that might be quite unfamiliar. Get to know these settings and how they affect Delphi's overall performance and behavior.

## Automatic Compiler Optimizations

The very first check box under Code Generation is the Optimization option. Clicking this box on activates a number of automatic compiler optimization techniques. Unfortunately, with this setting, it's an all-or-nothing affair. Turning this option off for debugging purposes is useful, but always turn this option on before performing a final build. When this option is on, it allows the compiler to perform a number of heavy-duty optimizations that can dramatically affect the performance of code. Some of these optimizations include register optimizations, call stack elimination, common subexpression removal, loop induction variables, and dead code elimination.

### Register Optimization

If Delphi determines that a particular variable is used heavily, it will store that variable in a hardware register. This eliminates the need to access the value of the variable by loading it from memory, resulting in much faster code. Delphi takes this one step further by determining if certain variables are used extensively in different parts of code. If so, a single register can be used for each variable.

### Call Stack Elimination

Delphi offers a number of different calling conventions that affect how parameters are passed to a function. Different calling conventions are required based on the task being accomplished, such as calling functions stored in C or C++ DLLs, or using Windows API functions. However, by default, Delphi uses a calling convention known as register. The register calling convention will pass up to three parameters to a function by using hardware registers. This makes it unnecessary to create a stack frame, eliminating quite a bit of initialization and cleanup code and improving application performance. However, if more than three parameters are passed, registers cannot be used and a stack frame will be created. Bear in mind that while a normal function can pass up to three parameters and still use this optimization, object methods can only pass two parameters, as Self is automatically passed as the third parameter. If a function requires more than three parameters, one way to still benefit from this optimization is to create a record structure defining all of the parameters. A single pointer to this record can then be passed to the function, allowing the function to access all of the required information while passing only one parameter in a register.

 **Tip:** A stack is also generated when a function returns more than a 32-bit number, such as returning a string. Try to write functions that don't return anything more than a single 32-bit number.

### Common Subexpression Removal

When compiling complex mathematical equations, Delphi will examine the equation to determine if any computations are performed more than once. If so, these common subexpressions are removed. Instead, Delphi will perform this calculation only once, and the resulting value will be used wherever the original calculation was located in the equation. The result is a mathematical computation that is reduced to a very compact, efficient form. This allows the developer to write computationally intensive code in a clear, concise manner without obscuring it by hand-optimizing the equation.

### Loop Induction Variables

If a variable is used only as an index into an array or a string, Delphi will instead replace the variable with a pointer that is incremented to directly access the string or array values. This eliminates multiplication operations and increases the speed at which array or string values are accessed. Additionally, using an index that is of a data type native to the hardware (such as a 32-bit integer type) will improve performance.

### Dead Code Elimination

While processing code, if Delphi detects that there is a block of code that is never called from the application, or code that ultimately has no effect, it will not be compiled into the final application. This is useful for reducing the size of the final build. However, during debugging, the compiler may remove code that would be useful to examine after a breakpoint.

## Additional Compiler Optimizations

While these automatic compiler optimizations are quite handy, there are several other options available under the Project Options dialog box that can affect the behavior of an application.

### Aligned Record Fields

When this option is turned on, all elements of record structures are adjusted so that they align on DWORD (32-bit) boundaries. The Intel architecture natively uses a 32-bit information format, and aligning the elements of a record so that each element begins at an address evenly divisible by 32 bits improves performance when accessing each element. The packed keyword can be used when declaring a record structure that will force alignment of the elements in that record structure to 32-bit boundaries.

**Caution:** Bear in mind that this can change the size of a record structure, which is a problem when reading in information that was previously saved as non-aligned records. This may also have an effect on function calls to Windows or other third-party DLLs that take a record structure as a parameter.

### Stack Frames

When this option is checked on, the compiler will always pass parameters to functions on the stack, creating stack frames for every function and defeating the stack frame elimination optimization. This can be turned on for debugging purposes, but should always be turned off for the final build.

### Range Checking

When this option is turned on, all array and string indexing expressions are verified as being within their defined bounds, and all assignments to scalar and subrange variables are checked to be within range. This generates additional code when accessing array and string elements, ultimately degrading application performance. Turn this option on only while debugging, and make sure it is off for the final build.

### Overflow Checking

Similar to range checking, overflow checking controls the generation of overflow checking code for certain integer arithmetic operations. The code for each of these integer arithmetic operations is followed by additional code that verifies that the result is within the supported range. Thus, when this option is turned on, additional code is generated for every arithmetic operation performed, degrading performance. Again, turn this option on for debugging purposes, but turn it off for the final build.

**Tip:** You can force any of these options on or off in your source code by including compiler directives. These directives, however, will override any settings made in this dialog box, which may cause confusion.

## Other Delphi-Specific Optimization Techniques

While these compiler optimizations help to improve overall application performance, there are several other tricks specific to Delphi that can dramatically increase application speed. Armed with a little knowledge about specific details about Delphi and the Object Pascal language, a developer can avoid common pitfalls that can completely negate the performance benefits realized by the compiler optimizations. Let's examine some very specific techniques that can improve performance in a number of ways.

### Exceptions

Exceptions are intended to inform both the user and the developer when something has gone wrong. Although they are very useful when employed correctly, they are incredibly slow. The developer should avoid trapping for exceptions at all costs, especially within a loop. The classic example is trapping for the EZeroDivide exception when performing division. If a number is divided by zero, it will raise an EZeroDivide exception. This could be put into a Try..Except block, simply swallowing the exception if it occurs. However, this is incredibly slow, and a simple example of this iterated as few as 10,000 times will take several seconds to execute on a Pentium 333 (on which the example was tested). If this Try..Except block is replaced by a simple If..Then to check if the divisor is zero before performing the math, 10,000 iterations take place in less than a millisecond (again, tested on a Pentium 333). Therefore, do not rely on exceptions for trapping errors when writing high-performance code. The following example demonstrates this technique.

 **Note:** You will need to turn off Stop on Delphi Exception for this example, located in Tools | Debugger Options | Language Exceptions.

*Listing 10-2: Exception handling in a loop*

```
procedure TForm1.Button1Click(Sender: TObject);
var
  iCount: Integer;
  Junk: Real;
  Divisor: Integer;

  StartTime,
  EndTime: LongInt;
begin
  {make sure that optimization is off}
  {$O-}

  {begin recording the time}
  StartTime := timeGetTime;
```

```
{perform a task that may or may not generate an exception (in this example
 it will always generate an exception). we don't want the user to see this
 exception, so we programmatically handle it}
Divisor := 0;
for iCount := 0 to 10000 do
begin
  try
    Junk := 10 / Divisor;
  except
    on EZeroDivide do;
  end;
end;

{recording the ending time...}
EndTime := timeGetTime;

{...and display the elapsed time}
Label1.Caption := 'Elapse Time (exception): '+IntToStr(EndTime - StartTime);

{begin recording the time}
StartTime := timeGetTime;

{perform the same task as before, but this time specifically check for
 instances that may create an exception}
Divisor := 0;
for iCount := 0 to 10000 do
begin
  if Divisor <> 0 then
    Junk := 10 / Divisor;
end;

{record the ending time...}
EndTime := timeGetTime;

{...and display the elapsed time}
Label2.Caption := 'Elapse Time (if..then): '+IntToStr(EndTime - StartTime);
end;
```

 *Tip:* Try..Finally blocks incur little to no overhead, so it is safe to wrap high-performance code within a Try..Finally block.

## Object Method Types

When declaring an object method, it can be defined as one of three types: static, virtual, or dynamic. Each one has its strengths and weaknesses. Static methods do not gain the benefits of inheritance or polymorphism, one of the corner-stones of object-oriented programming. Virtual and dynamic methods both allow for inheritance and polymorphism, but the way in which applications access these methods is implemented differently. Without expounding on the inner workings of Delphi too greatly, virtual methods create an entry in a Virtual Method Table that is stored with each object. Dynamic methods, on the other hand, use a different method call-dispatching algorithm. Where dynamic methods are optimized for code size, virtual methods are optimized for speed. However, static methods are the fastest of all, since they are called directly with no need for method dispatching or VMT lookups. In general, try to use static methods as often as possible, but definitely use virtual instead of dynamic when using object-oriented programming techniques.

## Variants

The variant data type is another new Delphi addition that makes certain programming practices incredibly easy. Using the variant type is almost essential when performing OLE or COM programming. However, because of its abilities to store just about any type of data, inexperienced programmers may be tempted to use only variables of type variant so as to avoid any data type incompatibilities. Unfortunately, because of its flexibility, the variant data type is very slow and should be avoided in high-performance code. With the variant being a 16-byte structure, it also wastes space. Unless you are doing some sort of OLE programming, avoid variants and use native data types.

**Listing 10-3:** *Variants versus native types*

```
procedure TForm1.Button1Click(Sender: TObject);
var
  iCount: Integer;
  Junk: Variant;
  Junk2: Integer;

  StartTime,
  EndTime: LongInt;
begin
  {turn optimization off}
  {$O-}

  {begin recording the time}
  StartTime := timeGetTime;

  {perform some standard task using a variant data type}
  Junk := 0;
  for iCount := 0 to 100000 do
  begin
    Junk := Junk + 1;
  end;

  {record the ending time...}
```

```
    EndTime := timeGetTime;

    {...and display the elapsed time}
    Label1.Caption := 'Elapse Time (variant): '+IntToStr(EndTime - StartTime);

    {begin recording the time}
    StartTime := timeGetTime;

    {perform the same function using a native data type}
    Junk2 := 0;
    for iCount := 0 to 100000 do
    begin
      Junk2 := Junk2 + 1;
    end;

    {record the ending time...}
    EndTime := timeGetTime;

    {...and display the elapsed time}
    Label2.Caption := 'Elapse Time (integer): '+IntToStr(EndTime - StartTime);
end;
```

## String Parameters

An entire chapter could be written on the internal operations performed when Delphi works with strings. Both string and variant local variables within a function or method require prologue and epilogue code to be generated around the function to initialize and deinitialize the variable. Temporary storage variables may be generated when passing string results from one function as the parameter to another (such as passing the result of an IntToStr directly as a parameter), further increasing the generated code. Variant and string local variables automatically generate a stack frame within a function, defeating register optimizations. In general, avoid creating small utility routines that work on or use strings. If necessary, string or variant data should be processed in fewer, large routines that do as much as possible. Never use string variables or parameters to process information where an integer variable or parameter could accomplish the same task.

## Data Types

The data types used by your application will impact its overall performance. Certain mathematical functions perform faster using certain data types; indeed, some data types are incredibly slow by comparison. In general, you'll achieve the greatest performance when using native data types, such as integer. The MathTest example on the CD in the directory for this chapter can be used as a benchmark for testing execution speed of different operations on different data types. All of the floating-point and integer data types are tested, and though the exact execution times will vary from machine to machine, it is easy to see which data types perform better under certain circumstances than others.

# General Optimization Techniques

We gain a lot of benefit from the automatic optimization that Delphi provides. We can also improve performance by being aware of the inner workings of certain Delphi code constructs. However, we should also be aware of general coding practices that can be used to improve performance in any language.

## Loop Unrolling

It is very common for the point of execution within an application to jump from one point to another during the course of execution. For example, an If..Then statement causes the point of execution to skip some instructions based on the expression value. The time required for the execution point to change a single time is minimal. However, when the execution point jumps around repeatedly, these minimal time increments can accumulate.

The biggest offenders in this category are loops, such as For..Next, While..Do, and Repeat..Until. Applications typically revolve around looping constructs such as these, performing the same functions on large amounts of data. This results in the execution point changing repeatedly. The amount of code and the task it performs within loops are prime targets for optimization. However, one technique you can use to improve loop performance is to unroll it.

The concept of unrolling a loop is simple. Instead of performing one block of operations several times, perform several blocks of the same operations a fewer number of times. For example, if you have a loop that performs one operation 10,000 times, try performing 10 of those operations within the loop, and reduce the loop to run only 1,000 times. This will reduce the number of execution point jumps by an order of magnitude, and can dramatically improve overall performance. The following example illustrates this technique.

**Listing 10-4:** *Unrolling a loop*

```
procedure TForm1.Button1Click(Sender: TObject);
var
  StartTime,
  EndTime,
  iCount: Integer;
  Accum: Real;
begin
  {turn optimization off}
  {$O-}

  {initialize our variable and start tracking the time}
  Accum := 0;
```

```
StartTime := timeGetTime;

{perform some task many, many times}
for iCount := 0 to 999999 do
  Accum := Accum + 0.5;

{record the ending time...}
EndTime := timeGetTime-StartTime;

{...and display the elapsed time}
Label1.Caption := 'Regular loop time: '+IntToStr(EndTime);

{rest the variable and start tracking time}
Accum := 0;
StartTime := timeGetTime;

{perform the same task as before, but this time repeat the task several
 times within the loop, and adjust the number of loops accordingly. note
 that the task is performed the same number of times as before, but now
 we've got an order of magnitude less jumps}
for iCount := 0 to 99999 do
begin
  Accum := Accum + 0.5;
  Accum := Accum + 0.5;
  Accum := Accum + 0.5;
  Accum := Accum + 0.5;
  Accum := Accum + 0.5;
  Accum := Accum + 0.5;
  Accum := Accum + 0.5;
  Accum := Accum + 0.5;
  Accum := Accum + 0.5;
  Accum := Accum + 0.5;
end;

{record the ending time...}
EndTime := timeGetTime-StartTime;

{...and display the elapsed time}
Label2.Caption := 'Unrolled loop time: '+IntToStr(EndTime);
end;
```

## Lookup Tables

Most game applications require the use of complicated or sophisticated mathematical functions. Functions such as Sin and Cos are common, and some games may require even more arcane trigonometry or calculus equations. Unfortunately, even with math coprocessors, these functions are quite slow, and if they are required in a loop, the application can slow to a crawl. However, if the total range of all inputs to a mathematical function or equation is known, you may be able to use a lookup table.

Simply put, a lookup table is an array that contains the results of a mathematical function or equation for all known input values, where the input value acts as an index into the table. For example, the Sin and Cos functions both take an argument in the form of a degree (actually they take radians, but the argument can be converted to radians and it's easier to think of it as a degree). The total range of inputs that return unique outputs is 0 to 359 degrees. Thus, you can create a 360-entry array and put the Sin or Cos value for each input in the range in its appropriate entry. Then, instead of calling the Sin or Cos function, you simply use the argument as an index into this array. Retrieving predetermined values in this manner is incredibly fast, usually much more so than actually running the equation or function. The table is generally initialized when the application starts. This technique can be applied to any area where a limited range of input values is known. The following listing illustrates this technique.

**Listing 10-5:** *Using lookup tables*

```
procedure TForm1.Button1Click(Sender: TObject);
var
  StartTime, EndTime, iCount: Integer;
  Lookup: array[0..359] of Real;
  SinValue: Real;
begin
  {turn optimization off}
  {$O-}

  {generate the lookup table}
  for iCount := 0 to 359 do
    Lookup[iCount] := Sin((iCount)*(PI / 180));

  {begin tracking the time}
  StartTime := timeGetTime;

  {perform a slow mathematical calculation}
  for iCount := 0 to 99999 do
    SinValue := Sin(50*(PI / 180));

  {record the ending time...}
  EndTime := timeGetTime-StartTime;

  {...and display the elapsed time}
  Label1.Caption := 'Sine Calculation: '+IntToStr(EndTime);

  {start tracking the time}
  StartTime := timeGetTime;

  {perform the calculation by finding the answer in the lookup table}
```

```
    for iCount := 0 to 99999 do
      SinValue := Lookup[50];

    {record the ending time...}
    EndTime := timeGetTime-StartTime;

    {...and display the elapsed time}
    Label2.Caption := 'Sine Lookup: '+IntToStr(EndTime);
end;
```

## Binary Bit Shifting

Every PC processor has built-in hardware to shift the bits in a register left or right. This has the result of effectively multiplying or dividing the number in this register by a power of 2. Applications can take advantage of this hardware through the use of the shl and shr functions. Shl shifts bits to the left, multiplying the number by two; shr shifts them to the right, dividing by two. This can be used for incredibly fast integer multiplication and division, as it bypasses the math coprocessor. The only drawback to this is that the multiplication or division has to be a multiple of two. However, if an equation can be broken down into components that use simple addition or subtraction with multiplication or division by a power of 2, performance can be dramatically improved. For example, the equation Y * 320 + X would require one multiplication and one addition by the math coprocessor. However, the equivalent function ((Y shl 8) + (Y shl 6)) + X requires two shifts and two additions. Although the number of functions performed on this equation has increased, additions take less time than multiplication, and the shifts are almost instantaneous, resulting in faster performance. The following example demonstrates how to use bit shifting for multiplication.

**Listing 10-6:** *Bit Shifting*

```
procedure TForm1.Button1Click(Sender: TObject);
var
  iCount: Integer;

  Result: Longword;

  StartTime,
  EndTime: LongInt;
begin
  {we must run this example with optimization turned on to see the
   performance gains}
  {$O+}

  {set up a dummy variable and begin tracking the time}
  Result := 1;
```

```
StartTime := timeGetTime;

{perform some function or task}
for iCount := 0 to 10000000 do
  Result :=  Result * 2;

{record the ending time...}
EndTime := timeGetTime;

{..and display the elapsed time}
Label1.Caption := 'Elapse Time (multiply): '+IntToStr(EndTime - StartTime);

{set up a dummy variable and begin tracking the time}
Result := 1;
StartTime := timeGetTime;

{perform some function or task using a faster method}
for iCount := 0 to 10000000 do
  Result := Result shl 1;

{record the ending time...}
EndTime := timeGetTime;

{...and display the elapsed time}
  Label2.Caption := 'Elapse Time (shl): '+IntToStr(EndTime - StartTime);
end;
```

# Additional Optimization Considerations

Developers are always discovering new tricks and techniques to squeeze a little more performance out of an application. The topics we've covered have only scratched the surface of the myriad of arcane programming constructs that programmers use to improve performance. Beyond the specific optimization techniques we've discussed in this chapter, developers should be aware of general coding practices that should help improve overall performance.

Memory allocation is one of those key areas that can dramatically affect the performance of an application. The task of dynamically allocating memory is an expensive one in terms of time. If possible, you should always dynamically allocate all memory up front, when the application starts. Of course, this is only possible if the total amount of required memory can be determined when it is allocated. If it is impossible to determine the total amount of required memory, try allocating the memory in larger blocks, using up the allocated memory until more is needed. For example, if you're using dynamic arrays, instead of allocating one entry at a time, try allocating 10 entries at a time and using those 10 until more are required. This results in fewer dynamic memory allocations, which in turn results in better performance.

As an alternative to dynamic memory allocation, you may want to try using only global variables. Global variables cause the system to allocate their memory when the application starts; by using only these global variables, you never have to dynamically allocate memory, and thus never incur the cost of such a task. Of course, this may only be applicable if the number of variables required is not too great. Otherwise, the hassle of managing such constructions in terms of coding and code maintenance may outweigh the speed benefits.

Another advantage to using global variables is that they can be used within local functions without creating a stack. In this manner, you could potentially pass hundreds of parameters to a procedure or function without creating and initializing a data structure as discussed above. You have all of the disadvantages associated with using global variables in such a manner, but you may be able to utilize this method in a limited fashion where you need both speed and a large parameter list.

Constant arrays are another area that one should look at. Constant arrays are easy to maintain, but their use incurs an array dereference. If possible, simply use several constants instead. This may be harder to maintain in the long run, but you avoid the array dereference, and ultimately it will improve performance where the constants are used.

However, where optimization is paramount and speed is critical, one may have to drop down to assembly language. It's hard to beat the speed of hand-optimized assembly. Unfortunately, assembly language, even verbosely documented, is both hard to maintain and hard to modify. It also takes a developer experienced in assembly language to do a decent job. Assembly language can be written right in the Delphi IDE; you simply have to enclose it within an asm..end block. An assembly language tutorial is beyond the scope of this book. However, several general Delphi books contain discussions of using assembly language within Delphi, and many good 32-bit assembly language references are available. Fortunately, with the speed of today's machines and Delphi's optimizing compiler, the use of hand-optimized assembly is not quite as necessary as it was just a few years ago.

# Summary

In this chapter, we discussed several techniques for improving the performance of games and applications. We looked at the optimizations that Delphi performs, as well as some Delphi-specific optimization techniques. We also examined some general optimization techniques that are language independent and discussed further optimization considerations. When optimizing your Delphi applications and games, it is important to keep these points in mind:

■ The most important step in optimization is knowing where to optimize. After you've determined where the bottlenecks are in application execution, the next step is to evaluate the problem and determine how to optimize the code. Never guess at where your bottlenecks might occur; either use a profiler or some technique for timing code execution.

■ Reevaluating an algorithm can have a greater impact on performance than any collection of singular optimization tricks or techniques.

■ The task of optimization has a diminishing margin of returns. Spending 10 hours to improve performance by 10% may be worthwhile; spending another 10 hours to improve performance by only 1% is probably a waste of time.

■ Optimization should be the last task in application development. Trying to optimize code halfway through the development cycle can be a waste of time, especially if the optimized code gets cut out in favor of another method.

■ Never spend time optimizing code that is only called once or twice throughout the entire execution of an application. The most common place to begin optimization is within loops, specifically inner loops that may be performed thousands of times.

■ Delphi itself offers a number of very useful optimization options. The compiler itself performs quite a few automatic optimizations, such as register optimizations, call stack elimination, common subexpression removal, the use of loop induction variables, and dead code elimination. Other optional compiler optimizations include aligned record fields, elimination of stack frames, range checking, and overflow checking.

■ Exceptions should only be used when an error occurs that must be responded to. Never use exceptions to account for errors (such as dividing by zero), as they are incredibly slow.

■ Virtual methods are optimized for speed, and dynamic methods are optimized for size. However, static methods are the fastest as they do not incur a dereference.

■ Never use a variant when a standard data type will do. Bear in mind that some standard data types are faster than others for certain operations.

■ Avoid using strings as parameters or as return values from functions, as this implicitly creates extra code that slows down the application.

■ Loops should be unrolled so as to reduce the number of jumps the application performs.

■ Lookup tables should be used for mathematical functions and equations when a finite range of input values is known.

■ When multiplying or dividing by a power of 2, using binary bit shifting, as this takes advantage of hardware available in every PC.

# CHAPTER 11: *Special Effects*

Although interactive computer games are slowly gaining ground, it is probably safe to say that movies and television are the most popular forms of entertainment among the masses. A good film or movie with Oscar-winning actors and exotic, beautiful sets and locations can be very enjoyable. Indeed, classic films such as *Ben Hur* and *Gone with the Wind* are timeless in their ability to enthrall and entertain.

Everyone enjoys a realistic, stirring performance by a good actor, and of course a good plot can make or break a movie (the same rule applies to games). Even so, when people watch movies, they want to be transported to another place and time, and it would be very difficult to achieve an effective illusion without the use of special effects. What would the *Star Wars* movies have been like without the massive space battles? Or *Star Trek* without the transporter? Special effects provide visualization of events or actions that could not take place in reality, and, in an ironic way, can add an air of "realism" to fantastic settings.

The same holds true for computer games. It is easy to portray exotic locations and creatures using computer graphics. Even so, you can accomplish only so much by just relying on the blitting functions to copy graphics from one surface to another. As we've already examined, the Lock method gives us the ability to directly manipulate the contents of a surface. This gives us incredible power, limiting game world visualization only to our imaginations.

This chapter examines how the Lock method can be used to produce effects that would be difficult to reproduce by using Blt or BltFast alone. While a comprehensive discussion of computer graphic special effects could probably fill several volumes, we'll examine a few selected case studies to demonstrate the power of directly manipulating surface contents and to spark our imagination for further applications of this technique.

**Caution:**   Always remember to call the Unlock method on a surface before it is used with other DirectDraw methods, such as Flip, or your application will crash.

# Bitmap Manipulation

Simply manipulating bitmaps in one way or another can produce many cool effects. The texture mapping that is performed in 3-D games could be considered a bitmap manipulation. Basically, by taking a plain, flat bitmap and drawing it in some way other than just blitting it to the screen in a plain, flat manner can give the bitmap an appearance of depth or texture. This can also stretch the art budget dollar, since producing visual effects programmatically will reduce the amount of artwork required.

There are thousands of ways that bitmaps can be manipulated to produce all kinds of interesting effects. In the interest of space, we'll examine only a small handful. Indeed, even the implementation of these examples can vary widely from programmer to programmer, but we'll examine some simplistic ways to produce some interesting effects by manipulating bitmaps. Specifically, we'll look at bitmap transformations, scaling, rotation, a cheap lighting effect, transition effects, and a very simple texture mapping routine to produce the illusion of a bitmap wrapped around a sphere.

## Bitmap Transformations

This rather broad title addresses techniques for transforming bitmaps and drawing them in a non-linear or non-rectangular manner. You could classify every effect in this section as a bitmap transformation. However, our discussion deals with techniques for using mathematical equations to modify the location of pixels as they are drawn to a destination. Specifically, we're going to look at using the Sin function to apply a sine wave to a bitmap of the Texas state flag in order to produce an animation of a flag blowing in the wind.

## Basic Theory

At the heart of this technique is the Sin function. If you've ever taken a trigonometry class, you should be very familiar with this function. Without going into a lot of detail, the Sin function takes a number, more specifically a degree on a circle (i.e., $0^\circ$ to $360^\circ$), and returns a value between –1 and 1. If you graphed out the result of the Sin function, it would look something like Figure 11-1.

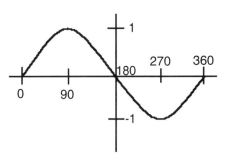

This produces what is known as a sine wave. It is a cyclic function that will return a result in the range of –1 to 1 for any value. If we scaled the resulting values from this function and used these as vertical offsets, we could easily produce a simple but effective wave animation with our bitmap.

**Figure 11-1:** *A graph of the Sin function results*

**Tip:** Remember that the trigonometry functions are notoriously slow, so you should probably use an optimization like a lookup table for trig function results in real-world applications.

We'll need to draw our bitmap as vertical strips of pixels in order to make this work. Beginning with a starting value of 0, we use the Sin function with this value to determine the vertical offset for the first strip of pixels. We then draw the first vertical strip of pixels within the bitmap at some starting point within our destination, with the top of this strip offset vertically by the return value of the Sin function. Iterating horizontally through our bitmap, we'll add 1 to the value passed to the Sin function as we draw each vertical strip of pixels, using this offset to modify the starting point of the top of the strip. This will produce an oscillating offset for the starting point of the top of each vertical line of pixels, as demonstrated in Figure 11-2.

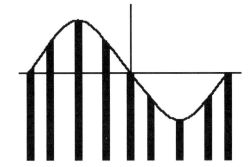

**Figure 11-2:** *Using Sin to modify vertical starting points*

If we increment the starting point each time we draw the bitmap, it will make the wave appear to move, and we'll produce an effective animation. Of course, we'll need to scale the values returned from the Sin function by some constant in order to produce a more pronounced wave effect. We'll also need to scale the values given to the Sin function in order to increase the frequency of the waves. The following listing demonstrates this concept.

**Listing 11-1:** *Producing sine wave patterns with a bitmap*

```
interface

const



  {controls wave magnitude}
  MAGNITUDE = 10;

  {controls wave frequency}
  FREQUENCY = 720;




var




  {the starting angle}
  AngleStart: Integer;


implementation




procedure TfrmDXAppMain.FormCreate(Sender: TObject);
begin




  {initialize our starting angle}
  AngleStart := 0;
end;
```

.
.
.

```
{ – this method initializes DirectX and creates all necessary objects – }
procedure TfrmDXAppMain.FormActivate(Sender: TObject);
begin


    .
    .
    .

  {create a palette based on this bitmap}
  FPalette := DDLoadPalette(FDirectDraw, ExtractFilePath(ParamStr(0))+
                            'texasflag.bmp');

  {attach the palette to the primary surface so that it takes effect}
  DXCheck( FPrimarySurface.SetPalette(FPalette) );

  {load in the bitmap containing the flag image}
  FFlag := DDLoadBitmap(FDirectDraw, ExtractFilePath(ParamStr(0))+
                        'texasflag.bmp');

    .
    .
    .

end;

    .
    .
    .

procedure TfrmDXAppMain.DrawSurfaces;
var
  DestSrfcInfo, FlagSrfcInfo: TDDSurfaceDesc2;
  DestPtr, FlagPtr: PByteArray;
  DestX, DestY, StartY, AngleBegin: Integer;
begin
  {erase the last frame of animation}
  ColorFill(FBackBuffer, 0, nil);

  try
    {lock the flag surface}
    FlagSrfcInfo.dwSize := SizeOf(TDDSurfaceDesc2);
    DXCheck( FFlag.Lock(nil, FlagSrfcInfo, DDLOCK_SURFACEMEMORYPTR or
                        DDLOCK_WAIT, 0) );
    FlagPtr := PByteArray(FlagSrfcInfo.lpSurface);

    {lock the destination surface}
```

```
DestSrfcInfo.dwSize := SizeOf(TDDSurfaceDesc2);
DXCheck( FBackBuffer.Lock(nil, DestSrfcInfo, DDLOCK_SURFACEMEMORYPTR or
                          DDLOCK_WAIT, 0) );

{this positions the initial starting point of destination drawing
 so that the flag will be centered horizontally and vertically}
DestPtr := PByteArray(integer(DestSrfcInfo.lpSurface)+
                      (DestSrfcInfo.lPitch*((DXHEIGHT div 2)-
                      (FlagSrfcInfo.dwHeight div 2)))+
                      ((DXWIDTH div 2)-(FlagSrfcInfo.dwWidth div 2)));

{increment our starting angle. this produces the motion of the wave,
 and a larger value will make the wave move faster. a negative value
 makes the wave move from left to right; positive values reverse
 this direction. incidentally, we never have to 'roll over' this
 value as Sin will return a value in the range -1 to 1 for any
 argument}
Inc(AngleStart, -5);

{begin iterating through each vertical strip}
for DestX := 0 to FlagSrfcInfo.dwWidth do
begin
  {we want to add 1 to the starting angle for each column in the bitmap}
  AngleBegin := DestX+AngleStart;

  {the FREQUENCY value increases the frequency of the wave across
   the bitmap. with a value of 360, the waves will peak and valley only
   once across the entire length of the bitmap. our frequency value is
   720, which causes 2 peaks and valleys, and makes a nice effect.
   increasing or decreasing this value accordingly may simulate wind
   strength.  this value is divided by the width of the bitmap to produce
   an 'angles-per-pixel' ratio so that the effect will spread evenly
   across the horizontal length of the bitmap.  this value must be in
   terms of radians instead of degrees, so we must multiply it by
   (PI/180).  finally, the MAGNITUDE value scales the results and produces
   offsets, in our example, between -10 and 10. this makes the peaks appear
   higher and the valleys appear lower.}
  StartY:=Trunc((Sin(((FREQUENCY/FlagSrfcInfo.dwWidth)*AngleBegin)*
                  (PI/180))*MAGNITUDE));

  {begin drawing the vertical strip of pixels}
  for DestY := 0 to FlagSrfcInfo.dwHeight do
    {the vertical offset is added to the vertical destination value, which
     may move this column of pixels up or down}
    DestPtr[DestSrfcInfo.lPitch*(DestY+StartY)+DestX] :=
    FlagPtr[FlagSrfcInfo.lPitch*DestY+DestX];
end;

finally
  {release all locks}
  FFlag.Unlock(nil);
```

```
      FBackBuffer.Unlock(nil);
    end;
  end;
end.
```

### Alternatives/Enhancements

The resulting animation from our bitmap transformation, while effective, is a little cheesy. We could produce a more realistic effect by applying another sine wave along the x-axis, perhaps at a 45-degree angle from horizontal. If we scaled the horizontal sine wave offset so that pixels moved left or right very little at the left side of the image, but they moved a large distance at the right side of the image, we could produce a more realistic wind effect. The result would make the flag look like it folded back on itself, and that it was attached to a flagpole.

## Scaling

Sometimes it may be necessary to draw a bitmap image at a size other than its original dimensions. For example, we could create the illusion of a creature getting closer to the user by drawing its image larger and larger as it draws nearer. By scaling an image in this manner, we can produce the illusion of depth, or even provide zooming functionality for things like sniper scopes.

### Basic Theory

Scaling a bitmap involves drawing the pixels of the source bitmap into the destination according to a specific ratio. This ratio determines the final size of the bitmap as it appears in the destination. The ratio is expressed as a fraction, or a floating-point number; the larger the number, the larger the bitmap, and vice versa. For example, a ratio of 2 indicates that the final bitmap will be twice as large as its original size, whereas a ratio of 0.5 indicates that the final bitmap will be half of its original size.

Specifically, the ratio indicates how each pixel is mapped into the destination. If we iterate through the pixels in the destination and divide their coordinates by the scaling factor, we can determine which pixel to select from the source. This is accomplished by the following equations:

```
Source_X := Trunc(Destination_X / Scale);
Source_Y := Trunc(Destination_Y / Scale);
```

A scaling factor less than 1 causes pixels in the source image to be skipped, thus resulting in a smaller final image. Similarly, a scaling factor greater than 1 causes pixels in the source image to be replicated, resulting in a larger final image. The following listing demonstrates this technique.

***Listing 11-2:*** *Scaling a bitmap image*

```
interface

  .
  .
  .

var

  .
  .
  .

  {this is used as an argument to the Sin function to
   create an oscillating scale factor}
  Angle: Integer;

implementation

  .
  .
  .

procedure TfrmDXAppMain.FormCreate(Sender: TObject);
begin

  .
  .
  .

  {initialize the angle variable}
  Angle := 0;
end;

  .
  .
  .

procedure TfrmDXAppMain.FormActivate(Sender: TObject);
begin

  .
  .
  .

  {create a palette based on this bitmap}
  FPalette := DDLoadPalette(FDirectDraw, ExtractFilePath(ParamStr(0))+
                            'Athena.bmp');
```

```
      {attach the palette to the primary surface so that it takes effect}
      DXCheck( FPrimarySurface.SetPalette(FPalette) );

      {load in the bitmap containing the image}
      FImages := DDLoadBitmap(FDirectDraw, ExtractFilePath(ParamStr(0))+
                              'Athena.bmp');
        .
        .
        .

end;

     .
     .
     .


procedure TfrmDXAppMain.DrawSurfaces;
var
  SrfcInfo, ImageInfo: TDDSurfaceDesc2;

  SrcPtr, DestPtr: PByteArray;

  DestX, DestY, SrcX, SrcY: Integer;

  Scale: Double;
begin
  {erase the last frame of animation}
  ColorFill(FBackBuffer, 0, nil);

  {increment our 'angle' variable}
  Inc(Angle);

  {using the angle variable with the Sin function to create a
   cyclic scaling value, compute a scale that oscillates between 0.5 and 1.5}
  Scale := 1+(Sin((Angle)*(PI/180))*0.5);

  try
    {lock the image surface}
    ImageInfo.dwSize := SizeOf(TDDSurfaceDesc2);
    DXCheck( FImages.Lock(nil, ImageInfo, DDLOCK_SURFACEMEMORYPTR or
                          DDLOCK_WAIT, 0) );
    SrcPtr := PByteArray(ImageInfo.lpSurface);

    {lock the destination surface}
    SrfcInfo.dwSize := SizeOf(TDDSurfaceDesc2);
    DXCheck( FBackBuffer.Lock(nil, SrfcInfo, DDLOCK_SURFACEMEMORYPTR or
                              DDLOCK_WAIT, 0) );
    DestPtr := PByteArray(Integer(SrfcInfo.lpSurface)+100*SrfcInfo.lPitch+100);

    {iterate through the destination pixels, with a maximum scale of 1.5}
    for DestY := 0 to Trunc(ImageInfo.dwHeight * 1.5) do
```

```
     begin
       for DestX := 0 to Trunc(ImageInfo.dwWidth * 1.5) do
       begin
         {compute the source pixels based on the scale and our current
          destination pixel}
         SrcY := Trunc(DestY / Scale);
         SrcX := Trunc(DestX / Scale);

         {if the source pixel coordinate is within the source image...}
         if (SrcX > 0) and (SrcX < ImageInfo.dwWidth) and
            (SrcY > 0) and (SrcY < ImageInfo.dwHeight) then
           {...copy this source pixel into the destination}
           DestPtr[DestX] := SrcPtr[(ImageInfo.lPitch*SrcY)+SrcX];
       end;

       {increment to the next line in the destination surface}
       DestPtr := PByteArray(Longint(DestPtr)+SrfcInfo.lPitch);
     end;
   finally
     {unlock both buffers}
     FImages.Unlock(nil);
     FBackBuffer.Unlock(nil);
   end;
end;
```

## Alternatives/Enhancements

Scaling is implemented by DirectDraw; it is emulated by the HEL, and some video cards provide hardware support for scaling. Thus, you do not really need this algorithm to scale a bitmap. However, when you use DirectDraw to perform scaling, you are relying on the implementation present in the current driver or hardware of the end user's machine. This could potentially lead to differing results from system to system. Using our own techniques, we can control the scaling, ensuring a consistent result on every machine. We could also employ interpolation techniques to determine the color of a scaled pixel from those around it. The resulting image could be of a much higher quality than that capable from DirectDraw, as it will not have the jagged edges produced by the DirectDraw scaling algorithms.

 *Tip:* To let DirectDraw perform scaling, use the Blt function and specify the desired size for the destination rectangle.

As with most of these bitmap manipulation effects, scaling a bitmap can be very computationally intensive. We could pre-compute the scaled pixel positions relative to an arbitrary starting point for the entire range of scaling values when the application starts. The resulting lookup table would be very fast, but it would probably take up loads and loads of memory, depending on the range of scaling values. It might be possible to provide several bitmaps at specific sizes and scale between them as needed. This might allow us to optimize the scaling routine, but it would require more storage space for bitmaps. However, this would allow us to improve the quality of the images as they get larger.

# Rotation

Most top-down, 2-D, sprite-based games feature sprite images that seem to be able to rotate in any direction. This could be accomplished by drawing the sprite image in all possible rotations, but this would be required for all frames of animation and would result in a large number of images for even one sprite. While this is a perfectly acceptable way of implementing rotation, we could use bitmap rotation equations to allow us to rotate images to any arbitrary angle while saving on memory space.

## Basic Theory

You may remember from trigonometry that it is mathematically possible to rotate a point about the origin by an arbitrary angle. Given an original x and y coordinate and an arbitrary angle, a point can be rotated using the following equations:

```
New_X := Original_X * Cos(Angle) - Original_Y * Sin(Angle);
New_Y := Original_X * Sin(Angle) + Original_Y * Cos(Angle);
```

This new point is rotated about the origin by the specified angle, as illustrated below.

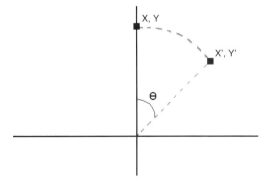

*Figure 11-3:*
*Rotating a point*

 **Caution:** A common mistake made when implementing these equations is to rotate the x coordinate, and then use this newly rotated value in the rotation equations for the y coordinate. The result will be a highly skewed image which will eventually shrink into nothing if rotations continue. This is why you must store the rotated values into separate variables.

If we treat each pixel in a bitmap as a point, we can use these equations to rotate the pixels in the bitmap. Now, most bitmap rotation algorithms map the pixels from the source bitmap to the destination bitmap, but most of the time, this results in a rotated image that contains holes. Therefore, we should iterate through the pixels in our destination image, determining the pixels we should draw from the source image. If we determine the center of the source image, like so:

```
CenterX := (SourceImageWidth / 2);
CenterY := (SourceImageHeight / 2);
```

then we can determine which pixels to pull from the source image based on the pixel being drawn in the destination image using these equations:

```
SrcX := Trunc(CenterX+(DestX-CenterX)*Cos(Angle)-(DestY-CenterY)*Sin(Angle));
SrcY := Trunc(CenterY+(DestX-CenterX)*Sin(Angle)+(DestY-CenterY)*Cos(Angle));
```

This will result in a perfectly rotated image with no holes.

Incidentally, we should load our source image into system memory as opposed to video memory. This will speed up the rotation, as it is much faster to access a surface in system memory than video memory. Also, we'll further optimize this by creating a sine and cosine lookup table instead of calling the Sin and Cos functions, using the angle as the index within these tables. The following listing demonstrates this technique.

***Listing 11-3:*** *Rotating a bitmap*

```
interface

    .
    .
    .

var

    .
    .
    .

  {the arbitrary angle}
  Theta: Integer;

  {these are used to create sine and cosine function lookup tables
   as an optimization}
  iAngle: Integer;
  SinTable: array[0..359] of single;
  CosTable: array[0..359] of single;

implementation
```

```
                .
                .
                .

procedure TfrmDXAppMain.FormCreate(Sender: TObject);
begin

        .
        .
        .

{initialize our starting angle}
  Theta := 0;
end;

        .
        .
        .

procedure TfrmDXAppMain.FormActivate(Sender: TObject);
begin

        .
        .
        .

  {load the palette from this bitmap}
  FPalette := DDLoadPalette(FDirectDraw, ExtractFilePath(ParamStr(0))+
                            'athena.bmp');

  {set the palette}
  FPrimarySurface.SetPalette(FPalette);

  {load the bitmap to be rotated}
  FImage := DDLoadBitmapSysMem(FDirectDraw, ExtractFilePath(ParamStr(0))+
                            'athena.bmp');

        .
        .
        .

end;

        .
        .
        .

procedure TfrmDXAppMain.DrawSurfaces;
var
  SrcInfo, DestInfo: TDDSurfaceDesc2;
```

```
    SrcPtr, DestPtr: PByteArray;

    DestX, DestY,
    SrcX, SrcY: Integer;

    SinTheta, CosTheta: Single;

    Area: TRect;
    CenterX, CenterY: Single;
begin
  {erase the last frame of animation}
  ColorFill(FBackBuffer, 0, nil);

  {increment our angle, making sure to roll it over if necessary}
  Inc(Theta);
  if Theta>359 then
    Theta := 0;

  {determine the sine and cosine of this angle by using our
   lookup tables}
  SinTheta := SinTable[Theta];
  CosTheta := CosTable[Theta];

  try
    {lock the source image}
    SrcInfo.dwSize := SizeOf(TDDSurfaceDesc2);
    DXCheck( FImage.Lock(nil, SrcInfo, DDLOCK_SURFACEMEMORYPTR or
                         DDLOCK_WAIT, 0) );
    SrcPtr := PByteArray(SrcInfo.lpSurface);

    {specify the rectangular area in the destination image to lock by
     determining coordinates that will center the image}
    Area := Rect((DXWIDTH div 2)-(SrcInfo.dwWidth div 2),
                 (DXHEIGHT div 2)-(SrcInfo.dwHeight div 2),
                 (DXWIDTH div 2)+(SrcInfo.dwWidth div 2),
                 (DXHEIGHT div 2)+(SrcInfo.dwHeight div 2));

    {lock the destination surface}
    DestInfo.dwSize := SizeOf(TDDSurfaceDesc2);
    DXCheck( FBackBuffer.Lock(@Area, DestInfo, DDLOCK_SURFACEMEMORYPTR or
                              DDLOCK_WAIT, 0) );
    DestPtr := PByteArray(DestInfo.lpSurface);

    {determine the center of the source image}
    CenterX := (SrcInfo.dwWidth / 2);
    CenterY := (SrcInfo.dwHeight / 2);

    {begin iterating through the pixels of the destination image}
    for DestY := 0 to SrcInfo.dwHeight do
    begin
      for DestX := 0 to SrcInfo.dwWidth do
```

```
      begin
        {determine the source pixel to use for this destination pixel}
        SrcX := Trunc(CenterX + (DestX - CenterX)*CosTheta -
                      (DestY - CenterY)*SinTheta);
        SrcY := Trunc(CenterY + (DestX - CenterX)*SinTheta +
                      (DestY - CenterY)*CosTheta);

        {if this pixel is within the source image...}
        if (SrcX > 0) and (SrcX < SrcInfo.dwWidth) and
           (SrcY > 0) and (SrcY < SrcInfo.dwHeight) then
          {...copy it to the destination}
          DestPtr[DestX] := SrcPtr[SrcY*SrcInfo.lPitch+SrcX];
      end;

      {move to the next line in the destination image}
      DestPtr := PByteArray(Longint(DestPtr)+DestInfo.lPitch);
    end;
  finally
    {clean up}
    FImage.Unlock(nil);
    FBackBuffer.Unlock(@Area);
  end;
end;


    .
    .
    .


initialization
  {we'll create lookup tables for the sine and cosine functions, using
  the angle as an index into these tables}
  for iAngle := 0 to 359 do
  begin
    SinTable[iAngle] := Sin(iAngle*(PI/180));
    CosTable[iAngle] := Cos(iAngle*(PI/180));
  end;
```

## *Alternatives/Enhancements*

Unlike bitmap scaling, rotation is not something that is emulated by DirectDraw. Some cards provide hardware support for bitmap rotation, but even these could be restricted to rotations by only 90-degree angles. Therefore, you cannot rely on DirectDraw for bitmap rotation on every machine; you must implement this functionality yourself.

Bitmap rotation can be very slow due to its mathematically intense nature. However, rotation could be optimized by the use of assembly language. A less dramatic approach may be to use lookup tables that contained the rotated pixel coordinates for all angles. The angle could then be used as an index into this lookup table. This would result in incredibly fast bitmap rotation, but it would be a memory hog.

## Lighting Tricks

In nature, the color of an object can vary according to the intensity of light to which it is subjected. When the lights go down, things appear darker; when an object moves into the shadow of another object, its color darkens. Modeling this in our graphics engines can make our game worlds appear much more realistic and dynamic. There are many ways to model realistic lighting, but one method in particular is easy to implement and produces acceptable results.

### Basic Theory

This technique works by imposing restrictions on the palette of an image. For example, say we want to display an image that will have four different levels of light intensity. We need to segregate our palette into four different segments, so 256 / 4 = 64 palette slots per segment.

Now, our artists need to draw the image using only the first 64 palette slots. These slots should contain the colors of the image at their brightest intensity. The other three segments of 64 palette slots contain exactly the same colors as those in the first 64 slots, but at darker and darker intensities. In other words, the second segment of 64 slots contains the colors of the first 64 slots at 75% of their original intensity, the third segment of 64 slots contains these colors at 50% intensity, and the final segment contains the colors at 25% of their original intensity.

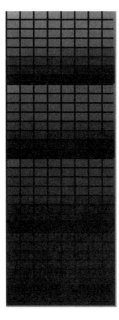

When the application draws the image, it needs to draw it one pixel at a time. Then, depending on the light level, we simply add 0, 64, 128, or 192 to the color of the original pixel. This will draw the pixel using the colors lower and lower in the palette, resulting in an image with darker and darker pixels. Using this technique, we can create a spotlight effect as demonstrated in Listing 11-4.

**Figure 11-4:**
*A segregated palette*

**Listing 11-4:** *Using lighting techniques to create a spotlight*

```
procedure TfrmDXAppMain.FormCreate(Sender: TObject);
begin

   .
   .
   .

  {position the mouse cursor to appear in the center of the screen}
  CurX := 320;
  CurY := 240;
  OldX := 320;
  OldY := 240;

   .
   .
   .

end;

   .
   .
   .

procedure TfrmDXAppMain.FormActivate(Sender: TObject);
begin

   .
   .
   .

  {load the palette for the image}
  FPalette := DDLoadPalette(FDirectDraw, ExtractFilePath(ParamStr(0))+
                            'image.bmp');

  {set the palette}
  FPrimarySurface.SetPalette(FPalette);

  {finally, load the image}
  Image := DDLoadBitmap(FDirectDraw, ExtractFilePath(ParamStr(0))+'image.bmp');

  {erase the background}
  ColorFill(FBackBuffer, 255, nil);
  ColorFill(FPrimarySurface, 255, nil);

   .
   .
   .
```

```
    end;

        .
        .
        .


procedure TfrmDXAppMain.DrawSurfaces;
var
  DestSrfcInfo, ImageSrfcInfo: TDDSurfaceDesc2;
  DestPtr, ImagePtr: PByteArray;

  ImgStartX, ImgStartY,
  PointX, PointY,
  Distance: Integer;

  iCount, iCount2: Integer;
begin
  try
    {lock the image surface}
    ImageSrfcInfo.dwSize := SizeOf(TDDSurfaceDesc2);
    DXCheck( Image.Lock(nil, ImageSrfcInfo, DDLOCK_SURFACEMEMORYPTR or
                        DDLOCK_WAIT, 0) );
    ImagePtr := PByteArray(ImageSrfcInfo.lpSurface);

    {lock the destination surface}
    DestSrfcInfo.dwSize := SizeOf(TDDSurfaceDesc2);
    DXCheck( FBackBuffer.Lock(nil, DestSrfcInfo, DDLOCK_SURFACEMEMORYPTR or
                              DDLOCK_WAIT, 0) );

    {this positions the initial starting point of destination drawing
     so that the image will be centered horizontally and vertically}
    DestPtr := PByteArray(integer(DestSrfcInfo.lpSurface)+
                          (DestSrfcInfo.lPitch*((DXHEIGHT div 2)-
                          (ImageSrfcInfo.dwHeight div 2)))+
                          ((DXWIDTH div 2)-(ImageSrfcInfo.dwWidth div 2)));

    {store the starting offset of the image}
    ImgStartX := (DXWIDTH div 2)-(ImageSrfcInfo.dwWidth div 2);
    ImgStartY := (DXHEIGHT div 2)-(ImageSrfcInfo.dwHeight div 2);

    for iCount := 0 to ImageSrfcInfo.dwHeight-1 do
    begin
      for iCount2 := 0 to ImageSrfcInfo.dwWidth-1 do
      begin
        {retrieve the current pixel coordinates and translate them such
         that the mouse cursor acts as the origin}
        PointX := (ImgStartX+iCount2) - CurX;
        PointY := (ImgStartY+iCount) - CurY;

        {determine the relative distance of this pixel from the mouse
         cursor, and restrain it to a range of 0-4}
```

```
          Distance := ((PointX*PointX)+(PointY*PointY)) div 600;
          if Distance > 3 then
            Distance := 3;

          {draw the destination pixel. the distance is used to determine
           which 64-slot segment of the palette is used to draw the
           destination pixel color}
          DestPtr[iCount2] := ImagePtr[iCount2]+(64*Distance);
        end;

        {increment to the next line in the image}
        ImagePtr := PByteArray(Integer(ImagePtr)+ImageSrfcInfo.lPitch);

        {increment to the next line in the destination buffer}
        DestPtr := PByteArray(Integer(DestPtr)+DestSrfcInfo.lPitch);
      end;

  finally
    {release all locks}
    Image.Unlock(nil);
    FBackBuffer.Unlock(nil);
  end;
end;
```

## Alternatives/Enhancements

This is a really cheap trick that is easy to implement and does not put too great a strain on your artists. However, another method for implementing lighting involves creating a lookup table for each level of light intensity desired. Specifically, the application creates a 256-entry array of integers, and begins iterating through each entry in the original palette. For each color, the application determines the color components at a darker intensity, and then searches the original palette for an entry that is the closest match for this darker color. The number of this matching palette entry is then placed into the array at the index of the original color. The pixels in the bitmap now act as an index into the new array, which in turn then act as an index into the original palette. It is possible to create many more light intensity levels using this technique as opposed to the one described above. It also allows your artists to use more colors, but they must be mindful to use a palette containing several shades of each individual color so that the color-matching step finds an appropriate match.

Alternatively, you could use a non-palettized video mode. Using a non-palettized color mode frees your artists to use whatever colors they wish, and the results of this trick can be much more spectacular than that shown here. The effect will take a little longer, depending on the chosen video mode, as the application must move double to quadruple the information. However, using this technique, the banding side effect of the technique shown above can be eliminated, and the lighting effect can be much more realistic.

**Tip:**  It is possible to lessen the banding effect using the above illustrated technique by using a mask for the lighted area instead of programmatically calculating the distance from the mouse cursor. The pixels in each band could be dithered somewhat around the edges of each band to help lessen the banding effect.

## Transition Effects

While it is perfectly acceptable to simply move from one scene to another with no fanfare, providing some sort of animation during scene transitions makes the software appear to have a smoother flow. We can take another lesson from the motion picture industry here. Typically, movies use a number of different wipes, fades, and other effects to smoothly transition from one scene to another. The next time you watch any of the *Star Wars* films, pay attention to how these transition effects create a smooth flow throughout the movie.

### Basic Theory

Each transition effect may be implemented in wildly differing ways or with only subtle, minor differences, depending on the desired effect. In this example, let's use three simple effects that are relatively easy to implement yet provide cool animation effects. Specifically, these transition effects will be melt, crawl, and dissolve.

*Melt*    This is the classic melting screen effect made popular by id software's Doom. It works by first drawing the next scene image to the back buffer, and then drawing the closing scene one column at a time into the back buffer. An array of integers, one entry per column of pixels, is used to track the vertical offset of the start of the pixel column. By starting some columns before others, we can create the illusion of the foreground screen melting away to reveal the next scene.

*Figure 11-5: The melt effect*

***Crawl*** This is a variation of the dissolve effect below. Starting from one side of the screen, we use two variables to track a beginning and ending column (or row), spaced some arbitrary distance apart. At each frame of the animation, we increment both the beginning and ending columns (or rows). These define an area into which several pixels from the next scene are drawn. Their coordinates are chosen at random and copied into the back buffer at the same position. Past the ending column (or row), the "exposed" portion of the next scene is drawn. The effect appears to eat away at the foreground image, revealing the image of the next scene underneath.

**Figure 11-6:** *The crawl effect*

***Dissolve*** This is a common effect that makes one image appear to dissolve, revealing the image beneath it. It works by randomly choosing a pixel from the next image and copying it to the back buffer (over the previous image) at the same position. However, it is rather slow to use the entire screen area for the range of random pixel selection. Thus, we constrain the random pixel selection to an 8 x 8 pixel area, and then replicate that throughout the entire image. In other words, the screen is divided into 8 x 8 blocks. The next pixel is chosen from the first 8 x 8 area, and we use this coordinate as an offset for each 8 x 8 block throughout the screen. This creates a fast, effective dissolve effect.

**Figure 11-7:** *The dissolve effect*

The following listing demonstrates a simple implementation of these three effects. Press the spacebar to move from one image to the next.

**Listing 11-5:** *Transition effects*

```
interface

    .
    .
    .

type
  TTransitionType = (transMelt, transCrawl, transDissolve);

    .
    .
    .

var

    .
    .
    .

  {holds the scene images}
  ScreenBackgrounds: array[0..2] of IDirectDrawSurface4;

  {tracks which background image is used next}
  NextBackground: Integer;

  {tracks the next transition effect to be used}
  NextTransition: TTransitionType;

implementation

    .
    .
    .

procedure TfrmDXAppMain.FormCreate(Sender: TObject);
begin

    .
    .
    .

  {initialize the next background}
  NextBackground := 0;
```

```
      {initialize the next transition effect}
      NextTransition := transMelt;
    end;

      .
      .
      .


procedure TfrmDXAppMain.FormActivate(Sender: TObject);
begin

      .
      .
      .


    {load the palette}
      FPalette := DDLoadPalette(FDirectDraw, ExtractFilePath(ParamStr(0))+
                              'begin.bmp');

      {set the palette}
      FPrimarySurface.SetPalette(FPalette);

      {load the three images to be used in the transition effect animations}
      ScreenBackgrounds[0] := DDLoadBitmap(FDirectDraw, ExtractFilePath(
                                    ParamStr(0))+'begin.bmp');
      ScreenBackgrounds[1] := DDLoadBitmap(FDirectDraw, ExtractFilePath(
                                    ParamStr(0))+'middle.bmp');
      ScreenBackgrounds[2] := DDLoadBitmap(FDirectDraw, ExtractFilePath(
                                    ParamStr(0))+'end.bmp');

      {copy the first image to the screen}
      DestRect := Rect(0, 0, DXWIDTH, DXHEIGHT);
      FPrimarySurface.BltFast(0, 0, ScreenBackgrounds[0], DestRect,
                          DDBLTFAST_NOCOLORKEY OR DDBLTFAST_WAIT);
      FBackBuffer.BltFast(0, 0, ScreenBackgrounds[0], DestRect,
                      DDBLTFAST_NOCOLORKEY OR DDBLTFAST_WAIT);

      .
      .
      .


  end;

      .
      .
      .


procedure TfrmDXAppMain.FormKeyDown(Sender: TObject; var Key: Word;
  Shift: TShiftState);
begin
  if Key = VK_ESCAPE then
```

```
    Close;

  {if the spacebar was pressed...}
  if Key = Ord(' ') then
  begin
    {move to the next transition}
    NextTransition := Succ(NextTransition);

    {rollover the transition effect if necessary}
    if Ord(NextTransition) > Ord(transDissolve) then
      NextTransition := transMelt;

    {perform the transition effect}
    CoolScreenTransition(NextTransition);
  end;
end;

procedure TfrmDXAppMain.CoolScreenTransition(TransitionType: TTransitionType);
var
  HeadCol, TailCol: Integer;
  iCount, iCount2, iCount3: Integer;
  Block, DestRect: TRect;
  RandBlock, RandBlock2: Integer;

  Worms: array[0..DXWIDTH-1] of Integer;
  StillGoing: Boolean;
begin
  {move to the next image}
  Inc(NextBackground);

  {rollover the image index, if necessary}
  if NextBackground > 2 then
    NextBackground := 0;

  {copy the foreground image into the back buffer}
  DestRect := Rect(0, 0, DXWIDTH, DXHEIGHT);
  FBackbuffer.BltFast(0, 0, FPrimarySurface, DestRect, DDBLTFAST_NOCOLORKEY or
                 DDBLTFAST_WAIT);

  case TransitionType of
    transMelt   : begin
                    {initialize the starting offsets for each column of
                     pixels}
                    for iCount := 0 to DXWIDTH-1 do
                      Worms[iCount] := 0;

                    {initialize the loop variable}
                    StillGoing := TRUE;

                    {begin the effect}
                    while StillGoing do
```

```
begin
  {assume that the effect will stop}
  StillGoing := FALSE;

  {for each column of pixels...}
  for iCount := 0 to DXWIDTH-1 do
  begin
    {if this column has not yet started to move...}
    if Worms[iCount] = 0 then
      {...give the column a 25% chance of starting}
      if Random(4) = 1 then
        Worms[iCount] := 1;

    {if this column has not yet reached to bottom,
     but is in motion...}
    if (Worms[iCount]<DXHEIGHT-1)and(Worms[iCount]>0) then
    begin
      {...there is still at least one column still
       'alive', so the effect has not yet stopped}
      StillGoing := TRUE;

      {copy this column of pixels into its new position}
      Block := Rect(iCount, Worms[iCount], iCount+1,
                    DXHEIGHT-3);
      FBackBuffer.BltFast(iCount, Worms[iCount]+3,
                          FBackBuffer, Block,
                          DDBLTFAST_NOCOLORKEY or
                          DDBLTFAST_WAIT);

      {copy the same column from the next scene above
       the currently moving column}
      Block := Rect(iCount, 0, iCount+1, Worms[iCount]+3);
      FBackBuffer.BltFast(iCount, 0,
                          ScreenBackgrounds[NextBackground],
                          Block, DDBLTFAST_NOCOLORKEY or
                          DDBLTFAST_WAIT);

      {move the column down a bit}
      Worms[iCount] := Worms[iCount]+3;
    end;
  end;

  {the back buffer now contains the next frame of the
   animation, so copy it to the screen}
  DestRect := Rect(0, 0, DXWIDTH, DXHEIGHT);
  FPrimarySurface.BltFast(0, 0, FBackbuffer, DestRect,
                          DDBLTFAST_NOCOLORKEY or
                          DDBLTFAST_WAIT);
end;

{the animation is over, so copy the final image to both
```

```
                          the front and back buffers to erase the last remains of
                          the animation sequence}
                      Block := Rect(0, 0, DXWIDTH, DXHEIGHT);
                      FBackbuffer.BltFast(0, 0,
                                          ScreenBackgrounds[NextBackground],
                                          Block, DDBLTFAST_NOCOLORKEY or
                                          DDBLTFAST_WAIT);
                      FPrimarySurface.BltFast(0, 0,
                                          ScreenBackgrounds[NextBackground],
                                          Block, DDBLTFAST_NOCOLORKEY or
                                          DDBLTFAST_WAIT);
                    end;
    transCrawl  : begin
                      {begin tracking the beginning and ending columns}
                      HeadCol := 0;
                      TailCol := -10;

                      {while the ending column is still on the screen...}
                      while TailCol < (DXWIDTH div 5)-1 do
                      begin
                        {iterate through the columns of pixels between the
                         beginning and ending column}
                        for iCount := TailCol to HeadCol do
                          {if this column is on the screen...}
                          if iCount > -1 then
                            for iCount2 := 0 to 20 do
                            begin
                              {choose a random block of pixels}
                              RandBlock := Random(DXHEIGHT div 5);

                              {copy this block of pixels from the next image
                               into the destination at the same coordinates}
                              Block := Rect(5*iCount, 5*RandBlock, 5*iCount+5,
                                            5*RandBlock+5);
                              FBackBuffer.BltFast(Block.Left, Block.Top,
                                          ScreenBackgrounds[NextBackground],
                                          Block, DDBLTFAST_NOCOLORKEY or
                                          DDBLTFAST_WAIT);
                            end;

                      {if the ending column is on the screen...}
                      if TailCol > -1 then
                      begin
                        {make sure we copy the entire column of pixels from
                         the next image into the destination so that the
                         final image will be complete}
                        Block := Rect(5*TailCol, 0, 5*TailCol+5, DXHEIGHT);
                        FBackBuffer.BltFast(Block.Left, Block.Top,
                                          ScreenBackgrounds[NextBackground],
                                          Block, DDBLTFAST_NOCOLORKEY or
                                          DDBLTFAST_WAIT);
```

```
                        end;

                        {increment the beginning and ending columns}
                        Inc(HeadCol);
                        Inc(TailCol);

                        {copy this frame of animation to the screen}
                        Block := Rect(0, 0, DXWIDTH, DXHEIGHT);
                        FPrimarySurface.BltFast(0, 0, FBackbuffer, Block,
                                          DDBLTFAST_NOCOLORKEY or
                                          DDBLTFAST_WAIT);

                        {pause for a short period}
                        Sleep(20);
                    end;

                    {the animation is over, so copy the final image to both
                     the front and back buffers to erase the last remains of
                     the animation sequence}
                    Block := Rect(0, 0, DXWIDTH, DXHEIGHT);
                    FBackbuffer.BltFast(0, 0,
                                      ScreenBackgrounds[NextBackground],
                                      Block, DDBLTFAST_NOCOLORKEY or
                                      DDBLTFAST_WAIT);
                    FPrimarySurface.BltFast(0, 0,
                                          ScreenBackgrounds[NextBackground],
                                          Block, DDBLTFAST_NOCOLORKEY or
                                          DDBLTFAST_WAIT);

                end;
transDissolve : begin
                    {we will copy 100 blocks of pixels for this effect}
                    for iCount := 0 to 100 do
                    begin
                      {choose a random block of pixels from our 8 X 8 area}
                      RandBlock := Random(8);
                      RandBlock2 := Random(8);

                      {this will be mirrored throughout the screen relative
                       to each segmented 8 X 8 block of pixels}
                      for iCount2 := 0 to 15 do
                        for iCount3 := 0 to 12 do
                        begin
                          {copy the relative block of pixels from the
                           next image into the back buffer}
                          Block := Rect((5*RandBlock)+(iCount2*8*5),
                                    (5*RandBlock2)+(iCount3*8*5),
                                    (5*RandBlock)+(iCount2*8*5)+5,
                                    (5*RandBlock2)+(iCount3*8*5)+5);
                          FBackBuffer.BltFast(Block.Left, Block.Top,
                                      ScreenBackgrounds[NextBackground],
                                      Block, DDBLTFAST_NOCOLORKEY or
```

```
                                        DDBLTFAST_WAIT);
              end;

          {copy this frame of animation to the screen}
          Block := Rect(0, 0, DXWIDTH, DXHEIGHT);
          FPrimarySurface.BltFast(0, 0, FBackbuffer, Block,
                                  DDBLTFAST_NOCOLORKEY or
                                  DDBLTFAST_WAIT);

          {pause for a short period}
          Sleep(20);
        end;

        {the animation is over, so copy the final image to both
         the front and back buffers to erase the last remains of
         the animation sequence}
        Block := Rect(0, 0, DXWIDTH, DXHEIGHT);
        FBackbuffer.BltFast(0, 0,
                            ScreenBackgrounds[NextBackground],
                            Block, DDBLTFAST_NOCOLORKEY or
                            DDBLTFAST_WAIT);
        FPrimarySurface.BltFast(0, 0,
                            ScreenBackgrounds[NextBackground],
                            Block, DDBLTFAST_NOCOLORKEY or
                            DDBLTFAST_WAIT);
      end;
  end;
end;
```

## Alternatives/Enhancements

The only thing limiting transition effects from one scene to another is the imagination of the programmer. While the three covered here are easy to implement, you can probably think of several dozen more that could be implemented just as easily. Many transition effects available from third-party products are little more than extensions of the effects implemented in the above example.

The effects demonstrated above rely on the fact that the images involved in the transition have the same palette. Using some palette manipulation, it may be possible to use images with two different palettes. This would require a new palette to be created for each frame of the transition animation, but this would result in a more flexible scene transitioning system.

*Tip:* Using a non-palettized display mode would, of course, eliminate this drawback.

## Simple Texture Mapping

We've seen how easy it is to blit rectangular sections of bitmaps onto the screen or into offscreen buffers. If you've done any basic Windows graphics programming, you also know how easy it is to draw geometric shapes. It would be cool if we could somehow draw geometric shapes but use a bitmap as the contents of that shape, as opposed to simply filling it with color. The technique of mapping a bitmap image onto a geometric shape is known as texture mapping.

**texture mapping:** A general term for algorithms that map a bitmap image onto a geometric shape.

Texture mapping techniques can be applied in many exciting ways. Texture mapping techniques allow us to produce very convincing graphical images of real-world objects, which would be very difficult or impossible to achieve otherwise. Algorithms that implement texture mapping range from the childishly simple to the absurdly complex. Let's look at a relatively simple texture mapping method that will allow us to wrap a bitmap around a circular shape to produce the illusion of a sphere.

### Basic Theory

Perhaps the first thing we will need is the texture to be mapped onto the shape. In this example, we'll create an animation of a planet spinning in space. Thus, our texture map should look like a planet, and will be rectangular in shape.

*Figure 11-8:* The texture map

Next, we need to define the circular shape itself. Specifically, we'll be using some of the scaling techniques described previously, so we need a series of points that define the perimeter of the circle. We can generate these points by using the equation for a circle:

```
MinorAxis := Sqrt((Radius * Radius)-(MajorAxis * MajorAxis))
```

The circle is generated at application startup and therefore does not have to be particularly fast. However, we'll make use of the symmetrical property of circles to generate points only for the first quadrant. These points can then be mirrored around the horizontal, vertical, and diagonal axes to form an entire circle, as illustrated in Figure 11-9.

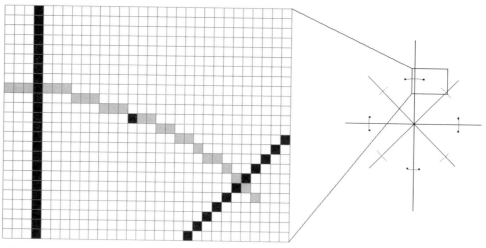

Pixels drawn in the first quadrant of a circle can be duplicated using symmetry.

**Figure 11-9:** *Using symmetry to mirror points around a circle*

Since our circular shape will be drawn one line of pixels at a time, the generated points serve as endpoints for each line of the circle. The actual texture mapping occurs by using the scaling techniques described above in conjunction with these endpoints to stretch each line of the texture bitmap between the endpoints of each line in the circle.

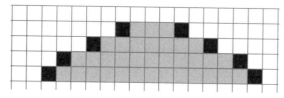

The circle is defined as a series of endpoints, each pair of which defines one 'line' of the circle.

**Figure 11-10:** *Defining a circle using endpoints*

By defining a rectangular area smaller than the texture map, and then using scaling techniques to stretch the defined rectangular area not only vertically across the circular shape but also horizontally between each pair of endpoints, the resulting image seems to warp and magnify at the center of the circle. This produces a convincing illusion of an image wrapped around a sphere. The following listing demonstrates this technique.

**Listing 11-6:** *Wrapping a texture around a sphere*

```
interface

const

      .
      .
      .

   {the position of the center of the screen}
   XPos = 320;
   YPos = 240;

      .
      .
      .


var

      .
      .
      .

   {tracks our endpoints}
   FEndptList: TList;

   {tracks the width of the portion of the texture to be wrapped
    around the sphere}
   FTextureSwatchWidth: Integer;

   {tracks the texture offset}
   TextureOffset: Integer;

      .
      .
      .
@code =
procedure TfrmDXAppMain.FormDestroy(Sender: TObject);
begin

      .
      .
      .

   {free the endpoint list}
   FEndptList.Free;
end;

procedure TfrmDXAppMain.FormActivate(Sender: TObject);
```

```
begin

    .
    .
    .

  {load the palette}
  FPalette := DDLoadPalette(FDirectDraw, ExtractFilePath(ParamStr(0))+
                            'Texture.bmp');

  {set the palette}
  FPrimarySurface.SetPalette(FPalette);

  {create the circle}
  GenerateCircle(100, ExtractFilePath(ParamStr(0))+'Texture.bmp');

  {initialize the texture offset}
  TextureOffset := 0;

  {erase the screen}
  ColorFill(FPrimarySurface, 255, nil);
  ColorFill(FBackBuffer, 255, nil);

    .
    .
    .

end;

procedure TfrmDXAppMain.DrawSurfaces;
var
  iCount, iCount2: Integer;
  SrcYRatio, SrcXRatio: Double;
  TextureX: Integer;

  SrcRect: TRect;
  SourceSrfcDesc, DestSrfcDesc: TDDSurfaceDesc2;
  iCol, iRow: Integer;
  SourceSrfcPtr, DestSrfcPtr: PBytePtr;
begin
  try
    {begin by locking the source buffer}
    FillChar(SourceSrfcDesc, SizeOf(TDDSurfaceDesc2), 0);
    SourceSrfcDesc.dwSize := SizeOf(TDDSurfaceDesc2);
    FTexture.Lock(nil, SourceSrfcDesc, DDLOCK_WAIT, 0);

    {now lock the destination buffer}
    FillChar(DestSrfcDesc, SizeOf(TDDSurfaceDesc2), 0);
    DestSrfcDesc.dwSize := SizeOf(TDDSurfaceDesc2);
    FBackBuffer.Lock(nil, DestSrfcDesc, DDLOCK_WAIT, 0);
    DestSrfcPtr := PBytePtr(Longint(DestSrfcDesc.lpSurface)+XPos+
```

```
                                     ((YPos-(FEndptList.Count div 2))*DestSrfcDesc.lPitch));

      {determine the ratio for stretching the texture map vertically}
      SrcYRatio := SourceSrfcDesc.dwHeight / FEndptList.Count;

      {increment the texture offset}
      Inc(TextureOffset);

      {rollover the texture offset if necessary}
      if TextureOffset > SourceSrfcDesc.dwWidth then
        TextureOffset := 0;

      {for each pair of endpoints in the endpoint list...}
      for iCount := 0 to FEndptList.Count-1 do
      begin
        {initialize the source pointer according to the next vertical pixel}
        SourceSrfcPtr := PBytePtr(Longint(SourceSrfcDesc.lpSurface)+
                    (SourceSrfcDesc.lPitch*Trunc(SrcYRatio * iCount)));

        {determine the ratio for stretching the texture map horizontally.
         the endpoints are stored as a single value relative to the center of
         the circle, so this value must be doubled to get the correct ratio}
        SrcXRatio := FTextureSwatchWidth / (Integer(FEndptList[iCount])*2);

        {for each pixel in this horizontal row...}
        for iCount2 := 0 to Integer(FEndptList[iCount])*2 do
        begin
          {retrieve the next texture pixel}
          TextureX := Trunc(SrcXRatio * iCount2)+TextureOffset;

          {roll this over if necessary}
          if TextureX >= SourceSrfcDesc.dwWidth then
            TextureX := TextureX-SourceSrfcDesc.dwWidth;

          {since the endpoint is a value relative to the center axis of
           the circle, we simply subtract the endpoint value from our loop
           counter to get the correct horizontal pixel coordinate}
          DestSrfcPtr^[iCount2-Integer(FEndptList[iCount])] :=
                    SourceSrfcPtr^[TextureX];
        end;

        {increment to the next line of pixels in the destination}
        Inc(DestSrfcPtr, DestSrfcDesc.lPitch);
      end;
    finally
      {unlock both buffers}
      FTexture.Unlock(nil);
      FBackBuffer.Unlock(nil);
    end;
end;
```

.
.
.

```
procedure TfrmDXAppMain.GenerateCircle(Radius: Integer; Texture: string);
var
  MajorAxis, MinorAxis: integer;
  YOffset: Integer;

  XOfsQuad1, XOfsQuad2: TList;

  iCount: Integer;
begin
  {create the endpoint list}
  FEndptList := TList.Create;

  {create the quadrant lists}
  XOfsQuad1 := TList.Create;
  XOfsQuad2 := TList.Create;

  {initialize the major and minor axes and the y offset}
  MajorAxis := 0;
  YOffset := Radius;
  MinorAxis := Radius;

  {using the symmetry of a circle, we will store endpoints as only a single
   value relative to the Y axis, or center, of the circle. when drawing
   the texture, we will simply use 0-EndPointValue as the first point in
   the pair of endpoints}

  {loop until the major and minor axes meet}
  while MajorAxis <= MinorAxis do
  begin
    {increment the major axis}
    Inc(MajorAxis);

    {find the minor axis according to the circle equation, adding a small
     offset to make a more rounded circle}
    MinorAxis := Trunc(Sqrt((Radius*Radius) - (MajorAxis*MajorAxis))+0.5);

    {add this value to the second quadrant}
    XOfsQuad2.Insert(0, TObject(MinorAxis));

    {in the first 8th of the circle, the Y value will not be incrementing
     each time, so only store this endpoint when the Y value increases}
    if MinorAxis < YOffset then
    begin
      {add this endpoint to the first quadrant}
      XOfsQuad1.Add(TObject(MajorAxis));
      YOffset := MinorAxis;
    end;
```

```
end;

  {define the width of the texture to be mapped as the major axis value. this
   will cause the texture to be shrunk near the top of the circle, and
   stretched near the center of the circle}
  FTextureSwatchWidth := MajorAxis;

  {finally, add the endpoints in our quadrant lists to the final endpoint
   list in the correct order (from the top of the circle to the bottom)}
  for iCount := 0 to XOfsQuad1.Count-1 do
    FEndptList.Add(XOfsQuad1[iCount]);
  for iCount := 1 to XOfsQuad2.Count-1 do
    FEndptList.Add(XOfsQuad2[iCount]);

  {these coordinates just list the top half of the circle, so we must
   mirror these and add them to the list to define the bottom half}
  for iCount := FEndptList.Count-1 downto 0 do
    FEndptList.Add(FEndptList[iCount]);

  {free the quadrant lists}
  XOfsQuad1.Free;
  XOfsQuad2.Free;

  {load the circle's texture map}
  FTexture := DDLoadBitmap(FDirectDraw, Texture)
end;
```

## Alternatives/Enhancements

There are hundreds, and probably thousands, of ways to map a texture onto a geometric shape. Texture mapping is an integral part of 3-D programming, unless you want your models to look like flat colors. Full 3-D texture mapping is beyond the scope of this book, but the idea behind it remains the same.

Using the lighting techniques described earlier, the spinning planet could be made more realistic by modifying the palette and drawing part of the texture using darker colors, creating a "night" effect. Additionally, you could use a second texture for the clouds, and use transparency techniques to make the clouds appear to move around while the planet stays still, or at least moves at a different rate. Alternatively, a bitmap with text could be used to create an interesting marquee.

# Dynamic Images

The ability to mold and shape a bitmap allows us to produce some pretty spectacular special effects. Creating an image on the fly can produce even more dramatic effects. Blitting sprite images on top of a background certainly creates a new image on the fly, but what we're concerned with here is creating an image based on some sort of algorithm or mathematical function as opposed to just creating a composited layer of bitmaps.

You could create dynamic images such as this in any manner imaginable. Fractal imaging comes to mind, which uses various mathematical equations to produce stunning graphics of everything from abstract forms to images that model natural objects, such as leaves or mountains, in an incredibly lifelike way. Full 3-D games use collections of points and polygons to produce realistic gaming environments. While this list could go on and on, we'll look at two methods for creating some pretty cool special effects: 3-D star fields and fire.

## Star Fields

Everyone has seen the Windows star field screen saver. At a fast enough velocity, it resembles something that you would see on the bridge of the *Enterprise* going at warp speed. Science fiction-based games are quite popular, and may benefit from the ability to produce a cool warp-speed star field animation that could be used when traveling from system to system.

### Basic Theory

This technique makes use of some very basic 3-D concepts. Specifically, each star is tracked as a point in 3-D space. Before we discuss how the stars are moved and how they are subsequently drawn to the screen, we must first understand some very basic 3-D graphics principles.

In a 2-D world, for which most of the examples in this book have been written, coordinates are typically based off of a flat grid. In mathematical terms, this can be considered a Cartesian grid, where the y-axis represents vertical placement and the x-axis represents horizontal placement. The origin, or where these two axes meet, is where the x-axis and y-axis are both at 0. The y-axis increases as you move upward and decreases as you move downward. Similarly, the x-axis increases to the right and decreases to the left. (For the moment, we'll ignore the fact that on a computer screen, the origin is in the upper left-hand corner and y increases as you move downward.) The figure at the top of the following page demonstrates a typical Cartesian coordinate system.

Using this system, simple 2-D sprites can be tracked by a simple x and y coordinate (as we've been doing throughout this book). They can move left and right or up and down, but this system has no method for tracking depth, or which sprites are on top of each other.

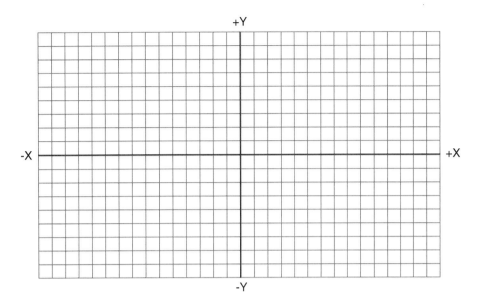

**Figure 11-11:** *A Cartesian coordinate system*

To track depth, we need to add another axis. This is known as the z-axis, and in concept, it is perpendicular to the x and y axes. You can think of it as another axis that runs straight into the computer screen. The z-axis increases as you go "into" the computer screen, and decreases as you come "out of" the computer screen. The following figure demonstrates this concept.

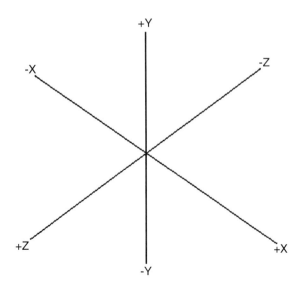

**Figure 11-12:** *A 3-D coordinate system*

A star can be effectively tracked as a single point, so one x, y, z coordinate will represent a single star. If we now initialize a star at a specific coordinate, and then modify its z coordinate, it will appear to move toward or away from the user as desired.

The values for each axis in a system such as this are somewhat arbitrary. In our example, each axis can range from –1000 to 1000. Stars can be positioned anywhere within this square area. Now, even though we've got an acceptable method of tracking star positions, we still can't draw them to the screen. How do we convert these arbitrary axis positions into actual screen coordinates that we can draw?

This is where perspective projection comes in. The equations are very simple, and will produce a correct 2-D coordinate for a 3-D point that will accurately reflect the perspective in relation to its depth on the z-axis. Skipping the lengthy derivation and proofs for producing these equations, they are:

```
Screen_X := XPos / ZPos * VIEWDISTANCE;
Screen_Y := YPos / ZPos * VIEWDISTANCE;
```

Dividing the horizontal and vertical positions by the depth is what gives us the correct perspective. The viewing distance constant is required because without it, the origin of the z-axis is effectively the glass of the computer screen. By multiplying by a constant viewing distance, we effectively push the origin of the z-axis into the computer screen. By modifying this, we can make things appear closer or farther away, depending on the size of this value.

To further enhance this illusion, we've dynamically created a grayscale palette and based the color of the pixel drawn to the screen on its z-axis position. This causes the stars to fade from black to white as they move toward the user, which further enhances the 3-D effect. The following listing demonstrates this effect.

**Listing 11-7:** *A 3-D star field*

```
const

    .
    .
    .

   {the total number of stars on the screen at once}
   NUMSTARS = 1000;

   {the viewing distance}
   VIEWDISTANCE = 350;

    .
    .
    .
```

```
type
  {tracks single point within our 3D world}
  TStar = record
    X, Y, Z: Single;
  end;

    .
    .
    .

var

    .
    .
    .

  {the palette interface}
  FPalette: IDirectDrawPalette;


implementation

    .
    .
    .

procedure TfrmDXAppMain.FormActivate(Sender: TObject);
var

    .
    .
    .

  {holds palette colors}
  PalColors: TColorTable;

  iCount: Integer;
begin

    .
    .
    .

  {define the colors for the palette. this produces a ranged palette,
   fading from black to white in the lower half, and all white in
   the upper half. this is used to make the stars appear to fade in as
   they move closer to the user}
  for iCount := 0 to 127 do
  begin
    PalColors[iCount].R := 255;
```

```
        PalColors[iCount].G := 255;
        PalColors[iCount].B := 255;
        PalColors[iCount].A := 0;
      end;
      for iCount := 128 to 255 do
      begin
        PalColors[iCount].R := 255-(2*(iCount-128));
        PalColors[iCount].G := 255-(2*(iCount-128));
        PalColors[iCount].B := 255-(2*(iCount-128));
        PalColors[iCount].A := 0;
      end;

      {create the actual palette}
      FDirectDraw.CreatePalette(DDPCAPS_8BIT or DDPCAPS_ALLOW256,
                                @PalColors, FPalette, nil);

      {attach the palette to the primary surface}
      FPrimarySurface.SetPalette(FPalette);

      {finally, initialize all of the stars}
      for iCount := 0 to NUMSTARS do
        InitStar(iCount);

        .
        .
        .

end;

        .
        .
        .


procedure TfrmDXAppMain.DrawSurfaces;
var
  SrfcDesc: TDDSurfaceDesc2;
  BytePtr: PByte;

  iCount: Integer;

  XPos, YPos: Integer;
begin
  {clear the back buffer}
  ColorFill(FBackBuffer, 255, nil);

  {lock the back buffer. all animation will take place on this surface}
  FillChar(SrfcDesc, SizeOf(TDDSurfaceDesc2), 0);
  SrfcDesc.dwSize := SizeOf(TDDSurfaceDesc2);
  FBackBuffer.Lock(nil, SrfcDesc, DDLOCK_WAIT, 0);
  BytePtr := SrfcDesc.lpSurface;
```

```
{move and draw all of the stars}
for iCount := 0 to NUMSTARS do
begin
  {a negative value here moves the stars closer to the screen. a positive
   value would move them away, giving the sensation of moving backwards}
  Stars[iCount].Z := Stars[iCount].Z - 15;

  {if the star's Z value is greater than zero...}
  if Stars[iCount].Z > 0 then
  begin
    {project the star onto our 2D computer screen in a perspectively
     correct manner.  note that since the origin of the computer
     screen is in the upper left-hand corner, we're moving the stars
     into the center of the screen to produce a more desirable effect.
     note that we're also reversing the sign of the Y coordinate so
     that it accurately reflects the movement in a Cartesian coordinate
     system}
    XPos := Round((DXWIDTH div 2)+
                (Stars[iCount].X/Stars[iCount].Z*VIEWDISTANCE));
    YPos := Round((DXHEIGHT div 2)-
                (Stars[iCount].Y/Stars[iCount].Z*VIEWDISTANCE));

    {if our stars are off of the screen...}
    if (XPos<0) or (XPos>DXWIDTH) or (YPos<0) or (YPos>DXHEIGHT) then
      {...re-create it}
      InitStar(iCount)
    else
      {otherwise, draw it at the correct position, using a color
       proportional to its Z axis position, making it appear to fade in
       from black}
      PByte(Longint(BytePtr)+XPos+(YPos*SrfcDesc.lPitch))^ :=
            Trunc(255*(Stars[iCount].Z/1000));
  end
  else
    {...otherwise, reinitialize the star}
    InitStar(iCount);
end;

{finally, unlock the buffer}
FBackBuffer.Unlock(nil);
end;

  .
  .
  .

procedure TfrmDXAppMain.InitStar(Index: Integer);
begin
  {place the star at a random position}
  Stars[Index].X := random(2000)-1000;
```

```
    Stars[Index].Y:=random(2000)-1000;

    {start the star as far back as necessary}
    Stars[Index].Z:=1000;
  end;

end.
```

### Alternatives/Enhancements

Allowing the user to specify the velocity of the stars through some sort of throttle control would create the perception of speed. By modifying the starting position of the stars, it would even be possible to create the sensation of turning. Coupled with a fast bitmap scaling algorithm, this effect could be used to create a pretty cool arcade-type space shooter.

 **Tip:** While this animation is pretty fast in its current implementation, there's really no need to use a three-dimensional coordinate system with perspective projection unless we're going to be creating a full 3-D game. This same effect can be reproduced using only x and y velocities and integer math, which could dramatically speed up the effect and leave more CPU time for more critical tasks. Remember, graphical effects do not have to be totally accurate; as long as it looks right, it is right.

Alternatively, if this was going to be used simply as a static animation or a transition from scene to scene, it may be faster just to create an actual animation using bitmaps drawn by an artist. However, the method by which stars are implemented could be considered a primitive particle system. By starting several "stars" at the exact same coordinate but giving each one a different heading and velocity and implementing a lifespan counter for each one so it disappears after a certain amount of time, a very realistic particle explosion system could be created. Adding gravity effects to the particles could produce an even more remarkable effect.

## Fire

The fire effect is a really cool trick that, when performed properly, can create a very convincing illusion of fire. This effect is well documented both on the Web and in various books on graphics programming, and has been around for quite some time. It is a very computationally intensive effect, but it can be highly optimized and runs quite fast when implemented in assembly code. There are numerous ways of implementing this effect, but we'll examine one that produces a nice effect at decent speeds.

## Basic Theory

The first thing we need to accomplish is creating an appropriate palette. For an effective fire, we'll create a palette that ranges from white in the upper slots (255-192), through yellow and orange, to red, and finally to black in the lowest slots (63-0). We could adjust the palette range somewhat and put some blues in, to simulate a cooler flame, or perhaps add some grays at the end, which would effectively simulate smoke.

This effect involves moving pixels that already exist in a surface. Therefore, we need to create a new surface that will contain the image of the fire. Since we'll be reading values from this surface, we'll place it in system memory. This algorithm is a CPU hog, so even though we'll create a surface that's the same size as the screen, we'll only use a small part of it for the effect. In our example, we've defined a starting and ending vertical position as well as a starting and ending horizontal position, which will confine the effect to the rectangle defined by these coordinates.

Now for the real work. Starting at the first row of pixels (defined by our starting vertical position) in the fire effect surface, we begin iterating through each column (as defined by our starting and ending horizontal position). We retrieve the current value of this pixel, subtract a random amount from this number, and then place the new value in the row of pixels <u>above</u> our current row. In effect, this produces an animation of pixels moving upwards on the screen. Additionally, we add a random number between –1 and 1 to move the pixels left or right in a chaotic manner.

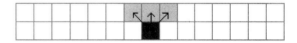

**Figure 11-13:** *Flaming pixels*

Relative to the colors we defined in our palette, the pixel colors will slowly move from white, through yellow and red, and finally to black as they move upward due to the subtraction of a random value from their current color. This produces a very effective illusion of flames. At each frame of the animation, we'll need to place some random pixel values on the bottom row of the effect to give the algorithm some starting values. Implementing this effect is very simple, as illustrated by the following example.

**Listing 11-8:** *The flame effect*

```
const
     .
     .
     .

 {define the rectangular area for the effect}
 XSTART = 200;
```

```
    XEND   = 440;
    YSTART = 100;
    YEND   = 400;

    {define the random decay value}
    DECAY  = 6;

type

    .
    .
    .

  TBytePtr = array[0..0] of Byte;
  PBytePtr = ^TBytePtr;

var

    .
    .
    .

  {the interfaces for the primary and backbuffer surfaces}
  FPrimarySurface,
  FBackBuffer,
  FireSurface: IDirectDrawSurface4;

  {the palette interface}
  FPalette: IDirectDrawPalette;


implementation

    .
    .
    .

procedure TfrmDXAppMain.FormActivate(Sender: TObject);
var

    .
    .
    .

  {hold the palette colors}
  PalColors: TColorTable;

  iCount: Integer;


  {this procedure stuffs the RGB values into the appropriate color table entry}
```

```
    procedure SetPalEntry(Idx, Red, Green, Blue: Integer);
    begin
      PalColors[Idx].R := Red;
      PalColors[Idx].G := Green;
      PalColors[Idx].B := Blue;
      PalColors[Idx].A := 0;
    end;

begin

    .
    .
    .


    {define the colors for the palette. this will produce a spread from white
     to yellow/orange to red, fading to black}
    for iCount := 0 to 63 do
    begin
      SetPalEntry(iCount, iCount shl 2, 0, 0);
      SetPalEntry(64+iCount, 255, iCount shl 2, 0);
      SetPalEntry(128+iCount, 255, 255, iCount shl 2);
      SetPalEntry(192+iCount, 255, 255, 255);
    end;

    {create the actual palette}
    FDirectDraw.CreatePalette(DDPCAPS_8BIT or DDPCAPS_ALLOW256, @PalColors,
                              FPalette, nil);

    {attach the palette to the primary surface}
    FPrimarySurface.SetPalette(FPalette);

    {create the offscreen buffer for the fire. we're going to be modifying this
     constantly, so we'll place it in system memory}
    FillChar(DDSurface, SizeOf(TDDSurfaceDesc2), 0);
    DDSurface.dwSize    := SizeOf(TDDSurfaceDesc2);
    DDSurface.dwFlags   := DDSD_CAPS or DDSD_HEIGHT or DDSD_WIDTH;
    DDSurface.dwWidth   := DXWIDTH;
    DDSurface.dwHeight  := DXHEIGHT;
    DDSurface.ddsCaps.dwCaps := DDSCAPS_OFFSCREENPLAIN or
                                DDSCAPS_SYSTEMMEMORY;

    {initialize the surface}
    DXCheck( FDirectDraw.CreateSurface(DDSurface, FireSurface, nil) );

    {initialize the offscreen buffer to all black}
    ColorFill(FireSurface, 0, nil);

    .
    .
    .
```

```
end;

            .
            .
            .

procedure TfrmDXAppMain.DrawSurfaces;
var
  SrcRect: TRect;
  SrfcDesc: TDDSurfaceDesc2;
  iCol, iRow: Integer;
  FireSrfcPtr,
  BottomLine: PBytePtr;
  CurPixel: Byte;
begin
  {begin by locking the fire surface buffer}
  FillChar(SrfcDesc, SizeOf(TDDSurfaceDesc2), 0);
  SrfcDesc.dwSize := SizeOf(TDDSurfaceDesc2);
  FireSurface.Lock(nil, SrfcDesc, DDLOCK_WAIT, 0);
  FireSrfcPtr := PBytePtr(Longint(SrfcDesc.lpSurface)+
                          (YSTART*SrfcDesc.lPitch));

  {we'll also need a pointer to the bottom line of the rectangular
   area for the effect}
  BottomLine := PBytePtr(Longint(SrfcDesc.lpSurface)+(YEND*SrfcDesc.lPitch));

  {initialize some new pixels in the fire}
  for iCol := XSTART to XEND do
    BottomLine^[iCol] := 255-Random(32);

  {perform the actual flame calculations}
  for iRow := YSTART to YEND do
  begin
    for iCol := XSTART to XEND do
    begin
      {retrieve the pixel from this column}
      CurPixel := FireSrfcPtr^[iCol];

      {if the pixel is less than the decay value or is at the far ends of
       the effect area, blacken it out...}
      If (CurPixel < Decay) or (iCol = XSTART) or (iCol = XEND) then
        {draw a black pixel on the row above the current one}
        PBytePtr(Longint(FireSrfcPtr)-SrfcDesc.lPitch)^[iCol] := 0
      else
        {...otherwise, draw a new pixel on the row above the current one,
         either directly above or to either side of the current pixel, but
         subtract a random value from its color. this causes the color of the
         pixel to slowly move from white, through yellow and red, to black}
        PBytePtr(Longint(FireSrfcPtr)-SrfcDesc.lPitch)^[iCol+Random(3)-1] :=
                CurPixel - Random(DECAY);
```

```
      end;

    {move to the next row in the fire surface}
    Inc(FireSrfcPtr, SrfcDesc.lPitch);
  end;

  {unlock the buffer}
  FireSurface.Unlock(nil);

  {finally, blit the fire surface to the back buffer to make it visible}
  SrcRect := Rect(0, 0, DXWIDTH, DXHEIGHT);
  FBackBuffer.BltFast(0, 0, FireSurface, SrcRect, DDBLTFAST_WAIT);
end;
```

### Alternatives/Enhancements

The strength of the blaze could easily be controlled by writing smaller starting pixel values on the bottom line, or perhaps writing values on only a few pixels and initializing the rest to 0. Because of the way this algorithm works, any pixels drawn into the fire canvas will become part of the blaze. By drawing text into the surface, the letters would appear to burn, creating a very cool effect.

Perhaps the easiest modification to this effect is changing the colors used in the palette. By defining a different range, we could make green fire, purple fire, etc. Indeed, by coupling this with some palette cycling, we could make the fire change colors on the fly. Employing a different method for moving the pixels could also dramatically change the effect. Various other plasma effects demonstrated in examples found throughout the Web use both of these techniques.

## Summary

In this chapter, we discussed several techniques for providing visual special effects that can enhance and complement a game application. We examined various bitmap manipulation methods, including lighting and simple texture mapping, as well as methods for dynamically creating images. When creating visual effects for your games, it is important to keep these points in mind:

■ Computer graphic special effect techniques can be used to produce visual images that would be difficult or impossible to reproduce using blitting techniques alone.

■ By drawing bitmaps using mathematical equations to modify the location of pixels as they are drawn to a destination, you can produce some very cool effects. Manipulating and transforming bitmaps in this way can give images a sense of texture or depth, and can stretch the art budget dollar.

■ Bitmaps can be easily scaled to a larger or smaller size. DirectDraw supports this natively, but by using our own methods, we can control certain aspects and produce images with much better resolutions.

■ Rotating an image is only supported by DirectDraw if it is available in the hardware. We can use our own techniques for rotating images, but most simple implementations are slow due to the mathematical intensity of the algorithm.

■ Lighting techniques can be used to create game worlds that are more realistic. A cheap, simple method is to segregate the palette into four segments of 64 slots, with the first segment containing the full intensity colors, and the other segments containing the same colors at darker and darker intensities. This results in banding, but the effect is quick and produces adequate results.

■ Transition effects give a game a better sense of flow. Pay attention to how modern movies transition between scenes for inspiration. Many transition effects are relatively easy to implement.

■ Texture mapping is a complex subject with intense math requirements. However, we can use scaling techniques in order to produce some simple texture mapping effects.

■ Using some basic 3-D mathematical algorithms, it is fairly easy to produce a realistic star field. The equations used in this effect are at the core of real-time 3-D graphics programming techniques.

■ By moving the pixels in an image, we can create a very realistic fire effect. It is possible to modify how these pixels move as well as perform a little palette rotation to produce some very interesting plasma effects.

# CHAPTER 12: *Artificial Intelligence Techniques*

There is no more dangerous opponent than a living, breathing human being. Humans can be incredibly unpredictable, and good game players can change tactics in a fraction of a nanosecond to take advantage of some new predicament within the game world. This is what makes multiplayer games so attractive; when facing real opponents, the replayability factor of just about any game is dramatically extended.

However, you can't always hook up with another human player. Some people may not even have the necessary hardware, and some may just want to play a game by themselves without worrying about the competition level introduced by battling other humans. In order for a single-player game to grab and hold the player's interest, it needs to be challenging, as good graphics and sound will entertain a user for only so long. This is where artificial intelligence techniques come in. In essence, artificial intelligence is the process of simulating intelligent thought and behavior through algorithmic methods.

As one would surmise from such a broad topic, a discussion of artificial intelligence could cover volumes upon volumes. Indeed, artificial intelligence is an area of specialty in the realm of computer science. Several large colleges and corporations spend millions of dollars (or more) yearly on furthering the research of artificial intelligence. Everything from simulating the thought process of an ant to accurately modeling the interaction of neurons in the human brain is being researched, with varying degrees of success.

Of course, most of these scholarly experiments employ technology that is either beyond the reach of game programmers or is simply "too much" for a game application. What we're interested in accomplishing is not an accurate model of living, thinking organisms, but a close facsimile thereof. We need game entities that appear to behave in an intelligent manner, but they do not have to truly be intelligent. As long as they challenge the player and provide a few surprises every now and then, we've done our job.

In this chapter, we examine various techniques for implementing simplistic artificial intelligence that will give our game's enemy units a sense of personality and behavior. Since we are concentrating on artificial intelligence programming, the examples in this chapter will use very simple graphics so we don't unnecessarily complicate the code.

# Movement

The most noticeable display of artificial intelligence is in the movement of enemy units. Indeed, in most action games, the user is going to be primarily concerned with the movement of enemy units, such as whether they are aggressively chasing the user's ship or running like cowards. Let's look at several techniques that can be used to breathe life into the movement of game world antagonists.

## Random Movement

Perhaps the simplest simulation of artificial intelligence is to introduce an element of randomness. When an enemy unit moves in a fashion that is unpredictable to the player, that unit can appear to exhibit a rudimentary intelligence. Consider the apparently random flight path of a common housefly. It darts about here and there, yet it always appears to have a mind of its own and to know where it's going.

Random movement is simple to implement. For example, say we have a very basic sprite structure defined as:

```
TSprite = record
  XPos, YPos: Integer;       // horizontal and vertical sprite position
end;
```

To implement random movement, we can simply use the Object Pascal function Random to return a number indicating the number of units to move in a particular direction. The Random function takes a single integer argument as the extent of the range of numbers to be returned, and returns an integer in the range 0<=X<Argument. If we specify a range of 3, which would randomly return the numbers 0, 1, or 2, and then subtract 1, our modified range of returned numbers would be –1, 0, or 1. By adding this translated number to the horizontal and vertical positions of our sprite, it would appear to move about randomly. The following listing demonstrates this technique.

**Listing 12-1:** *Random movement*

```
type

  .
  .
  .

  TSprite = record
    XPos, YPos: Integer;
  end;

var
  Enemy: TSprite;

implementation

procedure TfrmDXAppMain.FormActivate(Sender: TObject);
begin

  .
  .
  .

  {initialize the enemy's starting position}
  Enemy.XPos := 320;
  Enemy.YPos := 240;

  .
  .
  .

end;

  .
  .
  .

procedure TfrmDXAppMain.DrawSurfaces;
var
  SrfcDc: HDC;
  TempCanvas: TCanvas;
begin
  {erase the last frame of animation}
  ColorFill(FBackBuffer, clBlack, nil);

  {move the enemy randomly. this could be either no movement
   or movement by one pixel in a positive or negative direction}
  Enemy.XPos := Enemy.XPos + Random(3)-1;
```

```
      Enemy.YPos := Enemy.YPos + Random(3)-1;

      {check for collisions with the side of the screen}
      if Enemy.XPos < 0 then
        Enemy.XPos := 0;
      if Enemy.XPos > DXWIDTH - 1 then
        Enemy.XPos := DXWIDTH - 1;
      if Enemy.YPos < 0 then
        Enemy.YPos := 0;
      if Enemy.YPos > DXHEIGHT - 1 then
        Enemy.YPos := DXHEIGHT - 1;

      {retrieve a device context for use with GDI output techniques}
      FBackBuffer.GetDC(SrfcDc);
      TempCanvas := TCanvas.Create;
      try
        {initialize the canvas properties}
        TempCanvas.Handle := SrfcDc;
        TempCanvas.Font.Color := clWhite;
        TempCanvas.Pen.Style := psClear;
        TempCanvas.Brush.Style := bsSolid;
        TempCanvas.Brush.Color := clRed;

        {draw a small red circle at the current sprite position}
        TempCanvas.Ellipse(Enemy.XPos, Enemy.YPos, Enemy.XPos + 3, Enemy.YPos + 3);

        {draw some text}
        TempCanvas.Brush.Style := bsClear;
        TempCanvas.TextOut(0, 0, 'Random Movement')
      finally
        {clean up the temporary canvas and device context}
        TempCanvas.Handle := 0;
        FBackBuffer.ReleaseDC(SrfcDc);
        TempCanvas.Free;
      end;
    end;
```

This does indeed move our sprite around the screen randomly, but it merely jitters around the middle of the screen and doesn't really project an air of intelligence at all. We could improve this by waiting a random amount of time before changing directions, which would give us a more housefly-like behavior, but there is no real intelligence underneath, and this enemy would pose no true threat to the player.

## Aggression/Evasion

In order to portray a sense of intelligence, enemy units should react in a manner dictated somewhat by the actions of the player. This could be anything from the player's movements (or lack thereof) to the number of rockets or bullets the player launched to the status of a player's shields or hit points. When an enemy reacts to the player's actions or current status, its intelligence can be convincingly real.

This can also give an enemy a sense of personality. An enemy that actively hunts down the player can be perceived as confident, powerful, and aggressive. By contrast, an enemy that constantly eludes the player or turns tail can be perceived as cowardly, injured, or perhaps even cunning, like an assassin stalking its target.

*Tip:* Varying the velocity, perhaps according to the proximity of the player, will enhance this technique and improve the perceived intelligence.

Modeling aggression is simple enough. The application simply examines the horizontal and vertical position of the enemy unit and the player unit, and adjusts the enemy unit's horizontal and vertical positions to bring it close to the player. For example, if the player unit's horizontal position is less than the enemy's, subtracting 1 from the enemy's horizontal position brings it closer to the player. If the player's horizontal position is greater than the enemy's, adding 1 to the enemy's horizontal position brings it closer to the player. The same holds true for the vertical position. This is illustrated below.

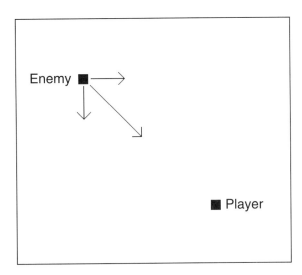

*Figure 12-1:*
*Chasing the player*

Modeling evasion is just as simple. Indeed, if we simply reverse the signs of the values being added to the horizontal and vertical position of the enemy, it will run from the player instead of chasing after it. This is illustrated below.

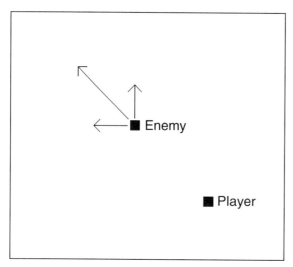

*Figure 12-2:*
*Evading the player*

Of course, most games would need to take into account obstacles and line of sight, but the basic principle holds true. The following example illustrates how to implement chase and evasion algorithms. The player's dot is controlled by the cursor keys, and the enemy dot will either chase or flee from the user based on its current status, which is toggled by the Enter key.

**Listing 12-2:** *Aggression and evasion in action*

```
type

   .
   .
   .

  TSprite = class
    XPos, YPos: Integer;

    procedure MoveSprite(XOffset, YOffset: Integer);
  end;

var

   .
   .
   .

  Enemy, Player: TSprite;
  Chase: Boolean;
```

```
implementation

        .
        .
        .


procedure TfrmDXAppMain.FormActivate(Sender: TObject);
begin

        .
        .
        .


  {create the two sprites}
  Enemy := TSprite.Create;
  Player := TSprite.Create;

  {initialize the enemy and player sprite positions}
  Enemy.XPos := 320;
  Enemy.YPos := 0;

  Player.XPos := 320;
  Player.YPos := 477;

  {start out in aggression/chase mode}
  Chase := TRUE;

        .
        .
        .

end;

        .
        .
        .


procedure TfrmDXAppMain.DrawSurfaces;
var
  SrfcDc: HDC;
  TempCanvas: TCanvas;

  EnemyOffset: Integer;
begin
  {erase the last frame of animation}
  ColorFill(FBackBuffer, clBlack, nil);

  {if the Enter key was pressed, toggle aggression/evasion}
  if (GetAsyncKeyState(VK_RETURN) and $8000) = $8000 then
```

```
    Chase := not Chase;

{move the player sprite based on the cursor keys}
if (GetAsyncKeyState(VK_LEFT) and $8000) = $8000 then
  Player.MoveSprite(-2, 0);
if (GetAsyncKeyState(VK_RIGHT) and $8000) = $8000 then
  Player.MoveSprite(2, 0);
if (GetAsyncKeyState(VK_UP) and $8000) = $8000 then
  Player.MoveSprite(0, - 2);
if (GetAsyncKeyState(VK_DOWN) and $8000) = $8000 then
  Player.MoveSprite(0, 2);

{determine the appropriate movement for chasing or evading}
if Chase then
  EnemyOffset := 1
else
  EnemyOffset := -1;

{move the enemy accordingly}
if Player.XPos > Enemy.XPos then
  Enemy.MoveSprite(EnemyOffset, 0);
if Player.XPos < Enemy.XPos then
  Enemy.MoveSprite(-EnemyOffset, 0);
if Player.YPos > Enemy.YPos then
  Enemy.MoveSprite(0, EnemyOffset);
if Player.YPos < Enemy.YPos then
  Enemy.MoveSprite(0, -EnemyOffset);

{retrieve a device context and create a canvas}
FBackBuffer.GetDC(SrfcDc);
TempCanvas := TCanvas.Create;
try
  {set up the canvas}
  TempCanvas.Handle := SrfcDc;
  TempCanvas.Font.Color := clWhite;

  {draw the two sprites as small dots}
  TempCanvas.Pen.Style := psClear;
  TempCanvas.Brush.Style := bsSolid;
  TempCanvas.Brush.Color := clBlue;
  TempCanvas.Ellipse(Player.XPos, Player.YPos, Player.XPos+3, Player.YPos+3);
  TempCanvas.Brush.Color := clRed;
  TempCanvas.Ellipse(Enemy.XPos, Enemy.YPos, Enemy.XPos+3, Enemy.YPos+3);

  {indicate which state the enemy sprite is in}
  TempCanvas.Brush.Style := bsClear;
  if Chase then
    TempCanvas.TextOut(0, 0, 'Chasing')
  else
    TempCanvas.TextOut(0, 0, 'Evading');
```

```
      TempCanvas.TextOut(0, 440, 'Press Enter to toggle state');
  finally
    {clean up}
    TempCanvas.Handle := 0;
    FBackBuffer.ReleaseDC(SrfcDc);
    TempCanvas.Free;
  end;
end;


procedure TSprite.MoveSprite(XOffset, YOffset: Integer);
begin
  {update the sprite's position}
  XPos := XPos + XOffset;
  YPos := YPos + YOffset;

  {clip to the screen boundaries}
  if XPos < 0 then
    XPos := 0;
  if XPos > DXWIDTH - 1 then
    XPos := DXWIDTH - 1;
  if YPos < 0 then
    YPos := 0;
  if YPos > DXHEIGHT - 1 then
    YPos := DXHEIGHT - 1;
end;
```

We could have just as easily made the chase/evade decision based upon whether or not the player was actively moving. If the player's sprite positioned has changed, we could have switched to evade mode; if the player hadn't moved, we could go right to chase mode. This would certainly keep players on their toes, and in the event our enemy units could kill a player, this would certainly discourage anyone from waiting around somewhere for very long!

## Patterned Movement

Chasing the player, running from the player, and moving around randomly can get pretty boring after a while. Typically, enemy units need to exhibit more complex movement, and one way to simulate this is through movement patterns.

For example, take the old arcade game Galaxian. When the enemies appeared in each round, they flew onto the screen in a complex flight path. Although their movements were a bit predictable, it made their appearance more menacing and deliberate. We can use patterned movement in our games to model similar complex, deliberate movements and make our enemies appear to move about more intentionally. Indeed, we could create several patterns and choose one randomly (or in a more context-sensitive manner), as illustrated in Figure 12-3.

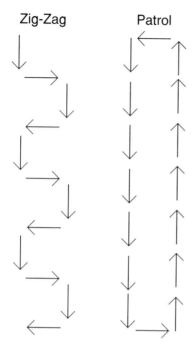

*Figure 12-3:*
*Movement patterns*

There are several methods by which patterned movement can be implemented based on the type of game and the sprite engine. If we had a simple, 2-D shooter, our patterns could simply be based off of a series of horizontal and vertical offsets that move the unit in the desired manner. These offsets would be relative to the current position of the sprite, so the patterns could be used anywhere within the game world.

**Tip:** It is relatively easy to flip the movement pattern horizontally or vertically, thus increasing the flexibility of this technique.

To implement this method of patterned movement, we could make an array of TPoints, filling each entry with the horizontal or vertical offset for that position within the pattern. As we move the sprite, we keep track of an index into this array of offsets, incrementing the offset at a preset time to advance to the next movement within the pattern. Once the pattern is complete, we can choose another array (or another row within a multidimensional array) and reset the index to 0, thus starting a new pattern. This technique is illustrated below.

*Listing 12-3: Implementing patterned movement*

```
TSprite = record
    XPos, YPos: Integer;
    CurPattern,
    CurPatternIdx: Integer;
```

```
      PatternIdxChange,
    CurTimer: Longint;
  end;

  TPatterns = array[0..5, 0..31] of TPoint;

const
  {in this example, the patterns are stored as direct X and Y offsets, but
   any method of specifying a direction and/or offset will do}
  Patterns: TPatterns = (
  ((x: 1; y: 0), (x: 1; y: 0), (x: 1; y: 0), (x: 0; y: 1), (x: 0; y: 1), ...
  ((x: -1; y: -1), (x: -1; y: -1), (x: -1; y: -1), (x: -1; y: -1), ...
  ((x: 1; y: 0), (x: 1; y: 0), (x: 1; y: 1), (x: 1; y: 1), (x: 0; y: 1), ...
  ((x: 1; y: 0), (x: 1; y: 0), (x: 1; y: 0), (x: 1; y: 0), (x: 0; y: -1), ...
  ((x: 1; y: 0), (x: 1; y: 0), (x: 1; y: 0), (x: 1; y: -1), (x: 0; y: -1), ...
  ((x: 0; y: -1), (x: 0; y: -1), (x: 0; y: -1), (x: 0; y: -1), ...

var

    .
    .
    .

  Enemy: TSprite;

implementation

    .
    .
    .

procedure TfrmDXAppMain.FormActivate(Sender: TObject);
begin

    .
    .
    .

  {initialize the enemy sprite}
  Randomize;
  Enemy.XPos := 320;
  Enemy.YPos := 240;
  Enemy.CurPattern := Random(6);      // start at a random pattern
  Enemy.CurPatternIdx := 0;
  Enemy.PatternIdxChange := 100;      // change the pattern index often
  Enemy.CurTimer := timeGetTime;

    .
    .
    .
```

```
end;


     .
     .
     .


procedure TfrmDXAppMain.DrawSurfaces;
var
  SrfcDc: HDC;
  TempCanvas: TCanvas;
begin
  {erase the last frame of animation}
  ColorFill(FBackBuffer, clBlack, nil);

  {if it is time to change the pattern index...}
  if timeGetTime - Enemy.CurTimer > Enemy.PatternIdxChange then
  begin
    {...move to the next step in the pattern}
    Enemy.CurPatternIdx := Enemy.CurPatternIdx + 1;

    {if we have moved the entire pattern...}
    if Enemy.CurPatternIdx > 31 then
    begin
      {...choose a new pattern}
      Enemy.CurPattern := Random(6);
      Enemy.CurPatternIdx := 0;
    end;

    {track for the next pattern index change}
    Enemy.CurTimer := timeGetTime;
  end;

  {update the enemy sprite's position based on the current step with
   the pattern}
  Enemy.XPos := Enemy.XPos + Patterns[Enemy.CurPattern, Enemy.CurPatternIdx].X;
  Enemy.YPos := Enemy.YPos + Patterns[Enemy.CurPattern, Enemy.CurPatternIdx].Y;

  {clip the enemy to the screen boundaries}
  if Enemy.XPos < 0 then
    Enemy.XPos := 0;
  if Enemy.XPos > DXWIDTH - 1 then
    Enemy.XPos := DXWIDTH - 1;
  if Enemy.YPos < 0 then
    Enemy.YPos := 0;
  if Enemy.YPos > DXHEIGHT - 1 then
    Enemy.YPos := DXHEIGHT - 1;

  {retrieve a device context and create a canvas}
  FBackBuffer.GetDC(SrfcDc);
  TempCanvas := TCanvas.Create;
  try
```

```
    {set up the canvas}
    TempCanvas.Handle := SrfcDc;
    TempCanvas.Font.Color := clWhite;

    {draw the enemy sprite}
    TempCanvas.Pen.Style := psClear;
    TempCanvas.Brush.Style := bsSolid;
    TempCanvas.Brush.Color := clRed;
    TempCanvas.Ellipse(Enemy.XPos, Enemy.YPos, Enemy.XPos + 3, Enemy.YPos + 3);

    {indicate the pattern number}
    TempCanvas.Brush.Style := bsClear;
    TempCanvas.TextOut(0, 0, 'Pattern: '+IntToStr(Enemy.CurPattern));
  finally
    {clean up}
    TempCanvas.Handle := 0;
    FBackBuffer.ReleaseDC(SrfcDc);
    TempCanvas.Free;
  end;
end;
```

This makes our enemy sprite appear to move in a more deliberate manner. We can adjust the offsets accordingly to make some patterns move the sprite faster or slower, and with some minor modifications we could make some patterns longer than others. By selecting different patterns, the movement appears more deliberate while at the same time reducing its predictability.

**Note:** In real-world situations, we should make sure that the sprite is not positioned such that a movement pattern will run it into a movement boundary immediately. In our example, we simply clip to the edges of the screen, but this can make a movement pattern almost useless. In a real-world situation, we should reverse the pattern when it detects a movement boundary, or even exit the pattern immediately and choose another form of movement.

## Finite State Machines

We've been examining methods by which intelligent movement can be modeled, and so far we've come up with some acceptable algorithms that can provide convincing, if somewhat limited, intelligent movement. However, we haven't discussed methods by which enemy units determine which movement technique to use.

We could just randomly pick something, but this would not model any sort of intelligent thought process. We need an algorithm by which an enemy unit can make a series of rational decisions based on various inputs from the game world, such as the current environment as well as the actions of the player. This can be accomplished through a method known as a finite state machine. A finite state machine is a logical construction that consists of several "states," each of which defines a specific behavior, and "state transitions," which define specific rules for moving from state to state.

**finite state machine:** A logical construction that contains a series of states defining specific behaviors and a series of state transitions defining rules for moving from state to state.

Using finite state machines, enemy units can have very complex behavioral models. These can include not only movements but also different tactics or other actions based on the actions of the player, the state of other game objects, and the overall situation. State machines also allow for the easy extension of behaviors, as all that would be required is the logic for the behavior under the new state and logic for moving into and out of this state. An arbitrary state machine could be visualized as illustrated below.

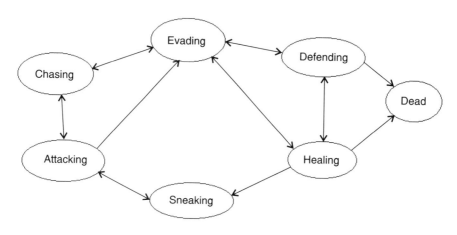

**Figure 12-4:**
*An abstracted finite state machine*

Each circle in the illustration represents a specific state, or behavior, and the lines connecting them represent the logic determining how one state leads to another.

One way to model this in software would be to define each state as an integer value or perhaps an enumerated type. A case statement could then be utilized to execute the appropriate code for the current state. The transitions from state to state could be controlled in a number of ways, from randomly choosing a different state at a specific interval to complex logic that considers the player's attributes versus the computer controlled adversary's. In the following example, we've used a case statement to control the logic for each state, and we simply choose a random state after a specific amount of time has elapsed.

While viewing the animation, you can definitely tell a difference in the sprite's movement behavior among the various states.

***Listing 12-4:*** *Movement behavior through a finite state machine*

```
type

  .
  .
  .

  TSpriteStates = (ssChasing, ssEvading, ssRandomMoves, ssPatternMoves, ssWait,
              ssPlayer);
  TStateNames = array[ssChasing..ssWait] of string;

  TSprite = class
    XPos, YPos: Integer;
    Direction: Integer;
    CurPattern,
    CurPatternIdx: Integer;
    PatternIdxChange,
    CurPatternTimer,
    StateChange,
    StateTimer: Longint;
    State: TSpriteStates;

    procedure ChangeState;
    procedure Move;
    procedure Draw(Canvas: TCanvas);
  end;

  TPatterns = array[0..7, 0..31] of Integer;

const
  {this array allows us to display the name of the state}
  StateNames: TStateNames = ('Chasing', 'Evading', 'RandomMoves',
                     'PatternMoves', 'Wait');

  {in this example, pattern movement is implemented as a direction, with 0
   indicating north, or upward movement. the directions increment in a
   clockwise manner}
  Patterns: TPatterns = (
  (0, 0, 0, 1, 1, 1, 7, 7, 7, 7, 7, 7, 1, 1, 1, 1, 1, 1, 7, 7, 7, 7, 7, 7, 7, 7,
   1, 1, 1, 0, 0, 0),
  (1, 1, 1, 2, 2, 2, 0, 0, 0, 0, 0, 0, 2, 2, 2, 2, 2, 2, 0, 0, 0, 0, 0, 0, 0, 0,
   2, 2, 2, 1, 1, 1),
  (2, 2, 2, 3, 3, 3, 1, 1, 1, 1, 1, 1, 3, 3, 3, 3, 3, 3, 1, 1, 1, 1, 1, 1, 1, 1,
   3, 3, 3, 2, 2, 2),
  (3, 3, 3, 4, 4, 4, 2, 2, 2, 2, 2, 2, 4, 4, 4, 4, 4, 4, 2, 2, 2, 2, 2, 2, 2, 2,
   4, 4, 4, 3, 3, 3),
  (4, 4, 4, 5, 5, 5, 3, 3, 3, 3, 3, 3, 5, 5, 5, 5, 5, 5, 3, 3, 3, 3, 3, 3, 3, 3,
```

```
    5, 5, 5, 4, 4, 4),
  (5, 5, 5, 6, 6, 6, 4, 4, 4, 4, 4, 4, 6, 6, 6, 6, 6, 6, 4, 4, 4, 4, 4, 4, 4, 4,
    6, 6, 6, 5, 5, 5),
  (6, 6, 6, 7, 7, 7, 5, 5, 5, 5, 5, 5, 7, 7, 7, 7, 7, 7, 5, 5, 5, 5, 5, 5, 5, 5,
    7, 7, 7, 6, 6, 6),
  (7, 7, 7, 0, 0, 0, 6, 6, 6, 6, 6, 6, 0, 0, 0, 0, 0, 0, 6, 6, 6, 6, 6, 6, 6, 6,
    0, 0, 0, 7, 7, 7)
  );

  {these indicate sprite positions in the array of sprites}
  ENEMY1IDX = 0;
  ENEMY2IDX = 1;
  PLAYERIDX = 2;

var

    .
    .
    .

  {tracks all of the sprites}
  Sprites: array[ENEMY1IDX..PLAYERIDX] of TSprite;

implementation

    .
    .
    .

procedure TfrmDXAppMain.FormActivate(Sender: TObject);
begin

    .
    .
    .

  {seed the random number generator}
  Randomize;

  {initialize the enemy sprites}
  Sprites[ENEMY1IDX] := TSprite.Create;
  Sprites[ENEMY1IDX].XPos := 15;
  Sprites[ENEMY1IDX].YPos := 240;
  Sprites[ENEMY1IDX].PatternIdxChange := 100;
  Sprites[ENEMY1IDX].State := ssRandomMoves;
  Sprites[ENEMY1IDX].StateChange := 500;
  Sprites[ENEMY1IDX].StateTimer := timeGetTime;
  Sprites[ENEMY1IDX].Direction := 2;

  Sprites[ENEMY2IDX] := TSprite.Create;
  Sprites[ENEMY2IDX].XPos := 625;
```

```
            Sprites[ENEMY2IDX].YPos := 240;
            Sprites[ENEMY2IDX].PatternIdxChange := 50; // this sprite will change pattern
                                                        // steps faster than the other...
            Sprites[ENEMY2IDX].State := ssRandomMoves;
            Sprites[ENEMY2IDX].StateChange := 250;      // ...as well as states
            Sprites[ENEMY2IDX].StateTimer := timeGetTime;
            Sprites[ENEMY2IDX].Direction := 6;

            {initialize the player sprite}
            Sprites[PLAYERIDX] := TSprite.Create;
            Sprites[PLAYERIDX].XPos := 320;
            Sprites[PLAYERIDX].YPos := 240;
            Sprites[PLAYERIDX].State := ssPlayer;


              .
              .
              .


          end;


              .
              .
              .


      procedure TfrmDXAppMain.DrawSurfaces;
      var
        SrfcDc: HDC;
        TempCanvas: TCanvas;
        iCount: Integer;
      begin
        {erase the last frame of animation}
        ColorFill(FBackBuffer, clBlack, nil);

        {move the player sprite}
        if (GetAsyncKeyState(VK_LEFT) and $8000) = $8000 then
          Sprites[PLAYERIDX].XPos := Sprites[PLAYERIDX].XPos - 2;
        if (GetAsyncKeyState(VK_RIGHT) and $8000) = $8000 then
          Sprites[PLAYERIDX].XPos := Sprites[PLAYERIDX].XPos + 2;
        if (GetAsyncKeyState(VK_UP) and $8000) = $8000 then
          Sprites[PLAYERIDX].YPos := Sprites[PLAYERIDX].YPos - 2;
        if (GetAsyncKeyState(VK_DOWN) and $8000) = $8000 then
          Sprites[PLAYERIDX].YPos := Sprites[PLAYERIDX].YPos + 2;

        {move all sprites. note that this simply performs screen boundary clipping
         for the player sprite, but we could have any number of enemy sprites}
        for iCount := ENEMY1IDX to PLAYERIDX do
          Sprites[iCount].Move;

        {retrieve a device context and create a canvas}
        FBackBuffer.GetDC(SrfcDc);
        TempCanvas := TCanvas.Create;
```

```
  try
    {set up the canvas}
    TempCanvas.Handle := SrfcDc;
    TempCanvas.Font.Color := clWhite;

    {draw the sprites}
    for iCount := ENEMY1IDX to PLAYERIDX do
      Sprites[iCount].Draw(TempCanvas);

    {indicate the current state for each enemy sprite}
    TempCanvas.Brush.Style := bsClear;
    TempCanvas.TextOut(0, 0, 'Enemy1 State:'+
                      StateNames[Sprites[ENEMY1IDX].State]);
    TempCanvas.TextOut(500, 0, 'Enemy2 State: '+
                      StateNames[Sprites[ENEMY2IDX].State]);
  finally
    {cleanup}
    TempCanvas.Handle := 0;
    FBackBuffer.ReleaseDC(SrfcDc);
    TempCanvas.Free;
  end;
end;


    .
    .
    .


{ TSprite }

procedure TSprite.ChangeState;
begin
  {set the state randomly}
  State := TSpriteStates(Random(5));

  {if this is the pattern move state...}
  if (State = ssPatternMoves) then
  begin
    {choose a random pattern}
    CurPattern := Random(8);

    {initialize to the start of the pattern}
    CurPatternIdx := 0;

    {retrieve the current time}
    CurPatternTimer := timeGetTime;

    {32 steps in a pattern multiplied by the time per each step should
     give enough time to complete the entire pattern}
    StateChange := PatternIdxChange * 32;
  end
  else
```

```
                {...otherwise, change state again in 1 to 3 seconds}
                StateChange := Random(2000)+1000;

           {begin timing the state}
           StateTimer := timeGetTime;
        end;

        procedure TSprite.Draw(Canvas: TCanvas);
        begin
           {draw enemy sprites in blue, player sprites in red}
           if State <> ssPlayer then
              Canvas.Brush.Color := clBlue
           else
              Canvas.Brush.Color := clRed;

           {draw a small dot for the sprite}
           Canvas.Pen.Style := psClear;
           Canvas.Brush.Style := bsSolid;
           Canvas.Ellipse(XPos, YPos, XPos + 3, YPos + 3);
        end;

        procedure TSprite.Move;
        const
           {initialize a horizontal and vertical velocity}
           XVel: Integer = 1;
           YVel: Integer = 1;
        begin
           {if this sprite is an enemy sprite...}
           if State <> ssPlayer then
           begin
              {if it is time to change the state, then change it}
              if timeGetTime - StateTimer > StateChange then
                 ChangeState;

              {for each state...}
              case State of
                 ssChasing     : begin
                                    {we're chasing the player, so move the sprite
                                     closer to the player sprite's position}
                                    if Sprites[PLAYERIDX].XPos > XPos then
                                       XPos := XPos + 1;
                                    if Sprites[PLAYERIDX].XPos < XPos then
                                       XPos := XPos - 1;
                                    if Sprites[PLAYERIDX].YPos > YPos then
                                       YPos := YPos + 1;
                                    if Sprites[PLAYERIDX].YPos < YPos then
                                       YPos := YPos - 1;
                                 end;
                 ssEvading     : begin
                                    {we're evading the player, so move the sprite
                                     farther away from the player sprite's position}
```

```
                                if Sprites[PLAYERIDX].XPos > XPos then
                                  XPos := XPos - 1;
                                if Sprites[PLAYERIDX].XPos < XPos then
                                  XPos := XPos + 1;
                                if Sprites[PLAYERIDX].YPos > YPos then
                                  YPos := YPos - 1;
                                if Sprites[PLAYERIDX].YPos < YPos then
                                  YPos := YPos + 1;
                              end;
          ssRandomMoves     : begin
                                {we're moving randomly, but we don't want to move
                                 each frame of animation or the sprite will look
                                 like it's having a seizure}
                                if timeGetTime-CurPatternTimer>PatternIdxChange*3 then
                                begin
                                  {modify the horizontal and vertical velocity}
                                  XVel := Random(3) - 1;
                                  YVel := Random(3) - 1;

                                  {reset the timer}
                                  CurPatternTimer := timeGetTime;
                                end;

                                {add the current velocity to the horizontal and
                                 vertical positions}
                                XPos := XPos + XVel;
                                YPos := YPos + YVel;
                              end;
          ssPatternMoves    : begin
                                {if it is time to change the current pattern step
                                 index...}
                                if timeGetTime-CurPatternTimer > PatternIdxChange then
                                begin
                                  {increment to the next step}
                                  CurPatternIdx := CurPatternIdx + 1;

                                  {if we've reached the end of this pattern...}
                                  if CurPatternIdx > 31 then
                                  begin
                                    {choose a new pattern}
                                    CurPattern := Random(8);

                                    {initialize to the first step of the pattern}
                                    CurPatternIdx := 0;
                                  end;

                                  {reset the pattern timer}
                                  CurPatternTimer := timeGetTime;
                                end;

                                {as stated above, pattern movement is implemented
```

```
                                  as a direction, so modify the sprite's position
                                  according to the direction at this pattern's
                                  movement step}
                                  case Patterns[CurPattern, CurPatternIdx] of
                                      0 : begin
                                              XPos := XPos + 1;
                                          end;
                                      1 : begin
                                              XPos := XPos + 1;
                                              YPos := YPos + 1;
                                          end;
                                      2 : begin
                                              YPos := YPos +1;
                                          end;
                                      3 : begin
                                              XPos := XPos - 1;
                                              YPos := YPos + 1;
                                          end;
                                      4 : begin
                                              XPos := XPos - 1;
                                          end;
                                      5 : begin
                                              XPos := XPos - 1;
                                              YPos := YPos - 1;
                                          end;
                                      6 : begin
                                              YPos := YPos - 1;
                                          end;
                                      7 : begin
                                              XPos := XPos + 1;
                                              YPos := YPos - 1;
                                          end;
                                  end;
                              end;
        end;
    end;

    {clip to the boundaries of the screen}
    if XPos < 0 then
       XPos := 0;
    if XPos > DXWIDTH - 3 then
       XPos := DXWIDTH - 3;

    {we'll keep sprites from moving up where the status is displayed}
    if YPos < 20 then
       YPos := 20;
    if YPos > DXHEIGHT - 3 then
       YPos := DXHEIGHT - 3;
end;
```

Implementing artificial intelligence as a finite state machine makes it easy to specify some very complex behavior and add new behavior if necessary. When coupled with some logic to control state changes based on the current game state, such as hit points, power, player hit points, etc., enemy sprites can appear to be very intelligent indeed.

However, the current implementation lacks personality. Enemy sprites may exhibit some fairly complex thought patterns, but they all think alike, and that can soon become boring to players. What is needed is a way to imbue enemy sprites with a little more character and individualism.

## Probability Machines

That's where probability machines come in. A probability machine is really just an extension of a finite state machine, allowing the application to simulate personalities based on a certain distribution factor. Using this technique, we can make some sprites appear more passive, some more aggressive, some a little bit sneakier, etc.

It works by choosing the next state based on a weighted distribution as identified by the type of personality we're modeling. For example, let's say we have five states, and we want to model an aggressive behavior. Whenever it comes time to change states, we want to choose the next state based on a percentage chance as illustrated below.

*Table 12-1:* *Aggressive personality percentage chance for state selection*

| State | Percentage |
|---|---|
| Chase | 50% |
| Evade | 10% |
| Wait | 10% |
| Random Movement | 10% |
| Patterned Movement | 20% |

So, in this example, an aggressive personality would choose the chase state 50% of the time. A more timid personality would likely choose the evade state more often. Other personality types would result in varying distributions.

One way to implement such a system would be to create an array of 10 elements, where each element holds a state (either as an integer index or an enumerated type). This array would then be populated by each state a number of times equal to its probability of selection divided by 10. Over time, each state would be selected according to its probability. For example, if the chase state had a 50% chance of selection, it would be in the array five times, and over time, it would indeed have a 50% chance of being selected when the state changed. This is the method by which personalities are implemented in the following example.

**Listing 12-5:** *Personalities through probability machines*

```
type

   .
   .
   .

   {this defines the different states}
   TSpriteStates = (ssChasing, ssEvading, ssRandomMoves, ssPatternMoves, ssWait,
                    ssPlayer);
   TStateNames = array[ssChasing..ssWait] of string;

   {this defines the different personalities}
   TPersonalities = (perAggressive, perDefensive, perTactical);
   TPersonalityNames = array[perAggressive..perTactical] of string;

   {this defines the probabilities tables that implement the personalities}
   TProbabilityTable = array[0..9] of TSpriteStates;
   TPersonality = array[TPersonalities] of TProbabilityTable;

   {our sprite class}
   TSprite = class
     XPos, YPos: Integer;
     CurPattern,
     CurPatternIdx: Integer;
     PatternIdxChange,
     CurPatternTimer,
     StateChange,
     StateTimer,
     PersonalityChange,
     PersonalityTimer: Longint;
     State: TSpriteStates;
     Personality: TPersonalities;

     procedure ChangeState;
     procedure Move;
     procedure Draw(Canvas: TCanvas);
   end;

   TPatterns = array[0..7, 0..31] of Integer;

const
   {these probability tables implement the behavior of each personality.
    each state is entered into each table a number of times equal to its
    percentage chance of selection divided by 10 (i.e., 50% chance of selection =
    5 times in the table)}
   AggressivePersonality: TProbabilityTable = (ssChasing, ssChasing, ssChasing,
                                               ssChasing, ssChasing, ssChasing,
                                               ssPatternMoves, ssPatternMoves,
```

```
                                                ssRandomMoves, ssWait);
    DefensivePersonality: TProbabilityTable = (ssEvading, ssEvading, ssEvading,
                                               ssEvading, ssEvading, ssEvading,
                                               ssRandomMoves, ssRandomMoves,
                                               ssPatternMoves, ssWait);
    TacticalPersonality: TProbabilityTable = (ssEvading, ssEvading, ssRandomMoves,
                                              ssRandomMoves, ssWait, ssWait,
                                              ssPatternMoves, ssPatternMoves,
                                              ssChasing, ssChasing);

    {this allows us to easily display the name of the current
     state and personality}
    StateNames: TStateNames = ('Chasing', 'Evading', 'RandomMoves',
                               'PatternMoves', 'Wait');
    PersonalityNames: TPersonalityNames = ('Aggressive', 'Defensive', 'Tactical');

    {this table implements patterned movement. moves are stored as directions
     in this example, with 0 equal to north (or straight up movement) incrementing
     in a clockwise direction}
    Patterns: TPatterns = (
    (0, 0, 0, 1, 1, 1, 7, 7, 7, 7, 7, 7, 1, 1, 1, 1, 1, 1, 7, 7, 7, 7, 7, 7, 7, 7,
     1, 1, 1, 0, 0, 0),
    (1, 1, 1, 2, 2, 2, 0, 0, 0, 0, 0, 0, 2, 2, 2, 2, 2, 2, 0, 0, 0, 0, 0, 0, 0, 0,
     2, 2, 2, 1, 1, 1),
    (2, 2, 2, 3, 3, 3, 1, 1, 1, 1, 1, 1, 3, 3, 3, 3, 3, 3, 1, 1, 1, 1, 1, 1, 1, 1,
     3, 3, 3, 2, 2, 2),
    (3, 3, 3, 4, 4, 4, 2, 2, 2, 2, 2, 2, 4, 4, 4, 4, 4, 4, 2, 2, 2, 2, 2, 2, 2, 2,
     4, 4, 4, 3, 3, 3),
    (4, 4, 4, 5, 5, 5, 3, 3, 3, 3, 3, 3, 5, 5, 5, 5, 5, 5, 3, 3, 3, 3, 3, 3, 3, 3,
     5, 5, 5, 4, 4, 4),
    (5, 5, 5, 6, 6, 6, 4, 4, 4, 4, 4, 4, 6, 6, 6, 6, 6, 6, 4, 4, 4, 4, 4, 4, 4, 4,
     6, 6, 6, 5, 5, 5),
    (6, 6, 6, 7, 7, 7, 5, 5, 5, 5, 5, 5, 7, 7, 7, 7, 7, 7, 5, 5, 5, 5, 5, 5, 5, 5,
     7, 7, 7, 6, 6, 6),
    (7, 7, 7, 0, 0, 0, 6, 6, 6, 6, 6, 6, 0, 0, 0, 0, 0, 0, 6, 6, 6, 6, 6, 6, 6, 6,
     0, 0, 0, 7, 7, 7)
    );

    {these indicate sprite positions in the array of sprites}
    ENEMYIDX = 0;
    PLAYERIDX = 1;

var

    .
    .
    .

    {track the sprites}
    Sprites: array[ENEMYIDX..PLAYERIDX] of TSprite;
```

```
  {our personality table}
  Personalities: TPersonality;

implementation

    .
    .
    .

procedure TfrmDXAppMain.FormDestroy(Sender: TObject);
begin

    .
    .
    .

  {free the sprite objects}
  Sprites[ENEMYIDX].Free;
  Sprites[PLAYERIDX].Free
end;

procedure TfrmDXAppMain.FormActivate(Sender: TObject);
begin

    .
    .
    .

  {seed the random number generator}
  Randomize;

  {initialize the enemy sprite}
  Sprites[ENEMYIDX] := TSprite.Create;
  Sprites[ENEMYIDX].XPos := 320;
  Sprites[ENEMYIDX].YPos := 240;
  Sprites[ENEMYIDX].State := ssWait;
  Sprites[ENEMYIDX].StateChange := 10;
  Sprites[ENEMYIDX].StateTimer := timeGetTime;
  Sprites[ENEMYIDX].PatternIdxChange := 100;
  Sprites[ENEMYIDX].Personality := perAggressive;
  Sprites[ENEMYIDX].PersonalityChange := 25000;
  Sprites[ENEMYIDX].PersonalityTimer := timeGetTime;

  {initialize the player sprite}
  Sprites[PLAYERIDX] := TSprite.Create;
  Sprites[PLAYERIDX].XPos := 320;
  Sprites[PLAYERIDX].YPos := 478;
  Sprites[PLAYERIDX].State := ssPlayer;

    .
    .
```

```
        .

  end;


        .
        .
        .


  procedure TfrmDXAppMain.DrawSurfaces;
  var
    SrfcDc: HDC;
    TempCanvas: TCanvas;
    iCount: Integer;
  begin
    {erase the last frame of animation}
    ColorFill(FBackBuffer, clBlack, nil);

    {move the player sprite based on which cursor keys are depressed}
    if (GetAsyncKeyState(VK_LEFT) and $8000) = $8000 then
      Sprites[PLAYERIDX].XPos := Sprites[PLAYERIDX].XPos - 2;
    if (GetAsyncKeyState(VK_RIGHT) and $8000) = $8000 then
      Sprites[PLAYERIDX].XPos := Sprites[PLAYERIDX].XPos + 2;
    if (GetAsyncKeyState(VK_UP) and $8000) = $8000 then
      Sprites[PLAYERIDX].YPos := Sprites[PLAYERIDX].YPos - 2;
    if (GetAsyncKeyState(VK_DOWN) and $8000) = $8000 then
      Sprites[PLAYERIDX].YPos := Sprites[PLAYERIDX].YPos + 2;

    {move both sprites (note that this simply clips the player sprite to
     the screen boundaries, as the player sprite's position has already
     been updated)}
    for iCount := ENEMYIDX to PLAYERIDX do
      Sprites[iCount].Move;

    {retrieve a device context and create a canvas}
    FBackBuffer.GetDC(SrfcDc);
    TempCanvas := TCanvas.Create;
    try
      {use the canvas for easy drawing functionality}
      TempCanvas.Handle := SrfcDc;
      TempCanvas.Font.Color := clWhite;

      {draw the sprites}
      for iCount := ENEMYIDX to PLAYERIDX do
        Sprites[iCount].Draw(TempCanvas);

      {display the current state and personality of the enemy sprite}
      TempCanvas.Brush.Style := bsClear;
      TempCanvas.TextOut(0, 0, 'Personality: '+
                         PersonalityNames[Sprites[ENEMYIDX].Personality]);
      TempCanvas.TextOut(0, 15, 'State: '+StateNames[Sprites[ENEMYIDX].State]);
    finally
```

```
      {clean up}
      TempCanvas.Handle := 0;
      FBackBuffer.ReleaseDC(SrfcDc);
      TempCanvas.Free;
    end;
end;


      .
      .
      .


procedure TSprite.ChangeState;
var
  Distance: Integer;
begin
  {set the state randomly based on the personality}
  State := Personalities[Personality][Random(10)];

  {if this is the tactical state...}
  if Personality = perTactical then
  begin
    {determine the distance to the player}
    Distance := Abs(XPos - Sprites[PLAYERIDX].XPos)+
                Abs(YPos - Sprites[PLAYERIDX].YPos);

    {if the player is too close, we'll evade the player}
    if Distance < 100 then
      State := ssEvading
    else
    {if the player is too far away, we'll move toward the player}
    if Distance > 300 then
      State := ssChasing
  end;

  {if this is the pattern move state...}
  if (State = ssPatternMoves) then
  begin
    {choose a random pattern}
    CurPattern := Random(8);

    {initialize to the start of the pattern}
    CurPatternIdx := 0;

    {retrieve the current time}
    CurPatternTimer := timeGetTime;

    {32 steps in a pattern multiplied by the time per each step should
     give enough time to complete the entire pattern}
    StateChange := PatternIdxChange * 32;
  end
  else
```

```
                {...otherwise, change state again in 1 to 3 seconds}
                StateChange := Random(2000)+1000;

            {begin timing the state}
            StateTimer := timeGetTime;
        end;

procedure TSprite.Draw(Canvas: TCanvas);
begin
    {draw enemy sprites in blue, player sprites in red}
    if State <> ssPlayer then
        Canvas.Brush.Color := clBlue
    else
        Canvas.Brush.Color := clRed;

    {draw a small dot for the sprite}
    Canvas.Pen.Style := psClear;
    Canvas.Brush.Style := bsSolid;
    Canvas.Ellipse(XPos, YPos, XPos + 3, YPos + 3);
end;

procedure TSprite.Move;
const
    {initialize a horizontal and vertical velocity}
    XVel: Integer = 1;
    YVel: Integer = 1;
begin
    {if this sprite is an enemy sprite...}
    if State <> ssPlayer then
    begin
        {if it is time to change the personality, then change it}
        if timeGetTime - PersonalityTimer > PersonalityChange then
        begin
            {change to the next personality}
            if Personality = perTactical then
                Personality := perAggressive
            else
                Personality := Succ(Personality);

            {reset the personality change timer}
            PersonalityTimer := timeGetTime;
        end;

        {if it is time to change the state, then change it}
        if timeGetTime - StateTimer > StateChange then
            ChangeState;

        {for each state...}
        case State of
            ssChasing      : begin
                                 {we're chasing the player, so move the sprite
```

```
                              closer to the player sprite's position}
                          if Sprites[PLAYERIDX].XPos > XPos then
                            XPos := XPos + 1;
                          if Sprites[PLAYERIDX].XPos < XPos then
                            XPos := XPos - 1;
                          if Sprites[PLAYERIDX].YPos > YPos then
                            YPos := YPos + 1;
                          if Sprites[PLAYERIDX].YPos < YPos then
                            YPos := YPos - 1;
                        end;
        ssEvading     : begin
                          {we're evading the player, so move the sprite
                           farther away from the player sprite's position}
                          if Sprites[PLAYERIDX].XPos > XPos then
                            XPos := XPos - 1;
                          if Sprites[PLAYERIDX].XPos < XPos then
                            XPos := XPos + 1;
                          if Sprites[PLAYERIDX].YPos > YPos then
                            YPos := YPos - 1;
                          if Sprites[PLAYERIDX].YPos < YPos then
                            YPos := YPos + 1;
                        end;
        ssRandomMoves : begin
                          {we're moving randomly, but we don't want to move
                           each frame of animation or the sprite will look
                           like it's having a seizure}
                          if timeGetTime - CurPatternTimer > PatternIdxChange*3
                                then
                          begin
                            {modify the horizontal and vertical velocity}
                            XVel := Random(3) - 1;
                            YVel := Random(3) - 1;

                            {reset the timer}
                            CurPatternTimer := timeGetTime;
                          end;

                          {add the current velocity to the horizontal and
                           vertical positions}
                          XPos := XPos + XVel;
                          YPos := YPos + YVel;
                        end;
        ssPatternMoves : begin
                          {if it is time to change the current pattern step
                           index...}
                          if timeGetTime-CurPatternTimer > PatternIdxChange then
                          begin
                            {increment to the next step}
                            CurPatternIdx := CurPatternIdx + 1;

                            {if we've reached the end of this pattern...}
```

```
                                if CurPatternIdx > 31 then
                                begin
                                  {choose a new pattern}
                                  CurPattern := Random(8);

                                  {initialize to the first step of the pattern}
                                  CurPatternIdx := 0;
                                end;

                                {reset the pattern timer}
                                CurPatternTimer := timeGetTime;
                              end;

                              {as stated above, pattern movement is implemented
                               as a direction, so modify the sprite's position
                               according to the direction at this pattern's
                               movement step}
                              case Patterns[CurPattern, CurPatternIdx] of
                                0 : begin
                                      XPos := XPos + 1;
                                    end;
                                1 : begin
                                      XPos := XPos + 1;
                                      YPos := YPos + 1;
                                    end;
                                2 : begin
                                      YPos := YPos +1;
                                    end;
                                3 : begin
                                      XPos := XPos - 1;
                                      YPos := YPos + 1;
                                    end;
                                4 : begin
                                      XPos := XPos - 1;
                                    end;
                                5 : begin
                                      XPos := XPos - 1;
                                      YPos := YPos - 1;
                                    end;
                                6 : begin
                                      YPos := YPos - 1;
                                    end;
                                7 : begin
                                      XPos := XPos + 1;
                                      YPos := YPos - 1;
                                    end;
                              end;
                            end;
                end;
              end;
```

```
  {clip to the boundaries of the screen}
  if XPos < 0 then
    XPos := 0;
  if XPos > DXWIDTH - 21 then
    XPos := DXWIDTH - 21;

  {we'll keep sprites from moving up where the status is displayed}
  if YPos < 30 then
    YPos := 30;
  if YPos > DXHEIGHT - 3 then
    YPos := DXHEIGHT - 3;
end;


initialization
  {set up the personality tables}
  Personalities[perAggressive] := AggressivePersonality;
  Personalities[perDefensive] := DefensivePersonality;
  Personalities[perTactical] := TacticalPersonality;
end.
```

As you can see from this simplistic example, the change in behavior of the enemy sprite is subtle, but you should be able to tell a definite personality, especially between the Aggressive and Defensive postures. Indeed, if we changed a sprite's personality based on game state (i.e., going from Aggressive to Defensive when hit points went below 30%), the sprite would seem a little more dynamic.

We could even change the distribution based on the success of a particular state within a personality during the game. For example, if the game timed how long it took to kill the player during each state and found that a particular state was more effective, it could modify the distribution so that that state was chosen more often. This would make the game grow with the player; the sprites would appear to "learn," and the game would become more challenging.

## Path Finding

Most games feature some form of entity or sprite that must move from one position in the game world to another. Usually, this is pretty simple, as we can determine an appropriate x and y velocity that will move the sprite in the direction of its goal and sit back until it gets there. This will work fine for game worlds that are flat and don't feature any obstacles that would hinder movement. Unfortunately, most game worlds tend to be a bit more complex, with several immobile or impassable objects. The presence of these objects negates the possibility of game entities always moving in straight lines to get from their origin to their destination, posing a problem that has been researched heavily over the years by both the academic world and the gaming industry alike.

When a game entity encounters an object that hinders its movement, it must find another direction of movement leading around the obstacle and toward the final destination. This is known as path finding. Technically, path finding describes algorithms for determining the shortest, most direct path from a starting position to an ending position, avoiding all impassible obstacles.

**path finding:** Algorithmic techniques for determining the shortest, most direct path from a starting position to an ending position based on terrain and obstacles in the game world.

There are numerous applications for such techniques. Real-time strategy games such as Age of Empires and WarCraft make heavy use of path finding algorithms. Indeed, any game that features entities moving through a world filled with impassible obstacles needs to implement some form of path finding. Path finding algorithms can be applied to real-world problems as well. We'll focus our discussion on path finding as it applies to 2-D game worlds, and we'll examine one well-known algorithm that produces acceptable results.

## Algorithms

The subject of finding a particular path over a specific terrain and algorithms for accomplishing this task have been researched almost as extensively as methods for producing graphical output. Several books have been published that cover this subject to varying degrees of depth. Many of these algorithms, while accurate, tend to be too slow for implementation in a game. However, three algorithms are well documented and well known in the game industry, and tend to serve as the basis from which most game implementations of path finding algorithms are drawn. These are known as breadth first search, depth first search, and A* (pronounced "A-Star").

### Breadth First Search

The breadth first search algorithm is very exhaustive, and while it can eventually find a very accurate, short path, it typically takes way too long for most games. It searches for the shortest path by choosing the next node in a particular direction and determining its distance from the destination. It performs this for all available directions, then it moves to the node closest to the destination and performs these calculations again. However, if two or more nodes are the same distance from the destination, it recursively performs these calculations for each of these nodes. Essentially, this algorithm explores all possible paths from the starting point to the destination, as long as those paths lead toward the destination. This can result in an exponentially increasing number of calculations depending on the size of the map and the position of obstacles. Calculation times for this algorithm are typically measured in seconds. While this may be completely appropriate for real-world problems, it is way too slow for a game application, which needs to calculate paths in milliseconds, if not faster.

### Depth First Search

By contrast, the depth first search simply chooses a direction toward the destination and begins moving along nodes in that direction until it reaches the destination. If it encounters an obstacle, it backs up one node and tries again in a different direction. While this algorithm can eventually find some path to the destination, it typically will not be the shortest or the most direct route. However, also unlike breadth first search techniques, path calculation times are much, much shorter. While this will find some type of path in a short amount of time, it will usually result in a path that makes game entities wander about almost aimlessly, and certainly in no logical or intelligent manner.

### A*

Perhaps the most widely documented solution for path finding problems is the A* algorithm. A* combines the best of both breadth first search and depth first search to determine the shortest path in a relatively minimal amount of time. Like the depth first search, it chooses a direction toward the destination, and begins moving along nodes in that direction. Like the breadth first search algorithm, it checks the distance of the next nodes in several directions to determine which is closest to the destination. It then moves to this next node and starts the calculations again. The result is a single path for which several directions were considered at each node. This typically produces a fairly intelligent looking path within an acceptable amount of time.

## Basic Implementation

In our example, we'll take a fairly typical approach and define a two-dimensional game world composed of square tiles. We'll need to define a starting point and an ending point, and populate this map with several impassible obstacles, like so:

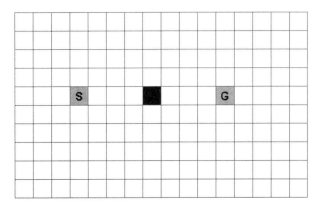

**Figure 12-5:**
*The game world*

Additionally, we'll need to set up a list that will hold information for the nodes we have selected on our path. We'll also need an array the size of the game world to mark nodes that have already been explored. We'll examine how these two requirements are utilized below.

We begin by determining the direction of the goal relative to our starting point. We'll use this to determine which nodes we should look at next. Based on this direction, we'll examine three nodes—the next node in the direction of the goal and the two nodes to either side of it. In this example, our goal is directly east of the starting point, so we'll examine the northeast, east, and southeast nodes relative to our starting point:

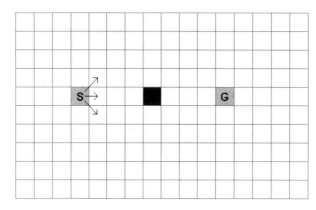

**Figure 12-6:**
*Examining nodes*

Now, for each of these nodes being examined, we need to determine their distance from the destination. If you remember your algebra, the distance formula is:

```
Distance := Sqrt(Sqr(X2 - X1) + Sqr(Y2 - Y1));
```

*Tip:* The Sqrt and Sqr functions are very slow. We could simply use multiplication in the case of the Sqr function, and perhaps utilize a lookup table for the Sqrt function in order to optimize this equation.

Using this equation, we find that the node directly to the east is the closest to the destination. We'll add this new node to our list of nodes along the path, as well as mark this new node as visited in our array of visited nodes (we also need to add the starting node to the list as well as mark it as visited before we start searching for a path). We then move to this new node, and begin the process again.

**Note:** The phrase "moving to the new node" indicates that we are simply tracking the current node we are processing in our algorithm. The actual movement of the game entity does not take place until the entire path is determined; it does not move in real time.

We'll continue this process until we encounter an obstacle. Even though the next eastward node would be closest to the destination, it is an impassible obstacle and cannot be selected. Therefore, we need to select one of the other two nodes that are closest to the destination and are not blocked. In this example, either of these nodes will work just fine, so we'll pick one at random.

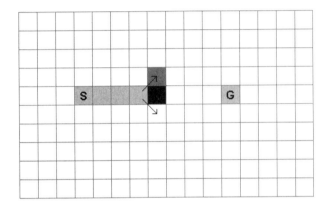

*Figure 12-7:*
*Moving past an obstacle*

Notice that we have now changed directions from east to northeast, which affects which nodes we'll examine on the next pass. Specifically, the next nodes we will examine will now be north, northeast, and east of the current node.

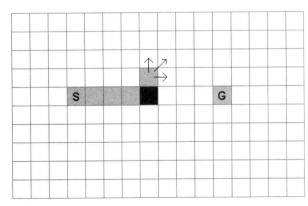

*Figure 12-8:*
*Examining nodes in a new direction*

Once again, we'll see that the eastward node is the closest to the goal. This entire process continues until the goal is finally reached.

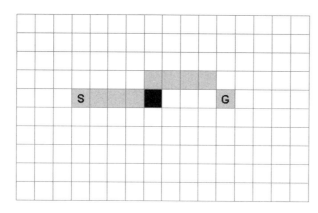

*Figure 12-9:*
*A path from start to finish*

## Back Stepping

This basic algorithm will get us there in simple game worlds, but what about situations where we run into larger obstacles, such as the one below.

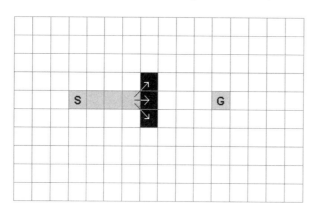

*Figure 12-10:*
*A large wall*

As we can see here, all three examined nodes are blocked, and thus the path cannot proceed any further. This is where the array that tracks which nodes have been visited comes in. We need to delete the current node we are on from our list of path nodes, and back up to the previous node. When we reexamine the next closest nodes, we'll treat the node we just visited as an impassible obstacle. This keeps us from choosing a node that we know will not work.

**Note:** When we back up to a previous node, we also need to reset our direction to the direction we were facing in this previous node.

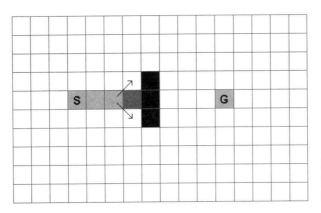

***Figure 12-11:***
*Backing up and reexamining nodes*

Continuing with this process, we see that our algorithm finds a relatively direct path to the destination.

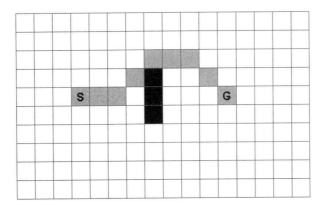

***Figure 12-12:***
*Pathing around a large wall*

Backing up and reexamining nodes in the previous direction really boosts this algorithm's intelligence. Indeed, while our implementation of this algorithm isn't totally infallible, it is pretty smart, and can get us around some fairly complex obstacles as illustrated below.

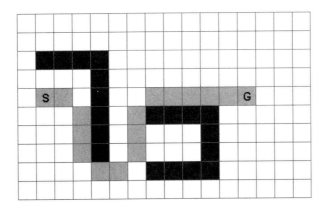

***Figure 12-13:***
*Navigating a complex game world*

## Case Study

Unlike most examples throughout this book, the path finding example is implemented using standard Delphi controls for the visual feedback. This was done to highlight the path finding algorithm and to make it easier to examine the algorithm at run time. You can't really set breakpoints and step through code once DirectDraw has exclusive access and has set the video mode to full screen. Implementing an A* path finding algorithm using standard Delphi controls allows you to step through it line by line to examine what's happening as it runs. This will also make it easier to improve the algorithm's performance and accuracy if you wish to play with it. In the output from this test application, the blue square is the origin, the red square is the destination, black squares indicate impassible obstacles, and purple squares indicate the final path. Green squares indicate nodes that were visited but did not belong on the final path.

The following listing demonstrates a simple, straightforward implementation of the A* algorithm.

**Listing 12-6:** *The A\* test bed*

```
interface

          .
          .
          .


  {defines the directions}
  TCompassDirection = (cdNorth, cdNorthEast, cdEast, cdSouthEast, cdSouth,
                     cdSouthWest, cdWest, cdNorthWest);

  {this defines node offsets relative to the current node for
   a particular direction}
  TDirectionOffset = array[TCompassDirection] of TPoint;

  {our node record, recording its coordinates and compass direction}
  TNode = record
    Direction: TCompassDirection;
    GridPt: TPoint;
  end;
  PNode = ^TNode;



  procedure ClearPathQueue;

var
  frmPathFinder: TfrmPathFinder;

  {tracks the origin and destination}
  StartPt, EndPt: TPoint;
  SetStart: Boolean;
```

```
      {tracks the list of nodes on the final path}
      PathQueue: TList;

      {defines the game world. nodes defined as 0 are clear,
       1 are obstacles}
      MapGrid: array[0..14, 0..14] of Byte;

      {tracks which nodes we've already visited}
      VisitedNodes: array[0..14, 0..14] of Boolean;

  const
      {this defines the actual node offsets at a specific direction
       relative to the current node}
      DirectionOffset: TDirectionOffset = ((X: 0; Y: -1),
                                           (X: 1; Y: -1),
                                           (X: 1; Y: 0),
                                           (X: 1; Y: 1),
                                           (X: 0; Y: 1),
                                           (X: -1; Y: 1),
                                           (X: -1; Y: 0),
                                           (X: -1; Y: -1) );

      {define each of our node types}
      NODECLEAR    = '';
      NODEOBSTACLE = '1';
      NODESTART    = '2';
      NODEEND      = '3';
      NODEPATH     = '4';
      NODEVISITED  = '5';

  implementation

  procedure TfrmPathFinder.FormCreate(Sender: TObject);
  begin
    {initialize the starting and ending node}
    StartPt := Point(-1, -1);
    EndPt := Point(-1, -1);

    {indicate that the left mouse button sets the start node by default}
    SetStart := TRUE;

    {create our list of path nodes}
    PathQueue := TList.Create;
  end;

  procedure TfrmPathFinder.FormDestroy(Sender: TObject);
  begin
    {free all existing nodes, and then free the path list}
    ClearPathQueue;
    PathQueue.Free;
```

```
end;

procedure ClearPathQueue;
var
  iCount: Integer;
begin
  {free each node in the list}
  for iCount := 0 to PathQueue.Count-1 do
    FreeMem(PathQueue[iCount], SizeOf(TNode));

  {empty the list}
  PathQueue.Clear;
end;

procedure TfrmPathFinder.grdPathMouseDown(Sender: TObject; Button: TMouseButton;
  Shift: TShiftState; X, Y: Integer);
var
  GrdRow, GrdCol: Integer;
begin
  {map the mouse cursor coordinates to grid cell coordinates}
  grdPath.MouseToCell(X, Y, GrdCol, GrdRow);

  {if the right mouse button was pressed...}
  if Button = mbRight then
  begin
    {...set or clear an obstacle node}
    if grdPath.Cells[GrdCol, GrdRow] = NODEOBSTACLE then
      grdPath.Cells[GrdCol, GrdRow] := NODECLEAR
    else
      grdPath.Cells[GrdCol, GrdRow] := NODEOBSTACLE;
  end
  else
  {...otherwise, we're setting a starting or ending node}
  if SetStart then
  begin
    {if a start node has already been placed, clear the previous node}
    if StartPt.X <> -1 then
      grdPath.Cells[StartPt.X, StartPt.Y] := NODECLEAR;

    {set the new start node}
    grdPath.Cells[GrdCol, GrdRow] := NODESTART;
    StartPt := Point(GrdCol, GrdRow);
  end
  else
  begin
    {if an end node has already been placed, clear the previous node}
    if EndPt.X <> -1 then
      grdPath.Cells[EndPt.X, EndPt.Y] := NODECLEAR;

    {set the new end node}
    grdPath.Cells[GrdCol, GrdRow] := NODEEND;
```

```
      EndPt := Point(GrdCol, GrdRow);
    end;

end;

procedure TfrmPathFinder.grdPathDrawCell(Sender: TObject; ACol, ARow: Integer;
  Rect: TRect; State: TGridDrawState);
begin
  {most squares should be colored white}
  grdPath.Canvas.Brush.Color := clWhite;

  {determine the color of the square based on its type}
  if grdPath.Cells[ACol, ARow] = NODEOBSTACLE then
    grdPath.Canvas.Brush.Color := clBlack;
  if grdPath.Cells[ACol, ARow] = NODESTART then
    grdPath.Canvas.Brush.Color := clBlue;
  if grdPath.Cells[ACol, ARow] = NODEEND then
    grdPath.Canvas.Brush.Color := clRed;
  if grdPath.Cells[ACol, ARow] = NODEPATH then
    grdPath.Canvas.Brush.Color := clPurple;
  if grdPath.Cells[ACol, ARow] = NODEVISITED then
    grdPath.Canvas.Brush.Color := clGreen;

  {fill this square with the appropriate color}
  grdPath.Canvas.FillRect(Rect);
end;

procedure TfrmPathFinder.shpStartPointMouseDown(Sender: TObject;
      Button: TMouseButton;
  Shift: TShiftState; X, Y: Integer);
begin
  {indicate we are setting a start node}
  SetStart := TRUE;
end;

procedure TfrmPathFinder.shpDestPointMouseDown(Sender: TObject;
      Button: TMouseButton;
  Shift: TShiftState; X, Y: Integer);
begin
  {indicate we are setting an end node}
  SetStart := FALSE;
end;

procedure TfrmPathFinder.btnClearMapClick(Sender: TObject);
var
  iCount, iCount2: Integer;
begin
  {clear out the map}
  for iCount := 0 to 14 do
    for iCount2 := 0 to 14 do
      grdPath.Cells[iCount, iCount2] := '';
```

```
end;

procedure TfrmPathFinder.btnFindPathClick(Sender: TObject);
var
  iCount, iCount2: Integer;

  CurPt, EvalPt, NewPt: TPoint;
  TempNode: PNode;
  Dist, EvalDist: Longword;

  Dir, NewDir: TCompassDirection;
  SearchDirs: array[0..2] of TCompassDirection;
begin
  {don't do anything until a starting and ending point have been set}
  if (StartPt.X = -1) or (EndPt.X = -1) then
    Exit;

  {clear out the visited nodes array}
  FillChar(VisitedNodes, SizeOf(VisitedNodes), 0);

  {populate the map grid with the specified impassible tiles}
  for iCount := 0 to 14 do
    for iCount2 := 0 to 14 do
      if grdPath.Cells[iCount, iCount2] = NODEOBSTACLE then
        MapGrid[iCount, iCount2] := 1
      else
        MapGrid[iCount, iCount2] := 0;

  {delete the current path}
  ClearPathQueue;

  {initialize the tracking variables}
  CurPt := StartPt;
  VisitedNodes[CurPt.X, CurPt.Y] := TRUE;

  {determine the initial direction}

  {destination left of origin}
  if EndPt.X < StartPt.X then
  begin
    if EndPt.Y > StartPt.Y then
      Dir := cdSouthWest
    else
    if EndPt.Y < StartPt.Y then
      Dir := cdNorthWest
    else
      Dir := cdWest;
  end
  else
  {destination right of origin}
  if EndPt.X > StartPt.X then
```

```
begin
  if EndPt.Y > StartPt.Y then
    Dir := cdSouthEast
  else
  if EndPt.Y < StartPt.Y then
    Dir := cdNorthEast
  else
    Dir := cdEast;
end
else
{destination directly above or below origin}
if EndPt.Y > StartPt.Y then
  Dir := cdSouth
else
  Dir := cdNorth;

{create a node object}
GetMem(TempNode, SizeOf(TNode));

{initialize the node object with our current (starting) node information}
TempNode^.Direction := Dir;
TempNode^.GridPt.X := CurPt.X;
TempNode^.GridPt.Y := CurPt.Y;

{add this starting node to the path list}
PathQueue.Add(TempNode);

{begin searching the path until we reach the destination node}
while (CurPt.X <> EndPt.X) or (CurPt.Y <> EndPt.Y) do
begin
  {reset the new coordinates to indicate nothing has been found}
  NewPt := Point(-1, -1);

  {reset our distance to the largest value available (new nodes should
   be well under this distance to the destination)}
  Dist := $FFFFFFFF;

  {determine the 3 search directions}
  SearchDirs[0] := Pred(Dir);
  if Ord(SearchDirs[0]) < Ord(cdNorth) then
    SearchDirs[0] := cdNorthWest;
  SearchDirs[1] := Dir;
  SearchDirs[2] := Succ(Dir);
  if Ord(SearchDirs[2]) > Ord(cdNorthWest) then
    SearchDirs[2] := cdNorth;

  {evaluate grid locations in 3 directions}
  for iCount := 0 to 2 do
  begin
    {get the coordinates of the next node to examine relative to the
     current node, based on the direction we are facing }
```

```
        EvalPt.X := CurPt.X + DirectionOffset[SearchDirs[iCount]].X;
        EvalPt.Y := CurPt.Y + DirectionOffset[SearchDirs[iCount]].Y;

        {make sure this node is on the map}
        if (EvalPt.X > -1) and (EvalPt.X < 15) and
           (EvalPt.Y > -1) and (EvalPt.Y < 15) then
          {make sure we've never visited this node}
          if not VisitedNodes[EvalPt.X, EvalPt.Y] then
            {make sure this isn't an impassible node}
            if MapGrid[EvalPt.X, EvalPt.Y] = 0 then
            begin
              {this is a clear node that we could move to. calculate
               the distance from this node to the destination.

               NOTE: since we're interested in just relative distances as
               opposed to exact distances, we don't need to perform a square
               root. this will dramatically speed up this calculation}
              EvalDist := ((EndPt.X - EvalPt.X)*(EndPt.X - EvalPt.X)) +
                          ((EndPt.Y - EvalPt.Y)*(EndPt.Y - EvalPt.Y));

              {if we have found a node closer to the destination, make this
               the current node}
              if EvalDist < Dist then
              begin
                {record the new distance and node}
                Dist := EvalDist;
                NewPt := EvalPt;

                {record the direction of this new node}
                NewDir := SearchDirs[iCount];
              end
            end;
  end;

{at this point, if NewPt is still (-1, -1), we've run into a wall and
 cannot move any further. thus, we have to back up one and try again.
 otherwise, we can add this new node to our list of nodes}

{we've got a valid node}
if NewPt.X <> -1 then
begin
  {make this new node our current node}
  CurPt := NewPt;

  {point us in the direction of this new node}
  Dir := NewDir;

  {mark this node as visited}
  VisitedNodes[CurPt.X, CurPt.Y] := TRUE;

  {create a node object}
```

```
    GetMem(TempNode, SizeOf(TNode));

    {initialize this node object with the new node information}
    TempNode^.Direction := Dir;
    TempNode^.GridPt.X := CurPt.X;
    TempNode^.GridPt.Y := CurPt.Y;

    {put this new node in the path list}
    PathQueue.Add(TempNode);

    {if we've recorded 50 nodes, break out of this loop}
    if PathQueue.Count > 50 then
      Break;
  end
  else
  begin
    {we've backed up to the point where we can no longer back up. thus, a
     path could not be found. we could improve this algorithm by
     recalculating the starting direction and trying again until we've
     searched in all possible directions}
    if PathQueue.Count = 1 then
      Break;

    {point us in the direction of the previous node}
    Dir := TNode(PathQueue[PathQueue.Count-2]^).Direction;

    {retrieve the coordinates of the previous node and make that
     our current node}
    CurPt := Point(TNode(PathQueue[PathQueue.Count-2]^).GridPt.X,
                   TNode(PathQueue[PathQueue.Count-2]^).GridPt.Y);

    {free the last node in the list and delete it}
    FreeMem(PathQueue[PathQueue.Count-1], SizeOf(TNode));
    PathQueue.Delete(PathQueue.Count-1);
  end;
end;

{at this point, we've found a path from the starting node to the destination
node, so we should populate the grid and allow it to display the final path}

{specify visited nodes}
for iCount := 0 to 14 do
  for iCount2 := 0 to 14 do
    if VisitedNodes[iCount, iCount2] then
      grdPath.Cells[iCount, iCount2] := NODEVISITED;

{specify nodes on the path}
for iCount := 0 to PathQueue.Count-1 do
begin
  grdPath.Cells[TNode(PathQueue[iCount]^).GridPt.X,
               TNode(PathQueue[iCount]^).GridPt.Y] := NODEPATH;
```

```
end;

{specify the starting and ending nodes}
grdPath.Cells[StartPt.X, StartPt.Y] := NODESTART;
grdPath.Cells[EndPt.X, EndPt.Y] := NODEEND;
end;
```

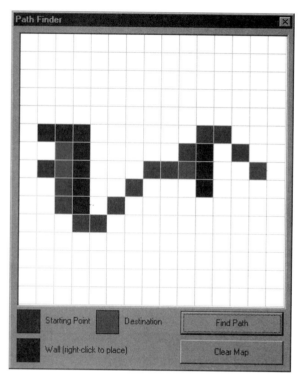

**Figure 12-14:**
*The A\* algorithm in action*

## Enhancements

Although this algorithm is relatively powerful, it is easy to bog it down and send it on a wild goose chase. In particular, large U-shaped sections of obstacles can make the algorithm calculate dozens or even hundreds of nodes that will not be part of the final path. This could potentially overflow the list of path nodes, or at a minimum cause a noticeable pause when a unit calculates a path over long distances. Therefore, your game world should avoid such constructions.

**Caution:** This implementation could potentially get the sprite caught in an infinite loop on some maps, resulting in an overflow situation which would most likely crash the machine.

One way to avoid an overflow on the path list would be to restrict the number of nodes in this list to some arbitrary number. Our example constrains the path to a total number of 50 nodes. This may need to be adjusted for large maps, but it will ensure that the path node list never overflows, and it will restrict pathing time to a maximum amount. If a unit tries to path to a destination, but the path node list reaches the limit before the destination is reached, you could just set a flag for that entity, and repath when the unit reaches the last node in its list. Allowing the user to set waypoints for a unit will further improve pathing, as the paths between each waypoint tend to be shorter and encounter fewer obstacles.

This algorithm is somewhat intelligent, but it can be easily fooled by certain obstacle constructions. Looking at nodes in the three directions relative to the direction of the destination is somewhat of an optimization, and cuts down on the number of calculations required at each node. However, this sometimes leads to paths that look less than intelligent, even downright stupid. The algorithm could be changed so that it checks all eight directions at each node. While this will dramatically increase the number of calculations, the overall path will tend to be much shorter and look more natural.

Additionally, this algorithm does not take into account nodes with different movement costs. For example, say that the game world was populated by terrain consisting of hard rock, grasslands, mud, swamp, and water. While water terrain might be impassable, the others can be moved through but at different degrees of difficulty. Hard rock or roads would certainly be the easiest to move over, but grasslands, mud, and swamp would all impose penalties to movement while not being totally impassable. Elevation could also be a factor. This algorithm would need to be modified somewhat if your game world features terrain with varying movement costs.

## Summary

In this chapter, we discussed techniques for implementing simplistic artificial intelligence routines that give our sprites the ability to display cunning and strategy when moving around the game world. We looked at different movement techniques, including chasing or evading the player and patterned movement. We also looked at controlling the movement decisions based on a finite state machine, as well as techniques for weighting the selected states as a method for implementing rudimentary personalities. When using artificial intelligence techniques in your games, it is important to keep these points in mind:

■ No matter how good your artificial intelligence algorithms may be, there is no greater challenge than playing another human being. However, some people may be unable to hook up with someone else to play a multiplayer game, or they may just enjoy playing by themselves. Therefore, it is important to include artificial intelligence algorithms in your games that make the antagonists at least moderately challenging.

■ The most noticeable display of artificial intelligence is in the movement of enemy units. In most action games, the user is going to be primarily concerned with the movement of enemy units, such as whether they are aggressively chasing the user's ship or running like cowards.

■ Perhaps the simplest simulation of artificial intelligence is to introduce an element of randomness. When an enemy unit moves in a fashion that is unpredictable to the player, that unit can appear to exhibit a rudimentary intelligence. Consider the apparently random flight path of a common housefly. It darts about here and there, yet it always appears to have a mind of its own and to know where it's going.

■ An enemy that actively hunts down the player can be perceived as confident, powerful, and aggressive. By contrast, an enemy that constantly eludes the player or turns tail can be perceived as cowardly, injured, or perhaps even cunning, like an assassin stalking its target.

■ We can use algorithms that make enemy units move about in a specific pattern. This can make antagonists appear to move in a very deliberate manner. Very complex movements can be modeled this way, where some patterns could be useful for evading the player, such as a zigzag pattern, and some patterns could be useful for chasing the player, such as a circular pattern to move around the player's flank.

■ A finite state machine is a logical construction that consists of several "states," each of which defines a specific behavior, and "state transitions," which define specific rules for moving from state to state. Finite state machines are a method by which an enemy unit can make a series of rational decisions based on various inputs from the game world, such as the current environment as well as the actions of the player.

■ A probability machine is an extension of a finite state machine, allowing the application to simulate personalities based on a certain distribution factor. Using this technique, we can make some sprites appear more passive, some more aggressive, some a little bit sneakier, etc. It works by choosing the next state based on a weighted distribution as identified by the type of personality we're modeling.

■ Most games feature a game world filled with moving sprites which must navigate around immovable or impassible obstacles. Path finding artificial intelligence routines must be utilized in order to make the sprite appear to move in an intelligent manner, selecting the most direct, shortest path available.

■ Breadth first search and depth first search techniques could be used, but these are typically too slow or too inaccurate for game applications. The A* (pronounced "A-star") algorithm combines the best of breadth first search and depth first search to find a fairly direct, short path in a short amount of time.

# CHAPTER 13: *Putting It All Together*

**THIS CHAPTER COVERS THE FOLLOWING TOPICS:**

- The Delphi Blocks game architecture
- User input implementation
- Sound and music implementation
- Graphics implementation
- Potential enhancements

Each individual piece of a game is interesting to study and can be downright fun to program. Sound and music programming is always interesting, as it's cool to programmatically control a sound's properties such as volume or panning, and perhaps even more interesting to output music from various sources. Input programming is also a lot of fun, especially when reading from devices other than the standard mouse or keyboard. Force feedback is especially cool, as it's unusual to control an external peripheral using code instead of the other way around. And, of course, graphics programming is never boring, and is limited to only what your imagination can stir up. However, while each piece is interesting individually, orchestrating them together into a digital masterpiece is incredibly rewarding and entertaining.

We've covered many useful game programming techniques throughout this book, and now it's time to put them together and make something useful. In this chapter, we will examine a full-fledged game written using the techniques and examples that we've developed throughout the course of the text. We'll break down several important aspects of the game, and see how all of these parts come together to make a working, playable game application.

## Delphi Blocks

Our case study game is called Delphi Blocks. If you remember the old Breakout game, this one will be very familiar. While we're not breaking any new technological ground with this application, it does serve as a working example of bringing graphics, sound, and input programming together to make a working, playable, and even fun game.

The basic idea is to destroy all of the blocks on the screen using a ball. This ball bounces around the screen, off of blocks and the screen sides. The user can control a small paddle at the bottom of the screen to deflect the ball toward the blocks. If the ball goes off of the bottom of the screen, it is lost and another ball is put into play. The user has three balls; when all of them are lost, the game is over. The game play is simple, but it is easy to learn without ever consulting a manual and can be addictive.

## General Game Architecture

This is a simplistic game with an equally simplistic architecture. The code is encapsulated into one unit, although we could have easily segregated several portions of the code into individual units in order to increase its readability and adaptability. In general, we decided to make the overall game level based to facilitate a more intuitive player advancement system, using a state-driven architecture to ease implementation and simplify game control.

## Player Advancement

As stated above, the player's goal is to destroy every block on the screen. We'll use a level based system of advancement, so that when all of the blocks have been destroyed, the level is increased and a new grid of blocks is generated. The score for each block is based on the level, so the higher the level, the more each block is worth. However, the speed of the ball is also based on the level, so at higher levels the ball will be moving at more and more rapid velocities, making the game harder and justifying the score increase for each block. This type of advancement is important, as it challenges the players and forces them to get better in order to play the game for longer periods of time.

## Game States

The game is state driven, using the basic state-driven architecture we covered back in Chapter 2. There are four specific states: Idle, Playing, Intermission, and Game Over. Game execution flows through the states in the following manner:

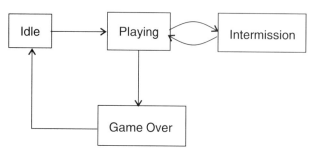

*Figure 13-1:*
*Delphi Blocks state flow*

*Idle*   This state is basically a demo state. All it does is sit and display a static image with a full grid of blocks and the game title while waiting for the user to start a new game. Unlike the other states, though, in this state we display two buttons, one for starting the game and one for quitting. We'll discuss how the buttons work when we cover user input.

*Playing*   This is the main game state, and includes the logic for moving the sprites and performing the graphics rendering. Additionally, it also checks to see if the current level has been cleared, and if so, it initializes a new level and puts the game in intermission.

*Intermission*   This state simply provides the player with a short pause between levels. This is important, as a twitch game like Delphi Blocks can get rather hectic at higher levels, and you really need to provide players with an opportunity to catch their breath every now and then. All this state does is display a full grid of blocks with an indicator of the next level.

*Game Over*   The game goes into this state when the player has lost all of the available balls. It serves to indicate to the user that the game has been completed, and a new one must be started. Like the intermission state, it simply displays a full grid of blocks with the words "Game Over" superimposed over them.

## User Input

During the idle state, the user has the choice of selecting two buttons, one for starting a game and one for quitting the application. While actually playing the game, the user has control over a paddle that can move left and right. At higher levels, the user needs to be able to move the paddle rapidly and intuitively. Thus, the most obvious form of control for this type of game would be the mouse. We've used a modification of the baseline application with mouse support in order to accomplish this task. Using this baseline, it was very easy to get mouse support up and running with little effort.

### Buttons

The buttons were actually very easy to implement. They are displayed only during the idle state, and it is in this idle state that we check for click events. If a click is detected, we simply check to see if the mouse cursor was located over one of the buttons, and take the appropriate action:

```
{determine if the mouse was clicked in one of the buttons}
if MouseClickList.Count>0 then
begin
  {while there are any events in the mouse click list, retrieve
   them all and empty the list}
  while MouseClickList.Count > 0 do
  begin
```

```
{free the current mouse data}
if MouseData <> nil then
begin
  MouseData.Free;
  MouseData := nil;
end;

{retrieve and delete the click event}
MouseData := TMouseData(MouseClickList[0]);
MouseClickList.Delete(0);
end;

{if the quit button was pushed...}
if PtInRect(Rect(416, 350, 544, 414),
          Point(MouseData.XPos, MouseData.YPos)) then
  Close;
{if the start button was pushed...}
if PtInRect(Rect(96, 350, 224, 414),
          Point(MouseData.XPos, MouseData.YPos)) then
  StartGame;
```

### Baseline Differences

While the baseline application with mouse support was functional, we needed to make some minor modifications. Specifically, we want to show a mouse cursor during the idle state, but we want to suppress the display of the mouse cursor during any other state. Therefore, we ripped all of the mouse cursor display code out of the mouse input thread and added a variable to control mouse cursor display. If the mouse cursor is to be hidden, only the horizontal position of the mouse cursor is updated, and it is clipped according to the dimensions of the paddle graphic.

## Sound and Music

Any game can be improved by using sound effects, and this game is certainly no different. We decided to use a few simple sounds to indicate when a ball hits a block, hits the side of the screen, hits the paddle, or falls off of the bottom and dies. There's not much opportunity for sounds to overlap, so we could have used regular Windows multimedia function calls to output the sound. However, we went with DirectSound in case we wanted to expand the sound functionality at a later date. DirectSound programming is relatively easy anyway, and this architecture certainly would support advanced sound functionality if we needed it.

We also wanted to have some music playing in the background, so the application uses MCI commands to continuously play a MIDI file while the application is active. We could have easily used DirectSound to stream a large WAV file to the sound card, which would have given us better sound quality, but this example shows how Windows multimedia functions and DirectSound can be used simultaneously.

## Graphics

The graphical requirements for this application are not very stringent, and were thus very easy to implement. This is a 2-D sprite game that doesn't feature very much animation, so all of the graphics easily fit into one file. We load this bitmap into an offscreen surface, letting DirectDraw determine its location; if there is enough video memory available, the surface will be located on the video card itself. Since we use nothing but simple blits, available hardware acceleration will dramatically improve the performance of the game. The game images are arranged in the single bitmap like so:

*Figure 13-2:*
*Delphi Blocks game*
*graphics*

The largest part of the graphic file is the background screen. The images for the block sprites are located below the background, including the image of the ball and paddle. We also see the button images as well as the cursor sprite image.

### Sprites

This game features a large amount of sprites in the form of the blocks and the ball. We could easily extend the block grid to be larger or smaller, and the game is already set up to support more than one active ball. In order to encapsulate this functionality, we will use an object to manage all of the block sprites, and another object to manage all of the ball sprites.

The block manager itself is pretty simplistic. It contains an array property that holds a 10 x 15 grid of TBlock objects, with each TBlock object representing one block sprite on the screen. The manager contains functions for initializing the entire block grid as well as drawing all of the blocks or deleting one specific block from the grid. This encapsulation allows us to deal with the large quantity of block sprites using one simple class. It is defined as:

```
{defines the manager that will track all of the blocks}
TBlockMgr = class
  {this static grid can be modified to increase or decrease the overall
   block area and size}
  BlockGrid: array[0..14, 0..9] of TBlock;
  NumBlocks: Integer;

  destructor Destroy; override;
  procedure Draw;
  procedure InitializeBlocks;
  procedure KillBlock(Row, Col: Integer);
end;
```

The ball manager object is very similar in functionality and design. It contains a list object that tracks several TBall objects. This allows us to add any number of active balls to the screen and track them all simultaneously. Additional methods move and draw all of the active balls, clear the entire list of balls, or delete a specific ball sprite. It is defined as:

```
{defines the manager that will track all of the ball sprites. note that
 this gives us the ability to add and track several active balls at once}
TBallMgr = class
  BallList: TList;

  VelCoefficient: Integer;

  FTotalBalls: Integer;

  function GetActiveBalls: Integer;

  constructor Create;
  destructor Destroy; override;
  procedure AddBall(XPos, YPos, XVel, YVel: Real; DecBalls: Boolean);
  procedure KillBall(Idx: Integer);
  procedure MoveBalls;
  procedure DrawBalls;
  procedure Clear;

  property TotalBalls: Integer read FTotalBalls write FTotalBalls;
  property ActiveBalls: Integer read GetActiveBalls;
end;
```

### Collision Detection

Collision detection really is the heart of this game. The entire idea is to make a ball collide with a block, and the balls must bounce off the walls and the paddle in a predictable manner.

Bouncing off the walls is a relatively simple behavior to implement. We simply check the horizontal and vertical coordinates of a ball after it has been moved, and if it has collided with the sides or top of the screen, its horizontal or vertical velocity is reversed as appropriate. A collision with the bottom of the screen results in a lost ball.

Collision with the paddle is a little more involved. To simplify matters, we use the bounding box collision detection technique covered in Chapter 6. To review, each ball has a bounding rectangle, as does the paddle. When these two rectangles intersect, a collision has occurred. The paddle is rectangular, and the ball is almost rectangular, so this collision detection technique is accurate enough for our purposes.

However, we would like to give the user some control over the ball so he or she can influence its direction. Therefore, the angle of deflection that the ball takes is dependent on the position at which the ball collides with the paddle. Towards the center of the paddle, the ball tends to deflect at a 90-degree angle to the paddle itself, or straight upward. As the ball collides nearer and nearer to the edge of the paddle, the deflection angle becomes more and more acute, as the following illustration shows:

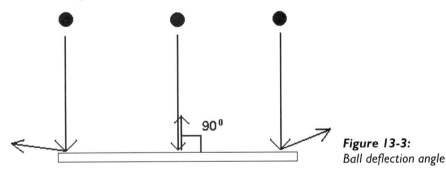

**Figure 13-3:**
*Ball deflection angle*

Collisions with the blocks are where things get kind of hairy. We first perform a bounding box collision test to see if they collided. However, we need to know if the ball hit the top, sides, or bottom of the block in order to determine which velocity to reverse. Unfortunately, it is impossible to determine this from a simple bounding box collision, as illustrated below:

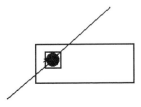

**Figure 13-4:**
*Which side was hit—the top or the left?*

Therefore, we need a more accurate method of collision detection that can determine which side of the box was hit. This can be accomplished by using a general line segment intersection algorithm. The specific algorithm used in the example is covered on page 199 of *Graphics Gems III* by David Kirk. The algorithm was deduced by Franklin Antonio. The math behind this algorithm is complex, and although it is documented thoroughly in the example code, please consult *Graphics Gems III* for a detailed explanation of this algorithm.

## Enhancements

We've created a complete game application that utilizes the vast majority of the techniques covered throughout the book. However, while it serves as a good case study, it certainly is not ready to be shrink-wrapped and put on store shelves. This is by design, as it leaves many opportunities for you, the reader, to exercise some creativity and take this basic game to the next level.

The first thing that should be enhanced is the collision detection code. While it is very accurate, it is incredibly math intensive, and a better, more optimized method could probably be implemented. We are also redrawing the entire screen each frame, which could be optimized by only drawing the paddle and any active balls in their new positions using dirty rectangle animation techniques.

Some general game enhancements might include the ability to track high scores, or perhaps show some skill statistics during the game over state. Additional balls can easily be activated in response to certain events, as the game already supports such functionality. It would be easy to tie such events to special blocks, where some blocks add another ball or perhaps increase/decrease the size of the paddle. You could even take this one step further and perhaps give the paddle a laser or other such weapon, or even make blocks that are indestructible or take multiple hits to destroy.

Perhaps the easiest modification would be to provide better graphics, or even different graphic sets depending on the level. These could even be themed; you could have an ice level, or a lava level, or even a water level. Techniques from the special effects chapter or the palettes chapter could be used to make some blocks glow, rotate, fade in and out, etc.

From a usability standpoint, it might be good to provide users with a configuration screen when the application starts so they can specify things like sound volume or skill level. This could include such things as a sound theme, utilizing better sound effects or different sound effects based on the user's preference or level. Context-sensitive music would also improve the feel of the game. You might also want to support input devices other than the mouse, such as the keyboard or joystick. Providing force feedback support would really add a new dimension to this game. If you want to provide this type of configuration while in full screen video mode, a more general architecture should probably be created to support user interface objects like buttons and menus.

A very fun enhancement for this game would be to include multiplayer support. One player could be at the bottom, and the other player could be at the top. This would also allow you to use some artificial intelligence techniques if you allowed the user to play against the computer. Using some of the incredible Internet technology now available in Delphi, it wouldn't be too hard to make this game playable over the Internet.

## The Case Study Code

The case study itself is presented here in its entirety so that you can see an entire game application laid out in all its glory. The code is heavily commented so as to make it easy to understand. This demonstrates how sound, user input, and graphics come together to form a complete, workable, usable game application.

**Listing 13-1**: *Delphi Blocks*

```
unit DelphiBlocksU;

{******************************************************************************

    Delphi Blocks

    Author: John Ayres

    Based on the baseline architecture with mouse support, this project
    is a 'Breakout' style of game.  The object is to hit the moving ball
    with the paddle and destroy all of the blocks on the screen.  If the
    ball goes off of the bottom of the screen, it is lost and a new one is
    created.  You have three balls before the game is over.  This is a simple
    implementation of a game that shows how to use the mouse input
    functionality of DirectInput in a real-world situation.

    ******************************************************************************

    Copyright © 1999 by John Ayres, All Rights Reserved

    This code is freeware and can be used for any personal or commercial
    purposes without royalty or license.  Use at your own risk.

    ******************************************************************************}

interface

uses
   Windows, Messages, SysUtils, Classes, Graphics, Controls, Forms, Dialogs,
   DDraw, DInput, MouseThreadU, MMSystem, DSound;

{these constants are used to modify specific attributes of the DirectX
 application, such as the color of the main form, the requested resolution,
```

```
  etc.}
const
  FORMCOLOR     = clBlack;
  FORMBORDER    = bsNone;
  FORMCURSOR    = crNone;
  DXWIDTH       = 640;
  DXHEIGHT      = 480;
  DXCOLORDEPTH  = 8;
  BUFFERCOUNT   = 1;
  COOPERATIVELEVEL = DDSCL_FULLSCREEN or DDSCL_ALLOWREBOOT or DDSCL_ALLOWMODEX
                     or DDSCL_EXCLUSIVE;
  SURFACETYPE      = DDSCAPS_COMPLEX or DDSCAPS_FLIP or DDSCAPS_PRIMARYSURFACE;

const
  {this user-defined message is used to start the flipping loop}
  WM_DIRECTXACTIVATE = WM_USER + 200;

type
  {controls the overall game state}
  TGameState = (gsIdle, gsPlaying, gsIntermission, gsGameOver);

  TBallMgr = class;

  {defines a ball sprite}
  TBall = class
    XPrev, YPrev,
    XPos, YPos,
    XVel, YVel: Real;

    BoundBox: TRect;

    Index: Integer;

    Manager: TBallMgr;

    procedure Move;
    procedure Draw;
  end;

  {defines the manager that will track all of the ball sprites. note that
   this gives us the ability to add and track several active balls at once}
  TBallMgr = class
    BallList: TList;

    VelCoefficient: Integer;

    FTotalBalls: Integer;

    function GetActiveBalls: Integer;

    constructor Create;
```

```
  destructor Destroy; override;
  procedure AddBall(XPos, YPos, XVel, YVel: Real; DecBalls: Boolean);
  procedure KillBall(Idx: Integer);
  procedure MoveBalls;
  procedure DrawBalls;
  procedure Clear;

  property TotalBalls: Integer read FTotalBalls write FTotalBalls;
  property ActiveBalls: Integer read GetActiveBalls;
end;

{defines the paddle sprite}
TPaddle = class
  XPos, YPos: Integer;

  BoundBox: TRect;

  procedure Move;
  procedure Draw;
end;

TBlockMgr = class;

{defines a single block}
TBlock = class
  GraphicIdx: Integer;

  BoundBox: TRect;

  procedure Draw;
end;

{defines the manager that will track all of the blocks}
TBlockMgr = class
  {this static grid can be modified to increase or decrease the overall
   block area and size}
  BlockGrid: array[0..14, 0..9] of TBlock;
  NumBlocks: Integer;

  destructor Destroy; override;
  procedure Draw;
  procedure InitializeBlocks;
  procedure KillBlock(Row, Col: Integer);
end;

{the primary form class}
TfrmDXAppMain = class(TForm)
  procedure FormCreate(Sender: TObject);
  procedure FormDestroy(Sender: TObject);
  procedure FormKeyDown(Sender: TObject; var Key: Word;
                        Shift: TShiftState);
```

```
  procedure FormActivate(Sender: TObject);
private
  { Private declarations }

  {necessary for our mouse input}
  FMouseThread: TMouseThread;

  {the block manager}
  FBlockMgr: TBlockMgr;

  {the player's paddle sprite}
  FPaddle: TPaddle;

  {the ball manager}
  FBallMgr: TBallMgr;

  {tracks the current level}
  FLevel: integer;

  {tracks the score}
  FScore: integer;

  {we will need to add an active ball both when the current ball dies as
   well as when the user completes a level and starts a new one. thus,
   sometimes we want to add a ball without decreasing the amount of balls
   available. this variable will track this state}
  FUseBall: Boolean;

  {the current game state}
  FGameState: TGameState;

  {the MCI device ID used for MIDI playback}
  MCIDeviceID: UINT;

  {the MIDI notify message handler}
  procedure MCINotify(var Msg: TMessage); message MM_MCINOTIFY;

  {flips back to the GDI surface to display the exception error message}
  procedure ExceptionHandler(Sender: TObject; ExceptionObj: Exception);

  {the main rendering loop}
  procedure AppIdle(Sender: TObject; var Done: Boolean);

  {intercepts certain messages to provide appropriate functionality}
  procedure AppMessage(var Msg: TMsg; var Handled: Boolean);

  {flips the DirectX surfaces}
  procedure FlipSurfaces;

  {restores any lost surfaces}
  procedure RestoreSurfaces;
```

```
      {draws the contents of surfaces}
      procedure DrawSurfaces;
    public
      { Public declarations }
      procedure InitLevel;
      procedure StartGame;
    end;

  procedure PlayGameSound(SoundNum: Integer);

var
  frmDXAppMain: TfrmDXAppMain;

  {the main DirectDraw interface}
  FDirectDraw: IDirectDraw4;

  {the interfaces for the primary and backbuffer surfaces}
  FPrimarySurface,
  FBackBuffer,
  FMouseCursors,                    // holds mouse cursor graphics
  FGraphics: IDirectDrawSurface4;   // holds the game graphics

  {the overall palette}
  FPalette: IDirectDrawPalette;

  {mouse cursor animation variables}
  FCursorFrame, FCursorFrameCount: Integer;

  {DirectInput objects for mouse functionality}
  FDirectInput: IDirectInput;
  FMouseDevice: IDirectInputDevice;

  {DirectSound object}
  DXSound: IDirectSound;

  {an array of sound buffers}
  Sounds: array[0..3] of IDirectSoundBuffer;


const
  {these are used in defining events for the mouse input functionality}
  MOUSEEVENT = 0;
  QUITEVENT = 1;

  {these identify the sounds in our sound array}
  BLOCKHIT = 0;
  LOSTBALL = 1;
  SIDEHIT = 2;
  PADDLEHIT = 3;

  {the names of the wave files to be used}
```

```
      FileNames: array[BLOCKHIT..PADDLEHIT] of string = ('bhump.wav',
                                                         'bigboom.wav',
                                                         'hitside.wav',
                                                         'bwik.wav');


implementation

uses
  DXTools, DDUtil, SyncObjs, Math, DSUtil{***}, gensuppt;

{$R *.DFM}


{ *-->>  BASELINE APPLICATION CODE <<--* }


{ - the callback function used to ensure that the selected graphics mode -
  - is supported by DirectX                                             - }
function EnumModesCallback(const EnumSurfaceDesc: TDDSurfaceDesc2;
                           Information: Pointer): HResult; stdcall;
begin
  {if the height, width, and color depth match those specified in the
   constants, then indicate that the desired graphics mode is supported}
  if (EnumSurfaceDesc.dwHeight = DXHEIGHT) and
     (EnumSurfaceDesc.dwWidth = DXWIDTH) and
     (EnumSurfaceDesc.ddpfPixelFormat.dwRGBBitCount = DXCOLORDEPTH) then
    Boolean(Information^) := TRUE;

  Result := DDENUMRET_OK;
end;


{ -> Events Hooked to the Application <- }

{ - this event is called when an exception occurs, and simply flips back -
  - to the GDI surface so that the exception dialog box can be read     - }
procedure TfrmDXAppMain.ExceptionHandler(Sender: TObject;
                                         ExceptionObj: Exception);
begin
  {disconnect the OnIdle event to shut off the rendering loop}
  Application.OnIdle := nil;

  {if the DirectDraw object was successfully created, flip to the GDI surface}
  if Assigned(FDirectDraw) then
    FDirectDraw.FlipToGDISurface;

  {display the exception message}
  MessageDlg(ExceptionObj.Message, mtError, [mbOK], 0);

  {reconnect the OnIdle event to reenter the rendering loop}
  Application.OnIdle := AppIdle;
```

```
end;

{ - handles certain messages that are required to make DirectX function -
  - properly within Delphi                                              - }
procedure TfrmDXAppMain.AppMessage(var Msg: TMsg; var Handled: Boolean);
begin
  case Msg.Message of
    WM_ACTIVATEAPP:
      {unhook the OnIdle event when the application is being deactivated.
       this will stop all rendering}
      if not Boolean(Msg.wParam) then
      begin
        FMouseDevice.Unacquire;
        Application.OnIdle := nil;
      end
      else
        {upon activating the application, send ourselves the
         user-defined message}
        PostMessage(Application.Handle, WM_DIRECTXACTIVATE, 0, 0);
    WM_DIRECTXACTIVATE:
      begin
        {upon activating, restore all surfaces (reloading their memory
         as necessary), hook up the OnIdle event, and redraw the contents
         of all surfaces}
        FMouseDevice.Acquire;
        RestoreSurfaces;
        Application.OnIdle := AppIdle;
        DrawSurfaces;
      end;
    WM_SYSCOMMAND:
      begin
        {do not allow a screen saver to kick in}
        Handled := (Msg.wParam = SC_SCREENSAVE);
      end;
  end;
end;


{ -> Form Events <- }

{ - initialize essential form properties - }
procedure TfrmDXAppMain.FormCreate(Sender: TObject);
begin
  {set up the application exception handler}
  Application.OnException := ExceptionHandler;

  {initialize form properties.  note that the FormStyle property must be
   set to fsStayOnTop}
  BorderStyle := bsNone;
  BorderIcons := [];
  FormStyle   := fsStayOnTop;
```

```
      Color     := clBlack;
      Cursor    := crNone;

      {initialize the mouse cursor to the top left of the screen}
      CurX := 0;
      CurY := 0;

      {hide the actual Windows mouse cursor}
      ShowCursor(FALSE);
    end;

    { - provides essential cleanup functionality - }
    procedure TfrmDXAppMain.FormDestroy(Sender: TObject);
    var
      iCount: Integer;
    begin
      {disengage our custom exception handler}
      Application.OnException := nil;

      {remember, we do not have to explicitly free the DirectDraw objects,
       as they will free themselves when they go out of context (such as
       when the application is closed)}

      {unacquire the mouse device}
      FMouseDevice.Unacquire;

      {fire the quit event so our mouse input thread will exit}
      SetEvent(FMouseEvents[QUITEVENT]);
      Sleep(100);

      {free any remaining data in the mouse click list}
      for iCount := 0 to MouseClickList.Count-1 do
        TMouseData(MouseClickList[iCount]).Free;

      {free the click list}
      MouseClickList.Free;

      {free our manager objects}
      FBallMgr.Free;
      FBlockMgr.Free;
      FPaddle.Free;

      {make sure that the MIDI device is closed before exiting the program}
      MCISendCommand(MCIDeviceID, MCI_CLOSE, 0, 0);
    end;

    { - this method initializes DirectX and creates all necessary objects - }
    procedure TfrmDXAppMain.FormActivate(Sender: TObject);
    var
      {we can only get a DirectDraw4 interface from the DirectDraw interface, so we
       need a temporary interface}
```

```
          TempDirectDraw: IDirectDraw;

          {structures required for various methods}
          DDSurface: TDDSurfaceDesc2;
          DDSCaps: TDDSCaps2;

          {flag used to determine if the desired graphics mode is supported}
          SupportedMode: Boolean;

          {mouse property structure}
          MouseProp: TDIPropDWord;

          SrcRect: TRect;
          iCount: Integer;

          {necessary structures for initializing MIDI output}
          OpenParms: TMCI_Open_Parms;
          StatusParms: TMCI_Status_Parms;
          SetParms: TMCI_Set_Parms;
          PlayParms: TMCI_Play_Parms;
        begin
          {if DirectDraw has already been initialized, exit}
          if Assigned(FDirectDraw) then exit;

          {create a temporary DirectDraw object. this is used to create the
           desired DirectDraw4 object}
          DXCheck( DirectDrawCreate(nil, TempDirectDraw, nil) );

          try
            {we can only get a DirectDraw4 interface through the QueryInterface
             method of the DirectDraw object}
            DXCheck( TempDirectDraw.QueryInterface(IID_IDirectDraw4, FDirectDraw) );
          finally
            {now that we have the DirectDraw4 object, the temporary DirectDraw
             object is no longer needed}
            TempDirectDraw := nil;
          end;

          {set the cooperative level to that defined in the constants}
          DXCheck( FDirectDraw.SetCooperativeLevel(Handle, COOPERATIVELEVEL) );

          {hook up the application message handler}
          Application.OnMessage := AppMessage;

          {call EnumDisplayModes and verify that the desired graphics mode is
           indeed supported}
          FillChar(DDSurface, SizeOf(TDDSurfaceDesc2), 0);
          DDSurface.dwSize   := SizeOf(TDDSurfaceDesc2);
          DDSurface.dwFlags  := DDSD_HEIGHT or DDSD_WIDTH or DDSD_PIXELFORMAT;
          DDSurface.dwHeight := DXHEIGHT;
          DDSurface.dwWidth  := DXWIDTH;
```

```
DDSurface.ddpfPixelFormat.dwSize := SizeOf(TDDPixelFormat_DX6);
DDSurface.ddpfPixelFormat.dwRGBBitCount := DXCOLORDEPTH;
SupportedMode := FALSE;
DXCheck( FDirectDraw.EnumDisplayModes(0, @DDSurface, @SupportedMode,
                                      EnumModesCallback) );

{if the desired graphics mode is not supported by the DirectX drivers,
 display an error message and shut down the application}
if not SupportedMode then
begin
  MessageBox(Handle, PChar('The installed DirectX drivers do not support a '+
                      'display mode of: '+IntToStr(DXWIDTH)+' X '+
                      IntToStr(DXHEIGHT)+', '+IntToStr(DXCOLORDEPTH)+
                      ' bit color'), 'Unsupported Display Mode Error',
                      MB_ICONERROR or MB_OK);

  Close;
  Exit;
end;

{set the display resolution and color depth to that defined in the constants}
DXCheck( FDirectDraw.SetDisplayMode(DXWIDTH, DXHEIGHT, DXCOLORDEPTH, 0, 0) );

{initialize the DDSurface structure to indicate that we will be creating a
 complex flipping surface with one back buffer}
FillChar(DDSurface, SizeOf(TDDSurfaceDesc2), 0);
DDSurface.dwSize  := SizeOf(TDDSurfaceDesc2);
DDSurface.dwFlags := DDSD_CAPS or DDSD_BACKBUFFERCOUNT;
DDSurface.ddsCaps.dwCaps := SURFACETYPE;
DDSurface.dwBackBufferCount := BUFFERCOUNT;

{create the primary surface object}
DXCheck( FDirectDraw.CreateSurface(DDSurface, FPrimarySurface, nil) );

{indicate that we want to retrieve a pointer to the back buffer (the surface
 immediately behind the primary surface in the flipping chain) }
FillChar(DDSCaps, SizeOf(TDDSCaps2), 0);
DDSCaps.dwCaps := DDSCAPS_BACKBUFFER;

{retrieve the surface}
DXCheck( FPrimarySurface.GetAttachedSurface(DDSCaps, FBackBuffer) );

{at this point, offscreen buffers and other surfaces should be created. other
 DirectDraw objects should be created and initialized as well, such as
 palettes. the contents of all surfaces should also be initialized at this
 point}

{load the palette for the game's images}
FPalette := DDLoadPalette(FDirectDraw, ExtractFilePath(ParamStr(0))+
                          'Images.bmp');

{attach this palette to the primary surface}
```

```
FPrimarySurface.SetPalette(FPalette);

{load the actual graphics used in the game}
FGraphics := DDLoadBitmap(FDirectDraw, ExtractFilePath(ParamStr(0))+
                          'Images.bmp');

{initialize the surface description structure to create the mouse
 cursor surface}
FillChar(DDSurface, SizeOf(TDDSurfaceDesc2), 0);
DDSurface.dwSize   := SizeOf(TDDSurfaceDesc2);
DDSurface.dwFlags  := DDSD_CAPS or DDSD_HEIGHT or DDSD_WIDTH;
DDSurface.dwWidth  := 224;
DDSurface.dwHeight := 32;
DDSurface.ddsCaps.dwCaps := DDSCAPS_OFFSCREENPLAIN;

{create the mouse cursor surface}
DXCheck( FDirectDraw.CreateSurface(DDSurface, FMouseCursors, nil) );

{copy the mouse cursor graphics into the mouse cursor surface}
SrcRect := Rect(256, 520, 256+(6*32)+32, 552);
FMouseCursors.BltFast(0, 0, FGraphics, SrcRect, DDBLTFAST_NOCOLORKEY or
                      DDBLTFAST_WAIT);

{set the transparent color in both the mouse cursor graphics as well as
 the game graphics}
DDSetColorKey(FMouseCursors, $00000000);
DDSetColorKey(FGraphics, $00000000);

{now that all of DirectDraw is initialized, begin initializing DirectInput}

{create our mouse click list object}
MouseClickList := TList.Create;

{create the DirectInput object}
DXCheck(DirectInputCreate(hInstance, DIRECTINPUT_VERSION, FDirectInput,nil));

{create a DirectInput device for the mouse}
DXCheck( FDirectInput.CreateDevice(GUID_SysMouse, FMouseDevice, nil) );

{set the appropriate data format for mouse data}
DXCheck( FMouseDevice.SetDataFormat(c_dfDIMouse) );

{set the cooperative level. note that we must set a nonexclusive cooperative
 level for mice as the mouse must be shared with other Windows applications}
DXCheck( FMouseDevice.SetCooperativeLevel(Handle,DISCL_FOREGROUND or
                                          DISCL_NONEXCLUSIVE) );

{initialize the structure to instruct DirectInput that we want an input
 buffer big enough to hold 64 pieces of input information}
MouseProp.diph.dwSize := SizeOf(TDIPropDWord);
MouseProp.diph.dwHeaderSize := SizeOf(TDIPropHeader);
```

```
MouseProp.diph.dwObj := 0;
MouseProp.diph.dwHow := DIPH_DEVICE;
MouseProp.dwData := 64;

{set the actual buffer size property}
DXCheck( FMouseDevice.SetProperty(DIPROP_BUFFERSIZE^, MouseProp.diph) );

{create our events, one for indicating new mouse input data, one for
 indicating that the application is terminating}
FMouseEvents[MOUSEEVENT] := CreateEvent(nil, FALSE, FALSE, 'MouseEvent');
FMouseEvents[QUITEVENT] := CreateEvent(nil, FALSE, FALSE, 'QuitEvent');

{create our critical section synchronization object}
FCritSec := TCriticalSection.Create;

{set the event notification}
DXCheck( FMouseDevice.SetEventNotification(FMouseEvents[MOUSEEVENT]) );

{create our secondary input thread}
FMouseThread := TMouseThread.Create(TRUE);

{we want it to be supremely responsive}
FMouseThread.Priority := tpTimeCritical;

{indicate it should free itself when it terminates}
FMouseThread.FreeOnTerminate := TRUE;

{post a message that will hook up the OnIdle event and start the
 main rendering loop}
PostMessage(Handle, WM_ACTIVATEAPP, 1, 0);

{now, initialize game management objects}

{create the ball manager}
FBallMgr := TBallMgr.Create;

{create and initialize the paddle}
FPaddle := TPaddle.Create;
FPaddle.YPos := 420;

{create and initialize the block manager}
FBlockMgr := TBlockMgr.Create;
FBlockMgr.InitializeBlocks;

{open the MIDI output device, loading the Canyon MIDI song}
OpenParms.lpstrDeviceType  := 'sequencer';
OpenParms.lpstrElementName := PChar(ExtractFilePath(ParamStr(0))+
                                    'custom16.mid');
MCISendCommand(0, MCI_OPEN, MCI_OPEN_TYPE or MCI_OPEN_ELEMENT or MCI_WAIT,
            LongInt(@OpenParms));
{save a handle to the device}
```

```
  MCIDeviceID := OpenParms.wDeviceID;

  {set the time format to milliseconds}
  SetParms.dwTimeFormat := MCI_FORMAT_MILLISECONDS;
  MCISendCommand(MCIDeviceID, MCI_SET, MCI_WAIT or MCI_SET_TIME_FORMAT,
                 LongInt(@SetParms));

  {commence song playback, indicating that we wish to receive an MM_MCINOTIFY
   message when the playback has completed}
  PlayParms.dwCallback := Handle;
  MCISendCommand(MCIDeviceID, MCI_PLAY, MCI_NOTIFY, LongInt(@PlayParms));

  {create the DirectSound object}
  DirectSoundCreate(nil, DXSound, nil);

  {set its cooperative level (we won't change the primary buffer format, so
   a cooperative level of Normal is all that is needed)}
  DXSound.SetCooperativeLevel(Handle, DSSCL_NORMAL);

  {load in the sounds}
  for iCount := BLOCKHIT to PADDLEHIT do
    Sounds[iCount] := DSLoadSound(DXSound, ExtractFilePath(ParamStr(0))+
                                  FileNames[iCount], FALSE);

  {finally, acquire the mouse and fire off the mouse input thread}
  FMouseDevice.Acquire;
  FMouseThread.Resume;
end;


{ -> Form Methods <- }

{ - the message handler for the MM_MCINOTIFY message - }
procedure TfrmDXAppMain.MCINotify(var Msg: TMessage);
var
  PlayParms: TMCI_Play_Parms;
begin
  {replay the song from the beginning}
  PlayParms.dwCallback := Handle;
  PlayParms.dwFrom     := 0;
  MCISendCommand(MCIDeviceID, MCI_PLAY, MCI_NOTIFY or MCI_FROM,
                 LongInt(@PlayParms));
end;

{ - this method is called in order to flip the surfaces - }
procedure TfrmDXAppMain.FlipSurfaces;
var
  DXResult: HResult;
begin
  {perform the page flip. note that the DDFLIP_WAIT flag has been used,
```

```
      indicating that the function will not return until the page flip has been
      performed. this could be removed, allowing the application to perform other
      processing until the page flip occurs. however, the application will need
      to continuously call the Flip method to ensure that the page flip takes
      place}
      DXResult := FPrimarySurface.Flip(nil, DDFLIP_WAIT);

      {pause until the flip has been performed}
      while FPrimarySurface.GetFlipStatus(DDGFS_ISFLIPDONE) <> DD_OK do;

      {if the surfaces were lost, restore them. on any other error,
       raise an exception}
      if DXResult = DDERR_SURFACELOST then
        RestoreSurfaces
      else if DXResult <> DD_OK then
        DXCheck(DXResult);
    end;

{ - this method is called when the surface memory is lost   -
  - and must be restored.  surfaces in video memory that    -
  - contain bitmaps must be reinitialized in this function - }
procedure TfrmDXAppMain.RestoreSurfaces;
var
  SrcRect: TRect;
begin
  {restore the primary surface, which in turn restores any implicit surfaces}
  FPrimarySurface._Restore;

  {reload the game images}
  DDReloadBitmap(FGraphics, ExtractFilePath(ParamStr(0))+'Images.bmp');

  {restore the mouse cursor surface}
  FMouseCursors._Restore;

  {copy the mouse cursor graphics into the mouse cursor surface}
  SrcRect := Rect(256, 520, 256+(6*32)+32, 552);
  FMouseCursors.BltFast(0, 0, FGraphics, SrcRect, DDBLTFAST_NOCOLORKEY or
                        DDBLTFAST_WAIT);
end;

{ - this method is continuously called by the application, and provides -
  - the main rendering loop.  this could be replaced by a custom        -
  - while..do loop                                                    - }
procedure TfrmDXAppMain.AppIdle(Sender: TObject; var Done: Boolean);
begin
  {indicates that the application should continuously call this method}
  Done := FALSE;

  {if DirectDraw has not been initialized, exit}
  if not Assigned(FDirectDraw) then Exit;
```

```
  {draw surface content and flip the surfaces. notice that we must use a
   critical section here, as we may need to access the mouse cursor coordinate
   variables, and we can't do that if the mouse input thread is accessing
   them at the same time}
  FCritSec.Enter;
  DrawSurfaces;
  FlipSurfaces;
  FCritSec.Leave;
end;


{ - this method is called when the contents of the surfaces need to be  -
  - drawn. it will be continuously called by the AppIdle method, so any  -
  - rendering or animation could be done within this method          - }
procedure TfrmDXAppMain.DrawSurfaces;
var
  SrcRect: TRect;
  SrfcDC: HDC;
  WorkCanvas: TCanvas;
  MouseData: TMouseData;

  iCount: Integer;
begin
  {copy the background into the back buffer, erasing the last
   frame of animation}
  SrcRect := Rect(0, 0, DXWIDTH, DXHEIGHT);
  FBackBuffer.BltFast(0, 0, FGraphics, SrcRect, DDBLTFAST_NOCOLORKEY or
                      DDBLTFAST_WAIT);

  {draw all of the blocks that are still alive}
  FBlockMgr.Draw;

  {based on the game state...}
  case FGameState of
    gsIdle : begin
              {if we are idle, we want to show our animated mouse cursor}
              ShowMouse := TRUE;

              {draw the Start and Quit buttons}
              SrcRect := Rect(0, 520, 128, 584);
              FBackBuffer.BltFast(96, 350, FGraphics, SrcRect,
                            DDBLTFAST_NOCOLORKEY or DDBLTFAST_WAIT);
              SrcRect := Rect(128, 520, 256, 584);
              FBackBuffer.BltFast(416, 350, FGraphics, SrcRect,
                            DDBLTFAST_NOCOLORKEY or DDBLTFAST_WAIT);

              {draw the game title}
              WorkCanvas := TCanvas.Create;
              FBackBuffer.GetDC(SrfcDC);
              with WorkCanvas do
              begin
                {set up the canvas to use the surface}
```

```
      Handle := SrfcDC;

      {initialize the canvas font attributes}
      Font.Name  := 'Arial';
      Font.Color := clRed;
      Font.Style := [fsBold];
      Font.Size  := 64;
      Brush.Style := bsClear;

      {draw the actual title}
      TextOut(320-(TextWidth('Delphi Blocks!') div 2), 125,
              'Delphi Blocks!');

      {unhook the canvas from the surface}
      Handle := 0;
    end;

    {release the surface device context}
    FBackBuffer.ReleaseDC(SrfcDC);

    {free the canvas}
    WorkCanvas.Free;

    {determine if the mouse was clicked in one of the buttons}
    if MouseClickList.Count>0 then
    begin
     {while there are any events in the mouse click list, retrieve
      them all and empty the list}
      while MouseClickList.Count > 0 do
      begin
        {free the current mouse data}
        if MouseData <> nil then
        begin
          MouseData.Free;
          MouseData := nil;
        end;

        {retrieve and delete the click event}
        MouseData := TMouseData(MouseClickList[0]);
        MouseClickList.Delete(0);
      end;

    {if the quit button was pushed...}
    if PtInRect(Rect(416, 350, 544, 414),
      Point(MouseData.XPos, MouseData.YPos)) then
      Close;
    {if the start button was pushed...}
    if PtInRect(Rect(96, 350, 224, 414),
      Point(MouseData.XPos, MouseData.YPos)) then
      StartGame;
```

```pascal
                        {free the current mouse data object}
                        MouseData.Free;
                        MouseData := nil;
                    end;
                end;
    gsPlaying : begin
                    {move and draw all of the active balls}
                    FBallMgr.MoveBalls;
                    FBallMgr.DrawBalls;

                    {display a ball for each one the player has left}
                    SrcRect := Rect(252, 507, 261, 516);
                    for iCount := 0 to FBallMgr.TotalBalls-1 do
                        FBackBuffer.BltFast(10+iCount*16, 440, FGraphics, SrcRect,
                                        DDBLTFAST_SRCCOLORKEY or
                                        DDBLTFAST_WAIT);


                    {create a canvas and retrieve a surface device context}
                    WorkCanvas := TCanvas.Create;
                    FBackBuffer.GetDC(SrfcDC);
                    with WorkCanvas do
                    begin
                        {hook the canvas up to the surface}
                        Handle := SrfcDC;

                        {initialize the surface font attributes}
                        Font.Name  := 'Arial';
                        Font.Color := clRed;
                        Font.Style := [fsBold];
                        Font.Size  := 12;
                        Brush.Style := bsClear;

                        {draw the number of balls remaining}
                        TextOut(10, 450, 'Score: '+IntToStr(FScore));

                        {unhook the canvas from the surface}
                        Handle := 0;
                    end;

                    {release the surface device context}
                    FBackBuffer.ReleaseDC(SrfcDC);

                    {free the canvas}
                    WorkCanvas.Free;

                    {if there are no more blocks alive...}
                    if FBlockMgr.NumBlocks < 1 then
                    begin
                        {increment the current level}
                        Inc(FLevel);
```

```
                          {initialize a new level}
                          InitLevel;

                          {and go to intermission}
                          FGameState := gsIntermission;
                       end;
                    end;
        gsIntermission : begin
                              {we are starting to play, so hide the animated
                               mouse cursor}
                              ShowMouse := FALSE;

                              {create a canvas and retrieve a surface device context}
                              WorkCanvas := TCanvas.Create;
                              FBackBuffer.GetDC(SrfcDC);
                              with WorkCanvas do
                              begin
                                {hook the canvas up to the surface}
                                Handle := SrfcDC;

                                {initialize the canvas font attributes}
                                Font.Name  := 'Arial';
                                Font.Color := clRed;
                                Font.Style := [fsBold];
                                Font.Size  := 64;
                                Brush.Style := bsClear;

                                {draw the level}
                                TextOut(320-(TextWidth('Level '+IntToStr(FLevel))
                                        div 2), 125, 'Level '+IntToStr(FLevel));

                                {unhook the canvas from the surface}
                                Handle := 0;
                              end;

                              {release the surface device context}
                              FBackBuffer.ReleaseDC(SrfcDC);

                              {release the canvas}
                              WorkCanvas.Free;

                              {flip the surfaces so that this new graphic
                               is displayed}
                              FlipSurfaces;

                              {pause for 2 seconds}
                              Sleep(2000);

                              {switch back to playing the game}
                              FGameState := gsPlaying;
```

```
                                 {add an active ball}
                                 FBallMgr.AddBall(DXWIDTH div 2, 300, -1, 1, FUseBall);
                        end;
      gsGameOver : begin
                        {hide the animated mouse cursor}
                        ShowMouse := FALSE;

                        {create a canvas and retrieve a surface device context}
                        WorkCanvas := TCanvas.Create;
                        FBackBuffer.GetDC(SrfcDC);
                        with WorkCanvas do
                        begin
                          {hook the canvas up to the surface}
                          Handle := SrfcDC;

                          {initialize the canvas font attributes}
                          Font.Name  := 'Arial';
                          Font.Color := clRed;
                          Font.Style := [fsBold];
                          Font.Size  := 56;
                          Brush.Style := bsClear;

                          {draw the Game Over text}
                          TextOut(320-(TextWidth('G A M E   O V E R') div 2),
                                  125, 'G A M E   O V E R');

                          {unhook the canvas from the surface}
                          Handle := 0;
                        end;

                        {release the surface device context}
                        FBackBuffer.ReleaseDC(SrfcDC);

                        {release the canvas}
                        WorkCanvas.Free;

                        {flip the surfaces to display the new graphic}
                        FlipSurfaces;

                        {pause for 2 seconds}
                        Sleep(2000);

                        {and go to idle}
                        FGameState := gsIdle;
                      end;
end;

{if we wish to display the mouse cursor...}
if ShowMouse then
```

```
  begin
    {increment the frame count}
    Inc(FCursorFrameCount);

    {when we need to increment the frame number...}
    if FCursorFrameCount mod 7 = 0 then
    begin
      {increment the current mouse cursor frame}
      Inc(FCursorFrame);

      {roll it over if necessary}
      if FCursorFrame > 6 then
        FCursorFrame := 0;
    end;


    {draw cursor to back buffer}
    SrcRect := Rect(FCursorFrame*CURSORWIDTH, 0,
                    (FCursorFrame*CURSORWIDTH)+CURSORWIDTH, CURSORHEIGHT);
    FBackBuffer.BltFast(CurX, CurY, FMouseCursors, SrcRect,
                        DDBLTFAST_SRCCOLORKEY OR DDBLTFAST_WAIT);
  end
  else
  begin
    {move the paddle and draw it to the back buffer}
    FPaddle.Move;
    FPaddle.Draw;
  end;
end;



{ -> Deletable Events <- }

///
{ - as a matter of convenience this framework will terminate when the -
  - Escape key is pressed, but this should probably be deleted and    -
  - replaced with your own terminate methods                        - }
procedure TfrmDXAppMain.FormKeyDown(Sender: TObject; var Key: Word;
  Shift: TShiftState);
begin
  if Key = VK_ESCAPE then
    Close;
end;
///


{ *-->>  END BASELINE APPLICATION CODE <<--* }

{initializes a level}
procedure TfrmDXAppMain.InitLevel;
begin
```

```
    {reinitialize all of the blocks}
    FBlockMgr.InitializeBlocks;
    {clear any active balls}
    FBallMgr.Clear;

    {set the ball manager's velocity coefficient based on the current level.
     this makes the balls move faster at higher levels}
    FBallMgr.VelCoefficient := FLevel div 2;
    if FBallMgr.VelCoefficient < 2 then
      FBallMgr.VelCoefficient := 2;

    {we'll be creating a new ball, but since we're at the start of a level,
     we don't want to decrement the available ball count}
    FUseBall := FALSE;
end;

{starts a game}
procedure TfrmDXAppMain.StartGame;
begin
    {initialize the level count}
    FLevel := 1;

    {initialize the score}
    FScore := 0;

    {initialize the level}
    InitLevel;

    {give the user 3 balls}
    FBallMgr.TotalBalls := 3;

    {upon starting a game, we want to decrement the overall ball count when
     we create a new one}
    FUseBall := TRUE;

    {go to intermission}
    FGameState := gsIntermission;
end;

{plays a sound}
procedure PlayGameSound(SoundNum: Integer);
begin
    {set the position of the sound to the start}
    Sounds[SoundNum].SetCurrentPosition(0);

    {commence sound playback}
    Sounds[SoundNum].Play(0, 0, 0);
end;
```

```
{ TBall }

procedure TBall.Draw;
var
  SrcRect: TRect;
begin
  {draw the ball to the back buffer}
  SrcRect := Rect(252, 507, 261, 516);
  FBackBuffer.BltFast(Trunc(XPos), Trunc(YPos), FGraphics, SrcRect,
                      DDBLTFAST_SRCCOLORKEY OR DDBLTFAST_WAIT);
end;

procedure TBall.Move;
var
  ISectRect: TRect;

  iRow, iCol: Integer;

  BlockCollision: boolean;

  DeflectAngle: Real;

  {assumes p1-p2, p3-p4 are the lines; returns true if the lines intersect}
  function CheckLineIntersect(P1, P2, P3, P4: TPoint): boolean;
  var
    A, B, C: TPoint;
    Denom: integer;
    Alpha, Beta: double;
  begin
    {assume the line segments do not intersect}
    Result := FALSE;

    {this uses an algorithm found in Graphics Gems III (ISBN 0-12-409673-5) by
     David Kirk (Academic Press) on page 199. the algorithm is by Franklin
     Antonio. basically, it is a quick way to determine if two line segments
     intersect}
    A := Point(P2.X-P1.X, P2.Y-P1.Y);
    B := Point(P3.X-P4.X, P3.Y-P4.Y);
    C := Point(P1.X-P3.X, P1.Y-P3.Y);
    Denom := (A.Y*B.X)-(A.X*B.Y);

    {must check to see if denom is 0 here}
    if Denom <> 0 then
    begin
      {determine the alpha and beta values}
      Alpha := ((B.Y*C.X)-(B.X*C.Y))/Denom;
      Beta := ((A.X*C.Y)-(A.Y*C.X))/Denom;

      {if both alpha and beta are in the range 0<=X<=1, then the lines
       intersect}
      if ((Alpha>=0) and (Alpha<=1)) and ((Beta>=0) and (Beta <= 1)) then
```

```
          Result := TRUE;
      end;
    end;
begin
  {if the game state is in game over, exit immediately}
  if frmDXAppMain.FGameState = gsGameOver then
    Exit;

  {record the previous position of the ball}
  XPrev := XPos;
  YPrev := YPos;

  {update the ball's position according to its velocity}
  XPos := XPos + XVel;
  YPos := YPos + YVel;

  {determine collision with sides}

  {left}
  if XPos < 5 then
  begin
    XPos := 5;
    XVel := 0 - XVel;

    {indicate we hit the side}
    PlayGameSound(SIDEHIT);
  end;

  {right}
  if XPos > DXWIDTH - 5 - 9 then
  begin
    XPos := DXWIDTH - 5 - 9;
    XVel := 0 - XVel;

    {indicate we hit the side}
    PlayGameSound(SIDEHIT);
  end;

  {top}
  if YPos < 5 then
  begin
    YPos := 5;
    YVel := 0 - YVel;

    {indicate we hit the side}
    PlayGameSound(SIDEHIT);
  end;

  {a collision with the bottom indicates that the ball has died}
  if YPos > DXHEIGHT - 5 - 9 then
```

```
begin
  {delete this ball from the managers list}
  Manager.BallList.Delete(Index);

  {play the lost ball sound}
  PlayGameSound(LOSTBALL);

  {if there are no more active balls...}
  if Manager.ActiveBalls < 1 then
    {...but there are balls left...}
    if Manager.TotalBalls > 0 then
    begin
      {indicate we will decrement the available balls when we create
       a new one}
      frmDXAppMain.FUseBall := TRUE;

      {go to intermission}
      frmDXAppMain.FGameState := gsIntermission;
    end
    else
      {...otherwise, the game is over}
      frmDXAppMain.FGameState := gsGameOver;

  {free this ball}
  Free;

  {the ball has died, so exit}
  Exit;
end;

{keep up with the bounding box}
BoundBox := Rect(Trunc(XPos), Trunc(YPos), Trunc(XPos+9), Trunc(YPos+9));

{check for collision with paddle}
if IntersectRect(ISectRect, BoundBox, frmDXAppMain.FPaddle.BoundBox) then
begin
  {the deflection angle is based on the point where the ball hits the paddle.
   the ball will deflect at a greater angle near the edges, but it will
   deflect almost straight up at the center. this gives the user the
   ability to control the direction of the ball. the deflection angle
   increases from 0 at the very tip to 90 degrees at the center}
  DeflectAngle := (180/92)*(ISectRect.Left-
                            frmDXAppMain.FPaddle.BoundBox.Left);
  if DeflectAngle > 90 then
    DeflectAngle := 180 - DeflectAngle;

  {reverse the vertical velocity}
  YVel := 0 - Sin(DegToRad(DeflectAngle))*Manager.VelCoefficient;

  {initialize the horizontal velocity based on the deflection angle and
   its current direction}
```

```
      if XVel >=0 then
        XVel := Cos(DegToRad(DeflectAngle))*Manager.VelCoefficient
      else
        XVel := 0 - Cos(DegToRad(DeflectAngle))*Manager.VelCoefficient;
      {indicate that we hit the paddle}
      PlayGameSound(PADDLEHIT);
    end;

    {now, check for collisions with blocks}
    for iRow := 0 to 9 do
      for iCol := 0 to 14 do
        {if there is an active block at this position...}
        if (frmDXAppMain.FBlockMgr.BlockGrid[iCol, iRow] <> nil) then
          {perform a quick bounding box collision test}
          if IntersectRect(ISectRect, BoundBox,
                         frmDXAppMain.FBlockMgr.BlockGrid[iCol, iRow].BoundBox)
                           then
          begin
            {the bounding boxes have collided. now, since we want to support
             balls that move at any velocity, we must check the line segment
             formed by the ball's current and previous location with each line
             segment of the current block. since a ball can strike a block from
             any direction, we must determine which side of the block was struck
             in order to determine which velocity value is to be reversed}

            BlockCollision := FALSE;

            {check bottom lines}
            if CheckLineIntersect(Point(frmDXAppMain.FBlockMgr.BlockGrid[iCol,
                                   iRow].BoundBox.Left, frmDXAppMain.FBlockMgr.
                                   BlockGrid[iCol, iRow].BoundBox.Bottom),
                                   Point(frmDXAppMain.FBlockMgr.BlockGrid[iCol,
                                   iRow].BoundBox.Right, frmDXAppMain.FBlockMgr.
                                   BlockGrid[iCol, iRow].BoundBox.Bottom),
                                   Point(Trunc(XPrev+5), Trunc(YPrev+5)),
                                   Point(Trunc(XPos+5), Trunc(YPos+5))) then
            begin
              {the bottom of the block was struck, so reverse the vertical
               velocity and signal a collision}
              YVel := 0 - YVel;
              BlockCollision := TRUE;
            end
            else

            {check top lines}
            if CheckLineIntersect(Point(frmDXAppMain.FBlockMgr.BlockGrid[iCol,
                                   iRow].BoundBox.Left, frmDXAppMain.FBlockMgr.
                                   BlockGrid[iCol, iRow].BoundBox.Top),
                                   Point(frmDXAppMain.FBlockMgr.BlockGrid[iCol,
                                   iRow].BoundBox.Right, frmDXAppMain.FBlockMgr.
                                   BlockGrid[iCol, iRow].BoundBox.Top),
```

```
                          Point(Trunc(XPrev+5), Trunc(YPrev+5)),
                          Point(Trunc(XPos+5), Trunc(YPos+5))) then
begin
  {the top of the block was struck, so reverse the vertical
   velocity and signal a collision}
  YVel := 0 - YVel;
  BlockCollision := TRUE;
end
else

{check right lines}
if CheckLineIntersect(Point(frmDXAppMain.FBlockMgr.BlockGrid[iCol,
                      iRow].BoundBox.Right, frmDXAppMain.FBlockMgr.
                      BlockGrid[iCol, iRow].BoundBox.Bottom),
                      Point(frmDXAppMain.FBlockMgr.BlockGrid[iCol,
                      iRow].BoundBox.Right, frmDXAppMain.FBlockMgr.
                      BlockGrid[iCol, iRow].BoundBox.Top),
                      Point(Trunc(XPrev+5), Trunc(YPrev+5)),
                      Point(Trunc(XPos+5), Trunc(YPos+5))) then
begin
  {the right side of the block was struck, so reverse the horizontal
   velocity and signal a collision}
  XVel := 0 - XVel;
  BlockCollision := TRUE;
end
else

{check left lines}
if CheckLineIntersect(Point(frmDXAppMain.FBlockMgr.BlockGrid[iCol,
                      iRow].BoundBox.Left, frmDXAppMain.FBlockMgr.
                      BlockGrid[iCol, iRow].BoundBox.Bottom),
                      Point(frmDXAppMain.FBlockMgr.BlockGrid[iCol,
                      iRow].BoundBox.Left, frmDXAppMain.FBlockMgr.
                      BlockGrid[iCol, iRow].BoundBox.Top),
                      Point(Trunc(XPrev+5), Trunc(YPrev+5)),
                      Point(Trunc(XPos+5), Trunc(YPos+5))) then
begin
  {the left side of the block was struck, so reverse the horizontal
   velocity and signal a collision}
  XVel := 0 - XVel;
  BlockCollision := TRUE;
end;

{if the ball collided with a block, kill the block}
if BlockCollision then
begin
  frmDXAppMain.FBlockMgr.KillBlock(iRow, iCol);

  {indicate that we hit a block}
  PlayGameSound(BLOCKHIT);
```

```
                   {increase the score}
                   frmDXAppMain.FScore := frmDXAppMain.FScore+5*frmDXAppMain.FLevel;
               end;
           end;
end;

{ TBallMgr }

procedure TBallMgr.AddBall(XPos, YPos, XVel, YVel: Real; DecBalls: Boolean);
var
  TempBall: TBall;
begin
  {if we are to decrement the total ball count, then do so}
  if DecBalls then
    Dec(FTotalBalls);

  {create a ball sprite}
  TempBall := TBall.Create;

  {initialize its position}
  TempBall.XPos  := XPos;
  TempBall.YPos  := YPos;
  TempBall.XPrev := XPos;
  TempBall.YPrev := YPos;

  {initialize its velocity}
  TempBall.XVel  := XVel;
  TempBall.YVel  := YVel;

  {initialize its bounding box}
  TempBall.BoundBox := Rect(Trunc(XPos), Trunc(YPos), Trunc(XPos+9),
                            Trunc(YPos+9));

  {hook it to the manager}
  TempBall.Manager := Self;

  {add the ball to the list}
  BallList.Add(TempBall);

  {set its index in the list}
  TempBall.Index := BallList.Count-1;
end;

constructor TBallMgr.Create;
begin
  {create the ball list}
  BallList := TList.Create;

  {initialize the velocity coefficient. increasing or decreasing this value
   will have a similar effect on the speed of the balls}
  VelCoefficient := 2;
```

```
end;

destructor TBallMgr.Destroy;
var
  iCount: Integer;
begin
  {destroy any balls in the list}
  for iCount := 0 to BallList.Count-1 do
    TBall(BallList[iCount]).Free;

  {free the ball list}
  BallList.Free;

  {finish the destruction}
  inherited Destroy;
end;

procedure TBallMgr.DrawBalls;
var
  iCount: Integer;
begin
  {draw each ball in the list}
  for iCount := 0 to BallList.Count-1 do
    TBall(BallList[iCount]).Draw;
end;

procedure TBallMgr.KillBall(Idx: Integer);
begin
  {if the index is not greater than the number of balls and there is a
   ball at the indicated index...}
  if (Idx < BallList.Count) and (BallList[Idx] <> nil) then
  begin
    {free and delete this ball}
    TBall(BallList[Idx]).Free;
    BallList.Delete(Idx);
  end;
end;

procedure TBallMgr.MoveBalls;
var
  iCount: Integer;
begin
  {move all of the balls in the list}
  for iCount := 0 to BallList.Count-1 do
    TBall(BallList[iCount]).Move;
end;

procedure TBallMgr.Clear;
var
  iCount: Integer;
begin
```

```
      {clear all of the balls}
      for iCount := 0 to BallList.Count-1 do
        KillBall(0);

      BallList.Clear;
    end;


    function TBallMgr.GetActiveBalls: Integer;
    begin
      {return the number of balls in the list}
      Result := BallList.Count;
    end;

    { TPaddle }

    procedure TPaddle.Draw;
    var
      SrcRect: TRect;
    begin
      {draw the paddle graphic to the back buffer}
      SrcRect := Rect(252, 500, 339, 506);
      FBackBuffer.BltFast(XPos, YPos, FGraphics, SrcRect,
                          DDBLTFAST_NOCOLORKEY OR DDBLTFAST_WAIT);
    end;

    procedure TPaddle.Move;
    begin
      {to move the paddle, we really just need to set its horizontal position
       based on that of the mouse}
      XPos := CurX;

      {update its bounding box}
      BoundBox := Rect(Trunc(XPos), Trunc(YPos), Trunc(XPos+92), Trunc(YPos+15));
    end;

    { TBlock }

    procedure TBlock.Draw;
    var
      SrcRect: TRect;
    begin
      {draw the indicated block graphic to the screen}
      SrcRect := Rect((GraphicIdx mod 15)*42, (GraphicIdx div 15)*20+480,
                      (GraphicIdx mod 15)*42+42, (GraphicIdx div 15)*20+20+480);
      FBackBuffer.BltFast(BoundBox.Left, BoundBox.Top, FGraphics, SrcRect,
                          DDBLTFAST_NOCOLORKEY or DDBLTFAST_WAIT);
    end;

    { TBlockMgr }
```

```
destructor TBlockMgr.Destroy;
var
  iCol, iRow: Integer;
begin
  {destroy all of the blocks}
  for iRow := 0 to 9 do
    for iCol := 0 to 14 do
      if BlockGrid[iCol, iRow] <> nil then
        BlockGrid[iCol, iRow].Free;

  {finish the destruction}
  inherited Destroy;
end;

procedure TBlockMgr.Draw;
var
  iCol, iRow: Integer;
begin
  {draw all of the blocks}
  for iRow := 0 to 9 do
    for iCol := 0 to 14 do
      if BlockGrid[iCol, iRow] <> nil then
        BlockGrid[iCol, iRow].Draw;
end;

procedure TBlockMgr.InitializeBlocks;
var
  iCol, iRow: Integer;
begin
  {seed the random number generator}
  Randomize;

  {create a block for each position in the block grid}
  for iRow := 0 to 9 do
    for iCol := 0 to 14 do
    begin
      {create the actual block}
      BlockGrid[iCol, iRow] := TBlock.Create;

      {randomly set it to one of 20 block graphics}
      BlockGrid[iCol, iRow].GraphicIdx := Random(20);

      {initialize its bounding box}
      BlockGrid[iCol, iRow].BoundBox := Rect(iCol*42+5, iRow*20+75,
                                        (iCol*42+5)+42, (iRow*20+75)+20);
    end;

  {initialize the number of blocks}
  NumBlocks := 150;
end;
```

```
procedure TBlockMgr.KillBlock(Row, Col: Integer);
begin
  {free the specified block}
  BlockGrid[Col, Row].Free;
  BlockGrid[Col, Row] := nil;

  {decrement the number of blocks}
  NumBlocks := NumBlocks - 1;
end;


end.
```

*Listing 13-2:* *The Delphi Blocks mouse thread unit*

```
unit MouseThreadU;

interface

uses
  Classes, Controls, Windows, SyncObjs;

type
  TMouseThread = class(TThread)
  private
    { Private declarations }
  protected
    procedure Execute; override;
  end;

  {this will hold mouse data for click events}
  TMouseData = class
  public
    XPos, YPos: Integer;
    Button: TMouseButton;

    constructor Create(X, Y: Integer; MButton: TMouseButton);
  end;

var
  CurX, CurY: Integer;
  MouseClickList: TList;
  FCritSec: TCriticalSection;
  FMouseEvents: TWOHandleArray;
  ShowMouse: Boolean;

const
  CURSORWIDTH = 32;      // we have a 32 X 32 pixel cursor
  CURSORHEIGHT = 32;
```

```
  NUMFRAMES = 8;          // with 8 frames of animation

implementation

uses DInput, DelphiBlocksU, DDraw;

{this creates and initializes one mouse data object for recording
 click events}
constructor TMouseData.Create(X, Y: Integer; MButton: TMouseButton);
begin
  XPos := X;
  YPos := Y;
  Button := MButton;
end;


{ TMouseThread }

procedure TMouseThread.Execute;
var
  EventNum: Integer;
  BufferEmpty: Boolean;
  NumElements: DWORD;
  DeviceData: TDIDeviceObjectData;
  DataResult: HRESULT;
begin
  {while the thread has not terminated...}
  while not Terminated do
  begin
    {pause this thread until either a mouse event or a quit event has fired}
    EventNum := WaitForMultipleObjects(2, @FMouseEvents, FALSE, INFINITE);

    {if the quit event fired...}
    if EventNum-WAIT_OBJECT_0 = QUITEVENT then
    begin
      {terminate the thread and exit}
      Terminate;
      Break;
    end;

    {enter the critical section. this prevents the main thread from accessing
     variables used within this block of code until the critical section
     is exited}
    FCritSec.Enter;

    {until the input buffer has been emptied...}
    BufferEmpty := FALSE;
    while not BufferEmpty do
    begin
      {indicate that we wish to retrieve only one element}
      NumElements := 1;
```

```
{retrieve one input data element}
DataResult := FMouseDevice.GetDeviceData(SizeOf(TDIDeviceObjectData),
                                        @DeviceData, NumElements, 0);


{if we did in fact retrieve data...}
if (DataResult = DI_OK) and (NumElements = 1) then
begin
  {determine what the data is}
  case DeviceData.dwOfs of
    {for horizontal or vertical mouse movements, record the new data}
    DIMOFS_X        : CurX := CurX + DeviceData.dwData;
    DIMOFS_Y        : CurY := CurY + DeviceData.dwData;

    {for all button presses (that is, a mouse button down only, as
     opposed to a mouse button up), add a click event to the list
     (mapping all mouse buttons to a mouse button left click event)}
    DIMOFS_BUTTON0,
    DIMOFS_BUTTON1,
    DIMOFS_BUTTON2,
    DIMOFS_BUTTON3  : if (DeviceData.dwData and $80) = $80 then
                        MouseClickList.Add(TMouseData.Create(CurX, CurY,
                                          mbLeft));
  end;
end
else
  {otherwise, if nothing was retrieved, we've emptied the buffer}
  BufferEmpty := TRUE;
end;

{if the mouse cursor is to be shown...}
if ShowMouse then
begin
  {clip the mouse cursor to the screen}
  if CurX < 0 then
    CurX := 0;
  if CurX > DXWIDTH-CURSORWIDTH then
    CurX := DXWIDTH-CURSORWIDTH-1;
  if CurY < 0 then
    CurY := 0;
  if CurY > DXHEIGHT-CURSORHEIGHT then
    CurY := DXHEIGHT-CURSORHEIGHT-1;
end
else
begin
  {...otherwise, we're only showing the paddle, so we only need to
   check the horizontal position of the mouse cursor}
  if CurX < 5 then
    CurX := 5;
  if CurX > DXWIDTH - 92 then
    CurX := DXWIDTH - 92;
```

```
    end;

    {finally, we must leave the critical section so that the main thread
     can have access to the mouse cursor location variables}
    FCritSec.Leave;
  end;
end;

initialization
  {initially, we want to show the mouse cursor}
  ShowMouse := TRUE;

end.
```

## Summary

In this chapter, we discussed how graphics, user input, and sound and music programming techniques come together to create a complete game application. We examined how each part of a game is implemented, including techniques for tracking several sprites as well as using DirectSound and Windows multimedia functions simultaneously. We also looked at various ways to enhance and improve the Delphi Blocks game. When using these techniques to create your own games, it is important to keep these points in mind:

■ The state-driven architecture is useful for many styles of games and is easy to implement. More complex games may require an equally more complex architecture, but the concepts are similar.

■ Always implement the most natural form of user input for the type of game being developed. For Delphi Blocks, this was the mouse, but for other games, it might be the joystick or keyboard. While not absolutely necessary, it is good programming practice to give the user a choice of input devices.

■ Sound and music always enhance a game. Sound for Delphi Blocks was implemented using DirectSound in order to allow for easier modification. However, music was implemented using Windows multimedia functions in order to show how the two can coexist gracefully. This should demonstrate how you can use whatever method is appropriate for your gaming application.

■ The simple 2-D graphics in this game use straightforward techniques for implementing the game animation. These techniques are acceptably fast, but could be optimized. However, bear in mind that optimization has a diminishing margin of returns, so only optimize those parts that truly need it.

■ While not a commercial quality game, this case study could easily be extended and molded into one within a few weeks. Remember, Delphi can do anything that C can do; you just have to have the knowledge and patience.

# APPENDIX: *Installing DirectX*

## THIS APPENDIX COVERS THE FOLLOWING TOPICS:

- Retrieving the version number of the currently installed DirectX
- Installing DirectX components, either in full or in part
- Overriding the default behavior of installation to provide custom status messages and feedback

Before a game written using the DirectX API can be run on a user's system, that system must have DirectX installed. Fortunately, Microsoft allows game developers to redistribute the DirectX run-time components and drivers at no charge. Additionally, they've included methods that make the installation of DirectX largely automated. In keeping with their naming convention for this technology, setup of DirectX components and drivers is accomplished through the DirectSetup API.

In this appendix, we'll examine how the DirectSetup API allows us to install DirectX with a minimum of hassle. We'll also examine ways to determine the current version of DirectX already installed, as well as how to override the default behavior of the installation in order to provide our own interface.

## DirectX Redistributables

DirectX is available from a number of sources. Many computer manufacturers are shipping machines with DirectX already installed. Indeed, future versions of Windows will include DirectX automatically. The DirectX run-time components are also available both online (at Microsoft's web site) as well as part of the installation for hundreds of commercial games and applications.

> ***Tip:*** You may want to suggest that users download the latest DirectX drivers straight from the Microsoft web site as part of your standard technical support. Users can retrieve the end user DirectX files from http://www.microsoft.com/directx/homeuser/downloads/default.asp at the time of this writing. Microsoft technical support should also be able to help users if they are having trouble installing DirectX drivers.

If DirectX is already installed on a user's system, it is not necessary to install it again when the user installs your application (unless, of course, the application uses a more current version of DirectX than that currently installed). Thus, if you are certain that your end users already have DirectX installed, there is no need to worry about the techniques described here. Unfortunately, although Microsoft is taking steps to make it simple for users to upgrade their Windows installation, we cannot always assume that users have DirectX installed on their machines.

Microsoft allows developers to redistribute the run-time portion of DirectX royalty free with our applications. This distribution is subject to the terms of their end user license agreement, also known as an EULA, which accompanies the DirectX SDK. Therefore, you'll need to obtain the DirectX SDK in order to get all of the information and rights necessary for redistributing DirectX. For more information on obtaining the latest DirectX SDK and other DirectX run-time components, please visit **http://www.microsoft.com/directx/developer/downloads/default.asp**.

**EULA:** End user license agreement; a legal document that details specific licensing issues concerning software.

The redistributable files themselves are located in the Redist directory of the DirectX SDK. The license agreement for redistributing DirectX run-time components instructs us that we must not modify DirectX in any way, nor change the files that must be redistributed, with one exception. The DirectX redistributable files come in several localized flavors, and we can leave out any specific language for which we will not support. Thus, if we only want to ship the English language version of DirectX, we need only include the 'eng' directory under the DirectX\Drivers directory of the redistributable files. This may be desirable, as the size of the entire redistributable file set is over 50 MB. Please see the DirectX SDK EULA.txt file that ships with the DirectX SDK for more details concerning redistribution of DirectX with applications.

> ***Note:*** At the time of this writing, the DirectX redistributables cannot be installed under Windows NT. DirectX can only be installed on NT through NT service packs.

# DirectSetup

As mentioned previously, DirectSetup is responsible for installing DirectX components on an end user's machine. Unlike the other DirectX subsystems, the DirectSetup API is rather small. There are only a few functions included in this API, and full installation of all DirectX run-time components and drivers can be accomplished by calling one simple function. Alternatively, the default behavior of the entire installation process can be overridden and monitored. The DirectSetup API can make installation of DirectX as simple or as complicated as necessary, giving developers plenty of flexibility in their installation programs.

## Features

DirectSetup provides several techniques by which an application can have a varying degree of control over the installation of DirectX. The following features are of interest to any developer implementing DirectX installation functionality:

- Quick, painless installation of the entire DirectX system, run-time components only, or drivers only through one simple function call

- Ability to override the default behavior of DirectX installation to provide custom status reports and installation query messages

- Testing of the DirectX installation without copying any files into system directories

- Determination of the version of the currently installed DirectX system

In the following sections we will see how DirectSetup is used to install DirectX components in an automated, default manner as well as techniques to override this default behavior to provide additional feedback.

## Functional Overview

The purpose of DirectSetup is to install DirectX in a manner such that it does not inadvertently affect the system. Therefore, it takes a very conservative approach, and by default, it will not replace any driver that is questionable or may impact the system in any negative way. In addition, it also backs up any driver that is replaced, so that the user may reverse the installation and restore the original drivers if necessary.

In contrast to other DirectX subsystems, the DirectSetup API is not a collection of COM components, but rather a small handful of functions. Indeed, our discussion of DirectSetup will encompass only three of these functions: DirectXSetupGetVersion, DirectXSetup, and DirectXSetupSetCallback.

The first function, DirectXSetupGetVersion, is rather simple. It merely retrieves the version and revision numbers of the DirectX components currently installed. This function can be used to determine if the current DirectX version is older than the one included with the application, or if DirectX is installed at all.

> **Tip:** You can also determine the version of DirectX currently installed on the user's machine using techniques from Chapter 4, An Introduction to DirectX.

The second function, DirectXSetup, is perhaps the most important. This function performs the actual installation of all of the DirectX components. Using this function, we can indicate if the entire DirectX system should be installed or only certain parts. Specifically, we can instruct the function to install only run-time components, audio drivers, or display drivers.

The final function, DirectXSetupSetCallback, is used to provide a callback function used by the installation procedure that notifies the application when an installation event occurs. This allows the application to customize the behavior of the installation process and display status messages and message boxes different from the default. This function must be used to install a callback function before the DirectXSetup function is called.

## Using DirectSetup

In what should be a very familiar theme by now, using DirectSetup involves some very specific steps performed in a specific order. Not surprisingly, some of these steps are optional, some are not. In order to use DirectSetup to install DirectX, the application must perform the following:

■ Locate the DirectX redistributables in the same directory as the setup application

■ Retrieve available drive space

■ Retrieve the current version of DirectX (optional)

■ Set a callback function (optional)

■ Call the DirectXSetup function

### Locate the DirectX Redistributables

More a requirement than a step, this is a task the developer must perform when packaging the application files for distribution. In order to use DirectSetup functions, the DirectX redistributable files must be placed somewhere on the distribution media (presumably a CD). Specifically, the dsetup.dll, dsetup16.dll, and dsetup32.dll must be in the same directory as the setup application so they'll be loaded when the application starts. The other DirectX redistributable files must be located in a directory named DirectX (not case sensitive) which may be located elsewhere, but typically it is more convenient to simply place them in the same directory as the setup application (see below for more details). In the example for this chapter, we placed the redistributables in the same directory as the example code, so refer to the accompanying CD for an example of directory structure.

### Retrieve Available Drive Space

Technically speaking, this step is not an absolute requirement, as the DirectX installation procedure will fail gracefully if it runs out of disk space. DirectX requires a minimum of 15 MB of free space (if you only use one language) on the drive in which Windows is installed. Out of courtesy to your customers, who may be computer novices that could get confused by insufficient disk space error messages during an install, you should always check and inform users if they do not have enough space to install DirectX.

### Retrieve the Current Version of DirectX

Since many machines now have DirectX already installed, either by another application or by the manufacturer, you may want to check to see if the currently installed DirectX version is older than that shipped with your application. If the installed version is more current than the one you are shipping, you can skip DirectX installation altogether.

In order to retrieve the version number, the application must call the DirectXSetupGetVersion function. The DirectXSetupGetVersion function is defined as:

```
function DirectXSetupGetVersion(
var lpdwVersion: DWORD;              // the version number
var lpdwRevision: DWORD             // the revision number
  : Integer;                       // returns non-zero if successful
```

The first parameter is a DWORD variable that will contain the major version number in the high-order word and the minor version number in the low-order word when the function returns. The second parameter is also a DWORD variable that will contain the release number in the high-order word and the build number in the low-order word. The minor version number reflects the "commercial" version of DirectX, and will be 6 for DirectX 6 or higher, 5 for DirectX 5, etc.

**Note:** There was no version 4 of DirectX.

### Set a Callback Function

If the developer wishes the DirectX installation to proceed using its standard, default behavior, this step can be skipped. However, in order to customize the behavior of the installation process, the application needs to inform DirectSetup that it should call a callback function during the installation process. This is accomplished by calling the DirectXSetupSetCallback function, which is defined as:

```
function DirectXSetupSetCallback(
Callback: TDSetup_Callback        // pointer to the callback function
) : Integer;                      // returns zero
```

Currently, this function only returns zero, whether it succeeded or failed. The only parameter for this function is a pointer to the callback function. This function will be called by the installation process at various times when certain events happen or the user needs to supply additional information. The callback function itself must be defined as:

```
function TDSetup_Callback(
Reason: DWORD;                    // reason flags
MsgType: DWORD;                   // message type flags
szMessage: PChar;                 // message string
szName: PChar;                    // driver name string
pInfo: Pointer                    // additional driver information
  : DWORD; stdcall;               // returns MessageBox return values
```

We'll examine this callback function in more detail below when we cover techniques for customizing the installation process.

### Call the DirectXSetup Function

To begin the process of actually copying DirectX system files onto the hard drive and configuring Windows with the new components, we must call the DirectXSetup function. The DirectXSetup function is defined as:

```
function DirectXSetup(
hWnd: HWND;                       // parent window handle
lpszRootPath: PAnsiChar;          // DirectX redistributables path
dwFlags: DWORD                    // installation control flags
  : Integer;                      // returns a DirectX error code
```

The first parameter is a handle to a window that will be used as the parent window for any dialog boxes that need to be displayed during the installation. The second parameter is the path for the location of the DirectX redistributable files. Setting this to nil causes DirectSetup to look for the files in the current directory, as described above.

The third parameter is set to a series of flags that indicate how DirectX is to be installed. This controls whether the entire DirectX system will be installed, or only certain parts. The available flags for this parameter are shown in Table A-1. The DirectSetup documentation recommends that applications perform a full install using the DSETUP_DIRECTX flag. However, an application could provide the user with a method to install only the run-time components or perhaps just audio and/or video drivers in the case of a malfunction or for troubleshooting purposes. Another very useful flag is DSETUP_TESTINSTALL, which runs through a test installation of DirectX but doesn't actually replace any drivers or copy any run-time components to the system. Using this in conjunction with a callback function allows the developer to make a detailed list of drivers that will be replaced during the installation, which could then be presented to the user in a summary format before the actual installation process began.

**Table A-1:** DirectXSetup control flags

| Flag | Description |
|---|---|
| DSETUP_DDRAWDRV | Installs display drivers only |
| DSETUP_DIRECTX | Performs a full installation of DirectX |
| DSETUP_DSOUNDDRV | Installs audio drivers only |
| DSETUP_DXCORE | Installs run-time components only |
| DSETUP_TESTINSTALL | Performs a test installation without installing files |

This function can return a number of error codes that indicate various problems such as insufficient disk space or missing source files. However, the application should specifically watch out for the DSETUPERR_SUCCESS_RESTART return value. This indicates that the machine must be rebooted before DirectX functionality will be available. DirectSetup does not automatically inform the user of this, so your installation application will need to do the job. A return value of DSETUPERR_SUCCESS indicates that installation was successful and no reboot is necessary. See the DSetup.pas file (part of the JEDI DirectX headers) for a complete listing of error codes returnable by DirectXSetup.

## Overriding Default Behavior

If the application did not specify a callback function, calling the DirectXSetup function will launch the installation of DirectX, and it will proceed to install DirectX drivers and components without any intervention from the user or the application. DirectSetup will provide a simple status window to the user, but this is the only feedback it outputs. The following illustration shows the default DirectSetup installation status box.

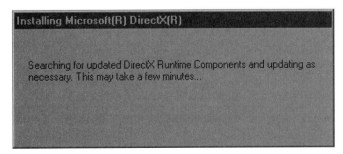

*Figure A-1: Default DirectSetup status message*

If any sort of error occurs, such as insufficient drive space, it will not display any message to the user, relying on the application to interpret the return value and display the appropriate message. It also will not ask the user for any sort of confirmation. If it encounters an unrecognized driver or other potential driver incompatibility problem, it simply skips the driver and returns success, without ever bothering the user. As mentioned before, this approach is taken so that the system is not left in an unusable state due to driver conflicts. However, this can lead to an unusable DirectX installation.

Therefore, it might be wise to provide a little more customized feedback to the user, especially if your application is to be widely distributed. As mentioned previously, we should set up a callback function using the DirectXSetupSetCallback function. For the sake of completeness (and so you don't have to flip back and forth in this section), the callback function itself is defined as:

```
function TDSetup_Callback(
Reason: DWORD;             // reason flags
MsgType: DWORD;            // message type flags
szMessage: PChar;          // message string
szName: PChar;             // driver name string
pInfo: Pointer             // additional driver information
  : DWORD; stdcall;        // returns MessageBox return values
```

The first parameter contains one of several flags that indicate why the callback function was called. These flags are listed in Table A-2 below. As you can see, this callback function is called on several occasions, notably when an error has occurred or when DirectSetup is about to install DirectX drivers or components. Of particular interest is the DSETUP_CB_MSG_NOMESSAGE flag. This flag is sent to the callback function merely to provide a method for updating a status bar. When this flag is received, none of the other parameters contain any useful information, and the callback function should return immediately.

**Table A-2:** Reason flags

| Flag | Description |
|---|---|
| DSETUP_CB_MSG_NOMESSAGE | Update pulse |
| DSETUP_CB_MSG_CANTINSTALL_ UNKNOWNOS | The operating system cannot be determined, and DirectX can't be installed |
| DSETUP_CB_MSG_CANTINSTALL_NT | Cannot install under Windows NT |
| DSETUP_CB_MSG_CANTINSTALL_BETA | Pre-release beta version of Windows 95 detected; cannot install DirectX |
| DSETUP_CB_MSG_CANTINSTALL_ NOTWIN32 | 16-bit version of Windows detected; cannot install DirectX |
| DSETUP_CB_MSG_CANTINSTALL_ WRONGLANGUAGE | The DirectX driver or component is not localized to the installed Windows language |

**Table A-2:** Reason flags (cont.)

| Flag | Description |
|------|-------------|
| DSETUP_CB_MSG_CANTINSTALL_ WRONGPLATFORM | The DirectX driver or component is for another type of computer |
| DSETUP_CB_MSG_PREINSTALL_NT | DirectX is already installed on this version of NT |
| DSETUP_CB_MSG_ NOTPREINSTALLEDONNT | DirectX cannot be installed on this version of NT |
| DSETUP_CB_MSG_SETUP_INIT_FAILED | General setup failure |
| DSETUP_CB_MSG_INTERNAL_ERROR | An internal error has occurred |
| DSETUP_CB_MSG_CHECK_DRIVER_ UPGRADE | A driver is being considered for upgrade |
| DSETUP_CB_MSG_OUTOFDISKSPACE | Insufficient disk space to install all DirectX components |
| DSETUP_CB_MSG_BEGIN_INSTALL | Installation has begun |
| DSETUP_CB_MSG_BEGIN_INSTALL_ RUNTIME | Installation of DirectX run-time components has begun |
| DSETUP_CB_MSG_BEGIN_INSTALL_ DRIVERS | Installation of device drivers has begun |
| DSETUP_CB_MSG_FILECOPYERROR | An error occurred copying a file |

The second and third parameters are used when a message should be presented to the user. These values are intended to be used with the MessageBox function, with the MsgType parameter indicating the flags to be used with MessageBox, and the szMessage parameter containing the text of the message to be presented. In any case when MsgType is not zero, the callback function should return a value commensurate with the values returned by the MessageBox function for the flags indicated in the MsgType parameter. Ideally, the callback function will just pass all of this to the MessageBox function, in turn passing its return value back as the return value for the callback. However, the application can display any form of dialog box desired with any type of feedback desired, as long as the callback return value matches that which would be returned by the MessageBox function for the given flags in the MsgType parameter. The sole exception to this rule is that the function can always return zero, in which case DirectSetup will act in a default manner as if no callback function had been specified.

In the case where MsgType is zero, the DirectSetup documentation states that we should always return IDOK. The IDOK return value, in this case, will suppress the default status window displayed by DirectSetup. However, if we return zero when MsgType is zero, the default status dialog box will be displayed. This allows us to display our own status indicator or use DirectSetup's default status indicator as desired.

**Caution:** It is possible through the use of the callback function to provide default responses and install DirectX without any intervention from the user, or even without the user being aware of the installation. This is very bad programming practice, and can potentially lead to an incorrect installation. Always inform the user that DirectX is being installed, and especially give the user the appropriate feedback and options when drivers are being upgraded.

## Verification of Driver Upgrade

The most interesting of all of the reason flags is DSETUP_CB_MSG_CHECK_ DRIVER_UPGRADE. This indicates that DirectX is considering upgrading a driver, and verification from the user is recommended. The MsgType and szMessage parameters will most certainly contain values indicating the type of message box to display as well as a text description of the problem and recommended user action. The fourth parameter, szName, will contain the name of the driver being considered for upgrade.

The final parameter, pInfo, is a pointer to a TDSetup_CB_UpgradeInfo structure that contains additional information about the driver in question. This simple structure is defined as:

```
TDSetup_CB_UpgradeInfo = record
  UpgradeFlags: DWORD;                    // driver upgrade information flags
end;
```

The only member of this structure, UpgradeFlags, can contain one or more flags from Table A-3 which indicate the status of the upgrade. Of particular interest are the DSETUP_CB_UPGRADE_FORCE and DSETUP_CB_UPGRADE_KEEP flags. DSETUP_CB_UPGRADE_FORCE indicates that Windows may not function correctly unless the driver is upgraded. In this case, DirectSetup will upgrade the driver regardless of the value returned by the callback function. The DSETUP_CB_UPGRADE_KEEP flag, on the other hand, indicates that Windows may not function correctly if the driver is upgraded. In this case, Direct Setup will not upgrade the driver, again regardless of the return value. Other flags indicate the type of driver being upgraded or other warnings that the user should take into account when deciding to allow or disallow the upgrade.

**Table A-3:** Driver upgrade information flags

| Flag | Description |
| --- | --- |
| DSETUP_CB_UPGRADE_KEEP | The system may fail if the driver is upgraded |
| DSETUP_CB_UPGRADE_SAFE | This driver is safe to upgrade; upgrading recommended |
| DSETUP_CB_UPGRADE_FORCE | The system may fail if the driver is not upgraded |
| DSETUP_CB_UPGRADE_ UNKNOWN | Existing device driver unrecognized; upgrading is not recommended |

**Table A-3:** Driver upgrade information flags (cont.)

| Flag | Description |
|------|-------------|
| DSETUP_CB_UPGRADE_HASWARNINGS | Upgrading the driver may affect one or more programs; upgrading is not recommended |
| DSETUP_CB_UPGRADE_CANTBACKUP | Existing system components cannot be backed up, and therefore cannot subsequently be restored |
| DSETUP_CB_UPGRADE_DEVICE_ACTIVE | The device driver is currently in use |
| DSETUP_CB_UPGRADE_DEVICE_DISPLAY | This is a display device driver |
| DSETUP_CB_UPGRADE_DEVICE_MEDIA | This is a media device driver (typically an audio device) |

The following example demonstrates how to use the DirectXSetup function in conjunction with a callback function to suppress the default status dialog box as well as provide custom feedback information to the user. It also illustrates how to perform both a test installation as well as a full installation of all DirectX components.

**Listing A-1:** *Installing DirectX*

```
interface

    .
    .
    .


  {declare the callback function}
  function DSetupCallback(Reason: DWORD; MsgType: DWORD;
      szMessage: PChar; szName: PChar; pInfo: Pointer) : DWORD; stdcall;

    .
    .
    .


implementation

{this function is called numerous times throughout the DirectX
 setup process}
function DSetupCallback(Reason: DWORD; MsgType: DWORD;
      szMessage: PChar; szName: PChar; pInfo: Pointer) : DWORD; stdcall;
begin
  {if the MsgType parameter is 0, return IDOK, otherwise let's
   display a message box and return the appropriate value}
  if MsgType = 0 then
    Result := IDOK    // setting this to 0 displays the standard status box
  else
    Result := MessageBox(frmDXSetup.Handle, szMessage, 'DirectX Setup',MsgType);
```

```
{display a message in our list box indicating the reason
 why the callback function was called}
case Reason of
  DSETUP_CB_MSG_NOMESSAGE :
    frmDXSetup.lbxStatus.Items.Add('NoMessage Pulse (could display '+
                                   'a progression indicator on this message)');

  DSETUP_CB_MSG_CANTINSTALL_UNKNOWNOS :
    frmDXSetup.lbxStatus.Items.Add('Can''t install, unknown OS');

  DSETUP_CB_MSG_CANTINSTALL_NT :
    frmDXSetup.lbxStatus.Items.Add('Can''t install to versions of Windows '+
                                   'NT prior to 4.0');

  DSETUP_CB_MSG_CANTINSTALL_BETA :
    frmDXSetup.lbxStatus.Items.Add('Pre-release beta version of Windows 95 '+
                                   'detected, cannot install.');

  DSETUP_CB_MSG_CANTINSTALL_NOTWIN32 :
    frmDXSetup.lbxStatus.Items.Add('DirectX is not compatible with Windows '+
                                   '3.x');

  DSETUP_CB_MSG_CANTINSTALL_WRONGLANGUAGE :
    frmDXSetup.lbxStatus.Items.Add('This version of DirectX not localized to'+
                                   ' the current language configured for Windows.');

  DSETUP_CB_MSG_CANTINSTALL_WRONGPLATFORM :
    frmDXSetup.lbxStatus.Items.Add('DirectX component or driver incompatible'+
                                   ' with current hardware.');

  DSETUP_CB_MSG_PREINSTALL_NT :
    frmDXSetup.lbxStatus.Items.Add('DirectX already installed on this '+
                                   'version of Windows NT.');

  DSETUP_CB_MSG_NOTPREINSTALLEDONNT :
    frmDXSetup.lbxStatus.Items.Add('Cannot install DirectX on this version '+
                                   'of Windows NT.');

  DSETUP_CB_MSG_SETUP_INIT_FAILED :
    frmDXSetup.lbxStatus.Items.Add('Setup of the DirectX component or '+
                                   'device driver has failed.');

  DSETUP_CB_MSG_INTERNAL_ERROR :
    frmDXSetup.lbxStatus.Items.Add('An internal error has occurred and '+
                                   'DirectX setup has failed.');

  {here, DirectSetup is considering upgrading a driver. the user will have
   already been asked for confirmation above, but here we can see how
   we can query the pInfo parameter for more information about the
   upgrade}
```

```pascal
DSETUP_CB_MSG_CHECK_DRIVER_UPGRADE  :
  begin
    frmDXSetup.lbxStatus.Items.Add('Upgrading driver: '+szName);
    frmDXSetup.lbxStatus.Items.Add(szMessage);

    {determine and display upgrade information}
    if (TDSetup_CB_UpgradeInfo(pInfo^).UpgradeFlags and
        DSETUP_CB_UPGRADE_KEEP) = DSETUP_CB_UPGRADE_KEEP then
      frmDXSetup.lbxStatus.Items.Add('Current driver cannot be upgraded');
    if (TDSetup_CB_UpgradeInfo(pInfo^).UpgradeFlags and
        DSETUP_CB_UPGRADE_SAFE) = DSETUP_CB_UPGRADE_SAFE then
      frmDXSetup.lbxStatus.Items.Add('Driver recognized, upgrade is safe');
    if (TDSetup_CB_UpgradeInfo(pInfo^).UpgradeFlags and
        DSETUP_CB_UPGRADE_FORCE) = DSETUP_CB_UPGRADE_FORCE then
      frmDXSetup.lbxStatus.Items.Add('Upgrade must be performed');
    if (TDSetup_CB_UpgradeInfo(pInfo^).UpgradeFlags and
        DSETUP_CB_UPGRADE_UNKNOWN) = DSETUP_CB_UPGRADE_UNKNOWN then
      frmDXSetup.lbxStatus.Items.Add('Unknown driver');
    if (TDSetup_CB_UpgradeInfo(pInfo^).UpgradeFlags and
        DSETUP_CB_UPGRADE_HASWARNINGS) = DSETUP_CB_UPGRADE_HASWARNINGS then
      frmDXSetup.lbxStatus.Items.Add('Upgrade is not recommended');
    if (TDSetup_CB_UpgradeInfo(pInfo^).UpgradeFlags and
        DSETUP_CB_UPGRADE_CANTBACKUP) = DSETUP_CB_UPGRADE_CANTBACKUP then
      frmDXSetup.lbxStatus.Items.Add('Driver cannot be backed up, '+
                                     'restoration impossible');
    if (TDSetup_CB_UpgradeInfo(pInfo^).UpgradeFlags and
        DSETUP_CB_UPGRADE_DEVICE_ACTIVE) =
        DSETUP_CB_UPGRADE_DEVICE_ACTIVE then
      frmDXSetup.lbxStatus.Items.Add('Driver being upgraded is currently '+
                                     'in use');
    if (TDSetup_CB_UpgradeInfo(pInfo^).UpgradeFlags and
        DSETUP_CB_UPGRADE_DEVICE_DISPLAY) =
        DSETUP_CB_UPGRADE_DEVICE_DISPLAY then
      frmDXSetup.lbxStatus.Items.Add('Driver is a display driver');
    if (TDSetup_CB_UpgradeInfo(pInfo^).UpgradeFlags and
        DSETUP_CB_UPGRADE_DEVICE_MEDIA) =
        DSETUP_CB_UPGRADE_DEVICE_MEDIA then
      frmDXSetup.lbxStatus.Items.Add('Driver is a sound driver');
  end;

DSETUP_CB_MSG_OUTOFDISKSPACE :
  frmDXSetup.lbxStatus.Items.Add('Out of disk space');

DSETUP_CB_MSG_BEGIN_INSTALL :
  frmDXSetup.lbxStatus.Items.Add('DirectX installation commencing');

DSETUP_CB_MSG_BEGIN_INSTALL_RUNTIME :
  frmDXSetup.lbxStatus.Items.Add('Installing DirectX run-time components');

DSETUP_CB_MSG_BEGIN_INSTALL_DRIVERS :
```

```
        frmDXSetup.lbxStatus.Items.Add('Installing DirectX device drivers');

    DSETUP_CB_MSG_FILECOPYERROR :
      frmDXSetup.lbxStatus.Items.Add('An error occurred trying to copy a file');
  end;
end;

procedure TfrmDXSetup.FormCreate(Sender: TObject);
var
  Version, Revision: DWORD;
begin
  {retrieve the version and revision number for the currently
   installed DirectX}
  DirectXSetupGetVersion(Version, Revision);

  {display the version and revision numbers}
  lblVersion.Caption := Format('%d.%d.%d.%d (Commercial Version: %d)',
                               [HiWord(Version), LoWord(Version),
                                HiWord(Revision), LoWord(Revision),
                                LoWord(Version)]);

  {set up our callback function}
  DirectXSetupSetCallback(@DSetupCallback);
end;

procedure TfrmDXSetup.btnTestInstallClick(Sender: TObject);
begin
  {clear the feedback list box}
  lbxStatus.Items.Clear;

  { - we'll use the ErrorString function located in the DSetup.pas unit  -
    - to retrieve a text string describing the success code returned by  -
    - DirectXSetup. we should specifically check to see if the system    -
    - must be rebooted.                                                  - }

  {perform a test installation}
  lbxStatus.Items.Add(ErrorString(DirectXSetup(Handle,nil,DSETUP_TESTINSTALL)));

  {indicate that installation has finished}
  lbxStatus.Items.Add('DirectSetup finished');
end;

procedure TfrmDXSetup.btnRealInstallClick(Sender: TObject);
begin
  {clear the feedback list box}
  lbxStatus.Items.Clear;

  {this time, we'll perform a full installation of DirectX. we're still
   using the ErrorString function as described above}
  lbxStatus.Items.Add(ErrorString(DirectXSetup(Handle, nil, DSETUP_DIRECTX)));
```

```
  {indicate that installation has finished}
  lbxStatus.Items.Add('DirectSetup finished');
end;

end.
```

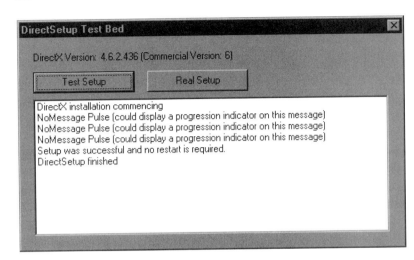

*Figure A-2:*
*The customized*
*DirectSetup*
*feedback*

## Summary

In this appendix, we discussed how DirectSetup can automate the task of install-ing DirectX onto an end user's machine. We examined various installation methods, including the standard, no-frills installation as well as a highly cus-tomized installation that overrides the default behaviors of DirectSetup. We also discussed retrieving the version of the currently installed DirectX, as well as some issues with redistribution of DirectX files. When writing an installation program that uses DirectSetup to install DirectX components, it is important to keep these points in mind:

■ If the version of DirectX installed on the target machine is equal to or more current than the version shipping with your application, there is no need to install DirectX.

■ Only those files located in the Redist directory of the DirectX SDK are redistributable with applications. Refer to the DirectX SDK EULA.txt file for more information, or visit **http://www.microsoft.com/directx/devel-oper/downloads/default.asp**.

■ The only change to the redistributable files that can be made is that lan-guages unsupported by your application can be left out. This can dramatically reduce the storage requirements for the DirectX redistributable file set.

■ Redistributables, and in particular the dsetup.dll, dsetup16.dll, and dsetup32.dll, must be located in the same directory as the installation program.

■ The minimum required disk space for DirectX is 15 MB, if you are installing only one language version.

■ The minor version number returned by DirectXSetupGetVersion reflects the commercial version of DirectX.

■ The DirectXSetup function can perform a full installation of all DirectX components, an installation of specific components (such as run-time components or drivers), or a test installation. The test installation acts like a real installation, except it makes no changes to the system.

■ By default, DirectSetup does not provide any feedback to the user other than a status dialog box, nor does it retrieve confirmation from the user concerning driver replacement. If any driver upgrade would cause any type of problem, it will simply be skipped and the DirectXSetup function will return success, with no indication to the user of any problems encountered.

■ A callback function can be specified, which will be called by DirectSetup at various times throughout the installation process. This allows the application to override default behavior and provide customized feedback to the user.

■ If the MsgType parameter of the callback function is anything other than zero, it should return a value commensurate with that returned by the MessageBox function.

■ If the MsgType parameter contains zero, the callback function should return a value of IDOK. However, returning a value of zero causes DirectSetup to perform the default action.

# Glossary

## A

**artificial intelligence (AI):** The concept of cognitive software that thinks and reacts to situations in a sentient manner. In relation to game programming, this is the section of code responsible for determining the actions and reactions of game antagonists in relation to the actions and reactions of the player.

**alpha channel:** A component of color that records levels of transparency/opacity as opposed to actual color data.

## B

**bitmap:** A collection of pixels arranged in a rectangular configuration in such a way that they form a recognizable shape, such as a picture or texture.

**BLT:** bit block transfer. Pronounced "blit," this is the act of copying the pixels of a bitmap image onto the screen or other graphical output surface for display.

## C

**coefficient:** A measurement of the strength of resistance output by a force feedback device in response to the movement of an axis, relative to the total maximum force available on the device itself.

**color depth:** A measurement of the number of bits per pixel required to describe the color of an individual pixel.

**condition:** A resistant force applied to one or more axes on a force feedback device in response to the movement or position of those axes.

## D

**device context (DC):** Represents the surface of an output device such as a monitor, printer, or plotter, allowing the application to perform graphical output.

**device-dependent bitmap (DDB):** An older bitmap image format that stores only height, width, color depth, and image pixels.

**device-independent bitmap (DIB):** A flexible bitmap image format that includes all necessary information to accurately reproduce the image on any device.

## E

**end user license agreement (EULA):** A legal document that details specific licensing issues concerning software.

**envelope:** A series of values that shape a force at the beginning and end of playback.

## F

**fade:** A transition effect where an image slowly appears out of a solid color, such as black or white.

**finite state machine:** A logical construction that contains a series of states defining specific behaviors and a series of state transitions defining rules for moving from state to state.

**frame:** A single image in a series of images to be animated.

**Frame animation:** The process of producing animation by rapidly displaying a series of images depicting an object or character in slightly different positions each frame.

**force feedback:** A method by which an input device can output tactile feedback to the user through various actuator motors.

## G

**gain:** A scaling factor for magnitudes and coefficients, measured in hundredths of a percent.

**Graphical Device Interface (GDI):** The Windows subsystem responsible for all graphical output during a Windows session.

## H

**HAL:** Hardware abstraction layer; the DirectX drivers responsible for direct interface to hardware capabilities.

**HEL:** Hardware emulation layer; the DirectX drivers responsible for emulating certain functionality if not present in hardware.

**hertz (Hz):** A measurement of samples per second.

**human/computer interaction:** The concept of techniques and methods by which humans and machines, primarily computers, exchange information.

## K

**kinetic force:** An active push on one or more axes on a force feedback device.

## L

**line:** A collection of pixels, usually arranged in a linear or connecting configuration.

## M

**magnitude:** A measurement of the strength of a kinetic force output by a force feed-back device, relative to the total maximum force available on the device itself.

**masking:** The act of using two bitmaps, an AND bitmap and an OR bitmap, along with raster operations to draw one bitmap over another while simulating transparent pixels in the source bitmap.

**Microsoft Foundation Classes (MFC):** Microsoft's object-oriented component hierarchy, similar to Delphi's VCL.

**mixing:** Combining several sounds in real time in such a way that they can be played simultaneously.

**MIDI (Musical Instrument Digital Interface):** A digital format for describing music.

## O

**overscan:** The area on a monitor that borders the usable display area.

## P

**path finding:** Algorithmic techniques for determining the shortest, most direct path from a starting position to an ending position based on terrain and obstacles in the game world.

**pixel:** The smallest, single element in a graphical image or on the display surface.

**polling:** A method for retrieving input or checking some data value manually (as opposed to letting a separate thread check it automatically), usually repeated often at regular intervals.

**polygon:** A collection of lines, arranged in such a way that the ends are connected to form a continuous, closed shape.

**POV hat:** The point-of-view (POV) hat is a device that typically rests on the top of a joystick, and can be used to indicate a viewing direction separate from movement direction.

**primary sound driver:** The audio output device selected by the user on the Audio tab of the Multimedia control panel applet.

**profiler:** A profiler is an application that typically measures application execution time. The level at which an application is timed usually varies, from timing the execution of individual lines to the execution time of functions, procedures, or the overall application.

**pulse code modulation (PCM):** An uncompressed audio format; the most common format for Windows WAV files.

## R

**raster graphics:** Graphics that are composed of a collection of pixels that together form a picture or image. Generally refers to bitmaps, icons, and other such graphical types.

**raster operation (ROP):** A Boolean function performed on pixels when they are copied from bitmap to bitmap that determines how the pixels from the source, the destination, and the destination device context's selected brush are combined.

**Red Book Audio:** The digital format used to store professional music on conventional audio CDs.

**resolution:** A measurement of the number of pixels displayed on the screen.

**Resource Interchange File Format (RIFF):** A complex, variable length file consisting of variable length "chunks." Each chunk can describe data or a header (which contains a description of the data following it). Commonly used for multimedia file formats, such as WAV files.

**RGB color:** Refers to the method by which colors are represented, usually in the form of a red, green, and blue component, respectively.

## S

**sprite:** An image that animates and moves around the screen in some fashion. Typically associated with images that the user can interact with, either directly or through interaction with other sprites.

## T

**texture mapping:** A general term for algorithms that map a bitmap image onto a geometric shape.

## V

**vector graphics:** Graphics that are represented by a series of connected points in a virtual 2-D or 3-D Cartesian (or similar) coordinate system. Generally refers to lines, polygons, curves, and other such graphical types.

**video mode:** The video hardware state that dictates the display resolution and number of available colors for graphical output.

## Z

**z-order:** The position along the z, or third-dimensional, axis. This is an imaginary axis that runs perpendicular to the screen, and gives the illusion of depth.

# Bibliography

There are a lot of great books out there on Windows graphics programming, game programming, and DirectX programming. The information contained in this publication is based in part on research and knowledge gleaned from the following books:

Abrash, Michael. *Michael Abrash's Zen of Graphics Programming*. Coriolis Group, 1996.

Ayres, et. al. *The Tomes of Delphi 3: Win32 Graphical API*. Wordware Publishing, 1998.

Bargen and Donnelly. *Inside DirectX*. Microsoft Press, 1998.

Kawick, Mickey. *Real-Time Strategy Game Programming*. Wordware Publishing, 1999.

Kirk, David. *Graphics Gems III*. Academic Press, 1992.

LaMothe, Andre. *Black Art of 3D Game Programming*. Waite Group Press, 1995.

LaMothe, Andre. *Teach Yourself Game Programming in 21 Days*. SAMS Publishing, 1994.

LaMothe, Ratcliff, et. al. *Tricks of the Game Programming Gurus*. SAMS Publishing, 1994.

Lyons, Eric R. *Black Art of Windows Game Programming*. Waite Group Press, 1995.

Swokowski, Earl W. *Fundamentals of Trigonometry*. PWS-KENT Publishing Company, 1989.

Trujillo, Stan. *High Performance Windows Graphics Programming*. Coriolis Group, 1998.

# *Index*

## welcome to
# gameTROPOLIS

### *Where the Fun Never Sleeps!*

Come seek the challenges of downtown competition and social interaction at the new **GameTropolis**! Play some games, chat with your friends and win some super-cool prizes. We offer multiplayer or individual game play, and you can also jump in and be a spectator at games in process. You can even chat with the players!

All games are written 100% in Delphi, including the front-end clients and back-end servers. Several new games will be appearing in the coming months using techniques outlined and described in this book. These are all multiplayer, Internet-only games that utilize either Win32 GDI functions or DirectX. Our flagship game, Beckett Football League (BFL), was written solely in DirectX using many of the techniques described herein and features an isometric tile-based scrolling map engine.

If you would like to see some super-cool, multiplayer, online games written in Delphi, check out Gametropolis at **http://gametropolis.com**.

# PROJECT JEDI

The Joint Endeavor of Delphi Innovators (Project JEDI) is an organization composed of volunteers from all over the globe. Their goal: to pool their combined talent and resources in an effort to extend the functionality of Delphi by bringing translations of Microsoft API headers and components that encapsulate these functions to the Delphi community. By extending Delphi's native access to Windows API functions for currently unsupported technologies, they bring more power to Delphi programmers everywhere.

The incredible effort of these volunteers has resulted in a cooperation agreement of sorts with Borland. A JEDI translated header was shipped with Delphi 5, and if this spirit of cooperation continues, the next version of Delphi will hopefully feature an astounding increase in access to a much broader range of technologies than what we've been previously offered. These generous programmers are working to make Delphi, already the greatest Windows development tool, even better.

The DirectX headers used in this book are a direct result of the accomplishments of Project JEDI. Delphi game programmers everywhere owe a big thanks to Erik Unger for translating the DirectX headers and to Project JEDI for bringing them to the masses. If you would like to know more about Project JEDI, please check them out at http://www.delphi-jedi.org/. They always need more volunteers, so if you've got some free time or some code to donate, please sign up!

# I don't have time for learning curves.

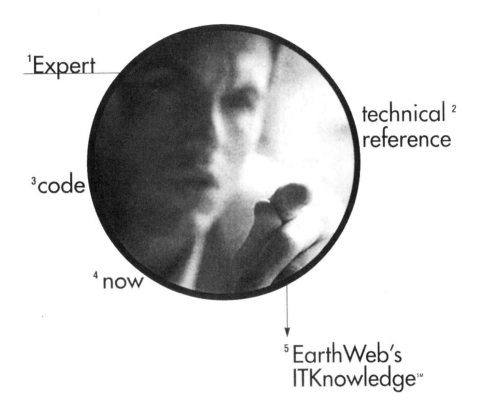

¹Expert

technical ² reference

³code

⁴ now

⁵ EarthWeb's ITKnowledge℠

They rely on you to be the ❶ expert on tough development challenges. There's no time for learning curves, so you go online for ❷ technical references from the experts who wrote the books. Find answers fast simply by clicking on our search engine. Access hundreds of online books, tutorials and even source ❸ code samples ❹ now. Go to ❺ EarthWeb's ITKnowledge, get immediate answers, and get down to it.

Get your FREE ITKnowledge trial subscription today at itkgo.com. Use code number 026.

 **EARTHWEB**
Go further *faster*

# On the CD

The CD accompanying this book contains all of the code referenced throughout the text. This includes both source code for the examples as well as precompiled executables so you can see how the example behaves right off of the CD. All examples were written and tested with Delphi 5, but should be usable under Delphi 4 with only minor modifications, if any.

Under the Book Resources directory, you will find the code examples organized by chapter. You will also find the JEDI DirectX header files in the dxsdk directory. These files must be placed in a directory included on Delphi's library path before any of the examples can be recompiled. Additionally, there is a Resources directory that contains several files that will be useful when extending the examples or creating your own applications. These files include several compositions by David Strahan, a selection of sounds from the *A Zillion Sounds 2.0* CD by Beachware, Inc., and the freeware sprite graphics library SpriteLib by Ari Feldman.

Also included are a full, retail version of Delphi 4 and a 60-day trial version of Delphi 5 Enterprise. To install Delphi 4, insert the companion CD and click on **Delphi 4**. Enter **100 004 2029** for the serial number and **4AX3 5FX0** as the authorization key.

Use Windows Explorer to access Delphi 5 and the Book Resources directory. To install Delphi 5, double-click on the **Delphi 5** folder and press **Setup**. Follow the on-screen steps to obtain the password needed to unlock the Delphi 5 trial version.

 **Warning:** Opening the CD package makes this book nonreturnable.